Food & Communication
Proceedings of the Oxford Symposium on Food and Cookery 2015

Food & Communication

Proceedings of the Oxford Symposium on Food and Cookery 2015

Edited by Mark McWilliams

Prospect Books
2016

First published in Great Britain in 2016 by Prospect Books, 26 Parke Road, London SW13 9NG.

ISBN 978-1-909-248-49-6

The illustration on the front cover shows Giovanni Bellini and Titian, Feast of the Gods, 1514-1529, oil on canvas, 170.2 x 188 cm, Widener Collection, National Gallery, DC. Courtesy: Nationa; Gallery of Art, Washington

The back cover illustration is by an unknown artist, Feast of Achelous, Venice, c. 1550-1560, tin-glazed earthenware, 30 cm diameter, Victoria and Albert Museum, London. © Victoria and Albert Museum, London

Design and typesetting in Gill Sans and Adobe Garamond by Catheryn Kilgarriff and Rebecca Gillieron.

Printed and bound in Great Britain.

Contents

8

Foreword

The most famous of food sayings must be Jean Anthelme Brillat-Savarin's fourth aphorism from *Physiologie du Goût*: '*Dis-moi ce que tu manges, je te dirai ce que tu es*'. Tell me what you eat, and I will tell you what you are. Brillat-Savarin's implication is that food communicates, but his command is to communicate about food.

With Food and Communication, 2015 was intended to be a 'broad' year – the Symposium alternates between broad and narrow themes – but even so paper authors stretched the theme in predictable and surprising ways. The Symposium had considered similar topics in earlier years, with 2009's Food and Language and 1998's Food and the Arts, but when the topic was chosen symposiasts clearly felt a need consider what seemed mushrooming communications about food.

In papers presented over three lovely July days in Oxford, symposiasts considered digital media (the new wave of multi-platform kid chefs, but also the unexpected resilience of the physical cookbook in an iPad age) and the explosion in televised food entertainment (the many iterations of *MasterChef*). But papers also explored food as an area of control and resistance in totalitarian societies; struggles between activists, corporations and bureaucracies over food labels; the use of food and cookery to explore the past and the exotic; the sounds of eating and selling food; and, as Brillat-Savarin predicted, the role of food in constructing and communicating aspects of individual and collective identity. These and many other fascinating takes on this year's theme were fortified, as always, by spectacular meals from the St Catz kitchen run by Tim Kelsey and his staff.

Communication about food is, of course, the heart of the Oxford Symposium. It takes a lot of smart, committed people to organize this annual meeting of this oldest and most interesting food studies conference. This year marked the first Symposium under the leadership of Bee Wilson, our new Chair, and Ursula Heinzelmann, our new Director. Those changes testify to the growing strength of the Symposium, but they also call for much celebration of the many years of leadership provided in those roles by Elisabeth Luard and, especially, the inimitable Paul Levy. Celebration, and even more gratitude. Preparing this volume takes many hands, too, and I would particularly like to thank – in addition to Bee, Ursula, Elisabeth and Paul – Andrew Dalby, Peter Hertzmann, Catheryn Kilgarriff, Tom Jaine, Helen Saberi and, of course, the many authors included here.

Mark McWilliams
Editor, Oxford Symposium on Food and Cookery

Fava Beans and Béchamel: Translating Egyptian Food as Modern Cuisine

Anny Gaul[1]

In Egypt in the early twentieth century, a new middle class was emerging. Collectively referred to as the *efendiyya* (singular *efendi*), its members hailed from a variety of origins and socioeconomic backgrounds but were united through a number of key common experiences and institutions.[2] The term *efendi* generally referred to men who had received Western or Westernized educations (as opposed to traditional religious educations) and tended to adopt Western clothing. Explicitly concerned with questions of modernity, the *efendiyya* engaged in a growing and vibrant print culture of books and newspapers, and they did so in Arabic – as opposed to the Turkish and European languages (French, Italian, Greek, English) that had previously dominated elite culture in Egypt. Nationalism was on the rise, and by the end of the First World War the *efendiyya* were articulating a new vision of what it meant to be modern and Egyptian, speaking from their new roles as leading citizens of the nascent nation.

Scholars of middle-class culture have observed that despite certain broad similarities, the 'local dimensions' of middle-class cultures are essential to understanding their emergence in specific geographic and historical circumstances.[3] This paper argues that food is a particularly apt way to draw out the specific and local dimensions of Egyptian middle-class culture during the first half of the twentieth century. In addition to the capacity of food to cut across such perceived divides as public vs. private and home vs. market, its material nature means that it can ground abstract nationalist narratives in the concrete stuff of everyday life – thus enabling deeper understandings of historical processes. By asking what the *efendiyya* were eating, and how their sisters, wives and daughters aspired to cook, we gain a glimpse of what major shifts in history spelled out for Egyptians in their daily lives – and what made the Egyptian case unique in a modernizing world.

Intersecting the new linguistic and literary practices of the *efendiyya* were changes in household structure and everyday life; some of the most prominent of these changes took place in the realm of kitchen and cuisine. Focusing on practices of writing and translation, this paper examines two dishes, *ful mudammas* and *macarona béchamel*, to explore how food was used by Egypt's *efendiyya* to signal their identity as modern subjects positioned as distinct from both existing elites and lower classes. Both of these dishes are essential elements of what might be called 'Egyptian cuisine', but their trajectories and cultural roles were quite different.

In analyzing the cuisine of the emergent Egyptian middle classes and an 'Egyptian cuisine', I draw on Raymond Williams's conception of newly dominant cultural formations in terms of dominant, residual and emergent elements. The last term, 'emergent', refers to a new set of practices, styles or conventions often associated with a new class, such as the culinary conventions of the *efendiyya*. Williams's conceptualization of 'residual' cultural material is particularly useful for thinking about food traditions, which are continually reinvented, reshaped and absorbed into national categories in such a way that obscures their historical trajectories (consider, for example, how New World foods like the tomato and the potato have come to be considered essential to 'Italian' or 'Irish' cuisine). As for 'residual' elements, Williams emphasizes that they are remnants of the past yet are 'still active in the cultural process [...] as an effective element of the present'.[4] These categories enable us to read the emergence of a new Egyptian national cuisine as a process and a negotiation, dispensing with binaries like modern-traditional to focus instead on how culinary material was used to communicate and consolidate distinctions between the new middle-class culture and the social strata above and below it. Thus, I am not attempting to identify a stable, canonical national cuisine so much as seeking the criteria and rhetoric that Egyptians themselves would have used to justify a particular ingredient or recipe as Egyptian, and why they might have done so. As kitchen technologies and cultural tastes changed, the definition of what counted as 'Egyptian cuisine' was a moving target.

Historical Context: Diverse Influences, New Print Cultures

The material discussed here dates to the 1920s, 30s and 40s, a crucial period for the *efendiyya* and for Egypt more generally. Egypt's 1919 Revolution had established formal political independence from Great Britain (Egypt's occupying colonial power since the early 1880s). The period witnessed explicit articulations of Egyptian identity understood in terms of the modern nation-state. Great Britain still wielded considerable influence in Egyptian politics and government, however, maintaining a strong military presence and control of the Suez Canal. The stakes for justifying and articulating Egypt as a modern, sovereign nation were therefore particularly high during this period, and always with an eye to the West.

Egypt had also been nominally a part of the Turkish Ottoman Empire from the sixteenth century through the First World War. Egypt's local ruling family and elites (along with their cuisines and language) were therefore Turkish at the time of the British occupation. While Ottoman cultural influence declined after the fall of the Ottoman Empire, it never receded entirely; its influence can still be seen in Egypt's foodways (as well as its dialect of Arabic) today. In addition to the Turkish-speaking elites and the British occupiers, Egypt's cities were home to large and influential communities of Syrians, Lebanese, Greeks, Italians, French and Armenians. The new Arabic-speaking Egyptian *efendiyya* class was coming to the fore amidst a markedly cosmopolitan social scene.

In addition to these diverse influences, shifts in literary culture were key forces shaping *efendiyya* identity. The introduction of the printing press and the rise of privately-owned periodicals and publishing houses created new modes of expression as well as new reading publics. In the late nineteenth and early twentieth centuries, hundreds of new privately-owned Arabic periodicals were founded in Egypt (many were short-lived, but some are still in print today).[5] Intellectuals began writing novels, a genre that typified modern literary culture in Europe, while popular fiction was also translated into Arabic and sold at unprecedented volumes.[6] Samah Selim describes how fiction and journalism transformed the Arabic language beginning in the nineteenth century, highlighting in particular the productive and creative role played by the translations and adaptations – which introduced new genres, ideas and modes of expression.[7]

These changes can be read against the backdrop of a series of processes aiming to 'Egyptianize modernity', to borrow a phrase from Lucie Ryzova, a scholar of *efendiyya* culture.[8] This was no unified process of rote adaptation of Western discourses or ideas, but a cluster of varied, hybrid and creative adaptations of cultural material into local vernacular idioms, which took place in a variety of sites, genres and modes. The kitchen was no exception: Egyptian chefs looked to Europe's *haute cuisines* for the latest techniques and recipes, transliterating French culinary terms into Arabic script and publishing cookbooks that translated the staples of continental cuisine into Arabic prose. Local foods were newly expressed as components of a national culture. Traditional domestic food preparation methods, which had long been transmitted orally and in local dialect, were transposed into a modern recipe format and printed in a new style of formal, modern standardized Arabic. All of these translations and transformations were essential to producing the cuisine of the new Egyptian *efendiyya*.

Starting with Cookbooks: Egyptianizing Modern Cuisine

Printed Arabic cookbooks are an excellent place to start understanding how the *efendiyya* were articulating and constructing their culinary culture. As most of the cookbooks from this era are out of print and difficult to locate in libraries, studying these cookbooks requires locating and purchasing used copies from the used book markets of Cairo. Thus far I have located about ten Egyptian cookbooks published between the 1930s and the 1950s, all of them in Arabic. They fall into two primary categories: the first comprises male professional chefs who trained under prestigious European chefs and worked their way to the heads of kitchens in the luxury hotels and elite residences of Cairo and Alexandria, including the royal palace. The second category incudes books written by expert Egyptian women who explicitly directed their cookbooks to the housewives and future housewives of Egypt.

The credentials of cookbook authors of both genders figure prominently in their cookbooks: the men typically describe where and with whom they trained, while the women's title pages include a brief note on their qualifications, often in home economics or domestic science, with many of them specifying the name of a British institution where they had studied. The structure of their cookbooks tends to reflect this training, mirroring that of European manuals for housewives at the time: they typically begin with prescriptive descriptions of the ideal kitchen, the tools a home cook needs and basic cooking techniques. Their recipes include a list of ingredients followed by precise measures and numbered instructions.[9]

As for the recipes themselves, both types of cookbooks include an eclectic mix of Middle Eastern and European foods. A typical dessert section, for example, would include both baklava and chocolate mousse, while the soup section would include both a French consommé and a traditional Egyptian lentil soup. Perhaps most interestingly, all of the authors frame their work explicitly in terms of service to the Egyptian nation. The men explain that they have acquired advanced culinary expertise and wish to make it available to an Arabic reading audience. The women frame their work in terms of the modern woman's essential role in producing and shaping the nation's families and coming generations, a theme that was frequently discussed in Egyptian public discourse at the time.[10] Women had played a prominent role in the 1919 Revolution, led by Huda Sha'rawi, Egypt's most prominent female activist, to whom one cookbook was actually dedicated.[11] Another woman author addressed her cookbooks to 'the young Egyptian woman who, in the spirit of the age, is contributing to our national awakening'.[12] According to these women, modernity was not merely the purview of statesmen and intellectuals. Modernity could be cooked up in the home kitchen.

Stewed Fava Beans: A Humble Dish Receives a Royal Makeover

Ful mudammas, a dish of slow-cooked fava beans (*ful*), is often cited as an unequivocally Egyptian food and an example of the continuity of Egyptian culture through history. According to a recent longitudinal study, it is one of very few dishes in Egypt that is still eaten regularly by families at all income levels – in other words, it is a persistently dominant food in Egypt.[13] And yet the way it is actually prepared has changed considerably over time. To trace this shift, it is useful to begin with the 1836 account of British Orientalist Edward Lane, who described the staple food this way: 'Beans slowly boiled during a whole night in an earthen vessel, buried in the hot ashes of an oven or bath. They are eaten with linseed oil or butter, and generally with a little lime juice. Prepared, they are sold in the morning in the souks (or markets) of Cairo and other towns'.[14]

With the rise of the domestic home kitchen, however, *ful mudammas* was increasingly prepared at home (although it also remains a staple of Egyptian street food as well). Home preparation, however, entailed a very different cooking technique than the one Lane describes – middle-class urban housewives did not have copious quantities of hot ash on hand. But they did increasingly have modern raised stoves and enclosed ovens, fuelled by charcoal, oil or gas. Recipes for *ful mudammas* appear in every Egyptian cookbook I have located from the 1930s, 40s, and 50s. The majority call for cooking the beans in a clay pot, which is left in the oven for a full day. At least one cookbook author, however, advises her readers that the dish can be prepared in half the time if it is cooked on the stovetop.[15] The same cookbook includes a short chapter on the ancient Egyptians, including their diet. The diet of the ancient Egyptians, she explains, was not only rich in vitamins; it included fava beans, the main ingredient in *ful mudammas*.[16]

Given the popularity of *ful mudammas*, it may come as no surprise that it merited inclusion in these cookbooks. But the way it is presented and contextualized represents a significant step in the process of Egyptianizing of modern cuisine, and is a telling example of how that process went about incorporating local foods that were already a part of the dominant popular culture. While its name may not have changed from colloquial usage, the dish was translated into the terms and norms of a modern form of domesticity that promoted the notion of a housewife as an efficient manager of time and money, educated in nutritionally sound dietary principles. At the same time, the assertion of a link between modern Egyptian cuisine and the food of the ancient Egyptians communicated the status of the *efendiyya* as participants in an Egyptian culture with primordial roots.

The periodical press offers additional insight into the ways that food played into the emerging culture of the *efendiyya*. One Egyptian weekly, focused mostly on lifestyle, current events, and celebrity news, featured an article about *ful mudammas* in 1936 that indicates the social significance that the humble fava bean had accrued by then. The article tells the story of an everyday Egyptian street vendor whose *ful mudammas* is reputed to be the best in the country. News of his excellent *ful* reaches Egypt's King Farouk himself, who requests a tasting. The dish is delivered to the palace with great ceremony, and the end of the story, the king and his distinguished guests are 'amazed by this national food (*al-ta'ām al-watanī*)'.[17] Thus humble *ful mudammas* is cast as a national dish, consumed by royalty, and documented and photographed in a middle-brow periodical. The new conventions of Egyptian print culture transformed and incorporated *ful mudammas*, a locally dominant food, into a national tradition, casting it as a link to the nation's ancient roots and adapted for the needs of the modern family.

Macarona Béchamel: A Continental Casserole, Rebranded Egyptian Modern

As its name suggests, *macarona béchamel* is an Egyptian dish with a very different story. A layered casserole with macaroni pasta, ground beef, tomatoes or tomato sauce, and béchamel sauce – often thickened with cheese or egg – it clearly has European roots. In the context of Egyptian food culture, it represents a residual element of the colonial era, but one that is very much a part of contemporary Egyptian cuisine, as a staple comfort food of middle class Egyptian cooking. How, then, did it make its way into Egyptian kitchens in the first place? The answer begins not with the brief Napoleonic invasion and occupation of Egypt at the turn of the nineteenth century, but rather with the changes that were taking place in Egyptian royal court culture a half century later.

After Napoleon's forces left Egypt, the territory remained an Ottoman province – but with its own ruling royal family, subject to the sultan in Istanbul. The Egyptian dynasty's founder, Muhammad Ali Pasha, was an Ottoman subject of Albanian origins, but his descendants gradually drifted away from these origins – as evidenced by King Farouk's well-publicized enjoyment of *ful mudammas*, described above. While initially the Egyptian court's culture modelled its practices and rituals on those of the imperial court in Istanbul, this began to change in the 1850s. Felix Konrad writes that in the Egyptian court during this decade, 'Ottoman patterns of representation receded, while European forms came to the fore'.[18] These 'European forms' included operas, ballets and, of course, banquets.

Court menus from the late 1890s show that by the turn of the twentieth century, court menus were thoroughly French – in language, content and ordering of courses. One menu from a ball at the royal palace in 1896, for example, begins with *consommé de volaille* and ends with *savarin aux fruits*.[19] This would have signified far more than a mere affinity with French culture: Rachel Laudan narrates how during the nineteenth century, French cuisine expanded globally as 'the preferred cuisine of monarchies [...] and of aristocrats and monied people everywhere, at least on those occasions when demonstrating membership in a cosmopolitan global elite was required'. She notes that as cooks and chefs from Mexico to Vietnam adapted elements of French cuisine to their local culinary practices, béchamel sauce was 'by far the most useful sauce for making a dish appear French'.[20]

It seems likely that male professional Egyptian chefs training in the palace kitchens were the first bearers of béchamel expertise into Egyptian food culture. Indeed, a 1932 cookbook written by such a chef includes a recipe for *Macaronis à la Grecque* which is practically identical to the dish known in Greece as *pastitsio* and in Egypt as *macarona béchamel*.[21] The fact that recipes titled *macarona béchamel* appear in seven of the eight women's cookbooks I have located indicates its popularity and acceptance among women who saw themselves as both taste-makers and instructors of the future housewives of Egypt. But the question remains how it migrated from the kitchens of Egypt's cosmopolitan elites to its new status as a bourgeois, middle-class phenomenon – and the role it played in establishing the cultural and social position of the *efendiyya* along the way.

Although the dish appears to be of Greek origin (not unusual given the large Greek populations of Cairo and Alexandria at the time), the components and techniques required to make it would have been familiar to the authors of the Egyptian women's cookbooks, particularly given their training in domestic science. The most famous of these authors, born Nazira Niqula but widely known as Abla Nazira, studied at the Gloucestershire Training College for Domestic Science in the UK from 1927-29.[22] There is no record of *pastitsio* among the school's cookery lessons from the time she studied there, but béchamel sauce and gratin-style casseroles appear to have been staples of its curricula.[23] Given the modern culinary expertise with which women like Abla Nazira were equipped, it would have been quite straightforward for them to rename a popular Greek dish and translate it into the proper format for the Egyptian housewife.

The process of compiling and constructing these cookbooks is of course a separate issue from the way that they were actually used in Egyptian kitchens, and an exploration of actual cooking practice entails a separate line of inquiry. But one thing is clear from *macarona béchamel*'s circuitous path from a leftover of Egypt's foreign milieu to a staple of home cooking: once a dish becomes a standard recipe used by mothers and grandmothers, it is well on its way to becoming canonized as a part of a national cuisine, no matter its provenance.

Conclusion

Tracing the trajectories of these two very different Egyptian dishes offers a glimpse into the dynamics by which the *efendiyya* asserted a new kind of middle-class culture through the practices of the home kitchen. *Ful mudammas* communicated the middle classes' connections to both the Egyptian everyman and the nation's ancient roots while bringing the dish into the modern kitchen by translating it into modern Arabic and a modern culinary writing style, thereby asserting forms of authority and authenticity that Ottoman elites lacked. Meanwhile, the adoption of a dish featuring béchamel sauce signalled a clear differentiation of the new middle strata from the classes that remained below them: as anyone who has attempted a béchamel sauce can attest, without some knowledge of the proper technique and timing it is all but impossible. Perhaps part of the appeal of *macarona béchamel* in particular was that it incorporated numerous elements of modern European cuisine (Italian pasta, French sauce, Greek recipe) while avoiding any overt connection with the British, Egypt's occupiers.

The assertion that nationalisms are recent and socially constructed phenomena is not a new or radical claim. Yet I suggest that the material and quotidian nature of food contributes a new kind of texture to the study of nationalism – one that does not always run along the grain of the hackneyed and overly general categories and labels that are so often used to interpret and describe cultures of nationalism (e.g. modern, Western, traditional, authentic). Family recipes and home cooking have no need to conform to the coherence of official narratives; they can sit and stew in their own contradictions – a street food made proper for the modern bourgeois home, an Ottoman dish for special occasions, a Greek dish as comfort food. Starting with cookbooks and kitchen scraps, we can chart the scaffolding upon which middle class narratives about Egyptian culture and identity were built.

17

Notes

1. I am grateful for the financial support provided by the Cherwell Studentship of the American Friends of the Oxford Symposium on Food and Cookery, as well as research assistance provided by the staff at the archives of the University of Gloucestershire, the Gloucestershire County Archives, and the Netherlands-Flemish Institute in Cairo.
2. For a thorough study of *efendiyya* culture in Egypt, see Lucie Ryzova, *The Age of the Efendiyya: Passages to Modernity in National-Colonial Egypt* (Oxford: Oxford University Press, 2014). For a discussion of

efendiyya as an analytical term, see Michael Eppel, 'Note About the Term Effendiyya in the History of the Middle East', *International Journal of Middle East Studies*, 41 (2009), pp. 535-39.

3. Jonathan Barry and C.W. Brooks, *The Middling Sort of People: Culture, Society, and Politics in England, 1550-1800* (New York: St. Martin's Press, 1994); Stuart Blumin, *The Emergence of the Middle Class: Social Experience in the American City, 1760-1900* (Cambridge: Cambridge University Press, 1989); Ryzova, pp. 4-17. Following Ryzova, I am defining 'middle class' as plural, emergent and culturally constructed, often marked by a set of aspirational ideas, rather than an already extant and empirically defined socioeconomic group (pp. 11-12).

4. Raymond Williams, *Marxism and Literature* (Oxford: Oxford University Press, 1977), pp. 115-133 (p. 122).

5. Samah Selim, 'The People's Entertainment: Translation, Adaptation and the Novel in Egypt', lecture at the Centre for Translation Studies at the American University in Cairo, 2 March 2015 < https://www.youtube.com/watch?v=s10_tahNYVM> [accessed 15 January 2016].

6. Samah Selim, 'The *Nahda*, Popular Fiction and the Politics of Translation', *The MIT Electronic Journal of Middle East Studies*, 4 (2004), pp. 70-89 <http://web.mit.edu/cis/www/mitejmes? [accessed 15 January 2016].

7. Selim, '*Nahda*', pp. 84-86.

8. Ryzova, pp. 24-25.

9. Nicole Humble notes that Eliza Acton (1799-1859) was the first to divide her recipes in this way (Introduction, in Isabella Beeton, *Mrs Beeton's Book of Household Management* (New York: Oxford University Press, 2000), pp. vii-xxx (p. xiv)). This format enabled housewives to plan and calculate not only portions, but costs; it contrasted with the 'aide-memoire' style more common in earlier cookbooks.

10. See Lisa Pollard, *Nurturing the Nation: The Family Politics of Modernizing, Colonizing and Liberating Egypt (1805-1923)* (Berkeley: University of California Press, 2005) and Mona Russell, *Creating the New Egyptian Woman: Consumerism, Education, and National Identity, 1863-1922* (New York: Palgrave Macmillan, 2004).

11. Basima Zaki Ibrahim, *Al-Ghidha' wa-l-matbakh wa-l-ma'ida* (Cairo: Wadi 'Abu Fadl, 1934).

12. Nazira Niqula and Bahiya, 'Uthman, *Usul al-tahy al-nazari wa-l-'amali*, 13th edition (Cairo: Maktabat al-Nahda al-Misriyya, 1981).

13. Habiba Hassan-Wassef, 'Food Habits of the Egyptians: Newly Emerging Trends', *La Revue de Santé de la Méditerranée orientale*, 10 (2004), pp. 898-915 (p. 905).

14. Lane, Edward, *The Manners and Customs of the Modern Egyptians* (London: J.M. Dent, 1908), p. 137.

15. Ibrahim, pp. 189-90.

16. Ibrahim, pp. 46-51.

17. 'Ful al-Haj 'Ali 'Assi', *al-Musawwar*, 21May 1936, p. 26.

18. Felix Konrad, 'Global and Local Patterns of Communication at the Court of the Egyptian Khedives (1840-1880)', in *Court Cultures in the Muslim World: 7th to 19th Centuries*, ed. by Albrecht Fuess and Jan-Peter Hartung (New York: Routledge, 2011), pp. 235-58 (p. 244).

19. 'Abbas II Hilmi Khedive of Egypt: 1896', *What's on the menu?*, New York Public Library Labs < http://menus.nypl.org/menus/26081> [accessed 15 January 2016].

20. Rachel Laudan, *Cuisine and Empire Cooking in World History* (Berkeley: University of California Press, 2013), p. 280, p. 288.

21. Muhammad 'Ali Abu al-Sanun, *al-Tabkh al-masri* (Cairo: Maktaba Madbouli, [n.d.]) [originally published as *Murshid al-tabakh al-hadith* (Cairo: Dar al-Kutub al-Misriyya, 1932)], p. 97. I am grateful to a 2015 Oxford symposiast who pointed out the similarities between Egyptian *macarona béchamel* and Greek *pastitsio* during the Q&A after my presentation.

22. University of Gloucestershire Archives, Cheltenham, England, UA 42/1/4, Bulletin of the College, December 1930; Gloucestershire County Archives, Gloucester, England, K1372, Minutes and Annual Reports, 1929. 'Abla' is a familial honorific used in Egyptian colloquial Arabic, which might be

translated as 'auntie'. Abla Nazira's cookbook saw several spinoff volumes and over a dozen editions in her lifetime; she is still a household name.

23. Gloucestershire County Archives, Gloucester, England, D10118 8/1, Cookery Demonstrations.

Secrets of the Great Chefs: Decrypting Untrustworthy Communications from the Kitchens of Carême, Escoffier and Guérard

Ray Sokolov

Chefs are not good communicators. Even the great ones are not good guides to their thoughts and intentions. People like you and me, food historians or food journalists, people who write about chefs, we express ourselves in words. Chefs normally let their food represent them, wordlessly, mute and cryptic as a lobster. Sometimes a chef speaks loud and clear, lashing out at an underling on reality TV. But mostly, chefs don't bother to explain their dishes' place in the gastroaesthetic universe. Their recipes and menus are terse and open to misunderstanding, even after a chatty waiter gives you the message he's heard in the kitchen about why vanilla brings out the best in *homard à la mexicaine*. And when chefs do make an effort to expatiate about their ideas, they can easily be misunderstood even by sympathetic listeners or traduced by journalists looking for a hook or an easy laugh.

The most revered of chefs, Carême, is conventionally regarded as the father and codifier of French cuisine. This is also how he hoped he would be viewed by posterity, but a modern reader of his work cannot fail to see his recipes as relics of a golden and aristocratic era that had almost vanished before he wrote them down in the early nineteenth century. The real meaning of his many books is their poignancy, their strenuous determination to act as if the grandiose foodways they tacitly imply, were not already fading out, but would go on forever. Nevertheless, Carême has paradoxically triumphed with this deliberately misleading and incomplete self-presentation. No one cooks like him today, but his reputation as the father of us all persists. Everyone wants a father, a culture hero, and Marie-Antoine Carême is that hero.

A child of the Paris streets, born in 1784, Carême rose to the pinnacle of *grande cuisine*, supervising extravagant banquets for Talleyrand, for Lady Rothschild, for pampered royalty, above all for Napoleon. He started out as an apprentice to a leading pastry chef, and with that man's permission, stole away to the royal library, soaking up knowledge about architecture and design, especially from antiquity, knowledge he would later turn into grandiose edible but never eaten sculptures of classical ruins and pastoral idylls, so-called *pièces montées*, that adorned his banquet tables, on low pedestals with an ancient name, *socle*.

Carême did not think these Piranesian images in sugar and flour were just props for his food. Drawings of them illustrate his books and his most famous utterance declares their importance: 'The fine arts are five in number: painting, sculpture, poetry, music, architecture – whose main branch is confectionery.'

He may never have actually said that, but it rings true as a proud declaration of his curious devotion to the aesthetics of table decoration. Still, the modern reader opens Carême's magisterial five-volume *L'art de la cuisine française au dix-neuvième siècle* without quite suspecting how important those engravings are to the great chef's concept of a fine meal.

In particular, the modern reader will not be prepared for this professional recipe book, which is not merely a vast record of a great chef's repertory, but also an elaborate piece of undeclared propaganda for a method of aristocratic food service that was controversial and already obsolescent when Carême presented it as a timeless expression of French culinary heritage. It was also an act of fealty to Carême's most revered employers, Napoleon and Napoleon's epicurean foreign minister Talleyrand. *L'art de la cuisine française* does not begin with a declaration of aesthetic principles or a general theory of cooking. After lengthy dedications, it disconcertingly devotes thirty-two pages to Napoleon, to praise for his gastronomic refinement and to bitter regret for the way he was mistreated and misfed by his British jailers before his death on St. Helena. This Bonapartolatry tacitly prepares for the book's ulterior programme of hostility toward Russian service, the radical and subversive method of food service brought to France from Russia, the nation that defeated Napoleon.

As Darra Goldstein has shown, Carême was publicly ambivalent in his dealings with Czar Alexander I after the fall of Napoleon, traveling to Russia to work for him but then hightailing it back to France.[1] In *L'art de la cuisine française,* the strained politeness he showed the Czar to his face gives way to an unvarnished anti-Russian campaign tacitly expressed in magnificent recipes magnificently unsuited for the newfangled method of bringing food to the table that had come from Russia: the streamlined, visually untheatrical *service à la russe*.

Recently, I opened Carême's volume two at random and landed on chapter eight, which contains twenty-five recipes for 'small' sturgeon weighing from '25 to 100, even 200 pounds'.[2] Carême's first few sturgeon dishes honour his hero Napoleon, Napoleon's empress Josephine (*Esturgeon Beauharnais*) and his vanished empire (*E. à l'impériale*). This last recipe covers two pages, beginning with detailed instructions on how to choose a good fish. The great man seems to have actually been able to persuade his fish man to sell him just a 30-inch section 'starting no closer than 6 inches from the head' and leaving the rest of the behemoth behind. Back in his kitchen, he cuts a fleshy piece from the belly side so that the sturgeon will eventually sit steadily on the platter. He ties up the fish 'like a roast beef' and sets it in an oval pot with a mirepoix moistened by bottles of Rhine wine and Madeira and two big spoons of consommé, cooks it gently, covered, for two hours, then lets it cool, skins it, glazes it entirely with a blond aspic enriched with crayfish butter and places it on a damask napkin, 'folded with art' and then arranges the package on a large platter. Then he surrounds it with big glazed crayfish on a bed of parsley with an '*entourage*' of carp roes prepared 'in the usual way' (*selon la règle*).

'Now' – he continues ominously – now, just before serving, he impales the sturgeon with eight *hâtelets* in aspic prepared 'in the customary way' (as indicated in the recipe for *salmon à l'impérial*), and serves it with mayonnaise and *ravigote* sauces. And as for the *hâtelets*, they impale shrimp and carp roe.

But what is an *hâtelets*? Carême doesn't think he needs to explain, but he shows many of them, in his illustrations. They are metal skewers, around eight inches long with ornamental handles at the top. And Carême was very proud of them. Speaking, it seems, from the heart, in a passage about cockscombs in the chapter on ragouts and garnishing, he boasts: 'Young cooks ought to exercise the greatest care in the preparation of cockscomb garnishes: they have become my work's most beautiful ornament; they give elegance to our *hâtelets*, which make our *grosses pièces* so sumptuous.'[3]

He kids you not. The king of classic cooks, author of recipes of intimidating elaboration and refinement, a master seemingly triumphant in his professional success, is bragging about decorative skewers holding cockscombs. With a baroque range of elaborately contrived oddments stuck on them, they bristle on almost all his dishes. They are his trademark innovation.

They also offer us a glimpse of the tempestuous world concealed behind the *calme*, *luxe* and *volupté* of Carême's recipes and the festive culinary utopia for which he intended them. In a footnote two pages before his preening *remarque* on coxcomb *hâtelets*, he confides ruefully that his *hâtelets* are a defence against a rampant gastronomic crisis:

> For many years, the culinary art has been in steady decline. I have called attention to this decadence in my works, without having stopped its sad effects. Not since the renaissance of French cuisine have we served so few *entrées* per guest in the opulent houses of Paris. We are serving eight instead of the dozen we should be providing. But such is the spirit of this century. One eats to live. There you have it. So bending to the parsimony that this way of life demands, I have found it more suitable, in order to save our science from shipwreck, to serve four *grosses pièces* with four *entrées* (something we have never done at any time before), rather than two *grosses pièces* with six *entrées*: through this new combination, my *grosses pièces* have balanced out the reduced number of *entrées,* with the additional result that, the *grosses pièces* and *entrées* now always served on oval dishes have created a need for new ragouts, so that these *entrées* and *grosses pièces* can be served with greater variety and elegance. The addition of my new *hâtelets* has given dignity to this new *service*.

Brave, humbled Carême has staved off professional shipwreck and shame by shuffling major dishes and minor ones, adding ragouts as ballast to his oval platters and tricking out his imperial sturgeons with *hâtelets*. But this lamentation makes sense only in the light of a much more fundamental crisis in elite dining than the reduction of *grosses pièces* from twelve to eight. And here we enter the dark and stormy night of the shift from the way rich people in France had eaten for more than two hundred years to the utterly different way French gentry and everyone else in the West began to eat some time in the nineteenth century and continues to eat today. I am talking about the gradual yet tempestuous switch from *service à la française*, French service, to *service à la russe*, Russian service.

French service is the central focus of the last book of the greatest of modern French food historians, Jean-Louis Flandrin (the mentor of those learned early Symposiasts Mary and Philip Hyman). In his technical and strenuous study, *L'ordre des mets*, Flandrin gave an accurately chaotic picture of an unsurvivably grandiose banqueting style conducted, like a grand opera, in three or more acts called *services*, services.[4]

French service was a pan-European phenomenon. Indeed, the front cover of Flandrin's book is a painting of a dinner given by the future Austrian emperor Joseph II at Frankfurt in 1764. Guests haven't sat down yet but the table is completely arrayed with the first *service*. Around the edge are place settings for twelve. Inside these covers are an equal number of covered silver serving dishes. Guests will have just entered the room and been surprised and delighted with the display, which included a silver centrepiece holding what look like coloured glass balls. Carême's *pièces montées* were far more spectacular but the Frankfurt dinner had the same dramatic visual purpose.

We don't know what was in those silver tureens, but soups or perhaps different dishes also called *potages* are likely in the first service. Flandrin reprints a circular menu for a four-*service souper* hosted by Louis XV at the chateau of Choisy on Thursday, 21 April 1757. The menu had a revolving circular cover with one quadrant cut through so that a diner could see one service at a time by turning the top disk. This preserved the element of surprise, from service to service. But experienced diners familiar with the rules of French service could anticipate at least the categories of food canonically prescribed for each service: *potages*, *entreés*, *entremets*, *rôts*, which were not roasts in our sense but spitroasted meats, often small birds.

For our purpose today, it should be enough to know that French service involved successive flights of many dishes without break. Imagine a tasting menu of twelve unrelated dishes all served at once. And then another flight of twelve dishes. And another. How could any diner make sense of it all? And even when these dishes were put on the table under glass bells (*cloches*), they were usually cold by the time a guest could taste them.

Russian service simplified the diner's life, replacing the polyphonic machinery of French service with a linear progression of first course, main course, salad, cheese, and sweet dessert – what we would recognize as a meal today. But Russian service also greatly reduced the potential for dramatic presentation of food. The table itself was no longer a 12-ring circus, repopulated completely with new 'acts' several times in the course of an evening.

Carême opposed Russian service. It threatened to destroy his flamboyant world. He fought a rearguard action against it until his early death. But you would barely notice this reading his florid masterpiece, which seldom mentions the function his recipes played on the tables of the antiquated banquets he staged. Was he deliberately ignoring the revolution in food service taking place all around him? Or did he assume that his readers knew all about it and would understand that a dish like sturgeon à *l'impériale* with its *hâtelets* was intended to be the gaudy centre of a throng of dishes on a French-service tabletop. It would have lost its point in a Russian service meal. Sliced in the kitchen and served on individual plates by waiters to individual diners, the sturgeon would arrive still hot but shorn of its sculptural magic, and of its *hâtelets*.

The complete triumph of Russian service, something Vladimir Putin has perversely neglected to claim as a victory for Slavic values in the decadent West, has made it difficult for most people today to look at Carême's encyclopedic masterwork for what it was: a handbook of dishes to be combined in groups on the same table as loci of edible architecture in French service. Instead, we look at those recipes and see them as a database of heritage food, something still relevant to us today, a relic, but an ancestral relic. Because he virtually eliminated the historical context of his recipes, Carême insured his own immortality. After his physical demise, a process of blind hagiography and misreading established Carême as the father of classic French cuisine – a pioneer – instead of its last true practitioner.

The slimming of haute cuisine continued under the modernizing leadership of a succession of nineteenth-century chefs, until it reached its last, superficially down-to-earth codification in *Le Guide culinaire – aide-memoire de cuisine pratique* of Auguste Escoffier.[5] This *'colossale besogne'*, with its 5000 concise recipes, remained the Bible of haute cuisine well into the postwar period and it is still studied by chefs wanting to ground themselves in classic (and now virtually extinct) French cooking. What they find in Escoffier is a Janus-faced compendium, respectfully revising the past but not fully committed to a new path. This ambivalence is openly declared in the four prefaces Escoffier wrote to successive editions of the book, which is still in print today.

In the preface of 1902, Escoffier saluted Carême and stressed the lasting importance of the fundamentals of the cuisine he established, but on the same page he wrote of making 'profound modifications' to bring classic cuisine in touch with the necessities of the 'ultra-rapid life' of today. And what is the first thing of these modifications and the only specific one he mentions: 'Before all else, I was led by the force of circumstance to suppress the *socles*. And, more generally, after abandoning Carême's cherished plinths, he eliminated the 'sumptuous presentations' of his predecessors.[6]

Escoffier explains his method more fully in the preface to the third edition of 1912. He has jettisoned not only *socles*, but also decorative borders and *hâtelets*. The number of garnishes has been reduced to three or four at the most, they will all be edible, and he recommends, in a silent bow to Russian service, that they be passed separately along with sauces, except at truly grand banquets. This has the advantage of making it easier to serve food that is hotter, lighter and healthier. For a moment, it is as though we are listening to Paul Bocuse extolling the virtues of the nouvelle cuisine. Bocuse would also have said something about his food being less stodgy than what came before. And even Escoffier seems to lean in this direction, when he insists that 'simplicity doesn't exclude beauty'.[7] But he also says that he has insisted on preserving 'a throng of dishes' abandoned by the modern repertoire but which any cook worthy of the name ought to know about so that he can recreate them when the occasion arises.

Here and elsewhere, Escoffier can sound a bit defensive about forsaking Carême and his world of culinary theatre and orotund garnishing. But to the modern eye, the recipes in the *Guide Culinaire*, by and large, do not seem streamlined and radically simple at all, except when they are directly compared with similar dishes in Carême. And then it becomes clear how much has been left out (and how many recipes are recent inventions, some of them imported from outside France, such as *Irish-Stew de mouton*).

Dozens of Carême's dishes have been silently dropped, including many created in homage to Napoleon. Sturgeon, as well as salmon, *a l'imperiale*, have vanished. But salmon coulibiac, salmon Riga and even cadgery make the cut.

Most revealing of all are the differences between Carême's and Escoffier's version of dishes with the same name. Carême's *filet de boeuf à la financière moderne* (!) is spit-roasted and dressed on a *ragout à la financière*, composed of a pound of truffles sweated in Madeira and then added to a *financiere* sauce (a 'small' sauce produced by combining *sauce espagnole*, the brown mother sauce, with lean ham, pepper, thyme, bay leaf, mushroom and truffle peelings, consommeé and dry Madeira) embellished with mushrooms and medium cockscombs as well as rooster kidneys, butter, tiny chicken quenelles, little *escalopes de foie gras* and lamb sweetbreads.[8] The assembled dish is additionally garnished with 'pretty' white cockscombs and big rooster kidneys.

In the Escoffier version, the beef is not spitroasted but slowly pot-roasted (*poélé*) in a covered casserole on a bed of vegetables, then garnished with veal or veal quenelles, mushroom buttons, cockscombs and rooster kidneys, thinly sliced truffle and olives, turned and blanched. There are no foie gras *escalopes* or lamb sweetbreads. There is also no ragout and no decorative garnish of cockscombs and rooster kidneys, both of which made sense only in an elaborate, French-service presentation. The *sauce financière* is a straightforward combination of reduced *espagnole* and Madeira spiked with truffle essence.

With such shortcuts, Escoffier tried to have it both ways. He posed as a radical but saved the essence of tradition. His prefaces put the best face they could on this, but he did not fool a new generation of chefs, trained in the kitchen of Fernand Point at Vienne south of Lyons. In the 1960s and 1970s, they opened their own restaurants in a France that had finally recovered from two world wars, a depression and a long postwar recovery. Michel Guérard, Paul Bocuse, the brothers Troisgros and Roger Vergé – these chefs re-examined French culinary tradition, throwing out garnishes almost completely, reducing sauces to their essence, so to speak, embracing Japanese plating and exotic ingredients from everywhere. They narrowly missed getting laughed out of business because of their passion for kiwifruit. But most of all, they deconstructed the glorious past of French cooking and invented a new, playful, ironic way of thinking about food, which spread all over the world, inspiring satellite nouvelle cuisines from Manila to Munich.

Bocuse got famous for cooking a sea bass inside a pastry shell that looked like a sea bass, a fish within a fish, afloat in *sauce choron* – a tomato-flavoured béarnaise, which is to say, a variant of a classic steak sauce served with a fish.

Guérard took vegetable purees that Carême would have used for adding colour to his fugal extravaganzas and let them shine on their own. He served a stunning and witty goose dish at his gritty debut restaurant just outside Paris, Le Pot-au-feu, *filet d'aile d'oie fraîche grillé saignant*. This was a goose breast (not a wing, *aile* means white meat of poultry in France) off the bone and, unlike almost all goose served in France, not preserved in goose fat, not confit but 'fresh.' And Guérard prepared it like steak, grilled, bloody rare (*saignant*), for two.

Then Guérard got famous for the wrong reason. *Cherchez la femme.* His wife, the heiress to a palatial spa in Southwest France, persuaded him to take an interest in healthy food and weight reduction. 'We will not get old and fat together,' she told a French journalist. To lure customers to the spa, Guérard wrote an international bestseller called *Cuisine Minceur*, which purported to let you eat great French food and lose weight. It had been hard enough to understand the tricky concept of nouvelle cuisine before *Cuisine Minceur*, but after it came out, the myth of nouvelle cuisine as a lo-cal version of Escoffier was impossible to eradicate. The nouvelle cuisine survived and conquered, but it was never adequately explained by the men who created it. Did they even understand how clever they had been? We will never know, because they haven't tried to say what was in their heads, beyond an oversimplified spiel about sauces without flour and a lightness distilled from French traditional cooking.

There was, of course, a superficial truth in the spiel. The nouvelle cuisine chefs were all students of tradition, which they undoubtedly manipulated brilliantly. Even the name nouvelle cuisine was a direct echo of the name given to an innovative band of French chefs in the 1740s, as onetime Symposiast Stephen Mennell taught us. But the young Turks of the 1970s were not food historians and didn't theorize in public or reliably reveal the sources of their dishes.

Roger Vergé was happy to take credit himself for the calf's ear he shocked people with at the Moulin de Mougins, even though he likely knew that both Carême and Escoffier had published several recipes for *oreilles de veau*. But Vergé's calf's ear was an unadorned dark organ on a bare plate, whereas Carême tricked out *oreilles de veau tortue* coquettishly with truffles and, in the cavity of each ear, he placed a garnish of cockscombs, kidneys and mushrooms.[9] One of six Escoffier recipes for calf's ear was an even more rococo *oreilles de veau tortue* than Carême's.[10]

Did Roger Vergé have these traditional recipes in mind? We will never know. Perhaps the offputting single ear he served to me in 1977 was meant as an in-joke for gourmets steeped in the traditional culinary literature. It does seem improbable that one day, out of the blue, he simply decided that calf's ear would make an interesting experiment.

If the *vedettes* of the nouvelle cuisine confused people by camouflaging their postmodern ideas behind a scrim of claims about health and weight loss, they were in a long tradition of chefs who did not communicate straightforwardly. But the cabal of worldbeating cooks who followed them into the limelight cast by The World's 50 Best Restaurants list, have been the reverse of reticent.

This latest group of chefs came together because of their interest in using science to inspire them in the kitchen. They convened in 1992 at a conference centre in Sicily at the invitation of the Oxford physicist and founding Symposiast Nicholas Kurti and of the French writer on food and science Hervé This, who many of you will recall made a brief and apprehensive appearance at the Symposium in 2006, during the *ancien regime* of Carolin Young. He fled perfidious Albion on the same day he had flow in from Paris to deliver his plenary address in this building.

At the 1992 conference in Sicily, in collaboration with foodminded scientists, chefs including Heston Blumenthal, later a Symposiast, and the Spanish-Catalan Ferran Adria decided to call the scientifically informed food approach they were taking in their restaurants 'molecular gastronomy'. This turned out to be a mistake, or at least, a public relations error. It confused the general public and earned Blumenthal *et al.* ridicule and hostility. Before long, the group announced they wanted to be known as culinary modernists.

Both Blumenthal and Adria have been outspoken, clear and unmisleading about their food and their ideas. Adria, in particular, has shared more information than, perhaps, any cook in the history of food. Every dish he ever served at El Bulli from 1983 to 2011, in an unprecedented stretch of creativity, has been documented in eleven volumes of recipes, photographs, discourses on method and service, on scientific procedures, sourcing of ingredients. In comparison to the chefs I have been discussing, Adria is a paragon of transparency. But even he has not managed to make his case to the world.

But then the world mostly never got to eat at El Bulli, so it depended on press reports, which fed the reflexive anti-science bias of many traditional gastronomes. And this prejudice crystallized around one narrow corner of Adria's repertoire that was easy to describe and to lampoon. I speak of the *espumas,* the foams of pure flavour he would pump out of siphons.

Journalists seeking to explain what was going on at El Bulli fastened on those foams as a shorthand for dealing with the constantly shifting target of Adria's menu. Ferran Adria became the foam man. Adria was a spectacular success, and a tireless communicator, but he failed to eradicate the twin public-relations stigmata of foam and of molecular gastronomy. Fortunately for him and for all the other miscommunicating chefs, there is a truth squad committed to setting the record straight. And we, my fellow food historians, are they.

27

Our job is to disperse the smoke and fog left by chefs, to scrutinize the shifty record they have left. And unlike other historians, we can re-enter the culinary past with all our senses in our own kitchens. In this digital age, Carême's cuisine, his kitchen, is only a few clicks away, cybernetically alive even on popular cooking sites. For example, the online version of the popular magazine *Marie Claire* offers you his recipe for *Pascaline d'agneau,* an Easter dish of baroque complexity, a weird fossil from the vanished tables of French service. It is a dizzy fantasy of decorative food presentation fit for Napoleon but available online to food historians or anyone else with four lamb's heads to hand and lots of time. I have just posted the URL to the *Marie Claire* text on Twitter at #pascalinerecipe.[11]

And that, ladies and gentlemen, is communication.

Notes

1. 'Russia, Carême, and the Culinary Arts', *The Slavonic and East European Review*, 73.4 (October 1995), pp. 691-715.
2. Only three of the five volumes of *L'art de la cuisine française* (Paris: Au Comptoir des Imprimeurs-Unis, 1847) were written by Carême before his death in 1833. A colleague, Armand Plumerey, prepared the final two.
3. Carême, vol. 3, p. 143.
4. Paris: Odile Jacob, 2002. And in English, *Arranging the Meal* (Berkeley: University of California Press, 2007).
5. Published in four editions between 1903 and 1921.
6. *Le Guide culinaire – aide-memoire de cuisine pratique*, Fourth Ed. (Paris: Flammarion), p. vi.
7. Escoffier, p. ix.
8. For *filet de boeuf à la financière moderne*, see vol. 3, pp. 282-83; for *ragout à la financière*, see pp. 246-47.
9. Carême, vol. 4, pp. 72-74. Plumerey edited this volume.
10. Escoffier, p. 480.
11. '*Têtes d'agneau à la pascaline, dites aussi pascaline d'agneau*', *Marie Claire* <http://www.cuisineetvinsde-france.com/,tetes-d-agneau-a-la-pascaline-dites-aussi-pascaline-d-agneau,55502.asp> [accessed 1 June 2015].

The Evolution of Cookbooks in the Digital Age

Ken Albala and Christine Larson

The past twenty years have witnessed a revolution in communication comparable in impact to the invention of the printing five hundred years earlier. Often, it has been cookbooks, rather than novels or other more 'important' cultural formats, that have served as the best bellwether of shifting societal attitudes and responses to new technologies. In examining the response of cookbooks to technological changes past, present and future, we can understand more about the cultural importance of both cooking and communication.

At first blush, the response of cookbook publication may seem a classic case of new technologies quickly rendering old forms obsolete. In fact, in key historic periods, cookbooks have offered an instance of the persistence, rather than obsolescence, of older technologies and traditions in the face of disruptive innovation. Thus, before we can understand the impact of technology of the present and future of cookbooks, we need to understand the history of technological change, publishing and the dissemination of recipes in much earlier periods, starting a mere twenty-five years after the publication of Gutenberg's Bible. In 1475, another bible of sorts was published: Platina's *De honesta voluptate,* which quickly became a bestseller among an increasingly literate public, clamouring for a more earthly kind of sustenance. The book quickly went through a dozen editions and was promptly translated into Italian, French and German. An English edition appeared, titled Epulario, under the pseudonym Rosselli.

By all accounts, the book was a runaway success, firmly associating Platina's name with fine dining – despite his intentions otherwise. Within a century, the printed cookbook had for the most part supplanted handwritten cookery manuscripts.

Surprisingly, however, handwritten cookbooks did persist in an important grassroots form: as personal collections of family recipes (some of which were copied from printed cookbooks). With a family manuscript of recipes no longer strictly necessary and required once printed cookbooks became commercially available, these family collections took on a new, more personal importance. Recipe manuscripts thus continued to hold a viable and valuable cultural position as a means of transferring family wisdom to one's progeny. For instance, Martha Washington kept a personal family cookbook, dating back to the seventeenth century, for some fifty years, handing the book to her granddaughter in 1799 as a wedding gift. The book moved through the family for nearly a hundred years before the family presented it to the Historical Society of Pennsylvania. (And you can buy a print copy online for $19.95). This and other examples demonstrate how technology rarely presents a simple story of one media replacing another outright. Rather, we see a complex interaction between old and new technologies, which in the case of cookbooks demonstrates societal attitudes and practical considerations around culture, society and food.

Today, similar patterns are playing out as print culture becomes digital culture. Much of the book industry was somewhat sheltered from the impact of information and communication technologies until the introduction of the Kindle in 2007; only recently has book publishing in general started to experience similar pressures as newspapers, music or other media which have suffered major transformation in the face of low cost digital production and distribution technologies. But cookbooks offer a special case: because recipes and cooking texts had long occupied a boundary-crossing space between magazines and books, they offer unique properties suiting them to adaption to interactive technologies early on.

Epicurious offered an early version of what editors thought the public would want as digital food offerings. Rather than putting each of its food-oriented magazines online, Condé Nast created a new brand, *Epicurious*, in 1995, drawing content from *Gourmet, Bon Appetit* and *Condé Nast Traveler.* While the move was prescient in many ways – after all, the first popular graphical Web browsers, Mosaic and Netscape had launched only a year or two before.

Like other early entrants in the Internet recipe space, ranging from recipe exchange databases to online providers like AOL and Prodigy to publications like *Reader's Digest*, the creators of *Epicurious* saw recipes as a key driver and a 'killer app' that would entice internet users, especially female users, to increasingly abandon print. Understanding that intrepid chefs would soon be able to share their own recipes, these companies tried to assert their authority by providing searchable, tested recipes on a mass scale. In many ways, then, recipes offered the perfect interactive content; rather than simply offering printed recipes online, many companies stored them in databases, allowing users to search by ingredient, health information or style.

What the early proponents of Internet recipes could not have anticipated, however, was that the sheer volume of information might prove stultifying rather than democratizing. Between the vast volume of recipes from traditional branded companies and the mass proliferation of cooking blogs that developed as Web publishing became dramatically easier with the rise of Web 2.0 technologies, users now may find it virtually impossible to find and trust recipes of high quality: Google 'lasagna recipes' and more than a million choices come up.

If Conde Nast had known in 1995 how online recipes would develop, they might well have stuck with their individual magazine brands rather than creating *Epicurious*. Media economists have observed that in an environment of massive choice, established brands often do better than newly minted ones because trusted brands offer a proxy for quality in the market for 'experience goods' (that is, goods that have to be fully used to up for their full quality to be known: you don't know if you really like a book until you read its ending; you don't know the quality of recipe until you've made and tasted it).

Fortunately, *Epicurious* had a 'first mover advantage', being very early to market and having time to establish itself from early on. As floods of recipes entered the online space, what had promised to be a democratic platform where home cooks and celebrity chefs alike could post their recipes became in fact a maelstrom of information. At first, this seemed like the end of the traditional gatekeepers – literary agents and powerful cookbook editors like Knopf's Judith Jones, who published Julia Child, who could make or break a book and change the way Americans eat. Rather, particularly with the rise of blogs after the turn of the twenty-first century, the crowd seemed to have replaced the agent and editor as arbiters of taste. Searching for that lasagna recipe, for instance, will yield the most popular entries, which may or may not be the most delicious. But as one recipe or author or source becomes popular (particularly before the field becomes crowded with wannabes), it becomes more likely to be displayed and clicked, and so on.

Sociologist Robert Merton calls this network influence the 'Matthew effect', where those who have been given much attention receive ever more of it. As Microsoft researcher Duncan Watts demonstrated with music, 'hits' often have less to do with high quality than with social influence; people rank highly what others have ranked highly, regardless of quality or taste. And as we have seen first hand, network technologies and search algorithms strongly favour early entries to the market. A few years ago a story about beef bungs was blogged on Ken Albala's *Food Rant*, posting an image that was probably one of the first online. Today, if you search on beef bung, the blog comes up first, for no other reason than it was first in line. That blog post is still the most consistently trafficked on the blog, getting about thirty or forty hits a day.

Not surprisingly, Internet users quickly realized the difficulty of sorting through recipes and finding high quality ones, and began to tire of the standard recipe search. They turned increasing attention to bloggers who managed with dogged determination to create a unique voice for themselves online. The most popular of them, of course, sought out book deals: for example, Julie Powell, whose cooking of Julia Child's recipes landed her a book and major motion picture deal. Thus, the crowd itself has generated from the maelstrom of recipes a new gatekeeping process, even replacing to some extent traditional literary agents. In some instances, the voice of the people seems to be a better predictor of sales than a single scout agent. And yet, though the crowd is now necessary for success, it is not sufficient; in the early twenty-first century, the traditional book deal remained the key to legitimization, not only because it offered more secure financial remuneration, through advances, but also because such books offer the imprimatur of quality in a market where quality is a large unknown. Thus, some oddballs managed to open up a print market that had been dominated by TV-driven cookbooks, superstar chefs and celebrities.

Surprisingly, though, one trend that many expected to emerge has not played out. Many expected that the e-book revolution would also democratize cookbook publishing by sweeping away the expensive printed full-colour cookbook. Had that happened, we might today see commercial publishers offering a wider range of cookbooks and profiting from the diversity of offerings. Instead, what has happened is a certain bifurcation of the market into high end, expensive, glossy colour cookbooks and a new boom in small publishing and self-publishing.

Startlingly, despite the early entry of recipes into the digital content world, print cookbooks continue to thrive. Although sales of print nonfiction books in general have dropped twenty per cent between 2007 and 2014, print cookbook sales have actually *grown* an impressive eleven per cent.

Why should this be? We would argue that digital cookbooks still aren't aesthetically pleasing despite the development of interactive apps and embedded content. There may be an important physical connection between the tactile, sensory nature of cooking and the flipping of pages, scribbling in margins, even staining for posterity, that can only happen with physical cookbooks. Further, if cookbooks are both a practical guide and a repository of future knowledge, one has to wonder what happens when the devices on which one reads the book become obsolete, as happened when music transitioned from cassettes to CDs to iTunes. It is completely conceivable that a cookbook on the Kindle or Nook may be unreadable in a decade. As a medium for recording and preserving favourite meals, then, the print cookbook offers enormous advantages that e-books can't duplicate and perhaps even undermine.

As sales of commercial print cookbooks expanded after 2007, so did an opposite development – self-publishing. In 2010, Amazon began offering self-published authors on its Kindle platform seventy per cent of sales revenues from their books, dramatically more than one can expect from a print book (which may yield seven to ten per cent in royalties for the author). A decade ago, to self publish, you had to contract a designer, an editor, a production manager, a printer, a warehouse and maybe a publicity agent, all financed out of your own pocket. This worked well for a handful of authors, including Amelia Salzman's *Santa Monica Farmers Market Cookbook*. But for Salzman, success came largely from dedicating herself to publicizing the book as a nearly full-time job; for people who want to research, test and develop recipes, this effort may represent a poor investment of expertise. But as self-publishing has become simpler, more widespread and less costly, the economics have started to look more attractive. After all, if you keep seventy per cent or a hundred per cent (if you don't go through Amazon and do everything yourself) of every sale, rather than less than ten per cent, your economic calculations become very different.

As another option, then and now, you can hire a company that prints on demand. Albala with coeditor Gary Allen tested this tactic with a book of short stories on cannibalism, replete with recipes. As you might imagine, this proved a tough sell to traditional publishers. So they contacted a company called Booksurge, which Amazon acquired in 2005 and merged with CreateSpace, its on-demand service provider. With this service, the Thyestian Press was formed. Costs were low, there was virtually no marketing, but the book still clears about $100 a year. Perhaps this doesn't sound impressive, but consider that ten times as many books would have had to be sold to earn that amount through traditional publishing.

Meanwhile, the hard and fast lines between publishers have been blurred in the past twenty years. University presses which once only published serious academic topics now publish food and cookbooks. Today you might see cookbooks from tiny outfits that do both scholarly and popular titles – say, Preston, or Berg before it was swallowed up by Bloomsbury. At the same time, library market publishers also began to seek popular audiences and sought out authors who might otherwise never have been able to publish with a large house. The series Albala edited with Greenwood was much like this before it was purchased by its competitor ABC-CLIO. Albala's current food series series with Rowman and Littlefield fits in the same category.

The point is that while sales of traditional cookbooks have risen, large commercial publishers have not opened up the market to new authors as much as smaller publishing options have. Such publishers are certainly not seeing the sales volume of large publishers, but somehow find they can make a profit selling to libraries or on Amazon. The larger point is that these developments, hinging largely on the lower cost of book production and distribution, have allowed a different cadre of authors to get into print, though often in a smaller way than in the past.

Still, however, we have the problem of a crowded market. Thousands of cookbooks can be found self-published through Amazon, and, frankly, many of them are garbage. But for a small few, authors can build a brand unto themselves and make a decent profit; this is already happening in romance and science fiction. For these authors, developing close, personal relationships with readers will be a core of their business and a key to their success. Thus, just as handwritten recipe manuscripts persisted in some form long after Gutenberg created a disruptive technology, so too have print cookbooks and other older technologies continued even as digital technologies offer new possibilities.

Our predictions for the future of cookbooks grow from observations of digital books and societal trends. On one hand, we feel the few big cookbook publishers will become increasingly hesitant to sign or promote untested or 'midlist' authors: continuing to publish celebrity chefs and heavy coffee table books. On the other hand, the business will be blown apart on the day that a beautifully designed and photographed e-book can be easily made at home and sold on Amazon for profit. That day is almost here.

Meanwhile, advances in what the industry calls 'enhanced ebooks' incorporating multimedia, images and unique interactive qualities could create a much more seamless experience. There is no reason why a good, inexpensive, authoritative cookbook for tablets cannot exist. For those of us who find tablets unwieldy, it's entirely possible we could see 3-D images and movies demonstrating techniques. Such a product might also have voice activation helping to simplify searches. For our lasagna recipe, we might ask our digital assistant to find recipes using fresh dough or sauce from scratch, or a shorter, simpler version. Such easy customizations might address what we feel is a great pitfall of digital books: they cannot gauge your skill level equipment or number of ingredients at hand. A recipe should encourage readers to experiment, to substitute ingredients, to play it by ear.

Perhaps, then, the cookbook of the future will not have an author, but a programmer. Perhaps it will know what pots you have, what kind of oven you use and what your tastes generally are. It may respond to dietary restrictions. As long as recipes are thoroughly tested, the technology exists to provide more and better recipes in more compelling ways. The future of the cookbook will be interactive, intuitive and personalized for every individual reader.

This way of cooking might offer something of an antidote to the call of convenience. The net effect should be exactly the opposite of what the past half-century of convenience foods has done to our skill set. Instead of keeping people out of the kitchen so they can buy mass-produced convenience foods, beautiful, compelling, easy to read or use digital cookbooks may offer new possibilities to readers and writers. All this would gently lead readers to new technologies and even new forms of cultural memory. And yet, as these more interactive or enhanced books gradually replace some print books, others will persist, if only for their sentimental values.

'Anything is possible!: *MasterChef,* World-Wide Illusion

Robert Appelbaum

A camera on a high overhead boom hovers over an island in the midst of a broad lake surrounded by mountains. Seated on the island is a magnificent seventeenth-century *palazzo*, whose steps lead down to the lake, and a huge, terraced Italianate garden, featuring stone-work follies, statuaries, hedge-work labyrinths, topiary evergreens and flourishing oaks. Percussive electronic music, at once familiar and exciting, plays in the background, as if informing us that a Jason Bourne-type figure, enacted by Matt Damon, was about to risk his life and crash a secret conspiracy of spies and thieves. The boom lowers to a terrace of the *palazzo,* where four youngish, meek, casually dressed people with the sun in their eyes stand opposite three older, more formally dressed men in sunglasses, one of them in a suit and tie, the others in blazers, posing there menacingly like Mafia bosses. The young people are being given instructions; they are being challenged to accomplish something that worries them. We are in the midst, in fact, of Series Four, Episode Twenty, of *MasterChef Italia*, and the four semi-finalists have to cook in the palazzo's kitchen, using local seafood as the main ingredient for three successive dishes each, an antipasto, a *primo* and a *secondo*.

The *MasterChef* franchise goes back to 1990, when it was shown on BBC One, but its current format, and worldwide success, only goes to 2005, when, after a hiatus of four years, the show was revamped with food entrepreneur Greg Wallace and chef John Torode as hosts, and shown on BBC Two. I was there, in the UK, not long after it started, and found not only myself and my wife getting hooked on it, but also many of my neighbours. One of the things that addicted us was the fact that unlike other series *MasterChef* was shown five days a week for eight successive weeks. Watching the show night after night we felt very much in the moment. It was as compelling as a major sports event. It was, in short, a species of reality television, making its own 'trans-reality', and getting us high on this trip away from the real.[1] But another thing that hooked us was the quality of the programme: this wasn't like so many other cooking shows we had seen. This one was expertly produced; it was intense yet jovial, featuring artful cooking combined with affability. Moreover, the hosts were enormously articulate; they knew how to describe and analyze food and cooking with a clarity I had never encountered before. When we watched the show we not only found that we were learning something about cooking, but also that the competitors and the hosts were learning something too. We were all together in this, it seemed: the hosts, the producers, the competitors and the audience.

A few years later *MasterChef Australia* came out. Although the basic elements of the British program were retained, the format was much revamped. The programme was larger, more theatrical. This one showed six nights a week. It began with fifty contestants, chosen out of an applicant pool of 7000. It had four hosts at first – all of them also articulate and lively personalities – and it was shot in a very large facility, a converted warehouse, with a balcony above and a tasting room in the rear. The pace of the competition was slowed down to introduce more kinds of competitions and intermittent steps toward elimination, including 'immunity pin' contests. A big part of the programme focussed on the personal lives of the competitors, and on their interactions with one another in the dormitory that was set up from them. *MasterChef Australia* was a feel-good show, celebrating the Australian character, its kindness, hopefulness and sociality, the unity of feeling among Aussies even in the midst of its cultural diversity and its competitive capitalist economy. Good food, in this programme, almost seemed as if it were an expression of a good soul, and advancing in the competition seemed for each individual not only a personal but also a collective effort. There was a lot of hugging and hand-holding, as well as confessions and tears and reassuring sentiments, not to mention hints about friendships that had taken an romantic turn. It was a huge hit, night after night coming in number one or two in Australian television ratings, and its finale becoming one of the most watched television programmes in Australian history. It would go on to be shown in syndication, with dubbing or subtitling as needed, in thirty-four countries.

In 2010 *MasterChef USA* debuted, featuring a mixture of the British and Australian formatting. Like the Australian show, *MasterChef USA* was large and theatrical, shot in a large opulently renovated warehouse, with a balcony so that contestants could watch, cheer, or – as was newly the case in the American show – taunt one another from above. It introduced some new format elements, for example a ritual of auditions to start off each series, where every plausible contestant had not only to make a very good dish of food but also make a spectacle of his or her personality. But like the British show, it emphasized individual competitiveness. Or even worse: it encouraged aggression. The American show was more about division than about unity; more about winning or losing than exploring the nature of fine dining or the camaraderie of cookery; more about making demands on oneself in order to succeed as an entrepreneur than about hospitality or the promotion of fine dining. It introduced a subtext of game theory, encouraging contestants to try cynically to 'game' one another in order to win, and often focusing on personal grudges that arose between contestants. (It also introduced the novelty of having youthful female competitors cooking in short skirts and high heels.) This programme, hosted by the histrionic team of Gordon Ramsay, restaurateur Joe Bastianich and Chicago chef Graham Elliot, was also a hit, though by no means as great a hit as the Australian programme.

By now *MasterChef* is shot in over forty countries, from China, India and Israel to France, Morocco and Brazil. Most of the shows I have been able to see adopt the American format, though each in its own way. *MasterChef Sweden* is a very sullen show, shot in a small studio. One of the hosts absolutely never smiles, and when contestants lose they act humiliated. *MasterChef Canada* is good-natured but very business-like; two of its hosts lack spontaneity, a third, who has the Bastianich role of playing the tough guy, seems to force his spontaneity, and some contestants seem uncertain how to behave in front of a camera. *MasterChef Italy* is over the top, almost a parody of itself, as is much Italian television. It is famous for the insults the hosts hurl at the contestants. 'Why do you give me food that makes me shit?' says one of the hosts to a contestant. 'You are an asshole', says another to the same person. 'I am convinced', says another host to a thirty-something aged woman with big red eyeglasses, 'that if you made this at home for your husband he would kick you out'. But there is a warmth in the programme as well, and the cooking I saw in one of the finals was the best cooking I have seen by any amateurs.

What does all this mean? The *MasterChef* franchise is owned by The Shine Group, an international production company based in London and chaired by Elisabeth Murdoch, the daughter of media mogul Rupert Murdoch. (Shine recently merged with the Endemol production company, makers of *Big Brother* worldwide, to become Endemol Shine.) Whatever it was at first, *MasterChef* is now the expression of a global media system which reaches into all continents and into many different kinds of national cultures; it appears in countries run by plutocratic dictators as well countries run by social democrats, in countries where the media are heavily censored as well as countries which guarantee free speech; it lands into countries where good food is historically a national obsession, like China and France, and into countries where good food is historically an afterthought, like Israel and Great Britain. If giving and receiving food is a form of communication, then a subject that cries out for attention is the role of the food communicator in the mediatization of the global world order. Some obvious topics suggest themselves. One is the adaptation of a universal format to particular cultures. One can look at this adaptation as a triumph of the global over the local, as the format gets repeated again and again with only minor adjustments: *MasterChef* is now an exemplification of what Jean Baudrillard called the postmodern system of reproduction, as opposed to what could be called an earlier ('modern') system of production.[2] The opening credits of *MasterChef Saudi Arabia* are a replica of the opening credits of *MasterChef Australia,* with the same facial gestures of the contestants welcoming the viewers to the programme, with similar upbeat music. The opening episode of *MasterChef China* is a replica the opening episode of *MasterChef USA*. When contestants audition before the three judges, who play the roles established by the American hosts, the judges take a few beats to tell a contestant 'My answer is yes', or 'my answer is no' – saying everything in Chinese, of course, except for the words 'yes' and 'no', which they say in English as if lovingly or jokingly quoting the American show.

Technically, *MasterChef* is what the trade calls an 'unscripted' programme, but there is actually a good deal of scripting involved, both directly and indirectly. Directly, the show follows a careful protocol, with rigorous blocking and camera placement, many prepared speeches and a good deal of input from producers. (I have independently confirmed in conversations with individuals who have taken part in the shows that the production is very much staged.) Hosts, judges and contestants know what kind of words and deeds are expected from them; they self-edit in order to satisfy what the producers require of them: and when they fail, or when anything else happens that upsets the values and customs of the program, either the producers make them do it over again or the material gets deleted.

Much of the show's success depends on editorial and technical innovation. First off, the hosts do not talk directly to the camera; they talk to each other and to the contestants, and they do so when looking at one another. This person-to-person approach makes their remarks seem more sincere, as well as more dramatic. Secondly, the programme is heavily edited and busily jazzed up with interjected material. The British *MasterChef* uses a voice over to explain dishes and add atmospheric effects; it combines that voice with dramatic background music, which heightens the show's sense of seriousness. In addition, it adds single-shot sequences of contestants after they have completed a task or have been driven out of the competition. We hear about the contestants' feelings, their hopes and frustrations, and we look at their facial expressions and body language, which often tell a different story. The Australian *MasterChef* added other elements of production. Most importantly, it added the technique of splicing in post-contest interviews with contestants, where in the present tense, in the midst of a close-up, the contestants explain what they are doing and thinking at almost precisely the same time we are watching them compete in the contest. Part of the realism of the show depends on this illusion that we are privy to the contestants' innermost thoughts. Part of the drama of the programme depends on this too: a rhythm is built up of shots where the contestant competes, and shots were the contestant is thinking about competing and worrying about the outcome. This enhances the effect of making *MasterChef* into a show about character as well as about cooking. The staged insights into private thought elicits the viewers' sympathies with these characters as well, if also at time their antipathies. There are heroes and villains in many *MasterChef* sequences, as well as vulnerable types who suffer in front of us and maybe even on our behalf.

A full treatment of the *MasterChef* would have to deal with the spin-offs: *MasterChef Professional*, *Celebrity MasterChef*, *MasterChef Junior* and *MasterChef All-stars*. But for now I will confine the discussion to the main, original show, especially in its British, Australian and American versions, of which I have seen almost every episode through 2014.

One thing the original *MasterChef* seems to do is to celebrate cookery itself. But that is not quite right. *MasterChef* celebrates a certain *version* of cookery. Most obviously, it celebrates cookery as *competition*. That means it examines cookery as an activity whose processes and outcomes can be rigorously judged. If you don't believe that, you cannot watch the show. You must believe that cookery is genuinely competitive, and that the judging of cookery is a valid, even objective enterprise. Nothing could be more antithetical to the spirit of *MasterChef* than the attitude of 'to each his own', or that 'there is no accounting for taste', or even that taste is relative to cultural and social values. Especially in countries like the United Kingdom and the United States, where food culture is a mish-mash of hybridities, the assumption must be made that at the highest level of critical judgment, British food, French food, Thai food, and so forth, are equally competitive with one another, and that this is no real divide so far as standards are concerned in food for different social classes – although, in fact, cultural partialities, social habits and professional preference inevitably enter into the tasting and the judging.

The purposes of competition, in any case, are multiple. For one can benefit from competing even if one doesn't win. Competition is sport: it is fun to participate in and fun to watch. Moreover, competition is a form of exercise; that is, it exercises one's skills, and thereby improves one's skills. And finally, being on television can be enjoyable – not for everyone of course, but those who make it onto programmes and thrive usually show themselves to be comfortable in front of cameras, even to blossom in front of them. But one can also think about the meaning of winning too. What does it meant to win *MasterChef*, or to come close to winning?

Some programmes offer what have come to be larger and larger awards for winning the series, thousands of dollars, a book contract, a car. But in smaller countries the awards tend to be token, and in the British series there is no monetary award at all. The winner gets a trophy. Many winners and runners-up also get new opportunities, of course, for example apprenticing in prominent restaurants, or being approached by business partners to open new ventures. And on the whole, most winners and runners-up have apparently found the experience of being on the programme life enhancing. But it is important to underscore that almost none of them find his or her life transformed in quite the way the programme would lead us to believe. (A judge in one of the European programmes told me that he and his colleague were very careful to tell contestants that they shouldn't set their hopes too high, whatever the hype surrounding the show.) *MasterChef* programmes develop narratives where people are shown to be determined to 'change their lives', to move from dead-end jobs or dissatisfaction – including dissatisfaction with high-end jobs like practicing medicine or law – to blazing careers doing something they love. Even in France, 'I need to change my life' is a mantra among *MasterChef* contestants early on. A big part of the life-change on almost all programmes is the development of a contestant from being an amateur to being a professional. By the rules of the game, at least in the English-language shows, all of the contestants are amateurs; they are either unemployed or working in some other capacity than as cooks. The implication is that they want to become professional chefs, and that this show is both teaching them how to do that and providing them with opportunities, including meeting, learning from and beginning to network with professionals. Being judged and winning means coming ever closer to the goal of professionalism and entrepreneurial independence. And there is no doubt what it means to be successful: it means to own

39

your own celebrated restaurant. It may even mean to own several celebrated restaurants, as many of the hosts actually do.

That, again, is seldom what happens.[3] The most melodramatic example comes from Season Three of *MasterChef America*. The winner was Christine Ha, a woman of Vietnamese descent from Houston who went blind in her twenties, after having earned a degree in business from the University of Texas. Ha was never going to follow the route the programme had laid out for contestants; she was never going to be a restaurant chef. Yet with the help of a seeing-eye assistant she was outstanding throughout the series. In the end, she wrote a cookbook, went back to the university, earned a degree in creative writing, worked as an editor for an obscure journal, published stories and poems in obscure journals, and in 2014 began work as the host of a cooking programme, on a Canadian non-profit network for the visually and hearing impaired. Meanwhile the runner-up on the programme was Josh Marks, an engaging young African-American from Chicago who was seven feet two inches tall. Within a year after his success on the programme, he was dead by suicide, having shot himself in the head.[4]

I find it encouraging to report on Christine Ha and very sad to have to report on the death of Josh Marks. But it points to some obvious and some not-so-obvious realities behind the facades of a reality TV programme like *MasterChef*. *MasterChef* creates a fantasy about what it means to be a successful professional. It generates a mystique about culinary excellence and with it a reassurance about the possibility of standards and goals and correspondent rewards in the world of food. It suffuses professional cookery with an aspirational aura, as if it were a kind of 'makeover' programme, and constructs simulacra of career development. But one thing it seldom does is create successful professional restaurateurs.

I don't for a second blame *MasterChef* for the death of Josh Marks. It appears that he was unable to cope with the stress of competing on TV, and that part of his problem was confusion about the reality in which he lived; he had become a celebrity, a simulacra of success but not the real thing; he is said to have told police officers after a violent incident of self-harming that he was possessed by Gordon Ramsay. Shortly before killing himself he was diagnosed with schizophrenia, and before then he had been diagnosed to be suffering from bipolar disorder.

I don't blame *MasterChef*, but *MasterChef* was part of Marks's problem. And it was part of his problem, apparently, because although *MasterChef* seldom creates successful restaurateurs, what it does create in abundance are minor celebrities. If you look at the results you find that many of the winners and runner-ups have gone on to become minor media personalities – the 'talent', as they are sometimes called in the trade. They produce books and blogs. They do cooking demonstrations. They appear from time to time on TV, including return visits to *MasterChef*, and they maintain a commercial presence on the Internet. They may even, like Ha, briefly host a TV programme. They may own catering companies or be the producers of brands of prepared food that their names help to sell; they may do special events. One winner of the UK *MasterChef*, Mat

Follas, after having opened a conventional restaurant that failed, now combines events, consultation and other activities with a two-day-a-week stint at a small restaurant in Dorset.[5] Mat Follas, in other words, has become a minor culinary talent, trading on his celebrity to earn an income, hard working perhaps in the food industry as a whole but not actually working as a full time chef. Meanwhile, Josh Marks, the odd man out, was unable to handle celebrity-hood, unable to deal with the difference of being a star in the media and just a person to himself, and so put a gun to his head.

What pleasures viewers get from watching *MasterChef* this *MasterChef* viewer finds it hard to say. Watching the programme is like watching a sport, but I seldom find myself rooting for someone to win with the enthusiasm I might invest in a sports team. The programme involves the vicarious pleasure of watching good food being cooked and eaten. I like to cook, and I like to watch people cook. I like to eat; and I like to watch people eat. It also involves education. I have learned a good deal about food from *MasterChef*, and I enjoy the challenge of imagining myself doing what the contestants do. What would I cook from that mystery box? Which ingredients would I identify from that stew? It would be convenient for me to claim that I enjoy those things but am indifferent to the special effects of the series, the melodramas of aspiration that get played out, the confrontations with judges, the visits to fabulous restaurants or strange locales, the background music, the personalities of the judges, the visits paid by celebrity chefs – but in fact, I confess that I enjoy most of these things as well. (I don't care for team challenges much, and especially those that include visits to military installations or television back lots.)

Still, I enjoy these things from a critical point of view, not just an adoring one, and I suspect that many viewers are the same. Is it not the case that though we find ourselves sympathizing with contestants, or at least some of them, and cheering them on, we are also made to know, by the programme itself, how hollow the whole process is? And aren't we supposed to find a certain satisfaction in seeing that? The programme teaches us a lesson that it at once harps upon and denies: these contestants are trying to short circuit the courses of their lives. They are trying to succeed in a profession without paying their dues. And few of them, we can see, actually have the wherewithal to succeed. Most of the contestants lack the skill, knowledge, physical stamina and drive to become professional chefs. Many of them have neither the need nor the nerve. Except at the very top end, working in kitchens is one of the worst paid professions in the Western world, and learning the ins and outs for most people takes many years of apprenticeship. Like some other reality programmes, *MasterChef* shows an alternative world, where people don't have to start at the age of sixteen washing dishes, or at eighteen going to cooking school, and then having to work double shifts at minimal wages. It shows a world where aspiration, pluck and television presence are more important than experience, ingenuity and labour.

It also shows a contrary reality, however. For the real winners in the show aren't the contestants, but the judges, hosts, and visiting chefs, and the system of dining they represent. My favourite example of how that works is negative, a situation that seems to arise at least once in every series on at least three continents. A contestant, not doing well or actually being eliminated, tells the camera or the judges, in tears, 'I am doing this for my kids. I want to show them that they can be anything they want to be. Anything is possible.' Now, since the contestant is losing or has just been eliminated, and is sobbing, the real lesson is the opposite. One cannot be anything one wants to be. Anything is not possible. For a lot of people the hard fact is that they will never be what they hoped. Going onto a television show to win a prize which itself is hollow, and then not even winning it, is an illustration of the fact that in the world of late capitalism, although aspiration is a nearly religious value, and everyone is encouraged to embrace it, aspiration is never really enough, and frequently ends up as a cause of disappointment.[6]

So there is a negative example. The contestants in the show are not, for the most part, the real winners, although they can go so far as to state publically that even when they lose, they have somehow won and proven themselves. But then there is the actual successful world of fine restaurants, which parades through the scenes of every *MasterChef* episode. Again, I believe that this differs from country to country. But it is notable how the *MasterChef* franchise has enabled networking among celebrity chefs around the world. It has made some stars into even bigger stars. It has made unknown chefs into known chefs. It has helped form a kind of fraternity among prominent chefs, a fraternity that may have been informally in place before, but which now has a media-fortified power. Especially in the UK, where Michelin stars are worshipped, the programme has confirmed the notion of a world hierarchy of restaurants and restaurateurs. It has made this hierarchy more visible to a wider public than ever before, and it has encouraged respect for this hierarchy. It has shown a wide public not only how hard most major chefs work, but how good they are. On the whole, the celebrity chefs are kind, congenial, articulate and generous, if also demanding. They know more about food and about cooking under pressure than most members of the public thought it was possible to know. And clearly they are very hard workers.

In the celebrity chef, as constructed by *MasterChef*, we thus find an ideal authority. A comparison might be made with a rock star or a movie star, but the celebrity chef is as even better sort of icon. One has access to a celebrity chef, even if the access is only virtual. A celebrity chef teaches us skills we can use, or hope to use, even on a daily basis, as well as attitude. Celebrity chefs encourage us, by and large, to embrace that which is creative without being tawdry, and that which is generous – hospitality, the making and serving of food – without hostility. In a world without heroes – where have you gone, Joe DiMaggio? – there are still Heston, Gordon and George, showing us how to filet a salmon and insisting that not all values and experiences are relative, that there is such a thing as excellence in the world, even in so humble a venue as a kitchen.

Yet between the ideal authority of the celebrity chef and the reality of both the contestants who strive and the viewers who observe the striving, there is an insuperable gap. I have given some negative and some positive examples of this: on the negative side, the failure of contestants to become what they claim they want to be, the death of Josh Marks, the insistence of losers that they are actually winners; on the positive side, the palpable success of hosts, judges and guest chefs, who are conferred not with an aura of aspiration but rather a benign and enviable authority, and whose own careers are shown to flourish all the more under the gaze of the camera and in accordance with the system of commercial confraternity that the media system encourages. What should we call this gap? My first choice is *fiction.* The difference between what actually happens and what we are shown to happen, or between the status of the aspiring contestants and the status of the celebrity chefs, seems to be reality itself; and it is. But it is reality itself, or maybe 'trans-reality' – as a fiction.

MasterChef is able to take us from the backstreets of London to the vistas of seaside Australia, from the inner lives of Americans trying to beat the system to the inner lives of mainland Chinese trying to prove themselves worthy of their parents. It takes us from our living room TVs to the most famous and glamorous restaurants in the world, and from the humdrum of our daily evening fare to fabulous four-course meals, prepared with the finest ingredients. But all the while, for all the pleasure and all the insight we get from the programme, we are really in a modern version of Plato's cave, where shadows play on a wall from a light source which we unable to look directly in the eye, and cast by a host of puppet-masters whose power over us we can only barely acknowledge.

Notes

1. See Jack Z. Bratich, 'Reality: Control Societies, New Subjects and the Powers of Transformation', in *Makeover Television: Realities Remodelled,* ed. Dana Heller (London: I.B. Tauris, 2007), pp. 6-22; *Trans-reality Television,* ed. Sofie van Bauwel and Nico Capentier (Lanham: Lexington, 2010); Beverley Skeggs and Helen Wood, *Reacting to Reality Television* (London: Routledge, 2010).

2. Jean Baudrillard, *Symbolic Exchange and Death,* trans. Iain Hamilton Grant (London: Sage, 1988). More specifics of the globalization of reality television, which are sometimes highly nuanced, are featured in the essays collected in *The Politics of Reality Television: Global Perspectives,* ed. Marwan M. Kraidy and Katherine Sender (London: Routledge, 2011).

3. Rather the reverse, as some argue. Contestants provide their cheap or free labour as 'amateurs' in the interest of the production companies that exploit them. See Kirsten Seale, '*MasterChef*'s Amateur Makeovers', *Media International Australia* 143 (2012): pp. 28 - 35. Also see See François Jost, 'When Reality TV Is a Job', in *The Politics of Reality Television,* pp. 31-43.

4. Rosemary Regina Sobol, 'Autopsy: Death of "MasterChef" Finalist Josh Marks Ruled Suicide, *Chicago Tribune* 12 October 2013 <http://www.chicagotribune.com/news/local/breaking/chi-author-ities-masterchef-finalist-josh-marks-dies-from-apparent-suicide-20131011-story.html>; Alan Duke, '"MasterChef" Runner-Up Josh Marks Loses "Battle of His Life", Commits Suicide', *CNN* 14 October 2013 <http://edition.cnn.com/2013/10/13/showbiz/masterchef-joshua-marks-suicide/>.

5. Mat Follas, 'Mat Follas at The Casterbridge', *Mat Follas* <http://www.matfollas.com/restaurant.html>.

6. With regard to a similar realty-television context, Brenda R. Weber thus writes of 'stories of failed or imperilled selfhood'. *Makeover TV: Selfhood, Citizenship, and Celebrity.* (Durham: Duke University Press, 2009), p. 5.

Tatattoouille on the Menu: Tats in the Kitchen, a Side of Ink, and Food as Communication.

Paula Arvela

Introduction

Food is as much solace for the body as is for the soul. What we eat becomes embodied, a veiled part of self. But food is more: as Roland Barthes argues, food is a system of communication that conveys broad meanings, ranging from taste, status, class and gender to emotions, beliefs, and cultural identity.[1] In recent years another nuanced layer of meanings has been ascribed to food, with the use of food iconography in the popular practice of body modification – tattooing. This study explores tattooing as a practice through which the permanent etching of food imagery on one's body becomes a form of communication, a narrative of self that highlights the prominent role of food in culture.

This project focuses on food iconography on tattooed bodies. Celebrity chefs and media representations of food have become an enduring and uncontested phenomenon of the twenty-first century. In recent years, media portrayals of chefs have been 'spiced up' by the sensationalist display of their tattooed arms and torsos. Selecting two specific cohorts – chefs and foodies – who are so closely associated with the production and consumption of food, this study seeks to explore the symbolic meanings communicated by this new form of food imagery, which becomes encoded with forms of power to act as markers of cultural identity and social belonging.

Using a line of inquiry that draws on textual and pictorial material collected from digital media sources, this study undertakes a textual and semiotic analysis of 'tats in the kitchen'. Thus, several questions guide this study: Why has food become an item of tattoo iconography? What are the encoded meanings communicated by food tattoos? Why are chefs and foodies adhering so passionately to this form of body modification?

This study is guided by a theoretical framework that views tattooing as a cultural practice with a broad range of connotations that are place- and time-specific. That is, whereas in some traditional cultures tattooing is still regarded as a ritual and a rite of passage, often specific to gender and status, its appropriation and increased utilization over recent decades by western societies has altered its meanings. Having shed its initial stigma, the practice no longer connotes deviance, rebellion and pathological social behaviour. Instead, tattooing, as a form of body modification, has acquired complex overlays of polysemic meanings. Associated with lifestyle choices, techniques of body management, hedonics enhancement and self-identification, tattooing 're-attaches' and grounds the self in a world full of uncertainties and risks.[2] Thus, by asserting that this form of body modification has in fact become culturally accepted and regarded as an integrative social practice, this study suggests that the permanent inscriptions of visual representations of food items on tattooees' bodies highlight the significant role of food as a marker of cultural identity and as a tool of cultural communication and social inclusion. By endorsing tattooing as a popular form of self-expression and creativity, chefs and foodies are further contributing to the endorsement of food as popular culture, as an artefact of consumer culture pertaining to processes of cultural identity.

Contextualizing Tattooing as a Cultural Practice

Tattooing is a form of body modification whose popularity has re-emerged in western cultures over the last thirty years.[3] Body modification includes a broad range of practices which have the purpose of altering the appearance and form of the body. Whilst some of these practices – tattooing, piercing, branding, cutting and binding – have usually been associated with some degree of stigmatization or stereotyping, others have not. For example, dieting, bodybuilding, plastic surgery and even routinized practices of makeup, hairdressing or hair removal have been normalized and even considered culturally desirable.[4]

Tattooing is one of the earliest and most common techniques of permanent body alteration.[5] Geometric patterns inscribed on mummies witness the use of tattooing by the Egyptians; likewise, Atkinson,' noting evidence of the practice being commonly used in India, China and Japan, claims that Tahitians, Samoans, Hawaiians and Maoris have been practicing tattooing for over 4000 years.[6] There is also documented verification that in the Americas, Aztec, Incan and Mayan cultures used tattoos as a form of body decoration.[7] In Europe, the popularity of the practice amongst the Greeks and Romans as well as in tribal groups in the British Islands debunks the preconception that tattooing is a practice unique to eastern cultures.[8] The Greeks and Romans used tattoos to connote social exclusion by marking outcasts or rival tribes. Roman soldiers scornfully referred to blue- or black-inked Celtic bodies as 'Picts', whereas Celtic warriors proudly ornamented their bodies with war-inspired tattoos.[9] In these cultures the practice was performed in ritualized ceremonies of group identity, and the tattoos were symbolic signifiers of social inclusion and in-group identification.[10]

45

Initial techniques of body inscription were customarily implemented with the use of serrated bones or shells dipped in pigment made from oily smoke or burning nut kernels. These painful procedures were usually associated with rites of passage to adulthood or higher hierarchical social ranking, thus denoting prestige, status and social identity, and at the same time documenting the tattooee's bravery and endurance.[11] Nevertheless, as a polysemic cultural practice, tattoos' meanings also differed across time and context. For example, amongst the Maoris and other tribal cultures, tattoos fostered 'in-group cohesiveness and mutual identification'; at times ascribed with religious and magical powers, tattoos would 'indicate spiritual filiations' or a protection against evil, as was the case with Fijian tattooed women seeking divine protection in their afterlife.[12]

Just as tattoos have been attributed with a wide range of meaning across time and space, their cultural acceptance has also undergone major shifts. Within the same culture, tattoos' acceptance has oscillated from periods of stigmatization and censorship to stages of approval and popularity. For example, in early Christianity tattoos were banned because they were seen as an alteration of the body made to God's image. Yet, during the crusades the practice was prevalent because the cross-etched on the crusaders' body ensured a burial according to Christian traditions.[13]

After centuries of dormancy in Europe, following Captain James Cook's eighteenth-century voyages in the Pacific, the practice was re-introduced to the continent as *ta-tu*, the name used by the local Pacific tribes. Loaded with racist overtones, stigmatized as a non-normative practice and a marker of deviance, tattoos also offered the allure of exoticism and difference. Since then, the practice's acceptance and popularity has undergone major shifts, especially after the 1960s Tattoo Renaissance when it started losing its negative connotations.[14] Increased social acceptance and, in particular, improvements in operating techniques, inks and pigments have decisively contributed to the current boom in tattooing practices and their cultural recognition. Currently, tattooing's socio-cultural acceptance and popularity are giving the practice's practitioners and supporters encouraging signs of successfully having tattooing recognized as an art form.[15]

Presently, there seem to be no limitations to what can be tattooed or who can choose to be tattooed. The practice's broad range of connotations indicates its cultural embeddedness, and its alternating patterns of social acceptance and refusal only reiterates the practice's cultural bearing, vitality and integration, reflecting its capacity to adjust to historical contexts and cultural milieus.

Currently, tattoos have a firm hold in popular culture and are a theme of scholarly research. Literature review gives evidence of the polysemic qualities of the practice, its cultural embeddedness and its ability to mould to historical and socio-cultural contexts. For example, expanding on Giddens's 'project of self' of the modern man, Paul Sweetman suggests that tattoos are a tool that re-anchors the postmodern self in environments of profound change and instability, further empowering tattooees with the capacity to exercise social agency and re-gain control over their bodies in the overregulated postmodern society.[16] In turn, B.S. Turner notes that in traditional societies tattoos were obligatory body marks with a fixed and culturally accepted meaning.[17] Usually associated with rites of passage, body inscriptions acted as markers of 'in-group' identity, group-membership, cultural affiliation and promoted social cohesiveness. Conversely, in postmodern societies, tattoos are 'optional, decorative, impermanent and narcissistic'; they refer to voluntary membership no longer connoting social bonding but rather an assertion of self.[18] If in some social cohorts, tattoos still represent alienation and disenfranchisement from mainstream values, in middle-class ranks, they function as a signifier of consumerism, a form of 'body capital' and an indicator of a culture that has commodified the body.[19] Tattoos have become polysemic codes invested with meanings ascribed by tattooees rather than social-cultural norms.

In this context, the use of food and culinary iconography in tattooing assumes scholarly relevance. Acknowledging the valuable contribution of previous studies to our current understanding of tattooing as a form of body modification, there is nonetheless a gap in the literature that this study addresses. By teasing out the meanings of food imagery in tattooing, this paper will further illustrate the communicative role of food and its cultural significance in the twenty-first century.

Methodology

Digital media made this study possible. From the start this study intended to use only secondary media resources. Acknowledging inherent shortcomings to this methodology, the advantages seemed to outweigh its limitations, as the plethora of available resources gave access to a much larger database than a qualitative study ever would. Moreover, this methodological design would bypass the bureaucratic protocol required by qualitative methods of research – ethics committee approvals, recruitment of respondents, interviewing processes and transcriptions – thus decreasing the duration of the investigative process. These benefits could not be overlooked when time and financial constraints had to be taken into account. Nonetheless, the drawbacks of this methodology also need to be acknowledged. It is particularly relevant to note the lack of the researcher's control over the choice of respondents and the gathering of first-hand primary data which qualitative methods of research may provide. However, given that this study constitutes a preliminary stage of research, the outcomes provide valid results, which can later be used as a platform for future investigation.

47

It is important to reiterate that the project's aim is not an exploration of tattoo as a form of body modification. Rather, it specifically analyzes food as a form of tattoo iconography. Its distinctiveness is twofold – the object and the subject of the study: the former exclusively exploring the use of food iconography in the practice of tattooing; the latter focusing solely on individuals that are either directly associated with cooking – chefs – or individuals 'very, very, very interested in food' – foodies.[20] Drawing on these principles, this study aims to establish the significant communicative role of food in a socio-cultural context where both food and the body have become highly commodified.

Guided by the research questions, a Google search using a selected range of keywords – 'chef', 'tattoo', 'foodie' and 'food' – revealed an abundance of material that surpassed initial expectations and provided a broad platform for research. It also made obvious the need to limit the amount of data analyzed by classifying it into two main groups, with group A constituted by renowned Australian celebrity chefs and group B comprising un-identified foodies. The preference given to the former cohort was based on the local popularity of celebrity chefs and food shows on Australian TV, which have created loyal audiences and a large pool of media resources. Accordingly, data will be clustered in two different sets – 'Chefs' Testimonials' centred on the chef and 'Food Tats as Communication' focusing on the tattoos of anonymous foodies.

Chefs' Testimonials and Kitchen Ink in Australia

Steve Dow's *Sydney Morning Herald* online series 'Kitchen Ink' publishes interviews with some of the more popular chefs in Sydney and Melbourne.[21] A photo gallery entitled 'Rockstars of the Kitchen' accompanies the text. From arms and hands to legs, torso and neck, chefs proudly display their body artwork to the camera. The iconography ranges from names of relevant people in the chefs' lives to text, pinups, star signs and mythological designs; some chefs also display food items, usually related to some of their signature culinary work. The variety is stunning, even amid just a few examples:

- Pastry chef Adriano Zumbo, who reached celebrity status after his participation on *MasterChef*, reveals a series of colourful tattoos on his arms and torso – a scorpion (his star sign); Willy Wonka, the classic character from Roald Dahls's children's novel *Charlie and the Chocolate Factory*; and a pinup wearing a frilly apron and holding one of Zumbo's trademark multi-coloured macaroons.
- Sardinian chef Giovanni Pilu of the Restaurant Pilu in Sydney's Freshwater displays the names of his three siblings on his left calf.
- Melbourne chef Brydie Smith, of Slowpoke Expresso in Fitzroy, poses with the wording 'Keep Calm and Carry On' her right forearm, and the words 'resolute' and 'strength' on the outer side of her hands.
- Chef Mike Patrick, from Melbourne's San Telmo, exhibits heavily tattooed forearms, a rose on his neck, and letters that spell out 'pots pans' on the knuckles of each of his eight fingers.
- Barcelona-born chef Olivia Serrano, at Bloodwood in the trendy Sydney suburb of Newtown, displays a tattooed jellyfish on her left arm, which she explains is a keepsake of the moment she was stung by one jellyfish on Clovelly beach in Sydney.

Also featuring in Dow's 'Kitchen Ink' are chefs Elvis Abrahanowicz and Ben Milgate from Restaurant Porteno in Sydney, who share their business partnership and their love for tattooing. Along with heavily tattooed arms and forearms, Abrahanowicz claims to have designed some of his tattoos, such as the word 'Esperanza' on his chest and a bandoneon on his abdomen. In turn, Milgate confesses to having had his first tattoo – an Incan design – when he was in Peru; now thirty-two, Milgate admits to having fifty per cent of his body covered in tattoos.

Mainstream media accounts of tattooed chefs are echoed in Steve Dow's visual and textual narratives. Portrayed as young school dropouts, chefs are described as rebellious individuals with artistic tendencies, creative dispositions, non-conformist attitudes and musical preferences that favour heavy metal and punk. For example, chef Zumbo was a dropout at fifteen; Zac Pauling (of The Anchor in Sydney's Bondi Beach) looked up to the controversial celebrity chef Anthony Bourdain (who loves tattoos and rock music) for inspiration and professional guidance. These same connotations work for female chefs too: for Claire van Vuuren tattoos connote toughness and resilience, attributes required in women working in a male-dominated industry. Nonetheless, acknowledging her 'female side', van Vuuren admits to using tattoos as a replacement for the jewellery that chefs are not allowed to wear at work. Rebellion, toughness, creativity and individuality of the 'not the normal nine-to-five class' – these themes discursively frame media narratives of 'kitchen ink' and conceptually underpin the tattooed celebrity chef phenomenon.[22] These accounts circulate abundantly in the media.

The heavily tattooed 'rockstar Aussie chef – Matt Stone' is another case in point.[23] Since being awarded the Best New Talent at the National Gourmet Traveller Awards in 2010, Stone rapidly ascended to stardom. After leading the kitchen at Greenhouse Perth in Western Australia, Stone took the helm as Executive Chef at Melbourne's Brothl, the first zero-waste food outlet in Australia. (Brothl closed down in March 2015 after a long battle with the Melbourne City Council over an industrial composter behind the restaurant.)[24] Stone claims to be an environmentalist at heart, a defender of 'small community farming and work with small producers'.[25] Portrayed as a young high-school dropout who loves surfing and skating, Stone started as a kitchen-hand at fifteen; at the age of twenty he was recognized as a talented and alternative chef, who creates 'recipes that rock', loves 'punk rock music', likes a 'bit of anarchy' and operates a restaurant that is a 'really fun place'. As media spokesperson for Western Australia, Stone currently promotes his hometown Margaret River's fresh produce and wines. Similarly, Stone spearheads the environmentalist movement by endorsing sustainable practices of food production and the consumption of alternative foods in the hospitality industry: Stone claims 'trying native Australian meats like wallaby and kangaroo […] and consuming insects like crickets, green ants […] is really an ethical way of consuming protein, vitamins and nutrients'.[26]

Like Stone's, media narratives of tattooed celebrity chefs frame their body artwork as representations of social agency, rebellion, innovation and artistic endeavour. In this context, tattoos become a signifier of individuality, a cultural marker that asserts difference and generates what has been described as an identification project of self.[27] For example, someone like Matt Stone becomes the embodiment of cultural values and a site of cultural representation where polysemic meanings are produced. On the one hand, his tattooed body constitutes a canvas where previously stigmatized meanings attached to tattooees (rebellion, non-normative) become normalized; yet, on the other hand, Stone's celebrity chef status equally flagships socio-cultural progressive dispositions. Stone's public persona is constructed in a way that stands for avant-gardism and cultural change, an association that has been described in the literature.[28] Concomitantly, from the individual's viewpoint, techniques of body modification connote social agency, become a tactic to re-assert control over one's body and a stance against the over-regulation and surveillance to which individuals are submitted in post-industrial societies.[29] As claimed in previous studies, to become part of mainstream culture tattoos needed to meet two conditions: the stigma attached to tattoos had to be removed and the practice of tattooing had to be veneered with glamour and cultural acceptability.[30] As this study demonstrates, the star status of these chefs has been a powerful tool to facilitate this process.

Arguably, and in time, the relentless circulation of these media narratives have multiple effects: they normalize body artwork, rubberstamp tattoos with social and cultural approval and encode the chefs' food with the fetish symbolism that the celebrity chef's body already carries. Thus, this study claims that the chef's tattooed body works as a 'silent' but highly visible semiotic icon in which three signifiers – chef, food and tattoo – come together to connote a fetishized style that is highly valued in commodity culture.

Thus, the overarching pattern emerging from the analysis of Steve Dow's 'Kitchen Ink' is that chefs use their skin as communicative human canvases on which they inscribe narratives that become projects of selfhood. Glamorized by media narratives, body artwork becomes body capital, and by association the chefs' food and ethical principles (e.g. environmentalism) become similarly invested with cultural capital.[31] Only time will tell if Stone's endorsement of kangaroo meat and insects as alternative sources of dietary protein will 'stick'. Nevertheless, these trends might successfully attain public endorsement, particularly in a media-saturated consumerist environment in which food's communicative power and chefs' cultural legitimacy inspire a large number of followers. Amongst these followers, foodies rank high. The next section emphasizes foodies and their tattoos, which noticeably are all images of food and/or food-related items.

50

Food Tats, Communication and Art Form

Whereas their tattoos are entirely food-related, these tattooees remain anonymous individuals who willingly display their bodywork and are described as 'people who love food' – that is, foodies. Indeed, the foodie's body becomes a site representing food as a fetish item of popular culture.

Foodie is a highly contested term. Ann Barr and Paul Levy define foodie as 'a person who is very, very, very interested in food. Foodies are the ones talking about food in any gathering – salivating over restaurants, recipes, radicchio. They don't think they are being trivial – foodies consider food to be an art, on a level with painting or drama'.[32] Josée Johnston and Shyon Bauman claim that the concept carries features that are dichotomous: foodie representing the democratization and accessibility of food knowledge, on one hand, and on the other foodie connoting taste, distinction, 'snobbery and the faddish trend-setting of elites'.[33] Expanding on Barr and Levy's previous work, Johnston and Bauman describe foodies as individuals with specific traits: the desire to learn about ingredients and cooking techniques, the need to make food a central identification marker, the craving for unusual foods and the tendency to evaluate food on the basis of its aesthetic attributes. Not surprisingly, many foodies are eager to etch a food-related tattoo on their skin. Tattoos on foodies claim cultural identity by marking difference, taste and style, by proclaiming an aesthetic value that sees food not as nutritional value but rather as an icon of consumer culture. Food becomes fetish.

Tattoos represent a wide variety of foods. The most common are vegetables and fruits. Some of these tattoos constitute colourful, meticulously crafted artwork. From aubergines, strawberries, pineapples and carrots to peas, bananas, corn and asparagus, these items are usually inscribed with vivid colours and sophisticated detail, representing highly refined still-lives imprinted on human canvas. The detail with which these tattoos are inscribed reflects current trends: tattoo enthusiasts are persuasively lobbying for tattooing to be recognized as an art form, and, in turn, tattooists as artists. These artistic representations on foodies' skins powerfully signify what food means to foodies – an item to be aesthetically valued, a fetish to be painted and tailored to individual specifications of colour, size and beauty. As a result, food iconography in tattooing is invested with personal values; each image becomes a signifier embedded with meanings that are arbitrary and personal. For example, food tattoos representing vegetables or fruit may as much signify aesthetic beauty as make statements about the tattooee's eating habits ('I am a vegetarian/vegan') or belief systems ('I eat ethically').

Pizza slices, ice-cream and small cakes, in particular cupcakes, are also popular. Animals are equally represented, with the pig being the most frequently depicted image, sometimes as a charming pet, sometimes as food (bacon slices) and sometimes as text ('I love bacon'). Chef Dustin Gardner explains the popularity of the pig in tattooing by asserting that 'every chef is obsessed with pigs'; indeed his own favourite tattoo is that of a pig 'labelled with all the primal cuts'.[34] Either way, the sheer frequency of pig tattoos raises questions that future studies should address, particularly in terms of the creature's cultural stigmatization as a 'dirty animal' and of the food's prohibition in some cultures and religions.

Foodies also display tattoos representing kitchen utensils. Most representations of culinary material culture are 'ordinary' items of everyday use, demonstrating that simple objects can still be represented as an object of art. The knife is the single most common representation in tattoo iconography. Knives are an essential part of the chef's toolbox and a fundamental tool in food preparation: they cut, carve, slice, chop, pierce, dissect, hack and tear food apart. Knives assist chefs to perform delicate tasks and give intricate shapes to food, as illustrated by the expert carving skills in the Japanese decorative garnishing practice of Mukimono. Knives' different applications are captured in tattooing, with explicit images of knives cutting through skin and piercing through hearts, reminding us, as Roland Barthes did, of the embedded violence associated with the practice of preparing food and transforming raw material into edible nutrients. Other kitchen utensils are also widely used as iconography – whisks, spoons and forks, and even bulkier utensils such as free-stand and hand-held cake mixers.

Such food iconography demonstrates foodies' desire to claim cultural identity through tattoos. These images represent food as a symbol of personal taste and style – the aesthetic values that go into the making of cultural identities. Food iconography in tattoos signify that food is more that an edible entity with a functional purpose; rather food tattoos communicate the fetishization of food in consumer culture.

Conclusion

Some patterns emerge from this study. The two researched cohorts – chefs and foodies – share common interests for food and tattoos. Chefs' tattoos reflect their professional association with the production of food; in turn, foodies's tattoos communicate their intense relationship with food. For both groups, skin representations of food iconography become markers of individual cultural identity and reflect a fetishized consumer culture. Thus, food iconography indicates the high currency that food culture and celebrity chefs currently have in popular consumer culture. Chefs and foodies use tattoos to re-claim their bodies as signifiers of social agency: these testimonials of self-identification on human canvas reiterate the communicative role of food as a commodified signifier of cultural identities.

Notes

1. Roland Barthes, *Mythologies* (London: Random House, 1993).
2. Maurice Patterson and Jonathan Schroeder, 'Borderline: Skin, Tattoos and Consumer Culture Theory, *Marketing Theory*, 10.3 (2010), pp. 253-67; Jill A. Fisher, 'Tattooing the Body, Marking Culture', *Body and Society*, 8.4 (2002), pp. 91-107; Anthony Giddens, *Modernity and Self-Identity: Self and Society in the late Modern Age* (Cambridge: Polity Press, 1991); Paul Sweetman, 'Anchoring the (Postmodern) Self? Body Modification, Fashion and Identity', in *Body Modifications*, ed. by Mike Featherstone (London: Sage Publications, 2000), pp. 51-76.
3. Michael Atkinson, *The Sociogenesis of Body Art* (Toronto: University of Toronto Press, 2003); Margo DeMello, *Bodies of Inscription: A Cultural History of the Modern Tattoo Community*, (Durham, NC: Duke University Press, 2000); *Body Modifications*, ed. by Mike Featherstone (London: Sage Publications, 2000); Clinton R. Sanders and D. Angus Vail, *Customizing the Body: The Art and Culture of Tattooing* (Philadelphia: Temple University Press, 2008); Sweetman.
4. Featherstone, p. 1.
5. Sanders and Vail, p. 9.
6. Atkinson, p. 30.
7. Sanders and Vail, pp. 9-10.
8. Sanders and Vail, p. 13.
9. Fisher.
10. Atkinson, p. 30.
11. Sanders and Vail, pp. 10-11.
12. Atkinson, p. 52; p. 30; Sanders and Vail, p. 11.
13. Sanders and Vail, pp. 13-14.
14. Sanders and Vail, p. 18.
15. DeMello.
16. Sweetman.
17. S. Turner Bryan, 'The Possibility of Primitiveness: Towards a Sociology of Body Marks in Cool Societies', in Featherstone, pp. 39-50.
18. Turner, p. 42.
19. Turner, p. 47; Featherstone, p. 3; Fisher.

20. Ann Barr and Paul Levy, *The Official Foodie Handbook. Be Modern – Worship Food* (Sydney: Doubleday, 1985), p. 6.

21. Steve Dow, 'Kitchen Ink: Chefs Reveal Bodies of Work', *goodfood.com*, 12 May 2012 <http://www.goodfood.com.au/good-food/kitchen-ink-chefs-reveal-bodies-of-work-20120512-1yizg.html> [accessed 12 January 2015].

22. Reid Hingston in Dow 2012.

23. Syarifah Syazana, 'Chef Matt Stone of 'Recipes that Rock' Interview', *Time Out Kuala Lumpur* <http://www.timeout.com/kuala-lumpur/tv-and-radio-guide/chef-matt-stone-of-recipes-that-rock-interview> [accessed 5 May 2015].

24. John Lethlean, 'City Bureaucracy Shuts down Joost Bakker's Brothl', *The Australian,* 3 March 2015 <http://www.theaustralian.com.au/life/food-wine/city-bureaucracy-shuts-down-joost-bakkers-brothl/story-e6frg8jo-1227245224605> [accessed 12 April 2015].

25. Syazana.

26. Ron J. Backus, 'Recipes that Rock: Oz Chef Matt Stone's New Show on Sustainable Foods', *The Star Online,* 27 April 2014 <http://www.thestar.com.my/Lifestyle/Food/Features/2014/04/27/Recipes-That-Rock-Oz-chef-Matt-Stones-new-show-on-sustainable-foods/> [accessed 12 April 2015].

27. Giddens; Sweetman.

28. DeMello.

29. Fisher.

30. DeMello; Fisher.

31. Turner.

32. Barr and Levy, p. 6.

33. Josée Johnston, and Shyon Bauman, *Foodies: Democracy, Distinction in the Gourmet Foodscape* (New York: Routledge, 2010), p. 54.

34. Gretchem McKay, 'Illustrated chefs: Why Kitchen Artists are Big on Tattoos. It Stems from the Artistic Self-expression of Their Profession, They Say', *Pittsburgh Post-Gazette,* 11 June 2011 <http://www.post-gazette.com/life/dining/2011/06/19/Illustrated-chefs-Why-kitchen-artists-are-big-on-tattoos/stories/201106190254> [accessed 20 December 2014].

Totalitarian Tastes: The Political Semantics of Food in Twentieth-Century Germany

Volker Bach

The idea that food has a political significance is hardly a new insight to anyone. From latte liberals and junk-food-gorging welfare recipients to real men who don't eat quiche, stereotypes of how the other side eats abound in the modern world, and they have a long history. As with all aspects of political symbolism, repression heightens its significance, and few countries have a more depressing history of well-planned, thoroughly considered political repression than twentieth-century Germany. In this article, I will try to give some insight into what symbolic significance food and eating took on under various governments, what official visions they propagated and what influence this had on eating habits. Given the size and complexity of the topic and the fact that it is still thoroughly under-researched, it will amount to no more than an impressionistic *tour d'horizon*, but as such I hope it can at least be amusing and stimulating.

What gave food and eating habits such a strong political charge was the fact that governments cared passionately about them. Without wanting to enter the contest over what constitutes a totalitarian system or which German governments could or could not be called such, we can clearly say that the dictatorships of twentieth-century Germany were trying to impose their political vision on all aspects of life. As a result, there was an officially sanctioned, politically correct way of dressing, travelling and eating from 1933 to 1989. In such an environment, small, private choices could become acts of resistance. Learning the political semantics of food became key to careers, social advancement, satirical commentary and in extreme cases even survival.

From Farm to Supermarket – Historical Background

To understand the food system in which the political symbolism is rooted, we must first look briefly at the historical development of Germany in the twentieth century. At its outset, we find a country just emerging as an industrial power, still heavily rural in many areas and with memories of subsistence crises and mass emigration barely a generation old. Agriculture had gone from accounting for almost half of the GDP to less than a quarter in two generations while industrial production exploded. For the first time, more people lived in cities than in the countryside – and did not grow their own food. Industrial food processing and the large-scale trade in foodstuffs created new forms of distribution and the need for new regulation. A nationwide law banning adulteration and mislabelling was passed in 1879 and revised extensively in 1927.[1]

At the same time, the phenomenon of mass pauperism that had dominated the eighteenth and nineteenth centuries ended. The diet of the broad mass of people was increasingly determined by choice rather than necessity, with potatoes, grain and legumes decreasing in importance while the consumption of meat, fats and sugar rose. The lives of industrial workers in the early 1900s may appear bleak and deprived from our perspective, but in comparison with what their parents and grandparents had known, these people were enjoying small but real luxuries.[2] The disapproval of moralists and economists predictably followed. Such rapid, unprecedented development would have been wrenching enough without the massive dislocation that would follow.

No aspect of modern German history can be understood without the impact of the First World War. In culinary terms, it erased the gains made in the years before 1914, curtailing food choices by creating shortages of many essentials and famine conditions especially in industrial cities. The *Steckrübenwinter* [turnip winter] of 1916-1917 merely represented the height of a food crisis that lasted past the end of the war into the early 1920s and may have killed upward of 800,000 people.[3] Meanwhile, businesspeople who could profit from the government's enormous war expenditures or the opportunities a patchy and poorly designed rationing system provided were living in ostentatious luxury.

With the end of the war came revolution, political instability and hyperinflation that wiped out savings and eroded wages. Hunger was once again a real, existential threat for working-class families even while there was work, and unemployment remained high. Tourists and businesspeople with access to hard currencies enjoyed great luxury while stunted German schoolchildren received free meals courtesy of foreign charities. Even the brief recovery of the late 1920s did not return the country to pre-war standards of living, and it was cruelly cut short by the global economic crisis that began in 1929. People came to different conclusions from these events, but almost all agreed that things could not stay as they were. Moderation was driven out of politics for a generation or more.

Both National Socialism and Communism had a vision of the foodways they wanted the German people of the future to adopt. Neither was particularly exclusive or innovative – they had long roots in their respective political traditions and social milieus – but both were pursued with remarkable earnestness. They were also the outcome of their competing visions of society at large, determined not by medical science or taste, but by economic policy, gender politics and the needs of a greater collective.

Feeding the *Volkskörper* - Nazi Eating

The most concise explanation of what Nazi foodways were about comes from the foreword of the 1938 cookbook *1000 Kochvorschriften* [1000 Cooking Rules]:

> We salute the German girls and women, especially those thousands who were our pupils.
> We hand to them our book with the honest wish that it may help them to serve

the people and the fatherland beyond the circle of their family or those they care for in their vocation.

A healthy diet produces health in body and mind.

A healthy family means a healthy people.

Guarding and improving the health of the people [*Volksgesundheit*] is the responsible duty of the German housewife.

In fulfilling this duty, may our book be a loyal comrade in their labour [*Arbeitskamerad*].[4]

This contains almost all the major elements of Nazi food ideology in one short, neat package: food is primarily envisioned as a bodily input to promote health. The health-giving properties of food are knowable and can be realized by following precise instructions. The purpose of this scientific cookery is to keep the body and mind functional in the service of a greater whole – the body of the nation, an almost mystical organic whole referred to as the *Volkskörper*. Working in support of this greater body is the duty of all its members. Feeding it and maintaining its health is specifically the duty of women – alongside the production of children, their only one. The book itself, a mass-market product turned out cheaply, comes with eight pages of advertising for household and health products and another eight of adverts for books on these matters. This is not unusual: Nazi propaganda was rarely conveyed through official channels, but by co-opting existing commercial ones and privileging them in return for their collaboration. The authors specifically identify as long-standing experts in home economics. Two are teachers at the cooking school attached to the German Museum of Hygiene in Dresden;[5] the third identifies with equal pride as a *Hausfrau*. This, too, is part of the Nazi vision of foodways: women should dedicate themselves to mastering its art and science, and many did. The state provided women who left employment on marrying an interest-free loan for household goods to encourage homemaking. Concerted efforts to disseminate knowledge about health and dietetics buttressed their claim to professional expertise that increased their standing in the family and in society at large.[6] Guida Diehl, a prominent early supporter of Hitler, even envisioned a concept of professional representations as organs of the state that would include one such body for women – the equals, in their capacity as carers and housewives, to engineers, soldiers and artisans, though equal only in their powerlessness.[7]

Since women, mostly as housewives, were expected to provide the food of the Nazi future, they were the primary target for its propaganda. In a concerted effort to educate young women for their future vocation, the *Deutsches Frauenwerk* took over hundreds of existing home economics schools and began offering systematic training. Until 1937, 1.14 million women had attended 54,000 courses, most of them the basic *Mütterschulungen*.[8] The *Frauenwerk* and its affiliates in other party organisations also issued literature, usually short, inexpensive or free booklets, including recipe collections. Yet in an arrangement that was typical of the way the Nazi state combined top-down control and private initiative, much of the material that circulated was the work of individual authors looking to capitalize on the boom, published commercially for sale to customers who aspired to enter this new culinary world. Erna Horn was one such successful home economics writer of her time and was able to continue her career in post-war West Germany.[9] Her *Der neuzeitliche Haushalt* [The Modern Household] of 1941 addressed the scientific management of home and hearth in the kind of detail that appealed to bourgeois housewives while reassuring them that, in the words of the Führer himself, 'Providence has assigned to woman the care of this her own world on which the world of man can be built and formed'.[10]

These works presented a cuisine they referred to as *fortschrittlich* [progressive] or *modern* [modern] with roots in the health food tradition of the *Lebensreform* movement and the economical recipes developed to deal with shortages and high food prices during and after the First World War. It extolled the virtues of vegetarian dishes and raw foods, not for spiritual of medical reasons, but because they were easy on the country's food and fuel resources. A booklet published early in the war sums up this view. Its main concern is *Nahrungsfreiheit*, 'food liberty', i.e. autarky:

> This book is to [...] serve to instruct not only the inexperienced, but also the already experienced housewife how to manage her kitchen schedule mainly with the products of our home soil while using meat almost not at all, eggs rarely, and fat only in the necessary quantities. As the following recipes show, the result is no nutritionally poor, unsatisfying fare. Rather, most of the listed dishes can fulfil the requirements of nutrition [*Nahrungsbedürfnis*] even without a starter or dessert.[11]

Preserving food, especially the still novel and exciting home canning, was a central concern of many writers, and the *Frauenwerk* regularly published instructions.[12] Erna Horn envisions the 'modern household' producing its own sausages, sauerkraut and pickles. Needless to say this is an unrealistic expectation for the majority of city-dwellers who would have lacked the storage space even if they had been able to afford the equipment, but it fits in with the quasi-rural homesteading that many senior Nazis saw as the ideal German way of life. A legacy of this vision is still found throughout Germany in many suburban *Siedlungen* of small homes surrounded by spacious gardens often laid out as long strips that the owners were to use for growing fruit and vegetables as well as keeping rabbits, chickens and even pigs. In such a home, kept busy by the demands of garden, livestock and her children (at least four), the wholesome German housewife would maintain her stock of hygienically preserved foods, cook nutritious but frugal dinners for her family and see to the moral and physical health of the *Volkskörper* in her little sphere.

Needless to say it did not happen that way. The semi-rural *Siedlungen* with their autarkic worker-farmers were given up in favour of apartment blocks as early as 1936. The appeal of Nazi foodways proved similarly limited. Public demonstrations of frugality were common, most prominently the monthly *Eintopfsonntag* [stew Sunday]

57

on which Germans were called on to replace their Sunday roast with a simple stew and donate the savings to the *Winterhilfswerk*, a party charity for poor relief. The *Kasseler Post* announced in 1934 that on 14 October, the first *Eintopfsonntag* of the autumn, restaurants were only permitted to serve the following: Pea soup with meat (pigs' ears, sausage, or salt meat), noodle soup with beef, or vegetable soup with meat.[13] Soup was often sold and eaten communally in the open to display support for the regime, despite the fact that *Eintopfsonntage* fell in autumn and winter. Those who decided not to participate would often still give their donation to the party *Blockwart*. Hamburg reported 65% of all households participating in 1934.[14] Still, sarcastic observers could not help notice that the lifestyles of their party leaders had little to do with frugality and health. Legend has it that Hitler himself was disgusted by the expanding waistlines of his party leadership, and the files of the political police preserve several versions of a satirical grace said over dinner:

> *Komm, Adolf Hitler, sei unser Gast, und gib uns all das, was du uns versprochen hast. Aber nicht Pellkartoffeln und dazu keinen Hering, sondern was du selber frißt und Hermann Göring.* [Come, Adolf Hitler, be our guest and give us all that you promised us. But not boiled potatoes and no herring with them, but what you yourself and Göring eat.][15]

At least one woman was executed for reciting this. Communicating about food could be perilous.

Enjoying the Fruit of Collective Labour – Real Socialist Eating

With the end of Nazi rule in 1945, a new dictatorship came to East Germany. Imposed by Soviet troops and run by a select group of German Communists, the KPD had drawn different lessons from the experience of the First World War and developed an entirely different concept of the politically desirable life and diet. Where Nazis and other right-wing parties even before 1933 had argued that Germany needed to refight the war and that its population had lacked the ability to withstand hunger and privation, the Communists believed that the primary problem had been the unequal sharing of suffering, and were determined not to fight another war. Well aware that they had not been elected and did not enjoy much popular support, the new government developed an enticing vision of the riches and comfort of future Socialist life from the beginning. *Wie wir heute arbeiten, so werden wir morgen essen!* [as we work today, so will we eat tomorrow] was a slogan that appeared immediately after the war and continued as a treasured legacy to the very end of the GDR, when it invited the mocking response 'I hope not'.

Though the early years of the young state were marked by shortages and rationing, exacerbated by a focus on developing heavy industry at the expense of consumer goods, the party always stayed true to its goal. Unveiling the 1959 'Seven Year Plan for Peace, Wealth and Happiness', Chairman Ulbricht addressed the party conference with a picture straight out of Cockaigne:

> Our table will be set with the best nature has to offer: High-quality meat and dairy products, fine vegetables and the best fruit, the earliest strawberries and tomatoes at a time when they do not yet ripen in our fields, grapes in winter, not just in times of their glut. As Socialists, we are aware that by 1965, a superfluity of food is to be reached in the Socialist camp. What the retailers are facing is an ever growing wave of foods and delicacies from all over the world![16]

Very few people could disagree with this. Providing this lifestyle, not for a select few, but for everybody equally, was defined as the ökonomische *Hauptaufgabe* [the main economic task] of the GDR, and its fundamental inability to realize that vision contributed greatly to its demise in 1989.

Initially, though, the East German government's food policy enjoyed a period of success. In the late 1940s, the country had barely emerged from acute famine.[17] By 1986, consumption had risen to a world-beating 96 kg of meat, 43 kg of sugar, 307 eggs and 15.7 kg of butter per capita.[18] This was a matter of pride to the state which never ceased to remind the citizenry of their collective good fortune and ended up astonished at the depth of their ingratitude.

The East German government had a propaganda apparatus at its disposal that dwarfed anything the Nazis could deploy. Television and radio, cookbook and magazine publishers, food manufacturers, wholesalers, retailers, even most restaurants and hotels had to toe the party line. The famous cooking show by celebrity chef Kurt Drummer was carefully vetted to ensure the week's recipes never included any articles currently in short supply. Advertisers, recipe publishers and retailers were told to boost demand for whatever could be offered in large quantities: eggs after the success of the industrial chicken farming programme KIM, fish in the 1960s before the introduction of economic exclusion zones limited the fishing fleet's options. Cholesterol awareness made an appearance in the press after egg production dropped, and when bratwurst output failed to keep pace with anticipated demand, the media were simply ordered to stop using the word. The import of coffee, bananas and cocoa were affairs of state managed at the Politburo level. This aspect of East German food history often descends into involuntary comedy as we read of coffee makers exploding after being fed with the latest legume-based substitute and entire factories spontaneously shutting down on the news of a banana delivery to the local shop, but to the people in charge it was a dead serious matter. Their food policy was made in the service of a grand scheme of social engineering.

The paradise the GDR envisioned for its citizens was a collectivized, industrial and egalitarian one. Food production at every level would benefit from economies of scale and improvement through specialization. Domestic cooking would eventually be reduced to a hobby, something people did purely for the pleasure. Women had to be freed from household labour as much as possible to integrate them into a workforce suffering from chronic skill shortage. As a result, much effort went into providing and advertising factory canteens, school lunches, child care services and processed food. A popular children's song, written, of course, at the behest of the party, began with the line *Wenn Mutti früh zur Arbeit geht* [When mummy goes to work in the morning].[19]

Accordingly, training food professionals was a priority, and East Germany was proud of the medals its chefs won in international competitions. Providing consistently high quality across the country, however, was beyond its abilities. Though industrial canteens, the military, schools and universities were given preferential food allocations, anecdotal evidence points to a fare that was at best adequate, and hygienic standards that often left much to be desired.[20] Nonetheless, the majority of people lived largely on this heavily subsidized institutional diet, and East German cookbooks reflect that fact. Complex recipes requiring long preparation times are rare and instructions for home canning disappear almost completely. Their signature dishes are quick to prepare so as to allow working parents to whip up a quick supper after their shift.

Providing its citizens with heavily subsidized basic foods at fixed prices as well as meeting their growing demand for the finer things in life was problematic for the GDR's top-down planned economy. The state allowed private restaurants, though they were strictly regulated. A few, like the *Waffenschmied* in Suhl offering Japanese cuisine or *Konnopkes Imbiß* in Berlin famous for its sausages gained cult status.[21] Most seem to have been as underwhelming as the state-run *HO Gaststätten*. The food trade, both retail and wholesale, was fully centralized. While moderately successful at providing industrially processed foods, bread and meat, it was forced to turn to private growers and foragers for fresh fruit and vegetables. Vegetarianism – discouraged as a bourgeois affectation – was unalloyed misery in the largely carnivorous country.

The politically correct proletarian foodways of East Germany were robust, hearty and communal, suggesting that there is something to the culinary habitus Bourdieu ascribes to the working class.[22] Suspicious of the exotic and overly refined, it appreciated rich, meaty and ample food enjoyed communally. Its ideal family left home early, the children to take breakfast and lunch in school, the parents to work where they ate with their *Brigade*. Only the evening meal was taken around the family table, a quick affair that did not require much preparation, but included high-value ingredients like meat, fish, butter and cheese as well as industrially processed convenience foods. The shared enjoyment of the product of joint labour was a key value. Sadly, as is often the case with maddeningly cheerful GDR propaganda, reality was less bright. As a result, people increasingly turned away from the communal experience to secure islands of privacy. This *Rückzug ins Private* also extended to the culinary sphere with an appreciation of bourgeois refinement over industrial efficiency, home cooking, gardening, home canning and the eternal quest for scarce imported delicacies. Especially the proverbially absent banana provided material for underground humour as in the doggerel based on a popular song: '*Zwei Apfelsinen im Jahr, und zum Parteitag Bananen*' [Two oranges a year, and bananas for the party conference].

Concluding Observations

If there is any broad conclusion to be drawn from these observations, it is that the political semantics of food is arbitrary. While the underlying ideologies are clearly placed on the right and left of the traditional political spectrum, the foodways they espoused are not linked to them by any necessity. The diet championed by Nazi *Bräuteschulen* and the *Rezeptdienst* with its reliance on local vegetables and whole-grain products, limited processing and frugal use of animal products is familiar to modern Germans as the hallmark of the bourgeois left, mostly urban, educated and sceptical of authority. Meanwhile, the East German love of rich, easy and highly processed foods seems to fit in much better with the conservative spectrum, people who are suspicious of anything organic, ecological or green, but happy to trust technological progress and the magic of consumer choice to deliver quality and convenience. Of course these adscriptions are stereotypical. There are nationalist vegans and hamburger-eating radical Socialists around today, and just as surely not everybody in the decades of Nazi and Communist rule fit the preconceived ideas. But the notion that a vegetarian diet was fit for nationalist race warriors is a strange one today.

Another interesting observation is that neither regime enjoyed much success in changing foodways against the wishes of the population. The twentieth century was a time of epochal culinary change, but this appears to be entirely driven by technology, not ideology. European habits changed together, almost regardless of the intentions of individual governments. In fact, for all the effort that went into propagating their vision, both the Nazi regime and the Politburo were frightened of the backlash that tampering with their people's food supply might create. Hitler's fear that the revolution of 1918 might repeat itself goes a long way towards explaining the reticence to put the German economy on a full war footing until 1944, and the cost of supporting an increasingly unaffordable standard of living contributed much to the demise of the GDR. However biddable and docile the German voter might appear to them, the German consumer, resentful, demanding and insistent on his accustomed fare, gave both the Gestapo and Stasi sleepless nights. There is a lesson to those who would impose dietary change from above here.

Appendix: Totalitarian Cooking at Home

Kale Pudding (Germany 1941)
¾ - 1 kg of kale leaves, 150 g bread, soaked in skim milk, 150 g raw ground meat or meat leftovers of any kind (bacon, smoked meat, sausage), sautéed onion, a little caraway, salt (celery salt), 1 egg. Serve with butter, tomato, or horseradish sauce.

The kale leaves are cooked in a small quantity of water or half water, half skim milk until almost soft, then drained and chopped finely. They are then mixed with all remaining ingredients and seasonings, worked into a smooth, not overly wet mass to which a little soybean flour may be added, filled into the prepared pudding basin and cooked in a water bath for ¾ - 1 hour.[23]

Szegedin Sauerkraut Chicken (East Germany 1981)

2 chickens, 75 g lard, 4 onions, 500g sauerkraut, 1 tbsp tomato concentrate, 1 ½ tbsp sweet paprika powder, 6 potatoes, ½ bottle yoghurt, 3 tbsp coffee cream, salt, bay leaf, caraway.

Quarter the chickens raw or divide them into two breasts and legs each, rub them with salt and sweet paprika powder, and fry together with the sliced onions in lard until very crisp. Add to the pan raw, coarsely chopped sauerkraut, tomato concentrate and sweet paprika, one bay leaf and a little finely chopped caraway, fill up with ¼ l of stock and cook in the oven, covered up. Cook raw, finely diced potatoes and add to the dish when it is almost done. Mix yoghurt and cream and add to the sauerkraut chicken at the end, bring to a boil once more briefly and serve immediately in the pot or pan, if possible.[24]

Notes

1. Jutta Grüne, '*Staatliche* Überwachung *der Lebensmittelqualität. Entstehung ihrer rechtlichen, wissenschaftlichen und institutionellen Prämissen*', in *Die Revolution am Esstisch*, ed. by Hans Jürgen Teuteberg, *Neue Studien zur Nahrungskultur im 19./20. Jahrhundert* (Stuttgart: Franz Steiner Verlag, 2004), pp. 249-62.

2. Peter Lesniczak, '*Derbe bäuerliche Kost und feine städtische Küche. Zur Verbürgerlichung der Ernährungsgewohnheiten zwischen 1880 und 1930*' in Teuteberg, pp. 129-47.

3. Gustavo Corni, 'Hunger' in *Enzyklopädie Erster Weltkrieg*, ed. by Gerhard Hirschfeld, Gerd Krumeich and Irina Renz (Paderborn: Schöningh (UTB), 2009), p. 565. Estimates vary, and data are hard to extrapolate since many victims died of disease brought on by poor nutritional status. Malnutrition remained a serious public health issue well into the mid-1920s.

4. Elisabeth Hegewald, Benita von Heimann and Margarete Schubert, *Tausend Kochvorschriften neuartig / vielseitig / wegweisend* (Dresden: Verlag Emil Pahl, 1938). The word *Kochvorschrift* [cooking rule or cooking regulation] is not unusual at the time. It also occurs, for example, in a home economics schoolbook published in Bremen in 1935 and reflects the belief that cooking was at heart a scientific effort (*Koch-Vorschriften für Schule und Haus, herausgegeben von Lehrerinnen der Berufsschule für Hauswirtschaft* (Bremen: Verlag Arthus Geist, 1935)).

5. This museum's association with Nazi ideology is a long and ignoble one. It organized travelling exhibitions on race and eugenics both in Germany and abroad, including *New Eugenics in Germany* that toured the United States in 1934, and its premises were home to several government and party agencies. Cf. *Das Deutsche Hygiene-Museum Dresden 1911-1990*, ed. by Klaus Vogel (Dresden: DHM, 2003).

6. Thomas Rohrkrämer, *Die fatale Attraktion des Nationalsozialismus. Über die Popularität eines Unrechtsregimes* (Paderborn: Ferdinand Schöningh Verlag, 2013), p. 188 f.

7. Guida Diehl, *Die Deutsche Frau und der Nationalsozialismus* (Eisenach: Neulandverlag, 1933), pp.III ff. For more on the role envisioned for women in the *Volkskörper*, see also Raffael Scheck, *Mothers of the Nation: Right-Wing Women in Weimar Germany* (Oxford: Berg, 2004).

8. Jürgen Schiedeck, '*Mütterschulung im Nationalsozialismus*', *Zeitschrift für Theorie und Praxis der Sozialen Arbeit*, 40 (1989), pp. 344-53 and Susanna Dammer, '*Kinder, Küche, Kriegsarbeit. Die Schulung der*

Frauen durch die NS-Frauenschaft in *Frauengruppe Faschismusforschung: Mutterkreuz und Arbeitsbuch. Zur Geschichte der Frauen in der Weimarer Republik und im Nationalsozialismus* (Frankfurt: Fischer TB, 1988), pp. 215-45.

9. Ilona Zubrod and Melanie Goldmann's book *Hier kocht die Frau! Von Kaltmamsellen und Küchenchefinnen* (Hildesheim: Gerstenberg Verlag, 2013) provides a brief overview of her career (pp. 134-35). Erna Horn's *Der neuzeitliche Haushalt. Ein* Führer *durch die gesamte Küche und Hauswirtschaft in zwei Bänden* (Munich: Lorenz Madl Verlag, 1941) saw several further editions in the 1950s that were very little changed, except for lacking the Adolf Hitler quotation in the introduction.

10. Horn, vol. 1, p. 5.

11. Rudolf Rösch, *Hausfrauen, jetzt verwendet was die Scholle spendet! Nahrhafte, gesunde Kost aus heimischer Scholle* (Munich: Verlag Ernst Reinhardt, 1941), p. 5.

12. For a history of the practice in Germany see *Mindestens haltbar bis... Konservieren und Bevorraten,* ed. by Astrid Bergmeister, in *Glasgefäßen, Schriften / Landschaftsverband Westfalen-Lippe, Westfälisches Industriemuseum Dortmund* (Essen: Klartext Verlag, 1998), vol. 20.

13. Claudia Hohmann, 'Die Volksgemeinschaft ißt Erbseneintopf', NordHessen (Blum-DE) <http://www.nordhessen-online.com/wp-content/data/hundert/1934/a1934.htm> [accessed 25 May 2015].

14. Peter Zolling, *Zwischen Integration und Segregation – Sozialpolitik im ,Dritten Reich' am Beispiel der NSV in Hamburg* (dissertation, Frankfurt/Main, 1986), p. 180.

15. Klaus Hansen, *Das kleine Nein im großen Ja. Witz und Politik in der Bundesrepublik* (Wiesbaden: Springer Fachmedien, 1990), p.36.

16. Jutta Voigt, *Der Geschmack des Ostens. Essen, Trinken und Leben in der DDR* (Berlin: Gustav Kiepenheuer Verlag, 2005), p. 48 f.

17. This is evocatively recounted in Rosemarie Köhler's *Falsches Schmalz und Wiesenwein. Ein sächsisches Nachkriegskochbuch. Rezepte, Erinnerungen und Zeitdokumente aus den Jahren 1945-49* (Leipzig: BuchVerlag für die Frau, 2006).

18. Voigt, p. 10

19. Susanne Kailitz, '*Wenn Mutti früh zur Arbeit geht. Kindererziehung in Ostdeutschland*', *Die Zeit* October 2011 <http://www.zeit.de/2011/10/S-DDR-Erziehung> [accessed 28 May 2015].

20. For examples of both, see Tobias Stregel and Fabian Tweder, *Deutsche Kulinarische Republik. Szenen, Berichte und Rezepte aus dem Osten* (Frankfurt (Main): Eichborn Verlag, 1998), p. 65 and *Alles Soljanka oder wie? Das ultimative DDR-Kochbuch 1949-1989*, ed. by Ute Scheffler, (Leipzig: Verlag für die Frau, 2000), p. 168.

21. The *Waffenschmied* offered Japanese cuisine and ambience improvised with locally available ingredients and is reported to have impressed even visiting Japanese businesspeople, cf. Voigt, p. 192 ff. The story of this restaurant and its founder, Rolf Anschütz, was made into the movie *Sushi in Suhl* (dir. by Carsten Fiebeler (Starcrest Media, 2012)). The *Suhler Waffenschmied* restaurant currently operating has no connection with it. The *Imbiß*, a family-owned street food stall, predates the GDR and became famous by introducing Currywurst to East Germany. It is still in business, though mired in a dispute about the right to use the family name (*Konnopke's Imbiß* <http://konnopke-imbiss.de/Home.html> [accessed 28 May 2015]).

22. Pierre Bourdieu, *Distinction: A Social Critique of the Judgment of Taste* (Cambridge, MA: Harvard University Press, 1984), pp. 169-225.

23. Rösch, p. 56

24. Kurt Drummer and Käthe Muskewitz, *Kochkunst aus dem Fernsehstudio. Rezepte – küchentechnische und ernährungswissenschaftliche Hinweise – moderne Garmethoden und Zubereitungsarten mit über 950 Rezepten und 48 Farbtafeln* (Leipzig: VEB Fachbuchverlag, 1981), p. 106 f.

Communicating Frenchness:
Escoffier and the Export of Terroir

Janet Beizer

Twenty-first-century theorists of what is now being called 'culinary diplomacy' may have invented the term, but not the concept. Similarly, the various Asian states today intent on 'nation branding' didn't found that practice, which has a history. My purpose is to look at one small part of that history, through a cross-section of the nineteenth- to early twentieth-century record that has been little examined from this point of view: Georges Auguste Escoffier's accounts of his own culinary mission as he took on an increasingly global role in the culinary world (circulating among the high kitchens of France, Monaco, Switzerland, England, Germany and the U.S.). Over the years, Escoffier edited two journals, wrote eight (cook and other) books and, finally, a posthumously published memoir, which will be my primary focus in what follows. I lead into Escoffier through a contemporary lens because I believe such a framework helps to highlight some unstated elements of his narrative, as, I will imply, Escoffier's rhetoric and practice might enlighten the diplomatic-economic work of our own era.

Setting the Table for Diplomacy

In 2012, a U.S. State Department initiative under Hillary Clinton ushered in the wide publicizing of a concept known as 'culinary diplomacy', a term already coined by the early years of this century. Culinary diplomacy has its theorists, notably Sam Chapple-Sokol, trained on the American east coast, and Paul Rockower, on the west. Chapple-Sokol, in an article in *The Hague Journal of Diplomacy*, defines culinary diplomacy as 'the use of food and cuisine as an instrument to create cross-cultural understanding in the hopes of improving interactions and cooperation'. Rockower, who distinguishes between culinary diplomacy as an elite, official practice, and gastrodiplomacy as a public or popular exercise, defines the second as 'winning hearts and minds through stomachs'.[1] I'll use the terms synonymously.

If culinary diplomacy has its official agents, that is, governments, to which we shall return, it also has its citizen practitioners. Notable is the 'Conflict Kitchen', an artist-run Pittsburgh take-out restaurant whose cuisine fluctuates to focus on regions with which the U.S. is in conflict: Afghanistan, Iran, North Korea, Venezuela. With each iteration there is a complete change in décor and menu, with accompanying programming that includes talks, interviews, films, discussions, performances and live webcam meals with diners in the area of focus. The Conflict Kitchen packages its food in wrappers printed with not only information about the region but also interviews with nationals on pertinent cultural and political subjects.[2]

Government ventures into culinary diplomacy run the gamut. There are efforts one might call foreign aid-related (current U.S. Culinary Ambassador José Andrés has been working with the Global Alliance for Clean Cookstoves to bring clean and energy-efficient cooking technologies to the people of Haiti, for example)[3] and then, on the other extreme, more elite, leader-directed strategies that play out on the gastro-symbolic level, as for instance, on the occasion of the Obama-hosted August 2014 dinner for 50 African heads of state. At that point White House chef Comerford explained the aims of culinary diplomacy on the level of a state dinner: 'If you have a wonderful meal [...] conversations are so much better.' She went on to summarize the strategic elements of such a meal, designed to 'showcase American food, including produce from the White House garden [...] highlighting whatever is wonderful and seasonal out there [...while] adding a hint of some of the wonderful African spices and different things that would be dear and near to all our guests [...taking] into consideration all of the dietary restrictions, the religious preferences of each country, so a lot of research and hard work [is involved]'.[4] At the pinnacle of official culinary diplomacy is Le Club des Chefs des Chefs, a top-secret organization assumed to discuss, at their annual meetings, the personal food preferences of the world leaders they work for so as to facilitate the work of the member chefs at state dinners.

Culinary diplomacy at the official level is not all about setting the table for summit meetings and visiting foreign dignitaries, however. Other examples figuring prominently in accounts of political commentators include the Thai government's launch, in 2002, of a 'Global Thai' program intended to build the number of Thai restaurants internationally and then to promote them through an educative culinary-historical website called 'Thailand: Kitchen of the World';[5] also the South Korean government's subsequent launch, through the Ministry of Food, Agriculture, Forestry and Fisheries, of a program called 'Korean Cuisine to the World' (often called 'Kimchi Diplomacy'), which includes efforts to establish courses in Korean cuisine in internationally-known cooking schools as well as the inauguration of a Kimchi Institute and a traveling Korean food truck.[6] Such gastronationalistic enterprises, known as 'nation branding' in language first used by Simon Anholt in 1996, clearly bring strong economic and, indeed, commercial interests to the table ostensibly being set for diplomacy.[7]

As Chapple-Sokol would be the first to signal, having placed his defining essay under an epigraph from Brillat-Savarin,[8] and having gone on to cite Carême in the body of his article, contemporary nation branding must trace its ancestry through nineteenth-century French *gastronomes*. Escoffier, I contend, is key.

Souvenirs Culinaires

In what follows, I'll assume some familiarity with Escoffier, one of the earliest celebrity chefs, and will give just a rough biographical sketch. Escoffier was born in 1846 in Villeneuve-Loubet, a village fifteen kilometres from Nice, still officially under the rule of Victor Emmanuel II. Child of a blacksmith father, he dreamed of being a sculptor, but was apprenticed at age thirteen to his uncle François who owned the upscale Restaurant Français in Nice. He had a meteoric rise, moving before he was twenty to the tiny Restaurant du Petit Moulin Rouge in Paris. He was then requisitioned as an officers' chef during the Franco-Prussian war, after which he split his time running restaurant and hotel kitchens in Paris, the French Riviera, Monte Carlo and Lucerne until teaming with Swiss hotel magnate César Ritz and moving to the new and fabulously modern Savoy Hotel in 1890, where he built up a royal clientele and illustrious reputation before mysteriously leaving in 1898. After a brief interlude at the Paris Ritz, he moved to the new London Carleton where he remained until 1920 except for guest appearances abroad, including one at the N.Y. Ritz and another on the SS Imperator, the flagship of the Hambourg-Amerika line.

Escoffier's memoir, posthumously published originally as *Souvenirs inédits* [*Unpublished Memories*], was a family effort. The souvenirs were in fact collected by his son and other family members from among autobiographical fragments Escoffier had written for this purpose but included also a selection of his published articles plucked from the *Art culinaire* and the *Carnets d'epicure* and recipes and menus scavenged from his cookbooks. For this reason the title was changed in a second edition to the more accurate *Souvenirs culinaires* [*Culinary Memories*]. The volume is a roughly chronological mosaic. There are accounts of his apprenticeship, his wartime feats, his years at the Savoy, the Ritz, the Carleton; a number of menus, a few recipes and a fair amount of name dropping. Escoffier's *Souvenirs* are a culinary variant of the classical model of biography: the book consists primarily of the feats of a great man (there's a bit about his brother and father; almost nothing about his mother and wife and children); there's a good deal about the excellence, gastronomic and otherwise, of the French, and about the fecklessness of the Germans and the tastelessness of the British; there's a heavy dose of thinly-disguised self congratulations on his resourcefulness and cleverness during the war and throughout his life.

To call Escoffier's *Souvenirs* self-promoting is probably a bit unfair: what author of an autobiography is not also its hero? And he does recount his numerous exploits with an occasional veneer of modesty. But it would be no exaggeration to call the book *French*-promoting. It speaks to the innate culinary superiority of the exceptional men of France who turn the natural bounty of French terroir, harvested from the earth, the sky, the sea and the vine, into exquisite French dishes piously preserved by the daily inventions of gastronomic genius as the regional treasures of French civilization. Lest you suspect my paraphrase of inflating Escoffier's rhetoric or of amplifying its emphasis on the natural and the inborn, let me cite one passage among many written in the same vein:

> On m'a souvent demandé pour quelles raisons les cuisiniers français sont supérieurs
> à ceux des autres pays. La réponse me paraît simple: il suffit de se rendre compte que

le sol français a le privilège de produire naturellement et en abondance les meilleurs légumes, les meilleurs fruits et les meilleurs vins qui soient au monde. La France possède aussi les plus fines volailles, les viandes les plus tendres, les gibiers les plus variés et les plus délicats. Sa situation maritime lui fournit les plus beaux poissons et crustacés. C'est donc tout naturellement que le Français devient tout à la fois gourmand et bon cuisinier. [I have often been asked the reason why French chefs are superior to those of other nationalities. The answer appears simple to me: it is sufficient to realize that French soil has the privilege of producing naturally and abundantly the best vegetables, the best fruits and the best wines in the world. France also possesses the finest fowl, the most tender meats, the most varied and most delicate game. Its maritime setting provides it with the finest fish and crustaceans. It is therefore completely natural that the Frenchman becomes at once a connoisseur and a creator of good food.][9]

This excerpt appears in the last chapter of the *Souvenirs*, '*Une Retraite active*' [An Active Retirement], which reports Escoffier's retirement at the age of seventy-four, in the summer of 1920, from the Carlton Hotel in London, and his return to his family in Monte Carlo after an absence of thirty years. He relates the ensuing boredom that prompts him to return to writing recipes and articles, and to begin his memoirs, with one overarching aim: '*Maintenir intacte la haute renommée de notre cuisine, et des vins exquis de France*' [To keep intact the high repute of our food and of the exquisite wines of France] (p. 229). Lest you imagine that the chef's note of fanaticism for all foods French is an attribute of nostalgia due to aging, retirement, the anticipated conclusion to his book or his life, let me assure you that it is a constant feature of his writing and that his ending merely continues the nationalistic fervour of his working days. As Timothy Shaw reminds us, 'this [...] was not only the age of Bergson; it was also the age of [...] Kipling, Péguy, Hillaire Belloc, Maurice Barrès, Lyautey and Cecil Rhodes.'[10] Enter Escoffier.

Is his jingoism in fact a displaced egotism? His prose comes close to suggesting this, as for example when he explains why he moved across London to the Carleton Hotel kitchens when forced to leave the Savoy, rather than returning home to family in Monte Carlo and the Edenic harvests adjacent in France: '*Il y avait dans ma décision une question d'amour-propre. Je ne voulais pas quitter l'Angleterre sans mener à bonne fin l'oeuvre commence au Savoy Hôtel: le développement de la cuisine française, non seulement en Angleterre, mais dans le monde entire*' [A note of vanity entered into my decision. I didn't want to leave England without successfully completing the work begun at the Savoy Hotel: the development of French cuisine, not only in England, but in the entire world] (pp. 152-53). As Escoffier recounts events, the story of his life and the history of France cannot always be neatly distinguished. So the founding and fostering of his London journal, *Le Carnet d'epicure*, is all in the service of publicizing (not to say propagandizing) the superiority of '*les meilleurs produits de notre sol et l'art de les accommoder*' [the best products of our soil and the art of preparing them], which takes in '*non seulement [...] la cuisine française [...] nos vins et fines liqueurs, mais aussi... argenterie, cristaux, verrerie, porcelaines diverses, nappes et serviettes*, éclairages, *fleurs, mais aussi des mille petites fantaisies qui complètent la toilette de la femme*' [not only [...] French cuisine [...] our wines and our fine liquors, but also [...] silver, crystal, glassware, a variety of porcelains, table linen, lighting, flowers and also a thousand caprices that perfect feminine beauty] (p. 198). In an ever-widening circle, Escoffier's journal aims to embrace the French table, French table arts, French women's fashion, and at the farthest reaches of the table, '*nos plus beaux sites, nos monuments historiques, nos musées*' [our finest sites, our historic monuments, our museums]. The distance between proclaiming this self-given responsibility to 'publicize' French gastronomy and elegant living and claiming the title of '*ambassadeur de la cuisine française*' is not great (p. 233). And for the self-appointed ambassador of gastronomy to declare that '*l'art de la cuisine est [...] une des formes les plus utiles de la diplomatie*' [the art of cooking [...] is one of the most useful forms of diplomacy] involves no stretch at all, simply a different turn of phrase (p. 236).

So, a century before Hillary Clinton, Auguste Escoffier came close to suggesting that he was setting the table for diplomacy. In fact he specifically observes that some of the dinners he hosted were the site of important political negotiations, at the very least what we might today call 'soft' ones. He recounts, for example, as *chef de cuisine* at the Restaurant du Petit Moulin Rouge in Paris, being asked in July 1874 to reserve a private salon and compose a special dinner menu for two notable epicures, Albert Edward, Prince of Wales, future King Edward VII, and Léon Gambetta. Looking back, he vaunts this dinner as having been politically pivotal: '*C'est probablement dans un salon du Petit Moulin Rouge que ces deux hommes ont posé les bases de la future 'Entente Cordiale' [réalisée trente ans plus tard, en 1907]*' [It was probably in a salon of the Petit Moulin Rouge restaurant that these two men laid the foundations of the future 'Entente Cordiale' (of 1907)] (*Souvenirs*, p. 109).

Escoffier's claims for diplomacy were both large and broad. Especially when they address his three decades in London, they might elicit another name...such as marketing. In a chapter extolling the triumph of French foodstuffs abroad ('*Le succès de nos produits alimentaires à l'étranger*' [the success of our food products abroad]), the chef writes, with habitual hyperbole, of the repute of French goods '*dans tous les marchés mondiaux*' [in all world markets] even in the face of '*la concurrence qui nous est faite par les autres pays*' [the competition of other countries]. In accounting for the acclaim of French products overseas ('*la vogue dont ils jouissent*'), however, he temporarily nuances his belief in the simple excellence of French soil and toil, necessary but not sufficient: '*C'est aussi que nos cuisiniers sont légion à l'étranger. Ces commis-voyageurs en toque blanche sont nos meilleurs agents commerciaux puisque, même loin de la France, ils conservent l'habitude de ne se servir que de produits de notre sol*' [Another factor is that our chefs are legion abroad. These traveling salesmen in tall white hats are our best commercial agents since, even far from France, they retain the habit of using only products of our soil] (p. 224).

Using a vocabulary of export and trade, Escoffier presents French chefs abroad as an economic corps embarked on a mission of public relations, marketing and sales for their country. Indeed, as he boasts of the legions of French chefs he has trained and dispersed to the world outside France – so many commercial boots on the ground spreading French cuisine to the far corners of the world like a superb Normandy butter or gastronomic manifest destiny – he evokes a kind of drawing off or draining of culinary talent from its native source. Just so his descriptions of the regionally-sourced French truffles, peaches, butter, ducks, asparagus, foie gras, sausages, oysters, oils, vinegars, plums, capons and scarlet-legged partridges that must be exported to London because their quality is without match not only outside the hexagon but even outside the boundaries of each individually circumscribed French terroir, be it a village or local pasture, field or forest.

The chef's Rabelaisian list of regions paired with delicacies is itself a verbal pouring forth of the bounty of France: *Le Périgord, ses dindes boursouflées de truffes; Nérac et Cahors, leurs terrines; Lyon, ses cervelas, Troyes, son indicible fromage de cochon; Strasbourg, ses carpes; Marseille, ses thons frais et marinés; Verdun, ses dragées; Niort, son angélique; Orléans, ses vinaigres; Bordeaux, son anisette; Sète, son huile de rose; Tours, ses pruneaux; Reims, son pain d'épice'* [Perigord, with its turkeys bursting with truffles; Nérac and Cahors, their terrines; Lyon, its sausages; Troyes, its indescribable headcheese; Strasbourg, its carps; Marseilles, its fresh marinated tuna; Verdun, its sugared almonds; Niort, its angelica; Orleans, its vinegars, Bordeaux, its anis liqueur; Sete, its rose oil; Tours, its plums; Rheims, its gingerbread] – and this is a very brief excerpt (pp. 234-35).

As might be guessed, this diffusion of goods being siphoned off from France to its expat chefs for the pleasure of foreigners (but ultimately for the greater good of the Nation) could conceivably lead to a depletion. Success, as we know, can be its own worst enemy. A case in point is Escoffier's invention, at the Savoy, of a dessert that was not at its origin as canned as what we find in many a bistro and café today: what he called '*ma création de la pêche Melba, maintenant de renommée mondiale*' [my creation of Peach Melba, now of world renown]. Perfect peaches, blanched and peeled, were placed on a bed of rich vanilla ice cream and blanketed by a raspberry coulis crowned by a veil of spun sugar. If almonds were in season, they could be scattered on top, slivered: fresh, never dried. Named for the Australian cantatrice Nellie Melba in honour of her role in *Lohengrin* at Covent Garden (1893), Pêche Melba was presented in a silver chalice nestled between the wings of a swan magnificently carved in ice, shrouded in vapours of dry ice. It quickly became the rage.

But not just any peach would do; what was needed was '*la pêche tendre… une pêche peu fragile… la pêche de Montreuil*' [a tender peach, firm, not fragile…a Montreuil peach] (p. 224). Escoffier had a real passion for Montreuil peaches, which featured on many a menu he composed, either *nature* or elaborated, but *la pêche Melba* was the summit. Predictably, the rush on tender Montreuil peaches took its toll: '*Depuis plusieurs années,*' relates Escoffier, '*cette qualité de pêches se fait rare*' [In the last several years this kind of peach has become rare], and he needs to search for a substitute (pp. 224-25). Similarly, the demand for green asparagus from Mérindol, in the Vaucluse, came to exceed the supply when Escoffier began to import vast quantities to London to satisfy his English customers at the Savoy, and he had to prevail upon growers in Lauris, a neighbouring town in the Vaucluse, to take up the cultivation of the vegetable for export.

What began as a trickle and then turned into a rush and in some cases even a drain of goods and labour was also a diffusion of Frenchness. For what was being exported to London (not insignificantly, the effective capital of the Western world at the time) along with chefs from Paris and truffles from Périgord, asparagus from Mérindol and peaches from Montreuil, were the recipes incorporating them: *Émincé de truffes à la crème* and truffle-studded *Poularde Sainte-Alliance*, layered with foie gras and garnished with ortolans; *Salade d'asperges aux truffes; Pointes d'asperges au beurre* and *Asperges sauce Mousseline*; *Pêches Melba* and *Pêches Alexandra* and in their most exquisite simplicity, *Les plus belles pêches de Montreuil.* What was being diffused to the outside world was a French identity itself being fused by the very process of this diasporic gastronomic outpouring. Priscilla Parkhurst Ferguson has quite rightly called French cuisine 'a national identity in the making'.[11]

The table was indeed being set for diplomacy. Just as we must read diplomacy here as nationalism, we should understand 'setting' as both laying out and casting: casting the table as a French table, casting the French table in a fixed form, creating what in today's lingo would be called a national brand.[12] (Other terms that come to mind are monument, *lieu de mémoire,* and propaganda: let us recall that the word 'propaganda,' like its cognate, 'propagate,' is derived from the Latin *propages*, something set out, spread out.)

On Communication

Anticipating the lavish contemporary 'spreads' that accompany contemporary state dinners at the White House and that characterize other high diplomatic tables, Escoffier was impresario to his own political-gastronomic table. He actively and purposefully took on a certain communicative role: that of setting out, spreading, making public – *propogandizing* – the idea of 'Frenchness' and his own place in its constitution. However, let us be clear: the idea of communication – derived from its root in the process of making common, making known, imparting knowledge, sharing information – overflows its neutral dictionary definition. For what is communicated, as psychoanalysis and other practices of reading teach us, may have at least as much to do with what is hidden, secreted, leaked involuntarily, as with what is deliberately divulged. Communication has also much to do with evasiveness and evasion. I have barely addressed Escoffier's personal flight, his thirty-year fugue from family and country. And

I haven't even mentioned the diversion of funds: the discovery by hotel auditors of the great chef's crime of embezzlement that led to his being silently sacked by the Savoy, along with his partner César Ritz and their head waiter, Louis Echenard, in 1898. Nor have I discussed the related disappearance and belated leaking of documents pertaining to this case: the signed confessions to the hushed-up crime which remained hidden for eighty-five years (doubtless to avoid a scandal that would have embarrassed Edward VII and the other royals), emerging and becoming public only in 1983 at the hand of food historian Paul Levy.[13]

How then do we know Escoffier beyond that monument to Frenchness he constructed in his *Souvenirs* and review articles? What do we say about his refusal to learn English during the thirty-year stint in England, his obstinate refusal to lose control of his mother tongue and his linguistic domain? There remains a good deal of ground for speculation about gaps, erasures, inconsistencies and evasiveness. The varied secondary sources I turned to handled gaps and secrets differently: alternately acknowledging and lamenting; resorting to filler material; writing a novel; falling back on the chronic biographical conditional to gloss over the unknown; or, in the case of the Escoffier Foundation website, run by the chef's heirs in Villeneuve-Loubet, crafting a narrative of circumlocution and indirection. Beyond the triumphant memoir and the celebratory biographies, there are unexpected traces of less congratulatory narratives; but they remain only stray threads.[14]

The loose ends of labyrinthine stories remain untied: the thirty-year exile from family while Escoffier cooked his fame (and eventual infamy) in London, while preaching in writing about how exquisite meals keep families under the same roof;[15] the lifetime friendship – or liaison – with Sarah Bernhardt and a host of other actresses and divas; the weekly siphoning of goods from his London restaurant orders, delivered to Southsea, to a certain 'Mr Boots' (– a code name for his wife, supporting a large household? a possible intermediary, who would then ship the packages to his wife? Or, as Paul Levy suggests, a second family?) We can only guess. Escoffier, known not only for codifying French cuisine but also for pioneering food preservation, recognized for opening restaurant doors to women, celebrated for reforming kitchen conditions and rehabilitating the status of chefs and of lesser kitchen workers, may in fact, according to little-heard reports, have worked some kitchen boys to their death.[16] Renowned as *le chef des rois et le roi des chefs* [the chef of kings and the king of chefs], Escoffier remains at the same time profoundly unknown to his modern public, an elusive celebrity, slippery, perplexing and troubling. As such he represents an emblematic predecessor to many a contemporary practitioner of culinary diplomacy, going forth boldly to brand nations, build economies, bolster commerce, foster community, all the while deploying strategies whose political-individual investments may be difficult to fully disentangle.

Notes

1. See for example, Sam Chapple-Sokol, 'Culinary Diplomacy: Breaking Bread to Win Hearts and Minds', *The Hague Journal of Diplomacy,* 8 (2013), pp. 161-83; Paul Rockower, 'Recipes for Gastrodiplomacy: Place Branding and Public Diplomacy', *Place Branding and Public Diplomacy,* 8.3 (2012), pp. 235-46; 'Projecting Taiwan: Taiwan's Public Diplomacy Outreach', *Issues and Studies,* 47.1 (March 2011), pp. 107-52. My gratitude to Bill Yosses for beginning the conversation on culinary diplomacy.

2. See Conflict Kitchen, 'About', *Conflict Kitchen* <http://www.conflictkitchen.org/about/>.

3. José Andrés, Public Lecture, Science of Cooking Lecture Series, Harvard University, 30 September 2013.

4. 'Culinary Diplomacy at the White House', Reuters News/USA, 5 August 2014.

5. According to the *Economist*, this 'will not only introduce deliciously spicy Thai food to thousands of new tummies and persuade more people to visit Thailand, but it could subtly help to deepen relations with other countries' ('Thailand's Gastro-Diplomacy', 23 February 2002, p. 84).

6. The Thai and Korean efforts were followed by gastrodiplomatic moves in Taiwan and Malaysia.

7. Simon Anholt, *Competitive Identity: The New Brand Management for Nations, Cities and Regions* (New York: Palgrave MacMillan, 2007). Anholt observes, 'the reputations of countries are rather like the brand images of companies and products' (p. xi). See too Michaela DeSoucey, 'Gastronationalism: Food Traditions and Authenticity Politics in the European Union,' in *American Sociological Review,* 75:3 (June 2010), pp. 432-55.

8. '*La destinée des nations dépend de la manière dont elles se nourrissent*' [The fate of nations depends on how they feed themselves] (Jean Anthelme Brillat-Savarin, *Physiologie du goût* (Paris: Flammarion, 1982 [1825], *Aphorismes*, p. 19. All translations from the French are my own.

9. Georges Auguste Escoffier, *Souvenirs culinaires,* ed. Pascal Ory (Paris: Mercure de France, 2011), p. 234.

10. Timothy Shaw, *The World of Escoffier* (London: Zwemmer, 1994), p. 140.

11. *Accounting for Taste: The Triumph of French Cuisine* (Chicago: University of Chicago Press, 2004), p. 5; see too Arjun Appadurai, 'How to Make a National Cuisine: Cookbooks in Contemporary India', *Comparative Studies in Society and History,* 31.1 (January 1988), pp. 3-24.

12. A national brand having to do with 'national identity and the politics and economics of competitiveness' (Anholt, p. xi)

13. See Paul Levy, 'The Master Chef who Cooked the Books', *The Telegraph* (9 June 2012). See also Michel Roux, Jr, *The First Master Chef: Michel Roux on Escoffier,* BBC 2013.

14. See Pierre Hamp, *Mes* Métiers (Paris: Gallimard, 1943), for a less than positive account of the author's internship with Escoffier in London, at the Savoy. For analogous accounts of the position of underlings in the restaurant trade (not concerning Escoffier) see George Orwell, *Down and Out in Paris and London* (New York: Houghton Mifflin Harcourt, 1966 (1933)). My other principle sources on Escoffier (not mentioned earlier) were the following: Jean Marc Boucher, *Auguste Escoffier: Préceptes et transmission de la cuisine de 1880 à nos jours* (Paris: L'Harmattan, 2014); Michel Gall, *Le Maître des saveurs: La Vie d'Auguste Escoffier* (Paris: Ed. De Fallois, 2001); Eugène Herbodeau and Paul Thalamus, *Georges Auguste Escoffier* (London : Practical, 1955); Kenneth James, *Escoffier: The King of Chefs* (London: Bloomsbury, 2002); N. M. Kelby, *White Truffles in Winter* (New York: W.W. Norton, 2012).

15. See James, p. 207.

16. See Hamp, p. 154 ff.

Nobody Said to Cook: The Chinese Food of Emily Hahn and Time Life Books

Lucy Bowen

Call it a Chinese Food Summit. On 21 March 1967, the editorial staff of *The Cooking of China* summoned a select group to dinner. Seated at a table for ten at the Mandarin East Restaurant, 1085 Second Avenue, in New York City, were Emily Hahn, the nominal author of the book, Theodore and Emily Kwoh, Florence Lin and Grace Chu, the stars of the Manhattan's Chinese restaurant and cooking scene. In ten years these refugees from Communist China had revolutionized the perception of Chinese food by introducing dishes that were more complex and challenging to the American palate than chop suey.

This is what they ate:

Salad of chrysanthemum leaves, Chinese sausage and shredded cucumber
Abalone, steamed egg, roast pork, shrimp, dried mushrooms and jellyfish
Chicken-in-snow – finely cut chicken served in a fluffy meringue of egg whites
decorated with delicately crisscrossed slices of ham and green vegetable
Lobster in tomato sauce
Scallops with water chestnuts and snow peas
Phoenix-tail shrimp and livers
Peking duck with meat, skin, scallion flowers, pancakes and bean paste smuggled
in from mainland China
Crispy sweet-and-sour sea bass
Winter melon balls and dried scallops
Eight treasure rice pudding

Hahn needed to understand the regional cooking styles of China, and this group were experts. For the expatriates, much was at stake: how to represent the culinary treasures of a nation they loved and had lost to Mao. The Time Life Books research staff suspected that the answers might require changes to the book's organization. For Hahn, the dinner meant a great meal and a round trip plane ticket from London to New York. Hahn was seated to the right of Emily Kwoh, and next to Theodore Kwoh, the owners of the restaurant.

To Americans, Hahn was a regular contributor to the *New Yorker*, author of more than three dozen non-fiction books on an encyclopedia of topics. Her expertise on the subject of China was based on personal experience. She had lived in Shanghai with a married Chinese lover from the late 1930s until the start of World War II. In the midst of

Japanese bombing she flew to Chongking to write the exclusive, authorized biography of the Soong sisters, one of whom was married to General Chiang Kai-Shek (Hahn 1941). In 1941, as an American with a Chinese passport provided by that Chinese lover, Hahn remained in Japanese-occupied Hong Kong. She smuggled food to Major Charles Boxer, a British intelligence agent, imprisoned by the Japanese. He was her infant daughter's father. Hahn was neither a suffragette, as her mother was, nor young feminist of the sort was emerging in the 1960s. She was independent, attractive and unconventional. Her scandal-filled memoir, *China to Me* (Hahn 1944), was a bestseller. Ken Cuthbertson's full-length biography of her is titled *Nobody Said Not to Go*. She did what she wanted.

My title, 'Nobody Said to Cook', might have been Hahn's answer to those questioning her credentials for writing a Chinese cookbook. In 1959, she had written 'A World of Rice' for *Gourmet* Magazine but she would have been the first person to tell you she cared little about food until she went to China. Hahn says so in her preface to *The Cooking of China*:

> It's amazing to think about. There was I, nourished on steak, pot roast, apple pie a la mode, banana split, and (on football days) waffles with a heathen mixture of sausages and syrup. There was I, suddenly face to face with the ancient, honorable and superlative cuisine of the world's oldest civilization. Inevitably the result of the confrontation was a complete transformation of one opinionated Midwesterner to whom all food, but especially Chinese food, suddenly became a brilliant revelation.

74

You could say that there was an additional host at the dinner, the ghost, if you will, of Henry R. Luce, Time Inc. founder and publishing giant. Even though Luce died in February, 1967, a month before the dinner took place, his presence was surely felt at the table. Luce was well known for his outspoken support of Chiang Kai-Shek's Nationalist Government in its struggle against the Communists. In New York, his China Institute continued to support the Nationalist government in Taiwan.

I'm not claiming that Luce played a direct role in *The Cooking of China*. He had retired from publishing operations three years earlier – and besides, he was a five-pack a day smoker, not much interested in food: Luce generally consumed a full American breakfast, and not much else (Herzstein 2005: 244).

I will argue, however, that Luce and his publishing empire created editorial formulas for the production of periodical magazines, and applied them to cookbooks. *The Cooking of China* was one of the first of the ground-breaking series, Foods of the World. Luce's views of the world were embedded in the process, and shaped the product in significant ways.

Luce's view of China was formed in his childhood. Luce was born in his parent's missionary compound in Dengzhou (now Penglai), a port city in Shandong Province, China, in 1895. In his teens he was sent to school in New England, first to a preparatory school, Hotchkiss, and then to Yale University. There, under the influence of his classmate Briton Hadden, he decided on a career in journalism. After graduation, Luce travelled extensively in Europe. In 1923, the pair founded *Time Magazine*, America's first weekly of national and international news. Hadden gave it an unforgettable shape. In addition to a much mocked sentence style – Wolcott Gibbs parodied it thus: 'Backward ran sentences until reeled the mind' – *Time* organized national and world events into Departments. Researchers and writers worked in teams to prepare short essays based on newspaper and wire service reportage. The magazine was a financial success.

Luce broke new ground in 1930 with *Fortune*, a graphically-stunning monthly, dedicated to in-depth reporting on the large corporations taking shape in all parts of the economy. In 1934, he founded *Life*, a weekly that told the news in photographs, charts and maps. By the early 1960s, Time Inc. had made Luce a very wealthy man and the largest and most prestigious magazine publisher in the world (Drucker 1997: 243).

In international affairs, Luce was an interventionist. He articulated his philosophy of America's obligation to provide world leadership in a February 1941 editorial entitled 'The American Century' in the pages of *Life*. Some distrusted his publications because of his politics, and with good reason: his opposition to communism, first in China and later in Vietnam, influenced both his philanthropy and his news coverage. His defenders pointed out that he gave his editors great latitude to cover events as they saw them (Baughman 2010:7) – but some intellectuals openly disparaged his 'group journalism' approach to reporting, quipping that Luce's researchers never knew the story, and his writers never knew the facts (Drucker 1997: 242).

In the sixties, in spite of its size and success, television ate into *Life*'s subscription base. When the idea of Time Life Books was first proposed, Luce resisted it (Drucker 1997: 237). He was anticipating his retirement in 1964 and didn't want to start a new venture. Yet he did want to educate the American public, and the resources of his publishing empire could make a contribution. Finally, he acquiesced. Illustrated with a mixture of fresh photographs and those from Time Inc.'s archive, the largest and most exciting in the world at the time, the books were backed by a research staff with access to the news morgue (Hatch 2001). Advertised and marketed nationally by direct mail to *Time, Fortune* and *Life* readers, the hardcover books sold by subscription for $2.95 each, plus shipping and handling. Series followed series and Time Life Books became Time Inc.'s cash cow.

In May of 1966, Time Life Books editor Richard L. Williams circulated a prospectus for a new series, Foods of the World. This series would be different from earlier ones: more than reading material, it would provide a socially necessary service in the kitchen and dining room. It must be mistake-free, lest hundreds of soufflés fall. In Williams's vision, the series covered the world by country by country, telling the origin of food and cuisine, culinary histories, habits and food preparation – 'why they do what they do and what they do best'. Williams argued the business and marketing case for the series. According to Williams, Time Inc.'s resources meant that 'Better than virtually anybody else, we can show and tell how to beat an egg'. As planned, subscribers would be offered a volume every two months and could subscribe to the entire series.

Time Inc. had the resources. The front material for each volume credits an author, consultants, photographers, editor, lead and additional researchers, two writers and a photography editor. The food critic Mimi Sheraton called them 'a virtual platoon' (1979). Each book in the series had its own team. All reported to Williams, who reported to two more layers of management.

For Foods of the World, something new was in store. Williams vetoed anonymous group-journalism, because 'a corporate point of view on how to stir mayonnaise doesn't necessarily make for a good cookbook'. Instead, a good writer 'with a point of view to which the reader can react' would be sought out, on staff or from outside. Williams did something even more radical.

He hired women, first M.F.K. Fisher, and then Emily Hahn.

This was a clear break with Time Life tradition. Luce's kingdom from top to bottom was decidedly male dominated – editors and writers were men, and women mere researchers. Williams' choice for *The Cooking of China* was a best-selling author, a famous and infamous China expert who revered Chinese food.

The earliest record of Hahn's involvement is the letter Williams wrote to her at her home in England, in June of 1966. (Hahn's copies of correspondence, Prospectus, notes and drafts are found in Hahn Mss.) He claimed that M.F.K. Fisher was already under contract to write *The Cooking of Provincial France* and Waverly Root, *The Cooking of Italy*. Four months later, Hahn's contract with Time Life Books was signed.

At first, Hahn's task went smoothly. In September and October, Emily and Editor James Wyckoff exchanged chapter outlines and summaries. After several revisions, the book took shape. The first chapter would describe in detail a banquet given by an imaginary official of the Qing Court. The next two chapters introduced cooking methods, tools and ingredients. The fourth chapter explored the extensive Chinese literature about food. The subsequent two described the staples of rice, wheat, tea and rice wine. The seventh chapter described the food associated with specific festivals, like the New Year and Moon Festivals. The final chapter explored the diffusion of Chinese food to the rest of the world.

In early 1967, at her home in rural Hertfordshire, Emily began drafting complete chapters. In each she recalled some aspect of her sojourns in Shanghai and Hong Kong. These personal recollections acted as a bridge into the subject for North American readers. To the staff, Hahn freely confessed her ignorance of certain crucial topics: in particular, how to accurately describe the regional styles of Chinese cuisine.

Hence the Chinese Food Summit at the Mandarin East in March, 1967. The book's researchers, Diane Kelly, Marjorie Chester and Iris Unger Friedlander planned it and attended to take notes. Luce once observed that in making researcher a serious occupation, he inaugurated 'a new order of female priesthood, the modern vestal virgin whom writers cajole in vain, and managing editors learn humbly to appease' (Jessup 1969:58-59). The researchers carefully plotted a seating chart, alternating the experts and researchers. Kelly noted to Hahn: 'Marjorie suggested a discussion of the regional breakdown and we might get each person to voice his opinion as to the specialty of his region. Theodore Kwoh on Shantung and Peking; Emily Kwoh on Shanghai and Szechuan; Florence on Fukien.' Emily Kwoh and her husband owned the hosting restaurant and several others in Manhattan. Florence Lin was famous for her cooking classes. Grace Chu's meals at the Chinese Embassy in Washington, DC in the 1940s had made her reputation as a hostess. She also taught, and in 1962 authored *The Pleasures of Chinese Cooking*. Both Lin and Chu were recipe consultants for the book.

Once again the book's content was being shaped by women.

Ironically, in China, professional chefs were men of low status who occasionally became famous. Well-born women like Florence Lin, Grace Zia Chu and Emily Kwoh never entered a kitchen until they were students or expatriates in the United States, forced to recall and reconstruct dishes they had eaten in their youth in order to make a living in their changed circumstances. The food critic Mimi Sheraton once referred to these three ladies as a 'group of Chinese girls who had studied at Wellesley, missionaries' (Weinraub 2009). By the time they gathered at the Mandarin East, they were, like Hahn, middle-aged and well-preserved. I call them the *Mesdames*, in deference to Madame Chiang Kai Shek, who was their friend.

Why was the topic of regional cuisine so troubling? For Chinese food aficionados in late 1960s New York, Regional was code for Authentic. Authentic appealed to those wishing to appear knowing, to rise above the ordinary. In preparation for the dinner the research staff had combed the extant English language Chinese cookbooks and translations of the voluminous Chinese literature about food. (These are listed in Appendix I, below.) They prepared a matrix of each region's specialty dishes and characteristics. By late March of 1967, Hahn's text must have been almost ready for her April 1 deadline. Still there was confusion. Were there eight regional cuisines? Five? Four? What about Tibet, which China had recently annexed?

The confusion of the Time Life staff may have stemmed from the structure of the other two volumes under development. For *The Cooking of Italy*, Waverley Root had no difficulty capturing the regional cuisines of Italy, and the book was organized accordingly. M.F.K. Fisher's *The Cooking of Provincial France* was not organized by province, and was attacked by Craig Claiborne for including recipes more *haute* Parisian than provincial (Claiborne 1968). Should *The Cooking of China* be organized by region? Could this be accomplished when Hahn and the Nationalist *Mesdames* were thousands of miles and two decades removed from mainland China? These questions were important enough to bring Hahn from England to New York.

What was the decision? The day after the banquet, Chester recorded the thoughts of the *Mesdames* of the question of 'How to divide Chinese Cuisine'. She reported that:

> The general opinion was that the original five schools should be mentioned and described *but* in terms of the cuisine as it is today. The regional description

dealing with the _four areas_ that Florence Lin refers to would be more helpful and accurate. The original schools of cooking are no longer the narrow specialized cuisines they were, and a considerable blending of dishes, even specialties has taken place, especially in the large cities.

In her introduction to the published book, Hahn warned that the volume described the cooking of the 'old China,' before the Communist takeover. She reported, 'Grace and Emily [Kwoh] felt that this blending was a good thing for the future of Chinese food, because a) the best dishes and traditions of the schools were kept and b) the trend resulting from this was the gradual formation of a more national cuisine' (Hahn 1968: 186).

As members of the Republican elite, the _Mesdames_, like the Emperor before them, knew and enjoyed each region's special foodstuffs and dishes. They framed their memories to represent a national cuisine. Mark Swislocki, in his _Culinary Nostalgia_, allows that during the Republican era in Shanghai, 'when civil war tore apart the Chinese body politic, Shanghai residents turned to food once again, this time the city's many regional Chinese restaurants, to connect with their country's rich heritage, and to imagine for themselves how such a culturally diverse country might be held together' (2009: 26). This politically charged imagining continued in exile on Taiwan, and in New York. When the book was published in 1968, the regional cuisines were presented in charts and maps, but the book was organized to reflect the common elements of a national cuisine.

Did this 'group journalism' compromise the individual author? Did it compromise Hahn's views...and ours? The three researchers, Kelly, Chester and Friedlander, had already forwarded many articles and interviews to Hahn throughout the spring of 1967. Hahn had seamlessly extended her authorial 'I' to encompass these materials, which included everything from Chinese philosophies of food to Kelly's interview with renowned Chef T.T. Wang of Shun Lee Dynasty. Kelly also forwarded menus and comments from consultants Florence Lin and Grace Zia Chu. _Time_'s far-flung correspondents contributed accounts of Chinese restaurants all around the world, and these, too, were incorporated into the narrative.

M.F.K. Fisher, with her distinctive trenchant style, had threatened to quit when she received multiple comments from multiple editors regarding her text for _The Cooking of Provincial France_ (Barr 2013: 36-37 and Reardon 2004: 344-345). Santha Rama Rau, writing _The Cooking of India and Pakistan_, also balked at changes suggested to her (Burton 2007: 115). Hahn accommodated additions and changes. She had no hesitation in refashioning material as needed. In 1970, for example, she cheerfully recycled over forty years of her _New Yorker_ 'Reporter at Large' columns into an autobiography she'd promised to publisher Thomas Crowell (Cuthbertson 2009: xix).

Why did Hahn proceed where others bridled at interference? Time Life paid good money. Hahn's contract specified ten thousand dollars, the equivalent of almost eighty thousand today, for forty thousand words. Hahn prided herself on making her own way financially. She had a husband and old house in England to maintain, and school fees for her daughters. She needed the money.

Hahn's sixty pages of text were less than half the volume. The other half of the book was produced by another platoon of photographers and graphic artists, working in parallel. On 19 October 1966, Kelly forwarded to Hahn a copy of the shooting script prepared by Friedlander for Mike Rougier, the photographer. The editors justified 'location' photography in real kitchens in Hong Kong and Taiwan as helping 'to remove cooking from an essentially isolated experience in the kitchen and places it in the context of the culture and people'.

The editors wanted reportage in the style of *Life*: process shots in the field, showing who was cooking. These would be run as 'picture acts'. Unscripted situations, illustrating the uniqueness and sophistication of Chinese cuisine, were to capture the precise moment where 'everything had jelled'. Again, the researchers had done their homework, producing a detailed list. Photographs were to be taken of Mrs. Fu Mei-Pei, a Taipai television chef; a family of 'landed gentry' of Taiwan, exemplifying the 'old' China; a family 'on one of the nicer junks in Hong Kong harbor'; a birthday celebration; a tea plantation; meatless cuisine of Buddhist monastery in Hong Kong's New Territories; noodle and soy sauce manufacture; cooking utensils and kitchens; Chinese crops and vegetables; and Peking Duck preparation and delivery. Less important were street vendors, novice chopstick use and restaurant situations.

This was no small assignment. To make sure that all went well, every precaution was taken. Time Life employed a Swedish photographer who could gain entry to the mainland. An examination of the volume, however, shows that Rougier was able to obtain almost all that was needed to illustrate Hahn's text in Hong Kong and Taiwan.

Foods of the World established new genres of food writing: cookbook as travelogue, cookbook as memoir. The series set a standard for instructional cookbooks. The recipes supplied by Lin and Chu were tested under the supervision of Michael Fields, concert pianist turned cooking school impresario. As published, a dozen or so recipes followed each chapter, in no apparent order. Emily's text is interspersed with pages of photographs, diagrams and captions written by the Time Life staff. The smaller spiral-bound book, suitable for use in the kitchen, contained additional recipes.

If Time Life's methods benefited readers aspiring to cook Chinese, Luce's politics had an impact on the popularization of the Nationalist Chinese *Mesdames'* elite versions of Chinese food. This was reinforced by beginning *The Cooking of China* with a description of a court banquet, with its focus on etiquette and ritual. The *Mesdames* gave cooking classes at the Luce-funded China Institute. These were publicized by the influential New York Times food critic, Craig Claiborne (Claiborne 1963).

Luce's abhorrence of Mao's revolution was reflected elsewhere in the book. Hahn quoted her friend Peggy Durdin, a China-watcher in Hong Kong, who said the Chinese would never forgive Mao for dismantling the beloved institutions of Chinese cooking in favour of communal kitchens (Durdin 1961). Hahn predicted that expatriates like the *Mesdames* would preserve the best of Chinese cooking, overseas. Was she accurate? Mao's Cultural Revolution soon began and took its toll on chefs and 'bourgeois' restaurants. Yet after Mao's death, regional Chinese food was revived on the mainland. In the United States, recent changes to immigration laws meant new arrivals and new regional specialties. The food critic Jonathan Gold recently listed no fewer than seventeen regional restaurants in suburban Los Angeles (Hallock 2013).

Whatever the limitations of *The Cooking of China,* whatever the sexism in Luce's organization, Emily Hahn, her platoon of vestal virgin researchers and the *Mesdames* changed what Americans cooked and ate, opening mouths and kitchens to a wider world of food.

References

Barr, Luke. 2014. *Provence, 1970: M.F.K. Fisher, Julia Child, James Beard and the Reinvention of American Taste* (New York: Clarkson Potter).

Baughman, James L. 2010. *Henry R Luce and the Rise of the American News Media* (Baltimore: Johns Hopkins University Press).

Burton, Antoinette. 2007. *The Postcolonial Careers of Santha Rama Rau* (Durham: Duke University Press).

Chu, Grace Zia. 1974. *The Pleasures of Chinese Cooking* (London: Faber and Faber). Originally published 1962.

Claiborne, Craig. 1963. 'Restaurant Review: Mandarin East Specializes in Spicy Food of Sichuan School of Cooking', *New York Times*, 19 April. <http://query.nytimes.com/gst/abstract.html?res=9C0CE3D71339 E43BBC4152DFB2668388679EDE> [accessed 30 May 2015].

Claiborne, Craig. 1968. 'Debut for Series of International Cookbooks', *New York Times*, 19 February. <http://query.nytimes.com/gst/abstract.html?res=9D07E3D71031E034BC4152DFB4668383679EDE> [accessed 30 May 2015].

Claiborne, Craig and Virginia Lee. 1972. *The Chinese Cookbook* (Philadelphia: Lippincott).

Cuthbertson, Ken. 1998. *Nobody Said Not to Go: The Life, Loves and Adventures of Emily Hahn* (Boston: Faber and Faber).

Drucker, Peter F. 1997. *Adventures of A Bystander* (New Brunswick: Transaction Publishers).

Durdin, Peggy. 1961. 'Mao's "Great Crime" Against Cuisine; China's Leader is Charged with Destroying that Great Pleasure of All Chinese---Good Food', *New York Times Magazine*, <http://query.nytimes.com/gst/abstract.html?res=9E00E1DA1630EE32A2575AC1A9659C946091D6CF> [accessed 30 May 2015].

Hahn, Emily. Hahn Mss. III. Manuscripts Department, Lilly Library, Indiana University, Bloomington, Indiana

Hahn, Emily. 1941. *The Soong Sisters* (New York: Open Road Integrated Media). Republished 2014.

Hahn, Emily. 1944. *China to Me* (Garden City: Garden City Publishing Company).

Hahn, Emily and the Editors of Time-Life Books. 1968. *The Cooking of China* (New York: Time-Life Books).

Hahn, Emily. 2000. *No Hurry to Get Home* (Seattle: Seal Press). Originally published in 1970 as *Times and Places: A Memoir* (New York: Thomas Y. Crowell and Company).

Herzstein, Robert E. 2005. *Henry R. Luce, 'Time', and the American Crusade in Asia* (Cambridge: Cambridge University Press).

Hatch, Denny. 2001, 'The Rise and Fall of Time-Life Books', *Target Marketing*. <http://www.targetmarketingmag.com/article/the-rise-fall-time-life-books-2-310-words-28269/> [accessed 30 May 2015].

Hallock, Betty. 2013. 'Jonathan Gold's Best Chinese Restaurants in L.A. by Region', *Los Angeles Times*, 15 February. <http://articles.latimes.com/2013/feb/15/news/la-dd-jonathan-gold-best-chinese-restaurants-in-los-angeles-20130215> [accessed 30 May 2015].

Jessup, John K. (ed.). 1969. *The Ideas of Henry Luce* (New York: Atheneum).

Lin, Florence. 1975. *Florence Lin's Chinese Regional Cookbook* (New York: Hawthorne).

Sheraton, Mimi. 1979. 'Flawed Start for a Major Cookbook Series' *New York Times*. <http://query.nytimes.com/gst/abstract.html?res=9F05EFDC1E39E732A25752C2A9659C946890D6CF> [accessed 30 May 2015].

Swislocki, Mark. 2009. *Culinary Nostalgia: Regional Food Culture and the Urban Experience in Shanghai* (Stanford: Stanford University Press).

Weinraub, Judith. 2009. 'Voices from the Food Revolution: People Who Changed the Way Americans Eat' Interview with Mimi Sheraton. <http://dlib.nyu.edu/beard/interviews/mimi-sheraton-interview-1> and <http://dlib.nyu.edu/beard/sites/dlib.nyu.edu.beard/files/Sheraton_Mimi-2009_07_02-transcript.doc> [Accessed 30 May 2015].

Appendix I: Sources Consulted by Time-Life Book staff in the production of *The Cooking of China*. Where publication information is listed, I have obtained and consulted a copy.

Burckhardt, V.R. 1958. *Chinese Creeds and Customs* (Hong Kong: [n. pub.].

Buck, John Lossing. *Land Utilization in China.*

Carl, Katherine A. 1986. *With the Empress Dowager of China* (London: KPI Limited). Originally published 1906.

Cameron, Nigel and Brian Brake. *Peking.*

Chao, Buwei Yang. 1963. *How to Cook and Eat in Chinese* (Random House: New York). Originally published 1945.

Chen, Joyce. *The Joyce Chen Cookbook.*

Cheng, F.T. 1962 *Musings of A Chinese Gourmet* (London: Hutchinson). Originally published 1954.

Chu, Grace Zia. 1974. *The Pleasures of Chinese Cooking* (London: Faber and Faber).

Chung, Su [Lucille Davis]. 1966. *Court Dishes of China: The Cuisine of the Ch'ing Dynasty* (Rutland, Vermont: Tuttle).

Feng, Doreen Yen Hung. *The Joy of Chinese Cooking.*

Giles, Herbert A. *A History of Chinese Literature.*

Hahn, Emily. *China Only Yesterday.*

Hahn, Emily. 1944. *China to Me* (Garden City: Garden City Publishing).

Johnson, Reginald F. *Twilight in the Forbidden City.*

Kaufman, William I. *The Tea Cookbook.*

Keys, John D. *Food for the Emperor.*

Kung, S.W. *The Chinese in American Life.*

Lee, Su Jan. 1962. *The Fine Art of Chinese Cooking* (New York: Gramercy).

Levy, Howard S. 1958. *Harem Favorites of An Illustrious Celestial* (Taichung, Taiwan: Chung-T'ai Printing Company).

Lin Yutang. *The Gay Genius,*

—.*The Importance of Understanding* .

—.*My Country and My People.*

Ling, Princess Der. *Two Years in the Forbidden City.*

Ma, Nancy Chih. 1961. *Mrs. Ma's Chinese Cookbook* (Rutland, Vermont: Tuttle).

Miller, Gloria Bley. *The Thousand Recipe Chinese Cookbook.*

Ouei, Mimie.1960. *The Art of Chinese Cooking* (New York: Random House).

Polo, Marco. *The Travels of Marco Polo.* Trans. William Marsden.

Schafer, Edward H. and the Editors of Time-Life Books. *Ancient China.*
Sia, Mary. 1956. *Mary Sia's Chinese Cookbook* (Honolulu: University of Hawaii Press).
Ukers, William. *The Romance of Tea.*
Waley, Arthur. *The Life and Times of Li Po.*
—. *The Life and Times of Po Chu-i.*
—. *Translations from the Chinese.*
Yang, Martin. *A Chinese Village.*
The Yellow Emperor's Classic of Internal Medicine. Trans. I. Veith.

Tablecloth and River: Dramatizing Historical Land Claims in Tomson Highway's *Ernestine Shuswap Gets Her Trout*

Shelley Boyd

Introduction

What meal do you prepare when you have been denied access to your traditional food sources by the very guest who is invited to dinner? What if there is no place for you at the table? These disempowering circumstances take centre stage in the play *Ernestine Shuswap Gets Her Trout: A String 'Quartet' for Four Female Actors* (2004) by Tomson Highway, one of Canada's most celebrated aboriginal playwrights. Highway dramatizes what he calls a 'mega banquet': an allegorical feast prepared by four women who personify both the voice of the Thompson River in the Canadian province of British Columbia and the local tribes as they anticipate the arrival of Prime Minister Sir Wilfrid Laurier for the presentation of the Laurier Memorial in 1910.[1] The Laurier Memorial is a narrativized document which was prepared and signed by the chiefs of the Shuswap, Okanagan and Couteau (or Thompson) tribes, and traces the history of native and non-native relations in the region from the time of the French fur trade to English settlement and asks that aboriginal land rights be respected. Although treaties were negotiated with the Crown throughout the colony since the eighteenth century, the province of British Columbia was the exception.[2] In order to renew the Memorial's message, Highway dramatizes an imagined food event that re-contextualizes the political process by exposing the fact that those who govern can be the very cause of inequality and starvation. The four Native women depicted in Highway's play face systematic exclusion from the land, the river and the table – places that should facilitate the collective care and well-being of their communities. To counter this injustice, Highway uses the women's transformational presence and the tablecloth-turned-river to offer a hopeful vision of both physical and spiritual nourishment for Native peoples. At the same time, he exposes a flawed Canadian democracy whose hierarchal governance fails to sustain community.

Historical Context

As an historical document, the Laurier Memorial is a compelling declaration of First Nations' rights as the original inhabitants of what is now known as Canada, and of the interrelationship between territory and cultural foodways. In their opening address, the chiefs welcome the Prime Minister to their country and state that both French trappers and English settlers have always been 'guests' in these lands: 'With us when a person enters our house he becomes our guest, and we must treat him hospitably as long as he shows no hostile intentions. At the same time we expect him to return to us equal treatment for what he receives.'[3] The term 'guest,' as Duane Thomson and Marianne Ignace explain, differentiates between those who have ancestral rights to tribal territories and those who do not.[4] First Nations were reassured for years by their 'guests' that 'the queen's laws would prevail in this country, and everything would be well for the Indians': tribal lands would be purchased by the government, reservations would be created, and aboriginal hunting, fishing and grazing rights would be upheld. Despite such promises, the Memorial details how this legally entitled form of reciprocity did not transpire (The Shuswap Nation). Restrictions on hunting and fishing rights and the founding of reserves on undesirable lands, over which the government claimed ownership, meant that the tribes were left 'landless' and living on territory 'unfit or inadequate to maintain' the health and well-being of their people (The Shuswap Nation). The Memorial is further evidence of what Margery Fee calls the 'nutrition transition': the history of colonization in North America is directly related to Native peoples' interconnected loss of traditional lands, foodways and cultural identities.[5] Significantly, the Memorial repeats the questions of tribal elders: '"How are we to live? If the government takes our food from us they must give us other food in its place"' (The Shuswap Nation). Because of the document's powerful recounting of the tangible effects of colonization, twenty-first-century commentators describe it as 'profoundly written, founded in history and law, and built around the force of ethical standards'.[6] As an historical event, however, the Memorial points to a failure of communication between nations. In 1910, Prime Minister Laurier pledged to help the chiefs, but his promise remained unfulfilled, and over one hundred years later, the First Nations of British Columbia continue to call for fair negotiations of unceded territories.

Speaking through Food on Stage

So why readdress the Laurier Memorial through a play that gives an ahistorical feast the central communicative role? When Highway was commissioned in 2003 by the Secwépemc Cultural Education Society and the Western Canada Theatre to commemorate the Memorial's one hundredth anniversary, the playwright described the document as 'undramatizable'.[7] Speaking in an interview, Highway relates that he drew his inspiration instead from a photograph of four Shuswap women featured in a Kamloops newsletter: 'Why are there no women in the picture? Who prepared the meal, and who set the table and worked in the background? Whoever that is, they are never recognized, their contribution to human history is never given recognition.'[8]

In the play, these women become the wives of the local chiefs as they prepare to welcome Prime Minister Laurier. Each is responsible for a different task: Ernestine Shuswap prepares the stuffed trout; Isabel Thompson, the Saskatoon berry pies; Annabelle Okanagan, the boiled beaver; and Delilah Rose Johnson, the tablecloths. Representing 'different reactions to colonization from complete assimilation to overt resistance' as one critic observes, the women also belong to groups that have experienced inter-tribal conflicts.[9] Their cooperative undertaking requires 'considerable political initiative', as did the original composition of the Laurier Memorial.[10] The women must address tensions amongst themselves over Catholic beliefs; recent Protestant alliances through interracial marriage; and the loss of their tribal lands, cultures and languages. The play culminates in the suicide of Delilah Rose Johnson, the youngest of the four, who is married to a cowboy who is the son of an English civil servant responsible for infringements on tribal rights. Pregnant with her first child, Delilah Rose is overwhelmed by her divided sense of loyalties, yet despite her tragic end, the women manage to create a meal from local ingredients that expresses their concerns.

The play centres on food gathering and preparations, concluding with the feast being served, but not consumed, as the women exit the theatre and copies of the Laurier Memorial are distributed to the audience. In an analysis of both historical and contemporary performances of the Laurier Memorial, James Hoffman notes that although 'there never was a First Nations feast served up to Laurier when he was in Kamloops, there *should have been* under normal, pre-contact protocols. By basing the play on the preparation for a meal [...] Highway re-inscribes the truth of the presentation by focusing on the exigencies of food gathering within local First Nations culture'.[11] Underscoring issues of food security is key, but the dramatized preparations for the feast also serve as an alternative mode of communication for those who historically have been silenced or relegated to the background.

Through food gathering tied to the land, the women speak anew through an embodied discourse that connects with conceptualizations of food as 'a system of communication', to use Roland Barthes's phrase, but through an aboriginal lens.[12] In her ethnographic research, Annie Hauck-Lawson describes what she terms a 'food voice' with an emphasis on social relations: 'people's ways with, words about, and meaning towards food' enable them to 'assert aspects of their identities, [...] forge cooperative links, extend hospitality and assert power over obligation'.[13] In the context of women's contemporary drama, Vivian Patraka similarly explores the notion of 'foodtalk': the 'way all aspects of processes connected to food – its production, preparation, consumption and excretion – are used to make meaning' on stage.[14] For Patraka, the 'language of food' is highly flexible in its 'weave of relationships – social, economic, emotional, sexual, and intellectual – that create and recreate us' (138).

Adding to Hauck-Lawson's and Patraka's lists of identity-related components, Highway generates a culturally encoded 'foodtalk' inextricably tied to the land. The Native women source local and symbolically charged foods, including 'wild onions, wild asparagus, wild beans, wild this, wild that'.[15] As the women gather their ingredients, their conversations converge with the sound of the Thompson River, which the opening stage directions describe as '*rich, evocative, the voice of a land*' (13). Far from simple background noise, the river is eventually connected to Delilah Rose's hand-made tablecloth, which grows with each of her sewing scenes, billowing out '*like a river with a "trout" "inside" it*' (66). At the close of Act One, as Isabel and Ernestine collect

Saskatoon berries, the river sounds, and the bushes '*shimmer across the two women's faces and bodies which, in turn, makes them look like spirits – the land is talking, through them*' (56). Personifying their tribes and the river, the four women become a unifying force and express a First Nations world view guided by balance: the land is not a commodity to be portioned off and greedily consumed, but is rather a sensate being through which all bodies are connected and sustained.

A Dialogue of Miraculous Meals

If the women offer an embodied 'foodtalk' through which the land speaks, then the impact of Highway's imagined feast rests particularly in its critical layering of a range of mythologies and traditions of commensality – that is, the act of sharing a meal. During the final scene, audiences witness both the First Nations feast and the Christian tradition of the Last Supper. In the documentary *Tomson Highway Gets His Trout*, which includes footage from the play's world premiere in Kamloops, the closing scene features an image of Leonardo da Vinci's *The Last Supper* projected onto the backdrop, with Laurier and the Chiefs superimposed as the Saviour and the apostles, respectively. It is important to note here that da Vinci's iconic banquet is, itself, a cultural composite. Carolin Young reveals that this Christian meal was ostensibly reimagined by fifteenth-century Italian artists who 'incorporated a rediscovered Platonic idea about dining as the symposium for men, a forum of conviviality, into the biblical narrative'.[16] Although Young describes da Vinci evoking a humanist vision, the scene is nevertheless a patriarchal gathering, quite at odds with the all-female cast of Highway's play.

Highway's creative solution is to create a confluence of food events. The Christian-Classical tradition served at the table and projected on the backdrop and the Native feast prepared along the river and served on stage create a veritable dialogue between communities and their values. In many ways, Highway's presentation is an extension of the 'complex communicative strategies' that Hoffman explores in relation to the historical performance of the Laurier Memorial, where the chiefs, who had been 'muted', still found ways to 'speak subversively' when using dominant discourse.[17] In the play, the women, previously excluded and silenced from the historical event, are given an opportunity to speak through food, reframing conversations surrounding the Laurier Memorial through a hybrid performance of commensality.

Throughout his career, Highway's abiding interest has been to address gender imbalances by creating transformational feminine presences and voices. His use of the women's imagined food event in *Ernestine Shuswap Gets Her Trout* intersects in revealing ways with what Margaret McFadden identifies as a particular genre of food performance exhibited across cultures in which miraculous meals are prepared by women who nurture and transform their communities. Food films such as Mexico's *Like Water for Chocolate*, Denmark's *Babette's Feast* or Hollywood's *Chocolat* in effect 'portray cinematically, the *imago Dei* as feminine and universal' as 'it is women who have created and served, women who have assumed the burden of Christlike suffering, women who have given all'.[18] Highway's re-visioning of history produces a veritable shift in the spiritual landscape, since giving voice to the feminine in all of his work is often about 'the return of God as a woman'.[19] Highway relates this guiding vision at length in his *Comparing Mythologies* lecture, in which he addresses the gendered politics of Christian, Greek and Native mythologies, noting that the monotheistic male god of Christianity is an 'angry male' who takes the garden away, whereas in Highway's Cree mythology the universe is created by a benevolent female force.[20] In Native North America there is 'no expulsion' because 'we are still in the garden' (45). Seeing the world anew from a feminine, life-sustaining perspective makes food a powerful means of expression since this is one resource that the women in Highway's play ought to direct according to the local tribes' 'cultural and social principles of the division of labour'.[21]

During the play, audiences witness over a hundred years of colonialism compressed into a single day through the abrupt meeting of distinct mythological views that initially result in a devastating reshaping of the landscape and, by extension, of aboriginal foodways. The imposition of a Christian mythology and a patriarchal form of governance appears most readily in scenes where the women confront laws and physical barriers that exclude them from the land. In the opening Prologue, Ernestine Shuswap voices her husband's plan to catch her a trout for the feast. Ernestine's monologue is directly followed by Isabel Thompson, who questions this presumption, since in their new reality, 'fishing's not allowed' (15). Later in Act One, Ernestine and Isabel encounter a sign that reads 'No' when picking Saskatoon berries; the scene closes with the shadows of a wire fence blocking the women's movement as tribal lands transform into English settlers' private property (55-56). These edicts are directly tied to the encroaching power of the Prime Minister and the local civil servants. Despite Laurier's physical absence from the stage, he is god-like in his influence, as Ernestine Shuswap relates: 'He rules like a king over millions of people [...], changing people's lives willy nilly billy [...]. He has so much power, it is said, that he can reach into the sky and move the sun about like a saskatoon pie' (54).

This Great Big Kahoona of Canada, as the women refer to him, is the angry male god that Highway describes in *Comparing Mythologies*, and they worry that their culinary efforts will not appease him. The women make preparations for the feast in accordance with Laurier's French tastes: serving trout, not salmon, and creating a stuffing for the fish (40, 42). Isabel fears that her 'agitated condition' will result in 'bloody awful wretched' pies followed by an 'unimpressed' Great Big Kahoona who will 'never listen to a word they say' (26). As for Delilah Rose Johnson, she must sew one hundred tablecloths for the 'sake of the Shuswap, Okanagan, and Thompson Indian Nations', as though their futures depend on her compliance with the Great Big Kahoona's dictates (28). In Act Two, when the trout has not yet been caught, Ernestine works herself into a frenzy with only three hours remaining before Laurier's arrival, crying out, 'The Great Big Kahoona of Canada will be furious. He'll destroy us, oh, for sure, he'll destroy us' (78). Time becomes increasingly pressured and linear, focused on a single event that threatens to be either the making or undoing of the Native communities, all at the whim of one dictatorial dinner guest.

To complicate matters further, the Great Big Kahoona's demanding persona is coupled with a monstrous appetite. This withholding male god of Christianity works in tandem with colonialism's and Canada's greed. Speaking of the Prime Minister, Ernestine Shuswap declares, 'You name it, he eats it,' and the women seem destined to become consumable objects themselves with Laurier 'gorging himself on beaver and tits' (34). Although Highway writes in the End Notes that the beaver is 'a staple of the Native diet' and that the English language is to blame for appropriating the term to mean something 'completely [...] inappropriate' (93), the bawdy humour *'spill[s]-over into horrifying tragedy'*, an aspect of the play that Highway details in the opening directions (11). A cannibalistic colonialism underlies the sexual word play in a way that threatens the women's transformative power. This exploitation brings to mind what Ojibway playwright Drew Hayden Taylor refers to as 'the metaphoric rape of Native culture' dramatized elsewhere in plays like Highway's *Dry Lips Oughta Move to Kapuskasing,* as a 'primarily patriarchal culture [...] forc[es] its way in, [...] basically eradicating everything else and forcing [a matriarchal] culture to do its will'.[22]

Adding further to Laurier's characterization are Isabel Thompson's repeated blasphemous allusions to Saint George and the Dragon. In this Christian legend, the crusading knight, Saint George, rescues a village from a monster that inhabits the nearby waterway and is appeased only by being fed sheep or young maidens. When the King's own daughter is about to be sacrificed to the dragon, Saint George slays the creature, saves the princess, and converts the town to Christianity. When this legend is re-contextualized within Highway's play, Laurier's divine-like role merges with the dragon, or devil, demanding constant feeding as he assumes dominion over the Thompson River. The young Delilah Rose assumes the role of the sacrificial maiden, but there is no white knight to rectify the situation. Delilah Rose succumbs to cultural isolation as she is torn between her Native community and her cowboy husband, whose father operates (according to Ernestine) as a 'cog in the machine' of the Canadian government as it devours the land and its original inhabitants (55). To counter Laurier's reduction of the women to animals, Highway's play offers an alternative food drama where women are divine producers of nourishment.

Shifting away from the domineering perspective of an angry male god and toward that of a benevolent female god, Highway infuses his female characters with a nurturing power that derives from and through the land and facilitates the kind of 'miraculous feeding' that McFadden sees recurring in women's food dramas.[23] One reviewer describes the play as 'the mother of all feasts', and the women certainly reassert their people's inherent relationship to the land as First Nations.[24] Confronted with the government's unjust prohibitions on trapping, Annabelle Okanagan transcends the near-impossible nature of her task: 'How am I supposed to feed 2000 people with one beaver!! Where's Jesus when you need him!' (60). A single smoked beaver is supplied by a female friend, with Highway attributing the miracle of provision to the women themselves. Similarly, Isabelle Thompson only has one Saskatoon berry per pie and her own children are starving, yet she delivers on her promise to bake 624 pies (71). And Ernestine Shuswap, tired of waiting for her husband Joe to catch her a trout when fishing is illegal, immerses herself in the river and catches the fish with her 'own sharp teeth' (91). As the spirit of the land and voice of their people, the women embody both resilience and a nurturing form of resistance. Throughout these preparations, the women are divine in their own right – Annabelle cooks with her huge ladle and 'cauldron' (57, 34); Delilah Rose emerges like a 'priestess' from the Thompson River (56, 86); Ernestine walks submerged at the bottom of the river bed (78); and Isabelle appears out of 'a huge cloud of flour', her face 'looking like a ghost' (71). These abilities enable the women to regenerate their communities' connections to the land, remaking the world through food.

In the final scene, when Delilah Rose Johnson's tablecloth transforms into the Thompson River, Highway's mega banquet is finally realized from the perspective of the land, its benevolent female creator, and the First Nations. Reviews of the Western Canada Theatre's production praised the 'two crescent-shaped runways' as the set 'enable[d] the characters to enact the continuous physical activity that living off the land entails'.[25] Eventually this landscape or waterway becomes the inclusive gathering place for inter-cultural communion. The dishes and trout are laid out by the embodied yet ghostly women in a never-ending cycle of time that is quite distinct from the foreboding countdown of Laurier's arrival. In the opening Prologue, Annabelle Okanagan describes the river as 'a-weaving its way [...] down, down, and down [...] right through our hunting grounds, right through our pastures, [...] right through our houses, [...] through our children, through our lives, through our dreams, our hearts, our flesh, our veins, our blood' (16). The river connects territories, generations and diverse communities, as the eyes of both Native and non-Native spirits float above the water alongside those of Delilah Rose following her death. Caroline De Wagter stresses the 'crucial role of the river in the cultural memory' of Native communities: the water 'brings the past into the present' and 'creates a new site [...] where history and mythology coalesce'.[26] The women embody and bring to life the river's creative energy, enabling Highway to counterbalance the patriarchal spirits of both Billy Boy, whose 'ghostly' cowboy hat rests near Delilah Rose throughout the play, and the Great Big Kahoona, whose 'legislative omnipresence hangs oppressively over [...] every action'.[27] Laurier may have demanded tablecloths, but in the end, the women – as spirits and priestesses – serve the feast 'on the ground', on the river – the place where, Delilah Rose declares, they have 'eaten [...] for [...] sixty thousand years,' reminding guests of their fundamental relationship to the earth and that this sharing of it unites them all at life's banquet (33).

89

Conclusion

In Highway's play, diverse traditions of commensality share the stage in the hope that this confluence of perspectives will lead to a community-sustaining vision. The four women create what seems impossible given their circumstances: a miraculous meal that will feed the multitudes. Combining the traditional First Nations feast with the Last Supper, the women's 'foodtalk' shifts the focus away from the historical predominance of colonizing guests, to the reciprocal vision of the First Nations hosts. In this way, Highway restores balance by countering Canada's immeasurable appetite for land and resources. The final scene becomes a reminder, ironically enough, of Christian mythology's own misconstrued values as part of colonialism's apparatus, since the tradition of communion, as Maggie Kilgour reveals, is supposed to be an act of 'reciprocal incorporation' and 'a model of relations that go beyond the binarisms which lead to cannibalism'.[28] In a final gesture of both assertiveness and profound generosity, the play's directions state that 'what's left *of "The Laurier Memorial"*' – a document that initially appeared as Annabelle Okanagan's recipe for her dish of boiled beaver – should be distributed to the audience (91). The original production featured the women facing the audience while serving the feast along one side of the tablecloth-turned-river, an arrangement that mimics da Vinci's painting, which incorporated a table 'similar to the ones at which the monks themselves would have eaten' in the refectory, so that they could be spiritually present at the Last Supper during their own daily meals.[29] The spirit of Delilah Rose, now merged with the river itself, kneels at the tablecloth waiting for the guests to receive the meal and to reciprocate in kind. The possibility for renewal exists as audience members become participants and 'guests' in an ongoing history. The women and their feast have brought the past to life, just as other food dramas use women's culinary powers and bodies to 'mediate between the earthly and the divine, between flesh and spirit'.[30]

Notes

1. *Tomson Highway Gets His Trout*, dir. by Tom Shandel (Getaway Films Inc., 2004).
2. The Royal Proclamation of 1763 guaranteed aboriginal title and prevented individuals from directly purchasing Native lands, as the Crown would negotiate treaties and grant titles for ceded lands. In British Columbia, the provincial government did not adhere to this legal course: 'Contrary to international and British laws (as well as Dominion Indian policy), the government [...] took possession of most of its lands without entering treaties' ('Native Land Claims – Backgrounder', *Law Connection*, Simon Fraser University, <http://www.lawconnection.ca/content/native-land-claims-backgrounder> [accessed 21 May 2015]). Although Prime Minister Laurier was prepared to help the tribes of British Columbia in 1910, he lost the federal election in 1911.
3. Shuswap Nation Tribal Council, 'The Memorial to Sir Wilfrid Laurier', <http://shuswapnation.org/wordpress/wp-content/uploads/2012/09/137543_ShuswapNation_Bro.pdf> [accessed 28 April 2015]. Subsequent citations are cited parenthetically.
4. Duane Thomson and Marianne Ignace, '"They Made Themselves Our Guests": Power Relations in the Interior Plateau Region of the Cordillera in the Fur Trade Era', *B.C. Studies*, 146 (summer 2005),

pp. 3-35 in *ProQuest* <https://ezproxy.kwantlen.ca:2443/login?url=http://search.proquest.com.ezproxy. kwantlen.ca:2080/docview/196880210?accountid=35875 > [accessed 15 January 2015] (n.p.). Thomson and Ignace explain that different terms signify varied relationships with tribal lands: 'In the secwepemc language, guests are called sexlitemc ("guests/those invited") to distinguish from kw'seltkten ("relatives/family"), who encompass the wide and intricate network of kinship that stretches over the entire nation, even between nations. Kw'seltkten are all those people who, by birth or affiliation, have title and/or access privileges to the nation's territory. Sexlitemc are individuals who are without such rights. They are considered to be at the mercy of their hosts and are expected to reciprocate their hosts' generosity (n.p.).

5. Margery Fee, 'Stories of Traditional Aboriginal Food, Territory, and Health', in *What's to Eat? Entrées in Canadian Food History*, ed. by Nathalie Cooke (Montreal: McGill-Queen's University Press, 2009), pp. 55-78 (p. 56).

6. John Ralston Saul, *A Fair Country: Telling Truths about Canada* (Toronto: Viking, 2008), p. 29.

7. *Tomson Highway Gets His Trout.*

8. Birgit Däwes, '"I Don't Write Native Stories, I Write Universal Stories": An Interview with Tomson Highway', in *Indigenous North American Drama: A Multivocal History*, ed. by Birgit Däwes (New York: State University of New York Press, 2013), pp. 141-55 (p. 154).

9. Isabelle Zufferey-Boulton, 'A Fuge for Three Voices: Q Art Theatre's Production of *Ernestine Shuswap Gets Her Trout*', *ALT.Theatre* 5.4 (2008), pp. 21-25 (p. 22).

10. James Hoffman, 'Political Theatre in a Small City: The Staging of the Laurier Memorial in Kamloops', in *Theatre in British Columbia,* ed. by Ginny Ratsoy, Critical Perspectives on Canadian Theatre in English, VI (Toronto: Playwrights Canada Press, 2006), pp. 186-202 (p. 196).

11. Hoffman, p. 196.

12. Roland Barthes, 'Toward a Psychosociology of Contemporary Food Consumption', in *Food and Culture: A Reader*, ed. by Carole Counihan and Penny Van Esterik (New York: Routledge, 1997), pp. 20-27 (p. 21).

13. Annie Hauck-Lawson, 'Introduction to Special Issue on the Food Voice', *Food Culture & Society* 7.1 (2004), pp. 24-25 (p. 24).

14. Vivian Patraka, 'Foodtalk in the Plays of Caryl Churchill and Joan Schenkar', *The Theatre Annual* 40 (1985), pp. 137-157 (p. 137). Subsequent citations are cited parenthetically.

15. Tomson Highway, *Ernestine Shuswap Gets Her Trout: A 'String Quartet' for Four Female Actors* (Vancouver: Talonbooks, 2005), p. 28. Subsequent citations are cited parenthetically.

16. Carolin C. Young, 'Depictions of the Last Supper', in *Food in the Arts: Proceedings of the Oxford Symposium on Food and Cookery 1998*, ed. by Harlan Walker (Devon, England: Prospect Books, 1999), pp. 223-36 (p. 222).

17. Hoffman, p. 193. Hoffman describes how the Laurier Memorial is a translation in a hybrid form of English that reflects aboriginal oratory (p. 199). During its presentation, the chiefs did not speak the text themselves, but stood by as a Catholic priest, Father Jean-Marie Raphael Le Jeune, performed the Memorial on their behalf for Prime Minister Laurier. As Hoffman notes, 'The Chiefs in effect put words in the mouths of others [...] ; [who] all now speak counter-discursively, not about a settler but an indigenous peoples' history. By disrupting the expectations of who is speaking, who is listening, and what the message ultimately means – in short by the giving the Memorial a multi-voiced enunciation – the authors/performers open the Memorial to continuing replay' (p. 194).

18. Margaret H. McFadden, 'Gendering the Feast: Women, Spirituality, and Grace in Three Food Films', in *Reel Food: Essays on Food and Film*, ed. by Anne L. Bower (New York and London: Routledge, 2004), pp. 117-28 (p. 124, 127).

19. Däwes, p. 154.

20. Tomson Highway, *Comparing Mythologies,* Charles R. Bronfman Lecture in Canadian Studies (Ottawa: University of Ottawa Press, 2003), p. 39. Subsequent citations are cited parenthetically.

21. Marianne Ignace and Ron Ignace, 'The Secwepemc: Traditional Resource Use and Right to Land',

in *Native Peoples: The Canadian Experience*, ed. by R.B. Morrison and C.R. Wilson (Toronto: Oxford University Press, 2004), pp. 377-98 (p. 383).

22. Drew Hayden Taylor, 'Storytelling to Stage: The Growth of Native Theatre in Canada', *TDR* 41.3 (autumn 1997), pp. 140-52 in *Jstor* <http://www.jstor.org/stable/1146613 > [accessed 3 September 2014] (p. 151).

23. McFadden, p. 126.

24. Adrian Chamberlain, 'Bawdy Women Enliven Tale of Native Hardships', *Times - Colonist*, 11 March 2005, C7 in *Canadian Newsstand Pacific* <https://ezproxy.kwantlen.ca:2443/login?url=http://search. proquest.com/docview/347990991?accountid=35875?> [accessed 19 February 2015].

25. Mike Youds, 'Highway's Ernestine Dishes Out Big Banquet of Food for Thought', *Kamloops Daily News*, 24 January 2004, A6 in *Canadian Newsstand Pacific* <https://ezproxy.kwantlen.ca:2443/ login?url=http://search.proquest.com.ezproxy.kwantlen.ca:2080/docview/358545705?accountid=35875> [accessed 19 February 2015].

26. Caroline De Wagter, 'Old Margins, New Centres: (W)righting History in August Wilson's *Radio Golf* and Tomson Highway's *Ernestine Shuswap Gets Her Trout*', in *Old Margins and New Centers/Anciennes marges et nouveaux centres: The European Literary Heritage in an Age of Globalization/L'héritage littéraire européen dans une ère de globalisation*, Nouvelle poétique comparatiste – New Comparative Poetics IX, ed. by Marc Maufort and Caroline De Wagter (Bruxelles, BEL: Peter Lang AG, 2011), pp. 307-23 (p. 319). ProQuest ebrary.

27. De Wagter, p. 316; Owen Percy, Review of *Ernestine Shuswap Gets Her Trout,* by Tomson Highway, *Canadian Ethnic Studies* 38.2 (2006), pp. 211-12 (p. 211).

28. Maggie Kilgour, *Communion to Cannibalism* (New Jersey: Princeton, 1990), p. 15.

29. Young, p. 230. Da Vinci's painting, which is incorporated on a refectory wall in a former monastery (Santa Maria delle Grazie, Milan) invites the viewer to the table as though one is dining alongside or across from the Savior (p. 233).

30. McFadden, p. 123.

Communicating Jewish Identity Through Taste: Jewish Flavour Principles as Culinary 'Midrash'

Jonathan Brumberg-Kraus

Jewish identity and values are communicated through the cultivation of certain tastes. There are Jewish taste preferences, shaped by Jewish historical experience and literary, religious and cultural heritage. They are not absolute, not every Jew has them at all times and in all places, but there are discernibly Jewish patterns of taste preferences for some foods, disgust for others. Indeed, these Jewish taste preferences have been prescribed or encouraged by Jewish religious and cultural traditions, by advocates with a stake in Jewish group identity and the continuity of the Jewish people as a group (e.g. rabbis, teachers, parents, Jewish recipe book writers, chefs, food producers and distributors, and other Jewish political and cultural leaders) – 'ethno-political entrepreneurs' in Rogers Brubaker's term.[1] They use taste to communicate Jews' historical experience and memories of their ancient Near Eastern Biblical origins and terroir, their dispersion among other peoples and nations throughout the world ('the Diaspora' or *galut* [Exile]) and a pattern of collective suffering and 'redemption', from the Exodus from Egypt to the Expulsion from Spain, from settlement of Eastern Europe to mass immigration to the US, from the Holocaust to the foundation of the modern Jewish State of Israel.

Jewish taste preferences are somewhat akin to what Elizabeth Rozin and John Prescott describe as flavour principles (really more than taste per se, i.e. the combination of certain patterns of preferred tastes, aromas, ingredients, textures, cooking methods, etc., characteristic of different regionally-based ethnic groups).[2] The principles can be traced back to sacred texts like the Bible and rabbinic literature that articulate them in religio-cultural prescriptions. Their effect makes some flavours pleasurable, others disgusting. For example classical Jewish texts and practices profess preferences for roasted, aromatic, salty, umami meat flavours; 'sweetening the bitter' (as in charoset and the 'Hillel Sandwich'); greens in certain circumstances; refined wheat bread (vs. rice or maize) as a staple; and abhorrence for certain flavours and flavour combinations: pork, seafood, meat with dairy, mayonnaise on white bread. And there are seasonally prescribed preferences, too – certain foods on certain holidays, like unleavened bread during Passover in the spring, sweets at Purim, fried foods in the dead of winter during Chanukah. Basically, Jewish scriptural and ritual traditions 'evaluatively condition' certain flavours or combinations of flavours into what I am calling 'Jewish flavour principles'.[3]

I have identified ten Jewish flavour principles, each to which I attach an exemplary

Biblical or rabbinic textual phrase suggesting why Jews ought to like or dislike them. Usually the texts evaluatively associate them with what *God* likes or dislikes Himself, or what God commands or encourages us to eat or not eat. And because Biblical sacrifices usually involve foods that God and the Israelites are to share, this is hardly surprising. Thus culturally specific Jewish language distinguishes between what tastes good and what does not: what God sees or says is good or not. Again, this should not be surprising in a culture whose foundation myth has humans learning to distinguish good from evil by tasting the fruit of the Tree of Knowledge of Good and Evil in the Garden of Eden. For God Himself acknowledges that after eating this fruit, humans have 'become like one of us, knowing good and evil' (Gen 3:22).

When I re-associate 'Jewish taste preferences' with representative classic Jewish texts that endorse these them, I'm engaging intentionally in culinary midrash. That is, I am interpreting and updating the meanings of verses of Torah in light of contemporary Jewish gastronomic experiences – these Jewish taste preferences. It's the reciprocal relationship between these tastes and Torah that I'm calling Jewish flavour principles.

So why take this to be anything other than one person's subjective, idiosyncratic interpretations about what's Jewish? I have two answers. First, I make these judgments as a Jewish 'insider', and more than that: I have certain relevant credentials and background to use my palate to make Jewish judgments. I am a Reconstructionist rabbi and an academic in comparative religious studies.[4] I keep a kosher home and observe Jewish holidays with my family and community, albeit in a liberal/progressive way, and I am actively involved in the so-called 'New Jewish food movement'. In other words, I am recognized as a professional Jewish leader and academic teacher, a Jewish 'ethno-political entrepreneur' with a stake in the game. Second, are you persuaded? Do the tendencies I label as 'Jewish flavour principles' accord with your experience and observation of the phenomena I'm describing? So without further ado:

Ten Jewish Flavour Principles

1. Preference for meat: 'Keep yourselves holy because I am holy. This is the Torah of beast and fowl...' (Lev 11:45-6ff); 'no one unlearned in Torah should eat meat' (b.Pesahim 49b)

2. Preference for roasted foods, especially umami, preference for cooked over raw foods: God likes '*Re'ach nicho'ach*' (pleasing smell of roasting meat and incense)

3. Preference for salted, aromatically assertive foods: 'Do not eat the flesh with the blood in it'; sacrifices (meat, grain, and incense) with salt in them

4. Qualified vegetarian preference: 'Better a meal of vegetables with love, than a fatted calf served in hate' (Proverbs 15:17)

5. Abhorrence of certain mixtures (like the Mishnaic idea of kelai'im): 'Do not boil a kid in its mother's milk'

6. Preference for bread, but as a cooked and refined everyday and 'sometimes' food, and not a stand-alone food: 'Not by bread alone' (Deut 8:3)

7. Preference for 'Song of Songs' flavour combination – Sweet with bitter: Passover food – *charoset*, with *maror*, bitter herb: 'Sweetening the bitter'

8. Preference for talked about food: 'Saying words of Torah about the table over the table' (m. Avot 3:4)

9. Preference for Middle Eastern vegetarian flavours: foods of 'the promised land' - The Seven Species: 'The Lord is bringing you into a land with wheat, barley, grape (wine), fig, pomegranates, olive (oil), and date (honey)' (Deut 8:7-8)

10. Preferences for seasonal food: 'Celebrate the Festival of Unleavened Bread; for seven days eat bread made without yeast, as I commanded you. Do this at the appointed time in the month of Aviv'

My brief discussion of each is meant to be suggestive rather than exhaustive, to keep within the constraints of this paper.

1. Preference for Meat: 'Keep yourselves holy because I am holy. This is the Torah of beast and fowl...' (Lev 11:45-6ff); 'no one unlearned in Torah should eat meat' (b.Pesahim 49b)

Implicit in the Biblical rules of kashrut in the list of clean and unclean animals in Leviticus 11 is that they apply only to the flesh of animals – meat. They do not specify which plant-derived foods are or are not fit for Israelites to eat. Though these rules apply to all Israelites, they come in the context of lists of *torot* detailing which animals and grain offerings are fit to be sacrificed ('made sacred', or literally, *hikrivu*, 'brought near') to God, and how to prepare and divide them among God, the priests, their families and ordinary Israelites. In other words, there is a hierarchy of foods associated with a social hierarchy where meat, God and the priests are at the top. Moreover, this accords with Michael Pollan's suggestion in *Cooked* that roasted meat is special food, with notable elaborations of rules and taboos associated with its preparation, under the supervision of male elites, as in the case of ancient Israelite sacrifices or modern American Southern barbecue.[5] Observing the 'Torah of beast and fowl and living creatures that move in the water' to distinguish between the *meat* of clean and unclean animals is what makes Israelites 'holy [like] I YHWH your God am holy' (Lev 11:45-47). Even after the rabbis of the Talmud reinterpreted this priestly torah about meat-eating to refer to the rabbinic Torah of text study, they kept meat elevated as a perk reserved for Torah scholars (b. Pesahim 49b).[6] Thus, the prominent role meat plays in Jewish cuisine around the world, especially in Orthodox Jewish diets, even today has the sanction of Judaism's most authoritative textual sources.

2. Preference for cooked over raw foods; roasted and stewed foods, especially umami: God likes 'Re'ach nicho'ach' (pleasing smoke/smell of roasting meat and incense)

Related to the preference for meat per se is a preference for the meat-like *umami* flavour of foods and methods of cooking them that bring out umami flavours, i.e. roasting and stewing. The ancient Israelites did not sacrifice raw foods on their altars, but rather *cooked* things. And according to the Bible, God took particular pleasure in the savoury aroma, the *re'ach nicho'ach*, of the burnt meat, grain, and incense offerings. A notable expression of this taste preference occurs in post-Biblical Sabbath dishes (slow-cooked in compliance with Sabbath legal restrictions on cooking) known among Sefardic Jews as *hamin* [hot dish] (as well as by other regional variant names, d'fina, ad'fina, etc.) and as *cholent* (or less commonly, *schalet*) among Ashkenazim, German and Eastern European Jews. Heinrich Heine's mock paean to *schalet* emphasized especially its aroma as food fit for the gods:

But at noon, as compensation,
There shall steam for thee a dish
That in very truth divine is –
Thou shalt eat to-day of schalet!

'Schalet, ray of light immortal!
Schalet, daughter of Elysium!'
So had Schiller's song resounded,
Had he ever tasted schalet,

For this schalet is the very
Food of heaven, which, on Sinai,
God Himself instructed Moses
In the secret of preparing,

At the time He also taught him
And revealed in flames of lightning
All the doctrines good and pious,
And the holy Ten Commandments.

Yes, this schalet's pure ambrosia
Of the true and only God:
Paradisal bread of rapture
…

Then the princess hands her golden
Box of spikenard to her lover,
Who inhales it, fain to revel
Once again in pleasant odours.[7]

The one explicitly Jewish flavour principle Elizabeth Rozin includes in her list: 'Onion-chicken fat (Eastern European Jewish Cuisine)' accentuates both the aromatic umami flavour and the process of cooking the onions in the animal fat until browned that produces it, as anyone who has rendered chicken fat to make *gribenes* (chicken skins sauteed with onions until crunchy) can attest.[8] Cooking buckwheat groats with browned onions and mushrooms achieves a similar effect even in vegetarian versions of the Eastern European Jewish dish *kasha varnishkes*.

3. Preference for salted, aromatically assertive foods: 'Do not eat the flesh with the blood in it'; sacrifices (meat, grain, and incense) with salt in them

In the Bible, God prefers his sacrificial offerings salted, presumably because it enhances their aroma ('a pleasing odour' to YHWH), and so should we. Thus the Israelites were commanded:

> 'You shall not omit from your grain offerings the **salt** of the covenant with your God; with all your offerings you shall offer **salt**.' (Lev 2:13)

> 'the firstborn of **a cow, a sheep or a goat**; they are holy. Splash their blood against the altar and burn their **fat** as a food offering, an **aroma pleasing to the Lord**. Their **meat** is to be yours, just as the breast of the wave offering and the right thigh are yours. Whatever is set aside from the holy offerings the Israelites present to the Lord I give to you and your sons and daughters as your perpetual share. It is an everlasting covenant of **salt** before the Lord for both you and your offspring.' (Numbers 18:17-19)

Salting meat to 'kasher' it became the way the post-Biblical rabbis assured subsequent generations of Jews could observe the biblical prohibition against eating meat with the blood in it (Gen 9:4; Deut 12:23). Hence, Jews acquired a taste for pungent, not bland foods – garlic, pickles, brisket, chicken soup, gefilte fish with horseradish, pastrami, corned beef, lox, etc.

4. Qualified vegetarian preference: 'Better a meal of vegetables with love, than a fatted calf served in hate' (Proverbs 15:17)

Biblically based preferences for meat were qualified. Originally human and animal diets were restricted to seed-bearing grasses and fruits (Gen 1:29-30). God conceded meat in the human diet only after the flood, to check human bloodthirstiness (Gen 9:3-6). But as the passage from Proverbs also suggests, it is more important to get along with your fellow diners than to eat meat, so even humble greens served with love are preferable to sacrificial calves.[9] Former Pharisee Paul suggested going veggie to ease tensions between Jewish and Gentile converts to Christianity caused by their divisive food preferences (Rom 14:21ff), and even today many Jews who eat meat in their kosher homes go vegetarian when they're eating out to socialize with their non-Jewish or non-observant friends and work companions. And it's nearly *de rigueur* in my Jewish circles to assume that some of our guests to Jewish holiday meals will be vegetarian and to accommodate them. And vice versa, when our Jewish culinary tour guide to the upper Galilee in Israel arranged for us to make and eat a meal at her Arab Muslim friend's home in Nazareth, it was to be vegetarian, to accommodate the kosher observance of some of us. Indeed, observing the flipside of the verse from Proverbs, I ate the one thing our host served us that was not vegetarian, a freekeh soup in a chicken broth, lest my usual practice of kashrut get in the way of connecting across politically fraught Arab-Jewish ethnic lines at our mostly veggie shared meal.

98

5. Abhorrence of certain mixtures (like the Mishnaic idea of kelai'im): 'Do not boil a kid in its mother's milk'

The Biblical prohibition against boiling a kid in its mother's milk has led to a whole range of Jewish culinary practices and preferences. Thus Jews typically use olive oil, goose or chicken fat instead of butter to cook meat. As olive oil is a staple component of most of the Mediterranean regional flavour principles Elizabeth Rozin lists, Jews in these lands found these flavour principles easily adaptable to kashrut-based preferences that avoided dairy-meat mixtures. And the Jews of Eastern and Central Europe easily substituted chicken, goose or beef fat for the lard in their neighbours' flavour principles. But I suspect a deeper abhorrence and sensitivity to certain mixtures underlies and reinforces the separation of milk and meat in Jewish food preferences. Jewish tradition developed a whole system and conceptualization of forbidden mixtures, *kela'im* (to which an entire tractate of the Mishnah is devoted) to be avoided in other spheres, such as the prohibition of sowing certain seeds together or of mixing no linen and wool together in garments (*shatnez*). In a people historically anxious about its own political and social boundaries, ritual concerns about forbidden mixtures might be ways to displace or attend to these anxieties, as Mary Douglas has suggested.[10] Is secular Jewish abhorrence for meat with mayonnaise on white bread a modern expression of this perennial Jewish concern?

6. Preference for bread, but as a cooked and refined everyday and 'sometimes' food, and not a stand-alone food: 'Not by bread alone' (Deut 8:3)

In the Bible, God definitely wanted grain-based offerings, but if we still went by the kind of bread God preferred, we'd be eating flour ground finely, cooked with oil and salt in an oven, in griddles, or pans, but without yeast or honey, i.e. savoury and unleavened. Even roasted whole grains, 'crushed heads of new grain roasted in the fire with oil' (not unlike freekeh in contemporary Arab cuisine) with incense, was acceptable to God and his priests as a food offering (Lev. 2:14). Apart from the basic ingredients of finely ground flour, oil and salt, they're a far cry from the braided, usually sweetened, egg-enriched and definitely leavened challah typically found on modern Jewish Shabbat tables.

Challah itself is a Biblical word, referring to one of the shapes of unleavened bread (*hallot matzah*!) fit for a *minhah* grain offering. Later, challah came to mean the portion of dough Jewish bakers (notably Eastern European Jewish women) separated from their loaves before baking them, to be burnt as God's portion, a memorial of the sacrifices Jews no longer practice since the destruction of the Temple. Technically, it's this separation that makes the Sabbath and holiday Jewish breads challah (even *matzah* has challah taken from it before being roasted), not its ingredients or shape. That comes from the braided sweet holiday breads Jews in medieval Germany adopted from their neighbours' celebratory propitiatory *berchisbrod* offerings made to their Teutonic crone goddess Berchta, also known as Holle, according to Gil Marks.[II]

99

Liturgically, a Jewish meal is not a meal unless bread is served over which the bread blessing *ha-motzi* is recited. The shapes of challah can vary seasonally (braided loaves weekly on Shabbat, round loaves often with raisins added at the New Year/Sukkot season, unleavened *matzah* during Passover and a special Mt. Sinai-shaped 'Seven Heavens' loaf for Shavuot). There are ordinary Jewish breads, too, Middle Eastern flat breads like pita (which non-Ashkenazic Jews probably used for holiday *hallot* until they adopted the Ashkenazic style loaves, especially in Israel) and the pungent pumpernickel and other ryes preferred by Eastern European Jews. The aromatic, earthy umami flavours of these whole grain breads seem closer to those of the Biblical minhah offerings.

Finally, Jewish breads (e.g. two loaves of challah on Shabbat) are associated with the miraculous manna the Bible says God provided us in the wilderness after our rescue from Egypt, suggesting not only bread's heavenly origin, but its being a particular expression of God's care for His people. The 'not by bread alone' quotation from Deut 8:3 refers to the miracle of manna; it is 'not by bread alone, but all that comes out of (*motza*) the mouth of the Lord' that one needs to live. Bread is pedagogical food: food for thought as well as food for the body. It is a collaboration between human effort and divine grace; even the manna was ground, seethed or baked into cakes (Nu 11:9; Ex 16:23). Let's say that there's a Jewish taste preference for bread as both ordinary and extraordinary food, a regular (plain, whole grain; daily minhah offerings) and 'sometimes' food (i.e. special variations for the holidays; the one-shot but remembered miracle of the manna). Bread is the Jewish 'go-with' starch; while one can make other ethnic groups' metonymic grains (e.g. rice, maize or millet) 'Jewish' by applying other Jewish flavour principles to them, wheat bread as described here is itself a Jewish flavour principle.

7. Preference for 'Song of Songs' flavour combination – sweet with bitter: Passover food – *charoset*, with *maror*, bitter herb: 'sweetening the bitter'

Jews have a Song of Songs-inspired sweet tooth, a preference for combining the sweet with the bitter or with other tastes unpleasant by themselves. Thus, for the Jewish Passover dish charoset, the Talmud views the verse 'Under the apple tree I aroused you' (Song of Songs 8:5) as both an allusion to the Exodus from Egypt and the starting point for a recipe. In the Talmud's view, apples have an 'acrid' taste which the aromatic spices and fruits of the Song of Songs temper. Thus around the world Jews have incorporated cinnamon, nuts, raisins, dates, figs and pomegranates into recipes for charoset. This Jewish flavour principle is virtually identical to Elizabeth Rozin's cinnamon-fruit-nut Central Asian flavour principle. Some Jewish communities' addition of clay dust as an ingredient – a mnemonic for the bricks Israelite slaves made – is a literal take on the word that may have given charoset its name; *cheres* is Hebrew for 'clay'.[12] The Hillel sandwich of matzoh, bitter herb, and sweet charoset eaten during the Passover seder explicitly spells out the flavour principle of sweetening the bitter, and subsequent Hasidic Jewish commentators turn this flavour principle in to a theological principle. The human condition necessarily combines the bitter and sweet.[13]

The principle of sweetening the bitter, or, better, of combining the sweet with other preferred tastes, can be expanded into a preference for 'good mixtures' that I call 'the *tzimmes* principle' (as opposed to abhorrent ones). The more festive the occasion, the more sweet, meaty, rich ingredients you add to the simple carrot dish *tzimmes*: On the harvest holiday of Sukkot, 'The Holiday', add meat and sweet dried fruits to it. On the festival of Passover, one can make *tzimmes mit a knaidl* (matzah ball). And every Jewish Sabbath and holiday meals is made more joyous by serving meat, and especially wine, as the Talmud says, 'there is no joy/celebration without wine!'. It's similar to the principle of meal elaboration in Mary Douglas's 'Deciphering a Meal'.[14]

8. Preference for talked-about food: 'Saying words of Torah about the table over the table' (m. Avot 3:4)

Jews preferred their food to be accompanied with talking. That both elevates it and makes it feel Jewish. Thus the rabbinic tradition:

If three have eaten at one table and have not spoken over it words of the Torah, it is as though they had eaten of the sacrifices of the dead, for it is written (Isaiah 28:8) 'The tables are full of vomit and excrement, no place [for anything else].' But if three have eaten at one table and have spoken over it words of the Torah, it is as if they had eaten from the table of God [lit., 'The Place'] , for it is written (Ezekiel 41.22) 'He said to me, 'This is the table which is before the LORD.'

Jewish celebrations are often meal rituals built around saying blessings or pertinent scriptural passages about foods before and after eating them, such as in a Shabbat dinner, the Passover seder, and the Tu Bishvat Seder on the New Year for the Trees, at which one recites blessings and scriptures praising tree fruits and the 'Seven Species' (the plant foods of the Promised Land mentioned next). The proliferation of Jewish cookbooks – far out of proportion to the world's Jewish population – is a modern, secular version of this preference for talked-about food.

9. Preference for Middle Eastern vegetarian flavours: foods of 'the promised land' – The Seven Species: 'The Lord is bringing you into a land with wheat, barley, grape (wine), fig, pomegranates, olive (oil), and date (honey)' (Deut 8:7-8)

The establishment of the state of Israel has revived Jewish preferences for the 'Middle Eastern' vegetarian flavours of the foods native to the land of Israel, and praised in the Bible as the seven species of 'wheat, barley, grape (wine), fig, pomegranates, olive (oil), and date (honey)'. Thus we have in Jerusalem today:

> The Eucalyptus Restaurant, owned and led by Chef Moshe Basson, serv[ing] a modern interpretation of biblical cuisine. Chef Basson's passions for biblical culture drove him to research and resurrect recipes, spices, and local and wild herbs that were part of the traditional cuisine, and were neglected and nearly forgotten for centuries. Every dish has its origins in biblical scenes and all the spices and herbs used grow, as in ancient times, in the surrounding hills of Jerusalem and Judea.[15]

And the tasting menus there have Biblically-themed names: the 'King David Feast', 'Shir Ha-Shirim [Song of Songs] Feast' and the 'Queen of Sheba Feast'. However, these Jewish Israeli taste preferences are also Palestinian Arab taste preferences, and Jewish cultural appropriation of them, unlike the cultural appropriation of all the other flavour principles from cultures in which Jews were subject minorities, are much more politically charged and sensitive. Since much of the Jewish Israeli population came from the Middle East and North Africa, they originally acquired their taste preferences as minorities in dominant cultures. Thus many Israeli Jews brought Rozin's Middle Eastern and North African flavour principles like 'Lemon-parsley (Middle East), Tomato-Cinnamon (Middle East, Greece), Garlic-cumin-mint (Northeast Africa), and Cumin-coriander-cinnamon-ginger + onion and/or tomato and/or fruit (Morocco)' to Israel, and indeed their Ashkenazi Jewish neighbours acquired them from them in turn. But if one lists the dishes Jews in and out of Israel identify as Israeli Jewish – such as hummus, felafel, 'Israeli Couscous' (like *maftoul* or *mograbieh*), *maqluba* (the featured, dramatically presented Biblical dish at Eucalytus) or baklava – they're all staples of Palestinian Arab cuisine.[16] This Jewish flavour principle thus communicates both belongingness and divisiveness among people, though in a sense, that's true of all of Rozin's ethnic terroir-based flavour principles. At the risk of sounding naively romantic, perhaps the missing ingredient is love.[17]

10. Preferences for seasonal food: 'Celebrate the Festival of Unleavened Bread; for seven days eat bread made without yeast, as I commanded you. Do this at the appointed time in the month of Aviv'

Finally, there's a strong preference for eating food in its Jewish season. Few Jews eat charoset except during Passover! So for Passover: matzah and charoset, no leaven, exceptional quantities of eggs, dense and crunchy textures, sweetness, maybe homemade gefilte fish for a change; fried crispy textures like latkes at Chanukah; hamentaschen at Purim; and dairy foods at Shavuot. It still weirds me out to see hamentashen available at some Jewish bakeries year round. Or better, I have no urge to eat them except around Purim. Where one eats Jewish food seasonally can make a difference. For the seven days of Sukkot many Jews eat outside in the *sukkot* they or others build, decorated with fall seasonal fruits. Easily conveyed one-dish casseroles or pies and harvesty fall foods predominate, warm and hearty foods, especially, as the nights can start to get colder. My point is that non-edible 'ingredients' can play a part in Jewish flavour principles – the timing and setting!

Conclusions

Jewish food and food practices need not be reduced to coercive dietary laws prescribing what to eat (or not), with whom and when. Jewish flavour principles, as opposed to Jewish food laws, provide a kind of script that maintains a basic sense of being grounded in our physical environment, the natural seasons, and our relationships with people, our own and Others. Jewish flavour principles are a diasporic strategy for maintaining cultural continuity and identity, while allowing for a great degree of flexibility and adaptability. Jewish flavour principles attach Jews to a kind of terroir, or better, terroirs:

1. Terroirs where the vagaries of Jewish history have placed and displaced Jews globally
2. Terroir of the fictive world of ancient Israel in the Bible, with its geography and seasons
3. Terroir of Torah – the Biblical and post-Biblical stories and rituals that 'evaluatively condition' the sensory topography of these other terroirs.[17]

Jewish flavour principles provide intrinsic rewards. The stories and rituals that shape them make the foods concocted through them taste better. The stories and rituals, that is, the 'religious' components of the Jewish flavour principles allow for a kind of role-playing that makes 'food a *flexible* symbolic vehicle for Self-identity, precisely through the invocation of "inflexible cultural stereotypes which link particular foodstuffs to particularized local identities"'.[19] Finally, Jewish flavour principles work as midrash, applying old wisdom to new situations in creative, dynamic, imaginative, adaptive and spiritually sustaining ways.

Grounding a Jewish culinary philosophy in certain taste preferences, or, for that matter, any culinary philosophy in specific flavours and combination of flavours, has two particular advantages for the groups that practice them. First, there is a built-in incentive for practicing the culinary philosophies communicated through evaluatively conditioned taste preferences: the pleasure in eating the foods that carry the cultural values. Not only are double braided challah loaves on Shabbat, cinnamon-nut flavoured charoset on Passover, pungent pastrami on rye at the Second Avenue Deli and freekeh-stuffed grape leaves shared by Muslims and Jews in Nazareth good to think, they are also good to eat!

Second, culinary philosophies grounded in taste preferences direct us to the foods that meet our biological-nutritional and social needs. In other words, our taste preferences are meant to be evolutionarily adaptive, so that time-tested Jewish (or Buddhist, Islamic, Christian, Meso-American, etc.) culinary philosophies should be 'good' for us, that is, nutritionally and ecologically sustainable.

In that sense, I hope what I've argued here suggests a way to re-couple what John Prescott calls the modern 'decoupling of pleasure and nutrition' with its detrimental consequences for both our health and our pleasure.[20] Jewish flavour principles, 'culinary midrash' – just as other time-tested culinary philosophies – can re-embed its practitioners in corporeal situations when they re-couple what tastes communicate through the mouth with what words communicate through the mouth, and to what the natural world (to which we often forget we belong) communicates to us through our mouths.

103

Notes

1. Rogers Brubaker, *Ethnicity without Groups* (Cambridge: Harvard University Press, 2004), p. 10.
2. John Prescott, *Taste Matters: Why We like the Foods We Do* (London: Reaktion Books, 2012), p. 150.
3. Prescott, p. 69. About evaluative conditioning Prescott says, 'it is possible that we automatically form associations between the context or environment in which the exposure occurs and the exposed item [....T]he context in which a food is consumed is obviously a crucial part of the eating experience and thus the degree to which a food or meal is pleasurable. It has been shown that a familiar food or meal will be enjoyed more if it is eaten in an environment that is highly regarded'.
4. That I approach the 'myth-ritual complex' of Jewish food from both insider and outsider perspectives is particularly important. Religious studies scholar and comparativist Jeffrey Kripal calls this interpretative dynamic the 'Insider-Outsider Möbius': 'There are no myths inside a religious worldview, but

every religious narrative is a myth to someone standing completely outside of it' (*Comparing Religions: Coming to Terms* (Chichester: Wiley/Blackwell, 2014), p. 139). As such I am 'aware of and sensitive to this insider-outside "flip", that is, whether [I am] "inside" or "outside" a particular myth-ritual complex […]. To the extent that we all inhabit a language and culture, we are all living inside a story and acting it out, be this religious or secular in nature. The central question then becomes: Are we aware of this?'. I think I am.

5. 'Barbecue is like kashrut for goys' (*Cooked: A Natural History of Transformation* (New York, Penguin, 2013), pp. 98-99).

6. See Jonathan Brumberg-Kraus, 'Meat-Eating and Jewish Identity: Ritualization of the Priestly "Torah of Beast and Fowl" (Lev 11:46) in Rabbinic Judaism and Medieval Kabbalah', *AJS Review*, 24.2 (1999): 227–62.

7. 'Princess Sabbath', trans. by Margaret Amour, in *The Standard Book of Jewish Verse*, comp. by Joseph Friedlander, ed. by George Alexander Kohut (New York: Dodd, Mead, 1917), ll. 97-144.(Sherry Ansky in her Hebrew book on cholent, *Hamin*, translates Heine's 'pleasant odors' as *re'ach nicho'ach* ((Jerusalem: Keter, 2008), p. 62).

8. 'Flavour Principles: Some Applications', *The Taste Culture Reader: Experiencing Food and Drink*, ed. by Carolyn Korsmeyer and David Howes (Oxford: Berg, 2005), p. 43.

9. See Jonathan Brumberg-Kraus, '"Better a Meal of Vegetables with Love": The Symbolic Meaning of Vegetables in Rabbinic and Post-Rabbinic Midrash on Proverbs 15.17', *Jewish Quarterly Review*, 104.1 (2014). pp. 46-56.

10. 'Deciphering a Meal,' *Daedalus* 101, no. 1 (January 1, 1972), pp. 61-81.

11. 'Challah', *Encyclopedia of Jewish Food* (Hoboken, NJ: John Wiley & Sons, 2010), p. 98.

12. Susan Weingarten, 'Charoset', *Authenticity in the Kitchen: Proceedings of the Oxford Symposium on Food and Cookery 2005*, ed. by Richard Hosking (Totnes, UK: Prospect Books, 2006), p. 424.

13. E.g. in the Sfas Emes's nineteenth-century commentary on the Passover haggadah: 'And therefore we need to eat the bitter herb because we are now in exile, and by eating the bitter herb [with the matzah and charoset] we are able to sweeten the bitterness on this night. And thus when swallowing the bitter herb, we will not feel the taste of the bitter herb more than the matzah, but the bitter herb is sweetened now'.

14. Douglas, pp. 67-68.

15. Ronny Basson, 'About Us', *Eucalyptus* <http://www.the-eucalyptus.com/restaurant/our-story/> [accessed 24 July 2012}.

16. Liora Gvion, *Beyond Hummus and Falafel: Social and Political Aspects of Palestinian Food in Israel* (University of California Press, 2012).

17. My culinary tour guide in Northern Galilee, Abbie Rosner, makes a compelling case for the power of shared Israeli Jewish and Arab taste preferences to bring people together, in her life and in her book, *Breaking Bread in Galilee: A Culinary Journey into the Promised Land*. Hilayon Press, 2012.

18. Jonathan Z. Smith, 'Earth and Gods', *Journal of Religion*, 49.2 (April 1969), pp. 103-27, and George Steiner, 'Our Homeland, the Text', *Salmagundi*, 66 (Winter-Spring 1985), pp. 4-25.

19. Allison James, 'Identity and the Global Stew', *The Taste Culture Reader*, p. 375.

20. Prescott, p. 167.

Defining 'Cuisine': Communication, Culinary Grammar, and the Typology of Cuisine

Anthony F. Buccini

Grandma... Chopped!

Food related television programming has become extremely popular. In the United States and elsewhere, there has been a gradual shift away from the traditional cooking show, where someone who presumably is an expert in some style of cookery teaches the audience how to make dishes in that style, to formats that are competitive in nature. The first of these to achieve great popularity in the US was an import from Japan, 'Iron Chef', which aired on the Food Network starting in 1999. The success of that show moved the network's management to create its own Americanized version, 'Iron Chef America', using essentially the same format but featuring as contestants celebrity chefs primarily from other programmes on the network. Two celebrity chefs are presented with a mystery ingredient which they must use to create a number of new dishes in a limited amount of time with the aid of a well-stocked pantry and elaborate kitchen facilities; their creations are then presented as a multi-course meal to a set of judges (including usually a well-known food critic) which then ultimately declares a winner.

The proliferation of competitive cooking shows in the US has been remarkable, fuelled by the general surge in interest in things culinary and the recent growth of the reality-television format. Thus, in addition to programmes featuring competitions between celebrity chefs, we find a vast array of programmes in which unknown contestants face off against one another in hopes of claiming a cash prize and in some cases of becoming themselves television cooking-celebrities. Typical of the genre is another Food Network production called 'Chopped', in which four aspiring chefs compete for a cash prize; their task is to compose first an appetizer, then a main course, and finally a dessert, using as principal ingredients the items presented to them in a basket, which usually contains at least one item that is not typically used in combination with the other ingredients or is generally regarded as inappropriate for the course in question. After each course, a panel of judges critiques the creations and then 'chops' or eliminates one contestant, leaving a winner after the dessert course.

From a culinary standpoint, many such competitive cooking shows share a number of encoded values of first-world culinary culture. Most importantly, the competitive food show is strongly commercial in nature: not only does the genre come to expression on for-profit networks (as opposed in the US to public television, which still offers old-style instructional cooking shows) and so are sponsored vehicles for advertisements hawking chain restaurants, prepared foodstuffs and mass-marketed individual ingredients (olive oil, cheeses, avocados, etc.), but in addition the hosts and celebrity contestants are chefs, cookbook authors and restaurateurs and themselves often enough also entrepreneurs whose names are borne by lines of prepared foods, kitchenware, etc. Unknown contestants in the reality-show variant of the genre are, moreover, typically small-time chefs or restaurateurs or else persons who aspire to become food professionals.

Within this strongly commercial context – and certainly related to it – is the general aesthetic orientation of competitive food-show cookery. Striking, though certainly not surprising in the context of a visual medium, is the attention that is paid to the appearance of finished dishes, with contestants going to great lengths to apply principles of modern culinary architectonics in stacking items and festooning them with patterns of differently coloured sauces applied with squeeze bottles in the final moments of their allotted cooking time.

Though competing chefs may often draw on some particular culinary tradition, the entire endeavour is in a real sense anti-traditional: the dishes offered in competition are to be expressions of the individual chef's creativity, of his or her personal culinary genius. Where, as in the case of 'Chopped', contestants must create dishes from ingredients imposed upon them, this creative element is built into the game through, for example, the required inclusion of chillies and olive oil in dessert or waffles in a main savoury course. But even when the ingredients are less at odds with general (American) culinary norms, it is clear from the comments of judges that the more dishes resemble well-known preparations the more they are disfavoured: the overriding aesthetic is one of novelty. Obvious, perhaps too obvious to be noted, is that the competitive food show is about food that exists outside of any cultural context but its own, producing food that is to be judged purely on its aesthetic qualities within a style of cookery that by and large eschews or is ignorant of traditional ethnic cookery of any background and revels in its own norms of presentation, its focus on novelty of combinations and its engagement with current culinary fads regarding ingredients and cooking methods. Of course, identifiable elements of traditional cuisines constantly appear here, but they do so as dislocated and appropriated tropes that serve first and foremost to highlight the individual chef's ability to co-opt, subvert or transcend the conventional.

Let us for a moment envision a different sort of a culinary competition, perhaps more of an experiment than a competition, where the contestants or subjects are grandmothers from some particular town or small region with a strong culinary tradition, very experienced cooks who are well versed in their local tradition but with little or no real knowledge of other cuisines. The grandmothers are presented with a basket full of ingredients, most of which are to varying degrees unfamiliar to them, and they are instructed to create a festive meal for their family or close friends that in their estimation would please the diners. To aid the cooks, they would be allowed to sample the unfamiliar ingredients (cooked in a neutral fashion where appropriate) and would be provided with a pantry of basic items, such as cooking fats, herbs, spices, aromatic vegetables, starchy ingredients (e.g. rice, pasta, potatoes, bread, corn meal), etc.

How would our traditional cooks go about their task? I think all would agree that they would most likely try to match the unfamiliar ingredients with analogues that are well-known to them from their traditional cuisine, and then to plug those new ingredients into recipes that they have at their command. In addition, they would likely seek to build a meal with an overall composition corresponding to the norms of their traditional cuisine. In both regards, they would be pushed in the same direction not only by their own competence as cooks but also by their sense of the expectations of their audience of family members and friends. But, depending on the traditional cuisine involved and the ingredients presented, one can imagine difficulties arising.

Let us say, for the sake of argument, that our grandmothers all hail from some town in southern Italy and that the basket includes the following items: black beans, blueberries, crayfish, collard greens, manchego cheese, mangoes, pork loin. It seems to me most likely that the blueberries and mangoes would either be used to create some sort of dessert or perhaps simply used as a fruit course to finish the meal and that the other ingredients would have to be fit into the usual southern Italian meal structure of first (*primo*) and second (*secondo*) courses, possibly with a preceding starter (*antipasto*). The pork loin would surely be regarded as the best candidate to be the basis of the second course or even to be the basis for both the first and second courses, by using it to make a *ragù* of pork, onion, and tomatoes or with less tomato and a full array of minced aromatic vegetables; the sauce from such preparations could be used to dress a first course of pasta and the meat then served with one or more side dishes and bread as the second course; an important consideration would be the availability in the pantry of an appropriate shape of dried pasta (e.g. *paccheri* or other large tubular form), or the availability of semolina flour to make an appropriate fresh form of pasta, e.g. *cavatelli* or *fusilli*. Another likely treatment of the pork for the second course would be to roast it simply with herbs and garlic, but with that choice the question of the first course would be unaddressed. The presence of the black beans in our hypothetical basket might suggest to our cooks a *primo* of *pasta e fagioli*, a universally consumed and beloved dish in southern Italy, but would the required substitution of black beans for the usual white cannellini beans render the dish visually too odd and objectionable? A greater problem with using the beans with pasta here would be that the meal is supposed to be festive and, as much as *pasta e fagioli* is beloved, it is generally speaking most decidedly not a festive dish in southern Italy. Instead, the beans could be paired with the collards and together form a reasonable side dish to the second course's pork, a *contorno* modelled after traditional dishes of beans with escarole or broccoli di rapa. As for the crayfish, little known or unknown in southern Italian cookery, they resemble other crustaceans that are popular there and could easily be adapted to traditional recipes and served either as an antipasto item or as the basis of a condiment for pasta; in either case, one could prepare them *in bianco* or with a tomato sauce, a choice one might make after deciding whether tomato sauce will be used elsewhere in the meal and thus avoiding repetition.

107

If the crayfish are made with pasta, a choice would have to be made regarding the form thereof; spaghetti or linguine are typical pairings with seafood, but for some the festive nature of the meal might incline one to use a less everyday form, such as tagliatelle or fettuccine. Finally, with regard to the manchego, which resembles Italian pecorino, our cooks might well choose to serve it before or after the two central courses of the meal, but if it is a more aged cheese, they might offer it to be grated on a pasta course, especially if the pasta is served with a sauce made from the pork, but they would surely not do so if they opt to make a pasta dish with the crayfish.

Now, it must be noted that within traditional southern Italian cookery, specific holidays demand meals that include particular dishes, with the links between holidays and dishes sometimes being widely observed (at the regional level) or more locally held or in some cases being a matter of family choices from an array of dishes regarded more broadly as appropriate. More generally, most families have templates for weekly meals, some even rather rigid schedules, and in addition many people faithfully follow recipes they've learned. Nonetheless, most cooks can and do improvise to varying degrees but do so within certain well-known parameters explicit or tacit. Our hypothetical situation is intended to emphasize the fact that beyond the level of set menus and recipes, traditional cooks – and their diners – are operating with a fairly elaborate set of 'unseen' rules and expectations, a set of communally shared ideas about what and how one properly eats in various situations.

Were we to repeat this experiment with the same basket of ingredients but with sets of grandmothers from various other places – south-western France, south-central Louisiana, northern Haiti, wherever traditional cookery survives well – we would surely see meals produced that reflected each group's background; in each case our cooks would necessarily make adaptive decisions shaped by their knowledge of their own community's rules and expectations.

Defining 'Cuisine'

Given that food studies, at least as a quasi-independent academic discipline, is relatively new, it is perhaps not surprising that there is no broad consensus regarding the definition of the term 'cuisine'. It is, however, also striking that the question of what we mean by 'cuisine' has not been more of a focal point for discussion in the field. Of course, one cannot expect food writers, academic or popular, to devote a part of each publication to definitions of fundamental terms, but in the absence of consensus on what is arguably the key technical term of the field, the colloquial and dictionary definitions of 'cuisine' can and do remain very much at play in specialized food discourse, whenever we as food scholars and writers fail to address the matter directly.

English-language dictionaries, reflecting common mainstream usage, all give as the primary meaning of 'cuisine' the phrase 'a style or manner of cooking' or some slight variation thereof. The word normally occurs with a modifier that falls into one of the following categories:

1) a geographical (especially national or regional) or ethnic designation, e.g.: German cuisine, Brazilian cuisine; Provençal cuisine, Szechuan cuisine; northern Italian cuisine, Mediterranean cuisine; Jewish cuisine, Italian-American cuisine.

2) a designation referring to an international and/or professional style of cooking, e.g.: haute cuisine, nouvelle cuisine, New Nordic cuisine, fusion cuisine.

3) a reference to the cooking of an individual chef or restaurant, e.g.: the cuisine of chef Paul Prudhomme, the cuisine of Noma.

It should also be noted that the dictionary definition of 'a style or manner of cooking' does not fully capture what is an extremely common and important aspect of how the non-specialist thinks about one or the other sort of cuisine: the usual way to conceptualize a cuisine is in terms of typical ingredients and typical dishes, perhaps also to a lesser degree salient methods of cooking, but all in all it is a decidedly concrete idea, perhaps elaborated with some qualification(s) of a general aesthetic nature, e.g. sophisticated, greasy, spicy, hearty, etc.

There is no arguing against common usage, even if it sometimes admits notions that bear little or no relation to culinary reality, as in the case of 'Mediterranean cuisine'.[1] The question at hand is, however, whether this popular sense of the term 'cuisine' is useful in the formal study of food and culinary culture. I believe it is not.

The popular conception of cuisine is strongly focussed on the physical manifestation of cookery – on ingredients and dishes and cooking methods. But, as illustrated in our hypothetical grandmother experiment, there are guidelines and rules that underlie any recipes or ingredients which direct the cook's decision making. In addition, there is also the question of the expectations of the intended audience which, while obviously standing in some relation to the eater's knowledge of ingredients and dishes, constitute an element that does not figure directly in popular conceptualizations of 'cuisine'. In discussing 'cuisine' in a serious way, we cannot disregard these non-physical elements.

Aside from this basic issue of the mental aspect of cuisine that lies behind its physical realization, there is a socio-economic dimension to the popular usage of the term 'cuisine' that renders it, at least to this writer, problematic for the scholarly discussion of food and culinary culture without being addressed explicitly. As a relatively recent borrowing from French (attested from the eighteenth century), a borrowing which surely was introduced by elite (wealthy, educated) speakers of English, the word 'cuisine', like many recent borrowings from French, is strongly coloured by its association with elite culture and, moreover, by its abiding strong association with French cookery in general and elite French cookery in particular. And indeed, one can see these associations clearly if we compare the uses of 'cuisine' alongside those of the partially synonymous but much older term 'cookery' (attested from the fourteenth century and built with a native English word and a nativized French suffix). Though the dictionary definitions of 'cuisine' and 'cookery' differ, in everyday parlance the two

109

terms overlap considerably, with 'German cuisine' or 'Portuguese cuisine' being roughly equivalent to 'German cookery' or 'Portuguese cookery'. But the elite or 'high culture' associations of 'cuisine', absent from 'cookery' (which is relatively neutral), render some pairings more common and preferable to others; thus, for example, 'peasant cookery' (or 'peasant food') seems preferable to 'peasant cuisine'. With regard to combinations with national or ethnic designations, the two words certainly both can be used broadly but while 'French cuisine' or 'Italian cuisine' seem utterly natural, in connexion with countries less internationally esteemed for their culinary cultures, 'cookery' seems to be the preferred term, as in 'English cookery' or 'Dutch cookery' versus 'English cuisine' or 'Dutch cuisine'. In the case of cultures which Westerners long described as 'primitive', use of the term 'cuisine' has been and remains even less usual; for example, 'Mohawk cuisine' has only recently come into use, as opposed to 'Mohawk food(s)'.

The point is that the term 'cuisine' can be used in a neutral way but the weight of historical popular usage lends it prejudicial nuances: a proper cuisine is for many people relatively more complex, sophisticated, admirable and desirable than the mere cookery or foods of less respected culinary traditions. But these are all for the greatest part purely aesthetic judgements and comparable to what we see in popular attitudes regarding languages: some are widely held to be beautiful, rich, subtle, precise, complex, etc., while others are said to be ugly, unsophisticated, harsh, inexpressive, primitive, etc. – judgements which derive not from actual linguistic qualities but from the prejudices of individuals, often enough conforming to prejudices more generally held in their own linguistic or cultural community. For linguists, French and Dutch and Mohawk are from a scientific standpoint equally 'languages'. To be sure, both linguists and laypersons make a distinction between languages on the one hand and dialects on the other but from a scientific standpoint the distinction expresses not a structural difference but a sociolinguistic difference – a dialect of a language stands in a certain sociolinguistic relation to its related, overarching and typically standardized (national) 'language' – and when regarded without reference to the sociolinguistic relationship, a 'dialect' is no less a genuine, full-fledged linguistic system than a 'language'.

For food scholars, then, the question is whether we have a scientific definition of what constitutes a 'cuisine'.

Cuisine as a Cultural Domain

The basis of human alimentation is indisputably and firmly biological: humans normally strive to fulfil the nutritional needs that nature has set for the body. And yet it is equally indisputable that under most circumstances, human alimentation involves behaviours that clearly transcend biological need; indeed, in some cases humans either unwittingly or even quite intentionally eat in ways that run counter to what nature requires for bodily well-being. Alimentary behaviours are by and large learned and thus shared at the least within the family but typically also throughout a community located in a specific time and geographical and/or social space. Such learned, communally-shared behaviours are propagated through various means – casual observation and explicit demonstration, incidental remarks and focussed conversation, the full range of sensory perception of shared food, etc. – and given that food preparation and consumption occur in social contexts, these activities and the food items involved can and commonly do accrue their own socially-determined meanings as well as associations with other aspects of a given community's activities, institutions, and ideological systems: in other words, a community's alimentary behaviours, taken together, constitute a domain of that community's culture with links to various other cultural domains, such as language, religion, medicine, etc. Culinary behaviour is part of culture.

The most reasonable term to use in a scientific context to refer both to this cultural domain of culinary behaviour and to its underlying ideas is, I believe, 'cuisine', with the caveat that we must do so while consciously stripping the word of its popular concrete conceptualization and associations with specifically French and generally elite cookery. From the recognition that culinary behaviour and knowledge, i.e. cuisine, is a cultural domain there follow some necessary implications:

1) Given that all human societies have culture and given the centrality of alimentation to human life, it follows that all societies have cuisine.

2) As a complex of behaviours and ideas that are learned by individuals in a social setting, cuisine necessarily relies upon communication and can itself be used as a means of communication.

3) Like other cultural domains, cuisine is a system, i.e. it is based on a complex of structured elements (ideas, beliefs, rules, etc.); these elements show a degree of hierarchical arrangement related in part to how and when they are acquired by the individual.

4) Cultural domains (language, religion, medicine, music, etc.) are interconnected and together form a higher order cultural system; generally speaking, elements of a given cultural domain are more stable (resistant to change) the greater the degree to which they are integrated into the network of cultural domains.

5) Cuisine, no less than other cultural domains, is an open system, with openings potentially at multiple points in its own structure and through its connexions to other cultural domains; consequently, like all open systems, it is subject to variation within a given community and to change across time.

6) As a cultural phenomenon dependent upon communication for its propagation and practice, cuisine is inextricably linked to the social structures that delineate networks of communication. Insofar as a community's discourse about cuisine is internally oriented, it will exhibit a higher degree of conservatism and, conversely, the denser the network of communication regarding cuisine is between communities, the greater the likelihood is that those communities' cuisines will come to share elements and structures.

Cuisine, Language and the Concept of 'Culinary Grammar'

As mentioned above, popular conceptions of specific cuisines are focussed very much on foods and how they are cooked. But while it is natural to think in terms of the concrete realizations of a given cuisine, it is important to recognize that the preferred ingredients and the dishes and meals made with them are manifestations or expressions of an underlying set of ideas, methodologies, rules and aesthetic principles which exist in the minds of individuals and are shared by those individuals who form a given cultural community. The distinction we make here coincides with a distinction that must be made in other cultural domains and is best known from linguistics, where one speaks of *langue* and *parole*: the latter is the actual individual utterance that can be heard or read, while the former is (the knowledge of) the underlying grammatical system and lexicon that allows a speaker to create a well-formed utterance and for a hearer to understand that utterance. In music, a given performance is typically the realization of a composition which has been constructed according to or at least with reference to a set of rules regarding tonality, harmony, rhythm, etc., as well as templates for preferred forms for musical genres, etc., and the performance is subjected to aesthetic judgement and analysis by the audience according to its own knowledge of musical 'grammar'. Likewise, in cuisine a meal is typically conceived and prepared according to the cook's knowledge of a culturally specific set of culinary rules, principles, etc. and each diner consumes the meal on the mental level in terms of his/her own culinary knowledge. In each of these instances, the greater the degree to which the performer and consumer share knowledge of the grammar of the cultural domain in question, the greater the likelihood is that the consumer will understand what the performer intended to communicate.

Recognition of the communicative aspect of cuisine has led some scholars to say that it is a language, but, while cookery often does serve to communicate in certain ways, it is only partly or secondarily a means of communication; its purpose and functions make it fundamentally different from language in various respects. For example, whereas with language, all speakers of a given dialect are able both to actively produce and decode utterances, with cuisine there is in most societies an asymmetry between a smaller group of those who can competently prepare foods and the whole group which consumes, enjoys and understands them; this mismatch resembles more what we see in music or other arts than what we see in language. Along similar lines, a dish or a meal produced by members of one culture can be thoroughly enjoyed, if not fully understood and appreciated from a cultural standpoint, by someone from a completely alien culture who encounters it for the first time; again, in this regard a stronger analogy can be made between cuisine and music or other non-verbal arts than with language, where utterances in an unknown language are simply incomprehensible to the alien. This point calls to mind an even more fundamental difference: whereas the linguistic sign and thus language as a whole is in a real sense arbitrary, cuisine has, alongside its arbitrary and culturally determined aspects (e.g. some taste preferences, meal structures, etc.), an essential connexion to nutritional requirements, physiological aspects of taste, and the availability of foodstuffs (conditioned by the environment, market constraints, etc.).

Given the important differences between language and cuisine, it is not surprising that attempts to draw far-reaching parallels between the two cultural domains' structures have only partial success, as in Montanari's (2002: vii) suggestion that ingredients correspond to the lexicon, recipes to 'grammar' (presumably morphology), meal structure to syntax and convivial comportment to rhetoric. While such an analysis may not work in detail, it is in a general sense very much correct in recognizing that the culinary knowledge that allows people to create and decode dishes and meals is hierarchically structured, an idea that has been rejected by some influential anthropologists, such as Goody (1982: 31ff.) and Mennell (1996:13ff.). These scholars clearly doubt the significance and utility of the concept of 'deep structure' in cuisine, though they are careful enough not to deny completely that it may exist; rather, they take the position that it is impossible to verify its existence, since what the analyst can derive as deep structure from the observable surface phenomena is – at least in their estimation – based on wholly circular argumentation: deep structure is derived from the surface phenomena but then used to explain the selfsame surface phenomena. Rather than resorting to such pernicious reasoning, they both argue that we can only understand how cuisine works by studying it in history – observing how it changes over time – and both ultimately focus their own analyses of culinary cultures on the dynamics of the social and economic contexts in which those cultures exist.

There are some observations to be made regarding the rejection of 'deep structure' by Goody and Mennell. First, the focus of their reaction is on Lévi-Strauss (e.g. 1965) and other structural anthropologists, who in their estimation were excessively concerned with discovering immutable structural universals, an issue which we will address elsewhere. Second, their conclusion, that a true understanding of how cuisine functions must centrally include historical and comparative analyses of cultures in their social contexts, is a view with which I whole-heartedly agree, but their further implications that internal structures of culinary systems are at best irrelevant to our understanding and further that there is necessarily some sort of opposition between the consideration of systemic structure and analysis of historical change are very much off the mark.[2] Indeed, it is in part precisely through study of culinary change that we can break through the circularity Goody and Mennell decry: on a small scale, we see how underlying principles and rules come to expression in a situation such as the one described above with our grandmotherly cooks and on a grander, community-wide scale we see much the same in the behaviours of immigrant communities all over the world, who upon finding themselves in new environments, confronted by new arrays of ingredients and cooking technologies and pressures from alien sociocultural standards, apply and, where necessary or desirable, adapt aspects of their culinary 'grammar' (cf. Fischler 1990: 148-49).

Detailed study of such immigrant communities' behaviour, as in Buccini's (2015 & forthcoming) analysis of the development of Italian-American cuisine, provides strong evidence for the necessity to analyze culinary change not only in terms of socio-economic conditions but also in terms of the systemic complexity of cuisine itself. In this and other similar cases, we see clearly that so long as the community and family structure allowed for full transmission of the culinary system through direct generational transfer, Italian-Americans maintained over two or sometimes even more generations a cuisine that was in all fundamental ways remarkably faithful to that which the original immigrants had brought to North America from southern Italy, faithful with regard to those elements which in a strongly family-oriented group involve prolonged exposure (aesthetics of taste and patterns of consumption) and are supported through multiple ties to other cultural domains entrenched in the ethnic community's life (other aspects of the patterns of consumption and non-aesthetic food ideology).

Telling also is how this southern Italian culinary culture among Italian Americans has broken down in a fashion parallel to (and in general temporally lagging only a generation behind) the linguistic shift from bilingualism with maintenance of the southern Italian 'heritage' language to total assimilation to Anglophone monolingualism with only residual knowledge of some Italian vocabulary. Just as the linguistic shift among Italian Americans has tended to be quite abrupt, with no prolonged (multi-generational) period of bilingualism, we can see an abrupt shift at the culinary level: once the tight bonds of family, extended family and ethnic community are loosened as a result of exogamy and the socioeconomic exigencies of American life, requiring stronger attachments to work and geographic dispersal, even individuals who strongly self-identify as ethnic Italian Americans do not acquire the deeper elements of Italian-American culinary grammar but rather those of the dominant American mainstream cuisine, maintaining knowledge only at a more superficial level of specific ingredients and dishes and then typically only those that are aesthetically and ideologically not at odds with the grammar of mainstream American cuisine and which have come to be thought of as ethnic markers both within and outside the ethnic community.

At several points in the above discussion I have referred to culinary deep structure as opposed to the surface manifestations of cuisine. Let us now consider in a systematic way what these aspects of cuisine consist of.[3] The following chart (Figure 1) provides a schematic overview of the basic structure, divided between the surface level of elements, which are easily observed and experienced even in a casual manner, and the deep structure, which consists of three sub-domains of elements represented in the minds of individual members of a given culinary culture which are not directly observable, elements which the individual acquires through prolonged exposure and/or through overt instruction from other members of the community. Though the analogy works only to a certain degree, it can nonetheless be said that part of what constitutes the surface level, ingredients and in some measure also composed dishes, forms a relatively more open set and in this way resembles the lexicon in language. The sub-domains of the deep structure then together correspond roughly to the complex of grammatical sub-domains in language, i.e. phonology, morphology, syntax, propositional semantics.

Figure 1: Overview of the Structure of Cuisine

SURFACE LEVEL
I Concrete Aspects of Cuisine
– ingredients (and to a degree composed dishes) represent a relatively open set
– surface elements are easily observed/experienced

INTERFACE BETWEEN SURFACE AND DEEP STRUCTURE

DEEP STRUCTURE
II Patterns of Consumption
III Aesthetics of Taste
IV Non-Aesthetic Food Ideology
– relatively closed sets
– not directly observable (requires long-term observation/experience and/or instruction to be acquired by an individual)
– II & IV: high degree of structuredness through relationships with elements of other cultural domains
– III & IV: enhanced stability on account of childhood acquisition and (partially) subconscious internalization/automaticization

A few terms introduced in Figure 1 require comment. First, we refer to 'stability', a notion that must be understood in the first place in terms of individual behaviour and thence can be applied in a more general way with regard to a community's culinary culture. For a given element in any cultural system, stability, i.e. resistance to change, is dependent upon various factors, among which figures crucially the degree to which that element is embedded in the system, the degree to which it supports and derives support from other elements within its cultural domain and in some cases also elements in other cultural domains. Thus, for example, patterns of consumption (daily, weekly, seasonally) are deeply embedded in the culinary system itself but then also are intimately connected to cultural elements that belong to other cultural domains (in Figure 2 such relationships are indicated with the symbol ⟺). Another factor that affects stability is the degree to which a given element is subject to automaticization, that is, internalization to the point where it normally exists or is triggered in the mind of the individual at a subconscious level. In language, for example, the complex movements involved in articulation are automatized and normally below consciousness and so deeply ingrained that a given speaker, when trying to learn to speak another language, naturally imposes on that target language his or her 'articulatory habits', rendering speech accented and foreign sounding or even 'incorrect' from the perspective of native-speakers of that target language; such articulatory habits can be so ingrained that they long remain despite conscious efforts by the speaker to suppress them. Somewhat analogous in cuisine are basic taste preferences and aversions, as well as other culturally-conditioned (through taboos or notions of hygiene, etc.) 'visceral' reactions to possible comestibles, which are typically acquired early in life, internalized, and thus can be difficult to unlearn or alter.

In Figure 2 we find a more detailed representation of our structural chart which includes lists of the elements typically found in each of the sub-domains of cuisine, as well as an explanation of the interface between the surface and deep levels; note that this chart is intended neither to be in all details universally applicable nor exhaustive with respect to the possible elements included.

Figure 2: Elements within the Culinary Sub-Domains

SURFACE LEVEL
I Concrete Aspects of Cuisine
• Ingredients
• Composed dishes and styles of dishes
• Cooking methods, preparation techniques
• Composition of individual meals

116   **INTERFACE BETWEEN SURFACE AND DEEP STRUCTURE**
Knowledge in the minds of individuals of ingredients, recipes, cooking methods & meal structures provide the mapping between deep structure and surface manifestations.

DEEP (ABSTRACT) LEVEL
II Patterns of Consumption
• daily meal patterns (⟺ gender roles, work patterns, family structure, etc.)
• seasonal patterns & food procurement and preservation
(⟺ agriculture, market structure, etc.)
• feasting and fasting (⟺ religion, ethnicity, etc.)
III Aesthetics of Taste
• preferences of basic tastes
• preferences of taste combinations
• preferences of taste with regard to meal patterns
• attitudes toward simplicity/complexity
IV Non-Aesthetic Food Ideology
• importance of food discourse
• nature of food discourse (⟺ family structure, marketing, etc.)
• attitudes toward tradition/novelty

- rôle of food in group identity (⟺ ethnicity, etc.)
- beliefs regarding food and health (⟺ medicine)
- taboos (⟺ religion, medicine (hygiene), etc.)

A detailed discussion of this material must be reserved for elsewhere but let us return briefly to the topic of Italian-American cuisine to illustrate some basic points.

To say that an immigrant group maintained its cuisine is not simply or even necessarily to say that it continued to consume a certain number of its traditional ingredients and dishes in its new environment. Rather, it is to say that it maintained *grosso modo* the fundamental rules, principles and aesthetics which form the deep structure or grammar of their cuisine. That southern Italian immigrants, mostly from poor backgrounds, increased their consumption of pasta, meat and fresh fish as their economic circumstances in the US improved clearly constituted a change in their cuisine but not a fundamental one. The immigrants and the first US born generations still prepared these foods in traditional ways, preferring, for example, their own methods of butchering meat (thin rather than thick steaks); such foods also continued to be fit into the weekly template for meals – e.g. soup on Monday, Wednesday and Friday meatless meals (even though the Church no longer required them to be so), Sunday meals necessarily festive and including special forms of pasta, elaborate ragùs and perhaps roasted meat as well. And traditional consumption of 'poverty' foods such as organ meats, salted and fermented fish, beans and bitter greens all maintained central places in the cuisine, tied as they were to firmly entrenched consumption patterns, aesthetics of taste, etc. In short, in those households in which food and family, cooking and culinary discourse and conviviality all remained tightly bound together, children were fully acculturated in a complex tradition.

Also instructive is the view from the opposite perspective, namely of how Italian-American and Italian food has been taken up by the American mainstream. It has been claimed, most famously by Mintz (1996: 106) that the United States does not possess a cuisine, a view that from my perspective is untenable but clearly depends upon how one defines 'cuisine'. As cuisine is defined here, the American mainstream clearly possesses one, though it is a cuisine that differs in a number of ways from the traditional cuisines of southern Italian and of the Italian-Americans. The grammatical structure of American cuisine can be seen at play in how it filters and alters elements that it accepts from other cuisines. A visit to a garden variety mainstream American 'Italian' restaurant offers ample evidence: Italian meal structure (*primo-secondo*) is rejected, and a main course typically conforms to the American presentation of protein/starch/vegetable together on one plate (with pasta often treated as a 'side'); salad is moved from its Italianate position toward the end of the meal to the beginning. The restraint and balance that characterizes traditional Italian cookery of all regions, conflicting with American culinary aesthetics, is set aside, and dishes that purport to be Italian(-American) are rendered unrecognizable through habitual over-saucing and inappropriate and profligate additions of garlic, cheese, chillies, etc. Not surprisingly, American takes on foods from other cuisines (Mexican, French, etc.) show the same general tendencies and specific adaptations, conditioned as they are by the mainstream's culinary grammar.

Toward a Typology of Cuisine

In this paper I have defined cuisine as the cultural domain that is principally concerned with the knowledge and behaviour of a given cultural community regarding the preparation and consumption of food; it has a complex internal structure like other cultural domains and in addition is interconnected with other cultural domains in important ways.

So far in the discussion I have not addressed other scholars' definitions but this neglect has been for the sake of brevity. There are, however, two such definitions which I would like to consider now for the light they shed on a crucial aspect of cuisine as defined here. They are diametrically opposed in a fundamental way and yet both scholars agree that the US does not possess a cuisine.

The first of these appears in Freeman (1977: 144-45) in the context of the history of Chinese food: 'Our definition is historical: the appearance of a cuisine, a self-conscious tradition of cooking and eating, implies the confluence of certain material factors – the availability and abundance of ingredients – with a set of attitudes about food and its place in the life of man.' Freeman elaborates on this idea and states that 'a cuisine does not develop out of the cooking traditions of a single region' for 'ingredients are apt to be too limited, cooks and eaters too conservative' (p. 144) and subsequently makes it clear that his notion of what constitutes a cuisine is limited to supra-regional, elite cookery: 'The appearance of a cuisine, then, involves the availability of ingredients, many sophisticated consumers, and cooks and diners free from conventions of region and ritual' (p.145). Writing almost forty years ago, Freeman was perhaps right in saying that the US did not have a cuisine according to his (narrow) definition, and perhaps that is still the case, but it is also abundantly clear that a kind of cookery that is not merely supra-regional but supra-ethnic is emerging in the US and elsewhere, which relies on a maximally wide array of ingredients, is prepared and consumed by people who believe themselves to be culinarily sophisticated and focussed on aesthetics and novelty, unfettered by 'conventions of region and ritual' – this is precisely the sort of food celebrated in the competitive cooking shows and served up in ever-increasing numbers of trendy restaurants and the home kitchens of 'foodies'.

Mintz's (1996: 104) definition contrasts sharply with that of Freeman for he not only rejects the strict association of 'cuisine' with elite cookery that Freeman embraces but also asserts that the only real cuisines are those that are regional in nature: '"Cuisine", more exactly defined, has to do with the ongoing foodways of a *region* [emphasis added], within which active discourse about food sustains both common understandings and reliable production of the food in question.' From this, it would seem to follow logically that Mintz rejects the notion of national cuisines: 'A "national cuisine" is a contradiction in terms; there can be regional cuisines, but not national cuisines. I think that for the most part, a national cuisine is simply a holistic artifice based on the foods of the people who live inside some political system, such as France or Spain' (p. 104). From Mintz's rejection of the notion of a national cuisine, it also follows that he would deny that there is such a thing as 'American cuisine', but his further observations on American eating habits show that there are three specific features of mainstream American foodways that help render the nation cuisine-less (pp. 108ff.): 1) Americans are exposed to a great many ethnic cuisines and are generally quite promiscuous in their eating habits, often consuming in a given week meals of very disparate origins, say, of Anglo-American origin one day, Chinese, Mexican, Italian and Thai origins on subsequent days; 2) an extraordinarily high percentage of the meals they eat are not home-cooked but rather purchased already prepared for home consumption or eaten in restaurants; 3) despite a recent rise in interest in local and seasonal foods, 'industrial' and seasonally independent imported foods purchased from grocery chains constitute the norm for the majority of the US population. These behaviours are increasingly common throughout the world but they have been especially prevalent in the US for a relatively longer time.

Mintz seems then to want to make central to his definition of cuisine a more prominent role of home cookery and a closer relationship between food consumer and food producer. Beyond that, he also lays particular emphasis on the role of communication in cuisine: 'I do not see how a cuisine can exist unless there is a community of people who eat it, cook it, have opinions about it, and engage in dialogue involving those opinions' (p. 117).

From my perspective, what Freeman and Mintz define in mutually exclusive fashion as the only kinds of cuisine are, in fact, both a kind of cuisine – where these two kinds of cuisine differ is not a matter of their status as cultural domains or their structural complexity with regard to sub-domains and specific elements within those sub-domains but rather of the differing social structures and patterns of food discourse of the communities that create and maintain them. Mintz clearly limits his notion of cuisine to traditional, regional culinary cultures; Freeman limits his to supra-regional elite culinary cultures. In a traditional regional cuisine the central locus of that discourse is the family, then the extended family and circles of friends and then the broader local, sub-regional and regional communities. Such discourse is not 'closed', and thus the cuisine remains to a degree open to external influence and change, but the higher the degree that culinary knowledge is passed on within familial or very local circumstances, the more it will show continuity across generations. A reasonable name for this sort of cuisine might be an ***endo-cuisine***, not in the limited sense that Levi-Strauss (2008: 42) first used the term, but rather to express the idea that the network of communication and culinary discourse that supports a cuisine is focussed locally.

Standing in natural contrast to the endo-cuisine would then be the ***exo-cuisine***, a cuisine supported by a network of communication and discourse that is more outward looking and diffuse, in which a significant part of the transfer of culinary knowledge is not limited to familial and local circles but extends outward, across ethnic and regional and national boundaries. These kinds of exchanges of knowledge go hand in hand with exchanges of trade goods, allowing for the sort of consumption of exotic and out-of-season foods that characterized only elite cuisines in pre-modern times, as in the case of the supra-regional elite cuisine that Freeman discusses in his article on the Chinese Sung dynasty. But the sort of long-distance exchanges of foods and culinary knowledge that formerly were available only to the elite have over the past two centuries become increasingly available to broader sectors of more and more societies around the globe.

In the case of mainstream America, there has been a wide range of socio-economic factors at work for a long time that have led to looser familial bonds, greater mobility of individuals and nuclear families and increased reliance on commercially prepared foods. In addition, some of the forces, *mutatis mutandis,* that Appadurai (1988) describes at work in the formation of an Indian national cuisine in the 1970s and 1980s were also at play in the development of a bourgeois supra-regional American cuisine earlier in the twentieth and even in the nineteenth century. And finally, there has been in the US a long-standing and pervasive intrusion of corporate marketing in all levels of food discourse. Thus, if we are to allow for the existence of national cuisines – which we must, insofar as modern mobility and ease of communication have forged national cultural discourse communities – then mainstream American cuisine can be seen as a somewhat precocious and extreme version thereof, a quintessential exo-cuisine.

Notes

1. The term 'Mediterranean cuisine', even if not originally of commercial origin, certainly has a strong commercial attachment through its use in marketing and is an excellent example of the concrete conception of 'cuisine' as a matter first and foremost of ingredients and dishes that are popularly thought of typical for a geographic zone – Mediterranean cuisine is a catch-all for those cuisines which use ingredients common around the Mediterranean region, such as olive oil, chick peas, fava beans, garlic, lamb, etc., or also a (primarily commercial) style of cooking of recent origin which draws promiscuously on various culinary traditions from countries around the Mediterranean Sea and that uses such ingredients. The term clearly serves a purpose in non-technical discourse but is, of course, difficult to justify in a more scholarly sense: 'Mediterranean cuisine' exists no more than there exists 'Mediterranean language', 'Mediterranean religion' or 'Mediterranean music', even if we can identify specific elements from these various cultural domains that are more or less widespread in lands around the Mediterranean Sea.

2. Note Goody's (1982: 34) criticism of Chang: 'There are important reasons of a theoretical and empirical kind for paying more attention to the time dimension. When anthropologists talk about the culture of food, they tend to see this as a continuing normative structure that, in the words of one recent writer on the subject, "absorbs or rejects foreign imports according to their structural or stylistic compatibility" (Chang 1977: 7).' Goody's comment here is odd. While there are some 'universal' structural constraints on culinary structure (e.g. the physiology of taste) – or the structure of any cultural domain, including language (e.g. the articulatory apparatus) – the more interesting structural aspects for this discussion, the cultural aspects, are themselves subject to change. But that said, it is also true that culture, by its very nature something shared by a community,

normally shows both openness to change and resistance to change, and communally shared cultural constructs do often function as filters regulating the acceptance or rejection of innovations. The necessity of considering structural aspects of cuisine (or language) when analyzing change over spans of time is to make sense of why some elements are (within a given culture but also cross-culturally) more liable to change and others less liable.

3.   This discussion is hardly the first in which the structure of cuisine or of 'culinary grammar' is presented as being a system with hierarchical structure. For example, Montanari's (2002) aforementioned comparison of cuisine to language is clearly an attempt to call attention to the internal structure of cuisine. Chang (1977: 1) writes explicitly of the need to relate 'food variables hierarchically' and his discussion of Chinese food culture bears similarities to the general views presented here. Though the focus of her discussion differs from mine, Rozin (1982: 201) presents an allied position: 'All cuisines, like other cultural systems, are sets of rules or prescriptions about how to organize our knowledge or beliefs of human behaviour.' My views seem to be very much in line with those of Fischler as presented in *L'Homnivore* (1990), though I read his work only after I had developed my positions from my own perspective as a linguist. Unfortunately, space restrictions here make it necessary to reserve a thorough discussion of other scholars' views for another publication.

Bibliography

Appadurai, Arjun. 1988. 'How to Make a National Cuisine: Cookbooks in Contemporary India', *Comparative Studies in Society and History* 30: 3-24.

Buccini, Anthony F. 2015. 'Italy', in Lucy Long (ed.), *Ethnic American Food Today. A Cultural Encyclopedia* (Lanham: Rowman & Littlefield), pp. 314-32.

_____. Forthcoming. 'Prejudice, Assimilation, and Profit: The Peculiar History of Italian Cookery in the United States', in Cynthia Chou and Suzanne Kramer (eds.), *Food, Identity and Social Change.* (Based on papers presented at the University of Copenhagen, Sept. 2014, and the Oxford Symposium, July 2015.)

Chang, K.C. 1977. 'Introduction', in K.C. Chang (ed.), *Food in Chinese Culture. Anthropological and Historical Perspectives* (New Haven: Yale University Press), pp. 1-21.

Fischler, Claude. 1990. *L'Homnivore* (Paris: Odile Jacob).

Freeman, Michael. 1977. 'Sung', in K.C. Chang (ed.), *Food in Chinese Culture. Anthropological and Historical Perspectives* (New Haven: Yale University Press), pp. 141-76.

Goody, Jack. 1982. *Cooking, Cuisine and Class* (Cambridge: Cambridge University Press).

Lévi-Strauss, Claude. 2008 (orig. 1965). 'The Culinary Triangle'. In Carole Counihan and Penny Van Esterik (eds.), *Food and Culture: A Reader* (New York: Routledge), pp. 36-44.

Mennell, Stephen. 1996. *All Manner of Food* (Urbana: University of Illinois Press).

Mintz, Sidney W. 1996. *Tasting Food, Tasting Freedom. Excursions into Eating, Culture, and the Past* (Boston: Beacon).

Montanari, Massimo. 2002. 'Introduzione: La cucina, luogo dell'identità e dello scambio', in Massimo Montanari (ed.), *Il mondo in cucina* (Rome: Laterza), pp. vii-xii.

Rozin, Elisabeth. 1982. 'The Structure of Cuisine', in Lewis M. Barker (ed.), *The Physiobiology of Human Food Selection* (Westport: AVI), pp. 189-203.

'That Was Good': Eating, Drinking and the Etiquette of Slurping in Japan

Voltaire Cang

Ramen is presently experiencing a worldwide boom, with restaurants specializing in this Japanese-improvised dish of noodles served in a broth sprouting in London, Paris and other European capitals and cities. Many ramen establishments have also opened and are expected to increase across Asia, the Americas, the Middle East and other regions in the world. In most of the restaurants outside Japan, ramen look and taste the same as their Japanese counterparts. Many, however, if not all of them, are eaten differently from Japanese ramen. In the first place, many customers in ramen restaurants outside Japan use the fork, unlike in Japan where chopsticks are *de rigueur*. There are also differences in the order of eating the noodles and drinking the broth: in Japan, the noodles and other ingredients are usually consumed first, with the broth drunk at the end; in other countries, the order varies. Most striking among the differences in eating styles, however, are the sounds of the meal: whereas in ramen restaurants outside Japan the diners – at least the non-Japanese – make little noise when eating, in Japan, slurping your ramen is encouraged, even mandatory.

The act and the accompanying sounds of the slurp are associated with ramen more than any other Japanese noodle dish or food, especially outside Japan. Barak Kushner's award-winning work on the social and culinary history of ramen was titled just that – *Slurp!* – while a recent listing of highly-rated ramen restaurants in New York by the *New York Times* called them 'slurp worthy' establishments.[1]

Indeed, slurping is imperative when eating ramen: 'all ramen-eaters, whether slow and contemplative, or fast and frenetic, still slurp.'[2] Most Japanese, however, employ the slurp not only for ramen, but for almost all kinds of noodle dishes. Although Japanese table manners generally prohibit slurping and chewing sounds at the table, '[t]he exception is noodles'.[3]

Several explanations have been given for this eating practice so closely identified with the Japanese and noodles. In his study on ramen, George Solt writes: 'In Japan […] slurping is considered a practical way to eat something hot and wet without burning oneself or making a mess, and when done correctly, it can be an impressive method allowing one to avoid burns and flying specks of soup.'[4] Japanese food research pioneer Ishige Naomichi explains that 'Noodle lovers attach great importance to the feeling of the noodles slipping smoothly down the throat, and consequently suck them down in a single breath without chewing well, an operation that inevitably produces some noise'.[5]

Technical explanations aside, the Japanese today would simply say that slurping is the tasty way to eat noodles. You are showing your enjoyment of the food when you slurp as well as communicating that enjoyment to those around you. You are also expressing politeness: 'In Japan, if noodles are not slurped it signals that they are not hot enough, or that they are not tasty [...] in short, this means that the ramen chef has failed in his mission to deliver something worth tucking into.'[6] In short, the slurp is a means of communication, an effective one at that.

While 'dignified' diners in Japan make sure that they make no noise at the table, the prohibition lifts for ramen and most noodle dishes, one major reason being that ramen especially had long been considered a 'poor person's meal for the day' and thus befitting the rather 'undignified' means it is consumed.[7] Ramen in Japan today, however, has become a food that straddles the divides of social class, with specialty shops catering to a diverse clientele, from labourers to salarymen to 'ladies who lunch'. The trend has led to the emergence of different classes of ramen connoisseurs; for all of them, the slurp remains an approved and recognized practice.[8]

The slurping noise is essential not only for ramen, however. It is also mandated in the rarefied, indeed dignified, and etiquette-laden practice of drinking tea, *Chadō*, or the Way of Tea tradition. In the Japanese tea ritual, specific situations require the guest to slurp when drinking the tea. Like ramen, slurping has its practical aspect in the ritual: you leave less tea in the bowl if you slurp it down instead of merely sipping it, thus finishing with a cleaner bowl and being polite in the process. More importantly, though, the slurp serves a critical function: in slurping the tea, you are deemed to be expressing your pleasure in it. Rather than mouthing the words, the slurping sound tells your host in the most minimal of means that you were pleased with the tea.

Slurping in the Way of Tea Tradition

In general, two types of tea are served in *Chadō*: thick tea [*koicha*] with the consistency of espresso coffee, and thin tea [*usucha*] which is lighter green in colour and foamy like cappuccino. (Each uses a different type of *matcha*, or powdered green tea.) The thick tea is served in a bowl containing enough tea for all the guests, who will take about three sips each as the bowl is passed around. The main guest who takes the first sip will do so by deliberately making a slurping sound that is loud enough for the host to hear, indicating that the initial tasting has just been made, and will prompt the host to ask the main guest about the taste of the tea. This is the first of very few instances during the serving of the tea when the host and the guest actually converse; there is little talking at this stage of the tea ritual.

Thin tea is served in a different manner, with the host whipping up a separate bowl of tea for each guest. The guests take turns receiving the tea in the prescribed manner, taking about three sips of the tea and finishing it all with a relatively loud slurp at the last sip. The Urasenke school of tea, the biggest in Japan, offers explicit instructions for drinking thin tea properly, with its guide telling beginners that 'for the last sip, make a sound as you take in all the tea'.[9] In the tea ritual, this specific act is called *suikiri* [*sui/*

suu=to suck or slurp; *kiri/kiru*=complete], which indicates that the tea must be totally slurped up. Expert slurpers manage to suck in all the tea, politely finishing with a clean bowl, not unlike the expert and well-mannered diner finishing with a clean plate. In the Way of Tea, the slurp also communicates an important message – that you enjoyed the tea, all the way to the last drop. Instructional manuals in Urasenke give two distinct reasons for the complete slurp, or *suikiri*: (1) It is a non-voiced expression of gratitude for and enjoyment of the tea; and (2) It cleans the bowl and prepares it for passing around for appreciation among the guests who may turn it over and otherwise cause a mess if tea is left inside.[10]

It merits mentioning that in the formal meals (i.e. *kaiseki* cuisine) served during tea gatherings, one of the main soup dishes is called *suimono* [literally, 'something to be slurped']. For this soup, however, there is no etiquette requirement to slurp it down, and guests generally drink it in silence.

Slurping in Early Modern Japan

The Way of Tea tradition was formalized and established in the sixteenth century, coinciding with the period during which many Jesuit missionaries visited Japan. Some of these visitors would later write about the country, publishing works that were essentially guidebooks for fellow and future sojourners that covered many aspects of the Japanese lifestyle, customs and traditions of the era. Their descriptions about Japan necessarily included local eating and drinking habits.

Among such accounts, the writings of the Portuguese missionary Luis Frois (1532-1597) have been particularly valued as a reference on life in early modern Japan. He wrote vivid descriptions based on first-hand observations of the country and its people, including detailed comments about Japanese food and drink traditions. Frois's writings had previously been translated into several languages, with several Japanese versions already released, but the English translation came out only recently, in 2014.[11] This latest publication includes critiques and notes by the translators, and is referred to here.

Concerning food in Japan, Frois writes, for example, about eating noodles: 'We [Europeans] eat our noodles hot and cut up; they put theirs in cold water and eat them in long pieces.' There are many other similar observations, including notes about drinking customs, cutlery, dining furniture as well as etiquette. For present purposes, the following comment about noises made during meals in Japan is particularly notable: 'Among us, making loud noises while eating and completely draining a cup of wine are considered slovenly; the Japanese consider both of these things to be refined manners.'[12]

Frois's English translators and editors commented on this particular observation. They agree with Frois, with their own notes following the translated text mentioning that Japanese even today pay little attention to eating and drinking noises, and that loud slurping is the 'correct' and 'best' way to enjoy noodles and soup while avoiding the dangers of scalding yourself in the mouth. Slurping is also explained away as a means to finish your meal quickly, which is 'good etiquette among this job-oriented culture'. As for drinking noises, the translators continue by commenting that 'the Japanese do often gulp aloud when they drink, simply because they are unconscious of such noises, having never been trained to avoid them'.[13]

One wishes that Frois's English translators limited their comments to Frois's observations and refrained from critiquing contemporary Japanese table manners while giving quaint and generalizing explanations for them. In any case, it is unclear which particular social strata or group of people Frois was observing. His description also contrasts with the rules of etiquette for the Japanese at the time, which were prescribed in several etiquette guides from the era and earlier.

One popular work published in the generation after Frois' work, which was read among different social classes, both urban and rural – though perhaps by the relatively higher-educated – was the *Secrets of the Three Rites* [*Sanrei kuketsu*] by the philosopher and herbal scientist Kaibara Ekiken (1630-1714).[14] In the section called 'Secrets of the Rites for Eating', there is a clear admonition against 'eating with a big mouth', that is, 'not chewing one's food with your mouth wide open'. This is immediately followed by explicit instructions that 'one should not eat soup dishes making loud and long noises with the mouth', meaning, simply, that slurping at the table is not allowed.[15]

It must be noted that since these were rules of etiquette, they were instructions and norms for behaviour that may or may not have been followed. None of the people Frois met may have been readers of any of the etiquette books of the day, but it is clear that slurping was frowned upon in early modern Japanese society. Frois may have referred only to the commoner class, who presumably did not consider slurping as taboo, while the higher classes who periodically engaged in ceremonial banquets and held festive gatherings – and where rules against eating and drinking noises were stricter – may have observed such etiquette rules. It has also been suggested that table manners may have changed in the years immediately following the visits of Portuguese missionaries, although such explanations are mere conjecture.[16]

Slurping in Modern Japan

The ban against slurping at the table continued to be written about in the centuries after Ekiken, with advice books proliferating in the Edo Period (1603-1868) that were directed at an even wider readership. Among the most representative and popular works of the era was Namura Jōhaku's *Record of Precious Treasures for Women* [*Onna chōhō ki*] from 1692 that was republished several times and became a reference work for later advice and etiquette books. One such later work, the 1801 *Chastity Bookstore House for Teaching Women Loyalty* [*Onna chūkyō misao bunko*], includes a section on 'How Women Should Eat the Ten Thousand Things' that has very detailed instructions on table manners, from properly using chopsticks to the formal serving order of dishes, as well as correct ways of offering and receiving all manners of food and drinks.[17]

Two pieces of advice from this particular section are pertinent for the present

125

discussion. One is about eating cold and hot noodles, the proper etiquette for which is as follows:

> While leaving the soup in its place on the eating table, one should take one or two chopstick's full of fine noodles out of the bowl, put them into the soup, then take up the soup and eat. Thereafter it is safe to hold the soup bowl in the hand, take up the noodles, put them in the soup and eat. Every time when one changes (i.e. fills up) the soup, one should at first place the soup on the table, take up the noodles, put them into the soup, then take up the soup bowl and eat.

The other instruction is for drinking tea: 'Tea that is served on a tray one should take with the right hand, drink, pass it to the left hand, and put it down. The serving woman takes the tea bowl, puts it on the tray, takes it up, and refills it. If the tea is too hot, one should not drink it by slurping it or after swirling around the tea bowl to cool it.'[18] The instructions for noodles were written in the era before ramen and were mainly for *sōmen* (fine noodles usually served cold) and *udon* (thicker noodles generally served hot). Both types of noodles are still eaten today and remain very popular in Japan. The eating style described above has been appropriated in the dish called *tsukemen*, which are noodles served separately from a dipping sauce or broth.

There is no admonition against slurping for noodles in these instructions, but the rules for drinking tea are clearly against it. The translator and researcher of these texts, however, indicated that 'eating or drinking noises were considered as repugnant' in other sections of this as well as in other etiquette books. Such noises were also prohibited more often for women than men but generally 'warn[ed] against noises when eating one dish or the other (noodles, grilled fowl, rice gruel, or bones among them)' for all genders.[19]

The same rules of etiquette that prohibited noises at the table continued to be written about in the Meiji Period (1868-1911), for a nation that was now looking toward the West and was desirous of assimilating others' 'civilized' ways. A prominent proponent of Japan's Westernization was Fukuzawa Yukichi (1835-1901), a social thinker who published volumes of essays and other discourses that outlined his teachings and visions for a modernized Japan. Fukuzawa was once described by a contemporary as someone who 'pointed out the weaknesses, defects, and errors of his countrymen' as 'an interpreter of Western ideas and life' while '[h]is books on "Western Manners and Customs," and his volumes of tracts and essays, have had an enormous circulation.'[20]

The cited books on Western manners would have included *Things Western* [*Seiyō jijō*] (1866) as well as *Western Clothing, Food, and Homes* [*Seiyō ishoku jū*] that was released in 1867 under the name of Katayama Junnosuke, presumably Fukuzawa's pseudonym.[21] The latter is a slim volume, with the section titled *Food* consisting of a short six pages that include illustrations of Western-style glassware and cutlery. It also contains very specific instructions against slurping, to wit: 'Soup is served on flatware and is eaten with a spoon. Slurping the soup and drinks like tea is considered bad manners.' Despite

Japan's Westernization in many respects, it is said that, even with clear instructions from influential writers such as Fukuzawa, 'the admonition not to slurp never really took hold in Japan', at least for noodles.[22]

Slurping in Contemporary Japan

In 1955, Japanese career diplomat Kawasaki Ichiro published a book that attempted to explain Japan and its people, called *The Japanese Are Like That*.[23] Described by the publisher as a 'down to earth scrutiny of the so called "inscrutable" Japanese', it is a clear-eyed but frequently irreverent and 'politically incorrect' guide to Japanese society and culture. The chapter titled *Boiled Octopus and Broiled Eels* about Japanese eating and drinking habits includes the following paragraph about slurping:

> Although it is considered bad manners in the West to make noises while eating or sipping, the Japanese do so, especially with soup. With us it is sometimes regarded as a mark of appreciation of the food or beverage. Whenever the members of our group touring the United States were invited to dinner by Americans, they nonchalantly made noises while partaking of soup or even coffee. The Americans were surprised. Knowing and appreciating the difference in customs, I was ashamed of my countrymen, but, fearing to offend them, I did not have the courage to warn them.[24]

The author explains simply that slurping in Japan is a means of communicating your enjoyment of food or drink. As someone who had lived years abroad and was skilful in the languages and customs of several places, Kawasaki was fully aware of the contrasting attitudes to the slurp between Japanese and Americans (and other non-Japanese). In this account, however, he is unable to bridge the divide on slurping manners or choose one side over the other. (Kawasaki subsequently published *Japan Unmasked* in 1969, which was another treatise on Japanese society and culture, though more provocative. His description in the latter book about Japanese people's appearance – 'the Japanese are perhaps physically the least attractive, with the exception of Pygmies and Hottentots' – was quoted in news releases that announced his forced resignation from Japan's Foreign Ministry following the book's publication.)[25]

127

Another Japanese author who, like Kawasaki, lived abroad for a considerable period and is fluent in foreign languages and customs, wrote a similar personal account about slurping. In his guide to men's etiquette, Yamasaki Takeya narrated an incident during a multi-course dinner at a fine dining restaurant. His group included Japanese and non-Japanese, but this time, the slurping offender was a 'well-educated and respected European friend'. In the author's account, his friend arrived just as the soup was served. Relieved that he had just made it in time, he promptly joined the others in taking his soup. However, he slurped his soup loud enough for everyone to hear, and 'for a split second, five or six others at the table held their breath'. The European friend 'immediately realized his faux-pas' and continued to eat his soup quietly.[26]

Although Yamasaki admits that for the Japanese, taking soup without making any slurping sound is 'extremely difficult', he instructs his readers that 'when dining at fine restaurants in Japan or abroad, they must follow Western manners and drink their soup without making any noise'. In fine Japanese restaurants and inns, however, 'when Western-style soup is brought to your table, it is all right to drink it with pleasure by making noise in the Japanese style'.[27]

With regard to noodles, particularly *soba* noodles, he recommends slurping, as follows:

> *Soba* is a dish that brims with Japan's common folk [*minzoku*] sensibilities. So, don't hold back – go ahead and make all the noise you want when you eat it. These days, even among the Euro-Americans who are not used to making any sound when eating, there are many who follow this 'chic Japanese' [*iki*] way of making noise when eating.[28]

Yamasaki would likely slurp ramen, too, if he eats it at all. He would definitely slurp his tea at tea rituals, being a teacher and active promoter of the tea tradition in the Urasenke school.

Recently deceased Shiotsuki Yaeko (1918-2015), widely considered as Japan's foremost authority on social etiquette and manners, also gave her tacit approval to the slurp for noodles.[29] In her guide to Japanese table manners, *Shiotsuki Yaeko no washoku no sahō* [*Shiotsuki Yaeko's Etiquette for Japanese Food*], she gives the following instructions: 'It is fine to make sounds while eating Japanese noodles, but pay attention to how you look while doing it, and do it elegantly.'[30] Shiotsuki does not elaborate, however, and the reader is left to her own devices on producing the elegant slurp.

Discussion

In the Japanese language, the slurping sound is rendered in onomatopoeia as *tsuru tsuru*. *Tsuru tsuru* is also used as an adjective meaning shiny or slippery, as in a shiny pate [*tsuru tsuru atama*]. Both the onomatopoeia and the adjective together perfectly encapsulate the pleasing experience of eating noodles. One derives pleasure from slippery noodles that are heartily slurped and made to glide smoothly down your throat, as Ishige explains above.

As for the act of slurping, the Japanese verb is *susuru*, which in its pronunciation also imitates the sound of slurping itself. It is an ancient Japanese term, found in literature from as early as the Kamakura Period (1192-1333), as in *A Collection of Tales from Uji*. In a popular tale, *Yam Gruel* describes a scene where a lord's retainer sat down to eat his favourite dish and promptly 'smacked his lips loudly as he sipped yam gruel'.[31] This manner of eating gruel is one of relish, by someone who loves his food and communicates his enjoyment accordingly.

Conclusion

This paper has briefly outlined the history of the slurp and attitudes toward it in Japan. As a form (or breach) of etiquette, slurping sounds at the table have been a concern for the Japanese throughout many centuries, with most etiquette rules admonishing against it. It is still of concern today: advice columns and discussion forums on the internet, for example, regularly run comments by users who complain about office colleagues or parents – usually the father – who eat their food and drink their tea with 'disgusting' slurping noises.

As a norm for eating and drinking, the slurp belongs to that group of bodily noises that are generally prohibited at the table. Whether in Japan or elsewhere, by controlling such noises, one is following 'established rules of social exchange […] that acknowledges (and heeds) the feelings, sensitivities, and thresholds of shame and repugnance of others'.[32] Such defines the world of table manners and etiquette in many places today.

Controllable as it may be, the slurp is nonetheless unleashed for ramen and other noodles dishes, as well as in certain situations in the Way of Tea tradition. On these occasions, slurping becomes a sign of connoisseurship: for ramen, you are showing – or showing off – the proper way of eating and expressing your enjoyment of the noodles, while in the Way of Tea, you are also exhibiting your expertise in the proper etiquette of the ritual. In both cases, you deliberately slurp to communicate your pleasure.

The key term is 'deliberately'. As one author explains in a discourse about early Japanese etiquette manuals, there had been a tendency in the Japanese character to stress the inner disposition – the 'heart' – in countering 'perfunctory subservience to etiquette rules'.[33] In Japan, this 'heart' that bears one's feelings of pleasure and similar emotions is brought to the fore during important occasions, away from and above the prescribed rules on manners. And the slurp could be simply that: an act communicating your pleasure, rising above the rules of etiquette.

Notes

1. Barak Kushner, *Slurp! A Social and Culinary History of RAMEN – Japan's Favorite Noodle Soup* (Leiden, The Netherlands: Global Oriental, 2012); Pete Wells, 'Slurp Worthy: The Top 10 Ramen Destinations in New York', *New York Times*, 4 March 2014, at <http://www.nytimes.com/2014/03/05/dining/slurp-worthy-the-top-10-ramen-destinations-in-new-york.html> [accessed 30 May 2015].

2. Kushner, p. 231.

3. Naomichi Ishige, *The History and Culture of Japanese Food* (London: Kegan Paul, 2001), p. 196.

4. George Solt, *The Untold History of Ramen: How Political Crisis in Japan Spawned a Global Food Craze* (Berkeley: University of California Press, 2014), p. 168.

5. *History and Culture*, p. 196. All Japanese personal names in the main text are written in the traditional order: family name or surname (Ishige) followed by the first or given name (Naomichi).

6. Kushner, p. 18.

7. Merry White, 'Ramen at Home and on the Road', *Japan Forum*, 27.1 (2015), p. 115. See also Emiko Ohnuki-Tierney, 'The Ambivalent Self of the Contemporary Japanese', *Cultural Anthropology*, 5.2 (1990).

8. Satomi Fukutomi, 'Ramen Connoisseurs: Class, Gender, and the Internet', *Japanese Foodways: Past & Present*, ed. by Eric C. Rath and Stephanie Assmann (Urbana: University of Illinois Press, 2010), pp. 257-74.

9. Urasenke Konnichian, '*Usucha no nomikata*' [How to Drink Thin Tea], *Hajimete no ocha* [*Tea for Beginners*] <http://www.urasenke.or.jp/textb/beginer/nomu.html> [accessed 30 May 2015]. Translated from the Japanese by the author.

10. *Chadō bunka kentei kōshiki tekisuto* [*Tea Culture Certification Official Textbook*], ed. by Konnichian (Kyoto: Tankōsha, 2013).

11. *The First European Description of Japan, 1585: A Critical English Language Edition of 'Striking Contrasts in the Customs of Europe and Japan' by Luis Frois, S.J.*, trans. and ed. by Richard K. Danford, Robin D. Gill, Daniel T. Reff (London: Routledge, 2014).

12. Danford, p. 135; p. 142.

13. Danford, p. 142.

14. Michael Kinski, 'Cold Norms and Warm Hearts: On the Conception of Etiquette Rules in Advice Books from Early Modern and Modern Japan', in *The Cultural Career of Coolness: Discourses and Practices of Affect Control in European Antiquity, the United States, and Japan*, ed. by Ulla Haselstein, Irmela Hijiya-Kirschnereit, Catrin Gersdorf, and Elena Giannoulis (Lanham, MD: Lexington Books, 2013).

15. Isao Kumakura, *Bunka toshite no mana-* [*Manners as Culture*] (Tokyo: Iwanami Shoten, 2014/1999), p. 26.

16. See Kumakura, p. 27.

17. Michael Kinski, '"How to Eat the Ten Thousand Things": Table Manners in the Edo Period', in, *Japanese Foodways: Past & Present*, ed. by Eric C. Rath and Stephanie Assmann (Urbana: University of Illinois Press, 2010), pp. 42-67.

18. Kinski, 'How to Eat', pp. 47-48; p. 48.

19. Kinski, 'How to Eat', p. 54.

20. William Elliot Griffis, *The Mikado's Empire* (New York: Harper, 1876), p. 320.

21. Both volumes are available at the Digital Gallery of the library of Keio University (founded by Fukuzawa) at <http://project.lib.keio.ac.jp/dg_kul/fukuzawa_title.php?id=3> and <http://project.lib.keio.ac.jp/dg_kul/fukuzawa_title.php?id=19>, respectively.

22. Kushner, p. 97.

23. Ichiro Kawasaki, *The Japanese Are Like That* (Tokyo: Charles E. Tuttle, 1955).

24. Kawasaki, *The Japanese*, p. 70.

25. Kawasaki, *Japan Unmasked* (Tokyo: Charles E. Tuttle, 1969), p. 26; 'Diplomat's Views Horrify Tokyo', *Schenectady Gazette*, 25 June 1969, p. 34.

26. Takeya Yamasaki, *Men's Etiquette: The Style of the Refined Adult* [*Otoko no sahō: Senren sareta otona no sutairu*] (Tokyo: PHP Interface), p. 163.

27. Yamasaki, p. 164.

28. Trans. in Jan Bardsley, 'The Oyaji Gets a Makeover: Guides for Japanese Salarymen in the New Millennium' in *Manners and Mischief: Gender, Power, and Etiquette in Japan*, ed. by Jan Bardsley and Laura Miller (Berkeley: University of California Press, 2011), pp. 114-35.

29. Shiotsuki was the firstborn child in the main family that heads the Urasenke school of the Way of Tea tradition. Her father was the school's Grand Tea Master who was succeeded by her younger brother, the eldest son. Shiotsuki wrote around one hundred books, mostly on etiquette and manners, including the *Kankon sōsai nyūmon* [*Introduction to Ceremonial Occasions*] series that have sold an estimated seven million copies in Japan.

30. Yaeko Shiotsuki, *Shiotsuki Yaeko no washoku no sahō* [*Shiotsuki Yaeko's Etiquette for Japanese Food*] (Tokyo: Kodansha, 1991), p. 41.

31. Douglas E. Mills, *A Collection of Tales from Uji. A Study and Translation of 'Uji Shui Monogatari'* (Cambridge: University of Cambridge Oriental Publications, 1970), p. 155.

32. Kinski, 'Cold Norms and Warm Hearts', p. 199.

33. Kinski, 'Cold Norms and Warm Hearts', p. 210.

Lessons from Generations Past:
Timely and Timeless Communication Strategies of Some Canadian Cooks of Note

Nathalie Cooke

Through the long twentieth century, the influence of individual home food authorities waxed and waned with the tides of changing times. What remained consistent across generations was the popularity of home food authority figures responding to a fundamental need for and appreciation of trusted advice, as well as a seemingly endless appetite for information on foodways.

This paper poses a series of thorny questions about the form, function and impact of communications about foodways, and it looks for possible answers in the careers of women who filled the role of trusted home authority figures for Canadians, each representative of her time and of a particular food communication paradigm.[1] My questions include the following:

1. How do communication technologies leverage influence?
2. How do food communications function as agents of change?
3. How might a food communication medium itself function as an agent of change?
4. Why are some communication formats eclipsed when others seem to endure?
5. Is the shift to internet-based communication a difference of degree or of kind in relation to other communication formats?
6. What is lost and gained as communications are translated across generations, cultures and languages?

Given the limited scope of this study, I provide only brief biographical snapshots, highlighting career elements that speak directly to questions about the nature and relative impact of food communication formats. This is intended as a preliminary overview of career implications of some Canadian figures of note, many of whom have not yet come to the attention of international food scholars. It will nevertheless be possible to draw tentative conclusions about key components of timely and timeless communication strategies. I hope to open new and productive avenues that will not find definitive conclusions but rather raise provocative questions that lead to future conversations about the what, why and how of food communication strategies.

How Do New Communication Technologies Leverage Influence?

The first Canadian cookbooks were published in the 1840s, with 1855 seeing the publication of the first cookbook devoted to documenting the foodways of the New World and intended for readers who were themselves Canadian settlers: Catharine Parr Traill's *The Female Emigrant's Guide*.[2] Traill herself was a British gentlewoman who, like many others of the period, settled in what was then Upper Canada, tempted by the promise of prosperity in the New World after her family in Britain came into reduced circumstances. The *Guide* brings together Traill's own recipes and tips on gardening and housekeeping, with the collected wisdom of her family, friends and neighbours. For example, it describes what to bring to the New World, namely a good pair of shoes; and what not to bring, namely one's best fine china. It also reintroduces the valuable skill of breadmaking to emigrants who were accustomed to buying their bread in England and includes a variety of methods and recipes. A printed book that incorporates excerpts from other useful texts that were prohibitively expensive for immigrants, the *Guide* shows the way that food advice circulated – passed by word of mouth, and through recipes and anecdotes shared in conversation and print. The same can be said today, of course. Is it not still a compliment to ask one's hosts for the recipe of a particularly tasty dish or the secret of a particularly good sauce or flavour combination? Now, just as then, one's host must decide whether to share culinary secrets or to keep them close to the chest. What has changed dramatically, however, is the way one shares recipes. Where one once resorted to paper and ink to copy a host's recipe, one is now more likely to take up a smartphone. In the blink of an eye, the recipe can be not only copied for one's personal use, but also circulated far and wide through social media. Between Traill's time and today what has changed is reach of communication technologies. The value of a cook's first-hand experience and the personal endorsement of those who prepare and taste the food remain constant.

132

How can new communication technologies leverage influence? One part of the answer is that they expand audience size and can therefore contribute to increasing an individual's influence over her contemporaries. While handwritten manuscripts circulated amongst a small coterie of individuals in geographical proximity, with each successive technological advancement the circle widened exponentially. In the nineteenth century, print technology improved such that typeset books, and later paperbacks, could be mass-produced to be more affordable. By the turn of the century, radio brought the wisdom of home food advisors into homes with bandwidths of increasing strength. As of the mid-twentieth century, television stations could broadcast cooking shows across the nation and beyond. At century's close, the internet expanded the reach of communications to the globe and gave individuals with basic computer skills the ability to share their opinions and thereby leverage influence.

Influence, however, depends upon more than appeal and audience size. For an individual to wield influence she – and I use the pronoun because all my examples of home food advisors are women – must have the right and ability to lay claim to the opinions she espouses. From Traill's day to today, this ownership is not without complication. As Nicola Humble has revealed, Isabella Beeton is perhaps the best-known example of a persona that casts a long shadow, but this persona had a longer and closer affiliation with Beeton's publisher husband, who continued the Beeton publishing empire long after his wife's death, than with the woman who was Isabella Beeton for the twenty-eight years before her untimely death. Happily, she did live to see the popularity of 'her' *Mrs Beeton's Book of Household Management,* which Humble explains sold 'over 60,000 copies in its first year of publication in 1861, and nearly two million by 1868'.[3] Despite the credit given her in the book's title, though, Humble underlines that even this early book was a combined effort.

Catharine Parr Traill's *Guide* is another example of a book of influence from which the author herself benefitted little financially. Traill initially published the *Guide* in serial form starting in 1854, with the complete book appearing on 12 March 1855, bearing Traill's title, *The Female Emigrant's Guide,* and crediting her as its author. Already by May 1855, another edition appeared, retitled *The Canadian Settler's Guide* without Traill's permission.[4] With this new title, publisher Henry Payne Hope shifted the spotlight to the book's 'Canadian' character and away from its role as a book targeting female emigrants. More true to his middle than his family name, Hope continued to give Traill considerable grief, acting as literary agent for the book and ensuring its reprinting and distribution but consistently reneging on his promises to pay her. By the time Hope produced a so-called tenth edition in 1860, this time entitled *The Canadian Emigrant Housekeeper's Guide*, most of Traill's recipes had disappeared.[5] Given the confusion of all these variant editions, it is disappointing, if not surprising, that when Canadian publisher McClelland and Stewart decided to honour this pioneering text by issuing an affordable paperback edition, it used Hope's retitled version, thus perpetuating an edition compiled by an unscrupulous publisher.[6] In 1880 Traill began to develop a second edition of the *Guide* with the intention of more directly benefitting from the popularity of her first book. By this time, however, she was wiser to the ways of the publishing world but without the necessary energy to see this project to fruition.

What, then, can one say about the extent of Traill's influence? Her *Guide* is still a valuable resource, with its distinctive voice and remarkably detailed recipes. Indeed, Fiona Lucas and I are currently producing a new edition of the *Guide* and highlighting the value of its insights for contemporary audiences. Ironically, however, while Traill saw little profit from her book thanks to Hope's practices, those same practices distributed the book widely. So Traill's *Guide* did find its way into the hands of many emigrants to Canada, but because Traill's presence in the book diminished with each edition, her influence arguably diminished as her book took on a life of its own.

Copyright laws have gained teeth since Traill's day so that appropriation and distribution of textual material is tightly regulated, and authors do not find themselves in a situation like Traill's. But there is one textual form that does not fall under copyright restrictions – recipes – and this has proved an obstacle for those food writers wanting to take credit for a particularly effective creation. Canadian baker and food writer Marcy Goldman was affected by this loophole and has subsequently used her writing to publicize the lack of protection for chefs and recipe developers as compared to writers.[7] In particular, she is beloved for two recipes. One is a Passover recipe that transforms the rather bland matzoh into a sweet treat: 'Matzoh Buttercrunch'. She first provided this recipe in various newspapers for which she was writing food columns and then published it in her *Treasury of Jewish Holiday Baking*.[8] Subsequently it has been downloaded by thousands of visitors to her website and, as she reports, 'presented to the Smithsonian as an example of a recipe that has become urban legend'. Explains Goldman, 'so many people make that recipe without knowing its origin. The only time it was bothersome was when it appeared in the cookbooks of colleagues and/or this company started manufacturing it'.[9] The second recipe is for a muffin that Goldman calls the 'Lawsuit' muffin. The story goes that Goldman scaled up her carefully developed recipe for industry-level production at a bakery called *Terre Étoile* in Montreal in which she worked. Sales flourished. However, one day when she came to work, the restaurant owners had claimed the formula as their own. Goldman was first disappointed but subsequently resilient. She began to distribute the recipe far and wide, along with the story, and she changed the name of the muffin recipe series from the 'Famous Buttermilk Muffin Collection' to 'Lawsuit Muffins'. There was no actual lawsuit involved, but the point was well made and, ironically, Goldman had more influence both in spreading the word and laying claim to the original recipe than had she remained toiling at *Terre Étoile*.[10] Today, when others mention and share either the recipe for Goldman's muffin or the matzoh caramel buttercrunch, they are careful to credit Marcy Goldman even though copyright law may not make this essential. When Marcy Goldman refers to the Passover recipe on *Epicurious*, she calls it, 'MY TRADEMARK, MOST REQUESTED, ABSOLUTELY MAGNIFICENT CARAMEL MATZOH CRUNCH'.[11]

How Do Food Communications Function as Agents of Change?

For their first audiences, cookbooks are largely prescriptive. They provide information about ingredients, cooking methods and more recently standard measurements. But their popular appeal also depends upon other factors: for example, affordability, the complexity of the recipes and what Susan Leonardi calls the 'recommendation', in addition to what Anne Mendelson sees as narrative elements of the sort she finds emerging in *The Joy of Cooking*.[12]

To some extent, because of their prescriptive nature, all cookbooks have the potential to influence foodways. But this is all the more true for the most prescriptive of all food communications, the advertisement and the textbook. Perhaps the most obvious way to explore whether food communications can themselves be agents of change would be to look at food advertising. Certainly strict regulations surrounding food marketing, especially to children, provide evidence that regulators, policy makers and our society perceive messages about food as very powerful indeed.[13]

Another way to answer the question involves scrutinizing a period between 1850 and 1920 in which change swept through kitchens and culinary thinking with remarkable force, even introducing a new field of culinary study. At the turn of the twentieth century, students trained in newly established classes in scientific cookery or, as it was eventually called, home economics, came to privilege emergent knowledge over the wisdom of their mothers and previous generations. Particularly relevant are the prescriptions just prior to and at turn of the twentieth century, a moment that saw so many advances in terms of bacteriology, epidemiology and later nutrition. Textbooks from the period provide detailed evidence of the nature of such change and of their own role, along with the role of institutions with which they were affiliated, as agents of change.

Figure 1. Adelaide Hoodless (in formal dress)

135

There are five significant textbooks published in Canada during this period of sea-change in culinary thinking, including Adelaide Hoodless's foundational textbook, *Public School Domestic Science*.[14] Hoodless is credited with introducing domestic science into Canadian schools and with forming the first classes to train teachers in the field. What constituted this new discipline? As Hoodless explains in *The Report of Mrs Hoodless on Domestic Science*, written at the request of the then Minister of Education, domestic science involved manual training and lessons in cookery, but 'it must not be inferred that cooking in the sense of pleasing the palate, and the ability to prepare new and elaborate dishes, is the ultimate object of such teaching. On the contrary, it is based upon scientific, hygienic and health principles'. Hoodless argued that domestic science functions as a kind of umbrella category, which includes 'the true principles of household management as related to health and income.' Not surprisingly, given Hoodless's emphasis on the 'scientific' nature of the discipline, *Public School Domestic Science* sheds light on emergent knowledge in nutrition and hygiene, referring to milk sterilization methods and arguing for milk pasteurization, as well as referencing new food products like cottolene and oleomargarine.[15]

Of the five household manuals published in Canada in the late nineteenth- and early twentieth-centuries Hoodless's *Public School Domestic Science* (1898) bookends a period of dramatic shifts in thinking.[16] Published after germ theory, largely acknowledging its sources, and serving as textbook for the new discipline of domestic science, Hoodless's textbook provides an excellent snapshot of thinking about nutrition and bacteriology at the close of nineteenth century in Canada. By focusing specifically on new ways of thinking about cooking, hygiene and the role of the home caregiver, it also provides evidence of the change effected by textbooks and teachers in the emerging field.

How Might a Food Communication Platform Itself Function as an Agent of Change?

Food radio garnered a loyal following of women listeners during radio's 'Golden Age' between 1920 and 1950. During radio's early years, and before strict marketing regulations, many programs were corporately sponsored. They might have included advertisements but they more frequently mentioned particular food products in the programs themselves. Perhaps the best-known examples included the programs starring Betty Crocker, who was created in 1923 by the advertising department of the company that would become General Mills, Washburn Crosby Flour. During her radio slots, Betty Crocker not only mentioned the virtues of Gold Medal Flour and affiliated products, but she also provided tips and stories about how they could be used. She also took on the role of teacher, leading 'Betty Crocker's Cooking School of the Air', which allowed her parent company to gain valuable information about customer demographics through their 'school registration forms'. An internal document reveals that between 1931 and 1932, there were '[t]en members of the Betty Crocker staff, 45 radio stations, 46,148 cooking school registrations [and] 135,819 mail volume'. Between

1939 and 1940, when the show discussed pioneer covered wagon days, 'which were a good background for discussions of thrift', there were sixty-five stations and 35,389 registrations – even though a 'fee was charged for registration' – and the year saw '151,952 mail volume'.[17]

What accounted for the number of listeners tuning in, and even paying for cooking school registrations? Surely the practical information that the shows provided was valued, alongside, perhaps, the opportunity to gain skills and educational certification at a time when few women pursued post-secondary education. Almost certainly Betty Crocker's friendly disposition and 'her' timely and informative responses to the many letters sent to her by what she called her 'radio friends' were also significant in allaying what Betty Friedan would call in her watershed book, *The Feminine Mystique,* 'the problem that has no name'.[18] That problem, of course, was the sheer loneliness of housewives who found themselves trapped in their homes, feeling unfulfilled in a role that, as Carol McFeely argues, was gaining symbolic value in direct proportion to the ways in which increasing possibilities of employment outside the home continued to threaten it.[19] However, if radio shows and advertising assuaged the housewife's loneliness, these positive effects were arguably slight, because both surely fuelled the very anxieties they claimed to assuage. While housewives found they had more technological aids at their disposal in the consumer age of the early twentieth century, the also found they were expected to produce dishes of greater complexity in this economy of rising expectations. Domestic work was involved in a vicious circle.[20]

By supporting the housewife in her task, however, food radio helped to reinforce the value of the housewife's role in the home. Ironically, women on radio, the very women speaking to housewives about their role, also modelled the possibility of women pursuing successful careers outside the home. With new radio channels available in the 1920s, producers quickly realized that content was needed for daytime hours when audiences were typically female. This need coincided nicely with a supply of highly trained personnel in the form of women trained in the emerging disciplines of household science and home economics who could supply radio stations with content that was appealing to the daytime audience. As T.J. Allard explains in unequivocal terms, the result was a positive step forward for women entering the workforce: 'Earlier than any other industry, private broadcasting provided senior employment opportunities for women. Few stations did not have one or more women's commentators who quite literally ran their own show.'[21] Consequently, even as radio entered homes, providing conversation and good company for women, this new communication industry was modelling and ushering in the winds of change.

Why Are Some Communication Formats Eclipsed When Others Seem to Endure?

Radio is one example of a communication medium that has remained surprisingly resilient in the face of television. Food radio has survived its own particular challenger, the *Food Network*.

One fascinating question is why talk about food on radio – where listeners cannot see, smell, taste or touch the food directly – is so popular? What about radio has makes it so persistent? Commentator Gill Murray is one convinced that radio has had a profound impact on society, but Murray ultimately perceives television not as an alternative to but rather an outgrowth of radio. 'If any cultural force reshaped the reality of living,' he writes, 'it was radio. Refinements such as television and cellphones intensified this reality.'[22] Kate Ramos, associate editor of 'Chow', instead perceives a growing distance between food radio and food television. She argues that food radio has made a comeback in recent decades because food television privileges entertainment over education: '[a]s the selection on TV became more varied, food programs on the radio eventually fell by the wayside. In recent years, however, as the hosts on the idiot box have become more interested in sizzle than substance, radio and podcast food shows have flooded the airwaves.'[23] I would situate my own answer between the two proposed here. I agree both with Murray, who sees radio's 'ubiquity and mobility' as key strengths of the medium, and with Ramos, who perceives the balance shifting towards food education in radio programming.[24] But I think we perhaps overlook one very basic point: conversation is familiar and pleasurable, and food radio effectively raises interesting topics and draws its readers into lively conversations.[25]

Is the Shift to Internet-Based Communications a Difference of Degree or Kind in Relation to Other Communication Formats?

The internet can bring historical figures back to public attention, seemingly without mediation, through textual, visual and audio formats. This has provided contemporary audiences with unprecedented ease of access to materials once requiring considerable expense, travel or luck to locate. For example, a quick web search brings up Julia Child's wonderfully informative and funny episode, 'To Roast a Chicken'.[26] In the Canadian context, a search reveals two beloved advisors, Mrs A. and Mme B. In the case of Mrs A., a Google query brings one to the Canadian Broadcasting Company's (CBC) digital archives to choose between ten radio clips and then hear Mrs A.'s distinctive voice once again.[27] Mrs A., or Kate Aitken, used to describe a variety of Canadian foodways in her wildly popular radio shows from 1934 to 1957, and her broadcasting career eventually moved her from the realm of culinary reporting to policy work for the government and even to one memorable interview with Mussolini. Gordon Sinclair notes that by 1950 Aitken received 5000 letters per day or 260,000 per year and, each year, she gave 'about 600 broadcasts and 150 speeches'.[28]

Similarly, a quick search for Mme B., or Jéhane Benoît, brings one to a selection of her television emissions, some uploaded on YouTube, and others from the CBC digital archives. In many ways, Benoît was the Julia Child of Canada. But while Child rendered transparent the longstanding culinary influence and intricacies of France's *cuisine bourgeoise,* Jéhane Benôit, cookbook writer and television star of the 1970s and

Figure 2. Kate Aitken on the CBC Radio Set

139

Figure 3. Madame Jehane Benoit with Paul Soles on the Take 30 *Television Set, 4 June 1964*

1980s, demystified both the history and the future of Canadian cuisine in French and English for North American audiences. Today, on computer and television screens one can watch the snowy black-and-white television show with its characteristic banter.

What is lost and gained through translation across generations, cultures and languages?

Despite the internet's illusion of direct access to the past afforded by sound and visuals, however, much is inevitably lost when one turns one's twenty-first-century attention to individuals who lived far away in terms of both time and place. So what is lost and gained through translation across generations, cultures and languages?

Let me explore my own favourite clips a bit more closely to expose the levels of mediation involved. For example, a clip that seems to be very representative of Benoît's insistence on eating local and healthy produce involves a lively discussion with Lucien Watier from 1959, where Benoît introduces Watier to the value of eating greens, or what Watier insists on calling '*des mauvaises herbes*' [weeds]. Watier's lack of acquaintance with all things culinary is an illusion, mind you, since at one point he acknowledges his familiarity with cooking terminology by telling the audience that '*fatiguer*' the salad means to toss it.[29] In other words, Watier is performing a role for the television audience, following a script intended both to entertain and to teach culinary skills.

Another way in which one's access to internet content is mediated involves curatorial decisions made by the program providers. For example, when one considers the ten clips readily available from Aitken's radio emissions, one sees in the selection of clips a heavy emphasis on shows providing key news of the day rather than just culinary banter. Of the ten clips, only one is dedicated to a meal. However, because the meal is heavily symbolic, the discussion of 'Sunday dinner' ventures beyond food and its preparation.[30] The other title of an Aitken radio emission containing a food reference is 'Fruitcake leftovers and international politics', which inserts the topic of cake amidst other pressing topics of 1953. In this emission, CBC explains 'Kate Aitken talks about world leaders, New Year's resolutions, and what to do with that leftover fruitcake'. The show's opening sequence provides one reason for this emphasis on politics, presumably targeting male listeners in addition to the usual audience, when Kate Aitken greets male audience members since 'they're not often in on the mornings when this broadcast hits the air'.[31]

As these examples illustrate, there seems at first to be a remarkable levelling of access to archival material thanks to the internet. But precisely because of this illusion of heightened transparency we must be more vigilant than ever in scrutinizing mechanisms of mediation, including editorial and curatorial controls. Why are particular clips selected for our internet viewing? How do such selections influence the way we perceive and remember figures of the past? To what extent can we accurately identify and interpret levels of fictionality in performances from previous generations?

Conclusion

One can point to certain communication mediums that have been remarkably tenacious over time, in Canada and elsewhere: the print cookbook and, despite the innovation of television, radio food programming. The influence of other communication formats, by contrast, has been fleeting. For example, where are the live cooking demonstrations and cookbooks by fictitious corporate spokespersonalities now? What accounts for the appearance, disappearance and more recent reintroduction of cookery classes in schools? One also notices remarkably different messages voiced by food advisors in different generations – Catharine Parr Traill advocates hard work and self-sufficiency, Adelaide Hoodless reliance on specific training or technological innovations, Kate Aitken the virtues of thrift, and Benoît the value of sourcing fresh food locally. Without exception, however, they all engage audiences by speaking in the first person, offering alongside cooking instruction anecdotes, insights and an invitation to connect – not over food itself, but rather through food communication. Over the years, readers, then listeners and eventually viewers have been eager to take up the invitation.

Notes

1. While most of the examples in this study are Canadian, I do pause to consider the example of Betty Crocker. While not a Canadian, she was nevertheless very popular with Canadian listeners.
2. Catharine Parr Traill, *The Female Emigrant's Guide* (Toronto: Maclear and Company, 1854). The book was released in 1855 but bears the publication date of 1854.
3. Nicola Humble, 'Introduction, ' in *Mrs Beeton's Book of Household Management, Abridged Edition*, ed. by Nicola Humble (Oxford University Press, 2000 [1861]), p. vii.
4. Fiona Lucas, 'Publication History of Traill's *Female Emigrant's Guide*' (unpublished draft, 2011).
5. Lucas; Catharine Parr Traill, *The Canadian Emigrant Housekeeper's Guide* (London: Edward Stanford of London 1860).
6. Catharine Parr Traill, *The Canadian Settler's Guide* (Toronto: McClelland, 1969).
7. For a broader discussion of this issue, see Cathy K. Kaufman, 'Recipes and Dishes: What Should Be Copyrightable?', *Food and Language: Proceedings of the Oxford Symposium on Food and Cookery*, ed. by Richard Hosking (Totnes: Prospect Books, 2009), pp. 189-97.
8. Marcy Goldman, *A Treasury of Jewish Holiday Baking* (Toronto: Whitecap, 2009).
9. Marcy Goldman, 'My Famous Matzoh Caramel Buttercrunch', *Marcy Goldman's BetterBaking.com* < http://www.betterbaking.com/viewRecipe.php?recipe_id=978> [accessed 27 May 2015]; Marcy Goldman, email to the author, 14 May 2015.
10. Marcy Goldman, 'My Muffin Story, Part One', *Marcy Goldman's BetterBaking.com* <http://www.betterbaking.com/viewRecipe.php?recipe_id=1031> [accessed 27 May 2015].
11. Marcy Goldman, 'My Trademark, Most Requested, Absolutely Magnificent Caramel Matzoh Crunch', *Epicurious* (New York: Condé Nast, 1998) <http://www.epicurious.com/recipes/food/views/my-trademark-most-requested-absolutely-magnificent-caramel-matzoh-crunch-109117> [accessed 27 May 2015]. See also Marcy Goldman, 'New Version Buttermilk Muffins - the Story Continues,' *Marcy Goldman's BetterBaking.com* <http://www.betterbaking.com/viewArticle.php?article_id=224> [accessed 27 May 2015].
12. Susan J. Leonardi, 'Recipes for Reading: Summer Pasta, Lobster à La Riseholme, and Key Lime Pie', *PMLA*, 104.3 (May 1989), pp. 340-47; Anne Mendelson, *Stand Facing the Stove: The Story of the Women Who Gave America the Joy of Cooking* (New York: H. Holt, 1996).

13. For further discussion of food marketing and its regulations in Canada, see Charlene Elliott, '*Taste Rules!*: Food Marketing, Food Law, and Childhood Obesity in Canada', *Cuizine: The Journal of Canadian Food Cultures*, 1 (2008) <http://www.erudit.org/revue/cuizine/2008/v1/n1/019371ar.html> [accessed 27 May 2015]; Charlene Elliott and Brian Cook, 'Not So Grrreat: Ten Important Myths About Food Advertising Targeted to Children in Canada', *Childhood Obesity*, 9 (2013), pp. 286-91.

14. Adelaide Hoodless, *Public School Domestic Science* (Toronto: The Copp, Clark Company, Ltd., 1898).

15. Adelaide Hoodless, *Report of Mrs. Hoodless on Domestic Science: Including a Recent Visit to the Schools of Philadelphia and Washington* (Toronto: Warwick Bros & Rutter, 1899), p. 5; p. 5; *Public School Domestic Science* pp. 30-31, p. 159, p. 35.

16. See also Nathalie Cooke, 'Canadian Cookbooks: Changing Ideas About Cooking and Contamination, 1854 to 1898', *Canadian Bulletin of Medical History* 32.2 (2015), pp. 297-318.

17. Mae Chesnut, 'Betty Crocker Chronology' (Minneapolis: General Mills Inc., August 1948).

18. Betty Friedan, *The Feminine Mystique* (New York: W. W. Norton 1963).

19. Mary Drake McFeely, *Can She Bake a Cherry Pie?: American Women and the Kitchen in the Twentieth Century* (Amherst: University of Massachusetts Press, 2000).

20. See also: Ruth Schwartz Cowan, *More Work for Mother: The Ironies of Household Technology from the Open Hearth to the Microwave* (New York: Basic Books, 1983) and Susan Strasser, *Never Done: A History of American Housework* (New York: Pantheon Books, 1982).

21. T J Allard, *Straight Up: Private Broadcasting in Canada, 1918-1958* (Ottawa: Canadian Communications Foundation, 1979), p. 54.

22. Gil Murray, *Nothing on but the Radio: A Look Back at Radio in Canada and How It Changed the World* (Toronto: Dundurn Group, 2003), p. 210.

23. Kate Ramos, 'Audible Edibles, Ten Radio Food Shows That Will Leave You Salivating' (CBS, 2008).

24. Murray, p. 210.

25. For additional hypotheses see Nathalie Cooke, 'Canadian Food Radio: Conjuring Nourishment for Canadians Out of Thin Air', in *How Canadians Communicate Vi: Food Promotion, Consumption, and Controversy*, ed. by Charlene Elliott (Edmonton, Alberta: University of Athabasca Press, 2016), pp. 107-28.

26. WGBH, 'Julia Child the French Chef: To Roast a Chicken', *The French Chef* (1971). <https://www.youtube.com/watch?v=fRZxaUuFA1Y> [accessed 30 October 2015].

27. See 'Kate Aitken', CBC Digital Archives (Toronto: CBC/Radio-Canada) <http://www.cbc.ca/player/Digital+Archives/CBC+Programs/Radio/Kate+Aitken/> [accessed 16 May 2015].

28. Gordon Sinclair, 'Busiest Woman in the World', *Maclean's Magazine*, 15 April 1950, p. 8.

29. See CBC / Radio Canada, 'La Salade De Jehane Benoît Avec Lucien Watier (Animateur)', in *Bonjour Madame* (Radio-Canada, 1959) <https://www.youtube.com/watch?v=uThAy2AjNek> [accessed 30 October 2015].

30. CBC / Radio Canada, 'Kate Aitken: Sunday Dinner', *Kate Aiken* (CBC, 1948) <http://www.cbc.ca/player/Digital+Archives/CBC+Programs/Radio/Kate+Aitken/ID/1811364216/> [accessed 30 October 2015].

31. CBC / Radio Canada, 'Fruitcake Leftovers and International Politics', *Kate Aiken* (CBC, 1953) <http://www.cbc.ca/player/Digital+Archives/CBC+Programs/Radio/Kate+Aitken/ID/1650555174/> [accessed 30 October 2015].

Common Senses: Sound and Touch in London Food Shopping

Anastasia Edwards

Contemporary food shopping in London has become an often silent, faceless enterprise. In supermarkets, and certainly on the Internet, it is possible to progress through the stages of browsing, selecting and finally purchasing without any form of communication with another human being. This anonymity is recent. Until World War II, the act of procuring food via shopping involved detailed communication and negotiation between buyer and seller, a mutual engagement that could be theatrical and noisy and tactile. Communications between buyer and seller involved most – and sometimes all – of the senses during even the simplest transaction.

This paper seeks to identify and outline some of the traditional forms of communication involved in selling and buying of food in London, many of which have either vanished or are becoming obsolete (or else are being consciously reborn in farmers markets). It also seeks to record that these vanishing forms of communication were considered important enough to serve as the inspiration for artists and musicians throughout the ages.

I have focussed mostly on fish because its perishability lends an urgency to communications about its desirability, and also because I have access to informants who are willing to speak to me about their work and its history. The four categories that follow – 'Noise', 'Music', 'Language' and 'Touch' – are not intended to be a conclusive comment on communication of food-selling, but rather constitute the beginnings of discussion. The research forms part of an on-going project to create a multi-dimensional and multi-disciplinary historical portrait of the foodways of London's City of Westminster.

Noise

Until Victorian times, buying fish – in fact buying anything – would probably involve a lot of noise. Most food was sold on the street, often by people selling from only one basket containing only one item. These street-sellers mostly lived by subsistence, seeking to dispose of everything that they had bought wholesale on a given morning before the end of the day and at the best price possible. Competition from other street-sellers created additional urgency. Their hands would be occupied with their baskets, and their clothes might be shabby, but they had their voices, and they deployed these until sometimes they lost them, temporarily or even permanently.

The din of these London street-sellers inspired a small but lively corpus of writing that concerns itself with the noise of selling. The earliest known comment on this phenomenon is a poem, 'London Lickpenny', by John Lydgate (*ca.* 1370-1451). Ostensibly about a man who comes to Westminster to seek redress for stolen property, it is actually a mini-epic journey through the cacophonous streets of the capital. The protagonist suffers many indignities, including having his hood stolen and later finding it for sale. He is too poor to buy anything, but comes away having been washed over with the noisy solicitations of the London street-sellers:

> Then unto London I dyd me hye,
> Of all the land it beareth the pryse:
> 'Hot pescodes,' one began to crye,
> 'Strabery rype, and cherryes in the ryse'
> One bad me come nere and by some spyce,
> Peper and safforne they gan me bede,
> But for lack of mony I myght not spede.

Some three hundred years later, not much had changed. On 18 December 1711, Joseph Addison (1672-1719), posing as one 'Ralph Crochett', communicated to *The Spectator* his ire at the noise:

> Vocal Cries are of much larger Extent, and indeed so full of Incongruities and Barbarisms, that we appear a distracted City to Foreigners, who do not comprehend the Meaning of such enormous Outcries. Milk is generally sold in a note above *Elah*, and in Sounds so exceeding shrill, that it often sets our Teeth on edge. The Chimney-sweeper is confined to no certain Pitch; he sometimes utters himself in the deepest Base, and sometimes in the sharpest Treble; sometimes in the highest, and sometimes in the lowest Note of the Gamut [...].
>
> It should be my Care to sweeten and mellow the Voices of these itinerant Tradesmen, before they make their Appearance in our Streets [...].
>
> And to take Care that those may not make the most Noise, who have the least to sell, which is very observable in the Vendors of Card-matches, to whom I cannot but apply that old Proverb of *Much Cry but little Wool.*

Juxtaposing these two pieces, some observations and speculations come to mind. The most obvious one is that there is a clear continuum between Lydgate, writing *circa* 1400, and Addison. Assuming that the phenomenon that the Lickpenny poem describes preceded Lydgate's lifetime by decades (if not centuries), and knowing as we do that cries were used to attract custom until only a few decades ago in London, it is safe to conclude that noise and the selling and buying of food were inseparable for at least half a millennium, at a conservative estimate.

Addison also sheds light on the distinction between soliciting and selling: noise can often be used to mask the fact that what is being touted is of dubious sales-worthiness. This dichotomy remains relevant in supermarkets, which, among other techniques, communicate visually 'loud' offers, often on price, of merchandise they want to clear.

Unsurprisingly, in England, class is not far from centre stage. Addison's posture of being just the right man to correct the flaws in street-seller communications reminds one of George Bernard Shaw's (1856–1950) Victorian play *Pygmalion* (1913), in which phonetics professor Henry Higgins trains a London flower girl, Eliza Doolittle, to shed her gutter talk and speak well enough to socialize with the elite. Class is a discrete, massive subject but, for the purposes of considering food and communication, it is worth noting that noisy communications about food could be considered undesirable by the elite, yet perfectible by the elite.

Music

Frances Grose (1731-1791), writing in *The Olio* some eighty years later than Addison but on the same theme, quotes Addison's *Spectator* piece and proceeds to offer advice to consumers wanting to navigate the maelstrom of street communications. For Grose, key to the cries is their inherent musicality. 'A good ear will be of more use than a knowledge of all the languages spoken at the confusion of Babel, as it is by their tune and at the time of day the modern cries of London are to be discriminated,' he states. By way of example of how not to emit sound, he cites a London milk maid: 'Milk is generally notified by the word *mew*, except by one wench whose walk was in the environs of Soho-square. Her note was an inarticulate scream, seemingly uttered as if her posteriors were then actually piercing by a cobbler's awl.'[1]

And yet the melodies of some of the London cries – presumably those emitted by sellers who would have met with Addison's and Grose's approval – were appealing enough that they formed the basis of a small, celebratory corpus of musical 'fancies', mostly from the beginning of the sixteenth century. Composers including Orlando Gibbons (1583-1625) and Thomas Weelkes (1576-1623) directly transcribed the cries and melodies of London street-sellers into such compositions. The cries in these pieces are clear, pleasant and distinct (and moving to the contemporary listener and food historian). Fanciful as a genre, perhaps, in the context of the more serious compositions of their creators, some of whom were official composers to royalty, they are actually very accurate and notable in their uniformity: the same intelligible cries and tunes crop up in several of the works by different composers.[2]

Although the fashion for fancies seems to have subsided after the sixteenth century, the musical cries lived on. London street cries and their melodies transcribed by the *Journal of the Folk-Song Society* in the early 1900s are virtually identical to those used by Gibbon and his fellow composers. There was thus a clear continuum in the musical cries for at least three hundred years.[3] Could it be that before the ubiquity of radio and television, and the possibility of round-the-clock access to music, there was an appreciation for music, in whatever simple and fleeting form it might take? Is there something about appetite and the anticipation of eating that responds positively to a snippet of musical expression? Street cries may have vanished but short melodies have for decades been used in advertising to communicate the desirability and particular identity of many a food product. As I write, the ditty to Cadbury's chocolate bar ad, 'Everyone's a fruit and nutcase', set to a musical snippet from Tchaikovsky's *The Nutcracker*, comes floating back into consciousness from a childhood in 1970s London.

By World War II, the number of street cries had radically diminished in London. This coincided, of course, with a reduction in food traded on the street and a gradual increase in shops and supermarkets. As the food industry became more 'efficient', in terms of everything from refrigeration to distribution, food required fewer people to deal in it and relied on means of communication other than human voice to solicit and sell it. As food-selling left the streets and occupied more enclosed places, the enterprise of selling food via the human voice was silenced. One wonders also if, as the availability and choice of food in London increased and satiety became a norm rather than an aspiration, there was less need for sounds to feed the senses.

Language

Another communication casualty of the shift away from the street-selling of food was an actual language of sorts. Backslang, widely used by Victorian street-sellers, involved crudely (and somewhat inconsistently) reversing the order of letters in a word so that they were spoken backwards. Henry Mayhew, a journalist who interviewed London street-sellers extensively in the mid-nineteenth century, recorded the following snippets, among others:

> *A doogheno or dabgheno?* Is it a good or a bad market?
> *A regular trosseno* A regular bad one
> *Cool the namesclop* Look at the policeman[4]

Mayhew noted that *kennetseeno*, or 'stinking', 'applied principally to the quality of fish'. According to John Norris, one of London's few remaining street-sellers of fish, *D-lo tish* ['old shit'], one of the last remaining shards of backslang, is very occasionally used on street stalls in London. It is, however, more widely used at Billingsgate wholesale fish market, especially when wholesalers are selling to non-trade customers whom they never expect to see again. (If the wholesalers try to pass off *D-lo tish* to John, he will send it back.) Lee Smith, who grew up helping his parents at their South London wholesale fish business in the 1980s, recalls that his family regularly used backslang, specifically to talk about getting older fish out of the refrigerator first, to try to sell it off before the fresher fish. 'Just talking to each other so people couldn't understand,' he explains. 'Like if we had fish left in the fridge... *D-lo tish*. Anything we had left, really. We just used it with each other. If people was in in the shop we would talk in our own language, that's all.'

Although specifically used to exclude customers, backslang is nonetheless noteworthy in a discussion concerning communicating about food. I suspect that it gradually subsided as modern refrigeration techniques kept food fresher – or at least looking fresher. John Norris claims that supermarket fish is of very dubious quality – *D-lo tish par excellence* (so to speak, in two languages) – and one wonders how quality-control experts for contemporary food concerns communicate with each other about evaluating merchandise for public consumption (and their own profit).

Touch

There exists a corpus of visual depictions of London street-sellers, many of which are stylized or idealized.[5] Among the works of Francis Wheatley (1747-1801), recognized for *not* idealizing his subjects, there is a 1796 painting which reveals a great deal about the importance of tactility in selling and buying fish.[6] Entitled 'New Mackrel', it depicts a female street-seller of fish who is showing her wares to a customer, a lady of some wealth and standing, and that lady's domestic, presumably a cook or someone closely involved in procuring and preparing food for the household.

The cook, let's call her, appears to be squeezing the mackerel's tail, while asking the street-seller a question, possibly related to its freshness or provenance. She seems excited about the prospect of cooking the fish and her mistress, holding out a coin for its purchase, seems equally excited at the prospect of eating it. The fish is at the centre of the composition, but the cook's almost affectionate touching of it is what gives the picture its vitality. The picture is a celebration of selecting ingredients for a meal, and of the importance of trustworthy communication in procuring these ingredients. Verbal communication with the seller is important. Also crucial is the act of, effectively, communicating with the fish itself via touch.

147

In contemporary London, John Norris is happy to allow customers to touch his fish, although he says these days 'most of them don't want to'. His fish is noted for its freshness (most is bought directly from fishing boats) but, when somebody has any doubt, he has a 'patter' that he does, picking up a fish and showing it off to the customer. He acts as a locum, vetting the fish's freshness on his customers' behalf, via touch: 'You'll just pick it up, show the colour, the firmness, maybe flip it open and show the gills,' he explains. His goal is to highlight the 'firmness, eyes, gills, just the general look of liveliness'. (While most customers delegate fish-touching to Norris, John Bussey, the fruit-seller a few stalls down, has to put up 'Don't touch!' signs, especially when soft fruits come into season, to prevent people's reflex-urges to squeeze fruit to assess its ripeness.)

In eviscerating and filleting his customers' fish, in effect touching it all over in front of their eyes, Norris further communicates with his customers on an even deeper level. 'Communication' has shared roots with many other words, such as communion, that imply a mutuality and a sharing. Whereas the cook in Wheatley's picture would have filleted the mackerel herself (older fishmongers bemoan the loss of such skills among contemporary customers and cooks), Norris is participating in their meal, albeit indirectly, by helping his customers prepare it, endorsing the food with his hands.

Conclusion and Further Questions

Norris never raises his voice to attract custom. 'Crying out: It's gone,' he says. 'Even the veg stands don't do it anymore.' Nonetheless, his transactions are not noiseless. He has established a bantering rapport with a large core of loyal, regular customers. 'I can set my watch by them,' he says. If one doesn't come for a few days, then Norris knows 'they have been on holiday', which he will ask them about next time he sees them. This familiarity is relished by people who have the option to buy their fish face to face, with the endorsement of touch. It stands in contrast both to buying fish as it was experienced for decades and even centuries on the very same Westminster spot as Norris's stall, and also to the manner in which fish is sold in the three major supermarkets that are within a one-or-two-minute walking radius of Norris's stall.

Notes

1. Francis Grose, *The Olio: being a collection of essays, dialogues, letters, biographical sketches, anecdotes, pieces of poetry, parodies, bon mots, epigrams, epitaphs, &c., chiefly original* (London: Hooper and Wigstead, 1796), p. 210.
2. For a terrific introduction to the genre, it is worth tracking down the *The Cries of London* by Theatre of Voices and Fretwork, conducted by Paul Hillier (Harmonia Mundi, 2006).
3. Lucy E. Broadwood, 'Some Notes on London Street Cries', *Journal of the Folk-Song Society*, 6 (1918–19), pp. 43–47.
4. Henry Mayhew, *London Labour and the London Poor: A Cyclopaedia of the Conditions and Earning of Those That Will Work, Those That Cannot Work, and Those that Will Not Work*, Volume I: The London Street Folk (London: Frank Cass, 1967) p. 28.
5. For a comprehensive introduction to the genre, see Sean Shesgreen, *Images of the Outcast: The Urban Poor in the Cries of London* (Manchester: Manchester University Press, 2002).
6. William Roberts, *The Cries of London* (London: The Connoisseur, 1924), plate 5.

Children's Culinary Culture: Why It Matters

Elizabeth Fakazis

In July 2015, First Lady of the United States Michelle Obama hosted the fourth annual Kids' State Dinner at the White House with fifty-four 'kid chefs' – one from each U.S. state, territory and the District of Columbia – as the honored guests. The dinner was part of a national initiative to 'promote cooking and healthy eating among young people across the nation', and was sponsored by the White House, the public broadcasting corporation PBS, the U.S. Department of Education and the U.S. Department of Agriculture. This event represented the growing and very public involvement of children in the politics, economics and material and symbolic culture of food, made possible by the growth of food movements around the world, the food media, new communication technologies and changes in education. In this essay, I reflect on the significance of children's culinary experiences, starting with my own, and on the growing importance of understanding how children make sense of what it means to 'cook' and to 'be a cook' in today's very public and politicized culinary landscape.

Beginning at Home

I found a photograph of three-year-old me with my grandmother in her kitchen in Athens, Greece, taken in 1968. It shows me sitting at the kitchen table, spoon in hand, smiling. An array of pots and pans are at the ready. From the looks of them, I'm guessing that it was early summer, and we were getting ready to use the June-harvest of apricots to make marmalade and Pasta Flora, a marmalade tart.

My grandmother always encouraged my presence in her kitchen, either allowing me to watch or help as she cooked or letting me play with pots, pans, spoons and bits of this and that from the pantry while she tended to other household tasks. She never took food for granted, having survived the hungry years of the World War II occupation of her city, and having heard the moans of a destitute shopkeeper dying slowly and painfully from starvation down the street.

Yet she also knew that I delighted in playing at cooking, and she must have deemed this kind of play valuable. So she would give me a cup of flour; a few teaspoons of cinnamon, nutmeg and oregano; and a handful of walnuts, and I would turn my attention to 'cooking', happily measuring, pouring, mixing. My Uncle Achilleas, always generous with a joke, would wander into the kitchen, take a 'taste' of my concoction, and declare it the best thing he had ever eaten. Then he would wink and smile before disappearing back into his room at the front of the house, leaving me feeling, somehow, special. In this way in my grandmother's kitchen, and along the stretch of Attica beach where my grandfather would take me on weekends, and where pails, shovels, sand, snails and shells stood in for pots, pans and pantry staples, pretend cooking and real cooking, play and work, childhood and adulthood, merged.

Food, and the procuring and cooking of food, was important in our family, beyond its vital role of sustaining life. It was understood as a source of pride in and manifestation of personal accomplishment, hard work, family cohesion and ethnic identity. My grandmother often told stories of her mother's culinary training in Istanbul, of her reputation as a superb cook, and of her ability to support her family by working as a cook in a wealthy Athenian home. My grandmother also took pride in her own ability to make savoury dishes and sweets that earned praise from friends and relatives, and that enticed neighbourhood children to her table for after-school treats. She also took pride in her husband who would wake up before dawn to cut out suit patterns on the kitchen table that he would later piece together in his workshop downtown, and in the fact that this hard work enabled him to bring home good food from the Athens Central Market, even during the war years. She often boasted of his ability to discern and negotiate for fresh fish, tender cuts of meat, ripe fruits and vegetables. He was proud of this ability, too, arriving home from work laden with bags, bellowing from the front gate, 'Kyria Fakazis, open the door!'. To which my grandmother would respond by hurrying to the porch landing and admonishing him to shush, embarrassed that he might wake the neighbours from their afternoon siesta, but also obviously pleased. Finally, my grandmother told stories of how it was the Greeks who returned to Greece as refugees from Asia Minor in the 1920s who were the best cooks in the country – a sentiment I often heard repeated even by Greeks who did not hail from Turkey.

So in our house, good food and good cooking (defined as well-executed, filling, flavourful, good-for-you dishes made with the best ingredients that were available and that we could afford) signified pride in self, family and ethnicity. (It also, of course, signified the pressure to figure out what to cook day after day, to scale fish and wash piles of dirty dishes by hand, to entice finicky children to eat something, to provide enough food for husband, children, children's friends and live-in in-laws on a limited budget and other obligations). These meanings came to us, were constructed by us, primarily through face-to-face interactions. The only cookbook we owned was the 1914 edition of *Nea Nea Mageiriki kai Zaharoplastiki* [*New Cooking and Pastry Making*] that my great-grandmother Eliso had used while attending cooking school in Istanbul at about the time this book was published, and which we kept tucked safely away on the top shelf of her armoire.[1] Neither did we entertain or educate ourselves with radio or television cooking programmes or magazines. Cooking at our house was largely unmediated. Even knowledge of the German-made cookware my grandmother valued came to her through friends and conversation. As a result, my formative understandings of what it meant to 'cook' and to 'be' a cook were constructed as I interacted with my grandparents and great-uncle in our small kitchen and on the sands of Faliro Beach through the ritual practices of cooking, whether 'pretend' or 'real' (these distinctions didn't mean much to my childhood self), and as I put to creative and prescribed use the material artefacts of pots, pans, spoons, walnuts, spices, pails, shovels and seashells.

Over the years, these interactions, somewhat preserved in fading photographs and memories, continued (and continue) to provide me with resources for developing an ever-changing repertoire of culinary values and practices that brush up against and leave impressions on the relationships I maintain with myself and others. Memories of these early interactions join new social experiences, face-to-face and mediated, that provide me with expanding resources as I develop aspects of my identity as a 'cook', a member of my changing family, and even as a professor, teaching culinary journalism, organizing an annual culinary study abroad program in Greece – and embarking on inquiries into the ways children today construct meanings of themselves and their worlds through cooking.

Contemporary Children's Culture and the Rise of the 'Child Celebrity Chef'

Reflecting on the significance of my own childhood culinary experiences has led me to give serious consideration to the importance of the culinary experiences children engage with today, and has alerted me to some of the aspects of such experiences that may be empirically and theoretically relevant. While a great deal of research has been conducted on how adults use food and cooking to construct individual and group identities and to build and maintain social relationships, less attention has been given to these processes in children.[2] Most research focusing on children and food has been concerned with the influences that marketing and advertising strategies exert on children's food choices and health, and on public policies governing access to certain foods and food advertising targeting children in schools, day care centres and other institutions where children spend considerable time.[3]

My own interest lies more in how children come to understand what it means to cook and to 'be' a cook, and on the symbolic and material resources they have available to them for constructing these meanings.[4] As representations of food and cooking occupy increasing shares of time and space in our media and other institutions, and as children spend more time accessing, interacting with and enacting these representations, food and cooking will continue to serve as important, perhaps increasingly important, sources for identity formation. Understanding the models for 'culinary selves' that are culturally available, and the social and economic advantages they require and confer, may also help us better understand contemporary private and especially public food-related engagements and performances that are becoming increasingly difficult to opt out of and that influence personal values, social status, gender roles and other central aspects of our private and public selves.[5]

In order to begin to understand how children comprehend and use diverse meanings of food and cooking to help make sense of themselves, their relationships and their place in their social worlds, I turned my attention to three teenagers who identify themselves and are identified by others as 'celebrity kid chefs'. This is a fairly new cultural identity that can be enacted and its benefits accessed in a limited way by many, while its full benefits can be harnessed and enjoyed by a privileged few. The cases briefly introduced below help highlight the culinary symbolic and material resources that are most widely circulating today, and that help set discursive 'conditions of possibility' for the kind of cooks that today's children can or cannot aspire to become.

In the Footsteps of Rachael Ray

Eliana de Las Casas was born 15 June 2000 in Gretna, Louisiana, to a multi-ethnic family. Her mother was born in the Philippines, and her grandparents hailed from Cajun Louisiana, the Philippines, Cuba and Honduras. Some of her earliest memories are of helping her mother with small cooking tasks in their Louisiana kitchen when she was just four years old. By the time Eliana was eight, she was publishing her own cooking blog, and shortly after that she began producing cooking tutorials for kids and posting them on the Web. Eliana told a reporter for the *Times Picayune* that she was greatly inspired by television shows. 'I'm obsessed with watching cooking shows,' she said. 'I love Rachael Ray and The Chew. I learned all kinds of things from them.'[6]

One of the things Eliana undoubtedly learned was the desirability of being a 'foodie', and the cultural cache of certain kinds of food and cooking values, knowledge and skills. With the help of her mother, a successful, well-travelled children's cookbook author and dramatic storyteller, and her older sister, a graphic designer, illustrator and promoter, Eliana was able to leverage this culinary capital, along with the economic opportunities made available by the expanding food entertainment industries, at a very young age. By the time she was thirteen, Eliana had garnered a reputation as a bona fide, professional, sought-after celebrity chef, attracting media coverage and guest spots on television shows – and commanding speaking fees starting at $5000 per day, plus expenses.

Now, at fourteen, Eliana has published two cookbooks, one of which, *Cool Kids Cook: Louisiana*, won the 2014 International Latino Book Award and a Parents' Choice Award. She hosts a weekly radio programme broadcast on Voice of America Kids, which reaches an international audience of listeners who can tune in to 'discover cuisine from around the world, cooking techniques, interviews with top chefs, and of course, recipes by Kid Chef Eliana'.[7] The show has won two awards from the Lifestyle Entertainment Industry, presented with much fanfare and glamour at a red carpet ceremony in Hollywood. Eliana also hosts her own web site, kidchefeliana.com, which she uses to promote herself as an author, radio show host and 'personality'. Directly below the banner on the site's home page is an endorsement by Andrew Zimmern, host of the Travel Channel's *Bizzare Foods* and *Bizarre Foods America*, that also appears on the cover of Eliana's first cookbook: 'Eliana is the real deal, a young cook with an amazing passion for sharing her knowledge and her appreciation of all that's edible. This is a straight shot from the heart, a labor of love from a Kid Chef who knows her way around the kitchen. Chefs and cooks of all sizes will appreciate what Eliana brings to the table. Literally.'[8]

Figure 1. Eliana de Las Casas, celebrity chef

Eliana also maintains a schedule of public appearances, offering 'celebrity chef' cooking demonstrations and classes at major events in cities across the United States. Three of her many engagements include appearing as a featured chef at a charitable fundraising event in New Orleans, helping to cook for and serve four hundred people, including the mayor of New Orleans; appearing as a speaker and menu curator for Dove's Self Esteem for Girls Conference in New York City; and appearing as a guest chef instructor at the New Orleans School of Cooking. She has held numerous book signings and has been featured in *Teen Vogue*, in the *New York Times Magazine* as a 'top teen chef', on *Fox News* as one of the '10 most famous kid cooks and food critics', on Nickelodean's news channel, on *Super Chef Kids* (the first Web reality cooking competition in the United States for children by the creators of the Food Network's *Iron Chef*) and in numerous other newspaper and magazine articles and television and Web programmes. Eliana can be hired to offer demonstrations and workshops in 'healthy living and cooking with fresh produce', to give motivational speeches 'encouraging kids to follow their dreams and pursue their passions', and to develop menus, recipes and videos for corporate events and marketing campaigns.

In the Footsteps of Thomas Keller

Eliana's success as a child celebrity chef, and the support and opportunities she has been able to harness, have been shared and surpassed by the internationally-known culinary prodigy, fifteen-year-old Flynn McGarry. While Eliana writes cookbooks for children and primarily addresses a young audience through her Web site, blog and radio show, Flynn moves in the very adult arena of brutally competitive, world-renowned culinary professionals. Most recently, Flynn was featured on the cover of the 2014 *New York Times Magazine* Food and Drink issue, with the accompanying teaser, 'Flynn McGarry Wants to Open The Best Restaurant in the World. So What If He's Only 15?'.

Flynn first garnered media attention for his supper club, Eureka, which he started hosting in his home when he was eleven years old. Guests, including adult celebrity chefs, actors, producers, editors, lawyers, real estate brokers and other well-heeled professionals paid $160 a head for tasting menus that Flynn spent days preparing and which he meticulously plated and served. Corina Chocano, the author of the profile that appeared in the 2014 *New York Times Magazine*, described the Eureka dinner she attended:

> McGarry emerged from the kitchen with each course, to both present it and finish it at the table. A snack of puffed trout skin was followed by blanched asparagus tips, wrapped in grilled asparagus gelee and garnished with the controversial petal. Served on a rustic slab of gray slate, they resembled an exotic species of snail. Diners praised the clean flavors and the way each ingredient was 'elevated' rather than obscured.[9]

Flynn attends an on-line private school which gives him the flexibility he needs to hone his culinary skills through his supper club, and the time to apprentice at some of the best restaurants in the United States, including Alinea in Chicago, Eleven Madison Park in New York and Alma in Los Angeles (he has also cooked for President Barack and First Lady Michelle Obama on the White House lawn). Early on, he supplemented his formal education by watching the Food Network and using the Internet, where he first learned about Michelin ratings, molecular gastronomy, sous vide and knife techniques. He has benefited from the support of his father Will, a professional photographer who works with the California film industry, and his mother Meg, an actor and screenwriter. They have used their professional skills and contacts to help promote their son and his work, and they have provided him with significant material resources. As Chocano writes, when the counters in Flynn's home kitchen proved too high for him, his parents built him a prep kitchen in the dining room that was:

> modeled after Keller's at the French Laundry. When McGarry decided he wanted a private space to create menu ideas, his dad constructed a kitchen in his bedroom to resemble Alinea's in Chicago. They redid the electricity, built the tables and removed the closet doors to convert it to a pantry; McGarry would get an induction burner for a birthday, a vacuum sealer for Christmas. When McGarry eventually visited the restaurant, he remarked, 'This is what I put in my bedroom!'[10]

In the Footsteps of Alice Waters

While Eliana promotes herself as a junior chef with popular appeal and Flynn promotes himself as a junior chef with formidable culinary skills and ambitions, twelve-year-old

Haile Thomas has committed herself to cultivating her culinary knowledge and skills in order to advocate for social change. Haile, from Tucson, Arizona, writes that she was inspired to educate herself and other children about the perils of a poor diet after her father was diagnosed with Type Two Diabetes when Haile was seven years old. Two years later, Haile enrolled in a media production workshop and developed *Kids Can Cook*, a YouTube video series that she hosts with her younger sister, Nia, that 'aims to empower kids with the skills, knowledge, and confidence to prepare healthy meals for themselves and their families'.[11] Since launching that first modest project, Haile has used her expanding skills to help people in her local community and nationwide. In addition to organizing a local healthy eating educational festival and interviewing public health advocates on her blog talk radio show, Haile serves as the executive director of the HAPPY Organization, which she founded to offer elementary school children classes that give them 'direct experience with healthy food in a fun, hands-on way', and that aim to 'prevent disease by highlighting the benefits and great taste of whole grains, legumes, fruits and vegetables, through kid-friendly delicious and nutritious recipes'.[12] The organization also helps lower-income Tucson families afford community supported agriculture shares by subsidizing half the cost, and hosts a community dinner and exposition that addresses childhood obesity, malnutrition and hunger. As a result of her successful community advocacy, Haile has been asked to serve on several advisory boards, including the Canyon Ranch Life Enhancement Program, and to serve as a taste-tester for organic meals developed for children by Chef Alice Waters for Hyatt Hotels in the United States, Canada and the Caribbean. Haile gained national recognition in 2013 when she was invited to sit with Michelle Obama during the President's State of the Union address as a representative of the First Lady's Let's Move initiative – and she was one of fifty-four 'kid chefs' invited to attend the Kids' State Dinner at the White House that same year.

Why Children's Culinary Culture Matters

While Eliana, Flynn and Haile are by no means typical children with typical experiences of food and cooking, they are also not alone, as shown by the fact that Michelle Obama was able to find 54 'kid chefs' to invite to the White House for dinner and by the many profiles of kid chefs that appear regularly in the media. Their experiences, while atypical, contain elements that many children either share in a much more restricted way as they learn 'cooking as a life skill' in school or as they watch television and visit shops awash in food and cooking products (including toys and children's cookbooks) – products they are made aware of and are influenced by even if they don't have the means or opportunities to take advantage of them and make them their own.

Juxtaposing the stories of Eliana, Flynn and Haile with my own has brought into relief some of the fundamental changes that have occurred over the past forty-five years, specifically: the economic and political opportunities opened up by the various public food movements; children's increased media access facilitated by the Internet, social media, reality television programming and the profitable advertising that culinary journalism and entertainment draws; the development of increased formal and informal institutional sites providing children with cooking and communication skills that they need to participate in the 'foodie culture'; and the increased circulation of diverse discourses of what it means to cook and to be a cook within numerous institutions beyond the family that are central in many children's lives. These discourses have enabled the emergence of new public personas, including the child celebrity chef, the child food critic and the child public health advocate – all of which allow children of means to actively participate in, take advantage of and/or change adult worlds. At the same time, by juxtaposing my personal experiences with those of Eliana, Flynn and Haile, I am able to see continuity, especially in the desire for children to participate in a meaningful way in the adult world, the importance of early cooking experiences in and out of the kitchen and the importance of family interactions.

All this raises a host of interesting and important questions. The meanings of 'cooking' and 'being a cook' are changing, with greater value being placed on de-privatized, public demonstrations of codified culinary knowledge and practices widely understood to be sophisticated (expressed in part by the ubiquitous use of words like 'chef' and 'gourmet'), and less value being placed on private, every-day cooking experiences. In the context of gender studies, this suggests that 'traditional masculine culinary discourses' are usurping 'traditional feminine culinary discourses' in many contexts for both boys and girls, men and women.[13] What does this imply for children's understanding of their gendered selves, relationships and practices, inside the home and out? The deployment of these new culinary meanings can require and confer new and powerful social, political and economic capital. But how are these meanings used and negotiated by children (perhaps the majority) who don't enjoy cooking, who don't aspire to be private or public cooks or chefs, or who have limited resources, including not enough food to keep hunger and disease at bay? How are these children and their families managing and negotiating discursive culinary environments that may be exerting new forms of social and political pressures that can't be ignored? Such questions may be fruitfully explored using a variety of research methods, including textual analyses of mediated representations of food and cooking either targeting or being regularly accessed by children, of changing material artefacts such as culinary toys and high-end kitchen tools desired or marketed to children and of the myriad strategies used to promote children's consumption of culinary products and experiences;[14] and by relying on ethnography and ethnomethodology to study the ways that different children construct what cooking and being a cook means to them as they interact with teachers, relatives, friends and others in a variety of institutional settings and social contexts.

Many contemporary food activists believe that our individual health, as well as the health of families, communities and even our planet, can be improved by the large-scale implementation of 'sustainable' food practices, rooted in culinary knowledges, attitudes, values and beliefs being promoted by organizations such as the International Slow Food

156

Movement and by food justice programs around the world. The procurement, cooking and eating of food – and how we think about what it means to cook and to be a cook – clearly have profound implications beyond what we experience in our kitchens and our tables. Children are not waiting until they grow up to participate in and shape local, national and even global culinary cultures, and so understanding their complex roles has become a worth-while critical endeavour. Mark Bittman has asked what might happen in twenty years if hundreds of thousands of children start taking an active interest in cooking.[15] Researchers, I believe, need to do our best to provide some answers to his and related questions.

Notes

1. Evangelos Malli, *Nea Mageiriki kai Zaharoplastiki* (Athens: Ioannis Kollaros, 1914).

2. For an excellent introduction to 'the significance of a range of food practices for childhood identities in the context of children's everyday lives in different cultural settings' that includes work by scholars working in a number of different disciplines from England, Scotland, Sweden, Norway and the United States, see *Children, Food and Identity in Everyday Life*, ed. by Allison James, Anne Trine Kjorholt and Vebjorg Tingstad (New York: Palgrave Macmillan, 2010); Rebecca O'Connell, '(How) Is Childminding Family Like? Family Day Care, Food and the Reproduction of Identity at the Public/Private Interface', *The Sociological Review*, 58.4 (2010), pp. 563-86; and *Children's Food Practices in Families and Institutions*, ed. by Samantha Punch, Ian McIntosh, and Ruth Edmond (New York: Routledge, 2011).

3. For examples, see Karine M. Charry, 'Product Placement and the Promotion of Healthy Food to Pre-Adolescents: When Popular TV Series Make Carrots Look Cool', *International Journal of Advertising*, 33.3 (2014), pp. 599-616; Andrew D. Cheyne, Lori Dorfman and Eliana Bukofzer, 'Marketing Sugary Cereals to Children in the Digital Age: A Content Analysis of 17 Child-Targeted Websites', *Journal of Health Communication*, 18 (2013), pp. 563-82; Anna R. McAlister and T. Bettina Cornwell, 'Collectible Toys as Marketing Tools: Understanding Preschool Children's Responses to Foods Paired with Premiums', *Journal of Public Policy & Marketing*, 31.2 (2012), pp. 195-205; Charlene D. Elliott, 'Packaging Fun: Analyzing Supermarket Food Messages Targeted at Children', *Canadian Journal of Communication*, 37 (2012), pp. 303-18; Jennifer A. Kotler, Jennifer M. Schiffman and Katherine G. Hanson, 'The Influence of Media Characters on Children's Food Choices', *Journal of Health Communication*, 17 (2012), pp. 886-89. For two general articles exploring ideological content of children's cookbooks, see Sherrie A. Inness, '"The Enchantment of Mixing-Spoons": Cooking Lessons for Girls and Boys", in *Dinner Roles: American Women and Culinary Culture* (Iowa City: University of Iowa Press, 2001) and Jan Longon. '"As Worthless as Savorless Salt"?: Teaching Children to Cook, Clean, and (Often) Conform', *Gastronomica*, 3.2 (Spring 2003), pp. 104-10.

4. See Frances Short, *Kitchen Secrets: The Meaning of Cooking in Everyday Life* (Oxford: Berg, 2006).

5. My theoretical and conceptual framework for understanding how 'culinary selves' are formed through social interaction in specific formal and informal institutional settings, and why such understanding is important, comes primarily from Jaber F. Gubrium and James A. Holstein, *The Self We Live By: Narrative Identity in a Postmodern World* (Oxford: Oxford University Press, 2000) and Jaber F. Gubrium and James A. Holstein, *Institutional Selves: Troubled Identities in a Postmodern World* (Oxford: Oxford University Press, 2001).

6. Judy Walker, 'Twelve-year-old Cooking Prodigy: Kid Chef Eliana Cooks in Harvey and Everywhere Else', *The Times-Picayune*, 1 April 2013. See also Eliana's Web site <www.kidchefeliana.com>.

7. Voice of America, *Cool Kids Cook with Kid Chef Eliana* < http://www.voiceamerica.com/show/2120/cool-kids-cook> [accessed 29 May 2015].

8. Eliana de Las Casas, *Cool Kids Cook: Louisiana* (New York: Pelican, 2013). Eliana has also published *Cool Kids Cook: Fresh and Fit* (New York: Pelican, 2014).

9. Carina Chocano, 'The Chef at 15', *The New York Times Magazine*, 28 March 2014 <http://www.nytimes.com/2014/03/30/magazine/the-chef-at-15.html?_r=0> [accessed 29 May 2015].

10. Chocano.

11. Information about Haile Thomas can be found on her Web site <www.hailevthomas.com> and at <www.thehappyorg.org>, <www.healthiergeneration.org> and <www.letsmove.gov>.

12. 'Happy Programs', *Happyorg.org* <http://www.thehappyorg.org/#!programs/cxxj> [accessed 29 May 2015].

13. For a discussion of gendered culinary discourses, see Michelle K.Szabo, '"I'm a real catch": The Blurring of Alternative and Hegemonic Masculinities in Men's Talk about Home Cooking', *Women's Studies International Forum,* 44 (2014), pp. 228-35 and Michelle K. Szabo, 'Men Nurturing through Food: Challenging Gender Dichotomies around Domestic Cooking', *Journal of Gender Studies,* 23.1 (2014), pp. 18-31.

14. See Jason Bainbridge, 'Fully Articulated: The Rise of the Action Figure and the Changing Face of Children's Entertainment', *Continuum: Journal of Media & Cultural Studies,* 24.6 (2010), pp. 829-42; Daniel T. Cook, *The Commodification of Childhood* (Durham, NC: Duke University Press, 2004); *The Children's Culture Reader,* ed. by Henry Jenkins (New York: New York University Press, 1998); David Machin and Theo Van Leeuwen, 'Toys As Discourse: Children's War Toys and the War on Terror', *Critical Discourse Studies,* 6.1 (2009), pp. 51-63; Allison J. Pugh, 'Selling Compromise: Toys, Motherhood, and the Cultural Ideal', *Gender and Society,* 19.6 (Dec., 2005), pp. 729-49; and Theo Van Leeuwen, 'The World According to Playmobil', *Semiotica,* 173 (2009), pp. 299-315.

15. Mark Bittman, 'Kitchen Little' *New York Times,* 7 May 2013 <http://opinionator.blogs.nytimes.com/2013/05/07/kitchen-little/> [accessed 29 May 2015].

When Menus Talk: The Bernard Fread Menu Collection

Rebecca Federman

Chinatown was crowded on the evening of 8 May 1977. Bernard and Ruth Fread had travelled forty-five minutes by bus from their apartment on the Upper East Side to celebrate Mother's Day in their favourite food neighbourhood. They wandered the narrow streets, ducking into busy restaurants to survey the clientele before leaving to find a more authentic experience. They finally chose to eat at New Lin Heong Restaurant at 69 Bayard Street. Ruth was dieting but allowed herself the night off to share egg rolls and suey kow soup with her husband. They also split the shrimp chow mein, sweet and pungent chicken with fried wontons and white rice. Like many of the restaurants in Chinatown, New Lin Heong was brightly lit, which Bernard, who had poor eyesight, especially appreciated. Except for one or two pictures on the walls, there were no decorations, nor were there any tablecloths. This was a paper napkin restaurant, but the service was good, the food was delicious and the portions were big. After dinner, the couple went across the street to the Carvel ice cream shop where Ruth ordered a vanilla soft serve cone and Bernard stuck to his favourite: a chocolate cone with chocolate sprinkles. Then, maybe because it was Mother's Day and Ruth had given birth to his five beloved children, Bernard suggested getting more ice cream at another Carvel store nearby on Canal Street, where, like two teenagers, Bernard and Ruth shared a chocolate sundae and double chocolate cup.

The details of the Freads' excursion to Chinatown were documented by Bernard later that night at home, but not in a notebook or day journal. Instead, Fread wrote about the evening – including the price of the bus fare – up and down the margins of the small, red menu he took from the New Lin Heong restaurant.

This is the story of Bernard Fread, an ordinary man who collected menus from ordinary restaurants in New York City. And while the Mother's Day meal in Chinatown was celebratory, Fread's precise recital of the outing is a consistent theme on nearly all the menus he collected. The evening of 8 May 1977 is just one story – one meal – among the many hundreds of annotated menus in his collection, now housed at the New York Public Library, which describe in detail what it was like for one man to eat and live in New York City in the middle of the twentieth century.

Restaurant menus are cherished by chefs, historians and food enthusiasts as valuable primary source documents. Menus reflect dining habits, food trends and prices, typography and designs that are rarely found elsewhere. But while there is much to learn from menus, there is also quite a lot that menus don't tell us. Spend enough time looking at bills of fare and you're likely to come away with more questions than answers. Who ate at this restaurant? What did the food taste like? What songs were playing? What happened at the table? How safe was the neighbourhood? Menus allow a diner in 2015 to observe what the person next to her was eating in 1885, or in 1977, but they're frustratingly lacking when it comes to providing detailed information about the restaurant, the food or the larger world in which they exist. Menus can't provide that level of detail because menus don't talk. But Bernard Fread's menus do.

The twenty-four boxes in Fread's collection span the 1930s through the 1980s, and the bulk of them answer the very questions that plague restaurant and food historians. His collection also provides a glimpse into his own personal world and a fascinating commentary on everyday life. When Fread annotated a menu, his musings ranged from a few sentences to many paragraphs. Besides carefully recording the date and exact address, Fread also mentioned the music that was played on the jukebox. He jotted down how many shrimp came with the order of shrimp cocktail. He took note of how many other diners were in the restaurant, and at what time. Fread remembered the colour and design of the waitstaff's uniforms, what the bill total was and how much he tipped. If Fread continued the evening with a movie, which was usually the case, he wrote down the name of film he went to see (e.g. *Zardoz*), the name of the theatre (e.g. Trans Lux East) and a two-line synopsis of the plot (e.g. 'science fiction, inane').[1] And if dessert or a snack was eaten later at home, he took note of what it was, how much it cost and where it was purchased (e.g. Keebler Town House crackers, 69 cents, Grand Union on 86th St).

But Fread rarely stopped there. He liked to describe his day's activities, who dined with him, how they arrived at the restaurant, how he planned on getting home and how much the entire trip might cost. His marginalia is so detailed and personal that it takes only a handful of menus for a portrait of this unique man to appear.

Dr Bernard Fread was a lifelong New Yorker. He was born in Manhattan in 1904, and died there in 1992. Fread was an ophthalmologist who practiced at Lenox Hill Hospital and lived with wife Ruth and their dog Isis nearby on Madison Avenue. He eschewed all alcohol and caffeine, but had a sweet tooth that he satisfied with frequent orders of ice cream, purchases of imported cookies from Zabars and fruit. He loved seafood.

And he was a frequent visitor to Chinese restaurants. Chinese restaurants make up the bulk of 'ethnic' food menus in his collection, and Chinese was the favourite cuisine to celebrate happy family occasions, which he did frequently with any and all of his five children: Cynthia, Richard, Gail, Amy and Wendy.

But while Fread enjoyed taking his wife and children out to lunch or dinner, the majority of his meals were eaten alone, usually after his hospital rounds on Saturday night. He was hungry, and he also had a mission: to collect a menu from every restaurant in New York City. He vowed he would never eat at the same restaurant twice – maybe because he started his dining-out life very differently, by eating in the same restaurant for ten years running.

The menu from the Fishermen's Net, on Third Avenue and 34th Street, is unassuming; but according to Fread's daughter Gail, this is where he ate for nearly a decade. He had the seafood cocktail, the Manhattan clam chowder, the broiled seafood platter, a Seven-Up and the Nesselrode pudding; and he had them so regularly that the restaurant knew to fire up the order before he arrived, so the plates of food would be waiting for him. Then Fread decided to cast a wider net than Fishermen's. Instead of eating in the same place every week, he would choose a new restaurant each time he went out. What's more, he would archive its menu for posterity. Now he wasn't just a doctor getting a late meal. He was a food adventurer with an eye on history.

It's clear from all those seafood platters and Seven-Ups that while Fread enjoyed eating, he was not by nature very curious about food. But a number of early menus in the collection indicate that he was a surprisingly eager traveller and a seeker of unique experiences. As a tourist he went all over the world, and everywhere he went he picked up a souvenir menu. Alas, he didn't annotate these, so we don't know whether he liked the food at the Rotisserie d'Alsace in Brussels, the Ristorante Stella d'Italia in Sicily, El Patio in Mexico City or the San Carlos Gran Hotel in Guatemala City. But he did consider it important to bring home the memory. Then, when he made his decision to collect menus from all over New York, he changed his approach. The menu per se was no longer memory enough. Now he had a yen to record his entire experience, not because it was an adventure in a foreign culture but because it was his own life. He was carving 'Bernard was here' on the trees of New York City.

As it turned out, his particular New York was a highly local one. The menus he collected tended to reflect a small world of restaurants from only a handful of neighbourhoods. Those most heavily represented include the Upper East Side (where he lived and worked), the Upper West Side (a cross-town bus away), midtown and Chinatown. While today's menu collectors and food enthusiasts might ferry across New York Harbour to see what restaurants Staten Island has to offer, or regularly attend new openings in the far reaches of Brooklyn or Queens, not so for Bernard Fread. He was not a foodie; he wasn't seeking out restaurants for their unusual cuisines or off-beat culinary philosophies. He gravitated towards the sort of places that appealed to him, in the sort of neighbourhoods he was comfortable in, and if he can be said to 'specialize,' it was in the everyday restaurants close to where he lived. The adventure, for him, seems to have been in the idea of such a project, not the countless real-world possibilities he could have followed up in every borough. And when he carefully recorded each adventure, the food was the least of it. Typically he used one of four words to describe the entirety of a meal: 'delicious', 'good', 'fair' or 'mediocre'. That's it. He didn't criticize the salt levels, or wonder why so many dishes featured the same sauce, or speculate about the chef's ideas.

And thank goodness he didn't. Fread's doggedly pedestrian approach to dining out is exactly what makes his collection so remarkable. Many menu collections, stored away in boxes in attics, garages or libraries, are made up of items kept from special events – a dinner in honour of a visiting politician, Christmas at a resort hotel, a birthday celebrated on shipboard. Most often these menus come from famous restaurants – the

Waldorf-Astoria, Le Pavillon or Tavern on the Green. But what about the places where people eat every day? Fread's collection is almost exclusively made up of this latter category. His menus come from some of the most ordinary restaurants imaginable – the restaurants where no one would think to ask for a keepsake menu. Here are the diners, luncheonettes, ice cream parlours, Chinese restaurants, delis, spaghetti houses and 24-hour cafeterias – all those places where everyone went and nobody noticed. These restaurants were not going to be immortalized in *Zagats*, the *New York Times*, *New York Magazine* or *Gourmet*; and the gastronomes who cherished their stash of favourite menus for decades certainly didn't keep any from Howard Johnson's or Sbarro. But Fread kept them, and today they tell a story that would be impossible to document elsewhere.

Fread's menus from the '60s and the early '70s represent places like Kellogg's Coffee Shop, 'Beautifully illuminated, mostly counter service, fair food';[2] the Park Avenue Luncheonette, 'Small, modest eating place. Good service, fair food.';[3] Kronk's Confectionary and Luncheonette, 'Modest, old fashioned ice cream parlor with luncheonette.';[4] and the Yorkville Luncheonette, 'Very modest place. Ice cream parlor, juke box in rear.'[5] He enjoyed these modest spots in part because he enjoyed simple food, and in part because they never closed. Fread was a night owl. He often emerged from Lenox Hill in the early hours of the morning, so his options were limited to the restaurants that were open. These counter restaurants also offered Fread an opportunity to be a bit of a voyeur, to perch on a stool anonymously taking in, and writing about, the city's early morning underworld.

Towards the end of the 1960s, Fread's menus change. The unassuming luncheonette and diner meals all but disappear from his evening routes. Ethnic restaurants begin to appear. The Chinese menus, which were always a favourite, show up even more frequently, and now there is representation from other cuisines, as well. 'Traveling around the world via many national restaurants is possible in New York City,' he wrote on 17 August 1968 after visiting the Lebanese restaurant Beirut on West 32nd Street.[6] During the next couple of years he also went to Topkapi on 58th Street, the Jamaican on Sixth Avenue, Cafe Sahbra on 72nd Street, Karachi on 46th Street, Tokyo-Bangkok on 79th Street and Mykonos also on 46th Street. He didn't have to travel to Flushing, Queens in order to experience his first taste of Korean food; he got it at Sam Bok on 43rd Street. Nor did he have to go to Jackson Heights to experiment with Indian food. These newly-opened ethnic restaurants were all within a comfortable distance of his usual stomping grounds. In 1979 he noted that one of his old favourites, the Press Box on East 45th Street, had been sold, and the new owners were Polish. They added Polish specialties to the menu, and the place was now called the Polonez Press Box. Two years later another old-timer, the October Restaurant on York Avenue, became a Thai restaurant.

We can't be certain whether this shift in the collection towards more varied cuisines reflects a genuine change in Fread's preferences or simply a change in New York's restaurant landscape. In many ways these new ethnic places in the neighbourhood were as unpretentious as the coffee shops and diners they displaced and they provided an opportunity for Fread to continue travelling the globe, temporarily leaving his order of shrimp cocktail and Carvel soft serve behind for baby cactus salad at Xochitl Mexican Restaurant, miso soup at Tsunuya Japanese Restaurant, couscous with chickpeas and lamb at Khalil Gibran Near Eastern Restaurant and baklava at Topkapi Turkish Restaurant.

A few years ago, Laura Shapiro and I organized an exhibition at the New York Public Library on the history of lunch in New York City. The Library holds the Jack Kerouac papers, so we decided to feature a manuscript from a Kerouac story called 'Last of the Old West', which he wrote in 1950 while sitting in Hector's Cafeteria in Times Square. Hector's was a famous Beat hangout, and we desperately wanted to display a menu along with the manuscript. I searched the menu collection but came up with nothing. Then I looked in Bernard Fread's boxes, and sure enough, Fread had eaten at Hector's on 30 November 1965 and come home with a menu. But this one was different from the others. Apparently Hector's didn't distribute paper copies of the menu – so Fread transcribed the entire menu, by hand. We showed his manuscript menu right alongside Kerouac's manuscript story.

Fread's menus, gathered so carefully over so many years, are valuable in all kinds of unusual ways. They document the hole-in-the-wall places that few other people take note of, and they record a changing restaurant culture from the point of view of a diligent non-gourmand with a hearty appetite. Even more distinctively, they're a by-product of one man's private mission: to observe his own life through the lens of dinner. The margins of Fread's menus are filled with information that no restaurant critic would bother jotting down: his wife's diet meal, the plotline of the newly released *Godfather* film, the street scene in SoHo, the fact that when he got home, he ate up the last scraps from a box of Danish cookies. Perhaps it's a testament to a life well lived that the food on these menus is often the least arresting part of the document. Fread may have had a sleepy palate, but he was not a passive participant in this restaurant project or in his own life. That's why his menus speak – unlike so many remnants of the culinary past. And that's why we listen.

163

Notes

1. New York, New York Public Library, Bernard Fread Menu Collection, 'Green Tulip Restaurant', 16 March 1974.
2. New York, New York Public Library, Bernard Fread Menu Collection, 'Kellogg's Coffee Shop', 19 June 1958.
3. New York, New York Public Library, Bernard Fread Menu Collection, 'Park Avenue Luncheonette', 16 August 1961.
4. New York, New York Public Library, Bernard Fread Menu Collection, 'Kronk's Confectionary and Luncheonette', 23 August 1961.
5. New York, New York Public Library, Bernard Fread Menu Collection, 'Yorkville Luncheonette', 10 September 1961.
6. New York, New York Public Library, Bernard Fread Menu Collection. 'Beirut Restaurant', 16 August 1968.

By Any Other Name

Priscilla Parkhurst Ferguson

How do things accrue the power to convince, to persuade, to impel belief and induce action? One answer lies in what things do for us, and what things do for us, in turn, depends on what we do with them. Through the discourse that articulates practice, things become part of the world about us, through words and deeds that communicate our ideas, ideals and principles, not forgetting our enthusiasms, fears and obsessions.

Discourse – language, or more simply what I call 'food talk' – transforms the material into the immaterial. Language intellectualizes the object by giving it a form that can be analyzed. Representation may well invest the object with properly aesthetic properties. Above all, the talk that we talk humanizes nature and socializes things. We rely on language to integrate things into our social universe, our lives.

Clearly, language transforms the object into something different from and yet governed by its material base. This constitutive duality of things – material and immaterial at one and the same time – connects people and things, or, more correctly, people through things. Just as things are always more than things, food is always more than food. It is symbol, ideology, discourse, image. At the same time, food is also always food, a material entity defined by its appeal to the senses and its claims on the body.

How do humans make things ours? How do we integrate things into the social world? If we consider systematically the many things that surround us, we will learn a great deal – about them, about ourselves and about the world we inhabit and shape. The answer lies in practice. It is the practice of things, and most especially the ways we talk about them, that makes them so important not only for us as individual beings in need of sustenance but also in the social world to which, willy-nilly, we belong.

Culinary Languages

Take food – no thing, surely, of greater importance for everyday life. Food means more still. Our connections to food represent an investment of self that is at once intellectual, aesthetic, affective and social. Food anchors our identity. (The much overused epithet 'foodie' does not begin to capture the intensity of our relationship to this 'thing'.) What, we ask, does food mean – for me, for others, for the world we inhabit? We are what we eat, to be sure, but how? with what effect? Language shapes our understandings and therefore our experience of food – as both culinary construct and cultural indicator. Without the language that allows sharing, without talk about food, consumption would remain a purely private, corporeal affair.

Few of us, it is safe to say, realize how very important what we say about food, how we talk about it, can be in defining our relationship to food. As the only means for humans to share gustatory experience, talk is crucial to any and every culinary connection. Foods by any other name might well taste as sweet. Or as sour, as salty or as bitter, as good or as bad. But, pace Shakespeare, they would not mean the same thing. Along with the stories to which they almost inevitably give rise, names create meanings and associations that give those names a life of their own.

Two components of this 'food talk' lay particular claim to our attention: the names bestowed upon culinary productions and the stories that connect word and referent, in this case, the dish and the larger cultural context.[1] Although French sources supply the examples, the model that I propose applies across the linguistic, cultural and culinary board. At the same time, the intense nominatory practices of French chefs have much to do with the ascendancy of French cuisine – professional cuisine, like ballet, speaks French, whatever the repast actually served. Baptism offers a cultural as well as culinary strategy to impose meaning and define practice. Names tell stories, and those stories in turn tell us how to 'read' the food that we consume. As we all know full well, recipes are not straightforward directives. Veritable instruments of society, recipes translate the material into the social and humanize the material world.

Names and Stories

It is hardly news that the cuisine that emerged over the nineteenth century in France offers the very model of a codified – that is, self-referential – cuisine. To the extent that the designations refer not to the actual food but to an external referent, dishes require translation into common parlance. Marie-Antoine Carême's '*potage à la Rothschild*' or '*potage de macaroni à la Bénévent*' (Carême's employer and mentor Talleyrand was Prince de Bénévent) give no clue as what is in the soup bowl before us. At the opposite end of the spectrum, a descriptive cuisine makes do with ingredients. Figuring out '*steak-frites*' requires no more than ordinary cultural competence. But '*sauce béarnaise*' requires extra-ordinary, specific knowledge to decode the preparation. It is of no gustatory help to know that Béarn is a French province or even the putative culinary connections of the sauce (see *Wikipedia* for one version). The culinary code is an independent culinary system.

Although all cuisines mix codes and descriptions, relentless linguistic formalization long set French cuisine apart. That formalization further contributed to the cultural power that for three centuries (and counting) made French cuisine the standard for formal dining in the West. 'Menu French' was, and to a significant extent still is, an international culinary language. The much bally-hooed decline of French cuisine in the early twenty-first century has to do with the competition from cuisines that celebrate difference rather than assert allegiance to what French tradition refers to as a 'universal' nature.[2]

Names lay claim to cultural space. Carême's codification of French cuisine depended substantially upon the names that designated its many different parts. Naming every variation of a basic preparation betrays a very different conception of culinary order than the contemporary practice of giving a basic recipe with open-ended suggestions of variations. So Carême's '*potage de purée de volaille*' comes *à la reine / à la Boieldieu / à la Montglas / à la française / à la princesse*. In the same chapter game purées are composed of *perdreaux à la duchesse / faisans à la royale / lapereaux à la Montglas / gibier à la française / cailles à la Rossini*.

For those who have mastered the code, names resuscitate a dish. Names produce a network of associations – of people, events and places – that work to counter the ephemerality of food.[3] As the examples above indicate, the names in Carême's final work, *L'Art de la cuisine française au XIXe siècle* (1833), include ingredients, honorific designations of individuals and recognition of places and their distinctive produce and preparations (as with truffles for Périgord).[4]

These names construct a true culinary France, a country that Carême identified with its great men, its landscape, its produce and its historic events. The names work as a self-referential system, but each name also connects the dish to a world beyond the kitchen and outside the code. Besides the 'great whose work has illustrated France', memories of great festive eras of the past and the landscape that is profoundly France, Carême looked to the future, always concerned with those entering the profession. He made a point, he made sure to tell us, to give his soups names derived from their composition 'to render the details easier to remember for young practitioners'.[5]

The more culturally specific the designations, however, the greater the odds that they will lose cultural currency. Among the examples above, a good many of us twenty-first-century moderns will recognize 'Rossini'. We may even know the composer's reputation as a gastronome and a talented amateur chef. But 'Montglas' will most likely draw a blank as it did for me. (Mme de Monglas was a seventeenth-century, literary-minded French marquise.) For whatever reasons (and assuming my identification is correct), Carême thought the name important. Should we? The more obviously local the designation, the less likely it will resonate beyond national or cultural boundaries. Dissociated from their personal or cultural origin, names turn into primarily culinary terms. How many of us think much about the name or wonder what it means or where it came from when we tuck into *steak-sauce béarnaise*?

And then there are the new dishes. The expansion of French cuisine in the nineteenth century, which owes so much to Carême's drive for codification and professionalization, put a premium on the new. Early in the century Jean Anthelme Brillat-Savarin already noted the competition that incited chefs to come up with a new dish at all costs.[6] Less than a century later, Carême's immensely influential successor Auguste Escoffier saw his *Guide to Modern Cookery* (1907: the quotations that follow are from the Preface) as a means of keeping up when 'everything is so unstable in these times of progress at any cost'. 'Novelty,' he lamented, 'is the universal cry – novelty by hook or by crook! […] Novelty! […] it is demanded by everyone,' most particularly those of 'inordinate wealth'. Competition among consumers sustained and exacerbated competition among producers and creators. The 'new-fangled habits' of the day required 'novel methods of Cookery'. Knowing himself to be in the forefront of the culinary revolution, Escoffier felt it imperative that he provide a record of the changes even as, 'judging from the rate at which things are going', he anticipated that a 'fresh selection of recipes' would be necessary in a few years.

On the one hand, as his incredibly influential *Guide* shows, Escoffier was an active modernizer. On the other, he firmly believed in 'the fundamental principles of the science, which we owe to Carême, and which will last as long as Cooking itself'. In contrast to Carême, who wrote his chapters as 'treatises', definitive statements of procedures and practices, Escoffier was imbued with, even overwhelmed by a sense of flux. Where Carême could say what he needed to say about sole in twenty-eight preparations, Escoffier required III recipes, just short of four times as many. Linguistic competition mirrored the competition among diners and restaurants. What name, what preparation would be remembered? How? Why?

A name is, or can be, a condensed story. The question is the meaning of the story, and, secondarily, its veracity. Anyone who has tried to pin down the origins of dishes knows how frustrating such research can be. There is no end of stories that connect a dish to its name and to the world beyond. Oral transmission has not altogether disappeared. Not only is 'fakelore' possible, it is inevitable. Repeated ad infinitum, absent credible evidence, fantastical tales of culinary creation enjoy no less long a life. It is no wonder that etymological dictionaries – not to mention *Wikipedia* – have recourse to hypotheticals. Names are slippery, stories unreliable. Joining word to a thing, person, place or event reveals the need for narrative. We want the story behind the dish. And, lexicographers and linguists aside, few of us spend much time worrying about veracity. We are concerned, for the most part, with the meaning beyond the food disappearing from the plate in front of us.

Humans are stubborn. Diners counter the all too evident ephemerality of food with the apparent permanence of narrative. We fervently want to believe that the names of things are not arbitrary, and we make good on that belief by invoking stories.

Take *tournedos à la Rossini*, which various sites on the Internet attribute to chefs (Carême, Escoffier, Adolphe Dugléré at the Café Anglais, Rossini's chef friend Casimir Moissons) as well as to Rossini himself (a talented amateur chef). Plausible? Unlikely? Impossible? We shall never know for sure.[7] Yet we should be wary of dismissing the stories, true or false. For true *and* false in whatever mix, these tales bring past culinary worlds to life and make them part of ours, in the twenty-first century.

Cultural Consequences

A great deal more could be said about specific nominatory practices and the ways that culinary systems use names and stories to define their food practices. The modes through which we understand and talk about the foods that we grow, produce, create and consume offer glimpses into our lives as individuals and as collectivities. Names and stories, criticism and conversation, prescriptions and proscriptions reconfigure things as fully as fully human and fully social.

How does this transformation occur? First, reflection recreates the object in a different guise. Thus it is the human investment that converts earth-bound agriculture into a cultural object. Terroir does not just measure properties of the soil, it defines a cultural attitude and associated practices, particularly but by no means exclusively with respect to wine. The more we attend to objects, the more we are bound to be struck by just how much things actually 'people' our lives, and they do so because they are constituents of, and embedded in, social relationships. As agents of sociability, things can provoke, sustain or break those associations. That is, the things that humans make reach beyond the material even as they derive their power from the material. Things are above all repositories of the investments – economic, cultural, intellectual and psychic – by which we as individuals and collectivities mark, express and claim our place in the world.

Transformation is what food is all about. Cooking, eating are always becoming. Physiologically food ripens and rots. Socially, it moves from raw to cooked to consumed and discarded. Language and the practice that it expresses produce a new social product and experience through the imposition of intellectual, aesthetic and social forms. Those forms distance the experience of food from the food itself. The specialization of culinary labour creates a separate social space, defined by its material props (knives, forks) and behavioural rituals (manners).[8]

168

Language further enables and fosters the communication that sustains a group. To the degree that the meal is a shared enterprise, it deemphasizes the individual's satisfaction in favour of conviviality, that is, a collective experience. The meal is a temporary gathering to be sure, but, however provisionally, it brings people together. As Brillat-Savarin observed almost two centuries ago, the goal of the meal is to translate private desire into a collective experience and to create an experience that is incomparably greater than the individual diners.[9] Food plays a role but never on its own.[10] Pleasure at table is a profoundly social experience: 'When need [*hunger*] begins to be satisfied, **reflexion** starts up, **conversation** commences, **another order of things begins**; and the one who until then was only a consumer becomes a more or less amiable companion [*convive*]' [emphases added]. It is worth keeping in mind that a *convive* is someone with whom one lives, if only for a while, and that a companion is someone with whom one breaks bread.

This subordination of self to others in the meal explains why Brillat-Savarin considers gourmandise as 'one of the principal social ties': 'It gradually extends the spirit of **conviviality** that brings the different social classes together every day, merges them in a single goal, animates conversation and **softens the angles of ordinary inequality**' [emphases added]. Conviviality is sociability, a model for living in society.

A good meal, that is, a proper meal that fulfils its potential, then, can only be a utopia, an ideal type, a model for social relations at their smoothest and least conflictual.

Obviously, any given meal falls of this ideal. Yet every meal is a social phenomenon that transforms the private ingestion of the individual into public consumption in company. Dependent on and a product of social interaction, the meal is a preeminently social construct, the construction of which occurs through language. Talk creates a social situation that directs the individual in one direction or another. Which is to say that all of these discriminations are so many vehicles of social control – the more forms, the greater the social control.

Finally, all the names we use and the stories that we tell about ourselves and food create, maintain and modify identities. As individuals we make our own 'tastescapes', as cultures, too. In each case the tastescape – that is, the foods and the foodways associated with the group – identifies that collectivity to itself and to others.

If food is always more than food, it is also always food. I would be remiss to those whom my mother called (approvingly) Eager Eaters and the French call Gourmands, if I talked only about food talk, about the words, images and representations that transform the material into the immaterial. For food remains gloriously material, obstinately private and profoundly sensual. To return to the question with which I began, food owes its power as a thing to this dual nature. Intellectual and instinctive, aesthetic and corporeal, social and private, mind and matter – food engages all of our being, the soul no less than the body, the body no less than the soul. This is its secret and, I hazard, the secret of the success and longevity of the Oxford Symposium where we gather to celebrate food, feasts and the fellowship of the table.

Notes

1. Priscilla Parkhurst Ferguson, *Word of Mouth: What We Talk About When We Talk About Food* (Berkeley: University of California Press, 2014).
2. For one reference out of many: '*notre cuisine reconnue universelle*' (Antonin Carême, *L'Art de la cuisine française au xixe siècle* (Paris: Payot, 1994 (1833)), p. 302 [IVe Partie, chapter 4: '*Observations sur les petites sauces, en gras et en maigre*']). On Carême's culinary nationalism, see Priscilla Parkhurst Ferguson, *Accounting for Taste: The Triumph of French Cuisine* (Chicago: University of Chicago Press, 2004), pp. 49-82.
3. The power trip afforded by baptism reaches back at least to Adam, to whom is given the naming of the birds of the air and the beasts of the field. Although Adam does not create the names he bestows make communication possible.
4. The identification of France with its land was a sign of the times. It acquired culinary standing with the publication in 1809 of the first gastronomic map of France which identified each region with its distinctive products. See Le Ministère de la Culture et de la Communication, *La gastronomie dans les guides de voyage : de la richesse industrielle au patrimoine culturel, France XIXe-début XXe siècle*, Figure 1, CultureCommunication.gouv.fr <http://www4.culture.fr/patrimoines/patrimoine_monumental_et_archeologique/insitu/image.xsp?numero=&id_article=csergo-1321&no_image=1> [accessed 6 March 2016].
5. Carême, p. 110 [IIe Partie, chapter 12: '*Traité des potages de profiterolles*'].
6. Jean-Anthelme Brillat-Savarin, *Physiologie du Goût* (Paris : Charpentier, 1839 (1826)), chapter 28: '*Des Restaurateurs.*'
7. Very much aware of the impossibility of fighting against plagiarism (already bemoaned by Auguste

Escoffier in the Preface to his *A Guide to Modern Cookery* (London: Bracken Books, 1994 (1907)), contemporary chefs rather obsessively document their culinary innovations. The extreme example is the celebrated Spanish chef, Ferran Adriá, who has recorded over 1800 of his creations over the past twenty years: see the study by Pilar Opazo, *Appetite for Innovation* (New York: Columbia University Press, 2016).

8. This is the now classic analysis of Norbert Elias in *The Civilizing Process – Part I The History of Manners*, trans. by E. Jephcott (Oxford: Blackwell, 1994 (1939)). Elias argues that beginning roughly in the Renaissance an increasing division of culinary labour both translated and fostered an increasingly interdependent relationship of self to society. Reading exemplary texts ranging from the Middle Ages to the nineteenth century, Elias contends that the increasingly elaborate table manners and table settings translate a distinct, and a distinctly new relationship both between the diners and between the individual and the food. The more elaborate the manners and the setting, the greater the distance from the body and from other diners. My place at table is emphatically mine, delimited and defended by the veritable barricade of knives, forks, and glassware that came to define formal dining in the West.

9. Brillat-Savarin, *Physiologie du Goût*, chapter 14: '*Du Plaisir de la table*' and '*Portrait d'une jolie gourmande*'.

10. Brillat-Savarin's conditions for a good meal emphasize cultural production (conversation) equally with consumption: decent food, good wine, agreeable guests, and time to enjoy it all (*Physiologie du Goût*, chapter 14: '*Du Plaisir de la table*').

The Past on a Plate: Images of Ancient Feasts on Italian Renaissance Maiolica

Allison Fisher

By the nature of their subject matter, illustrations of feasts of the gods include perfect, divine bodies consuming the best of earth's bounty. Elite members of society sought to achieve such idealized bodies through a healthy diet and lifestyle, which would enable them to guide and defend their realms morally and effectively. By examining the communicative power of images of ancient feasts on maiolica, this paper seeks to uncover the critical intersections between the artistic appeal of ancient culture and the changes in eating habits that governed the behaviour of the socially-conscious elite of Renaissance Italy. Drawing on case studies of ancient imagery on *istoriato* maiolica, I will reveal how these utilitarian objects convey a wealth of information through three means: the technical process of ceramic production, the usage at tables of elite patrons and, finally, the erudite iconography embedded in the imagery itself.

The term 'maiolica' broadly describes earthenware vessels covered in a lead glaze, which is made white through the addition of tin oxide.[1] Spurred on by the development of new glazes that did not blur when the vessel was fired, maiolica painters at the turn of the sixteenth century began to explore the possibilities of painting narratives on their ceramic wares. They developed a figurative style, known as *istoriato*, 'storied'.[2] For the first time, maiolica artists represented scenes of increasing visual complexity, using subject matter from pagan mythology, ancient history and biblical episodes. In contrast to paintings in fresco or panel, maiolica decoration has the advantage of never fading with age. The process of firing the glazes renders the decoration permanent, and thus the same brilliant colours and crisp figures are as apparent as they were originally five centuries ago.

The physical production of maiolica communicates much information about the sources of artistic inspiration used by maiolica painters. During the Renaissance, artists sought to emulate the artists of the classical world by combining the antique style and lofty pagan subject matter.[3] Thus, artists flocked to Rome to study the few examples of classical art that survived, sketching the Roman Forum, Trajan's Column and sculptures in the collections of antiquarians and erudite patrons. In contrast to architects, sculptors and painters in the Renaissance, ceramic painters had very few extant classical models to follow.[4] Accounts of ancient ceramics in Renaissance collections are few, though several were known to be in the collection of Lorenzo de' Medici (1449-1492).[5] Moreover, in his *Lives of the Artists*, Giorgio Vasari noted that 'So far as we are aware, the Romans did not know of this method of painting on pottery. The ones found containing the ashes of their dead or other things have the figures hatched, with only black, red or white colouring, and never glazed or containing the modern charm and variety of painting [seen in our day]'.[6] Thus, even the few known examples of narrative classical pottery lacked the vivid colour and scenes that appealed to Renaissance audiences and artists. Because of this, and because maiolica artists often worked in pottery centres far removed from sites rich in ancient models, they sought inspiration from other sources.

Many maiolica painters did not, in fact, design their own subjects. Rather, they turned to popular works by leading artists of the day, especially Raphael, whose compositions circulated widely through drawings and engravings.[7] The *Banquet of the Gods* (Figure 1) is a prime illustration of a maiolica painter adapting a work by Raphael. The fresco was created as part of the vault decoration of an open-air loggia in the suburban villa of the merchant-banker, Agostino Chigi, around 1518 (Figure 2). The *Banquet of the Gods* depicted the celebration of the marriage of the divine Cupid with the mortal woman Psyche, related by the author Apuleius in *The Golden Ass*. Although the fresco was located in a private space, many artists came to view the work. Indeed, the sculptor Benvenuto Cellini wrote in his *Autobiography* that as a young man, he sometimes came to draw 'in the house of Agostino Chigi of Siena, where there were many beautiful paintings done by that splendid artist Raphael of Urbino'.[8] Unfortunately, there is no concrete evidence that maiolica artists, including the painter of this dish, went to Rome to study Raphael's painting directly.

Raphael's designs were available, however, to maiolica artists in the form of engravings that circulated widely across Italy. In the case of the *Banquet of the Gods*, this composition was engraved by the Master of the Die around 1530-1535 (Figure 3). Prints such as this would have been transferred from a paper drawing to the tin-glazed surface of the vessel through the method of 'pouncing'. This entailed tracing the original design on thin paper and pricking the outlines of forms with a pin. The tracing would then be placed on top of the vessel and dabbed with a cloth bag filled with charcoal dust. The charcoal passed through the pin-holes onto the ceramic, creating faint spots for the painter to connect.[9] Any evidence of the pouncing technique is, regrettably, obscured on the case studies of this paper because the outlines of the figures and spaces were filled in with pigments by the artist.[10]

The painter of the *Banquet of the Gods* dish does not follow the engraving exactly, likely indicative that he did not trace an engraving, but rather modelled his version more loosely, either drawing an image of the engraving, or drawing from a sketch of the original fresco. Regardless of his method, the artist translated a recognizable image of the *Banquet of the Gods* onto his work. On the reverse of the dish, an inscription further explains the imagery represented.[11] Any sophisticated viewer, who would know of Raphael's fresco, could therefore have easily recognized the visual quotation based on their familiarity with both the text and the image portrayed.

Beyond examining artistic sources for *istoriato* maiolica, consideration of ownership offers fruitful insights to the appeal of these objects and how they were utilized in the

Figure 1. Unknown Artist, Banquet of the Gods, *Urbino, 1541, tin-glazed earthenware, 28 cm diameter, Victoria and Albert Museum, London. © Victoria and Albert Museum, London*

Figure 2. Raphael and Workshop, Banquet of the Gods, *1518-1519, fresco, Loggia of Psyche, Villa Farnesina, Rome. Courtesy: Scala / Art Resource, NY*

173

Figure 3. Master of the Die after Raphael, Banquet of the Gods, *1530-1535, engraving, 29.4 x 49.7 cm, British Museum, London. © Trustees of the British Museum*

Renaissance. For patrons, to eat from a dish decorated with a scene from a classical text – and to espouse their knowledge of the story – reinforced their erudition to fellow diners. Specific imagery could be ordered by the patron in order to display their learnedness in classical culture, or even to ally their reputation with the heroes of antiquity. Rulers who commissioned maiolica were some of the very people most concerned with the humanist ideas of eating and health, as they needed to govern their realms morally and effectively.

Maiolica artists sourced the imagery of many dishes from classical texts, including Virgil's *Aeneid* and Ovid's *Metamorphoses*. The artists often chose texts that were widely read, and which were available in both the original Latin or in vernacular translations, making stories such as the *Aeneid* readily accessible. One example in the Louvre, portraying the *Banquet of Dido and Aeneas* (Figure 4), was created by the maiolica master, Nicola da Urbino, as part of a service ordered by Isabella d'Este, the wife of the marquis of Mantua.[12] Isabella was, in fact, one of the most discerning female art patrons of her time, commissioning works from artists such as Mantegna, Pietro Perugino and Leonardo da Vinci. In addition, she was one of the best-known maiolica patrons, ordering services of dishes from workshops in Urbino, through the intermediacy of her daughter, Eleonora Gonzaga, Duchess of Urbino.

Of the maiolica dishes considered in this paper, only the *Banquet of Dido and Aeneas* can be concretely connected with a patron. A letter from Eleonora in 1524 informs her mother about a shipment of '*vasi di terra*' from Urbino that she believes would be appropriate for Isabella's Palazzo di Porto. It is likely that this letter refers to the service produced by Nicola da Urbino for Isabella, which included the *Banquet of Dido and Aeneas*.[13] Even disregarding the letter connecting Isabella to the service, the dish is covered in her personal symbols that mark her as owner, including her coat-of-arms prominently displayed above the seated figures.[14]

Interestingly, the dish represents a particular scene from the *Aeneid* that underscores the identity of the patron.[15] In Book I of Virgil's tale, Dido, the Queen of Carthage,

174

Figure 4. Nicola da Urbino, Banquet of Dido and Aeneas, *Urbino, c. 1524, tin-glazed earthenware, 27 cm diameter, Musée du Louvre, Paris. © RMN-Grand Palais / Art Resource, NY*

gives a splendid feast for Aeneas, the wandering Trojan hero. Not only does this dish represent a virtuous female leader from antiquity with whom Isabella could identify, but the story itself derives from the *Aeneid*, written by the famed Roman poet Virgil. Virgil held a personal significance for Isabella, and the Gonzaga family that she married into, because the poet was born in the town of Mantua, where the Gonzaga ruled.[16] Guests who dined with Isabella would have immediately recognized the connection between the author of the subject-matter on the dish and their hostess, thus this interactive object was intended to foster learned dinner conversation.[17]

Maiolica dishes including the *Banquet of Dido and Aeneas* were not created as individual objects. Rather, this piece is one of twenty-four known dishes from a service ordered by Isabella for use at her rustic villa, the Palazzo di Porto.[18] The service consisted of a variety of forms, ranging from large plates to small, shallow bowls, which is typical for maiolica services commissioned in the sixteenth century.[19] Such a diversity of form is evidence of changing dining habits in Renaissance Italy. During the late Middle Ages, communal bowls and platters were used, from which diners picked out their portions with their fingers and placed their morsels on trenchers of dried bread.[20] Growing prosperity in the mid-fifteenth century led to larger quantities and greater variety of foodstuffs available, which, in turn, required a 'proliferation of forms [of tableware…] for different types of food and particular activities'.[21] Later inventories list the wide repertoire of maiolica dishes subsequently produced; the 1596 inventory of the Ducal Palace in Urbino, for example, lists maiolica wares according to their function: eggcups and salts, basins for washing hands, wine flasks, fruit bowls, plates for salads, and dishes for sweetmeats are among those vessels described.[22]

Cookbooks likewise reflect a complex array of serving dishes and an increased number of courses at which these vessels would be used.[23] Diners were now served a greater variety of foods, presented on smaller dishes; one example in Bartolomeo Scappi's cookbook of 1570, *Opera*, describes a three-course modest banquet given on a meatless Friday, at which forty guests dined. The first two courses consisted of fifty dishes, served on four hundred pieces of gold, silver and maiolica tableware. This was followed by twenty-seven desserts served in 216 bowls and dishes.[24] Through the huge number of dishes in every course, the host could announce his wealth and status to fellow guests.

The expansion of the repertory of serviceware to include many types and sizes of serving vessels and utensils reflect what the historian Richard Goldthwaite calls the 'culture of consumption' that grew to pervade Italian Renaissance culture.[25] Elite patrons like Isabella d'Este demanded all kinds of new objects to decorate their palaces and villas, from secular pictures complete with picture frames for their walls, to portraits, to forks, and elaborately-painted dishes on the table. By owning *istoriato* maiolica, and, either by displaying the dishes on a *credenza* [sideboard] or physically using the dishes at meals, an ambitious Renaissance patron could publically present their refined tastes to viewers, highlighting both new dining habits and their passion for ancient literature and culture.

Feasting iconography is the mode through which *istoriato* maiolica best represents and communicates a breadth of information about Renaissance dining habits and knowledge of classical convivial episodes.[26] Drawing on Erwin Panofsky's iconographic method of analysis, larger cultural values are suggested through considerations of the motifs popularized on maiolica dishes in the three case studies explored in this paper.[27] Beginning with the *Banquet of Dido and Aeneas*, the artist depicts the feast recounted in Virgil's *Aeneid*: Dido clutches a disguised Cupid and stares into Aeneas' eyes as the pages bring forth platters of wine and food.[28] No food is specifically represented, though the two lion-footed tables are set with small, round objects. The round objects likely correspond with small bread loaves, or buns, which would have been found on all Renaissance tables, both rich and poor. In addition to the long tradition of religious symbolism, bread was, at its most basic level, a food staple in the Mediterranean region for thousands of years. In Ovid's myth of Anius, his three daughters received a magical gift from Bacchus: whatever they touched transformed into grain, wine and oil, the foundational triad of nutrition in the ancient Graeco-Roman world.[29]

In one of the best-known dietetic texts of the Renaissance, *De honesta voluptate et valetudine* [On Right Pleasure and Good Health] by Bartolomeo Sacchi, known as Platina, the author extolls the virtues of bread, writing that 'Among the fruits of earth discovered for man's use, grain is most useful'.[30] He highlights wheat as the best grain available for human consumption, stating, 'Nothing is more productive and pleasant or more nourishing than wheat.'[31] Platina then offers advice to his reads on how to best leaven and bake the best, and he even provides a recipe for making buns of the same type that might be represented on Dido's table.[32] Platina's text was intended for elite audiences who would be concerned with the health properties of food. Maiolica artists would not necessarily have read the work, especially considering that it was written in Latin.[33] Nevertheless, Platina writes about many of the same foodstuffs that the maiolica painters would have encountered and eaten on a daily basis, including bread and buns made of wheat.

Platina's text was, in fact, part of a long literary tradition commenting on diverse foodstuffs, not simply bread. Ancient physicians, particularly Galen, linked diet with medicine. In the Galenic system, a person's physical body is dominated by four humours – blood, phlegm, yellow bile (choler) and black bile.[34] Each individual is inclined toward an excess of one particular humour, which can make them more susceptible to certain diseases or extreme humoral imbalances. Food can be used to help balance these four humours, as all comestibles have certain humoral qualities of their own.[35] The Galenic tradition was preserved in the Byzantine world, and brought to the West in Arabic texts in the eleventh and twelfth centuries. By the late fourteenth century, this information circulated across Europe through treatises and manuscripts which presented the information about food in tabulated form for the elite audiences of Northern Italian courts.[36] In an age when life expectancy was low and diseases rife, dietetic writings provided advice to elite members of society on a healthy diet and lifestyle, which would enable them to optimally guide and defend their realms.

A final example of *istoriato* maiolica provides further insight into the aesthetic and alimentary tastes of elite Renaissance diners. Two versions of the *Feast of Achelous* survive, one in London and a second in New York (Figures 5 and 6). According to Ovid's *Metamorphoses*, when the hero Theseus returned home from hunting the Calydonian boar, he was invited to dine with the river god Achelous.[37] Ovid does not focus on the meal served by the deity; rather he describes that the guests were served by nymphs, and 'a feast was set upon the tables, and then when the food had been removed, [the nymphs] set out the wine in jewelled cups'.[38] The artists of the two dishes did not have a composition by Raphael on which to base their illustrations and, while I suspect there is a common visual source for the two examples, I have yet to uncover a model in my research.[39] The London dish portrays Theseus and his companions, all dressed in *all'antica* muscled cuirasses, in the company of Achelous, identified by a rippling yellow drapery. The diners are served not by the naked nymphs described by Ovid, but rather by two satyr-like figures, whose lower bodies curl into vegetal tendrils. On the table is a platter of small fish, two larger fish and two nautilus shells. All of the foodstuffs and tableware have associations with water, which is fitting for a banquet hosted by a river god.

177

Figure 5. Unknown Artist, Feast of Achelous, *Venice, c. 1550-1560, tin-glazed earthenware, 30 cm diameter, Victoria and Albert Museum, London. © Victoria and Albert Museum, London*

Figure 6. Unknown Artist, Feast of Achelous, *Venice, second half of sixteenth century, tin-glazed earthenware, 39.7 cm diameter, Metropolitan Museum of Art, New York. Courtesy: www.metmuseum. org*

The New York *Feast of Achelous* offers further variety of comestible delicacies on the table. Scattered between the shell serving platters of fish are a number of varieties of ripe fruits, including cherries, grapes, pears and plums. Considering that the dish represents the banquet of a marine god, the viewer might not anticipate the breadth of terrestrial fruit rendered. However, fruit are found in many other Renaissance paintings of ancient banquets. For example, in Piero di Cosimo's *Battle of the Lapiths and Centaurs* (Figure 7), the picnic celebration of the human Lapiths has been interrupted by a group of intoxicated satyrs, one of whom wears a girdle of grapes. A basket of flowers and fruit has been forgotten by the revellers in the violent foray between the two groups. One of the most famous paintings representing a *Feast of the Gods* is Giovanni Bellini's canvas of 1514-1529 (Figure 8). This work shows a convivial group of nymphs and deities enjoying wine in the out-of-doors. Prominently featured in the foreground is a blue and white bowl, possibly in the style of Chinese ceramics, filled with grapes and peaches. Fruit, during the Middle Ages and Renaissance, was associated with the elite and considered a status symbol at wealthy tables. The natural order of the world held that because vegetables, particularly onions and beans, grew either underground or low to the ground, they should therefore be eaten by the poor, the lowest levels of human society. Fruit, in contrast, which grew in trees, was prized for the tables of the elite. The more aerial the origin of the food, the more appropriate that it be consumed by the highest members of society.[40] Although, as the ancient authors reveal, the Olympian gods ate ambrosia and drank nectar, virtually all of the images of ancient feasts in Renaissance art represent the classical deities consuming earthly fruit. Such foods would only have been available to human diners when in season, but their presence in these utopian images of immortals serves as another reminder that the gods are not bound by terrestrial limitations.

By the very title of his treatise, Platina links the themes of pleasure and health in the diet of his intended audience of sophisticated elites, corresponding to the examples of maiolica explored in this paper. As Platina announces at the beginning of his text, he aims to 'speak about the pleasure which derives from continence in food and those things which human nature seeks': a pleasure which Renaissance patrons of maiolica clearly sought.[41] Such linkages between food, health, pleasure and knowledge underscore the themes that antique feasts represented on *istoriato* maiolica communicate to the viewer. Although perceived as utilitarian tableware, *istoriato* maiolica dishes reveal to us a wealth of information about Renaissance dining habits, social and alimentary hierarchies and classical tastes. Examining the technical process of creating maiolica furthers our present understanding of how artists were influenced by the *all'antica* compositions of Raphael. In addition, explorations of the patronage and practical usage of maiolica at elite tables, such as those of Isabella d'Este, underscore how maiolica reflects the transformations in eating habits, which became more varied and individualized, requiring vast numbers and forms of vessels. This paper has also demonstrated that, through feast iconography, we can read into these dishes attitudes towards specific foods, like fruit and bread. Like the food described in *De honesta voluptate et valetudine*, maiolica dishes with scenes of ancient feasts embody both pleasure and health through the beautiful, elaborate imagery of the past on a plate.

Figure 7. Piero di Cosimo, Battle of Lapiths and Centaurs, *probably 1500-1514, oil on wood, 71 x 260 cm, National Gallery, London. © National Gallery, London / Art Resource, NY*

179

Figure 8. Giovanni Bellini and Titian, Feast of the Gods, *1514-1529, oil on canvas, 170.2 x 188 cm, Widener Collection, National Gallery, Washington, DC. Courtesy: National Gallery of Art, Washington*

Notes

1. Lisa Boutin, 'Displaying Identity in the Mantuan Court: The Maiolica of Isabella d'Este, Federico II Gonzaga, and Margherita Paleologha' (PhD dissertation, UCLA, 2011), p. 6. This is in contrast to majolica, which refers to lead-glazed earthenware pottery produced during the nineteenth century in Britain, Europe and the USA.

2. J.V.G. Mallet, *Xanto: Pottery-Painter, Poet, Man of the Italian Renaissance*, exhib. cat. The Wallace Collection, London, 25 January-15 April 2007 (London: Paul Holberton, 2007), p. 10.

3. David Cast has written extensively on the comparison between Renaissance artists and Apelles, including *The Calumny of Apelles: A Study in the Humanist Tradition* (New Haven: Yale University Press, 1981).

4. John Varriano, *Tastes and Temptations: Food and Art in Renaissance Italy* (Berkeley: University of California Press, 2009), pp. 164-65.

5. Varriano, p. 165; also Laurie Fusco and Gino Corti, *Lorenzo de' Medici: Collector and Antiquarian* (Cambridge: Cambridge University Press, 2006), pp. 72-73.

6. Giorgio Vasari, *The Lives of the Painters, Sculptors and Architects*, trans. A.B. Hinds, ed. William Gaunt, 4 vols. (London: Dent, 1963), IV, p. 20. For the Italian, see Vasari, *Le Vite de'più eccellenti pittori, scultori, ed architettori*, ed. G. Milanesi (Florence: Sansoni, 1906), VI, pp. 581-82.

7. For a discussion on the use of engravings of Raphael's work by maiolica artists, see Giuseppe Liverani, '*La fortuna di Raffaello nella maiolica*', in *Raffaello, L'opera, le fonti, la fortuna*, ed. Mario Salmi, 2 vols. (Novara: Istituto geografico De Agostini, 1968), II, pp. 671-708.

8. Benvenuto Cellini, *Autobiography*, trans. George Bull (London: Penguin Books, 1956), p. 28.

9. Elisa Sani, *Italian Renaissance Maiolica* (London: V & A Publishing, 2012), p. 30.

10. However, pricked engravings associated with maiolica dishes from the seventeenth and eighteenth centuries survive in a variety of collections. See, for example, nos. 202-03, 205-07, and 217-22 in Catherine Hess, *Maiolica in the Making: The Gentili/Barnabei Archive* (Los Angeles: The Getty Research Institute, 1999).

11. '*Fanse le noze splendide e reale / non senza molt festa e allegrezza / Lalato iddio con la pharetra e istrale / En grenbo a psiche nel ambrosia apprezza / Gioye Giunone egli altri dei inmortali / Tuti hor ragionan di lor gran bellezze / E cosi a mensa stando spargon le ore / Fiorette intoneno di souaue odore 1541*', as transcribed in Bernard Rackham, *Catalogue of Italian Maiolica*, 2 vols. (London: HMSO, 1977), I, no. 903, p. 301.

12. The maiolica collecting habits of Isabella and her family, including her son Federico Gonzaga, have been explored in great detail by scholars, such as Mallet and Boutin, who stress her *all'antiqua* taste and personal interest in commissions. See, for example, Boutin, 'Displaying Identity'; Boutin, 'Dining in the Gonzaga Suburban Palaces: The Use and Reception of *Istoriato* Maiolica', *Predella Journal of the Visual Arts*, 33 (2013), pp. 103-15; J.V.G. Mallet, 'Mantua and Urbino: Gonzaga Patronage of Maiolica', *Apollo*, 113 (July 1981), pp. 162-69.

13. Boutin, 'Displaying Identity', p. 40. Eleonora Gonzaga to Isabella d'Este, 15 November 1524, Archivio Stato di Mantova, AG, b. 1070, c.41 Or. Letter originally published in Mariarosa Palvarini Gobio Casali, *La ceramica a Mantova* (Ferrara: Belriguardo, 1987), pp. 211-12. See also Mariarosa Palvarini Gobio Casali, '*Ceramiche a Mantova al tempo dei Gonzaga*', in *Una 'credenza' istoriata per Isabella d'Este. Il servizio di Nicola d'Urbino interpretato da Ester Mantovani*, eds. Daniela Ferrari and Mariarosa Palvarini Gobio Casali, exhib. cat. Madonna della Vittoria, Mantua, 30 November 2014-18 January 2015 (Mantua: Universitas Studiorum, 2015), pp. 7-49 (p. 21).

14. The Louvre dish is compared with a similar example in the Petit Palais in Paris. See the entry by Françoise Barbe in *Majolique: La faïence italienne au temps des humanistes 1480-1530*, eds. Françoise Barbe and Thierry Crepin-Leblond, exhib. cat. Musée national de la Renaissance, château d'Ecouen, 11 October 2011-6 February 2012 (Paris: RMN-Grand Palais, 2011), no. 67, p. 126.

15. The Louvre *Dido and Aeneas* was also adapted from an engraving after a design by Raphael. See Christian Kleinbub, 'Raphael's *Quos Ego*: forgotten document of the Renaissance *paragone*', *Word and Image*, 28 (2012), pp. 287-301; Lawrence Nees, '*Le "Quos Ego" de Marc-Antoine Raimondi: L'adaptation d'une source antique par Raphael*', *Nouvelles de l'estampe*, 40-41 (1978), pp. 18-29.

16. Indeed, Isabella was so fond of her adopted city that she promoted other works to commemorate Virgil, including a campaign in 1499 to replace a lost statue of the poet. Boutin, 'Displaying Identity', p. 115.

17. On *all'antica* banquets, see Guendalina Ajello Mahler, '*Ut picture convivial*: Heavenly Banquets and Infernal Feasts in Renaissance Italy', *Viator*, 38.2 (2007), pp. 235-64. For a detailed discussion on the literary tradition of erudite table talk, see Michel Jeanneret, *A Feast of Words: Banquets and Table Talk in the Renaissance*, trans. Jeremy Whiteley and Emma Hughes (Oxford: Basil Blackwell, 1991).

18. Palvarini Gobio Casali, 'Ceramiche a Mantova al tempo dei Gonzaga,' p. 33; Boutin, 'Displaying Identity,' p. 4 presents a table detailing the subject matter, shape, and diameter of twenty-three pieces from the service.

19. Richard Goldthwaite cites the example of a service of 84 pieces commissioned in 1517 for Filippo Strozzi's wife: Goldthwaite, 'The Economic and Social World of Italian Renaissance Maiolica,' *Renaissance Quarterly*, 42 (1989), p. 20. Other services ordered by the Gonzaga family have only a handful of known extant pieces, as demonstrated by Boutin, 'Displaying Identity,' p. 5.

20. Varriano, p. 160; also Norbert Elias, *The Civilizing Process*, trans. Edmund Jephcott (Oxford and Cambridge, MA: Blackwell, 1994), pp. 45, 53-54.

21. Sani, pp. 117-119; also Mallet, 'Mantua and Urbino,' p. 167.

22. Sani, p. 116.

23. Sani, p. 119.

24. Varriano, pp. 15-16; also Bartolomeo Scappi, *The Opera of Bartolomeo Scappi* (1570): *l'arte et prudenza d'un maestro cuoco*, trans. Terrence Scully (Toronto: University of Toronto Press, 2008), pp. 397-400.

25. Varriano, pp. 160-161; also Richard Goldthwaite, *Wealth and the Demand for Art in Italy*, 1300-1600 (Baltimore: Johns Hopkins University Press, 1993), pp. 212-43.

26. Interestingly, as Marcia Reed explores in her paper at this symposium, images of feasting and food during the Renaissance do not tend to show specific foods or ingredients. See also Marcia Reed, 'Court and Civic Festivals', in *The Edible Monument: The Art of Food for Festivals*, ed. Marcia Reed, exhib. cat. The Getty Research Institute, 13 October 2015-13 March 2016 (Los Angeles: Getty Publications, 2015), pp. 27-72, at p. 33.

27. Erwin Panofsky, *Studies in Iconology: Humanistic Themes in the Art of the Renaissance* (Oxford: Oxford University Press, 1939; rpt. New York: Harper & Row, 1972), pp. 3-31.

28. Virgil, *Aeneid*, trans. H. Rushton Fairclough, Loeb Classical Library (Cambridge, MA: Harvard University Press, 1999), I, 695-722.

29. Ovid, *Metamorphoses*, trans. Frank Justus Miller, Loeb Classical Library, 2 vols. (London: William Heinemann, 1916; 2nd ed. 1984), XIII, 650-654. See also Massimo Montanari, 'Food Systems and Models of Civilization', in *Food: A Culinary History from Antiquity to the Present*, eds. Jean-Louis Flandrin and Massimo Montanari, trans. Clarissa Botsford et al. (New York: Columbia University Press, 1999), pp. 69-78 (p. 71).

30. Platina, *On Right Pleasure and Good Health*, ed. and trans. Mary Ella Milham, Medieval and Renaissance Texts and Studies, 168 (Tempe, AZ, 1998), I, 14. For a thorough study of Platina, see Bruno Laurioux, *Gastronomie, humanisme et société à Rome au mileu du XVe siècle: autour du De honesta voluptate de Platina* (Florence: Edizioni del Galluzzo, 2006).

31. Platina, I, 14.

32. Platina, I, 15.

33. Although five Italian editions had been printed by 1515, as explored by Timothy Tomasik, 'Translating Taste in the Vernacular Editions of Platina's *De Honesta Voluptate et Valetudine*', in *At the Table: Metaphorical and Material Cultures of Food in Medieval and Early Modern Europe*, eds. Timothy Tomasik and Juliann Vitullo (Turnhout: Brepols, 2007), pp. 189-210.

34. Humoral theory is derived from Hippocratic sources (5th century BCE), Plato (426 -347 BCE), Aristotle (384-322 BCE), and was later promoted in the teachings of Galen (131-201 CE). In addition to the physical body of humans, the whole universe operates on these imbalances, including the seasons,

the natural world and the planets. For a history of the humoral theory, see Raymond Klibansky, Erwin Panofsky and Fritz Saxl, *Saturn and Melancholy: Studies in the History of Natural Philosophy, Religion and Art* (London: Nelson, 1964).

35. See, for instance, Ken Albala, *Eating Right in the Renaissance* (Berkeley: University of California Press, 2002), pp. 19-20; p. 49.

36. Cathleen Hoeniger, 'The Illuminated *Tacuinum sanitatis* Manuscripts from Northern Italy c. 1380-1400: Sources, Patrons, and the Creation of a New Pictorial Genre', in *Visualizing Medieval Medicine and Natural History, 1200-1550*, AVISTA Studies in the History of Medieval Technology, Science, and Arts, eds. J. Givens, K. Reeds, and A. Toutwaite (Aldershot, UK: Ashgate, 2006), pp. 51-81.

37. Ovid, VIII, 547-576.

38. Ovid, VIII, 571-573.

39. One possibility is the 1497 vulgate edition of Ovid's *Metamorphoses*, which was illustrated. On maiolica artists using book illustrations, see Ilaria Andreoli, '"*Fabulae Artificialiter Pictae*": *Illustrazione del Libro e Decorazione Ceramica nel Rinascimento*', in *Fabulae Pictae: Miti e Storie nelle Maioliche del Rinascimento*, ed. Marino Marini (Florence: Giunti Editore, 2012), pp. 110-25.

40. Allen Grieco, 'The Social Politics of Pre-Linnaean Botanical Classification', *I Tatti Studies in the Italian Renaissance*, 4 (1991), pp. 131-49 (pp. 131-34).

41. Platina, I, Preface.

Dinner Isn't Served! : The Use of Historic Cookery as a Method of Interacting with Visitors to Hampton Court Palace

Richard Fitch

Dinner Isn't Served

For twenty-four years, the Tudor Kitchens of Hampton Court Palace have planned, cooked and presented a plethora of historical dishes for visitors to view but not consume. A veritable feast for all of the senses bar taste, historic recipes, ingredients and techniques have been used as a lens through which to view the past and as tools with which we can better interact and engage with our visitors.

In the summer of 1991, the then Historic Royal Palaces Agency concocted a marketing plan for the newly interpreted Tudor Kitchens at Hampton Court Palace. The new display in the kitchen had been conceived by curator Simon Thurley as a radical departure from the norm: while kitchens at other heritage sites had been interpreted before, his aim was to provide a display that gave the impression that the visitor was entering a working kitchen and not a static display, that they had entered the space just after the cooks had left through another other door, with fires lit and the rooms filled with food and utensils and with minimal use of barriers between object and visitor. The result was described by the *Daily Telegraph* as 'Quite the most stunning exhibition of its kind in the world'; the live interpretation which would follow this redisplay was intended to match these lofty ambitions and provide something that had not been seen before.[1]

Over four days after Christmas that year, a team of men would interpret Tudor recipes whilst dressed as cooks from the reign of Henry VIII, using period equipment and methods to show a microcosm of the kitchens in their heyday. Although open to the public, this event would be pushed heavily towards the press and media; the plan was a one-off event designed to advertise the static kitchen representation in order to attract future visitors. The team was to be overseen by the food historian Peter Brears, then Director of Leeds City Museum and responsible for the food research used in the static interpretation of the kitchen. He would be joined by three costumed interpreters, brought in from the Chiltern Open Air Museum in Buckinghamshire, who had helped to manufacture some of the replica items now adorning the newly presented kitchens. Neither food historian nor interpreters had any concept of what to expect over those four days, or in reality even what they were expected to do.

The brief was a loose one: provide costumed interpretation of recipes from the sixteenth century and cook in front of the public. Brears had minimal costumed interpretation experience, though a lifetime of experience in presenting to the public in the form of talks, presentations and lectures. In contrast, the interpreters had a wealth of experience in presenting to visitors whilst in costume and in portraying roles from the past, but absolutely no experience with the sixteenth century and extremely minimal interest in food and cooking. Similarly, the public, whose view of historic food owed more to TV and film than it did to actual history, had no idea what to expect.

The one thing that was clear from the start was that this was to be a method of interpreting and discussing history through the use of food and cooking, not an exercise in public catering. The food that would be produced was not intended for public consumption; instead, the recipes and cooking were to offer a lens through which to view the history of the kitchens and their cooks. With food and cooking not having reached the levels of mass popularity they enjoy today and with no celebrity chefs to champion the cause of historic recipes or ingredients, the notion that you could cook recipes from history and produce workable final dishes was an alien concept to most potential visitors; even as late as 2000 Gordon Ramsay declared that there was 'nothing to be learned' from historic recipes.[2]

Why Use Food and Cooking as a Focus for Interpretation?

Since a kitchen is being interpreted, food is an obvious choice to form part of the interpretation, but it could easily be relegated to being merely a bit player in a story which includes tools, equipment, people, clothes and architecture. Other areas within Hampton Court Palace and in other Historic Royal Palaces sites such as the Tower of London benefit from costumed interpretation that covers a multitude of subjects in many differing styles, but none have concentrated their efforts on the use of one single topic for as long as the kitchens have.

Food is a subject that links us; interpreter, historian and visitor alike rely on food to survive; all have at least a basic understanding and concept of cooking and recipes, and this common bond makes the use of food unique as a medium for discussion of any and all topics. Through food one can link and discuss language, politics, economics, design, mathematics, trade and geography amongst many other subjects as well as, of course, history. Like it or not, discussing mid-sixteenth century court politics within the Great Hall of Hampton Court Palace is not as easy for visitors to empathize with as it is for them to discuss food imports into England under Henry VIII whilst within the Great Kitchen; they eat imported foods, cook them in their kitchens, read about them in recipes and watch them being used by cooks on television, even if they don't often own a Great Hall themselves. Without such an initial hurdle for visitors to overcome, the interpretation staff in the kitchens have a much easier life than their counterparts working within the Tudor processional route, though of course the complete story of the building and its occupants can only be understood by both interpretation systems working together for the visitor.

In the early years of the live interpretation, the simple premise of using food and cooking as the way to disseminate historical and other information to the public took a fairly basic approach: essentially a didactic presentation of information, with cooks on one side of a line of tables and visitors on the other, purported experts presenting to an unenlightened, passive audience. This methodology established a degree of separation between visitor and interpreter that, whilst allowing for clear, unobstructed views of the cooking as well as a safety barrier between visitors and potentially dangerous heat sources and sharp tools, also built a more intangible barrier to intimate conversation and questioning. Furthermore, the onus for recipe interpretation and information in these early years fell exclusively to Brears; he was the expert and sole provider of recipe information to the visiting public and the other members of the team.

Historic recipes and information were presented orally to visitors in a manner that often reinforced the effect of reducing visitor interaction or engagement to simple questioning related solely to what had been communicated to them. Recipes were written longhand in a modernized form and kept in a back storeroom along with spare equipment and ingredients, necessitating (for all but Brears) frequent trips away from the kitchen and visitors in order to check the instructions.

That is not to say that this approach was not successful or unsuited to the visitor demographic for Hampton Court Palace at that time. Over the Christmas week of 26 December 1992 to 3 January 1993, the first true incidence of live interpretation as a visitor attraction within the kitchens, some 18,665 visitors came to see the cookery demonstration, with 2536 venturing out for the first ever opening of the palace on New Year's Day; compared to the same period the year before, revenue rose 98.9%. With figures like this the fate of the cookery demonstration was sealed and what began as a one-off event was transformed, by increasing the duration and expanding the team, into the Christmas cookery that was to continue into the foreseeable future.

Over the next several years, as the team expanded and contracted, interpreters dallied with other aspects of material culture but generally continued to acquiesce to Brears for all food research, along with the bulk of the food presentation responsibility. Visitors came, they watched a recipe being cooked, they asked questions about what they saw, then they left. In an attempt to illustrate the fate of the food in the sixteenth century, the great table within the kitchens would be laid at three o'clock as if it was in the Great Hall, the main dining room of the period, and the food prepared over the course of the day was set for a meal. The interpretation team would gather at the table, give a short presentation covering table manners and etiquette of the time and then sit down and consume the food before the eyes of the visitors.

Acting as surrogates for the visitor's taste buds, the team spent about an hour each day eating the meal whilst conversing with the assembled public, explaining the taste and texture of the dishes whilst allowing only the aromas to be sampled by them. As interesting as this was for those that could interact directly with it, or for those who came back to the display after visiting earlier in the day and who thus understood that the food being consumed before them had actually been prepared within the same kitchen, the vast majority of visitors took away an image of costumed staff eating their fill at a groaning table all day long, an image that reinforced the erroneous view of late medieval and Tudor food and dining that persists amongst the public to this day and that the interpretation at Hampton Court Palace was supposed to be countering.

Although the Brears years were undoubted fun, and thanks to the publication of his book, *All the King's Cooks: The Tudor Kitchens of King Henry VIII at Hampton Court Palace* certainly the most well-known, that period was low on specific learning outcomes for both the public and the interpretation team.[3] Despite cookery being labelled as an experimental archaeology project, those years were also devoid of any true experimentation, and they should be considered as an apprenticeship for the interpretive cooks that formed the cooking team. Things changed in 1998 when Brears left the project in order to concentrate on writing and other ventures, leaving the other members of the team to fill the vast void that his departure left with regards to knowledge of food history and recipes. In effect, being forced to begin again from scratch allowed the interpretation methodology and the food research to work much more closely together than previously, which was first put to the test with moves away from simply running cookery interpretation once a year and from sixteenth-century interpretation as well.

In 2001, an opportunity arose to look at the kitchens of Hampton Court during the second quarter of the seventeenth century. That opportunity allowed recipes to be placed at the centre of all the work that was being done with this chance at a reinvigorated interpretation. With no detailed records specific to the kitchens at Hampton Court regarding meals cooked or recipes followed, a broad selection of recipes published during the first half of the seventeenth century were chosen and compiled into a number of period-effect recipe books that would be worked from when in front of the public. (See Figure 1.) This change removed the reliance upon memorizing recipes and all of the attendant errors that followed. Unlike much recreation of historic recipes, the team decided to only work from copies of the original texts rather than from modernized versions. The hope was that having a recipe book full of transcribed original recipes would not only lead to a more faithful recreated end dish, without the errors brought about by having to memorize the recipe, but would also allow visitors to see the same information used by the interpretation team.

No longer did the audience have to be passive consumers of information presented in a didactic manner; instead, the interpretation could become much more two-way, with visitors suggesting methods and approaches and discussing the recipes and their language in ways which had not been possible before. For the first time, visitors could read the recipe as cooks of the past might have and watch the text be transformed into finished dishes before them. The recipes became central to the work of interpretation: they drove the choice of equipment and ingredients and to some extent the choice of work being done. However, the layout of the interpretive space remained as it had

*Figure 1: Facsimile seventeenth century recipe book created for public interaction.
Photo R. Fitch*

been from the very first year: a row of tables from behind which interpreters presented information to a passing audience.

Some experiential elements were included in the interpretation, such as allowing visitors to turn the spit and roast meat before the great fire or experience churning butter in a dash churn, but, although the new period of cookery being interpreted provided extended learning outcomes for the interpretation team, visitors were, in the main, left behind on this matter. That is not to say that visitor numbers were poor, or that there was a desire for a more interactive, learning based approach that was not being provided; that was simply not the case. This approach to food history was a common one, helped in no small part by the rise in historical re-enactment at sites run by English Heritage throughout the 1990s. In addition, Brears and many of the team helped to push this form of interpretation to a wider audience by providing interpretation to newly opened or reinterpreted kitchens across the country, such as those at Petworth, Harewood and Dyrham Park.

The next few years saw an expansion in the time periods recreated, from Elizabeth I through James I to George II, all with the common theme of periods that had used the Hampton Court kitchens to prepare food for the court in general, rather than focusing on specifically royal foods. All the interpretation continued to centre on the recipe as the core element; take a recipe, collect the required ingredients and tools to make it, proceed to cook that recipe in front of the visitors and discuss whilst working. While this methodology continued to produce positive feedback from visitors, it was clear that the practice would be difficult after the 2006 return to interpreting the kitchens of Henry VIII: there simply weren't enough surviving recipes to work with. That said, change was slow to evolve, as is often the case with long running projects and a team very much set

187

in their ways. Gradually elements were altered or removed, most often to fit into other palace-wide projects, but these changes were often considered experiments that would not be long lasting. It wasn't until 2010 that real changes were implemented with the removal of the meal interpretation during the Christmas cookery event that year.

By this time, the visitor demographic for the kitchens in particular and Hampton Court in general had subtly changed. Whereas the previous decade had seen visitors mostly interested in entertainment, that portion of our visitors had diminished substantially, and those attuned to expression were now the majority.[4] These visitors want more interaction: they seek to be involved during their visit rather than simply being passive consumers. This increase in those keener to question and seek out answers may have been driven by the popular rise in the fashion of food and cooking. Famous names were bringing the ideas and ingredients found in historic recipes to a much wider audience, access to better cookery information from TV shows and books flourished and the live presentation of historic recipes had to evolve and change to meet the challenges of using food as an explanatory tool for this well informed and inquisitive group.

Visitors were now coming with a level of knowledge about food that was not present before, and both the interpretive cooks and the format of the cookery events had to take this change into account. The older, didactic presentational methodology had simply had its time. The main question to be asked was: how could we improve the interpretation to capture the imagination of our new visitor segments whilst retaining the elements that made the events popular? The answer was to experiment with a new layout of the working tables: we decided to dispense with the practice that saw interpreters and audience separated by a table. By 2015 we introduced a new interpretation event to the Tudor kitchens unlike those that had come before it.

From the outset of interpretation in 1991, it was clear that any interpretation would have to involve a healthy dose of compromise if it was to involve integrating history and public access; from 2010 to the present, that awareness has been ever more present in the cookery interpretation. Professor Christopher Woolgar was quite correct when he wrote that 'the false emotion of nostalgia and the accidents and inventions of heritage must not be confused with the realities of medieval society'.[5] Yet that invention of heritage is precisely what must happen for visitors to engage in any meaningful way when visiting a heritage site such as Hampton Court Palace, a building which was the epitome of exclusivity when operating as the home of Henry VIII's court, yet is now operating as a fully inclusive visitor attraction. The kitchens were never an intended destination for visitors originally so any interpretation of that space that includes them will always be an invention of heritage; at best we must strike a delicate balance between compromise and authenticity. This comes even more to the fore when considering the actual historic use of the only large space available for use today, the Great Kitchen, which in its heyday was used purely for the roasting of meat for the court and not the delicate, more complex cookery that surviving recipes allow to be demonstrated; yet it is these recipes which are of most interest to the visiting public.[6]

The Compromise

Clearly if the building was designed and used for roasting, yet the more complex surviving recipes are the more publicly interesting, then the obvious solution is to interpret both: since this approach has been used from the very beginning of interpretation back in 1991, what has changed? First, the old-fashioned arrangement of working tables separating interpreter from visitor has been dispensed with. In part, this layout had been utilized to keep the public away from the actual cooking area and the charcoal fires burning within the cooking range. (See Figure 2.) However, the use of the seventeenth-century range and the damage that this use incurred had always sat uneasily with the Conservation and Collections Care Department, and any change that could reduce possible damage and increase the life of the building fabric in line with our principal Cause should be considered a good one.[7] With that in mind, the line of tables keeping visitors on one side and forming a barrier across the room has been altered to an island of tables within the middle of the space, giving the public three hundred and sixty degree access to the cookery interpretation.

This simple alteration has had remarkable implications to the way food and cooking are now interpreted, as with this new layout visitors can literally see what the interpreter sees when reconstructing a recipe; they can now stand next to or behind the cook. (See Figure 3.) Allowing visitors to view the work from these different angles has helped to promote a deeper level of information exchange. In addition, a revamped risk assessment and a fresh look at the recipes chosen to be interpreted has had just as profound an effect: now, except for working with knives or directly manipulating the heat sources (which now sit safely in the middle of the tables), visitors can interact with the cookery tasks themselves if they wish. Such interaction was simply not possible with the previous arrangement of tables, but it springs naturally from having the interpreters work within their audience rather than presenting towards them.

This change has not been an easy one for the interpretation team to accommodate; having people immediately beside and behind you, entering personal space and suddenly being able to touch and engage directly with the objects you are working with is no small matter, especially whilst presenting information and cooking at the same time. If an interpreter steps away to get fresh ingredients, equipment or simply take a break, it is often very difficult to negotiate a way back through the crowd or to ensure a clear workspace. Similarly, visitors are no longer afforded clear, uninterrupted views of the cookery work.

However the plus points far outweigh these minor negative ones. The interpretation feels fresher and less old fashioned, a feeling which is passed on to the visitors by the interpreters;. Conversations regarding food, history and associated topics have become more in-depth with no detrimental effect on visitor satisfaction. Most interestingly, the actual levels of cookery have diminished: it is the interaction and information exchange that is important rather than the food itself.

The second change is the implementation of a new series of interpretation events

189

Figure 2: Original arrangement of working tables, separating visitors from interpreters. Photo R. Fitch

Figure 3: Working 'in the round' with working tables forming an island giving all round access. Photo T. Love

focussing on roasting, the principal task of the kitchens at Hampton Court Palace. Unfortunately, the current approach distracts from that fact: surviving recipes from history make it possible to display a more interesting, varied and exotic look at food and cooking from the past with a broad spread of ingredients, tools and techniques. Yet the kitchens at Hampton Court were originally designed for the primary task of roasting meat, the main foodstuff for the court of Henry VIII.[8] The largest surviving building and the principal area available for live interpretive cookery is the Great Kitchen with its six large roasting fireplaces; one is still in a useable condition and contains a fire almost every day of the year. Since 1991, the roasting fire and its use in history has featured in all of the cookery interpretation and is always popular with visitors, especially on cold wet days! In that time, though, it has been treated in a supporting role to the more instantly interesting recipe based interpretation. That position is now in the process of being reversed; as Professor Woolgar implied, we must strive to show visitors what was done in the building, not what we would like to have been done. Thus, taking the mantra of history where it happened, the aim is to deliver interpretation that clearly shows the visiting public what the original function of the building was – roasting meat on a large scale – rather than for the complex recipe based work that previous interpretation gave the impression as being the norm.

To that end, a plan has been conceived to conduct daily roasting for the five summer months of 2015. Unlike previous interpretation, this project will see meat roasted daily in front of the great fire within the kitchens, bringing food and cookery interpretation to a much wider audience than before. The roasting will allow visitors to interact with the task and turn the spit themselves, experiencing the heat of the fire first hand. This personal contact with the task engenders a greater level of interaction with the interpretation staff, which in turn allows for a greater level of information transfer or, at the very least, a greater opportunity to take part compared to passive viewing. It also concentrates interpretive efforts on a cooking task that, whilst fundamental to the public's view of food and feasting as well as synonymous with Henry VIII, is rarely shown to the same scale at the majority of heritage sites within the country.

Public Consumption of the Food

So why not allow the food to be consumed? In essence, the interpretation was never set up with public consumption in mind; it was and is an exercise in history, not catering. The aim is to try to learn from practical experience, as well as traditional research methods, how the spaces could have been utilized in the past, and to allow the public to view and interact with this learning process. However, part of the planning work for the daily roasting considered the possibility of providing food for the public, starting with investigating what was believed to be the desire of most of the visitors. In actual fact, though, surveys have shown us that while 73% of our visitors would like there to be food sampling, only 11% actually ask about trying the food they see being prepared and only 36% thought there would be sampling of the food, an expectation that was only considered after prompting to find their opinion. In short, the majority of visitors have no thoughts as to eating the food cooked during cookery interpretation, and it is only after prompting that they express an opinion one way or the other. This is fortunate, because investigations into providing roasted meat to visitors have shown that meeting current health and hygiene requirements whilst delivering a high quality, high accuracy interpretation is close to impossible, especially for an organization which prides itself on providing a better than gold standard product for the visiting public. That is not to say that the roasting or indeed any of the other regular cookery interpretation through the year is lacking in an end result. The one-hundred-and-fifty-one days of roasting and thirty-nine other cooking days in the interpretive year 2015 will provide ample opportunity to interact with visitors as well as to collect new data on roasting times, temperatures, fuel expended etc. that will help us to learn more about these fascinating buildings.

Final Thoughts

It is important to understand that food and cookery used for interpretation purposes do not have to be used solely for eating. The ubiquitous nature of these subjects and items allows them to function as a link to a wealth of other topics, in turn opening these up to an audience far wider than might normally be considered. The work done on public history and food interpretation within the kitchens at Hampton Court Palace shows that, when used as a catalyst for discussion and questioning rather than simply as a meal, food has the ability to link together a wide and diverse number of subjects and audiences, and that although the vehicle for a message is an important choice, it is the message that is the important thing to pass on, all of which food can do without being served.

Notes

1. Simon Thurley, 'Historic Royal Palaces', SimonThurley.com, 2014 <http://simonthurley.com/historic-royal-palaces/> [accessed 15 May 2015].
2. *Ever Wondered? : Food*, Open University, BBC2, 2000, various dates.
3. Peter Brears, *All the King's Cooks: The Tudor Kitchens of King Henry VIII at Hampton Court Palace* (London: Souvenir Press, 1999).
4. These categories come from the Culture Segments system developed by Morris Hargreaves McIntyre to analyze audiences like those of Hampton Court: see 'Entertainment Pen Portrait | Morris Hargreaves McIntyre' <http://mhminsight.com/articles/a-pen-portrait-of-one-of-the-8-culture-segments-enter-tainment-495> [accessed 15 May 2015] and 'Expression Pen Portrait | Morris Hargreaves McIntyre' <http://mhminsight.com/articles/expression-pen-portrait-505> [accessed 15 May 2015].
5. Christopher Woolgar, *The Great Household in Late Medieval England: A Life* (New Haven, CT: Yale University Press, 1999), p. 204.
6. Simon Thurley, 'The Sixteenth-Century Kitchens at Hampton Court', *Journal of the British Archaeological Association*, 143 (1990), pp. 1-28 (p. 15) <http://dx.doi.org/10.1179/jba.1990.143.1.1>.
7. Thurley, 'The Sixteenth-Century Kitchens at Hampton Court', p. 9; Historic Royal Palaces, 'Cause and Principles | Historic Royal Palaces' <http://www.hrp.org.uk/aboutus/whoweare/causeandprinciples> [accessed 15 May 2015].
8. *A Collection of Ordinances and Regulations for the Government of the Royal Household, Made in Divers Reigns: From King Edward III to King William and Queen Mary, Also Receipts in Ancient Cookery* (London: Society of Antiquaries, 1790), pp. 174-92.

Framework for a New Culinary Arts Curriculum

Peter Hertzmann

Modern chef training resembles an informal version of the traditional apprentice system. Unfortunately, most culinary schools graduate students are ill prepared to work in a commercial kitchen environment. Even graduates who are able to successfully work in novice kitchen positions are seldom able to actually cook. The culinary schools producing these weak graduates have their curriculum partly to blame. In this paper, a framework for a new culinary school curriculum is proposed that follows a modern medical education model rather than an apprenticeship model.

The old method of learning a skilled trade was to be apprenticed to a master. After many years of training, the skilled apprentice was promoted to the position of journeyman. Additional experience and testing was then required before the journeyman advanced to being a master. Today, building-trades apprentices cannot earn a license solely with fieldwork. They must endure a prescribed number of hours of classroom work and pass written tests. Apprentices must learn job-related science, customs and codes besides learning how to use their tools.[1]

In a similar manner, physicians and surgeons commence their training with two years classroom work followed by two additional years of observation with minor hands-on experience before they begin their true practical training.[2] The final portion of their training, the part that takes place after they legally become medical doctors, may last as little as three years for physicians entering the practice of internal medicine or as long as six years for surgeons learning neurosurgery or plastic surgery.[3] Some doctors add to their knowledge by completing supplementary subspecialty training as part of a multi-year fellowship.[4]

The major difference between training a carpenter and training a physician, other than actual course content, is that a significant portion of medical training involves both the overt and covert training of the students to think like doctors. Depending upon the realm of medicine of interest to the candidate, future physicians are trained to think like physicians and surgeons are trained to think like surgeons.[5]

Current Training Methods

Restaurant cooks follow one of two paths to attain their position in the kitchen. Either they enter the kitchen as a novice and learn their trade 'on the job', or they attend a cooking school and then enter the kitchen as a novice doing the same work they would do without their diploma. I have yet to meet a chef who has hired a culinary school graduate with no previous restaurant experience where the new cook didn't need to start at the bottom of the kitchen hierarchy. Many chefs tell me that they avoid inexperienced graduates because they often 'think they know it all'.[6]

There are chefs that require new cooks to have some form of certification or diploma to be hired as most culinary schools provide classroom work in sanitation and food safety before drilling the principles into the student's mind during the practical portion of their program.[7]

Cooking schools may be for-profit or non-profit organizations. They may be publicly operated or privately owned. An individual cooking school may have no accreditation and issue a simple diploma or certificate of completion, or the school may be fully accredited as a university and have both degree and certificate programs. The formal program may be as short as a few months of part-time participation or as long as four years of full-time attendance. The emphasis at some schools is all aspects of restaurant work or even the entire food industry while others spend all their time in the kitchen preparing recipes.[8]

Modern Culinary Education Problems

'Because someone goes into culinary school doesn't mean they're wired for it.'[9]

'We have a generation [of graduates] that's not passionate about what they're doing.'[10]

'It's hard to find motivated students.… Students from City College have a better attitude.'[11]

Young cooking school graduates are often unwilling to put in the long hours required by fine-dining restaurants. The range of students completing cooking school is as great as the differences in the individual students modified by the program they attended. Mature students tend to take better advantage of the educational opportunities provided by the schools and have more realistic expectations of the work opportunities awaiting graduation. As one chef put it, 'If you don't have a base of life going [into cooking school], you're not going to get it in school.'[12]

In the class environment, students usually work as groups to produce a few dishes for the class to taste, or they work singularly to produce two or three complete dishes. Whatever their range of education, 'most students are rarely ready to work in a [restaurant] kitchen'.[13] They are unprepared to work a station by themselves on even a moderate evening.

Most cooking schools ignore large sections of the food preparation industry. One chef noted, 'Schools prepare students to cook in restaurants or hotels, not other food-industry jobs'; another said, 'I would be reluctant to hire a recent cooking school graduate. Six months is too little time to learn what you need to know.'[14]

Unfortunately, when most students finish their culinary school education, they still do not know how to cook; as one chef explained, 'It took ten years after school to learn how to cook.'[15] Students have learned how to prepare recipes but not how to cook. When I get into discussions with recent cooking school graduates and even some chefs, I pose a couple of challenges for them to think about. The first is to choose any primary ingredient, such as a meat or a vegetable, and quickly tell me ten ways to cook it without resorting to simply changing a sauce or some other simple variation. I want ten totally different preparations. The second challenge is to take ten recipes for different types of dishes and tell me, if there is one, the non-flavour or taste purpose of each ingredient. Knowing how to cook is not a matter of knowing how to complete recipes, it is knowing how to prepare complete meals given a basket of raw food without having to first find a recipe. As one culinary instructor I work with always says, 'You cook with the ingredients you have, not the ones you wished you had.'[16]

Students today are expected to understand basic arithmetic when they enter cooking school, yet many cannot multiply two fractions or even two decimal numbers when they graduate. Worse, they are incapable of estimating numerical results without the use of a calculator. Students today do not understand weights and measures or the concepts of accuracy and precision. Culinary school graduates have, at best, a rudimentary knowledge of ingredients and usually no knowledge of their interaction. They don't understand heat transfer and heat flow. They don't understand how proteins react to heat, or the difference between non-enzymatic and enzymatic browning. Students do not understand how basic appliances work. Yes, they can turn a blender on and off, but they do not understand how blade design, motor horsepower and tip speed can affect the minimum particle size in a puree or how particle size affects mouth feel. Today's graduates do not know the difference between hype and reality. They do not understand that the terms 'kosher' and 'sea' have no meaning past their marketing benefits when used as adjectives for salt. Most do not understand how to choose the right whisk, or even how to properly use a cook's knife.

A Proposal for a New Curriculum

The education received by students in the culinary arts needs to be closer in process to the education afforded medical students. The culinary student should receive an extensive education in the fundamentals of cooking, supported by appropriate laboratory experiences, before moving into the kitchen to prepare dishes.

The remainder of this paper is a proposal for a framework for a new curriculum to be taught in culinary schools.[17] The new curriculum framework is based on the fundamentals of food and its preparation rather than learning a series of recipes without an understanding of why the steps of a particular recipe matter. As a matter of completeness, baking in all forms is considered integral to the culinary arts and not treated as a separate subject. The curriculum framework does not distinguish between pastry and cooking. The new curriculum framework also contains elements designed to motivate and challenge the culinary student to be more responsible and mature upon graduation.

The first phase of the proposed curriculum framework emphasizes the fundamentals of cooking without reverting to food preparation. Laboratory work completed by the student is designed to complement the student's classroom work. For example, to complement the discussion about heat transfer, an exercise shall be performed to look at the relationship of hob type to pan materials. Each student would be responsible to run the exercise for different configurations and illustrate the results. The goal would be for the student to learn that the best heat transfer coefficient may not produce the most even heating of the surface of the pan. Because this is a test that cannot be rushed, the student needs to learn patience. Because multiple tests can be run simultaneously, the student needs to learn multi-tasking since it is rare for a cook in a professional kitchen to perform only one task at a time.

The first phase is also meant to be rigorous. Satisfactory completion of all classwork, laboratory exercises and course tests would be required to progress to the next level of learning. This will be difficult for many potential students who lack the prerequisite skills. For this reason, parts of the coursework, such as the mathematics, are intended to be somewhat remedial, and students already well versed in portions of the coursework would be able to 'test out' of these portions. Even with extra effort, it is expected that many students will not advance to Phase 2 of the program.

This coursework is designed to be part of an all-inclusive program. There are programs designed specifically to be the opposite. As one cooking school course syllabus states: 'The whole purpose of the course is to get you a job in the culinary field. The purpose of the course is NOT to teach you how to cook'.[18] Upon starting the course at the school, each student acknowledges this statement in writing. The primary goal of this proposed curriculum framework *is* to teach students how to cook with the secondary goal of learning to do so in a professional environment. Most of what is taught during the first phase of the curriculum framework cannot be learned 'on the job' through *staging* or apprenticing. It must be taught in a classroom and laboratory environment.

The second phase of the curriculum framework immerses the student in the different techniques of cooking but still without recipes. For example, to learn how to braise a dish, the student would combine the just-learned principles of braising with information about ingredients, flavour, heat, equipment, etc., and propose a plan for a preparation. After discussion with the instructor, the student would complete the preparation and critique the results. The process would be completed multiple times using a variety of ingredients for each technique.

The final phase of the curriculum framework has the student preparing many classical preparations from recipes provided by the instructor and or researched by the student. The student would, at the same time, create a variation of the dish intended to be simpler or modern. Part of the grading would be based on how far from the original the new dish journeyed while still being recognised as being that dish.

Additionally, as part of their last phase of training, students will be required to prepare the full gamut of culinary dishes using the ingredients provided by the instructor and no written recipes. Class after class, the students will demonstrate that they truly know how to cook.

During the entire program, students will be required to wash and maintain all equipment used during classes and or laboratory exercises. They will be responsible for storage of unused food items, sweeping and mopping the floor and disposal of waste.

Missing from the program is training for the student in how to work a station during a meal rush. This can be best learned in the real situation and not one simulated in the classroom. Students may participate in some form of externship as part of the course requirements, but the externship may not be used as an alternative to completing the curriculum.

The most common complaint that I heard from chefs who could and or do hire the graduates of culinary schools was that the current supply of students are not passionate about cooking. Being able to cook competently is not enough. Thus an additional goal of this curriculum framework is to produce graduates who are, ultimately, both passionate about food and passionate about cooking.

Framework Phase I

Kitchen Math
    Longhand arithmetic of decimal numbers
    Longhand arithmetic with currency
    Longhand arithmetic of fractions
    Conversion of fractions to and from decimal numbers
    Longhand arithmetic of time
        Reading analogue clocks and timers
    Division of shapes
    Graphing
    Calculating yield
    Calculating concentration
    Understanding simple statistics
        Correlation vs. causation
    Estimation
    Measuring
        Units of measure
        Archaic units
        Geographical differences
    Scaling
    Precision and accuracy
Microbiology for cooks
    Microbes [bacteria, fungi, protista, viruses, parasitic worms, prions]

Foodborne illness
    Viruses sicken, bacteria kill
    Contamination sources
    Symptoms vs. microbe
    Determining infectious dose
    Role of personal hygiene
Common misconceptions
Food-related pathogens [worms, fungi, protists, bacteria, viruses, prions]
    Avoidance
    Suppression
    Extermination

Food safety
    Understanding relevant sections of national food codes[19]
    Understanding HACCP[20]
    Food safety misconceptions
    Hygiene [personal, kitchen]
    Food storage [temporary, long-term]
    Food handler certification
    Enforcement [jurisdiction][21]

Worker safety
    Posture [lifting, walking, standing]

    Protective equipment
    First aid [cuts, burns, falls, fainting]
Thermodynamics
    What is heat
    Specific heat capacity
    Heat transfer
    Heat flow
        Radiation [black body, line-of-sight]
        Convection [gas, liquid]
        Conduction [solids, interfaces]
States [solid, liquid, gas]
    Phase change [triple point, sublimation, reversibility]
Bulk heating
Heat flow [contours]
Introduction to heat sources [efficiency, paths of heat flow]
Relationship to power and energy
Fluid forms [non-Newtonian fluids]
    Gels
    Emulsions
    Suspensions[non-Newtonian fluids]

Foams
Food politics
    Sustainability
    Organic
    Hybridization vs. genetic modification
    Industrial vs. small farms
    Heritage animal and plant programs
    Additives and adulteration
    Understanding processed foods
    Labelling [regulated, marketing]
    Husbandry [certification systems]
Diet systems
    Historical perspective
    Types of diets [evolutionary, proactive]
    Relationship to science [epidemiology, medically prescribed]
    Food pseudoscience [beliefs vs. facts]

Framework Phase 2

Common kitchen axioms
    Truths
    Partial truths
    Falsehoods
Flavour theory
    Flavour vs. taste
    Perspective
    Maillard (non-enzymatic browning) reactions
    Flavour pairing [prospective, analysis]
    Seasoning
Planning [integrated with the Ingredients, Equipment, and Cooking Techniques
    and Methods sections]
    Time management
    Ingredient sourcing
    Labour allocation
Ingredients[22]
    Animal [sources, physiology, life cycle, heat effects]
        Mammals [cattle, sheep, pigs, rabbits]
        Poultry [chickens, ducks, geese, pigeons, guinea fowl, pheasants]
        Seafood [fish, molluscs, crustaceans, echinoderms]
        Eggs [poultry, fish]

Vegetables [source, physiology, life cycle, heat effects]
    Leafy and salad vegetables [arugula, beet greens, bok choy, Brussels sprout, cabbage, celery, chard, collard greens, endive, fiddlehead, grape leaves, kale, lettuce, mustard, napa cabbage, pea sprouts and leaves, radicchio, sorrel, spinach, turnip greens, watercress]
    Fruits [apple, apricot, aubergine, avocado, banana, bell pepper, berries, breadfruit, chayote, citrus fruit, courgette, cucumber, dates, durian, grape, jackfruit, lychee, mango, melon, nuts, olive fruit, pear, pepper, persimmon, pineapple, quince, squash, tomatillo, tomato]
    Flowers and flower buds [artichoke, broccoli, caper, cauliflower, courgette flowers]
    Podded vegetables [beans in pods, peanuts, peas, lentils, okra, shelled beans]
    Bulb and stem vegetables [asparagus, cardoon, celery, fennel, garlic, kohlrabi, leek, lotus root, onion, shallot]
    Root and tuberous vegetables [bamboo shoot, beetroot, burdock, carrot, cassava, galangal, ginger, Jerusalem artichoke, jicama, parsnip, potato, radish, salsify, sweet potato, taro, turnip, water chestnut, yam]
    Sea vegetables [aonori, hijiki, kombu, nori, wakame]
Herbs [allspice, anise, basil, bay, borage, caraway, cardamom, celery seed, chives, cilantro, cinnamon, clove, coriander seed, cumin, dill, fennel, ginger, grains of paradise, horseradish, hyssop, juniper berry, kaffir leaves, lavender, lemongrass, liquorice, lovage, mace, marjoram, mint, mustard, nutmeg, oregano, parsley, pepper, prickly ash, rosemary, saffron, sage, sassafras, savoury, shiso, star anise, sumac, tarragon, thyme, turmeric, vanilla, wasabi]
Minerals
    Edible minerals [table salt]
    Sources
    Politicization
Additives [functions, issues, application]
    Anti-caking agents [calcium silicate, iron ammonium citrate, silicon dioxide]
    Colour additives [artificial colourings, natural colourings]
    Dough strengtheners and conditioners [ammonium sulphate, azodicarbonamide, L-cysteine]
    Emulsifiers [soy lecithin, mono- and diglycerides, egg yolks, polysorbates, sorbitan monostearate]
    Enzyme preparations [transglutaminase, lactase, papain, rennet, chymosin]

Fat replacers [olestra, cellulose gel, carrageenan, polydextrose, modified food starch, microparticulated egg white protein, guar gum, xanthan gum, whey protein concentrate]

Firming agents [calcium chloride, calcium lactate]

Flavour enhancers [monosodium glutamate (MSG), hydrolysed soy protein, autolysed yeast extract, disodium guanylate or inosinate]

Flavours and spices [natural flavouring, artificial flavour, and spices]

Gases [carbon dioxide, nitrous oxide]

Gelling agents [gelatine, agar, sodium alginate, pectin, egg protein]

Humectants [glycerine, sorbitol]

Leavening agents [baking soda, monocalcium phosphate, calcium carbonate]

Nutrients [thiamine hydrochloride, riboflavin (vitamin B2), niacin, niacinamide, folate or folic acid, beta carotene, potassium iodide, iron or ferrous sulphate, alpha tocopherols, ascorbic acid, vitamin D, amino acids (L-tryptophan, L-lysine, L-leucine, L-methionine)]

pH control agents and acidulants [lactic acid, citric acid, ammonium hydroxide, sodium carbonate]

Preservatives [ascorbic acid, citric acid, sodium benzoate, calcium propionate, sodium erythorbate, sodium nitrite, calcium sorbate, potassium sorbate, BHA, BHT, EDTA, tocopherols (Vitamin E)]

Stabilizers and thickeners, binders, texturizers [gelatine, pectin, guar gum, carrageenan, xanthan gum, whey, methylcellulose]

Sweeteners [sucrose (sugar), glucose, fructose, sorbitol, mannitol, corn syrup, high fructose corn syrup, saccharin, aspartame, sucralose, acesulfame potassium (acesulfame-K), neotame]

Yeast nutrients [calcium sulphate, ammonium phosphate]

Equipment [description, design, usage (both demonstration and hands on)]

Hand tools [baking sheets, baking tins and plates, ballers, blow torch, bowls, brushes (bristle, high temperature), chocolate working tools, citrus juicers, cleavers, cooling racks, cups (prep, measuring), cutters, cutting boards, dough scrapers, egg slicer, fish scaler, food mills, graters (box, mouli, microplane*), grinders (meat, nuts, cheese), knives (chefs, paring, slicer), ladles, mandolins, meat pounder, openers (bottle, jar, can), pastry bags and tips, peelers, pH meter, pots, pressure cooker, ricers, rolling pins, sausage stuffer, scales (spring, balance, digital), scissors, scoops, skillets, spatula (flexible, stiff), spoons (solid, slotted, measuring), storage containers, strainers (chinois, sieves, colanders), syphon jar, thermometers (dial, digital, oven), Thermomix*, tongs, whisks]

Small appliances [blender, chocolate tempering warmer, circulator, crepe maker, dehydrator, food processor, homogenizer, hot plates, ice machine, immersion blender, microwave oven, panini grill, rice cooker, rotary evaporator, sausage stuffer, sealer (impulse, end, vacuum), stand mixer, thermal immersion circulator, toaster, waffle iron, water bath]

Large appliances [bowl chopper, centrifuge, cooktops (flattop, French-top, griddle, multi-hob), dough sheeter, floor mixer, freezers (walk-in, reach-in, flash), fryers, grills (gas, wood-fired, charcoal), ovens (conventional, convection, water vapour, combined, radiant, bread, brick), ranges, broilers (over-fired, cheesemelter), refrigerators (walk-in, reach-in, cabinet, flash), steam kettles, tilting cookers, warmers (cabinets, steam table)]

Cooking techniques and methods [description, demonstration, hands-on experience]
    Wet-heat methods
    Boiling [water, fat]
    Simmering [water, fat]
    Blanching [water, fat]
    Low-temperature [active, passive]
    Braising
    Steaming
    Pressure cooking
    Shallow frying
    Pan frying
    Dry-heat methods
    Baking and roasting
    Grilling
    Hot smoking
    Cold methods
        Fabrication and assembly
        Cold smoking
        Maceration
           Acid cooking
        Cryogenic cooking
    Preservation methods
    Drying [water-activity level]
    Fermenting
        Brining
        Pickling
    Auxiliary methods

Thickening [sauces]
Extraction [stocks]

Framework Phase 3

Kitchen accounting
    Principles of double entry bookkeeping
    Balance sheets
    Net vs. gross profit
    Cash flow
Calculating labour expense
    Cost of benefits
Waste management
Personal development
    Personal finance
        Banking
        Budgeting
    Consumer credit
    Insurance
    Investments
    Retirement planning
Stress management [meditation, tai chi, yoga]
Résumé and cover-letter writing
Interviewing skills
Survey of world foods and cooking methods
    Asia [China, Korea, Japan, Vietnam, Thailand, India]
    Mediterranean [Spain, France, Italy, Greece, Egypt, Tunisia, Morocco]
    The Americas [Mexico, Peru, the Caribbean, Brazil, Argentina, Chile]
Cooking with all five senses [rate of cooking, doneness, seasoning, flavouring, portioning, proportioning]
Classic dishes [original preparation and modernisation, savoury and sweet]
Select classic-dish recipes
    Analyse ingredients [then vs. now]
    Analyse techniques and methods [then vs. now]
Prepare dishes per original recipe
Prepare dishes per modern interpretation [simplified, rethought, deconstructed]
Improvisational cooking
Prepare complete meals in a fixed time period given a preselected group of major ingredients and access to a reasonably stocked larder

Conclusion

The current methods of training future cooks, whether on-the-job or in a classroom, fail to produce workers who truly know how to cook. Current methods are geared towards producing workers who can follow instructions, whether written or verbal, but not towards employees who can truly create greatness out of the ordinary.

The framework proposed above for a new culinary school curriculum is designed to produce graduates who understand all aspects of cooking. Students who successfully complete the program will have a true understanding of professional cooking and all that the profession demands including a broad knowledge of materials, methods and techniques, equipment, planning, achieving goals and objectives, and interpersonal relationships.

Notes

1. National Electrical Contractors Association, 'Professional Development: State Code & Licensing Requirements' <http://www.necanet.org/professional-development/careers-in-electrical-contracting/licensure/state-code-licensing-requirements> [accessed 3 March 2015].
2. In actuality there are five types of doctors: physicians, surgeons, radiologists, pathologists and psychiatrists. There are also crossover doctors such as gynecologists that often treat patients both as a physician and a surgeon. Peterson's Nelnet, LLC, 'A Brief Synopsis of Medical School' <http://www.petersons.com/graduate-schools/synopsis-medical-school-requirements.aspx> [accessed 3 March 2015].
3. American College of Surgeons, 'How many years of postgraduate training do surgical residents undergo?' <https://www.facs.org/education/resources/medical-students/faq/training> [accessed 3 March 2015].
4. American College of Surgeons, 'Post-Residency Fellowships' <https://www.facs.org/education/resources/medical-students/postres> <accessed 3 March 2015].
5. American College of Surgeons, 'Section I: Surgical Traits' <https://www.facs.org/education/resources/residency-search/traits> [accessed 3 March 2015].
6. Roland Passot (Executive Chef and Owner, La Folie Restaurant, San Francisco, CA), in discussion with author, 2 March 2015.
7. Adam Weiner (Culinary Instructor, JobTrain, Menlo Park, CA), in discussion with author, 5 March 2015.
8. Information collected from the individual websites and or catalog of a number of schools including Art Institute of California, City College of San Francisco, Culinary Institute of America, Johnson & Wales University, Institute of Culinary Education, International Culinary Center, JobTrain and Mission College.
9. Christian Hallowell (Customer-Dedicated Executive Chef for Delta Airlines, Gate Gourmet, College Park, GA), in discussion with author, 3 March 2015.
10. Simón de Swaan (Food and Beverage Director, Four Seasons Hotel, New York, NY), in discussion with author, 6 March 2015.
11. Passot. City College of San Francisco is a public, two-year institution.
12. Charles Vollmar (Chef and Owner, Epicurean Exchange, Orinda, CA), in discussion with author, 2 March 2015.
13. Passot.
14. Hallowell; Vollmar.
15. Vollmar.
16. Weiner. Weiner has a similar line that he tells his students often: 'Cook with the equipment you have,

not with the equipment you wish you had.'

17. In preparing the framework, as well as relying heavily on personal experience, a number of works were consulted: *Academic Catalog 2014–2015* (Hyde Park NY: Culinary Institute of America, 2014), pp. 46-70; James Beard, *James Beard's Theory and Practice of Good Cooking* (New York: Alfred A Knopf, 1977); *The Science of Good Cooking*, ed. by Jack Bishop (Brookline MA: America's Test Kitchen, 2012); Glynn Christian, *How to Cook Without Recipes* (London: Portico Books, 2008); Marian Cole Fisher, *Twenty Lessons in Domestic Science* (Chicago: Calumet Baking Powder Company, 1916); Harold McGee, *On Food and Cooking: The Science and Lore of the Kitchen* (New York: Charles Scribner's Sons, 1984); Nathan Myhrvold, Chris Young, Maxime Bilet, *Modernist Cuisine: The Art and Science of Cooking* (Bellevue WA: The Cooking Lab, 2011); Barb Stuckey, *Taste: What You're Missing* (New York: Free Press, 2012).

18. Adam Weiner, *JobTrain Culinary Arts Program Adult and Out of School Youth (Full Time) Course Syllabus* (Menlo Park CA: JobTrain, 2015), p. 12.

19. It is important that students be familiar with the national food code for the country they plan to work in.

20. The student should understand what a HACCP plan is and how to comply with one. Creating a HACCP plan is beyond the scope of this program.

21. Food safety enforcement may be the responsibility of multiple organizations with different jurisdictions.

22. The detail level of the discussion of ingredients will vary with ingredient importance, frequency of use, and complexity.

Deep-frying the Nation: Communicating about Scottish Food and Nutrition

Christine Knight

Introduction

Since the mid-1990s, the UK media and popular culture have associated the Scottish diet with unhealthy, deep-fried foods, notably the notorious deep-fried Mars bar. The Carron Fish Bar in Stonehaven, near Aberdeen, claims to have invented the deep-fried Mars bar in the 1990s (Dow, 1995). A light-hearted survey of Scottish fish and chip shops by Glasgow public health researchers, published in the Christmas 2004 edition of the *Lancet,* found that twenty-two per cent of Scottish chip shops currently sold deep-fried Mars bars, and seventeen per cent had done so in the past (Morrison and Petticrew, 2004). The deep-fried Mars bar is now widely available in tourist areas such as Edinburgh's Royal Mile, although publicity from journalists and travel writers (e.g. Rough Guides, 2015) has no doubt increased demand, and thus availability. Although anecdotal evidence suggests that Mars bars were deep-fried in several countries apart from Scotland before they first appeared in Stonehaven, my focus in this paper is not the origins of the deep-fried Mars bar as an actual food, but rather its origins and use as a cultural symbol and stereotype.

The *Daily Record* first reported the deep-fried Mars bar in 1995 (Dow, 1995), and the story 'went viral' in the British media (e.g. Arlidge, 1995; Low, 1995). Since then there has been an on-going trail in the UK press about the deep-fried Mars bar, to the point where it seems virtually inevitable that any media report about the Scottish diet will include a reference to it, sometimes alongside references to other notorious deep-fried Scottish foods, such as deep-fried haggis and deep-fried pizza. Further examples of media coverage will be discussed in the second half of this paper, but to illustrate this, a recent report in the *Daily Mail* online about a study on beliefs about fruit and vegetables in Scotland provides an ideal opportunity for the journalist to make reference to the deep-fried Mars bar, describing Scotland as '[t]he nation that gave the world such culinary obscenities as the deep-fried Mars Bar and the pizza fritter' ('A Fifth of Scottish People', 2013).

In this paper I consider how and why the deep-fried Mars bar has become the icon for the Scottish diet over the last twenty years, the implications of depicting the Scottish diet in these terms and alternative narratives that have emerged in opposition. To begin, I review the history of stereotyping of the Scottish diet over the last several centuries, suggesting that far from being a novel phenomenon, the deep-fried Mars bar is the latest in a line of stereotypes of the Scottish diet that have emerged during periods when the relationship between Scotland and England has been changing and uneasy. Drawing on interdisciplinary food scholarship about 'food slurs' and the cultural representation of fat, I then consider why the Scottish diet stereotype has taken this particular form since the mid-1990s. Finally, I discuss two key modes in which journalists and others use the deep-fried Mars bar to communicate messages about Scottish culinary culture, diet and health, and the Scottish nation more broadly. Namely:

1. Journalists introduce the deep-fried Mars bar into news and feature articles about Scottish public health as a symbol of the poor Scottish diet, simultaneously communicating derogatory messages about taste, class, morality and the Scottish nation.

2. Scottish journalists and food industry representatives have increasingly contested this pattern in an effort to break a vicious cycle which negatively affects eating habits in Scotland, as well as the image of Scottish food products and culture.

Thus I will examine how a specific food – the deep-fried Mars bar – is deployed and redeployed by different people to communicate varied messages about Scotland, its diet and cuisine.

While the deep-fried Mars bar is undeniably comic, it is important to note that the deep-fried stereotype of the Scottish diet has become part of a vicious circle with real, negative effects on eating habits, and therefore health. Previous qualitative research has shown that this stereotype has shifted at least some people's beliefs about nutrition and dietary norms in an unhealthy direction: participants reported the belief that their diet is healthy and does not require attention provided they are not eating deep-fried foods on a regular basis (Fuller, Backett-Milburn and Hopton, 2003, p. 1045S). Separate research with young people from minority ethnic groups shows that the stereotype can encourage deep-fried food consumption as a way of 'claiming' Scottish identity (Hopkins, 2004, p. 265). Thus a critical examination of the deep-fried Mars bar stereotype is not only about contesting negative perceptions of Scottish food, culture and people, but also intervening in a vicious circle of representation to improve diet and health.

Analysis of mass media communication about food, diet, weight and health is a significant body of research in sociology, media and cultural studies, as well as psychology. (Recent UK studies include: Cooper et al., 2011; Gough, 2007; Hilton, Patterson and Teyhan, 2012; Hollows and Jones, 2010; Inthorn and Boyce, 2010; Ries, Rachul and Caulfield, 2011; Riesch and Spiegelhalter, 2011; Warin, 2011.) There is also an enormous body of academic research about the symbolic messages food carries, notably in anthropology (Mintz and Du Bois, 2002), as well as across the humanities and social sciences; indeed, this could be said to be the unifying concern of food scholars. This paper aims to contribute to these literatures via detailed empirical analysis on a topic of social, cultural and political importance in the contemporary UK. I examine

207

communication about the deep-fried Mars bar to make new points about how food is used in the public sphere to negotiate the relationship between Scotland and the rest of the UK, and build Scottish national identity – highly contemporary issues given the 2014 Scottish independence referendum. This is the first research project to examine the popular association of deep-fried foods with Scotland. It builds on food and folklore scholar Joy Fraser's research about stereotyping of the Scottish people and nation through images of food in the eighteenth and nineteenth centuries, notably in relation to haggis (Fraser, 2011). Thus this paper illuminates contemporary UK patterns of communication about Scotland through food, as well as the historical weight that these bear.

Historical Stereotyping of the Scottish Diet

In his famous *Dictionary* (1755), Dr Johnson notoriously defined oats as '[a] grain, which in England is generally given to horses, but in Scotland supports the people' (n.p.). However, Dr Johnson's quip is only one example of pervasive derogatory stereotypes of the Scottish diet that circulated during the eighteenth century, in particular. Writing about the history of the cultural symbolism of haggis in eighteenth- and nineteenth-century Britain, Fraser shows that haggis came to be associated specifically with Scotland by the middle of the eighteenth century, even though people continued to eat haggis elsewhere in the UK throughout the nineteenth century (2011, pp. 22-23). Fraser bases her argument on analysis of a range of English publications from this period, including cookbooks, satirical poems and cartoons and political tracts. These documents use haggis as a pejorative symbol of Scottishness, and as a way to communicate broader stereotypes of the Scots that were emerging at the time, especially the stereotype of the so-called 'beggarly Scot' said to be poor, dirty, and diseased. As Fraser writes, '[i]n the English context [haggis was just one of] a range of culinary stereotypes and metaphors that were used to stigmatise and satirise the Scots' (p. 13).

A further example of historical 'food slurs' against the Scots is the following recognizably contemporary urban myth about food contamination. Written around 1760 by an anonymous author, who purports to be an Englishman reporting on a journey around Scotland, it describes the disgusting food practices that he supposedly witnessed north of the border:

> when I asked for Bread, some *Baunock was given to me, which the* slattern Landlady, and as nasty as Filth could make her, told me was excellent in its Kind, and that they were baking more in the next Room. Hunger having compelled me to eat a Little, which I took Care to frequently moisten with my Rum and Water; then Curiosity egged me, to have a Peep through a Hole in the Partition, to view their Manner of baking. The Object that presented itself to me, was the Landlady wiping with her Hand, the scabby Arse of a young Child, covered with Squitter [diarrhoea], *which, to save her Laziness the Trouble of getting a Cloth to* wipe her

own Hand with, she dabbed into the Dough. This is a new Kind of *Scotch Yeast*, *discovered for the Art of baking, unknown to us of the* South. I laid down my Money to pay for what I had, ran out of the House, and have since almost puked my Guts out. (English, c. 1760, pp.56-57, quoted in Fraser, 2011, p.106)

Drawing on Fraser's work by way of historical foundation to my own research on the late twentieth and early twenty-first centuries, I suggest that in order to understand current stereotypes of the Scottish diet we need to understand this history, as well as the broader context of Scottish political history and the relationship between Scotland and England. Fraser points out that the 'marketability [of satirical fictions about Scotland] increased whenever the relationship between the two nations was at its most turbulent' (p. 33), for example around the Act of Union in 1707, the Jacobite Rising in the 1740s and the appointment of Lord Bute as Britain's first Scottish-born Prime Minister in 1762. This may partly explain why the late twentieth and early twenty-first centuries have seen stereotypes of the Scottish diet (re-)emerge so strongly: since the mid-1990s the political relationship between Scotland and England has been changing in ways certainly not entirely easy, with the establishment of the Scottish Parliament and recent referendum on Scottish independence. While it is inherently difficult to prove a link between devolution and the independence movement, and recent stereotypes of the Scottish diet – at least without the benefit of historical hindsight – there are clear and suggestive historical parallels.

209

Deep-Fried Foods and Fat in the Contemporary Era

Setting aside the political timing, there remains the question of the deep-fried Mars bar itself: why have deep-fried foods, and the deep-fried Mars bar in particular, replaced haggis in political cartoons and satires about Scotland? The deep-fried Mars bar was certainly in the right place at the right time, but it was also an ideal candidate to be picked up as a national food slur against Scotland in the late twentieth century. As the passage I cited above from *John English's Travels through Scotland* (c. 1760) may suggest, this is partly due to the 'yuck factor' associated with the deep-fried Mars bar and other deep-fried foods. Rozin and Fallon's work (1987) suggests that our disgust response to certain foods may relate to their resemblance to bodily fluids and body parts, especially faeces, pus, vomit and genitalia. The deep-fried Mars bar combines visual and textural similarities to all of these elements in a single package, with partially melted chocolate, oozy caramel, pale lumpy batter and a phallic profile. Such resemblance to the taboo and the abject (in the Kristevan sense) goes some way to explaining why the deep-fried Mars bar is so often interpreted and represented as grotesque or obscene. These associations, and their deployment in the UK media, are perhaps best illustrated by the ironic use of the phrase 'deep-fried Mars bar supper' (a deep-fried Mars bar with chips) as a metaphor for anal rape by political sketch-writer Simon Hoggart in the *Guardian*: "'let's gie 'im a Mars Bar supper" may be some terrible Scottish slang expression meaning male rape' (Hoggart, 1999).

However, to understand fully why the deep-fried Mars bar can be considered 'obscene', and why (two centuries on) it has replaced haggis as the ultimate Scottish diet stereotype, we also need to consider changing ideas about nutrition and fat in the contemporary period, including the specific significance of deep-fried foods. While it can now seem common sense that fat, and saturated fat in particular, are unhealthy and 'bad', historically this idea is quite recent, emerging in the 1960s. Deborah Lupton summarizes the shift in attitudes during the twentieth century:

> Animal fat, which was once considered a valued component of food (and indeed earlier this century was often eaten as 'dripping' spread on bread), is now almost uniformly represented in medical and popular discourses as an evil substance [...].' People routinely describe fat or fatty foods as 'unhealthy', particularly if the fat is visible, either in its solidified form, or as a greasy or oily residue. (Lupton, 1996, p. 82)

Although Lupton specifically refers to animal fat, similar arguments can be made about the fats used in deep-frying. Nutritionally, deep-fried foods today are considered unhealthy junk foods and therefore 'bad', so that eating them attracts moral (and class) judgement (Everett, 2009; McPhail, Chapman and Beagan, 2011, p. 302). The deep-fried Mars bar can seem especially 'obscene' because it takes something that is already a junk food (a Mars bar), and literally adds an extra layer of unhealthiness or 'wrongness' by battering and deep-frying it. Moreover, deep-fried foods in Britain are closely tied to the fish and chip shop, which has been associated since it first emerged in the late nineteenth century with the working classes and the industrial north (Walton, 1992). Until well into the twentieth century chip shops were considered places that respectable people, women in particular, did not go (Walton, 1992) – and some of this class stigma continues to attach to their products today.

As with fat in food, it can seem common sense today that overweight and obesity are unhealthy and 'bad', but understanding that these concerns are culturally specific and relatively recent is also part of the jigsaw in understanding where the deep-fried Mars bar stereotype has come from and why it has any purchase on the public imagination. It is no coincidence that it is since the early-to-mid 1990s that obesity has attracted increasing public health concern and media attention, initially in the United States but within a very short time around the world (Boero, 2007; Coveney, 2006, pp.143-144; Herndon, 2005). In recent OECD figures, Scotland ranked sixth in the world for obesity (Castle, 2015, pp. 19-20); notably, the nation also faces one of the world's highest rates of heart disease. Arguably, until the UK media and public began to associate Scotland with having a particular problem with obesity and heart disease, the stereotype of the deep-fried Mars bar could never have taken root. To illustrate this rather starkly, we are now used to seeing stereotypes of the Scottish body such as the character Fat Bastard in Mike Myers's series of *Austin Powers* films (*Austin Powers: The Spy Who Shagged Me*,

1999; *Austin Powers in Goldmember*, 2002), but 250 years ago the visual stereotype of the Scottish body was one of emaciation and famine (Churchill, 1763, cited in Fraser, 2011, pp. 46-47). Thus while stereotyping of Scottish bodies and Scottish food have been constant themes in the relationship between England and Scotland since the eighteenth century, the form those stereotypes have taken has depended on historical context, including changing ideas about fat in food and on a person's body.

Media Narratives
In the second half of this paper I examine how the deep-fried Mars bar is deployed by different writers and spokespeople in the press to communicate two competing messages about Scotland and its food. As I indicated in the introduction, the two narratives I will focus on are:

1. the use of the deep-fried Mars bar as a shorthand or symbol for poor Scottish nutrition, health and obesity rates, simultaneously communicating derogatory messages about taste, class, morality and the Scottish nation itself; and

2. a competing narrative which I call 'gastronomic Scotland', emerging over the last fifteen years in part as an explicit response to the deep-fried Mars bar stereotype, which focuses on high-quality Scottish produce, chefs and restaurants.

My research is based on analysis of articles from UK and Scottish newspapers between 1995 and 2014. Newspapers referred to here are the two national Scottish broadsheets, the *Herald* (Glasgow) and the *Scotsman*, in order to focus on the conversation in the Scottish public sphere. In this conversation, Scottish national identity and cultural and economic aspiration (as well as, implicitly, political aspiration) coalesce around the issue of Scotland's food – or alternatively, we might say that food is used to communicate Scottish national identity and aspiration. One side of this conversation emphasizes Scotland's well-publicized public health problems, while the other highlights its increasingly successful food and drink sector. Throughout, the deep-fried Mars bar resurfaces again and again as the emblem of Scotland's notoriously poor diet, and the stereotype against which the Scottish food industry must battle. Indeed, the deep-fried Mars bar trope functions as a kind of 'return of the repressed' in aspirational economic and cultural narratives about Scottish food.

The Deep-Fried Mars Bar, Scottish Health and Nutrition
I begin with several examples of newspaper articles from the mid- and late 1990s in which overweight and disease in Scotland are blamed directly on alleged national consumption of the deep-fried Mars bar, as well as metonymic fried or high-fat foods. For example, a report about people in Scotland choosing plastic surgery to address overweight and obesity opens with the claim that '[a] penchant for deep-fried Mars bars and living off the fat of the land means that seven out of ten Scotsmen are overweight'

(Jourdan, 1997, p. 17). Likewise, a report highlighting that a high-fat diet increases skin cancer risk begins with the claim that 'Scots' love of chips, pies and deep-fried Mars Bars is behind the country's skin cancer epidemic' (O'Donnell, 1998, p. 22). These examples are both from the *Scotsman*, but similarly, in the *Sunday Herald*, a report about workplace food links the deep-fried Mars bar, workplace catering and poor Scottish health outcomes: 'Here in the land of the deep fried Mars bar, workplace food is not something we do well. [...] We have higher blood pressure, more strokes, and higher cancer rates than almost everywhere, but what we really excel at is heart disease' (Bradshaw, 1999, p. 20).

This claim is less direct than the two previous examples: the suggestion does not seem to be that workplace canteens actually serve deep-fried Mars bars. Rather, the deep-fried Mars bar is used here (as it frequently is) as an emblem or shorthand for an unhealthy national diet, the implication being that this causes cardiovascular disease and cancer. Although the London-based UK press certainly make these kinds of statements too, I highlight examples from the Scottish press to show that this is not by any means simply a stereotype imposed on Scotland from outside, but also a powerful instance of national self-flagellation. Although similar patterns continue into the new millennium, this is a narrative that is most dominant in the 1990s.

The Deep-Fried Mars Bar and the Scottish Food Industry

Over the last fifteen years a much more confident Scottish food narrative has emerged and established itself in the pages of Scotland's broadsheet press. Indeed, it appears that political devolution, and the establishment of the Scottish Parliament in 1999, represented a turning point in Scotland's public narratives about its food. This can be attributed in part to increasing cultural confidence, but also (and importantly) to the opportunities that devolution created for the establishment of public sector bodies with the mandate to grow and promote the Scottish food sector – notably the industry leadership body Scotland Food & Drink, established in 2007. However, these political and institutional developments only built on the longstanding independent efforts of several key 'champions' for Scottish food (notably food writer Sue Lawrence and chef Nick Nairn). Examples from the press chosen at intervals every few years give an indication of how this narrative develops.

By 2001 (two years post-devolution), senior figures in the Scottish food arena, such as the food writer Sue Lawrence, begin to call publicly in the Scottish broadsheets for the establishment of a Scottish food industry body, along the lines of the Irish Food Board, to promote Scottish produce, especially abroad. In the interim, Lawrence calls on the Scottish Tourist Board to do more to promote Scotland's 'fantastic produce and cuisine': 'There are still the deep-fried Mars bar and McHaggis burger jokes, but there continues to be a great deal of ignorance about our wonderful produce; we too have stunning farmhouse cheeses, beef, game, lamb, seafood and the best home-baking around' (Lawrence, 2001, p. 36).

Moving forward, a business column in April 2004 opens by highlighting Scotland's 'natural advantages in producing fish, high-quality meats and soft fruits', contrasting this (inevitably) with the claim that '[m]any Scots seem happy to go along with the joke that the deep-fried Mars bar is the summit of our culinary achievements' (Friedli, 2004, p. 7). The reporter calls for initiatives to take advantage of opportunities overseas for quality Scottish products, pointing out that this will have spin-off benefits for tourism.

By 2008, signalling a step-change in Scottish gastronomic confidence, a Scotsman editorial about gastro-tourism encourages Scotland 'to start promoting itself as a gastro-destination'. The deep-fried Mars bar stereotype is briefly dismissed in order to move on: 'All talk of deep-fried Mars Bars aside, Scotland produces some of the greatest meat, vegetables and seafood in the world, and the whisky speaks for itself. The future marketing of Scotland as a visitor destination should make greater use of our cuisine and restaurants' ('Leader', 2008, p. 29).

And by 2011, an article in the *Herald* reports that Scottish food exports have exceeded £1 billion per annum for the first time, an increase of nearly fourteen per cent. In keeping with the narrative I refer to as 'gastronomic Scotland', this achievement is 'hailed as evidence of increasing international awareness and appreciation of the quality, provenance and heritage of Scottish food' (Ross, 2011, p. 9).

In a final example, an extended interview in the *Herald* in early 2014 with James Withers, Chief Executive of Scotland Food & Drink, focuses almost entirely on Scotland's high-quality produce and the impressive progress made by the Scottish food sector – in line with the official messaging of Scotland Food & Drink. (Indeed, it could be argued that the organization's official communications line, promoting Scotland internationally as a 'Land of Food and Drink', has successfully populated the Scottish broadsheets.) Quoted here, Withers quickly dismisses an inevitable opening gambit from the reporter about the deep-fried Mars bar, using it as an opportunity to compare national and international perceptions of Scottish cuisine: '"We are a bit self-deprecating about our crisps and fizzy drinks, but overseas Scotland is noted for its salmon, fresh fruit, oats and other natural produce." [...] In a nod to Robert Burns, he adds: "We need to see ourselves as others see us"' (Murden, 2014, p. 37).

213

Discussion and Conclusion

The narrative of 'gastronomic Scotland' is not just an alternative to the deep-fried Mars bar stereotype. Rather, as the examples above show, the deep-fried Mars bar is used *within* the 'gastronomic Scotland' narrative as a springboard for Scottish self-imagination in the realm of food: the deep-fried Mars bar must repeatedly be dismissed in order to move on. Yet arguably these continued references to the deep-fried Mars bar, even by way of dismissing it, actually reinforce the stereotype of the Scottish diet as much as its use as a slur. This may be part of the reason for the deep-fried Mars bar's enduring place in the cultural imaginary, despite the establishment of alternative, more positive narratives about Scottish food and diet. A further risk of the 'gastronomic Scotland' narrative is that conversations about nutrition and cuisine become disconnected from one another, as the 'gastronomic Scotland' narrative addresses the deep-fried Mars bar primarily as a problem for the Scottish food industry. This focus might indirectly benefit nutrition and public health via changes to the representation of the Scottish diet and thus eating behaviour. Yet a focus on quality produce and cuisine risks skipping over serious questions of health and inequality within the nation, and who can afford high-quality, healthy Scottish food.

Thus connecting discussions about food and nutrition in Scotland is key to improving national cultural and economic confidence and public health simultaneously – a connection attempted in the Scottish Government's recent 'Good Food Nation' national food and drink policy. Moreover, the new Scottish Food Commission tasked with delivering the Good Food Nation vision includes wide-ranging experts from the food industry, nutrition and community organizations. It remains to be seen how far these initiatives can address issues of poor diet across the Scottish population. One requirement of intervening effectively is to recognize the damaging effects of the national dietary stereotype not just on the Scottish food sector and economy, but also on public health, as noted above. Although Scotland arguably cannot change patterns of external representation, the media produced and consumed in Scotland – as well as everyone who speaks or writes about Scottish food and diet – have the power and responsibility to decide which images and stories circulate within the nation.

References

'A Fifth of Scottish People Think that Jam Is One of Their Five a Day Despite Containing Two Thirds Sugar'. 2013. *Daily Mail*. 11 August. <http://www.dailymail.co.uk/news/article-2389234/A-fifth-Scottish-people-think-jam-day-despite-containing-thirds-sugar.html> [accessed: 2 June 2015].

Arlidge, J. 1995. 'The Scots Get a Taste for Fried Mars Bar and Chips'. *Independent*. 2 October. p. 9.

Austin Powers in Goldmember. 2002. Film. Directed by Jay Roach, written by Mike Myers and Michael McCullers. [DVD] US: New Line Cinema.

Austin Powers: The Spy Who Shagged Me. 1999/ Film. Directed by Jay Roach, written by Mike Myers and Michael McCullers. [DVD] US: New Line Cinema.

Boero, N. 2007. 'All the News that's Fat to Print: The American "Obesity Epidemic" and the Media'. *Qualitative Sociology*. 30. pp. 41-60.

Bradshaw, A. 1999. 'You've Had Your Chips'. *Sunday Herald*. 14 March. p. 20.

Castle, A. (2015) *Obesity in Scotland* (Edinburgh: Scottish Parliament Information Centre).

Churchill, C. 1763. *The Prophecy of Famine: A Scots Pastoral* (London: Printed for the author).

Cooper, B. E. J. et al. 2012. 'The Quality of the Evidence for Dietary Advice Given in UK National Newspapers'. *Public Understanding of Science*. 21. pp. 664-73.

Coveney, J. 2006. *Food, Morals and Meaning: The Pleasure and Anxiety of Eating*. 2nd Ed. (London: Routledge).

Dow, B. 1995. 'Mars Supper, Please'. *Daily Record*. 24 August. p. 9.

English, J. [pseud.]. c. 1760. *John English's Travels through Scotland, Containing a Curious and Entertaining Account of the Manners and Strange Customs of the Inhabitants* (London: Printed for W. Morgan).

Everett, H. 2009. 'Vernacular Health Moralities and Culinary Tourism in Newfoundland and Labrador'. *Journal of American Folklore*. 122 (483). pp. 28-52.

Fraser, J. 2011. *A Taste of Scotland? Representing and Contesting Scottishness in Expressive Culture about Haggis* (Unpublished PhD dissertation, Memorial University of Newfoundland).

Friedli, D. 2004. 'Tell the World Scots Food is More Than Haggis and Mars Bars'. *Scotland on Sunday*. 11 April. p. 7.

Fuller, T., Backett-Milburn, K. and Hopton, J. 2003. 'Healthy Eating: The Views of General Practitioners and Patients in Scotland'. *American Journal of Clinical Nutrition*. 77 (Supplement). pp. 1043S-47S.

Gough, B. 2007. '"Real Men Don't Diet": An Analysis of Contemporary Newspaper Representations of Men, Food and Health'. *Social Science & Medicine*. 64. pp. 326-37.

Herndon, A. M. 2005. 'Collateral Damage from Friendly Fire?: Race, Nation, Class and the "War against Obesity"'. *Social Semiotics*. 15.2. pp. 127-41.

Hilton, S., Patterson, C. and Teyhan, A. 2012. 'Escalating Coverage of Obesity in UK Newspapers: The Evolution and Framing of the "Obesity Epidemic" from 1996 to 2010'. *Obesity*. 20.8. pp. 1688-95.

Hoggart, S. 1999. 'Scots and Peers Whinge Away'. *Guardian*. 28 April. p. 13.

Hollows, J. and Jones, S. 2010. '"At least He's Doing Something": Moral Entrepreneurship and Individual Responsibility in *Jamie's Ministry of Food*'. *European Journal of Cultural Studies*. 13.3. pp. 307-22.

Hopkins, P. 2004. 'Young Muslim Men in Scotland: Inclusions and Exclusions'. *Children's Geographies*. 2.2. pp. 257-72.

Inthorn, S. and Boyce, T. 2010. '"It's Disgusting How Much Salt You Eat!": Television Discourses of Obesity, Health and Morality'. *International Journal of Cultural Studies*. 13.1. pp. 83-100.

Johnson, S. 1755. *A Dictionary of the English language*. Vol. 2 (London: Printed for A. Millar).

Jourdan, T. 1997. 'Knife and Easy Does It'. *Scotsman*. 11 June. p. 17.

Lawrence, S. 2001. 'Homage to Caledonia'. *Scotland on Sunday*. 10 June. p. 36.

Leader: 'It's Just Litter – But It Will Cost Us the Earth'. 2008. *Scotsman*. 10 April. p. 29.

Low, V. 1995. 'It's Mars for Batter or Worse'. *Evening Standard*. 3 October. p. 17.

Lupton, D. 1996. *Food, the Body and the Self* (London: SAGE).

McPhail, D., Chapman, G. E. and Beagan, B. L. 2011. '"Too Much of that Stuff Can't Be Good": Canadian Teens, Morality, and Fast Food Consumption'. *Social Science & Medicine*. 73. pp. 301-07.

Mintz, S. W. and Du Bois, C. M. 2002. 'The Anthropology of Food and Eating'. *Annual Review of Anthropology*. 31. pp. 99-119.

Morrison, D. and Petticrew, M. 2004. 'Deep and Crisp and Eaten: Scotland's Deep-Fried Mars Bar'. *Lancet*. 364. p. 2180.

Murden, T. 2014. 'Monday Interview: James Withers'. *Scotsman*. 6 January. p. 37.

O'Donnell, F. 1998. 'High-fat Diet Link to Skin Cancer'. *Scotsman*. 2 November. p. 22.

Ries, N. M., Rachul, C. and Caulfield, T. 2011. 'Newspaper Reporting on Legislative and Policy Interventions to Address Obesity: United States, Canada, and the United Kingdom'. *Journal of Public Health Policy*. 32. pp. 73-90.

Riesch, H. and Spiegelhalter, D. J. 2011. '"Careless Pork Costs Lives": Risk Stories from Science to Press Release to Media'. *Health, Risk & Society*. 13.1. pp. 47-64.

Ross, D. 2011. 'Food Firms Enjoy Taste of Success as Exports Soar'. *Herald*. 13 July. p. 9.

Rough Guides. 2015. *Scotland: Food and Drink* <http://www.roughguides.com/destinations/europe/scotland/72520-2/> [accessed: 2 June 2015].

Rozin, P. and Fallon, A. E. 1987. 'A Perspective on Disgust'. *Psychological Review*. 94.1. pp. 23-41.

Walton, J. K. 1992. *Fish and Chips and the British Working Class, 1870-1940* (Leicester: Leicester University Press).

Warin, M. 2011. 'Foucault's Progeny: Jamie Oliver and the Art of Governing Obesity'. *Social Theory & Health*. 9. pp. 24-40.

Messages of Subversion: Communicating Czech Nationalism through Culinary History

Michael Krondl

In the early summer of 1944, Czech food writer Marie Úlehlová-Tilschová walked into the offices of her Prague editor carrying a thick, heavy manuscript. The book, *Česká strava lidová* [*Czech Folk Food*], seemed innocuous enough that the publisher, still under the iron strictures of the Nazi censors, would have no problems printing it. It was after all about women's stuff: food and cooking. Certainly there couldn't be even a breath of dissent here, certainly nothing that could threaten the rule of the Third Reich.

Under normal circumstances the manuscript could be read as nothing more than a remarkably comprehensive catalogue of ethnic Czech foodways, but circumstances were anything but normal. The Allies had just barely landed in Normandy, and German V-1s were raining down on London. Tens of thousands were being transported from Terezín to Auschwitz. In the Nazi protectorate of Bohemia and Moravia, it wasn't at all clear what the outcome of the war would be. Yet oddly, there was a veneer of normalcy to life in the Czech lands. Though the Nazis had shuttered Czech universities long ago, they tolerated a Czech-language popular culture as long as it didn't step over the official line. Czechs sidled up to that line as close as they dared, with novels and films that explored Czech history and folklore, with a barely concealed subtext of national survival. In this respect, a book of culinary history fit right in. It's hard to pick up *Česká strava lidová* and not see it in the context of the war, as a subversive rejoinder to the ideology of 'master race'.

As Úlehlová-Tilschová was preparing the manuscript, Czech identity was under an even greater existential threat than of her countrymen realized. While not widely publicized, Hitler's long-term plan was to either forcibly remove Czech speakers to points east or to fully assimilate them. Nazi ideology saw the Czechs as a nation of backward peasants; civilization could only be found in the German speaking cities of Bohemia; culture, religion and industry were all German imports. During the war, countering this narrative in any public form would have got you shot. But Czechs have a deep repertoire of subverting authority, and what could be more stealthy than culinary ethnography?

There was nothing especially new or novel in the use of culinary history for nationalist purposes. Úlehlová-Tilschová drew heavily on the work of earlier generations of food historians, most notably Zikmund Winter and Čeněk Zíbrt, who are discussed below. Though neither her work, nor that of Winter and Zíbrt, can or should be read primarily as propaganda, the message that Czech culinary culture is at least equal if not superior to its German equivalent is never far from the surface. Like her predecessors, the some-time journalist lived in a small nation fearful of being inundated by its vastly more numerous neighbours, and, like the scholar-patriots that preceded her, she looked to food and especially culinary history as the language that spoke to the distinctive identity of her people.

Nations Are Built of Stories

Although the contributions of all three authors to their field is invaluable, it is ironic that their projects are all constructed on the basis of a flimsy, even quixotic premise, mainly that cuisine is contiguous with ethnicity or, even more problematic in the central European context, that people speaking the same language eat the same kind of food. In a country that was roughly one quarter German-speaking, Úlehlová-Tilschová's well-fed peasants have no German (never mind Jewish) neighbours, Winter's Italianate renaissance banquets exist with only a fleeting acknowledgement of foreign influence, and when Zíbrt chooses to excerpt a Bohemian aristocrat's cookbook he actively disregards the majority of recipes written in German. Yet the reality is that the region has seen centuries of culinary miscegenation between Czechs, Hungarians, Austrians, Bavarians, Saxons, Italians and others. Certainly Czech speakers in Western Bohemia had more dishes in common with the Bavarians in the next valley than with their countrymen in Northern Moravia.

Not that Czechs are any different from other ethnic groups in their self-absorption. Identity is fabricated in an echo chamber. Nations are built of stories told and retold by their own people; it's why a common language is so important.

The three food writers all share a sensibility forged in the nineteenth-century Czech national revival. The movement's publicists kept returning to certain tropes. The foremost of these nationalist principles was formulated by František Palacký in his magisterial *Dějiny národu českého* [*History of the Czech Nation*] (1848–1876). He posits that the organizing feature of Bohemian history is the struggle between Czechs and Germans. The latter are associated with Catholicism and repression, the former, enlightened, egalitarian even democratic; the Germans are corrupt, cosmopolitan courtiers while the Czechs are honest, down-to-earth peasants, or occasionally, enlightened rural aristocrats.[1] In part, nineteenth-century Czech nationalism was a Europe-wide project of nation building. It was certainly aware of a parallel drive by Germans toward Grossdeutchland, a union of all German-speakers, whether they resided in Prussia, Austria or, more worryingly, in Bohemia. In 1862, German-speaking historians in Bohemia had gone so far as to organize their own *Verein für Geschichte der Deutschen Böhmen* [Society for German-Bohemian History] to promote a German-centric version of Czech history, something the Nazis would later embrace.[2]

A second trope was that Czechs' subservient status was the result of the 1620 battle of White Mountain, where the Czech aristocracy was wiped out and replaced by Hapsburg tyranny. Nationalist historians including Zikmund Winter devoted almost

217

all their writing to the era prior to the battle, a period widely seen as the nation's golden age.

A third trope concerned the character of the Czech people. Here the idea was that Bohemia (especially its border regions and cities) had been infiltrated by German elements and the only way to reclaim the nation was to turn to the uncontaminated Czech rural populus.[3] In this view the peasants' *koláče* and *buchty*, that Úlehlová-Tilschová would later describe, were no mere tasty sweet buns, but edible bulwarks against the Germanic tide.[4] It wasn't long before scholars and artists of every metier would embrace an idealized rural culture with open arms. In Prague, the movement led to the building of a 'national' Czech-language theatre filled with murals of Czech country folk and featuring operas such as Bedřich Smetana's *Bartered Bride* filled with happy, dancing peasants. Božena Němcová, Karolina Světlá and other novelists turned their attention to village grandmothers and mountain shepherds. The culmination of the pastoral idyll came in 1895 with the Czechoslavic [*sic*] Ethnographic Exhibition of 1895 (which explicitly excluded the German Bohemians) where visitors could indulge in an orgy of folklore, including exhibits with model kitchens and parlours reproduced in a variety of regional rural styles.[5]

The Hungry Antiquarian

One of the happy consequences of the nationalist impulse was the attention paid to the history of material culture, especially to the period prior to Hapsburg hegemony. This was Zikmund Winter's stomping ground. In his day job Zigmund Winter (1846-1912) taught at an academic high school (*gymnasium*), but his real passion was digging through fifteenth and sixteenth century archives. His eclectic output included books on fashion, on merchants and tradesmen, on domestic life, as well as the 1892 *Kuchyně a stůl našich předků: líčení dějepisné ze XVI. století* [*The Cuisine of Our Ancestors: A Historical Exposition from the Sixteenth Century*]. He was more antiquarian than academic, more populist than scholar, which may be why he wears his ideology on his sleeve. He grew up during the period of German-Bohemian resurgence so perhaps he had good reason to be thin-skinned.

Winter is no expert on renaissance cuisine, and the catalogue of recipes he presents gives the impression of a cabinet of curiosities. He is enthused about the abundance, something he sees as indicative of Czech culinary sophistication, but far from thrilled about what was actually served. His reaction to the actual recipes is in turns horrified and bemused. There is, as he explains, nonetheless good reason to bring the peculiar tastes of his forebears to the attention of the nineteenth century patriot:

> While the cuisine of the Czech nation certainly has its own attributes, it has, since ancient times, been influenced by both the West and the East. Some of our foods were nurtured here, others were brought by the West while yet others we appropriated from the East. But we do not intend to discuss that here. We are

218

intrigued by sixteenth century Czech cuisine, that is a cuisine long fully-formed, of an established character and nature, even then renowned beyond the border of this famed kingdom. Let us discover old Czech culture in gastronomic matters, and if we, the mendacious children of the nineteenth century, do not find it all to our taste, then we need not follow our ancestors, and let us act more wisely, we are after all three hundred years older. Early Czech cuisine merits our attention for these two reasons: because through it you will discover the character of your fathers, but also due to its fame.[6]

He then goes on to list how the cuisine was appreciated and appropriated by Germans, pointing out the presence of 'heidnisch' and 'behaimisch' [Bohemian] recipes in such collections as the 'Würzburg manuscript' (Das Buch von guter Speise) and pointing out how, in a book by the Styrian Archduke Maximilian Ernest (1607), the cook is advised to prepare the calf's head in the Czech fashion.[7] Winter notes how donuts (koblihy) have been appropriated by Germans, citing a volume from 1712 that posits the invention of the donut by a Viennese baker named Cecilie in 1615. 'No such thing!' writes the incensed nationalist:

As early as the fourteenth century, Štítný [an early proponent of the Czech reformation] is angered by Czechs who eat so many donuts during Lent, and in the following century in Rakovník [in western Bohemia] there was a grim trial involving "poisoned donuts!"[8]

Following his lengthy justification for focusing on food, he launches into an examination of sixteenth-century Czech cookery, dietetics, table settings and specific cookbooks. He begins the first chapter by identifying the characteristics of the national diet as consisting primarily of peas, meat, cheese, porridge, dumplings and especially bread. He contrasts this with the Germans who supposedly gorged on giant hunks of meat and the Italians who subsisted on bread and vegetables. He compares the abundance of the pre-White Mountain era, when everyone could afford meat, to what came next: 'The tastes of the common people turned to buchty and porridge, even while they still pined for a meatier diet.' But there was more deprivation to come: 'soon after the beginning of the last century, German potatoes were imposed upon the Czech stomach, even as they continue to be today.'[9]

After briefly noting contemporary local criticism of the sixteenth-century Italian fashions that had swept through the Prague court, he turns to three sixteenth-century cookbooks heavily indebted to those same fashions: an anonymous volume likely printed by Jan Severin the younger in the early part of the century; a second authored by the famed alchemist, Bavor the younger Rodovský of Hustiřan; and a third, the so-called Kantor cookbook, which was mostly cribbed from Severin and is generally dated to the middle of the century.[10] From an outsider's perspective the recipes reflect the cosmopolitan style then current throughout aristocratic Europe; there's nothing especially Czech in the abundance of spice or the fondness for blancmange and similar mushy preparations. Yet in a passage that recounts a lamprey recipe that requires the cook to repeatedly stab the poor living creature, Winter can't help but to contrast this with even more brutal contemporary German recipes that call for cooking geese alive. He quips, 'It would seem that our old Czech cuisine was more humane than its German equivalent, which is to be expected given the character of each nation.'[11]

The next section is mostly devoted to the Czech-language version of the dietetic oeuvre of Ferdinand I's physician Jan Kopp (Johannes Copp von Raumenthal), and here Winter shows himself more the antiquarian than the chauvinist, sympathizing with the German doctor's dietary mission impossible, despite his Teutonic origin.[12] Then comes a chapter on table settings which sets about to prove how advanced Czech civilization was in this respect prior to White Mountain. In some ways this is the most original part of the book, drawing on a noteworthy set of sources. Winter is certainly more impressed by the gilded steins and Venetian glass of Prague inventories than the spiced dishes of renaissance cooks. Next he turns to menus and the quantities of food eaten. Citing dozens of sources, he depicts a diet abundant and cheap, even for the labouring classes. Another chapter is devoted to banqueting and its Czech critics. Needless to say, any decadence in eating and drinking could be blamed on the Germans: 'The described excesses, from which the sixteenth century suffered, arrived in Bohemia from Germany.'[13] The final section is devoted to (women) cooks, kitchens and their equipment. Luckily for today's historian, Winter's disapproving account is full of granular detail that includes specific menus, inventories and prices.

The Omnivorous Archivist

A generation younger than Winter, Čeněk Zíbrt (1864-1932) was much more the professional historian: he served as professor of cultural history at Charles University and later as director of the Czech National Museum library. Coming of age in an era of increasing Czech self-confidence, he stands out even from his generation's ethnographic enthusiasts in his attention to just about every aspect of Czech popular culture, pivoting from old Slavonic mythology to histories of popular song and dance, from vernacular Czech peasant architecture to an account of old-time hunting customs and superstitions. He devoted several historical books to food and drink, including a history of brewing, a study on brew masters, a similar monograph on millers, another on beer in popular song as well as a slim volume devoted to gingerbread.[14] In *Staročeské umění kuchařské* [*The Culinary Art of the Early Czechs*] (1927), he transcribed and annotated a series of culinary manuscripts, providing them with a thirty five-page introduction that traces the cuisine of Bohemia starting with the earliest medieval sources.

Zíbrt keeps the historian's distance, hardly ever commenting on the palatability of what he transcribes. Written in the euphoric first decade of an independent Czechoslovakia, the book lacks the occasionally jingoistic passages interspersed throughout Winter's book. That said, after a two-page discussion of early Italian and

220

French sources, he dismisses German cuisine in a single sentence. And he doesn't neglect to mention that the fourteenth-century religious reformer Jan Hus 'concerned himself with the use of proper, indigenous Czech food words, reproaching Prague residents for not using the original, old Czech work *šiška* [for dumpling] and instead using the Germanized *knedlík* [from *knödel*]'. For shame! However, the reputation of Czech cooks did deserve attention:

> Even the food-loving Italians and French with their gourmet palates praised Czech cuisine. In 1464, the Czech nobleman Albrecht Kostka 'invited, on the Thursday preceding the festal day of St. Peter and Paul, the advisor to the Duke of Milan (Francesco Sforza) and some elders of Aquila to lunch'. At the time, in the aftermath of the Hussite wars, Czechs didn't have a good reputation, whether in terms of education, morals, way of life or manners. The Czech nation was disparaged and subjected to vicious rumours. The Italian gourmets were accordingly surprised. 'And they were all surprised that the Czechs had such estimable and attractive food'.[15]

The core of Zíbrt's almost 600-page volume, and his inestimable contribution to culinary history, is a transcription of several recipe collections as well as a scattering of other sources (such as regulations issued in 1562 concerning food served in public houses as well as its price and an extensive description of the 1578 wedding feast of Vilém of Rožmberk, among others). The overwhelming majority of his book, however, is devoted to recipes, starting with a fifty-three page anonymous manuscript dating to the late fourteen hundreds and ending with a 1712 book credited to Kateřina Koniášová (this collection turns out to be a catchall of recipes going back as far as the sixteenth century).

All told *Staročeské umění kuchařské* contains more than a dozen manuscripts and printed codices, many transcribed in full, including all the Severin and Bavor of Hustiřan recipes only briefly described by Winter. Zíbrt's only qualification for including a text seems to be that it is written in the Czech language. He shows no interest in making connections with the international culinary style mirrored in the early collections (typical are recipes such as Severin's salt cod with almond milk, pepper, ginger and saffron, or Bavor's instructions for a deer meat puree seasoned with 'pepper, ginger and all the spices'). Even more oddly, the Czech historian leaves without comment the rise of certain 'national' dishes. For example, a manuscript collection of recipes from early seventeenth century noble households written in multiple hands includes a lengthy repertoire of rich cakes (*dorty*) and a diversity of dumplings (*knedle*), including what are perhaps the first boiled bread dumpling recipes, a quintessential Czech staple.[16] When he turns to recipes collected by Alžběta Lidmila of Lisov around 1661, written in both Czech and German, Zíbrt transcribes only the Czech language sections, remarking that that there are enough of those that he need not bother with those written in German. As it is there is too much that is German, he sniffs: 'The influence of German cookery is evident in both the Germanized names and the culinary terminology for kitchen implements and procedures as well as in the general way German, French and Italian cooking intruded into the aristocratic kitchens that were once home to a distinctive Czech, old-world cuisine.'[17] Any Czech reading Zíbrt's book would understand this fall from culinary grace was yet one more regrettable consequence of the defeat at White Mountain.

The Accidental Historian

Marie Úlehlová-Tilschová (1896-1978) may not have had any background as a historian, but she did come from Prague's intellectual elite. Her father was Emanuel Tilsch, a professor of law at the Czech Charles University (the university was divided by language), and her mother Anna Marie Tilschová was a widely published novelist.[18] Following studies in botany at Charles University, Marie eventually found her niche as a nutritionist, a field she would eventually explore not merely from a health but also a social, economic and ethnographic perspective.

During the war, even as she was employed in the protectorate's State Institute of Health, she wrote a food column in *Lidové noviny*, one of the country's remaining dailies. Despite the arrests, censorship and the imposition of racist Nuremberg laws, the Czech press continued to muddle on. Anything with a whiff of politics was heavily censored of course, but the more ordinary stuff that fills newspapers was left mostly untouched. Accordingly Úlehlová-Tilschová was let be when, in 1940, she invited her readers to send in culinary memories for a project the newspaper called '*Hledáme kořeny lidové výživy*' [Searching for roots of the popular diet].[19] The response was overwhelming. She received thousands of letters that would eventually form the core of her book. The result would be a loving and exhaustive study of the Czech folk diet, a 650-page volume that is arguably the most in-depth study of rural food culture in any language.

To the censor's eye, *Česká strava lidová* shows no evidence of propaganda; there are certainly no anti-German screeds à la Winter: in fact, Germans barely seem to exist at all. Nonetheless, for anyone who can read the code, the book's nationalism seeps out of every chapter. For one, it specifically covers all the territory of the Czech crown, including the border regions ceded at Munich, provinces that were now officially German *Länder*. The author had to tread carefully to circumvent the censors. In an afterward appended to the book just prior to its 1945, post-liberation publication, Úlehlová-Tilschová apologizes for some of her awkward territorial terminology. Since it was illegal to use Czech names for Sudetenland towns, and the author refused to use the German ones, she had to make do with contorted regional neologisms. What's more, the book focuses entirely on the foodways of Czechs, even in regions with significant minority populations. Though her focus is on Bohemia and Moravia, when she does occasionally venture abroad it is primarily to 'neighbouring Slovakia' and less frequently to Slavic lands to the east. Hardly ever does she reference the German-speaking neighbours to the north, west and south. She spends more time on the maple-syrup-consuming North Americans (in a section on birch and maple sap consumption in the Czech lands) than she ever does on Bavarians or Silesians. In a regrettable internalization of racial ideas she posits Czechs as part of a Slavic 'race' with the implication that food (like language) is a race-specific phenomenon. A typical formulation that echoes in many variants throughout the book is 'We are a people, just like other Slavs' who have particular traditions – such as mushroom hunting, for example.[20]

The book is divided into five sections, the first three to ingredients – gathered, cultivated and raised – while the final two are dedicated to holiday dishes and everyday foods. She draws on an enormous range of written sources well beyond her crowd-sourced archive. She looks to culinary historians such as Winter and Zíbrt, botanists, folklorists, herbals, cookbooks and even folk songs and sayings. She even plunders German-language sources when it helps her cause.[21] Her interest in nutrition is a returning leitmotif. Thus we don't merely learn how wild rosehips were made into fruit butter or their pips dried and roasted as a coffee additive (apparently imparting a vanilla-like flavour) but we are told of the abundance of vitamins C and A the fruit contains.[22] The subtext is how much more healthful the folk diet was compared to contemporary urban foodways.

Her peasants eat dumplings with mushroom sauce for Christmas, donuts on Shrove Tuesday and *koláče*, large and small, at weddings, christenings and funerals. They dry their fruit in smoke houses, sweeten their porridge with powdered, desiccated carrots and press oil from beechnuts. They drink a milky 'coffee' made of roasted wheat or barley for breakfast, caraway soup (little more than roux-thickened water) for dinner and flour-thickened applesauce with bread for supper.

Given its astonishing breadth and depth, any summary of the book is impossible, but a brief passage pertaining to the two staples of the Czech diet, bread and beer, can give the English-speaker a taste of Úlehlová-Tilschova's prose. She begins with a quotation from one of her correspondents:

> An essential person and a frequent visitor to the village was the yeast woman, called the *kvasníčářka* [from the Czech *kvasnice* or yeast].' This yeast woman used to go pail in hand from village to village, much like herb or vegetable women do or any other peddler for that matter. Kvasníčářky used to walk for miles to get to the breweries, then distributed the yeast from their pails, selling it by the *máz* [about two litres]. But now they're quite gone.[23]

She continues to explain how the yeast women's demise was in part caused by the shift by brewers from top to bottom fermentation [that is from ale to lager] signalling the end of the kvasníčářka's curious lifestyle. Apparently bottom-fermented yeast was unsuitable for home baking, leaving a bitter taste and producing little or no foam.

Other than its nationalistic message, there is another theme that runs through the book, mainly an awareness that many of the foodways the armchair ethnographer describes have, or are, rapidly disappearing. And this was something you couldn't

223

blame on the Germans. In the end it wasn't the Nazi war machine that would do in Czech peasant foodways but rather the cumulative effects of industrialization and then, following 1948, the forced collectivization of all food production. Now socialist worker and comrade farmer could indulge in a national dish of pork, cabbage and dumplings day in and day out. It's just that meat and cabbage were produced on a factory farm, the dumplings manufactured to centrally mandated norms and all of it was cooked (or reheated) in a government-run commissary. Food lost most of its old meanings. Now it spoke the language of industry.

Food Is the Message

It bears repeating that reading too much of an ideological message into their texts would be unfair to the three authors. Above and beyond any political component, their work is a valuable contribution to European culinary history. Nevertheless it is hard to imagine any of these books being written without a nationalist impulse, without the inferiority complex of a colonized nation. But it is just this partisan motivation that we can thank for prodding scholars to explore culinary history at a time when it was most definitely not in style elsewhere. The nation's foodways became a medium of communication, not merely about the past but about the present. Renaissance aristocratic menus recounted the tale of a deep-rooted nation, five hundred-year old recipes told the story of a people's stubborn survival.

And today? Following 1989 Czechs rushed to join the civilization they felt had left them behind. At first, this required studying the language of Tuscan extra-virgin olive oil and global supermarket chains, next it meant parsing Punjabi and Palestinian menus and finally it turned to shopping for pasture-fed lamb at city farmer's markets and searching out pubs with microbrews – or, just as likely, feeding on KFC and doner kebabs. That Czechs might be able to resist the onslaught of global civilization, especially by drawing on their culinary heritage, seems almost quaint, a little like the Slow Food Don Quixotes who tilt at Parmelat.

Or it may be that just the opposite is true. That an impossible task is just what is needed. The story Czechs have long told themselves is that they are the victims, whether as a Hussite snubbing Rome or as the hardworking everyman under the thumb of Brussels' bureaucrats. There was a time when this urge to prove their worth led some to document the nation's culinary roots, today, with luck, it might lead to better sausages and beer.

Notes

1. See, for example the discussion of Palacký's work in František Kutnar and Jaroslav Marek, *Přehledné dějiny českého a slovenského dějepisectví. Od počátků národní kultury až do sklonku třicátých let 20. století* [*A Historical Overview of Czech and Slovak Historiography: From the Beginnings of the National Culture to the End of the 1930s*] (Prague: Nakladatelstvý Lidové noviny, 1997), pp. 224-26.
2. Kutnar and Marek, pp. 351-52.

3. Kristina Kaiserová and Jiří Rak, *Nacionalizace společnosti v Čechách 1848-1914* [*The Nationalization of Society in Bohemia, 1848-1914*] (Ústí nad Labem: Univerzita Jana Evangelisty Purkyně, 2008), p. 32.

4. *Koláče*, pizza-like disks of enriched dough with a sweet topping (ground poppy seed, pot cheese and prune butter are typical), used to be central to most country celebrations. *Buchty* resemble rectilinear buns, also typically with a sweet filling. In Czech folklore they are closely linked to a character called '*hloupý* Honza' or simple John who inevitable leaves home to find his fortune with a satchel of mother's *buchty* slung over his shoulder.

5. Kaiserová and Rak, p. 113.

6. Zikmund Winter, *Kuchyně a stůl našich předků. Líčení dějepisné ze XVI. století* (Prague: František Bačkovský, 1892), p. 8.

7. Winter, p. 9. I have not been able to identify the book he mentions.

8. Winter, p. 9.

9. Winter, p. 14.

10. The books are: (1) *Kuchařství, o rozličných krměch, kterak se užitečně s chutí strojiti mají* [*Cookery, Concerning Diverse Dishes, How These May Be Usefully and Tastefully Prepared*], (Prague: Jan Severin, [before 1535]). The book was republished around 1535 by Sevenin's uncle, Pavel Severin. Incidentally this same book was the source of the oldest Polish-language cookbook, *Polské Kuchmistrzostwo* (1535); (2) *Kuchařství o rozličných krmích, kterak se užitečně s chutí strojiti mají, jakožto zvěřina, ptáci, ryby a jiné mnohé krmě, všelikému kuchaři aneb hospodáři, knížka tato potřebná a užitečná. A ocet jak se dělá, také radu najdeš* [*Cookery, Concerning Diverse Dishes, How These May Be Usefully and Tastefully Prepared, such as Game, Poultry, Fish and Many Other Dishes, This Book Necessary and Useful to Every Cook and Housekeeper. Also Here You Will Find Advice on How to Make Vinegar*] (Prague: Kantor, n.d.); and (3) Bavor Rodovský z Hustiřan. *Kuchařství, to jest: Knížka o rozličných krmích, kterak se užitečně s chutí strojiti mají: jakožto zvěřina, ptáci, ryby a jiné mnohé krmě* [*Cookery, Concerning Diverse Dishes, How These May be Usefully and Tastefully Prepared, such as Game, Poultry, Fish and Many Other Dishes*] (Prague: Nygrin, 1591).

11. Winter, p. 24.

12. Johann Kop von Raumenthal, *Knijžka o nakaženij mornijm sepsaná skrze Jana Koppha z Raumentálu, Doktora ec.* (Prague, 1542).

13. Winter, p. 128

14. *Z dějin piva a pivovarnictví v zemích českých* [*From the History of Beer and Brewing in the Czech Lands*] (1894); *Sladovnické obyčeje, zábavy, slavnosti a pověry v nákladnických domech a pivovarech českých* [Brewmasters' Customs, Amusements, Celebrations and Superstitions in Czech Warehouses and Breweries] (1910); *Staročeské obyčeje a pověry mlynářské* [Early Czech Customs and Superstitions of Millers] (1897); *Pivo v písních lidových a znárodnělých* [Beer in Popular and Naturalized Songs] (1909); *Staročeský perník. 107 návodů z rukopisův a knih kuchařských staročeských* [*Early Czech Gingerbread: 107 Recipes from Early Czech Cookbooks and Manuscripts*] (1916).

15. Čeněk Zíbrt, *Staročeské umění kuchařské* (Prague: Nákladem Staré gardy mistrů kuchařů, 1927), p. 99. Interestingly, the first cookery manuscript transcribed by Zíbrt included a recipe for the sort of bread dumpling his readers would have been familiar with. It is made by mixing shredded bread with eggs and a little wine. It is fried in butter (or ghee), however, rather than being boiled as it would be now. The boiled version comes later (see next note).

16. Zíbrt, p. 343. The section includes a baker's dozen dumpling recipes, most of which are made from left-over bread mixed with cream and eggs then boiled (a common approach in contemporary Bavaria). A similar recipe is also enriched with plums. There is, however, a dumpling recipe that most Czechs today would recognize as iconic of their national pantry: 'Large good dumpling. In a bowl or tray, take some white flour and mix with milk and two or three egg yolks, some leaven, salt, and make a dough as for *koláče*. Let it rise, form into a round loaf and roll out like a thick pancake. Have ready a finely grated white bun [breadcrumbs] fried in butter. Beat an egg yolk with saffron, brush the pancake with this and sprinkle with the breadcrumbs, roll into a sausage shape, put into boiling water. When it's

225

cooked, set in a dish. You can leave it whole or slice it if you wish, pour over butter and sprinkle with fried breadcrumbs. Some finely chop onion, cook and use it as a topping instead of the breadcrumbs.'

17. Zíbrt, p. 446.

18. Libor Vikoupil, '*Ecce Homo-Marie Úlehlová-Tilschová*', Český rozhla*s*, 9 August 2008 <http://www.rozhlas.cz/brno/upozornujeme/_zprava/482538> [accessed May 11, 2015].

19. *Lidová kultura: národopisná encyklopedie Čech, Moravy a Slezska* [*Popular Culture: An Ethnographic Encyclopedia of Bohemia, Moravia and Silesia*], ed. by Stanislav Brouček and Richard Jeřábek, 3 vols. (Prague: Etnologický Ústav Akad. Věd České Rep., 2007), vol. 1, pp. 237-323.

20. Marie Úlehlová-Tilschová, Česká strava lidová (Prague: Triton, 2011), p. 45.

21. Admittedly, one of her favourite sources was the botanist Adam Maurizio, who was Swiss, not German.

22. Úlehlová-Tilschová, p. 34.

23. Úlehlová-Tilschová, p. 499.

Dragon on a Platter: The Art of Naming Chinese Dishes

Kian Lam Kho

Naming dishes seems generally quite straightforward in most parts of the world. In China, however, it is not so simple. Go to a Chinese restaurant, and you will find menu items such as Dragon and Phoenix Platter (龍鳳拼盤) and Stir-Fried Squid with Magnolia Slices (玉蘭炒魷魚). In fact, these dishes are a cold platter of lobster and chicken, and stir-fried squid with dried bamboo shoots, respectively. To most Chinese diners these names are understood through their regular usage. But these names can be confusing to those unfamiliar with Chinese cuisine and are often difficult to translate for foreigners (Zhu 2011). To demystify how the Chinese communicate descriptions of their food to diners, one must examine Chinese naming customs, focusing on the poetic qualities of the names, the use of metonyms and homophones and the symbolic meanings of ingredients and cooking methods.

Naming ingredients and finished dishes has developed into a uniquely Chinese art form. Culinary art in China has a very long history of mingling with literature and poetry. Many Chinese historical records on food and cooking were penned by well-known scholars and poets. For example, during the Tang Dynasty around the sixth century, Li Bai (李白) and Du Fu (杜甫), who were renowned drunkards, wrote legendary poems in praise of wine and food. Su Dongpo (蘇東坡), who wrote during the Song Dynasty around the tenth century, and Yuan Mei (袁枚), who wrote during the late Qing Dynasty in the nineteenth century, were poets, scholars and administration officials as well as celebrated epicureans. And in his Qing Dynasty era novel, *Dream of the Red Chamber* (紅樓夢), Cao Xueqin (曹雪芹) detailed descriptions of dining rituals and foods served at different meals that are crucial to the narrative. It is not surprising then that many Chinese names given to food ingredients and dishes contain elaborately poetic and flowery language.

A metonym, which transforms an ingredient's name by a lyrical and often romantic metaphorical substitution, is the most commonly used technique in Chinese food naming conventions. For an example: phoenix claws (鳳爪), which describe chicken feet, perfectly removes the unpleasant image of limp chicken feet and elevates them to the status of an elegant delicacy. In addition, homophones are often used to symbolize prosperity, happiness and other aspirations. Fish (魚), which is pronounced *yu* in Mandarin, has the same pronunciation as leftover (餘), and hence is commonly used as a symbol for abundance.

Furthermore, this naming system includes giving dishes auspicious titles, which are often associated specifically with celebrations such as birthdays or weddings. The dish names can be full of subtle meanings. For example Mandarin duck (鴛鴦), or *yuanyang*, is a very common term used in menus for weddings because these birds mate for life (Yang 2014).

The practice of creating symbolic menus for celebratory meals is considered to have originated from the palace and aristocratic customs during the Sui and Tang Dynasties between the sixth and the tenth centuries (Chen 2001). In the *Book of Rites* (禮記), which was compiled around the tenth century BCE, the *Nei Ze* [*Pattern of Family*] section describes cooking techniques and the composition of dishes. Here the dish names were made up solely of cooking techniques and ingredients. Dishes are similarly named in the *Zhao Hun* (招魂) [*Summoning of the Soul*] a poem in the *Verses of Chu* that is believed to have been written around the third century BCE. (Chen 2001). However, by the Tang Dynasty a celebratory banquet menu recorded by Shu JuYuan (書巨源) in 708 to honour students who passed the Mandarin entrance exam shows that the dish names have already dramatically changed to include the now familiar lyrical language.

The common people also started adopting this custom gradually during the Sui and Tang Dynasties when commercial dining establishments became popular and began promoting their menus. To cater to the increasing demand for elegant business and celebration banquets, sumptuous menus heavy with symbolism were created to attract customers by offering them a sense of sophistication during their dining experience. Symbolic menus have become more popular than ever in contemporary China, and Chinese naming conventions remain a very rich and interesting way of conveying to diners how the dishes are prepared as well as their symbolic meaning.

Basic Naming System

In spite of the many elaborate ways of naming Chinese dishes, the conventions are based on a simple standard. Rudimentary names are constructed by combining cooking techniques, ingredients, and/or the ingredient's final shape or the cutting method used to create it. Both B. Zhou (2011) and Wei (2010) describe how these combinations are employed to create dish names.

A cooking technique combined with a main ingredient is considered the most common way of naming a dish. For example Red Cooked Pork (紅燒肉), Steamed Sea Bass (清蒸鱸魚) and Stir-Fried Asparagus (清炒蘆筍) are all straightforward descriptions of a cooking technique and main ingredient.

In order to describe a dish in more detail, supplementary and sauce ingredients are often included in addition to the main ingredient. Green Pepper Beef (青椒牛肉) and Chinese Broccoli in Oyster Sauce (蠔油芥藍) are examples of this approach. However, simply combining the two ingredients does not always sufficiently convey the idea of the dish itself. So a cooking technique is sometimes inserted into the name to clarify how the dish is cooked. Using this more elaborate method we can describe dishes such as Flash-Fried Lamb with Leeks (蔥爆羊肉) and Braised Chicken Wings With Shiitake Mushrooms (香菇燜雞翅).

Some names, such as *gongbao* (宮保) or *kung pao*, refer to a specific combination of technique and supplementary ingredients which produce a specific flavour. Although the main ingredient may change to create *Gongbao* Chicken (宮保雞丁), *Gongbao* Shrimp (宮保蝦球) or *Gongbao* Squid (宮保魷魚), the dish is always a dry stir-fry with chillies, spices and peanuts. Oftentimes, a specific combination of techniques and ingredients becomes established, and then it is named after the associated person, place or legend. *Gongbao* was the nickname given to a late Qing Dynasty magistrate who, according to legend, had a private cook who created this spicy chicken dish to welcome him home whenever he returned from an official tour of his domain.

Finally the shape of the main ingredient or the cutting method used to obtain it can be used to more accurately describe a dish. Moo Goo Gai Pan (蘑菇雞片), which literally means 'mushroom chicken slices' in Cantonese, is a good example. The *pan*, or *pian* in Mandarin, means 'slices'. The addition of this cutting shape immediately explains what the ingredients will physically look like in the dish. In Chinese knife technique there is a specific name for each type of cutting shape. In the case of Moo Goo Gai Pan, the *pan*, or *pian*, immediately means that the chicken and shiitake mushrooms are served sliced.

At times the shape of the ingredient does not fall into any of the standard knife-cutting categories. When this happens a metaphorical description is often used. Prawn, for example, is almost always described as prawn ball (蝦球) because it curls up into a round shape when cooked. Certain ingredients, such as chicken gizzards, are often scored in a crisscross pattern for easy cooking. When quickly stir-fried they open up into a flower shape. Therefore they are always called 'gizzard flowers' as in Flash-Fried Chicken Gizzard Flowers (爆炒雞胗花).

229

Shape Name	Chinese Name	Description
Pian	片	Bias cut into slices
Si	絲	Thin julienne into fine strands
Tiao	條	Thick julienne into baton shapes
Duan	段	1½-inch pieces of long ingredients, such as scallion or string bean
Ding	丁	Large dice of about 1-inch thick
Mi	米	Fine dice about the size of a rice grain
Kuai	塊	Rolling cut into irregularly shaped large pieces
Mo	末	Fine mince into very small pieces
Sui	碎	Finely minced until almost a paste

Table 1. Chinese Knife-Cutting Shapes

Metonyms

Naming ingredients using metonyms, or metaphorical substitutions, makes a dish name more lyrical. This is a common practice in naming both the final dish and in identifying ingredients in markets. The main purpose for substituting an ingredient name with a metonym is to transform the ingredient from a common item to a more palatable or luxurious one.

Elevating the image of ingredients is a common practice in Chinese menus. One of the most familiar substitutions is to label chicken feet as phoenix claws (鳳爪). Phoenix (鳳凰), a mythical bird with a regal and powerful image often associated with the imperial court, has become the de facto substitution for chicken. A whole chicken is often portrayed as a phoenix in the menus of elegant restaurants or at banquets (Yang 2014).

Another example of a metonym that conjures up an image of luxury or prosperity is one used to describe *gailan* (芥藍), a common Chinese broccoli. When used to accompany expensive main ingredients such as prawn or ham, these pedestrian stalks are often referred to as 'jade trees' or *yushu* (玉樹).

Wu (2012) and G. Zhou (2008) write that metonyms used in Chinese dish names are often divided into three main groups: animals, plants and precious jewels, whether real or imaginary. Animal names are generally used for meat or protein ingredients, while plant and flower names are conversely used for vegetable and fruit ingredients. Precious stones are regularly used to describe ingredients with the appearance or shape of jewels.

In addition to the phoenix, there are many other animal metonyms used in Chinese dish names. Dragon (籠) is often used to connote the authority of the imperial court. Since dragon is the symbol of the emperor, it is widely used at official government banquets or important business functions (Yang 2014). Generally used to describe snake or lobster, dragon is the ultimate metonym around which a lavish menu is crafted.

An animal name does not always simply refer to an ingredient. Lion's head, for example, is used to refer to a large meatball dish from the Shanghai region. The meatballs are made into large spheres of about one to two inches in diameter that, when cooked in a clay pot sitting on a bed of napa cabbage, resemble lion heads. The metonym in this case does not refer to meat itself but to a final shape when the pork is transformed into meatballs.

Just like meats, vegetable names are similarly replaced by metonyms in some Chinese dishes. These metaphors often refer to more attractive plants or flowers. For example *yulan* magnolia (玉蘭), a delicate white variety of magnolia, is used to represent dried bamboo shoot slices because, when sliced, the rehydrated bamboo shoots appear yellowish white and are shaped like petals. Because of its white colour, *yulan* is often used by authors and poets to represent beauty and purity, which gives this dish a feminine overtone.

Lastly, the use of precious stones and jewellery in describing dishes can truly raise the bar in transforming a dish name into a posh delicacy. Pearl studded meatballs (珍

珠丸子) is a dish of steamed pork balls covered with sticky rice. When cooked the dish looks as if the meatballs are covered with tiny white seed pearls. Another dish, Stir-Fried Emerald Shrimp (翡翠蝦仁), is made with small tender shrimp covered in a green sauce made with spinach juice. The glaze on the shrimp makes them look as though they have been made from green emeralds. In these cases the metonyms are not used to describe a particular ingredient, but rather to highlight the shape of the main ingredient and appearance of the final dish.

Homophones

In the daily life of the Chinese people, homophones are regularly employed for seeking good fortune. For example, the number eight (*ba* or 八), which thymes with prosperity (*fa* or 發) in many Chinese dialects, has always been considered a lucky number; whereas the number four (*si* or 四), which is pronounced just like death (*si* or 死), is avoided at all costs. So it is only natural that this same practice is carried over in naming dishes.

In the culinary realm, the characters for fish (魚) and abundance (餘), although written as two distinct characters, are pronounced exactly the same when spoken. Only the context will tell you which meaning is being referred to. So 'fish' has become synonymous with prosperity and is a must-serve item in a Chinese New Year dinner. In fact, fish is almost always served at many major celebration banquets when prosperity is a major theme.

Examples of homophones abound and they are regular tools in naming dishes for the purpose of making the dishes more auspicious and desirable (Li 2002). Ingredients or cooking methods are both candidates for substitution by homophones. The practice of using homophones resulted from the fact that the Chinese language has many fewer unique syllables compared to other languages. For example, there are only about 400 in Chinese as compared to more than 10,000 in English. This dearth of syllables produces a large number of homophones with a variety of meanings (Y. Zhou 2003). Given this language characteristic, it is natural that homophone usage has become common practice in dish naming.

231

Auspicious Names and Symbolism

Ultimately, the main objective of all these devices for naming dishes is to make sure that the final names seem auspicious and prosperous. This is especially important for major celebrations such as birthdays, weddings and holidays. Each type of celebration requires different symbolism, and dish names are created using a combination of the various conventions described above.

For birthday celebrations, longevity is the central theme; hence the dish names should reflect this particular motif. As an example, a noodle dish, Longevity Noodles (長壽麵), is made from a single strand symbolizing hopefulness for a long life. It is in fact quite common to create a new dish along with a unique name specifically designed for a special event. Another example of a dish for a birthday celebration is known as Happy Family Together (全家福), a standard name for a braised dish with exotic ingredients (Christensen 2013). Many different variations of this dish are known to exist with ingredients such as prawns, sea cucumbers, lobster, chicken or wild mushrooms. Although the ingredients may vary widely, when served for a birthday banquet it indicates that the entire family is gathered together with the birthday celebrant. Other dishes that symbolize longevity include those made with turtle because of its long lifespan. Sweet steamed buns (壽桃) made into the shape of peaches are also a symbol of long life.

Happiness and fertility are the dominant themes of wedding banquets. Dishes with complementary paired sauces or ingredients have become symbols of the coupling of the bride and groom. An example is Mandarin Duck Prawns (鴛鴦蝦仁), which normally is a stir-fried prawn dish with two sauces. Despite its name, there is no Mandarin duck in this dish. Instead the fidelity of these ducks, which mate for life, is compared to the union of the two sauces. Foods with seeds are often included in the meal to represent fertility. In fact, a sweet soup of jujubes, peanuts, dried longan and lotus seeds is known as 'Early arrival of children' (早生貴子). In Chinese the pronunciation of the dish is *zao sheng gui zi*, and each character's sound is represented in the dish by a homophone ingredient: *zao* for jujube (*hong zao* 紅棗), *sheng* for peanuts (*hua sheng* 花生), *gui* for dried longan (*gui yuan* 桂圓), and *zi* for lotus seeds (*lian zi* 蓮子).

232 During Chinese New Year, symbolic foods are even more plentiful. In addition to fish dishes, other examples include dumplings shaped like gold ingots, symbolizing hoped for prosperity, and 'sticky rice cake' because it sounds like 'New Year cake'. The Mandarin pronunciation of 'sticky cake' (黏糕) is *nian gao* which happens to be the exact homophone of 'year cake' (年糕), which can be interpreted as 'New Year cake' in Chinese. Similarly, *nian gao,* the homophone of 'better every year' (年年高), becomes the symbol of prosperity. With all these auspicious qualities 'sticky rice' cake has become a must-serve dish in any Chinese New Year celebration.

Complete Menus

One of the clever concepts that the Chinese have incorporated into menu writing is to mimic the cadence of classic Chinese poetry. The rhythm of Chinese poetry is accomplished by using a set number of characters per line. The same practice is employed in naming of many Chinese dishes. Four and five characters per line are the most widely used standard, according to Zhang (2014). Based on her analysis of more than one thousand Chinese dish names, 33% are made up of four characters, and 31% have five characters. Zhang's finding reinforces the notion that Chinese dish names evolved closely with ancient Chinese poetry. Four-character poems originated during the Zhou Dynasty around the tenth century BCE, and five-character poems became popular during the Sui and Tang Dynasties about sixth century CE. Before the Sui and Tang period dish names used a realistic description identifying ingredients and techniques, which regularly used four characters. Poetic and lyrical names did not become popular until after the five-character poems proliferated and developed into one of the most common ways to name dishes. Seven characters dish names also developed later, in tandem with the appearance of seven-character poems, but they are not as common as the four and five character forms.

As the use of these symbolic names became prominent, chefs and cooks would start with auspicious phrases such as the 'Early arrival of children', or *zao sheng gui zi* (早生貴子), mentioned above. Then they would identify food related homophones of the characters to select ingredients for new dishes.

Another celebrated dish known as 'One hundred birds paying court to the phoenix', or *bai niao chao feng* (百鳥朝鳳), is often served during a banquet to pay respect to a business superior or an elder. The dish name is based on Chinese legend in which the phoenix is the leader of birds; the other avian subjects come to pay respect to their ruler. Although the same name is used in many different restaurants, large variations exist in the dish itself. Some restaurants create a dish of roasted chicken surrounded by little decorative radish pieces in bird shapes. Other interpretations include a braised chicken ringed by a multitude of bird-shaped dumplings.

Finally, the epitome of Chinese menu writing is achieved when the menu is written in the format of acrostic poem. A list of dishes is compiled into a menu: each item is composed of a Chinese idiom or auspicious saying, and the first character of each menu item also in turn forms a separate idiom. As an example, consider this snippet in a wedding banquet menu describing four hot dishes:

233

龍騰虎躍
鳳凰展翅
呈祥前程
祥和團圓

These four lines describe four dishes, and each name is derived from a Chinese idiom. The first item is 'Soaring dragon and leaping tiger', or *long ten hu yue* (龍騰虎躍), which symbolizes that the newlywed couple will stand together through a good life. A chef would interpret this dish as braised fresh ham hock with tiger prawn, where the ham hock represents the tiger and the prawn substitutes for the dragon. The second dish is 'Phoenix extending its wings', or *feng huang zhan chi* (鳳凰展翅), which means that the young couple will become independent and extend their wings to succeed in their new life. Here a chef could make fried chicken wings with fragrant spices. The third line reads 'Successful future together', or *cheng xiang qian cheng* (呈祥前程). This dish can be translated as a vegetable stir-fry of asparagus, spring bamboo and baby carrots, where only the tips of the vegetables are used to signify future growth and a forward outlook. Finally, the last item is written as 'Harmonious together', or *xiang he tuan yuan* (祥和團圓), which is a hope for happy life together. Since togetherness in Chinese literally translates to circling back to get together, a chef would most likely create a dish of meatballs with a flavourful sauce accompanied by vegetables. But simply using these auspicious names is not enough. The first character of each dish, which forms *long feng cheng xiang* (龍鳳呈祥), in fact means 'Dragon and phoenix happy together'. That is the main theme of the menu celebrating the forming of a happy family between the groom (or dragon) and the bride (or phoenix).

Similar examples abound in other types of celebratory banquets. Milestone birthday celebrations for the elders are especially important and there are many traditional symbols used to put together the menu.

Summary and Conclusion

While describing the composition of a dish is normally not a very complicated process in most other culinary cultures, the Chinese dish naming tradition is very sophisticated. Not only do the Chinese name their ingredients with metonyms and use homophones to create auspicious dish names, but the menus are also laden with symbolism and can be as lyrical as poetry. Chinese scholars and poets have a longstanding connection with the enjoyment of food and wine. What started out most likely as the practice of palace official scholars naming dishes for the emperor or aristocratic patrons was later adopted by the commoners and flourished.

The tradition of naming dishes using these conventions continues into contemporary China and thrives in an increasingly affluent Chinese society. Restaurants in China and in Asian countries with large Chinese populations still pay a great deal of attention to their menu writing. Faced with rapid globalization and the rush to adopt the trappings of Western culture, hopefully the Chinese people's belief in the power of auspicious symbolism, and respect for the ancient sages' clever and playful conventions, will continue to perpetuate and amplify the Chinese art of naming their foods.

Bibliography

Chen, Jinbiao. 2001. 'Study on Chinese Dishes Naming' (中國菜餚命名研究 — 陳金標). *Cuisine Journal of Yangzhou University* 3: 13-17.

Christensen, Matthew B. 2013. *Decoding China* (Rutland, Vermont: Tuttle Publishing).

Li, YouQing. 2002. 'Cultural Connotation of Chinese Dish Names and Its Translation' (中國菜式命名的文化內涵與翻譯 - 李憂青). *Journal of Jianghan University (Humanities and Social Science)* 21.1: 102-04.

Lin, Hsiang Ju, and Tsuifeng Lin. 1969. *Chinese Gastronomy* (New York: Hasting House).

Wei, Yun. 2010. 'Analysis of Chinese Dishes Naming Model' (中國菜命名模式分析 — 魏雲). *Modern Chinese* 3: 91-92.

Wu, WangXin. 2012. 'Discussion of Cultural Connotation of Chinese Dish Name' (趣談中國菜名的文化內涵 — 吳望新). *Business Culture* 6: 394.

Yang, Huijuan. 2014. 'A Cognitive Analysis on Chinese Dish Names' (中國菜名的認知語言學分析 - 楊會娟) (master degree dissertation, Xihua Universitu, Chengdu, Sichuan).

Zhang, Jing. 2014. 'Chinese Dish Name Structure and Naming Characteristics' (中國菜名的結構及命名的語言文化特征 — 張婧). *Modern Enterprise Education* 24: 544.

Zhou, Bei. 2011. 'Chinese Dishes Naming Convention and Research' (中式菜名的認識研究及其命名

啟示 － 周貝). *Literature Education* 113-15.

Zhou, Guiying. 2008. 'Chinese Dishes Naming Theory and Translation Method' (中國菜的命名理據及翻譯策略 － 周桂英). *Journal of Zhengzhou Institute of Aeronautical Industry Management (Social Science Edition)* 27.1: 112-13.

Zhou, Youguang. 2003. *The Historical Evolution of Chinese Languages and Scripts.* Translated by Liqing Zhang (Columbus, Ohio: National East Asian Languages Resource Center, Ohio State University).

Zhu, Li. 2011. 'The Characteristics of Chinese Dish Names and Their Translatability' (中國菜名的特點與文化可譯性實踐 － 朱莉). *Journal of Ningbo University (Liberal Arts Edition)* 24.4: 70-73.

Communicating Superfoods: A Case Study of Maca Packaging

Jessica Loyer

Introduction

In recent years there has been an explosion onto the health food scene of exotic 'superfoods': food products celebrated for their purported extraordinary nutritional and medicinal values, derived from indigenous culinary and healing traditions and inserted onto the shelves of wealthy Western marketplaces. These products are presented as something between medicine and food; the very word 'superfood' indicates that these are superlative edibles. Goji berries, açai, maca, quinoa, chia seed – these, among others, have become the superheroes of the grocery store. Placing these novel food products on the shelves of health food shops – and, increasingly, supermarkets and chemists – around the world has required that the concept of superfood be constructed and communicated to new consumers. Product packaging is one significant site at which such information is communicated.

This paper takes a closer look at the packaging of one particular superfood product available in Australia, the Peruvian root maca. Drawing upon my own fieldwork in the central Andes in 2014, I offer a case study of one point at which the superfoods concept is constructed and communicated by evoking contemporary discourses about the relationship between food and health. With their dual emphases on scientifically substantiated health benefits and long histories of indigenous use, superfoods represent the intersection of two popular discourses regarding how food and health are best understood and approached. The first is the discourse of 'nutritionism', a term coined by Gyorgy Scrinis to refer to the reductionist view of foods as made up of the sum of their nutrients.[1] The second is the discourse of what Christine Knight calls 'nutritional primitivism', which privileges ancient or indigenous knowledge and 'natural' production practices in a nostalgic search for authenticity in the diet and its related health outcomes, in contrast to those food and health cultures and regimes seen as 'tainted' by complex modern technologies.[2] Both themes are represented in food and nutrition elsewhere, but come together in the concept of superfoods.

In addition, superfood products have increasingly incorporated discourses of critical consumption into their representations by showcasing environmental and ethical certifications such as 'organic' and 'fair trade'.[3] The use of such certifications on product packaging provides consumers with information about the circumstances of production, which is presented alongside information about how consumers should understand and use superfood products. The large quantity of information presented on superfood packaging serves not only to produce and reproduce the concept of superfoods, but also to communicate geographical knowledges about products sold far from their places and cultures of origin. The package in question is presented with a variety of knowledge claims, which should be read critically as representations that serve particular interests rather than as an unproblematic attempt to 'defetishize' the commodity. Points of disjuncture between these knowledge claims open up spaces for contestation by other actors involved in the production and consumption of these food products.

Case Study: Maca Packaging

We begin with an image: a beautiful illustration of a bucolic scene featuring plump women in traditional Andean dress, bent neatly at the waist and cradling in their arms big round baskets full of pink, black and cream coloured root vegetables. With felt hats perched atop their heads and black braids hanging either side of calm, dark skinned faces, the women are plucking turnip-like vegetables from sparse soil. The uniform tan colour of the earth contrasts with the brightness of the women's outfits, a cheerful array of blue, red, green, yellow and orange. In the background, snow-capped mountains rise to meet a clear blue sky scattered with fluffy clouds.

Figure 1. Power Super Foods maca packaging

237

This image is not a Diego Rivera painting hanging in an art gallery; it is featured on a plastic package of maca powder on the shelf of a South Australian health food store, 500 grams for forty dollars.[4] The package declares that this beige powder is 'The Inca Superfood' and that it is 'a source of vitamins, protein and minerals' alongside claims of 'certified organic' and 'fair trade'. Further information about the product's healthfulness, origins and uses are provided on the back of the package. The back of the package notes that it is a product of Peru, packed in Australia by the Australian company Power Super Foods. The company is based in New South Wales but sells their products nationwide both via their own website and through distributors.[5]

Maca is a relatively new product in Australia, having only become widely available within the past ten years. It has no history of use in Australia before the late 1990s, and the entirety of the maca available in the country is imported from Peru. As such, Australian consumers have had to learn how and why to use maca. Maca has been *placed* in the Australian health food market in two senses: it has been physically put there, and it has been imaginatively constructed as a useful product for Australian consumers.

Defining Superfoods

There is a relationship between these physical and imaginative placements. Maca is positioned on the shelf grouped with other superfood products such as cacao powder, chia seeds and goji berries. Behind this physical placement is an imaginative connection between maca and these other products that informs how maca should be encountered and used by new consumers. These foods have been collectively cast as 'superfoods', a category in between dietary supplement and ordinary foodstuff. This category is constructed in the retail setting by grouping these products together. It is also constructed for each individual product by communicating how the product should be used.

The packaging establishes the appropriate setting in which maca should be consumed by providing 'Suggested Uses': 'Mix ¼ teaspoon up to 1 heaped teaspoon into daily smoothies, cereal, yoghurt, juice, baked goods, etc.'. Thus maca powder is established as an ingredient to use in food preparations, not a supplement to be taken on its own. Despite the fact that mixing maca powder into a smoothie or sprinkling it over cereal is a food preparation to be consumed as part of a meal or snack, there is a similarity between the idea of adding a daily teaspoon of maca to one's breakfast and taking a multivitamin supplement each morning. By communicating how consumers should use maca, it is placed in an ambiguous category between food and medicine – the category of superfoods.

Placing maca as a superfood implies that it is beneficial for the consumer on two accounts: it is extremely healthy as proven by science, and its healthfulness is also supported by a long history of indigenous knowledge. Its health benefits are thus doubly verified through two different, but not necessarily oppositional, knowledge frameworks regarding what qualities make a food 'healthy'.

Nutritionism

The first knowledge framework referenced on the maca packaging is that of nutritionism, which Scrinis defines as 'a reductive *focus* on the nutrient composition of foods as the means for understanding their healthfulness, as well as [...] a reductive *interpretation* of the role of these nutrients in bodily health'.[6] Under the paradigm of nutritionism, the invisible actions of nutrients on the body dominate understandings of food and health. In particular, superfoods have arisen against a backdrop of what Scrinis calls the 'era of functional nutritionism'. Since the mid-1990s, nutritional research, dietary advice and popular discourse has moved beyond the avoidance of 'bad' nutrients such as saturated fat and has shifted focus to increasing consumption of 'good' nutrients such as antioxidants.

In communicating maca's healthfulness, the packaging uses the language of nutritional science, describing the product as 'a source of vitamins, protein, and minerals'; 'high vegetarian protein (20+ amino acids), vitamins, and too many minerals/ trace elements to list'; and as a 'nutrient-rich food'. The communication of this kind of scientized health information to consumers is typical of the era of functional nutritionism, in which foods are increasingly viewed not only in terms of their macro- and micronutrient contents, but also in terms of the impacts of particular nutrients on bodily functions and health outcomes as measured by biomarkers.[7] Similarly, the production of this kind of information is the focus of scientific studies, many of which are at least partially funded by industry.[8] By communicating maca's excellent nutrient profile, the package argues for the 'functional' benefit of consuming maca. In this sense, superfoods such as maca can be seen as a type of 'functional food' in that they tend to be marketed using nutrient content or health benefit claims.

However, unlike many other functional foods, superfoods are not nutritionally engineered, fortified or enhanced; rather, they are whole foods such as chia seeds or minimally processed foods such as dried and powdered maca. They are a product of functional nutritionism in that their development, promotion and consumer popularity relies on an understanding of the relationship between food and health in terms of the sufficient consumption of the right nutrients. But they are also a backlash against formulated functional foods, a 'natural' way to get those nutrients without relying on a technological fix. Like other functional foods, their healthfulness is validated through a framework of scientific knowledge. But they also skirt the problem of consumer distrust of technologically developed and highly processed foods by further validating their healthfulness through frameworks of folk and indigenous wisdom and naturalness.

Primitivism and the Natural

While the concept of superfoods embraces the premise of functional nutritionism – that foods are made up of specific nutrients that directly impact health outcomes – they also challenge the reductive aspect of this discourse that equates the health value of supplemental nutrients with those occurring naturally in foods. Superfoods challenge the discourse of functional nutritionism in two ways. The first is by offering an alternative framework for validating knowledge about food and health, which I call the framework of folk and indigenous wisdom. Within this framework, knowledge about food and health is valued not because it has been demonstrated using the scientific method but because it has been passed down through generations and carries an aura of tradition and authenticity. In superfoods discourse, the framework of folk and indigenous wisdom does not displace the paradigm of functional nutritionism; rather, the two types of knowledge are often presented side by side.

The maca packaging presents the framework of folk and indigenous wisdom in addition to that of nutritionism by declaring that maca is 'The Inca Superfood' and describing it as 'truly ancient'. Further, it refers to the purported Peruvian 'belief' that it is 'a powerful enhancer of well-being and vigor' that enables Peruvians 'not just to exist but thrive in the stressful intensity of their high altitude climate'. Language is important here and suggests that knowledge in this framework is produced and valued differently than it is within scientific frameworks; knowledge takes the form of 'beliefs' rather than 'facts' and refers to general 'well-being and vigor' and 'thriving' rather than specific nutrients and their particular bodily impacts.

The image also communicates this framework by depicting indigenous women wearing traditional dress harvesting maca by hand into woven baskets. The indigenous appearance of the harvesters, the manual harvest method, the way in which the women are dressed and the baskets they carry suggest a sense of tradition and authenticity. Through this combination of words and images, maca's healthfulness is presented as validated via its authenticity. However there is a gap between this image and practice which calls into question the origins and purposes of this representation. During fieldwork I observed that harvesters rarely wore traditional dress, they gathered harvested roots into large plastic sacks rather than carrying baskets, and they did not harvest entirely manually but used a small hand tool to loosen roots from the soil.

240

Figure 2: Harvesting maca in Junín province, Perú

The second challenge to the discourse of functional nutritionism is in the valuing of the natural over the technological. This naturalism presents a challenge to the material manifestation of functional nutritionism in the form of fortified, enhanced or otherwise modified functional foods, rather than to the premise of functional nutritionism as a whole. The appeal to nature and the natural in relation to food and health is not unique to superfoods discourse. Christine Knight has observed similar use of the natural/ unnatural dichotomy in low-carbohydrate diet discourse, and movements privileging culinary authenticity in opposition to industrialized, highly processed foods such as Slow Food also employ naturalist discourse.[9] Associations with nature and the natural are also used frequently in the marketing of food products, and consumer studies have shown a preference for natural.[10] The primary way in which the maca packaging communicates a sense of naturalness is through the romantic imagery of production. This image not only places maca production in nature, but also places it in opposition to technological production. In the picture, maca is harvested by hand under a blue sky. Notably absent are the tractors that turn over the soil and the machinery where maca is milled and packaged. In the text, as well, maca is described as natural by what is omitted: maca is described as 'grown in the mineral-rich volcanic soils' but not as processed in factories and shipped around the world. Further, in the 'ingredients' section of the packaging, maca is elaborately described as '100% pure certified organic maca root powder', further emphasising the naturalness of the product.

While the meaning of the word 'natural', both in relation to food and in general, is far from clear, it tends to be used discursively to set apart those foods 'that had not been changed in any significant way by contact with humans' from those that humans have deliberately manipulated through either production or processing.[11] The nature/technology dichotomy is problematic; even what we consider to be very basic agricultural practices, such as the process of selective breeding whereby humans sow seeds from cultivars with qualities that they consider favourable, are forms of technologies. The concept of superfoods is man-made, as are the technologies for cultivating, preserving, transporting and retailing them. Thus the appeal to the natural in superfoods and other food and health discourses raises the question of where to draw a line between the natural and the unnatural, and 'illustrates the extreme malleability of these concepts in different nutritional paradigms'.[12]

In their critique of science-based knowledge frameworks and their technological applications, superfoods also draw upon a discourse of primitivism. Bell defines primitivism as 'the nostalgia of civilized man for a return to a primitive or pre-civilized condition', which manifests in a romanticization of the ways of life of remote, isolated indigenous peoples and a celebration of their material culture.[13] As Marianna Torgovnick observes, primitivism can only exist in opposition to a post-industrial present, and thus she calls it 'a discourse fundamental to the Western sense of self and the Other'. The primitive becomes a foil through which to voice discontent with the 'civilized' present; therefore 'the needs of the present determine the value and nature of the primitive'.[14] Dissatisfied with the medicalization of food and health and the techno-fixes offered by big food manufacturers, superfoods consumers can look towards the primitive for ostensibly more intuitive and natural ways of pursuing health through foods.

The image of production on this maca package displays primitivist ideas through the depiction of maca being harvested by hand, by indigenous-looking women wearing traditional dress. There is a tension here between celebrating indigenous culture and employing racist stereotypes, and I illustrate this point by drawing attention to the similarities between this image and many of Diego Rivera's paintings. Similarities include the portrayal of female peasants in colourful traditional dress with dark skin and long dark braids, carrying produce in baskets against a mountainous landscape. There is more than a little irony in appropriating such imagery on product packaging, because while Rivera's paintings celebrated the culture and aesthetics of Mexico, they also expressed the oppression of Mexican peasants and Rivera's own communist leanings. Further, Rivera's work depicted Mexicans, while maca comes from the Peruvian Andes – a very different place in many ways. By conflating these two places and cultures, the image underscores Torgovnick's observation that primitivist discourse is not about representing a specific culture, set in real time and space, but rather about expressing dissatisfaction with the place and time from which the primitivist representation originates.

Maca is also connected with its 'primitive' heritage through words. The package declares that maca is 'the Inca superfood', but does not explain that it was the Pumpish people, not the Incas, who domesticated the root. The Pumpish occupied the lands where maca has historically grown long before the Incas came into power for a brilliant but fleeting historical moment. There is no evidence outside of legend that the Incas themselves had much to do with maca; however the image of the Inca warrior is powerful.[15] Drawing on existing representations of South America, maca producers have, probably correctly, assumed that 'Inca superfood' has a more resounding impact than 'Pumpish superfood', and therefore have forgone historical accuracy to deploy this imaginative geography.

An image of a mountainous South American landscape and connection with the legendary Inca and their dark-skinned descendants combine to create a sense of place that is timeless, untouched by the forces of modernity. This is an example of what Torgovnick calls 'the persistent Western tendency to deny a plenitude of time and time-layers to the primitive'.[16] The very idea of the primitive is, Johannes Fabian explains, 'essentially a temporal concept, is a category, not an object, of Western thought'; the construction of the category 'primitive' depends upon this placing of the Other outside of intersubjective time.[17] The packaging reinforces this idea by employing an image of maca production being done as it always has been done, without the aid of heavy machinery or the intellectual inputs of agricultural science. Maca is pictured being harvested by hand, by women in traditional dress, creating an image of nostalgic pastoralism, in which little has changed for thousands of years. The hyperbolic claim on the back of the package – 'Peruvian men and women passionately love this heart-shaped tuber, believing it to be a powerful enhancer of well-being and vigor, to not just exist but thrive in the stressful intensity of their high altitude climate' – gives a sense of continuous ancient wisdom handed down through generations. This further reinforces ideas of historical continuity and of production processes that occur outside of time, by timeless people.

Within a discourse of nutritional primitivism, superfoods are desired because they are not modern. This places a strong emphasis on foods that have a long history of indigenous culinary and medicinal use, and thus are seen as traditional and authentic. It also emphasizes foods that are natural, that is, perceived as not obviously altered by technology in either field or factory. It is those superfoods that were not already known as foods in the West and have entered the Western market as superfoods, such as maca, that rely most heavily upon the use of primitivist discourse. However, the use of primitivist discourse in relation to superfoods is not simply a matter of how Western consumers justify their purchasing decisions; it may have consequences for many superfood producers and their communities that are worth closer examination. While primitivist discourse valorizes superfoods because of their seemingly timeless, pristine origins, it is important to remember that these foods are being produced in places and by people that exist in the tangible, temporal, real world.

Critical Consumption

Many superfood consumers are, indeed, aware that some of the products they purchase are acquired through a global system of provision that has widespread and diverse social, economic and environmental impacts. Therefore a third discourse often employed in representing superfoods is critical consumption. Luke Yates explains that 'critical consumption can be read as a way of participating that renders consumption behaviour conscientious and diligent, over a multitude of political and ethical agendas' and therefore 'refers to cases where consideration of the implications of a product or service's production or consumption result in a consumer decision to boycott or buycott'.[18] The maca packaging communicates a discourse of critical consumption through the display of organic and fair trade certifications. Through these labels, some of the social and environmental facts of maca's production are communicated to consumers. The assumption is that because the product is certified organic, it is not harmful to the environment, and because it is certified fair trade, it is socially beneficial to the people who produce it.

Whether or not certified organic production is, indeed, a benign practice with regard to the environment is a contentious question beyond the scope of this paper. However, the question of maca production's environmental impact is not as simple as whether or not chemical inputs are used. Most maca production in the Junín area does not require the use of pesticides, herbicides or fungicides for the simple reason that few pests, plants or fungi thrive at the extreme altitude at which maca grows. Fertilizers have not historically been required because, although maca production does deplete the soil, traditional cultivation practices dictate long fallow periods between crops. But not only has increased demand for maca outside of Junín led to some growers practicing shorter fallow periods, which may eventually lead to the need to use fertilizers, it has also led to the geographical expansion of maca cultivation, and thus more land which has historically been used for grazing or has been the habitat of native vicuñas (a wild camelid) is now growing maca. Some locals have observed hair loss on vicuñas and attribute this to the animals both eating the maca leaves and experiencing stress from the noise of tractors and trucks. Certifying the product as 'organic' does not absolve its production from all negative environmental impacts. Of course there is also the question of whether or not consumers even think about organic certification in terms of environmentalism; many studies of consumer behaviour suggest that consumers purchase organic foods primarily for health, rather than environmental, reasons.[19]

Fair trade certification is also more contentious than it may appear. Not only does it attempt to solve the problem of fetishization created by capitalist exchange through the very type of exchange that has led to the obfuscation of the circumstances of production,[20] but it also has been shown that the certification process can be exclusionary and serve to exacerbate existing power dynamics.[21] However what I find problematic about the fair trade label on this maca packaging is that its very use is in conflict with the romantic, timeless image of production used to construct a discourse of primitivism. If maca production is actually as idyllic as the package imagery suggests, why does the need for a fair trade label exist?

244   There is an inbuilt friction in these two knowledge claims regarding maca production. In the primitivist account, maca production occurs in an imaginative geography placed outside of real time or space. In the fair trade account, it takes place in a real geography, where things like poverty due to forces of cultural imperialism and political inequalities are experienced and need to be remedied – in this case through the 'benevolent' market intervention of fair trade exchange. The paradox is that the product's value is linked to both its association with the imaginative geography in which maca production is placed outside of real time and space, and its association with the real geography in which maca production is rooted in an imperfect global food provisioning system. It is important to question to what extent these representations serve as genuine attempts to connect worlds of production and consumption through knowledge, and to what extent they serve as points of differentiation to sell a product, points through which consumers can build their identities as people who value natural or inherent knowledge about health in opposition to mainstream allopathic medicine and as people who resist the inequality of the free market and who wish for a more just world.

Conclusions

This paper has demonstrated how the packaging of one superfood product sold in Australia constructs and communicates a concept of superfoods by bringing together popular discourses about food, health and values through the use of knowledge claims.

It has probed the disjunctures and contradictions within and between these knowledge claims, such as the limitations of organic and fair trade certifications and the information about contemporary maca production that is left out in communicating a discourse of primitivism. It is these disjunctures that I suggest open up spaces for contestation of both the claims themselves and the concept of superfoods more broadly by other actors involved in maca's production and consumption.

While this paper has focused on one way in which knowledges are constructed and communicated to new consumers by the intermediaries who bring maca to the Australian market, these actors do not have a monopoly on the representational practices that give maca meaning as a superfood. While they often play the powerful role of voicing and translating knowledges between primary producers and consumers, other actors – including producers, consumers, government officials, health professionals, educators and the media – are also active constructors and interpreters of knowledges. Further studies should investigate the roles that such actors play in the construction of knowledge about superfoods in general and about individual foods in particular. For example, what is the role of the Peruvian government, who has declared maca a 'flagship product' of Peru and has encouraged the development of export markets, in this process? Do growers themselves influence the primitive geographies communicated on maca packaging by promoting a particular image for their product to importers or by taking pride in sharing some of their inherited cultivation practices? How do new consumers challenge these knowledges, both by the uses to which they put products and by the sharing of information that occurs at breakneck speed via electronic media?

One way in which knowledges of maca production are currently being challenged is through the creation of a geographical indication for maca production in the Junín and Pasco regions of Peru. A Denomination of Origin (DO) for 'Maca Junín-Pasco' was officially declared by the national intellectual property organization INDECOPI (Instituto Nacional de Defensa de la Competencia y de la Protección de la Porpiedad Intelectual) in 2011.[22] This is an important way in which maca producers have employed their own practices of place-making in relation to maca's origins, for the geographical zone described under the DO is not defined by political boundaries created by government. Instead, the boundaries of the DO have been drawn collectively by growers, historians and scientists who have pooled their expertises in defining an area historically, culturally and agronomically appropriate for the production of the high quality maca distinctive to the region. While the DO is not currently active because a regulatory body has not been formed, a potential application for this geographical indication is to create a certification that communicates production knowledges constructed by producers themselves. Further studies examining the role that other actors play in constructing knowledges in maca's, and other superfoods', production-consumption circuits may reveal other points at which the representations presented here are challenged, constructed and redeployed.

Notes

1. Gyorgy Scrinis, *Nutritionism: The Science and Politics of Dietary Advice* (New York: Columbia University Press, 2013).
2. Christine Knight, '"We Can't Go Back a Hundred Million Years": Low-carbohydrate Dieters' Responses to Nutritional Primitivism', *Food, Culture & Society,* 18 (2015), pp. 441-61.
3. Luke S. Yates, 'Critical Consumption', *European Societies,* 13 (2011), pp. 191-217.
4. Power Super Foods, 'Maca Powder', (Murwillumbah, NSW, Australia, 2015).
5. 'Maca Powder' <http://www.powersuperfoods.com.au/maca/maca-power-powder.html, 2013> [accessed 19 December 2014].
6. Scrinis, p. 2.
7. Scrinis, p. 2.
8. For a review of scientific studies on maca, see Gustavo F. Gonzales, 'Ethnobiology and Ethnopharmacology of *Lepidium meyenii* (Maca), a Plant from the Peruvian Highlands', *Evidence-Based Complementary and Alternative Medicine,* 2012 (2012), pp. 1-10.
9. Christine Knight, '"An Alliance With Mother Nature": Natural Food, Health, and Morality in Low-Carbohydrate Diet Books', *Food and Foodways,* 20 (2012), pp. 102-22.
10. Paul Rozin et al., 'Preference for Natural: Instrumental and Ideational/Moral Motivations, and the Contrast between Foods and Medicines', *Appetite,* 43 (2004), pp. 147-54.
11. Rozin et al., p. 148.
12. Knight, '"An Alliance With Mother Nature"', p. 119.
13. M. Bell, *Primitivism* (London: Methuen, 1972), p. 1.
14. Marianna Torgovnick, *Gone Primitive: Savage Intellects, Modern Lives* (Chicago: University of Chicago Press, 1990), p. 8; p. 9.
15. Michael Hermann and Thomas Bernet, 'The Transition of Maca from Neglect to Market Prominence: Lessons for Improving Use Strategies and Market Chains of Minor Crops', *Agricultural Biodiversity and Livelihoods Discussion Papers 1* (Rome: Bioversity International, 2009) <https://www.bioversity-international.org/fileadmin/_migrated/uploads/tx_news/The_transition_of_maca_from_neglect_to_market_prominence__nbsp_lessons_for_improving_use_strategies_and_market_chains_of_minor_crops_1318.pdf> [accessed 19 December 2014].
16. Torgovnick, p. 244.
17. Johannes Fabian, *Time and the Other: How Anthropology Makes Its Object* (New York: Columbia University Press, 1983), p. 18.
18. Yates, p. 192.
19. Stewart Lockie et al., 'Eating 'Green': Motivations Behind Organic Food Consumption in Australia', *Sociologia Ruralis,* 42 (2002), pp. 23-40; Maria K. Magnusson et al., 'Choice of Organic Foods is Related to Perceived Consequences for Human Health and to Environmentally Friendly Behaviour', *Appetite,* 40 (2003), pp. 109-17.
20. Gavin Fridell, 'Fair-Trade Coffee and Commodity Fetishism: The Limits of Market-Driven Social Justice', *Historical Materialism,* 15 (2007), pp. 79-104.
21. Sarah Besky, 'Can a Plantation be Fair? Paradoxes and Possibilities in Fair Trade Darjeeling Tea Certification', *Anthropology of Work Review,* 29 (2008), pp. 1-9; Raymond L. Bryant and Michael K. Goodman, 'Peopling the Practices of Sustainable Consumption: Eco-Chic and the Limits to Spaces of Intention', in *Green Consumption: The Global Rise of Eco-Chic,* ed. by Bart Barendregt and Rivke Jaffe (London: Bloomsbury, 2014), pp. 37-55.
22. Perúbiodiverso, 'Reconocimiento de la Denominación de Origen MACA JUNIN-PASCO Desafío y Oportunidad', INDECOPI (2011).

A French Culinary Figure in the Anglosphere: Translating Édouard de Pomiane for English Books and Television

Katherine Magruder

The archives of the Pasteur Institute in Paris hold a photograph from 1950 of a group of women posing outside the Institute's front entrance. Standing in front of the group is Doctor Édouard de Pomiane – a square-jawed man with deep-set eyes and white hair, wearing a lab coat, tie and an ample Hussar-style moustache. Despite the suggestion of his jaunty upturned moustache, it is difficult to know if he is smiling, and shadows obscure what might be a gleam in his eyes. If at first glance Pomiane's image projects an aura of charm and good nature, it also signals a sense of knowingness and mystery.[1] Born in Montmartre, Paris in 1875, Édouard de Pomiane (d. 1964) was the son of Polish émigrés, and he eventually married another medical researcher by the name of Wanda Pozerska. In addition to his position as physician and researcher at the Pasteur Institute, Pomiane was a university lecturer on gastroenterology, amateur ethnographer, the host of a radio show about food and cooking on Radio-Paris in the 1920s and 1930s and the author of twenty-two books on gastronomy.[2] These books apparently sold well and received substantial attention from critics in France, and Pomiane eventually gained a substantial readership elsewhere when his titles were translated into German and English. However, Pomiane's persona, biography and ideas changed in these various translations. In contrast to the Pomiane of the 1950 photograph, for example, the 1995 BBC Two television adaptation of Pomiane's book *La cuisine en dix minutes* (1930) – first translated into English in 1948 – transforms Pomiane into a portly, giddy, clean-shaven man with half-moon glasses. This Pomiane speaks English with a heavy Polish accent, darting around a studio kitchen as he assembles a four- or five-course French meal in ten minutes. Around the nine-minute mark, a mute woman joins Pomiane for supper, wearing a long black dress and carrying a bottle of what Pomiane calls 'the finest claret'.[3]

Finding differences between source texts, translations and television adaptations is neither a rare phenomenon nor a novel enterprise – each form responds to particular pressures of audience, funding and genre. Conveying a sense of 'fidelity' to the original text may not be a priority. Nevertheless the question here concerns the effects of the English translations of Pomiane and how they might have supported the interpretations demonstrated by the BBC series. This inquiry relies on the notion that the impressions and, in some cases, misinformation built up around Pomiane in the Anglosphere did not arise naturally or spontaneously; they resulted from the practices of particular reading and interpretive communities. Surveying the publication history of the four Pomiane titles translated into English, analyzing the translations and their commentators and considering the effects of moving Pomiane out of the French language and onto the television screen for BBC viewers will outline the Anglophone rendering of this French culinary figure and evaluate the stakes invested therein. These efforts scrubbed the translations of biographical, geographical and historical context, both exoticizing and demystifying 'French' gastronomic concepts for the Anglophone reader and viewer. In effect, Pomiane was reinterpreted for Anglophone audiences as a twentieth-century visionary for food media who was charming, timeless and empathetic to Anglo-American cooking and eating practices.

Theoretical Framework and the Question of Translating Food-Focused Texts

This analysis borrows concepts from cultural historians who have contributed to the effort to reconstruct various modes of reading in the history of Western societies. Their efforts push past purely semantic notions of the text, emphasizing the changes in meaning and status texts undergo when readership changes. This is not simply a question of general reading competence, but of the many particularities of reading practices, including language, interpretive norms, materials, and readers' interests and expectations.[4] Reading presents the opportunity to invest a text with particular meanings and expectations, even though the extent of this appropriation is limited. The text presents itself to the reader as one of a limited range of choices; there has already been a careful selection and curating process in authoring, editing and publishing the text that did not directly involve the reader.[5] In the case of translation, this pre-shaping of the text has passed through even more hands. However, the meanings of these texts are not necessarily foregone conclusions; readers are still in a position to defy readership targets or override intended readings of translated texts.

Stanley Fish offers the concept of 'interpretive communities' to illustrate how a collective group of people confers meaning to a text. Fish's notion emphasizes the social and cultural aspects of reading and knowledge production, suggesting that 'if the self is conceived of not as an independent entity but as a social construct whose operations are delimited by the systems of intelligibility that inform it, then the meanings it confers on texts are not its own but have their source in the interpretive community (or communicates) of which it is a function'.[6] For the translations of Pomiane, an important interpretive community is spearheaded by a group of non-French food writers, including Elizabeth David, M.F.K. Fisher, Jehane Benoît, Ruth Reichl and Claudia Roden, who have given warm endorsements to the translated Pomiane. Reichl calls Pomiane 'thoroughly modern' and claims she has trouble understanding 'why [the book] is not on every cook's shelf'; she quotes David's claims that Pomiane has 'the vital touch of the artist' and that his 'brief explanations […] are worth volumes of weighty expertise'.[7] Elsewhere David calls Pomiane's work 'the best kind of cookery writing. It is courageous, courteous, adult'.[8]

In contrast, Pomiane was derided as well as embraced in France. His gastronomy books sold well, and his medical and scientific professional appointments held a certain prestige.[9] However, the institution of high French cuisine did not necessarily welcome Pomiane and his non-doctrinaire message about French cooking. Pomiane disdained the demands and regimentations of classical French cuisine and displayed a kind of irreverence to tradition, exclaiming, for example, that *sauce blanche*, a cornerstone of French cooking, is a '*horrible sauce. Mais elle a ceci de bon, qu'elle se laisse améliorer à volonté*' [horrible sauce, but at least it may be improved to your taste].[10] At another point, Pomiane defended himself against critics who balked at the proposition that French cooking could be learned in six lessons through the application of a few general principles and scientific laws; conventional understanding was that it took many years of professional tutelage in order to reach the height of culinary practice.[11] Elizabeth David made note of Pomiane's ambivalent status in the French culinary sphere, calling him 'a learned, high-spirited, infinitely stimulating mixture of *grand seigneur* and *enfant terrible* of the gastronomic world'. But for David, this position was desirable, as it allowed him to deflate so many 'grave pontiffs of that world'.[12] Therefore, the changes, and to some extent, aggrandizement that Pomiane's work underwent through English translation was partly an effect of the decisions made by translators and editors, and partly the work of the interpretive community constituted by non-French food writers.

It is worth briefly contextualizing Pomiane's example within the larger market of food-related literature, translated cookbooks and world literature. It is uncommon for cookery books to be translated unless they are deemed of historical interest or the author is a well-known figure. More often a native of one country becomes an 'expert' in the cooking practices of another region either by travel or research, or an expatriate author will write about the food and cooking traditions of their family and where they grew up. If cookbooks are translated into English, their foreignness and national provenance are usually pointed up, likely as an effort to create categories and marketing opportunities for cooks and readers looking for new ideas. This is evidenced by Philip and Mary Hyman translating Pomiane's title *La cuisine en dix minutes* as *French Cooking in Ten Minutes* (1977), rather than the preceding, more literal translation *Cooking in Ten Minutes* (1948). Interestingly, this runs against a larger trend toward the denationalization of literary production in the world market of translation, which is arguably an outcome of globalization ideology and publishers' hopes for producing a global bestseller.[13]

Alongside the trend of associating food literature with particular nations, the English-language food writing market tends to adapt foreign or historical cookbooks so that they are 'practical' or 'usable', despite the potential loss of primary material that would be useful for the scholar. Elizabeth David confirms this translational norm when she comments on the quality of Peggie Benton's 1962 translation of *Cooking with Pomiane*: 'Dr de Pomiane's recipes have been admirably transposed into English usage and the spirit of his writing accurately conveyed by Peggie Benton. An entrancing book to read, and to cook from a highly instructive and successful one.'[14] Here the value is placed on practical usability, instructiveness and the 'accurate' conveying of Pomiane's spirit, rather than producing correlations of language and form between the source text and the translation. The underlying question at the centre of this discussion concerns the responsibilities carried by people involved in the translation of cookbooks and food literature. When the source text involves something so seemingly quotidian as cooking instruction and recipe formulation, does translating it need to be as vexed and exacting as some of the more insistent translation theorists might have it? When does food writing enter the realm of literature, and when is it simply a set of practical instructions that must be manipulated to fit a kitchen with different equipment and ingredients, for a cook with a different set of culinary knowledge?

A Brief History of Pomiane Publications in the Anglosphere

In the case of Pomiane, translation and adaptation helped elevate his writings into the realm of literature within the Anglosphere. The early translations of Pomiane were based on source texts that were predominantly dry and technical, carrying little of the warmth and charm for which he came to be known after further translations were published. The latter translations reveal Pomiane as witty, curious and open-minded, and the cooking instructions he recommends appear modern. To begin, a general genealogy of the movement of Pomiane's texts through the United States and Britain will be offered, followed by close analyses of the BBC series and the text that inspired it.

Le code de la bonne chère: 700 recettes simples publiées sous les auspices de la Société d'hygiène alimentaire (1925) was translated as *Good Fare: A Code of Cookery* (1932) by Blanche Bowes with G. Howe Publishers of London. The book was intended to offer young housewives simple, scientifically sound formulas for cooking that were inexpensive and practical. Pomiane suggested that this text inaugurated a new genre in the cookery book market that targeted neither the wealthy nor the professional chef, but the new class of home cooks and eaters who had elevated tastes and diminished budgets after the World War.[15] The English edition of this text, now long out of print, contains numerous footnotes explaining the logistical differences between French and English kitchens and ingredients.

The next Pomiane title to leave France was *La cuisine en dix minutes; ou l'adaptation au rhythme moderne* (1930). This book contains menu plans and recipes that can be cooked quickly, often by using ready-made convenience products. Bruno Cassirer first published a German translation of this book in 1935; Cassirer published it again in 1948, this time in English, after having fled to Oxford from Nazi Germany. Peggie Benton also worked on the English translation, which remained the standard until Philip and Mary Hyman re-translated the work in 1977. This text became Pomiane's most widely read and available English-language book; Ruth Reichl pointed out that it was perhaps the first cookbook of its kind, and has also become the most widely imitated cookbook form of the twentieth century.[16]

The graceful, generous, literary Pomiane arrived when radio transcripts from his weekly broadcasts on Radio-Paris were loosely adapted and translated. The transcripts of his broadcasts from 1931 to 1932 and from 1935 to 1936 were collected into manuscripts titled *Radio-Cuisine* (2 volumes). On the radio, Pomiane told personal anecdotes, dictated recipes, embraced culinary shortcuts and spoke frequently about '*gastrotechnie*', a phrase he coined to indicate the scientific reasoning explaining why certain cooking methods work.[17] Pomiane offered cooking advice to listeners through the rationing efforts of the early 1940s, and he continued to broadcast on the radio throughout the 1950s. His style on the radio was more intimate and chatty than his written cookery book persona, though those distinctions blurred upon the publication of *Radio-Cuisine* and its subsequent translations, which do not mention that originally these were scripts read on radio broadcasts. Cassirer first published a German translation of *Radio-Cuisine* vol. 1 (1933) in Berlin in 1935, titled *Die fröhliche Kunst den Kochens*. In Oxford, Cassirer and Benton worked together once again for the English translation of this work, loosely adapting *Radio-Cuisine* vol. 1 and 2 for *Cooking with Pomiane* (1962). Cassirer and Benton's translation is still used in re-issues of *Cooking with Pomiane;* Serif Books in London published the latest edition in 2009.

Finally, *Cuisine Juive: Ghettos Modernes* (Albin Michel, 1929) was translated and self-published by Josephine Bacon in 1985 as *The Jews of Poland: Recollections and Recipes*. Unlike the majority of Pomiane's books, which were based on his own cooking and eating experiences, *Cuisine Juive: Ghettos Modernes* is a collection of recipes, stories and observations gathered from the Jewish communities in Poland in 1928. The English translation proved important to several Jewish social historians, who commended Bacon for bringing this book to their attention and cite her translation in their bibliographies.[18] *Cuisine Juive* is part cookbook, part ethnography, part personal reflection on Polish identity and overall a vivid depiction of Jewish life in Poland in the interwar years. This complexity comes across even though the Bacon translation contains some typographical errors and curious translation choices. For example, she translates *boudin de farine* as 'Flour sausage', though what was probably indicated was a form of Kishke, a beef intestine stuffed with matzo or flour, spices and chicken fat.[19]

Translating *La cuisine en dix minutes*

The remaining analysis will focus on the translations of *La cuisine en dix minutes,* both in text and onscreen. The book offers recipes, etiquette advice, menus and personal anecdotes about the benefits of cooking quickly and eating well. The Hyman 1977 translation is most readily available in the United States market, while the Benton 1948 translation remains the standard in the UK. Along with *Cooking with Pomiane*, these texts form the core of the Anglophone perception of Pomiane, as they are the most frequently cited, mentioned and published of his English-language texts.

The Benton translation of *La cuisine en dix minutes* reflects an effort to Anglicize the text and appeal to a general readership. For example, in the French edition, Pomiane opens the section on pasta cooking: '*Rappelez-vous qu'en France, macaroni, spaghetti, lazagnes et nouilles sont toujours servis trop cuits, comme une pâtée informe. D'ou leur peu de success'* (p. 87). The Benton translation applies this idea directly to the British, translating the passage: 'Remember that in England spaghetti, tagliatelle and other forms of pasta are almost always cooked too long and served as a shapeless mass. This is why they are not particularly popular.'[20] The translation by food historians Philip and Mary Hyman keep with the original geographic indication, writing, 'In France, macaroni, spaghetti, lasagna, and noodles are always overcooked and served in a formless mass. That's why they are not very popular here.'[21] Indeed much of the Hyman translation demonstrates an effort to appeal to a readership that is non-specialized, but intrigued by the prospect of learning how the French manage quick cooking, despite the fact that the narrator is someone who, in certain respects, breaks all the 'French' rules. Anglophone adaptations of French cuisine for home cooking often aim to streamline and demystify what is assumed to be a time-consuming, demanding and overly elaborate – but desirable – way of preparing meals. The same is true here for Pomiane's translations, which manage to modernize and Anglicize the text in certain ways, as if their main purpose is to allow readers to quickly comprehend and approximate Pomiane's recipes in their own kitchens.

Translating Pomiane's French into English presented both linguistic challenges and opportunities to compose an interesting, even enriched prose that signals its status as a translation in various ways. In some cases, the Hyman translation appropriates the French in order to produce something smooth and comfortable for the English reader, which gets punctuated by words and phrases that do not fit this frame. For example, in the recipe for salt cod the Hyman translation proceeds as follows: 'Pour some melted butter over it and serve with a slice of lemon. Drink a glass of white wine with it – or two, because they say that codfish has a thirst for butter and gives a thirst to anyone who eats it' (p. 70). Compare this to the original French: '*Arrosez de beurre fondu. Ornez avec une rondelle de citron. Servez. Buvez un verre de vin blanc bien sec ; plutôt deux verres, car la morue a soif de beurre, dit-on, et assoiffe ceux qui en mangent*' (p. 104). The first sentence of the translation is a synthesis of Pomiane's more truncated syntax. The second phrase, about a piece of cooked fish having thirst and giving thirst to the person who eats it, ends up sounding stilted. It is unclear why the qualifier was altered to white wine rather than '*bien sec*', but the unconventional usage of having thirst/giving thirst, combined with the little wink about being justified to two glasses of wine with this meal, lends an overall sense that the text has been translated, and that the translated author is rather charming.

Another example comes from Pomiane's preferred way to eat oysters. In the Hyman: 'Alternate sensations: burn your mouth with a hot, crunchy sausage, then soothe your burns with a cool, smooth oyster. Continue in this way until you have finished off both the sausages and the oysters. Cold white wine, of course' (p. 74). The original French reads: '*Faites alterner les sensations. Brûlez-vous la bouche avec une saucisse croustillante. Pansez vos brûlures avec une huître bien fraîche. Continuez ainsi, jusqu'à disparition et des huîtres et des saucisses. Vin blanc bien entendu*' (p. 110). In this example, the translation takes more license with adjectives and sentence structure to emphasize the contrasting sensations in the combination of sausages and oysters. But the translation of 'croustillante' to 'crunchy' to describe eating a hot sausage is an extraordinary and effective phrase. The Benton translation also brings in the idea of burning your mouth with a 'crackling sausage' (p. 90). Here the texts allow the foreign in, illuminating a certain French style of cooking and speaking, rather than forcing the English into something that does not fit. It reads as a creative and enticing way to give cooking instruction.

In the case of *French Cooking in Ten Minutes,* it is clear that the translators altered some of Pomiane's recipes according to what kitchens and markets might have had in the place and at the time of translation. For example, *fromage de Hollande* becomes American cheese, and *jambon cuit, d'York ou de Paris* becomes Virginia ham in the Hyman US edition (p. 109, p. 129; p. 81, p. 52); *fromage blanc* becomes cream cheese, and *thon à l'huile* becomes tunny fish in the Benton UK translation (p. 212, p. 150; p. 40, p. 46). These substitutions cloud the sense of what Pomiane was recommending and was available to him in Paris in 1930, and it would seem that delivering that kind of information was not a priority for the translations. However, the rule of substitution is not consistently applied: lamb's brains, acacia flowers, larks, foie gras, veal kidneys, sorrel and boudin noir are all called for without apology in the English translations. The texts appropriate when they can and foreignize when they do not have a choice.

Following this attempt to toe the line between fidelity to Pomiane's text and opening it up to different readerships, the translations change the format of some recipes. When Pomiane describes a recipe in paragraph form, the Hyman translation usually pulls the ingredients forward into a list, in line with modern cookbook conventions (p. xxvi). Furthermore, if Pomiane elaborated on something that might be tedious for the casual Anglo-American reader, such as where to buy bacon, how to ask for it and how to tell the difference between bacon and *lard fumé,* this section is cut from the translation (p. 52). While this changes the text and obscures its provenance as a historical, translated document, it manages to familiarize itself to readers.

Finally, there are two instances where the text of the translation is altered perhaps as a way to minimize uneasy historical difference. In the preface, Pomiane writes: '*Mon livre s'adresse* [...] *à tous ceux qui ne disposent que d'une heure pour déjeuner ou pour dîner et qui veulent avoir, quand même, une demi-heure de liberté pour contempler la fumée de leur cigarette, tout en buvant gorgée une tasse de café qui n'a même pas le temps de refroidir*' (p. 4). Pomiane's cigarette disappears in the Hyman version: 'I am writing this book for [...] everyone else who has only an hour for lunch or dinner but still wants thirty minutes of peace to enjoy a cup of coffee' (p. xxvi). Later, Pomiane talks about the pleasure of listening to the radio, which is playing '*un tango ou un chant nègre*' (p. 37). The Hyman edition translates *chant nègre* as 'jazz' (p. 25), and the Benton translation calls it a 'tango or a rhumba' (p. 44). As historian Jeffrey Jackson demonstrates, race and the idea of 'black music' were among the main categories some people in interwar France used to define jazz, but in the 1930s '*chansons nègres*' more likely referred to folk

253

tunes and spirituals from black America and Africa, including France's colonies.[22]

It is reasonable to surmise that the translations of *La cuisine en dix minutes* intended to inspire new, practical cooking ideas and to expose a wide, but conservative audience of cooks, enthusiasts and academics to this French culinary figure. Perhaps it can be assumed that the scholar who is interested in the breadth of Pomiane's work and his historical moment would be convinced to find and study the original French, making a rigorous, historically minded translation less useful and potentially alienating the recreational cookbook reader. However, crib translations and light introductions may introduce problems even in the scholarly realm. Researchers looking for a quick reference to Pomiane might be led to think that *French Cooking in Ten Minutes* is evidence that Pomiane is one of the first great modern cookery writers, far ahead of his time, and so naturally accessible to a wide audience, while in fact much of this work was done by and through translation.

Several decades after Pomiane's work began circulating in the US and the UK, there was a flurry of activity around *La cuisine en dix minutes* in the early 1990s. Serif Books of London first published its edition of Benton's *Cooking in Ten Minutes* in 1993; in 1994, North Point Press, a division of Farrar, Strauss and Giroux, published a new edition of the Hymans' translation, *French Cooking in Ten Minutes*. And in 1995, BBC Two broadcast a six-episode dramatization of the Benton translation titled *French Cooking in Ten Minutes* (screenplay written by Nicholas Cooper, directed by David Giles, and produced by John Ellis of Large Door Productions). Édouard de Pomiane is also listed in the writing credits, and a Polish-English actor, Christopher Rozycki, played Pomiane.

In the series, Pomiane is described as a Polish physician and research scientist in Paris who cooks meals for his mysterious guest, Madame X. Pomiane indeed dedicated the book to a Madame X, and it is not clear in either the text or the television series whether Madame X and Pomiane are married. The nine-minute episodes play out as a series of meals that Pomiane enthusiastically prepares for this woman. In each episode, Pomiane greets the viewers as if they are students in a tutorial session. He reads the daily menu slowly in French in a heavily decorated style with long rolled Rs. The first episode features a menu of prawn omelette, veal with *petit pois*, a green salad and cheese and fruit. A more elaborate menu is prepared in episode four, including *moules marinieres*, chicken à la crème, potato salad, cheese and apple fritters. Pomiane accomplishes this menu in part by using purchased, pre-cooked chicken and cold, leftover boiled potatoes. Pomiane's Polish-accented voice, the muffled sounds of unattended cooking, amplified sounds of active preparation and ambient on-set noise are the only sounds in these episodes. Pomiane's direct harried tone is juxtaposed by static visuals and silences between his directions. There is an intent auditory and visual focus on Pomiane, as he provides all of the movement and all of the dialogue. The silent Madame X glides in at the end, almost like a phantom.

Toby Miller has argued that television helped popularize French cuisine in English-speaking countries through the process of demystification. Noting a 'cosmic ambivalence about French culture, an oscillation between contempt and admiration', Miller suggests that UK television hosts like Delia Smith and Graham Kerr made French cuisine seem more approachable both by substituting ingredients and displaying an air of frivolity and playfulness in their on-air presentations.[23] Nigella Lawson's programs occasionally air this attitude as well. When she makes her mother's bearnaise sauce, she explains that the recipe in *Larousse Gastronomique* calls for a reduction of shallots, chervil, tarragon, wine and 'various other things', but that she does not do it that way.[24] In a segment on mustard pork chops, Lawson describes her first 'grown-up holiday' without her parents. She went to Normandy and ordered pork chops with mustard, cider and cream at a bistro, feeling 'so sophisticated'. As she demonstrates how to cook the chops, she explains that one can either cut off the rind or leave it attached, but admits that she skips a step when it can be skipped.[25] The BBC Two Pomiane series fits this template – his recipes call for canned asparagus, pre-boiled potatoes, instant soup powder, cream cheese, etc. – though the series is particular in its arbitrary overemphasis on Pomiane's Polishness, giddiness and intention to seduce a mysterious woman. When the on-screen Pomiane uses a convenience ingredient, he often defends himself by saying that he is a physician who is pressed for time, not a *chef de cuisine*. While the real Pomiane was interested in destabilizing the institute of French cuisine and advocated for an explicitly flexible, healthful approach to cooking, the decision to skew his persona as an outsider to France and an outsider of the French culinary world serves to make his cooking method seem eminently doable and unfussy, despite the fact that it still has the general elegance and desirability of being 'French'.

255

In 2010, the *Guardian* named *Cooking in Ten Minutes* one of the '50 best cookbooks of all time'.[26] The list refers only to English-language (including English-translated) cookbooks. The Benton translation effectively fuses with Pomiane's writing in this context, even with all of its interpolations, erasures and adaptations. The intentions of Benton and her editors are upheld even as the visibility of those intentions-qua-intentions fade and become forgotten. The translated Pomiane is simply Pomiane; the efforts that were made to modernize and Anglicize the texts, and to make French cooking seem both exotic and approachable, appear natural. But not only on these relatively local levels was Pomiane reinterpreted by his adaptors. As we could expect in a trans-national context, politics also intervened. Or rather, in this case, was purposefully made not to intervene. An area for further study, and a focus of my own forthcoming work is the de-politicization of Pomiane in the hands of his Anglophone translators, particularly in the adaptation of *Radio-Cuisine*. Allusions to Radio-Paris, which became a mouthpiece for Nazi ideology during the Occupation, and other potentially contentious issues, are conspicuously absent in Cassirer and Benton's *Cooking with Pomiane*.

Notes

1. Margaret McArthur went on a quest to discover more about the mysterious and intriguing Pomiane ('Desperately Seeking Edouard: A Passion for de Pomiane', *Gastronomica: The Journal of Food and*

Culture, 4.4 (2004), pp. 62-65).

2   'Edouard Pozerski', *Institut Pasteur*, n.d. <http://www.pasteur.fr/infosci/archives/pozo.html> [accessed 25 May 2015].

3.   'Episode 5', *French Cooking in Ten Minutes*, 1.5, BBC2, 17 May 1995.

4.   Gugielmo Cavallo and Roger Chartier, *A History of Reading in the West*, trans. Lydia G. Cochrane (Amherst: University of Massachusetts Press, 1999), pp. 1-4.

5.   Cavallo and Chartier, pp. 34-35.

6.   Stanley Fish, *Is There a Text in This Class? The Authority of Interpretive Communities* (Cambridge: Harvard University Press, 1980), p. 335.

7.   Ruth Reichl, 'Foreword', in Edouard de Pomiane, *Cooking with Pomiane*, ed. by Ruth Reichl, trans. by Peggie Benton (New York: The Modern Library, 2001), p. ix, p. xiii.

8.   Elizabeth David, 'A Kitchen Was His Laboratory', *Gourmet*, March 1970 <http://www.gourmet.com/magazine/1970s/1970/03/kitchenwashislaboratory.html> [accessed 25 May 2015].

9.   The *Guide du Médecin* established the Prix Édouard de Pomiane in 1969 to honor the memory of Pomiane, nicknamed the '*Prince des médecins gastronomes*': see Hervé This, *Cours de gastronomie moléculaire no.2: Les précisions culinaires* (Paris: Belin, 2010), p. 104.

10.   Edouard de Pomiane, *La cuisine en dix minutes* (Paris: Calmann-Lévy, 1969 [1930]), p. 61. Subsequent references will be cited parenthetically.

11.   Edouard de Pomiane, *Le code de la bonne chère: 700 recettes simples publiées sous les auspices de la Société d'hygiène alimentaire* (Paris: Albin Michel, 1925), p. 5.

12.   Elizabeth David, *French Provincial Cooking* (New York: Penguin Classics, 1999), p. 322.

13.   Gisèle Sapiro, 'French Literature in the World System of Translation', in *French Global: A New Approach to Literary History*, ed. by Christine McDonald and Susan Rubin Suleiman (New York: Columbia University Press, 2010), p. 317.

14.   David, *French Provincial Cooking*, p. 474.

15.   Pomiane, *Le code de la bonne chère*, pp. 5-7. Pomiane overstates the novelty of *Le code*, as cookery books offering practical information about cooking, aimed primarily at housewives or domestic servants, arose in France around the turn of the nineteenth century with titles such as Menon's *La Cuisinière Bourgeoise* in 1790 and Saint-Ange's *La Cuisine de Madame Saint-Ange* in 1827; see Amy Trubek, *Haute Cuisine: How the French Invented the Culinary Profession* (Philadelphia: University of Pennsylvania Press, 2000), pp. 11-13.

16.   Reichl, p. x.

17.   Hervé This argues that Pomiane was not the first to come up with this method of culinary instruction (pp. 104-06); for further reference, see Caroline Lieffers, '"The Present Time is Eminently Scientific:" The Science of Cookery in Nineteenth Century Britain', *Journal of Social History*, 45.4 (2012): pp. 936-59.

18.   For examples of scholars who have integrated Pomiane's observations of Jewish life in Poland into their work, see: John Cooper, *Eat and Be Satisfied: A Social History of Jewish Food* (Northvale: Jason Aronson, 1993), p. 171, p. 187; Eve Jochnowitz, 'Flavors of Memory: Jewish Food and Culinary Tourism in Poland', in *Culinary Tourism*, ed. by Lucy Long (Lexington: University Press of Kentucky, 2004); Leonid Livak, *The Jewish Persona in the European Imagination: A Case of Russian Literature* (Stanford: Stanford University Press, 2010); and Claudia Roden, *The Book of Jewish Food* (New York: Knopf, 2008), p. 58, p. 66, p. 111.

19.   Pomiane, *The Jews of Poland: Recollections and Recipes*, trans. by Josephine Bacon (Garden Grove: Pholiota Press, 1985), p. 97.

20.   Pomiane, *Cooking in Ten Minutes*, trans. by Peggie Benton (London: Serif Books, 1993), p. 75. Subsequent references will be cited parenthetically.

21.   Pomiane, *French Cooking in Ten Minutes or Adapting to the Rhythm of Modern Life (1930)* trans. Philip and Mary Hyman (New York: North Point Press, 1994 [1977]), p. 57. Subsequent references will be cited parenthetically.

22. Jeffrey H. Jackson, *Making Jazz French: Music and Modern Life in Interwar Paris* (Durham: Duke University Press, 2003): pp. 26-28, p. 89.

23. Toby Miller, 'Screening Food: French Cuisine and the Television Palate', in *French Food on the Table, on the Page, and in French Culture*, ed. by Lawrence R. Schehr and Allen Weiss (London: Routledge, 2001), p. 223.

24. 'Family Food', *Nigella Bites*, 1.3, BBC4, 2000.

25. 'Everyday Easy', *Nigella Express*, 1.1, BBC2, 3 September 2007.

26. 'The 50 Best Cookbooks of All Time', *The Guardian,* Observer Food Monthly, 15 August 2010 <http://www.theguardian.com/lifeandstyle/2010/aug/13/50-best-cookbooks-ofm> [accessed 25 May 2015].

The Language of Food Gifts in an Eighteenth-Century Dining Club

India Aurora Mandelkern

On 27 October 1743, eight well-to-do gentlemen founded a new dining club in London. Every Thursday thenceforth, they convened for dinner in one of the swank private dining rooms at the Mitre Tavern, which was patronized by the likes of Johnson and Boswell and where the food was served on silver plate. There, they enjoyed a hearty commons: fresh fish, boiled fowls, generous chops of butchers' meat, greens, pies and puddings washed down with pints of claret and port. Word of the dinners spread quickly; before long the club had evolved into the semi-official social adjunct of the Royal Society of London, where it entertained powerful statesmen and intellectuals from all over the globe.[1] Over the second half of the eighteenth century, these dinners were attended by princes and politicians, explorers and Eskimos, scholars and celebrities. The diners styled themselves, rather grandiosely, as the Thursday's Club call'd the Royal Philosophers.[2]

Meals were taken very seriously at the Thursday's Club. For over thirty years, the club's secretary painstakingly recorded each week's bill of fare in what came to be volumes of leather-bound, pocket-sized, gold-trimmed dinner books.[3] The vast majority of the food was supplied by the tavern, and varied with seasonal rhythms. But sometimes there were additional items – foods given as gifts – that were carefully set apart from the rest. Between 1748, when the records begin, and 1785, when the club ceased to record its weekly meals, the Thursday's Club received 242 gifts of food: approximately five per year, usually exchanged over the spring and summer.

The club never devised any rules governing what counted as a gift and what did not. Nor did it ever set a calendar or season for gift giving. Yet there was nothing random or arbitrary about these practices. Gifts tended to be hunted rather than bred, cultivated rather than purchased. Partridges, pheasants and Scottish pickled salmon were exchanged as gifts, but never bread or ale. White currants and Carolina strawberries could count as gifts, but not when preserved in pies and tarts. Certain gifts warranted special privileges and honorary toasts, while others garnered no further remark.

Table 1

Types of Food Gifted to the Thursday's Club: 1748-84

Food never gifted	*Food always gifted*
Livestock	Venison
Domesticated fowl	Partridge, pheasant
Saltwater fish	Freshwater fish
'Garden stuff'	Exotic vegetables
Cooked fruit	Fresh fruit

Some aspects of this gift lexicon may be familiar to scholars. Once the English landscape began to be enclosed, and starvation gradually brought under human control, the fruits of the wilderness began to rise in social status. Little wonder that game and freshwater fish were given as gifts, while livestock and saltwater fish were not.[4] Moreover, given the clear cultural boundaries between commodities and gifts, bread's absence from the gift repertoire should come as no surprise.[5] Yet other patterns are harder to explain. Why fresh fruit but not vegetables? Why were some gifts valued more highly than others?

Gift transactions often escape the historical record, leaving scholars little opportunity to treat them much quantitative rigor. The Thursday's Club's unusually meticulous records, however, make possible this kind of analysis. Altogether, the Club left thirty-two years of consecutive dinner records behind: over seven thousand meals in all. By reading this data within the broader social histories of food in eighteenth-century London – asking not only who gave what sorts of gifts, but also when, where and why – I illustrate how food gifts helped solidify relationships and values that could not be communicated by other means.

***

Food gifts have long been familiar fixtures of English social life. Deer hunted in private game parks were tokens of elite power and privilege, reinforcing the mutual obligations between patrons and clients. Sixteenth-century household accounts are rife with records of fruits, jams and marmalades given by poorer tenants: small and toothsome tokens to remind the powerful of their presence. Yet gift-giving in the Thursday's Club was a noteworthy act. Of over 1200 men who dined at the Club's table between 1748 and 1785, only around four per cent of the club's attendees – forty-one men – ever gave a gift. Even within this small sample, it is hard to describe the typical giver. A couple of these men gave gifts on the same week each year, like clockwork. A third of these men gave a gift only once. Either way, gift-givers selected from a limited repertoire. Venison comprised over half of all gifts made to the club, and was distantly followed by turtle (twenty-one gifts), pickled salmon (fifteen gifts), fresh fruit (twelve gifts) and small game (nine gifts).

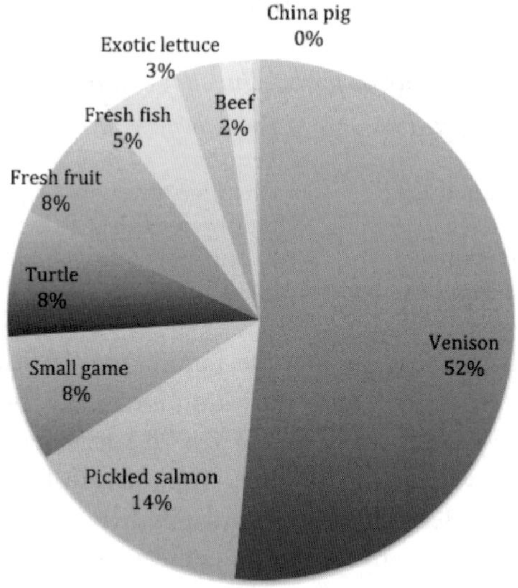

Figure 1 Men selected gifts from a limited repertoire of food categories

Not all gifts were created equal. Gifts of venison, turtle and extraordinarily large haunches of beef granted their donors special privileges: honorary membership in the club for one year and into perpetuity so long as the gift continued to be given annually, a toast to the donor's health in claret and an official word of thanks delivered to his door. While never elaborated in the club's minutes, there were important political and cultural reasons why these three foods were so valuable. Since the fourteenth century, when the first hunting laws were implemented in England, venison had been a tangible manifestation of landed privilege as well as the respective obligations that such privilege entailed.[6] Sixteenth-century conduct manuals described the stag hunt as a school of honour that inculcated the juridical and magisterial skills required to rule.[7] These understandings were at the heart of the 1723 Waltham Black Acts, which legislated the nobility's control over these food sources by making poaching a hanging offense. They were unlikely to have been lost on the club when its gifting tradition began in 1748.

Venison historically had been a powerful proxy of the giver's physical presence. The expense and difficulty of transporting a heavy stinking carcass over long distances underscored the giver's wealth and influence. This was also true of the Thursday's Club. Of the three men who gifted venison with any regularity – indeed, on the very same week for eighteen, twelve, and nine years respectively – two of these men were high-ranking peers who never attended the weekly dinners at all. The third, the well-known physician William Heberden, attended club dinners regularly, yet his venison gifts were consciously subordinate to his peers. Instead of presenting an entire buck, as titled aristocrats did, Heberden unfailingly gave only single haunches, wordless acknowledgements of his non-noble blood.

Gifts of sea turtle brought other kinds of cultural baggage to the table. Introduced to the English public as the sustenance of Indians, slaves and shipwrecked sailors who had no recourse to anything better, the animal became known as an exotic delicacy among cosmopolitan elites during the 1740s and 1750s. Virtually impossible to procure without connections to West Indian enterprises, anonymous parvenus went so far as to put ads in London newspapers in their quests to obtain one. The club was hardly immune from these pressures. After the first turtle promised to the club died as it crossed the English Channel in the autumn of 1750, it took another four years before the Club received another specimen.[8]

It was only partially thanks to its rarity that turtle gifts elicited such powerful emotions. The sea turtle had never been subject to ancient hunting restrictions; it defied the edible strictures of custom and tradition. For some, the strange reptile perfectly embodied the culinary consequences of foreign enterprise and the corrupting effects of fashion and luxury. Yet for the Club, the sea turtle represented something far more optimistic: the unfathomable reaches of an ever-growing empire. This is evident in the 1755 dinner that honoured Commodore George Anson (1697-1762), who had attained celebrity and riches from his swashbuckling exploits during the War of Jenkins Ear, where the green sea turtle, consumed on a remote island in the Pacific, had nourished a hungry and exhausted crew.[9] When word got out that Anson would present one to the club, invitations were sent out to all forty members by penny-post. The animal's unique, indescribable flavour – some thought it tasted like beef, some like chicken, some marvelled at its texture, with the consistency of butter – fostered a shared sense of vicarious participation in the empire's overseas expansion. Even the shell mimicked a large communal bowl, evincing a forgotten form of fellowship that seemed to predate history and time. 'Never was turtle eaten with *greater sobriety and temperance,* or more good fellowship', the inventor James Watt wrote to his wife in 1780, as it was at the Thursday's Club.[10]

261

Unlike the innumerable quantities of domesticated cows, sheep and pigs that passed anonymously through the Mitre's kitchen, venison and turtle evoked the masculinized *exo-cuisine* of the hunt. Size was critical to their value – hence the careful records of the freights and portages charged for transporting slaughtered bucks, and the weights and measures applied to haunches of beef. (Although beef was not hunted, the 'Homerian' size restrictions on it transformed it into a non-commercial food; throughout the club's history, only one man managed to meet this criterion.[11]) Rumours of turtles so large that they dwarfed kitchens and dining rooms circulated in newspapers and coffeehouses; the Club learned this the hard way in 1749, when it was moved to an adjacent room in the Mitre because of a 400-pounder bestowed on another unnamed association. Rare, monstrous and culturally loaded, these food gifts celebrated the Englishman's conquest of nature.

Such optimism also inhered in the numerous ancillary gifts that imparted no special privileges on their givers. These came in the form of exotic fruit raised in hot houses and physic gardens – pineapples, cantaloupes, Malaga watermelons and Egyptian lettuces – as well as strawberries, peaches, apricots and white currants. As opposed to the preserved apple, pear and damson pies, tarts and puddings proclaimed on the common bill of fare, the fragility of fresh fruit underscored one's intimacy within the Club. Gifts of freshwater fish – perch, pike, carp and potted char – followed similar patterns. There was nothing particularly rare or exotic about them aside from the fact that they were fished in local ponds and streams rather than obtained commercially.[12] Ancillary gifts also presupposed a different kind of giver. Unlike givers of venison and turtle, givers of these lighter, less caloric foods came from all social ranks, ranging from titled peers to lowborn writers and gardeners admitted to the club on the merits of their wits and connections. What these givers shared was some degree of seniority in the Thursday's Club, many having attended dinners faithfully for years.

***

Given the food gift's close associations with custom and patronage, it is tempting to regard these rituals as vestiges of a crumbling social order: a system mediated by title and privilege rather than enlightened free enterprise. Some of the Thursday's Club's own members certainly shared this sentiment. Shortly after the election of Joseph Banks to the Presidency of the Royal Society in 1778, causing leadership of the Thursday's Club to change hands, a new rule soon appeared in the club's minutes: 'no person in the future be admitted a member of this society in consequence of any present he shall make to it.' It is not difficult to surmise why this rule was passed. Banks understood how easily food gifts masqueraded as freely given largesse.[13] He himself had presented venison on several occasions in order to ingratiate himself with the group.[14] (Even after the rule's passage, Banks twice gifted haunches of venison, and once entertained members with a turtle feast.)

Yet relegating food gifts to self-interested bribes or favours oversimplifies the cultural work they performed. In many ways gifts worked as symbolic social contracts, solidifying bonds of trust and fellowship across far-flung social ranks. As a 1757 dispute over the honorary admission of Philip Dormer Stanhope, the Fourth Earl of Chesterfield (1694-1773) reveals, members did not take these functions lightly. The Chesterfield dispute was simple: instead of presenting the club with a food gift, the nobleman had written a satirical petition to the king, a copy of which had been read aloud to the club members over dinner. Chesterfield's cousin, a long-time member of the Thursday's Club, proposed that Chesterfield should be elected an honorary member on the spot. The present company unanimously agreed.

But the club's secretary, who had missed dinner that night, was deeply unsettled by the nomination. In a three-page diatribe written in the dinner books, he asked whether any piece of writing could truly substitute for a food gift. He pointed out that everyone knows what venison or turtle tasted like, calling them 'substantial forms' known through the senses. Wit and humour, by contrast, worked only on the mind, making the petition vulnerable to changing fashions. And while, given the time and the resources, he believed that members of the club could agree upon a 'standard' of wit, it would always lack the unconscious immediacy of a remembered taste or smell. 'Every one knows the meaning of the words venison, turtle, and chine of beef,' Colebrooke argued, 'the things are objects of our own senses, we know the tast [sic] of them.' In many ways, substituting a petition for a food gift was a double failure on the Earl of Chesterfield's part. Not only did Chesterfield fail to play by the gift economy's rules, but he also violated his inherited duties: displays of hospitality and largesse were practically mandated by his birthright. Should word get out that a nobleman was admitted on these terms, Colebrooke warned, the club would not only 'be much embarrassed', but it also would find itself flooded with new applicants. (In fact, posterity would most likely consider the 'petition' a name of a new dish, Colebrooke went on, so much did the proposal violate the strictures of custom.)

***

They say that a picture can speak a thousand words. So can a gift of food. Clothed in unspoken traditions, dancing to deeper cultural rhythms, food gifts articulated nuances of rank, politics, friendship and history in ways that language could not. This doesn't mean that a food gift's meanings were always obvious; they were sometimes ignored, sometimes transgressed and sometimes misunderstood. Still, there was something deep and venerable about the ritual that commanded a gentleman's respect. Procured, prepared and presented on the table, food gifts connected eaters to the kingdom's past and future. Chewed, swallowed, digested and absorbed, they made disparate eaters more alike. Food gifts in this way, proved powerful agents of identity, nourishing bonds of fellowship in an increasingly market-driven world.

263

Notes

1. Excluding the first few years of the club's existence, each club member was also a fellow of the Royal Society, although membership in the Royal Society by no means guaranteed membership in the club. Since the club's beginnings, the president of the Royal Society always became the *de facto* President of the Thursday's Club, although this rule was not codified until 1766.
2. Three histories of the club have been written to date, all of which have been authored by former members: Admiral Smyth's *Sketch of the Rise and Progress of the Royal Society Club* (London, 1860), Sir Archibald Geikie's *Annals of the Royal Society Club* (London, 1917), and T.E. Allibone's *The Royal Society and Its Dining Clubs* (Oxford: Pergamon Press, 1976). Renamed the Royal Society Club in 1795, the club continues to meet today.
3. This practice was highly unusual. Many clubs recorded attendance and the costs of each meal, yet the contents of the bill of fare were rarely mentioned.
4. During the eighteenth century, saltwater fish were shipped to London in large quantities from the

coast, and were purchased at the Billingsgate fish market; see Joan Thirsk, *Food in Early Modern England* (London: Hambledon, 2007), p. 159.

5. See Felicity Heal's work on gifts – 'Food Gifts, the Household, and the Politics of Exchange in Early Modern England', *Past and Present*, 199 (2008), pp. 41-70 and *The Power of Gifts: Gift Exchange in Early Modern England* (New York: Oxford University Press, 2014) – for a fuller explanation of the historical demarcations between gifts and commodities in early modern England.

6. See Daniel Beaver, *Hunting and the Politics of Violence before the English Civil War* (Cambridge: Cambridge University Press, 2012); Roger Manning, *Hunters and Poachers: A Social and Cultural History of Unlawful Hunting in England 1485-1640* (Oxford: Oxford University Press, 1993), pp. 5-17; and Susan Whyman, *Sociability and Power in Late Stuart England: The Cultural World of the Verneys 1660-1720* (Oxford: Oxford University Press, 2000).

7. Beaver, p. 11.

8. Turtle feasting became so popular that, while the exclusivity of venison consumption gradually declined over the eighteenth century, turtle maintained its novelty for decades.

9. For the broader study of the navy's significance to eighteenth-century cultural politics, see Nicholas Rogers and Gerald Jordan, 'Admirals as Heroes: Patriotism and Liberty in Hanoverian England', *Journal of British Studies*, 28:3 (July, 1989), pp. 201-24. For the significance of turtle feasting in Anson's *Voyage Around the World* (1748), see India Mandelkern, 'The Politics of the English Turtle Feast', *The Appendix: A New Journal of Narrative and Experimental History*, 1:4 (2013) <http://theappendix.net/issues/2013/10/the-politics-of-the-turtle-feast> [accessed 30 November 2015].

10. James Patrick Muirhead, *The Life of James Watt: With Selections from his Correspondence* (New York: Appleton, 1859), p. 20.

11. After receiving a chine of beef that measured '34 inches in length and a weight of 140 pounds', in 1750, the club deemed the gift equal to 'half a buck' and entitled the giver to the same benefits.

12. These meanings are present in the diary of Parson Woodforde, who frequently recorded giving tench caught in local ponds and streams to family and friends. See the entry dated May 26, 1768 in *The Diary of a Country Parson,* ed. by John Beresford (London: Oxford University Press, 1924). This might have something to do with fish's greater availability as opposed to meat, as well as its symbolic inheritance; fish has stood as a Judeo-Christian symbol of fertility since Biblical times.

13. D.P. Miller, 'The Hardwicke Circle: The Whig Supremacy and its Demise in the 18th-Century Royal Society', *Notes and Records of the Royal Society of London*, 52:1 (Jan., 1998), pp. 73-91.

14. Banks presented the club with venison in 1773, 1774, 1776 and 1777. According to T.E. Allibone, the latter two occasions might well have been peace offerings. In November 1775, Banks formed his own dinner club for his own circle of friends, although he continued to attend the Royal Philosophers' dinners several times a year. See 'The Thursday's Club Called the Royal Philosophers, and its Relation to the Royal Society Club', *Notes and Records of the Royal Society*, 26:1 (June 1971), pp. 73-80.

Hot, Sour, Salty…Write: *Saveur* Magazine, Thai Food Culture and the Communicative Potential of Food and Travel Journalism

Robert McKeown

The texts of food and travel journalism provide a unique perspective in which personal experience, the foreign, the edible and the exotic play central roles. The texts of *Saveur,* in their depiction of Thai food culture, have the potential to offer critical information and consumer-friendly ideas, and to encourage active audience participation and cross-cultural engagement. Mobilizing Hanusch's definition of travel journalism – and adapting it for the more specific field of food travel – this paper puts into conversation themes of globalization, cosmopolitanism, otherness and representation, as theorized by Appadurai, Robbins and Hall, and applies the research of Livingstone to consider the role of the audience in both historical and modern media contexts. Issues of power/knowledge, as defined by Foucault, complicate the idea of otherness, and help demarcate a place for the individual. Extending Schudson and Anderson's position on journalistic ideals and challenging Witschge's position on professional standards, this paper further offers a normative set of practices for food travel journalism, illustrating ways we – as readers, journalists and food travellers – can take it more seriously. This paper makes the argument that, though it is has been paid little attention academically, food and travel journalism provides an unlikely but powerful alternative for counter-balancing the excesses of traditional, legacy or corporate news journalism as we know them.

Shaping and Defining the Field

While it is sometimes derided as a market-driven medium, food and travel journalism is actually one of the most robust and healthy forms of the craft alive today. Titles like *Saveur* (and *Food and Wine* and *Bon Appetit* in the US, or *Gourmet Traveller* in Australia, etc.) continue to expand and emphasize their international coverage as they push for worldwide sales and web presence. It could even be argued that food and travel is among the oldest operating types and topics for journalism, with everyone from Marco Polo to Mark Twain occupying varying spaces along a food and cultural writing continuum dating back many centuries. While foreign news reporting has fallen in quality and quantity in the last decade, food and travel content has proliferated online and off, in the Global North and South alike.

For the purposes of this paper, mobilizing a solid definition of food and travel journalism is crucial. Folker Hanusch's book, *Travel Journalism* (2014), provides a jumping off point in his important arguments for the political economy of such a specific strain of journalism. With a billion-plus tourists and the multi-trillion dollar yearly economy of travel as fuel, tourist advertisers demand spaces for reaching their target markets. Websites, programs, magazines and media outlets as a whole have expanded to meet this demand (2014: 5). From an audience point of view, the ensuing texts have become an important source for the representation of Others – an important site for witnessing the 'dynamics of globalization' (2014: 6).

Hanusch connects the dots between traditional journalistic norms and ideals and travel journalism's relationship with foreign places and cultures. He asserts that foundational ideas of verification, fairness, independence and truth seeking are also adopted by travel journalism. He further defines journalism as a greater textual system that helps connect to audiences, and in some cases to create readers as publics (2014: 7). This distinction is an important one, as the seriousness of journalism is often correlated with its ability to motivate audiences to act and, in certain cases, to create moments of 'publicness'. Through its interaction with foreign food cultures and its complex relationship with the culinary Other, this paper argues that *Saveur*, at times, accomplishes this with as much seriousness and brio as traditional journalism.

Hanusch identifies several salient features of travel journalism, which can also be applied to *Saveur's* hybrid of food and travel journalism. First, he highlights the importance of representing Others, their cultures and their countries as 'the main purpose' of this medium (2014: 9). Second, he emphasizes that media can fundamentally shape the way tourists think about other cultures. Third, he stresses the sheer expense of travelling to, working in, reporting from and producing journalism about foreign places. Fourth, he underlines concerns raised by the market-driven stance of lifestyle journalism – of which food and travel is a specific subset – in which some editors and publishers approach audiences as consumers rather than citizens (2014: 9-10).

It is important to accurately place *Saveur* on this continuum of journalistic concerns, with its dual focus on food and travel. As a global title that publishes articles from numerous places around the globe, it is in a unique position to represent the cultural and culinary Other. With healthy ad sales, *Saveur* can still afford to support expenses and trips for their photographers and writers, providing a strong ethical base from which to write about their experiences. Though there is inevitably an influence from advertising and publishing, to art and editorial, *Saveur* generally protects the ideals of their writers and photographers. These defining characteristics and circumstances form a base from which *Saveur* is able to operate with efficacy at a level that rivals – and sometimes surpasses – that of corporate news journalism. Extending the reach of Hanusch's definition to food and travel journalism, we will consider the unique aspects of *Saveur* within what he further defines as 'factual accounts that address audiences as consumers of travel or tourism experiences, by providing information and entertainment, but also critical perspectives' (2014: 11).

266

Globalization and Cosmopolitanism – The Context

Two decades ago, the media was, predominantly, nationally oriented. Media outlets addressed audiences within their own borders, and the discourses they created stayed largely within those confines. In the current media environment – one shaped by the world-flattening force of the Internet and the future-creating speed of telecommunication innovation – this is no longer the case. Media are now global: one can read a magazine from any place in the world about any culture in the world, while sitting in any corner of the world, with the potential to be anywhere else in the world in a matter of hours. The consequences for readers, journalists, eaters, audiences and subjects are substantial.

Global tourism numbers help to illuminate the transnational setting in which these groups operate. Two decades ago, in 1990, there were 435 million tourist arrivals worldwide. Since 2012, tourist arrivals have eclipsed 1 billion yearly (World Tourism Organization 2013). Thailand alone hosted 24.77 million tourists in 2014 and received some 2,654,634 in January of 2015 alone (Tourism Authority of Thailand 2015a, 2015b). On a macro level, tourism is the world's biggest industry, collecting some 6.6 trillion US dollars in receipts or 9% of the world GDP, creating some 260 million jobs in total (World Tourism and Travel Council 2014).

The ever-changing nature – the process and site – of food travel means that ideas of place, person, culture, taste and perception are in constant flux. For this reason, embracing and understanding the concept of globalization is crucial for understanding what food travel journalism stands for. This is especially true when still-developing countries like Thailand are the subject matter, as their language, culture, history and viewpoints are very different from those of the Global North.

Marking the era of globalization as a crisis for the nation-state, Appadurai sees the current era as a 'world of flows' whose intellectual current includes 'ideas and ideologies, people and goods, images and messages, technologies and techniques' (2001: 4). He champions this object-driven process through the promotion of 'the role of the imagination in social life'. Through its interaction with daily Thai experiences like markets or street food, the texts of *Saveur* initiate a conversation with the same world that Appadurai aims to describe. They give agency to the social imaginaries of Others and breech the levee in a stream of thoughts and experiences that can flow from one culture and people to another.

Appadurai hints at these fluid experiences by emphasizing that 'we need to make a shift away from what we call trait geographies to what we would call process geographies' (2001: 7). He proposes a shift in priority and focus – in optical, social and academic senses – towards a study of areas that takes foregrounds process geographies against different types of action and reaction – including travel, import/export, migration and warfare (2001: 7-8). How does a noodle soup cook in Chiang Rai's morning market perceive Western food? How does she think of other Thais in her capital, Bangkok? By representing such views in direct quotations and providing a space in which to let them circulate, *Saveur* becomes a medium through which such global flows of information and ideation can happen.

Appadurai's recipe for globalization has many complex and cultured levels and viewpoints. Unpacking the idea of social imagination, he emphasizes that we must recognize that in every corner of the world – the mountains of Northern Thailand, the Chinese trading towns of the Andaman Sea – different inhabitants bring different conceptions to bear on the world. For him, we must 'recognize the global capability to imagine regions and worlds is now itself a globalized phenomenon. That is, due to the activities of migrants, media, and capital, tourism, and so forth the means for imagining areas is now globally widely distributed' (2001: 8).

With a monthly international readership of 1.2 million readers, many of whom spend thousands per year on travel, *Saveur* prompts many readers to action, travel and consumption. They might call on native speakers or celebrity and chef-correspondents to collaborate with local stylists, photographers and editorial teams to create a feature on Southern Thai food. Or perhaps commission a series of smaller pieces on Thai market specialties. This border-dissolving process helps engender conversation and initiates trips for and between cultures. Appadurai outlines some of the benefits of this process: 'The potential payoff is a critical dialogue between world pictures, a sort of dialectic of areas and regions, built on the axiom that areas are not facts but artifacts of interests and our fantasies as well as of our needs to know, to remember, and to forget' (2001: 9).

268

Delineating public spheres in the most plural and trans-national senses of the world, he makes an impassioned call for the coming-together of 'symbolic analysts' (2001: 9). Though this statement is made in the context of research and teaching, the idea could easily be applied to the potential of *Saveur*'s publishing model, a world where art directors, writers, stylists, photographers, editors, sources, cooks, travellers and journalists all should come together to create articles for subjects and audiences that are global.

Robbins (1998) provides a different viewpoint on the same subject matter, aiming to re-define the idea of cosmopolitanism, a concept that initially implied a growing set of global elites who moved freely in their roles as expatriates, capitalists and diplomats, all living in a world of dissolving borders. Citing the anthropologist James Clifford, Robbins re-jigs his definition in a way that is inclusive and future appropriate (1998: 1). He rolls in some of the same groups that contribute to Appadurai's globalization from below – twenty-something travellers from emerging economies like Mainland China and urban India, backpackers chasing noodles in Hong Kong, young chefs working for free in Thai kitchens. These cohorts, Robbins argues, have specific, important and ultimately cosmopolitan viewpoints and should not be excluded (1998: 1). 'This change in personnel implies a change in definition,' he argues, and 'like nations, cosmopolitanisms are now plural and particular [...] they are weak and under-developed as well as strong and privileged' (1998: 2).

The tension between the plural and particular is of great importance in food and travel journalism. As Robbins puts it, 'instead of an ideal of detachment, actually existing cosmopolitanisms is a reality of re-attachment, multiple attachment, or attachment at a distance' (1998: 3). It is from this platform that the many origins of *Saveur*'s articles can locate an opportunity – to represent the pluralistic state of cosmopolitan thoughts in a way that is appropriately diverse in a global sense. Stories written from, say, the viewpoint of modernist cooks in Bangkok, emerging organic farmers in Esarn provinces or street food vendors in Phuket, can help to represent the multi-faceted world as many people may not know it, as well as how others may want to know it.

Highlighting the emotional connections implicit in Benedict Anderson's concept of print-capitalism, Robbins believes that we are now living in an era of 'electronic- and digital-capitalism, and now that this system is so clearly transnational it would be strange if people did not get emotional in much the same way, if not necessarily to the same degree about others who are not fellow nationals, people bound to them by some sort of transnational fellowship' (1998: 7). By linking the border-dependent process of nation building in the past to the transnational and emotional attachments of his cosmopolitanism, Robbins re-constitutes Anderson's idea of an imagined community. Here, where borders dissolve like ice in a Thai market, the readership of *Saveur* creates their own imagined communities, transcending borders, pursuing new ideas, fomenting cross-cultural understanding in the context of food, travel and journalism. As Robbins describes, cosmopolitanism is fast becoming an 'effort to describe, from within multiculturalism, a name for the genuine striving toward common norms and mutual translatability that is also a part of multiculturalism' (1998: 11-12).

Representation and the (Culinary and Cultural) Other

One of the most crucial ideas in cultural studies is the system of representation that helps construct the 'Other' – in short, the way we help demarcate and delineate ourselves from one another in relation to ethnicity, race, culture and perceived difference. By taking other cultures, tastes and places as its central subject matter, food and travel journalism has a unique and important relationship with this notion. In a time when foreign news coverage is in rapid decline, periodicals like *Saveur* occupy an increasingly important position in the world of news flows. Through a unique blend of experiential and fact-based reporting about predominantly foreign places, it can at best offer crucial, enlightening and positive information about Others to their readership. This is in stark contrast to the often reductive – and shrinking – coverage of these binaries in legacy journalism outlets.

Stuart Hall's (1997) seminal work, 'The Spectacle of the Other', guides readers through various counter-strategies of representation. Focusing on race in photographic representations of black athletes, he focuses on the binary relation of Us and Them, unpacking discourses through historically-informed observation, semiotic analysis and anthropologically-rooted commentary (1997: 228). His core ideas present an area of opportunity for food and travel journalism. Indeed, as a magazine that presents highly personal viewpoints and experiences in diverse settings, *Saveur* is a case study for multiple potential meanings, letting their presentation of food journeys be shaped and re-shaped in the interactions – and acts of consumption – between journalist/eater, subject/cooks and audience/readers. Hall tables a way to interpret these situations: 'Meaning Floats. It cannot be finally fixed. Attempting to fix it is a work of a representational practice, which intervenes in the many potential meanings of an image in an attempt to privilege ones' (1997: 228).

A quick glance at some scenarios: the locally-educated reader in Taipei will bring to their reading of an article on regional Esarn Thai food a different set of preconceptions than a Thai, perhaps educated in London, perusing a piece on where to find 'authentic' regional Thai food in Las Vegas. Here, the unique set of circumstances is evident and applied to a highly specific subject matter, where meaning is constantly re-defined via audience activity and action.

Foucault's writings on the subject and power record many of the same issues within the process of identifying Others, shedding light on the origins of power and the re-imagined role they play when looked at with the media and journalism as subjects. Foucault focuses on 'dividing practices' both within the personality of the subject and in relation to the subject's role vis-à-vis others (1983: 208). His concern lies less with macro ideas foisted from one dominant group onto another weaker one than with the individual/subject themself (1983: 209). He takes as his objects of debate a 'series of oppositions' – men and women, parents and children – with a broad focus on authoritative power.

Foucault frames these struggles in a cross-cultural way – ethnic, social and religious – that departs from that of Hall. Interestingly, these categories reflect the same social class concerns that inform the globalization work of Appadurai and the cosmopolitan approaches of Robbins. Foucault assigns social agency to the 'knowledge of man around two roles: one, globalizing and quantitative, concerning the population; the other, analytical, concerning the individual' (1983: 215). The tension between these duelling roles, in an operating theatre defined by power, should be a focus of *Saveur*'s editors. Questions editors might ask themselves while writing story briefs include: How might we empower those different from us? How might we diffuse the imbalances endemic in covering developing countries such as Thailand? How can we engage with and represent the cultural and culinary other in a positive way?

Hall presents several useful strategies for battling negative representation. Broadly defined as trans-coding, they include actively reversing stereotypes, expanding the range of complexity and representation and rocking the boat of representation by contesting it from within (1997: 272-74). This between-worlds space of power and representation offers *Saveur*'s editorial and publishing team's alternatives for change. By having editors demand that writers include quotes from varying types of native speakers or indigenous peoples, they can give an active voice to Others. By applying greater depth to subjects that range from the historical experience of the Burmese in Thailand to the gastro-political history of the South and its cooking, they can provide a space where audience members can engage with difference, circulate ideas, and re-distribute power in active and public discussion of – and approaches to and with – Others.

Audiences, Publics and Cultures – From Subservience to Independence

Examining the roles of audiences, the public and their on-going conversations and conditioning through the media, Sonia Livingstone (2005) provides a useful and modern perspective on journalistic structures. Hers is a nuanced argument built on examinations of audiences, content and the media practices that create them. Livingstone highlights systemic issues that include political, economic and professional influences on journalistic institutions, and the multiple aspects of meaning endemic in media texts (2005: 27). In the context of these continuing problems. Livingstone highlights matters of interest for the field of food and travel journalism: the complex interplay between audiences and texts and the public friction created by dual tendencies between 'centralization/standardization and diversification/innovation' by the current environment of technology (2005: 27). Theoretically, this idea can be extended and applied to include all current forms of information and journalistic distribution. It strikes at the heart of how we as audience members can influence the relations between content and reception.

It is in this environment that *Saveur* and its audiences operate. As a well-funded publishing house with large travel budgets for writers and photographers and a global network of readers, the magazine has an opportunity to deliver well-researched and well-formed stories to an audience that is, by nature of reading a title with a food and travel focus, highly motivated. With a multi-platform approach that allows readers to consume information across boundaries as well as interact through social media platforms, *Saveur* influences the process of action and ideation that sweeps magazine readers from the status of audience to that of a public – and into the spaces in-between. Livingston argues for the commingling of 'public and audience,' asserting that 'media appear to be simultaneously expanding the scope of the audience and diminishing the realm of the public, leaving few if any aspects of social or personal life unaccompanied by or independent of the media' (2005: 19).

Saveur readers do frequently engage on a personal and social level. They clip articles and act upon information to decide how to use their leisure time – that afforded to them by capitalist systems when work is completed. They plan trips based on such information. Livingstone's elucidation of the most current phase of audience development provides a framework for the *Saveur* audience as a citizen-consumer: 'the diffused audience is no longer containable in particular places and times, but rather is part and parcel of all aspects of daily life, certainly in industrialized nations and increasingly globally' (2005: 26). Here, in a space that can be as transnational as it is driven by special interests, the highly globalized, obsessed-with-the-foreign-food structure of *Saveur* has room to grow.

Standards, Practices…and Opportunities

Although the still-evolving practices of *Saveur* are, in many ways, divergent from the structures of traditional news journalism, there is still a strong link between the standards and practices of the latter and the professional norms of the former. Relying on cultural theories and a historical approach to the development of journalistic professionalism, Schudson and Anderson's discussion of concepts such as objectivity and truth seeking identifies core ideas which food and travel journalism should adopt as their own (2004: 92). They underline the normative importance of such ideals as the bedrock on which journalism should be structured as a respected and important profession. As pillars of the craft, these ideals serve the same role for food and travel journalism, albeit with a divergent set of story structures, audience relationships and approaches to representation than the more classical stance of news.

In mapping various levels of professionalism across international borders and foreign strains of the profession, Schudson and Anderson cite Hallin and Mancini, noting that while professionalism might be consistent, 'the social bases of their professionalism' and 'the specific content of their values' diverge (2004: 94). While splitting socio-cultural foundations, they again invoke Hallin and Mancini in a future context that opens the door for new strains of journalistic professionalism: 'professional journalism might have different bases cross-culturally, historically, and even in the future. The end of objectivity, even if it arrives, may not signal the end of professional journalism' (2004: 94).

It is within this context that food and travel journalism operates. Like another nation's social system, it exists with different ethical bases and the opposing (to traditional journalism) idea of oft-subjective, narrative-based, first-person stories focused on the cultural and the culinary. Heavily freelance-based, food and travel journalists should set common goals for discovering other food cultures and revealing their subtleties through personal experiences. They should include inspiring the reader/audience to act, while actualizing food travel and forming emotional connections.

Examining how journalists – and the vocation as a whole – have reacted to the new forms of media birthed by emerging technologies and their adoption by audiences around the globe, Tamara Witschge (2013) provides a current analysis of journalism as a professionalized craft. She looks at the different strands of thought in the newsroom, evaluating how traditional values are point-counterpoint with fluid systemic changes and challenges. One of her main issues is trying to square 'high standards versus low practices' with the idealistic nature of journalists in a commercially-driven, time-tight environment with unrelenting deadlines (2013: 161). Witschge pinpoints journalists as 'knowledgeable people working with certain standards', and she emphasizes that standards are regarded as professionalize ones that serve commercial and entertainment aspects, but also ones of public service or political value. According to interviews, things cherished by journalists include providing good information and expert commentary, as well as long-form and original stories – though in traditional newsrooms these are also in decline (2013: 164-65).

So where does food and travel journalism fit into this journalistic landscape, and how can the re-appropriation of such norms benefit *Saveur*? The conception of well-informed people with high standards fits neatly. To balance against the commercial and entertainment aspects of their business, *Saveur* should develop more robust structures, practices, and standards. Fairness, truth, verification, independence – these values should be evident in their content production. Ethics should be fortified with ample travel and production budgets, while local correspondents spread around the globe can provide valuable foreign culture input.

Re-activating practices that are waning in traditional journalism, *Saveur* should place a focus on long form and original features. As a monthly periodical they are not bound by the 24/7 news cycle that is seen as a diluting factor in much of Witschge's interviews. Indeed, *Saveur*'s may be a different service to the public, but it should still take as a starting point the same journalistic values cherished by the profession as a whole.

Towards a Set of Normative Practices

This ultimate section looks to prime food and travel journalists for the future by suggesting an evolved and specific set of practices that might benefit their unique strain of coverage. Each practice addresses a set of themes representative of the ideas discussed in this paper. They have been developed for immediate editorial play, but possess a normative function that can contribute to a more robust definition of their specific mission.

273

> *A New Foreign Correspondence*: The importance of food and travel journalism as a site for interaction with cultures of different origins grows stronger each week. Food and travel journalism should appoint foreign correspondents for their localized expertise and language, as well as the ability to present more complex representations of the Other. As Smith and Higgins observe, the specialized orientation of glossy magazines affords opportunities for content that can amplify a sense of community 'driven by mutual interest, shared beliefs, or a common national or regional identity' (2014: 49).

> *Symbolic Analysts in Journalism:* Inspired by Appadurai's call for symbolic analysts to collaborate, *Saveur* should re-contextualize this idea in the way they commission long-form articles and provide briefs to both textual and visual journalists (2001: 9). They can call on foreign correspondents, mixing and matching talents, linguistic capability and viewpoints to enrich the content that drives their magazine and lures their readers in a more culturally muscular and

sensitive assembly of coverage teams.

Audience Platforms – Extended and Global: As Thompson points out, the media now have a 'mediated worldliness' that is fed by the 'growing importance of forms of communication, and interaction which are not face-to-face in character' (1995: 5-6). *Saveur* should capitalize on the growing power afforded by extended media platforms to engage their audience in a way that makes them as active and potentially public in character and action as possible. It is here, in these overlapping circles of communication, that opportunities for cross-cultural experiences and shared conversation can be found.

Activating Voices: Just as Robbins (1998) called for a re-definition of cosmopolitanism to recognize the changing nature of the global experience, so too should *Saveur* re-adjust its journalistic practices to demand that writers, through techniques such as interviews employment of local-language scribes, give voices to different people from different points along the socio-cultural continuum of the foreign food cultures that are the taken subject of *Saveur*.

A Positive and Open Othering Process: Magazines such as *Saveur* place the representation of the foreign food culture and the edible Other at the centre of their work. By incorporating these practices, they should endeavour to make constructing a more complex, learned, positive and accurate picture of others a prime concern. By seeking out new voices and viewpoints, experiences and cultural entry points, they should demand a more open and aware representation process from their writers, thus re-distributing the power and knowledge that theorists such as Hall (1997) and Foucault (1983) have placed on the side of the Western or dominant classes. As Rojek and Urry underline in their work on tourism, the current 'culture of flows produces spaces of "in-betweenness" inhabited by various types of tourist and traveller' (1997: 11). It is in these gaps that common ground should be found.

Enactment of Professional Journalistic Codes: Taking cues from the professional norms outlined by Schudson and Anderson (2009), *Saveur* should permanently enshrine the journalistic codes of truth, verification, independence, and fairness into their working process. While it is understood that some ideals – specifically, objectivity and representation – are re-cast by the singular circumstances presented by food and travel journalism, the aforementioned ideals will help command respect and create continued impact and achievement.

Bibliography

Appadurai, Arjun. 2001. 'Grassroots Globalization and the Research Imagination', in Arjun Appadurai (ed.), Globalization (Durham: Duke University Press), pp. 1-21.

Clifford, James. 1988. The Predicament of Culture: Twentieth-Century Ethnography, Literature, and Art (Cambridge: Harvard University Press).

Foucault, Michel. 1983. 'The Subject and Power', in Hubert L. Dreyfus and Paul Rainbow (eds.), Beyond Structuralism and Hermeneutics (Chicago: University of Chicago Press), pp. 208-26.

Hall, Stuart. 1997. 'The Spectacle of the "Other"', in Stuart Hall (ed), Representation: Cultural Representations and Signifying Practices (London: Sage), pp. 225-79.

Hanusch, Folker and Elfriede Fursich. 2014. 'On The Relevance of Travel Journalism: An Introduction', in Folker Hanusch and Elfriede Fursich (eds.), Travel Journalism: Exploring Production, Impact and Culture (New York: Palgrave Macmillan), pp. 1-18.

Livingstone, Sonia. 2005. 'On the Relation Between Audiences and Publics', in Sonia Livingstone (ed.), Audiences and Publics: When Cultural Engagement Matters for the Public Sphere (Bristol: Intellect), pp. 17-41.

Robbins, Bruce. 1998. 'Introduction Part I: Already Existing Cosmopolitanism', in Pheng Cheah and Bruce Robbins (eds.), Cosmopolitics: Thinking and Feeling Beyond the Nation (Minneapolis: University of Minnesota Press), pp. 1-19.

Rojek, Chris and John Urry (eds.). 1997. Touring Cultures: Transformations of Travel and Theory (London: Routledge).

Said, Edward W. 1979. Orientalism (New York: Vintage).

Schudson, Michael and Chris Anderson. 2009. 'Objectivity, Professionalism, and Truth Seeking in Journalism', in Karin Wahl-Jorgensen and Thomas Hanitzsch (eds.), The Handbook of Journalism Studies (New York: Routledge), pp. 88-101.

Smith, Angela and Michael Higgins. 2014. The Language of Journalism: A Multi-Genre Perspective (New York: Bloomsbury).

Spivak, Gayatri. 1988. 'Can the Subaltern Speak?', in Larry Grossberg and Cary Nelson (eds.), Marxism and Interpretation of Culture (Urbana: University of Illinois), pp. 271-313.

Thompson, John B. 1995. The Media and Modernity: A Social Theory of the Media (Stanford: Stanford University Press).

Tourist Authority of Thailand (TAT). 2015a. 'Asian Source-Markets Lead as Thailand Visitor Arrivals End 2014 on a High Note', TATNews.org, 16 January <http://www.tatnews.org/asian-source-markets-lead-as-thailand-visitor-arrivals-end-2014-on-a-high-note/> [accessed 20 May 2015].

Tourist Authority of Thailand (TAT). 2015b. 'Asian Visitors Lead Strong Thai Tourism Comeback in January 2015', TATNews.org, 18 March <http://www.tatnews.org/asian-visitors-lead-strong-thai-tourism-comeback-in-january-2015/> [accessed 20 May 2015].

Witschge, Tamara. 2013. 'Transforming Journalistic Practice: A Profession Caught Between Change and Tradition', in Chris Peters and Marcel Broersma (eds.), Rethinking Journalism: Trust and Participation In a Transformed News Landscape (London: Routledge), pp. 160-72.

World Tourism Organization (UNWTO). 2013. UNWTO Annual Report 2012 (Madrid: UNWTO).

World Travel and Tourism Council. 2014. Travel and Tourism: Economic Impact 2014 World <http://www.wttc.org/-/media/files/reports/economic%20impact%20research/regional%20reports/world2014.pdf> [accessed 20 May 2015].

Food Fight: Survival and Ideology in Cookbooks from the Spanish Civil War

Maria Paz Moreno

Cookbooks are, just like any other type of texts, products of the time and circumstances in which they are written. This is particularly true in the case of the cookbooks published in times of war, as has been shown by critics.[1] In the following pages, I will present several cookbooks from the Spanish Civil War (1936-1939), considering their multiple purposes and looking at their role as historical documents and important testimonies of their times. As we will see, these texts reflect the extremely difficult circumstances endured by the populations of major Spanish cities during the conflict. Not only do they contain incredibly ingenious recipes to feed entire families when there was little to eat, but they are also tremendous sources of historical information about life during the Civil War. This essay aims to show the importance of these books as historical documents, as well as to highlight the underlining ideological discourse that is embedded in them. The consideration of their authors' intentions and their purposes constitute a key element to fully understanding the significance of these cookbooks. As Jessamyn Neuhaus states, 'the purpose of a recipe collection may not be "unmistakable". Cookbooks contain more than directions for food preparation.'[2]

There is no question that the Spanish Civil War period and the decades that followed were years of hunger. From the beginning of the war, as Miguel Ángel Almodóvar points out in his book *El hambre en España*, the Republican zone was the hardest hit by food shortages.[3] This situation was worsened by the fact that the majority of big cities were Republican, while the rural areas, that had the ability to produce food, belonged to the Nationalist side. It is not surprising, then, that the few cookbooks published during the war years instructed their readers on how to survive in a time of scarcity and how to make do with very little. Their titles bear testimony to their intention: *Menús de guerra* [*War menus*] and *El menjar en temps de guerra. Problemas alimentaris que planteja la guerra* [*Eating in a Time of War. Food Problems Posed by the War*] were both published by the Catalan government during the civil war. Another example is *Platos de guerra. 60 recetas prácticas, acomodadas a las circunstancias, para la conservación y el condimento de la sardina* [*War Dishes: 60 Practical Recipes, Adapted to the Circumstances, for the Preservation and Seasoning of the Sardine*], published in Alicante, in the south-eastern region of Spain, in 1938.

The propagandistic nature of these texts is epitomized in the prologue to *Menús de Guerra*, which reminds citizens that they should not let themselves be defeated by the circumstances. On the contrary, these circumstances should be taken as an obligation and even as an opportunity: 'War imposes restrictions on us that we need to accept as our moral duty. It is not a sacrifice to deprive ourselves at the table of what is superfluous, especially if we keep in mind that satisfying our gluttony is not everything. Satisfying our appetite is enough. [...] The big cooking masters always spoke of the convenience of creating delicacies with the most simple elements.' The brief prologue ends with a reference to the legendary French gastronome Brillat-Savarin who asserted in *The Physiology of Taste* that 'A good meal consists only of the indispensable'.

The reference to bearing hunger as a 'moral duty' illustrates the symbolic connection between food and morality, one that is deeply rooted in religious beliefs, where fasting is associated with moral rectitude, while gluttony and indulgence are viewed as sinful.[4] By appealing to the patriotic and religious values of their audience, the argument for hunger as a noble type of suffering becomes unquestionable. This desire for simplicity – clearly born out of necessity – is reflected in the recipes contained in the book, which often have just a handful of basic ingredients and aim to maximize the amount of food available to feed a large number of people. Most dishes in the book follow a similar pattern of ingredients and directions, combining different vegetables with milk, flour and butter, making with them a type of béchamel sauce. This technique increases the volume of the dish, adding caloric value, thus contributing to the feeling of satiation with less food.

Besides recipes, *El menjar en temps de guerra. Problemas alimentaris que planteja la guerra* contains abundant advice regarding how to deal with the worst consequences of food scarcity. In addition to several sections devoted to the caloric and nutritive content of different foods, the index contains sections with titles such as 'Being a little hungry after eating is healthy', 'Being a little hungry never killed anyone' and 'It is possible to resist hunger for a long time'. There is also an entire section on substitutions, explaining how to substitute certain foods for others when the needed ones are unavailable. But there are also sections that show us the most difficult aspect of hunger: sections like 'Diseases caused by deficiencies' provide instructions on how to recognize a number of these diseases, such as rickets, anemia and the so-called war edema, caused by a deficiency of protein in the diet. Here, readers are given symptoms and nutrition advice to both prevent and remedy these diseases.

Perhaps a more important marker of ideology in this work is the fact that it is written both in Catalan and in Castilian; by publishing this booklet in bilingual form, the Republican government in Catalonia was no doubt making a statement about their strong sense of regional identity to distance itself from the central Spanish government of Madrid. The Franco regime would eventually ban the use of regional languages, such as Catalan and Basque, during the years of the Dictatorship, in an attempt to repress resistance to being assimilated into the 'One, Great and Free' Spain. ('*Una, Grande y Libre*' was the motto of Franco's regime for Spain, encompassing Franco's nationalist concept of Spain as an indivisible, unified country. Clearly, regional differences would have no place in Franco's Spain).

277

A similar statement was made in *Platos de guerra. 60 recetas prácticas, acomodadas a las circunstancias, para la conservación y el condimento de la sardina* (1938) when the author, José Guardiola y Ortiz, signs the book under a clever pseudonym. '*Un cocinero de la retaguardia*' ['A cook from the rearguard'], combining an allusion to the armed conflict through the military term '*retaguardia*' with a reference to the well-known gastronomical writer José Castro y Serrano. Neither reference was gratuitous; rather, the allusions aimed to establish a clear historical and ideological frame for the book, placing its author within an important tradition: Castro y Serrano was a popular writer in Spain during the nineteenth century, who signed his own works with the pseudonym of '*Un cocinero de Su Majestad*' ('His Majesty's cook'). He achieved notoriety for his newspaper articles dealing with gastronomic issues, which reflected also his political and ideological views. Castro y Serrano became especially known for his debate with another gastronomic giant of nineteenth-century Spain: Mariano Pardo de Figueroa, better known by his pseudonym, Doctor Thebussem.[5] Their correspondence, dealing with a wide array of controversial gastronomic issues, was published in 1888 as *La mesa moderna. Cartas sobre el comedor y la cocina cambiadas entre el Doctor Thebussem y Un Cocinero de S. M.* Their debates about a number of issues related to gastronomy and food customs during the nineteenth century became famous; Doctor Thebussem's influence even reached Spanish monarchs Alfonso XII and Alfonso XIII, who were convinced by him to have the menus for their official banquets written in Spanish instead of French, as it had been customary during the eighteenth century.[6]

278

This reference to Castro y Serrano would not be lost on the more educated of Guardiola's readers. Clearly, the author seeks to align himself within a well-respected tradition of gastronomes, who thought and wrote about the philosophical and ideological implications of food and cooking. This identification could be seen as a legitimatization mechanism, in order to give authority to his own opinions, but one also contextualized by replacing '*Su Majestad*' with '*la retaguardia*' with its implication of elevating those supporting the fight from behind the lines.

The note that opens Guardiola's book reiterates the same idea seen in other cookbooks published during this period of hunger as patriotic duty. We are reminded here that 'war brings along a number of deprivations and sacrifices, among them not the least important are those regarding nutrition, and it is our patriotic duty to endure them'.[7] According to the author, the purpose of the book is none other than to provide the readers with a practical manner to prepare the foods that chance may bring to them, whether at the battlefront or in the rearguard. For example, in recipe n. 26, he gives instructions on how to feed an unexpected guest if the only thing in the pantry is a can of sardines: hence, the recipe calls for preparing the sardines with some butter, mustard and breadcrumbs, and baking them in the oven on top of slices of fried bread. What is most remarkable about Guardiola's cookbook, however, is that it is entirely devoted to a single ingredient, for which the reader is presented with sixty different recipes. Once again, the historical background helps explain such a peculiar choice:

the author justifies choosing this product by the fact that 'among the very few kinds of fish with which markets are stocked, the sardine is the most affordable for people of modest means' (p. 24). Throughout the book, Guardiola offers options for substituting some ingredients with others, since it would be likely that some of them would not be available to readers. The tone of the book is surprisingly light-hearted and optimistic, often even humorous despite the difficult circumstances of its origin and the food scarcity that it portrays. The political ideology of its author comes through the book in numerous comments and references to the war, emphasizing the need to resist the advance of Franco's fascism. In addition, the text offers much information about the supplies available in coastal cities like Alicante, a city on the Republican side of the war, and therefore very much affected by shortages. The fact that the book is entirely devoted to the sardine is an accurate reflection of what the majority of the population had access to and could afford during the war.

Thus, as the title of the work indicates, *Platos de guerra* is very much tied to the historical context of the Spanish Civil War, as well as to the needs and survival strategies of the population at that time. The voice of the author is clearly present in this book – unlike in the other cookbooks mentioned earlier. As he explains, he abstains from using milk and eggs in these recipes, given that such ingredients were out of reach for the majority of the population: 'if right now we tell any housewife or any cook to put in some milk or so many eggs into a dish, they would think we are being sarcastic and they would rightly cry "but where are those precious items?!!" (p. 24).

Food scarcity appears as a clear indicator of the hardships caused by the war in *Cocina de recursos. Deseo mi comida* [*Resourceful Cooking. I Desire My Food*], a remarkable cookbook written by Ignasi Doménech i Puigcerós (1874-1956) and published in Barcelona in 1941. Well-known and respected in his lifetime, Doménech built his career in Barcelona, Paris, London and Madrid, working at the service of aristocrats and ambassadors. He was also the founder and editor of a legendary gastronomic journal, *El gorro blanco* [*The White Hat*], and he worked as a cooking instructor as well. He published over thirty cookbooks, many of which are still considered classics. *Cocina de recursos. Deseo mi comida* is arguably the most interesting cookbook published in Spain during this time, due to combining the classic role and structure of a cookbook with elements of biography and essay. Furthermore, under the appearance of a cookbook, it contains a devastating depiction of Spain during the war and postwar years, and as a result it offers an implicit criticism of Franco's dictatorial regime. However, its author employs a double discourse in order to outsmart the censorship of the regime that had to approve its publication. All books published in Spain during Franco's regime were thoroughly examined by a team of censors, who decided whether or not the work questioned the values of the regime or presented it in a negative light. References to political dissidence, discussion of sexual matters and attempts to damage the image of the Catholic Church or the figure of the *Caudillo* were eliminated, and the authors of such works could be severely punished, even sentenced to prison. Considering the

279

denunciation embedded in the pages of Doménech's book, it is surprising that it passed the censors' examination. As we will see, its author mastered the art of rhetoric in order to succeed.

Even though *Cocina de recursos* appeared in 1941, two years after the Civil War had ended, it was clearly written during the war, as the recipes and stories included in the book reflect. The title of the book is telling of its content, with the word *'recursos'* ['resources'] and the very expressive *'deseo mi comida'* ['I desire my food']. Obviously, the book originated in the hunger suffered during the war and after, and this experience is presented from the point of view of a cook and a food lover. The amount of historical information that can be obtained from these pages is staggering, since it is an honest, thorough and detailed account about how people ate – and how they cheated hunger – during such a critical time. The voice of the author guides us through heartbreaking pages, in which we witness with him the suffering of the Spanish people. The book aims to offer advice and help fellow citizens survive the times of hunger, as the author states in his prologue, and it provides readers with advice on how to detect food adulterations and frauds that were common at the time, and that could pose a health risk to the population. Adulterated foods, ranging from flour to coffee, were sold *de estraperlo* [in the black market] by unscrupulous – and desperate – individuals seeking to make a profit off the food shortages endured by the population.

Cocina de recursos contains amazing recipes, but their singularity does not come from their flavours or complexity, but rather from their ingenuity, which reveals much information about their historical circumstances. Here are some of these recipes: *'Calamares fritos sin calamares'* ['Fried calamari without calamari'] –basically fried onion rings – *'Mayonesa falsa'* ['Fake mayonnaise'], *'Selecto café de guerra'* ['Select wartime coffee'] – made from carob beans and roasted peanut shells – *'Girasoles rebozados fritos'* ['Fried Sunflower heads'], and *'Chuletas de arroz'* ['Rice chops'] – made by forming a paste of cooked rice that was then put into a mould in the shape of a pork chop, coated with breadcrumbs and fried. The simulation and deceit of these dishes consisted of an ingenious switch of ingredients, substituting those that were not available to the majority of the population, such as eggs or potatoes, with others that had a similar consistency. After all, the real goal was to emulate familiar flavours, textures and shapes to fill the stomach, a goal that was attained with recipes like the ones mentioned above, and like the *'Tortilla sin huevo'* [Eggless omelette], which reads as follows:

Take a few potatoes, onions, green beans, zucchinis and artichokes. Cut/chop in small pieces. Place in a container that has been rubbed with garlic, add 1 tablespoon of finely chopped parsley, a pinch of paprika, 1 tablespoon of baking soda , 6 soupspoons of flour, some salt, 10 or 12 soupspoons of water, 1 tablespoon of oil. Let the mixture rest for 15 minutes, mix everything well and make the omelet.[8]

According to Doménech, this type of omelette became extremely popular during the war years, made by the thousands and almost replacing traditional omelettes made with eggs. With this peculiar recipe, which uses flour, water, spices and vegetables to hide the absence of the egg, success was guaranteed – says Doménech – and dinner guests would not notice the difference at all. Taking this idea a step further, Doménech gives us the recipe for '*Tortilla de guerra con patatas simuladas*' ['War time omelette with fake potatoes'], a potato omelette made without eggs or potatoes. Instead of using sliced potatoes, as in the traditional Spanish recipe, potatoes are replaced by orange pith – the white substance found between the peel and the flesh of an orange – which had to be soaked in water for two or three hours to eliminate any possible bitterness or orange flavour before frying it as if it were potato.

Cocina de recursos is a complex book with more than one purpose. The author declares several intentions throughout the book; on one hand, he repeatedly emphasizes his purpose of portraying that particular moment in history; on the other hand, he expresses his desire to help his fellow citizens in such difficult circumstances, providing them with solutions to the everyday problem of what to eat in a time of hunger. Both of these purposes stem from a common cause: the uprising by General Franco that resulted in the civil war. By showing the terrible consequences of the war, the author articulates an implicit criticism of the Franco regime. However, this criticism is never expressed directly; much to the contrary, the author includes frequent conventional formulas of praise to the regime and its leader, in an effort to mask the critical nature of his portrayal of postwar Spain.

281

Reading this cookbook presents us with a new portrayal of the Spanish Civil War, one that had systematically been silenced during the years that followed the war until the end of the dictatorship in 1975, hence the miraculous fact of its publication. In *Cocina de recursos,* the main protagonists are hunger and food scarcity, and war is not only the context, but more importantly – and although it is never said explicitly – the cause of those ailments. Written between the style of a memoir and a journalistic report, the book seeks to present us with a thorough account of the calamities endured by Spaniards during the war years.

To this end, Doménech sets out to visit a long list of eating establishments in Madrid and Barcelona to assess the situation for the readers. From 1937 to 1938, he visited a wide variety of places, from upscale to humble, and recorded what he ate, its quality and how much it cost. Thanks to his thorough eye, we learn about a place in Barcelona with an eloquent sign hanging at the door, which read in capital letters: 'Wartime Meal. We only serve one plate. It is useless to ask for more.' Doménech also tells us how he observed that in most restaurants there was no bread available, which resulted in most people bringing their own bread along, carrying it in their back pockets or, in the case of the ladies, in their purses, well wrapped in white paper. The author recommends avoiding meat at any restaurant during this time, because, he says, 'even though they would call it beef or ox, I knew that it came from horse, donkey or mule, which were then very often used for this purpose' (p. 153). He expresses his indignation about the high prices of basic foods such as milk, eggs and bread, constantly comparing prices of before and after the *Alzamiento* (Franco's uprising).

Pointing out that the *Alzamiento* is the turning point for things to deteriorate constitutes a direct accusation to the regime, which could have caused the author much trouble. How did this book, which presented Franco's Spain in a very negative light, make it pass the censors?[9] The answer lies in the combination of different factors. Because the work is presented as a cookbook and not essays or memories of the war, it is likely that the genre itself helped avoid the suspicions of the censors, who probably considered it as a mere manual of recipes with some comments in between.

In addition, Doménech engages in a clever double discourse, beginning with the prologue and continuing throughout the book. In the most prominent parts of the text – the prologue and the introductions to the different sections – there is high praise to the *Caudillo* and the 'New Imperial Spain'; these were formulas repeated everywhere, such as 'Thank God for our Great Caudillo' and 'God Bless the Glorious Imperial Spain'. Furthermore, the author cleverly appropriates the discourse of the regime, declaring Franco to be the 'saviour' of Spain, and using terms favoured by the regime, such as '*Patria*', '*Nueva España*', '*Imperio*', '*Caudillo*' and '*Dios*'.

The prologue that opens the book, by Yago Cesar de Salvador, praises the work as a useful resource, emphasizing that its purpose is to help Spaniards who were loyal to Franco in such difficult times. The usefulness of the book is mentioned as its greatest asset, 'especially in these difficult times, when good Spaniards happily offer their sacrifice in favour of the resurrection of the Glorious Imperial Spain' (p. 73). The reference to Franco's ideals, along with the insistence that this is merely a cookbook with no other motive than to help his fellow citizens, help to understand the censors' approval. To today's readers, *Cocina de recursos* is an invaluable resource of information about both the author and his circumstances. The autobiographical quality of cookbooks, as explored by Janet Theophano in her classic study *Eat My Words,* resonates in the book, which constitutes one of the best examples of a hybrid gastronomic text; in this case, blending different genres – memoir, documentary and recipe book – clearly makes it stand out.[10]

Another fascinating text, unknown outside of Spain despite being a direct product of the Spanish Civil War, is *El cocinero español.* Published in 1938 to aid the Spanish Republican cause, the particularity of this book is that despite its title, it was not published in Spanish, or even in Spain, but rather written in English and published in Boston, Massachusetts, by the Milk Fund for Spanish Babies and the Medical Bureau to Aid Spanish Democracy.[11] Its economic purpose was the real motivation behind its publication, since it was put together to raise funds to fight against Franco's Nationalist Army. The Medical Bureau to Aid Spanish Democracy was one of the pro-Loyalist fund-raising agencies created in the United States to help the Republican cause in Spain. The Bureau, created shortly after the beginning of the war with the support of doctors from the Harvard Medical School, joined the North American Committee, a sort of umbrella organization that included several other groups. According to Merle Curti, the Bureau 'was a pioneer in getting a medical unit off to Spain early in 1937' and it sent three additional ones before summer. By midsummer the Bureau had sent eighteen ambulances and ninety-nine surgeons, nurses and drivers, and had established six hospitals at a cost of $118,000. Perhaps the most remarkable fact is the total amount of the contribution that this effort was able to make to the Republican cause: 'Together, the North American Committee and the Medical Bureau to Aid Spanish Democracy contributed, in cash and kind, aid totalling over $800,000'.[12]

El cocinero español is a perfect example of community cookbook, a genre with a long tradition in the United States since the American Civil War.[13] These cookbooks are written by a group of people, usually with the goal of raising funds for a specific cause. In the case of *El cocinero español*, we are told that the Chef of the Spanish Embassy in Washington is one of the contributors to this volume; the names of those providing some of the other recipes are given as well. The book was clearly intended for an American audience, as one of the sections, entitled 'Special for New Englanders', suggests. In addition, all recipes are written in English, although the names of the dishes are given both in Spanish and English. It is clear that the transcriber of these recipes did not speak Spanish, since some of the translations are inaccurate or misspelled: '*Lenguados al graten espanol* [*sic*]', is translated as 'Spanish Sole with Cheese', despite not having any cheese in its ingredients or in the Spanish name; likewise, '*Langostinos*' are translated as 'lobsters', and almost all of the Spanish names for the dishes are misspelled. We also have recipes that do not correspond to any traditional Spanish dish, such as the '*Plato espanol* [*sic*]' 'recommended by Miss Beatrice Beasley', which is a pretty unusual concoction made with butter, peppers, milk, flour, tomato soup, crab meat and egg. A second example is the 'Convent pie', made with several layers of spaghetti covered with peppers, butter, cheese and dry bread, which does not correspond to any Spanish dish, conventional or otherwise. Despite its errors, however, the value of this book is clear: its purpose was not to offer an accurate compendium of Spanish cooking, but as a community cookbook it fulfilled its mission of gathering the community behind a fundraising effort.

Much more research work remains to be done in the area of cookbooks published in Spain during the war. The fact that these texts, all of which reflect the hunger and difficulties endured by the population, were published by the Republican side – be it the Republican government in Catalonia, or authors affiliated to the Republican cause both in Spain and in the US – could perhaps be read as a good indication of the direction that the war was taking. As we know, the armed conflict eventually ended with the victory of the Nationalist Army. Interestingly enough, the cookbooks published in the decades after the war continued the theme of economical cooking, using leftovers and making the best of the strict food rationing imposed by Franco's government. In addition, patriotic duty continued to be presented as a powerful argument to accept rationing and food shortages, much as it happened in the countries involved in the Second World War, in which Spain remained neutral. Even though the Spanish war ended in 1939, food scarcity remained a difficulty over the following decade.

All these texts show that food writing, especially in the case of cookbooks, is not necessarily devoid of ideological bias. Quite the contrary, that is almost never the case: there is always an embedded ideological discourse. In the case of these particular cookbooks, their ideological content and the reality they portray make them valuable documents that help deepen our knowledge of the Spanish Civil War; they complement the collective memory and are therefore of unquestionable importance as repositories of information for the use of historians, sociologists, anthropologists and students of the human condition. The very existence of these texts raises issues of how food writing can be –and often is – a powerful vehicle to propagate ideas, whether political, religious, social or any other kind. In sum, these humble cookbooks are powerful reminders of a dark episode in our history. They bear witness to the resilience of the human spirit.

Notes

1. For example, see *In Memory's Kitchen. A Legacy from the Women of Terezin*, ed. by Cara deSilva, trans. by Bianca Steiner Brown (Northvale: Jason Aronson, 1996); Jessamyn Neuhaus, *Manly Meals and Mom's Home Cooking: Cookbooks and Gender in America* (Baltimore: Johns Hopkins University Press, 2003); and Celia Kingsbury, '"Food Will Win the War": Food and Social Control in World War I Propaganda', in *Edible Ideologies: Representing Food and Meaning*, ed. by Kathleen Lebesco and Peter Naccarato (Albany: State University of New York Press, 2008).

2. Neuhaus, p. 1.

3. Miguel Ángel Almodóvar, *El hambre en España. Una historia de la alimentación* (Madrid: Oberón, 2003). All translations in this paper are by the author.

4. Among the many studies that have dealt with this topic, especially useful are Elizabeth Luard's *Sacred Food: Cooking for Spiritual Nourishment* (Chicago: Chicago Review Press, 2001); Felipe Fernández-Armesto's *Near a Thousand Tables: A History of Food* (New York: Free Press, 2002); Jacinto García Gómez's *Un convento de aromas* (Toledo: Junta de Comunidades Castilla-La Mancha, 2002); and the seminal *The Raw and the Cooked* by Claude Lévi-Strauss (New York: Harper and Row, 1969).

5. The name 'Thebussem' is the result of rearranging the syllables of the word '*embustes*' ['lies' or 'fabrications'] backwards.

6. Maria Paz Moreno, *De la página al plato. El libro de cocina en España* (Gijón, Trea, 2012), p. 187. For a detailed account of Dr. Thebussem's life and achievements, see Andrés Ruiz Cobos, *Doctor Thebussem* (Madrid: Est. Tip. de Ricardo Fé, 1890); Dorotea Newell, *Dr. Thebussem (Mariano Pardo de Figueroa), Historian of Spanish Customs* (dissertation, University of California, 1921); and Íñigo Ybarra, *Doctor Thebussem, la realidad de la ficción* (Sevilla: Renacimiento, 2009.)

7. Guardiola, p. 5. Subsequent references are cited parenthetically.

8. Ignacio Doménech, *Cocina de recursos. Deseo mi comida* (Barcelona: Quintilla, Cardona y Ca. Editores, 1941), p. 62. This book has been recently reissued by Editorial Trea (Gijón, 2011). Subsequent references are cited parenthetically.

9. The copy of this book available at the National Library in Madrid and consulted by the author of this essay shows on its cover the approval stamp from the Censorship.

10. Janet Theophano, *Eat My Words. Reading Women's Lives Through the Cookbooks They Wrote* (New York: Palgrave, 2002). For a more detailed classification of recipe books and the common combinations of

genres and purposes, see Moreno, *De la página al plato,* Chapter 5: '*Cómo leer un libro de cocina*'.

11. The Medical Bureau published other books to help raise funds, although *El cocinero español* was the only cookbook. The other books were clearly political in their focus and nature, as their titles suggest: *From a Hospital in Spain, Adolph Hitler and Francisco Franco: Two minds but a Single Thought, A Negro Nurse in Republican Spain,* and *Shop talk in Spain: The Trade Unions and the War in Spain,* among others.

12. Merle Curti, *American Philanthropy Abroad* (New Brunswick, NJ: Transaction Books, 1988), p. 396.

13. For a detailed study of community cookbooks, see Carol Fisher, *The American Cookbook* (Jefferson, NC: McFarland & Company, 2006).

On Food and Fascism: Plating up Oral Histories

Karima Moyer-Nocchi

The oral transmission of traditional recipes, the alchemy and magic of food preparation handed down from sage to novice, is an affective experience. The multiple layers inherent in the communal act of cooking, when funnelled into a list of measurements, ingredients and instructions, flatten into a sterile replica. When the topic of food is used as a vehicle to draw out an oral transmission of history, however, its intrinsic largesse has the power to unveil a unique perspective onto the past. Foodways are inextricably embedded in history and imbued with nostalgia, each force exerting influence over the other, and together forging a continuum of culture and identity. The multifarious nature of oral history brings to life the colours and textures of those experiences that would otherwise fade if itemized as dates and facts.

While the volatile and unpredictable nature of oral history as a research method may be unwieldy, it is also its animus and the basis of its utility. However, indulgence in anything perceived as whimsy does not fare well on the academic stage: as Anthony Portelli notes, 'There seems to be a fear that once the floodgates of orality are opened, writing (and rationality along with it) will be swept out as if by a spontaneous uncontrollable mass of fluid, amorphous material.'[1] What makes oral history so unsavoury is the factual, quantitative measuring stick used to invalidate it as 'quaint' and 'anecdotal', read: unreliable, particularly given its indecorous association with spotlighting the unsung and the unschooled. Oral history, as ethnographic qualitative research, emphasizes meaning and perspective over the event itself. It is an investigation of perception, as opposed to reportage of data: 'Oral sources tell us not just what people did, but what they wanted to do, what they believed they were doing, and what they now think they did.'[2]

Objective and subjective sources of historical evidence are often perceived as being mutually exclusive, opposing sides of a coin. A more accommodating viewpoint would recognize that the two faces complement each other, allowing us to make both heads and tails of an event. However entrenched a work of historical literature may be in verifiable fact, it is, regardless, the product of a human mind and, as such, not immune to contamination by personal perspectives and underlying agendas. As Paul Thompson notes, 'Most historians make implicit or explicit judgments – quite properly, since the social purpose of history demands an understanding of the past which relates directly or indirectly to the present.'[3] By the same token, orally transmitted historical accounts, non-linear and memory-based, cannot be discounted as devoid of fact insofar as they are not, and are not intended to be, fictional yarns, but collaborative efforts working toward the selfsame purposeful objective of social cognizance. In this light, subjective and objective are not value assessments, but perspectives. They do, however, beg an examination of the concept of truth.

The continuum of Truthfulness is bookended by Fallacy and Truth. As interdependent social beings, we require truthfulness, but are sceptical of the existence of truth, given the fallibility of the human mind, projections of cultural perspective, and the inevitability of experiential filters. Oral histories offer a window onto truthfulness, regardless of their grounding in indisputable fact. Wherever they may fall on the continuum of truthfulness, the value of oral accounts lies in the tellers' sincerity, in the belief that they are telling the truth and nothing but, in the hope that their experience might be validated, respected and understood, and contribute to our ever-evolving sense of social purpose and self-awareness. They are larger than a sum of their parts, as Ronald Grele explains: 'The interviews that we gathered, and the people we talked to, told us more than simple information about the past. We began to argue that they were richer than repositories of information or archival documents. They were texts themselves'.[4]

Orally transmitted history cannot be dismissed from the historical realm as biography or memoir, though it contains elements of both. It also shares commonalities with journalism, but whereas the journalist interviews for current events, the oral historian investigates past events, though both are concerned with issues of empathy, ethics and evidence.[5] Oral histories enrich and complete the historical landscape by championing what Portelli euphemistically calls the 'non hegemonic strata', those who made history by forming the foundation upon whose backs movers and shakers built their empires, the very people without whom there would have been nothing to move or to shake.

The oral historian is responsible for forging the two sides of the coin onto a single medallion, bringing both the quantitative and qualitative, the prosaic and the poetic perspectives to bear. It is they who are charged with the task of crafting a work that will give a voice to the voiceless and of transmitting it far and wide.

Chewing the Fat – Bringing Italy's 'Ninetysomethings' Out of the Shadows.

In the spring of 2013, I got a bug in my bonnet. In the twenty-five plus years I have lived in Italy, I have witnessed the unfolding of a curious concomitance: a bewildering decline in the quality and craftsmanship of Italian food together with a skyrocketing deification of it. In a vicious circle, the decline stimulated the explosion of the gastronomic nostalgia industry, which, in turn, hastened the very process it claimed to quell. This cyclonic state of affairs roused a parallel fundamentalist food frenzy bent on saving supposed traditions one bean at a time, giving rise to yet another market profiting from the propagation of gastronomic mythology.

There is a fantasy about Italy, a seductive enchantment, which sells countless tour packages and millions of delectable meals in the myriad 'rustic', 'authentic' restaurants peppered throughout Italy. It has mesmerized not only starry-eyed foreigners, but also unwitting Italians under fifty, who devour it wholesale. It is the pastoral delusion of the idyllic, simple abundance of yesteryear, of country folk whiling away the days in lush fertile fields under the Tuscan sun, chalices brimming with ruby red wine, and plates piled high with sauce-laden pasta.

If only it were true.

Human credulity rushes in where scholars fear to tread. The annals of Italian food history say nothing of a glorious yesteryear of Italian food, at least not one enjoyed by any more than a miniscule, fortunate minority belonging either to society's upper crust or the high end clergy. But even so, with the exception of a few signature dishes, what was then standard fare is only vaguely similar to the culinary wonders that are daily plated up and touted, even in Italy, as traditional Italian cuisine. Contrary to history, Italian food is now considered to be one of the few classless cuisines, that is, rich and poor alike partake of the same sorts of foods (albeit not of the same quality). And many believe that it has always been that way.

Befuddled, I decided to go to the authorities for some answers.

Although the pool of experts is ever dwindling, there were still a handful of ninety-year-old women who had lived through the *Ventennio fascista*, the twenty-year reign of fascism. Surely they would be able to shed some light on the evolution of Italian food from their own experiences. Oral history was the ideal vehicle to bring these details to the fore because the tale they would divulge was indeed stark, highly personal and vastly different from glossy travel brochures and the rustic-porn memoirs, films and cookbooks that so titillate consumers. As Thompson insists, 'History should not merely comfort; it should provide a challenge and understanding which helps towards change. [...] It has to encompass the complexities of conflict.'[6] Theirs are memories of an Italy that the modern collective has cavalierly reinvented, photoshopped and romanticized, not only to sell products, but to whitewash the unpleasantries of the past. In a matter of a few years, the unsung voice of a generation of courageous women who lived that past firsthand will be silenced. These women are the last witnesses to a fundamental chapter in Italian history, one that is being rewritten while they live and breathe. It is imperative that history be recorded in their words, from their perspective, and retold. Otherwise it will vanish as if they had never been here.

Thus began my project to assemble a compendium of oral histories and transform them into narratives that would become the core of the book *Chewing the Fat – An Oral History of Italian Foodways from Fascism to Dolce Vita* (Perrysburg, OH: Medea, 2015). At the risk of cliché, hyperbole or both, this project has enriched my life exponentially. It has deepened the way I experience my adopted homeland, broadened my perspective of Italy's culinary heritage and altered my perception of aging. As with any true passion, it was arduous travail wrought with joy, discovery and suffering. Although my purpose here is to illuminate the considerations involved in such an undertaking, in order to encourage others to pursue this type of venture, I cannot offer a precise template to follow, given the individual requirements of each oral history quest. Each and every premise and context differs to the degree that suggesting a rigid program of methodological execution would not only be misleading, it may also prove counterproductive. At the same time, however, there is much that can be gleaned from examining a framework exemplifying a project successfully brought to fruition. The procedure and process outlined below details the specific variables involved in my research investigating foodways of the fascist era and concludes with notes on the construction of the final text.

Defining Ethnographic Parameters

While oral history is a distinct form of qualitative research from ethnography, borrowing and overlapping between the two approaches occur.[7] For my purposes, establishing parameters in ethnographic terms allowed me to delineate my pool of informants. Ethnic groups are socially defined, and as such, share a set of collective characteristics that establish and demarcate their identity. History neatly packages the fascist era into a timeline from 1922 to 1943, referred to as the Ventennio. It is not merely a timespan, but represents a period of concerted sociopolitical upheaval, during which the population, particularly children and young adults, was subjected to purposeful indoctrination aimed at forging and imposing a cultural identity through school, youth groups and the Church. Political agendas and consequent proselytization touched every aspect of daily life. The fascist ideology influenced beliefs about taste, diet and nutrition and instilled a stalwart value for enduring dearth. Food policies were set in motion to placate the nation's basic needs in accordance with political aspirations for self-sufficiency. Mussolini reasoned that the adjustment would be minor as Italians were already not used to having much to eat.

289

The delineated ethnic group must, of course, be able to respond to the premise of the research. As outlined above, the quest sought to illuminate the discrepancy between the invention and propagation of highly marketable culinary myths and the less glamorous historical experience of foodways of the Ventennio, as disseminated through firsthand accounts. Stated as a question: What resemblance does the modern commercial packaging of Italian culinary lore bear on the actual experiences of those who lived that history before it morphed into 'tradition'? In essence, what is fakelore, and what is folklore?

Having defined the commonalities of the ethnicity, a representative sample must provide a range of exemplars embodying the chief variables within the group. These sub-ethnicities provide the inter-contextual basis from which to cross-reference the implications of macro (representative of the sub-group) and micro (pertaining to the individual) variants. In the specific case of foodways in the fascist era, the foremost delineating features are geographical location and social class. Having only become a unified nation in 1861, at the onset of fascism in 1922, Italy was little more than a geographic expression. A comprehensive cultural exploration would, therefore, need to cover a vast amount of territory and include various extant strata of socioeconomic milieus. The eighteen narratives selected for *Chewing the Fat* cover eight regions spanning from Italy's Swiss border to Sicily, and include the ex-Italian colony Libya and the territory Istria, both lost in WWII. The subdivisions of the urban context – city, town, village and burg – feature a range of social classes from royalty to slum-dweller, while the rural context partitions in accordance with the long-established agricultural hierarchy that ranged from wealthy landowners to sharecroppers to homesteaders to farmhands.

Recruiting Participants

There is a well-worn expression in Italy: *Fidarsi è bene. Non fidarsi è meglio.* [Trusting is good. Not trusting is better.] All of the interviewees had lived out their entire youth in an environment saturated with fascism. Indeed, in spite of the impressive line-up of despotic tyrants throughout history, totalitarianism is a descriptor that arose specifically from fascism for the way in which it wholly structured one's life and thinking in line with the dictates of the state. Dissention was not tolerated and was dealt with summarily. Once the regime fell, the young men and women whose formative years had been imprinted with the fascist stamp were expected to do an about face, move forward and erase the programming that had been pummelled into them for years. They were, in effect, being asked to lose their religion, posthaste.

Fast-forward seventy years. A 'young' American university professor wants to come to the house and ask some questions about food 'from the old days', the days of the Duce. In spite of the universal pretext of food, the intervention of a trusted go-between to set up the meeting between the *signora* and myself was an absolute necessity. There was no question of handpicking interviewees; I interviewed anyone who fell within the ethnic definition. Many were intimidated because of their lack of schooling. On average, they had about four years of elementary school, and therefore didn't know what they could possibly have to say that might interest me, or they feared embarrassing themselves or their family with their ignorance. As for food, it was mostly a question of daily survival, of having something to put in their stomach and taking great pains to get through to the next season. There was a wide gap between the concept of 'provisions' and that of 'cuisine'. Once they understood that I did not want a history lesson with names and dates, that I 'just' wanted to talk about food (even the lack thereof), the doors opened, cookies were brought out and the interviews were underway. Within a year, I had conducted thirty interviews covering the expanse of Italy and had amassed a vast enough sample from which to choose.

Preparing to Interview

I was seeking answers to my premise, as well as confirmation of certain hypotheses of my own, but at the same time I was open to the will of the interview itself as an organic entity. In accordance with my culinary research, I prepared a list of questions that I thought would serve as a template for the entire interview process. I used the list twice. In preparing this paper, I looked back at my list of questions compiled early in 2013 and was almost aghast. Although I do not travel in the same circles as ninety-year-olds,

I consider myself well integrated into the fabric of the Italian community. I have lived in Italy for twenty-six years; I've taught at the University of Siena for nineteen years; my husband is Italian. And yet looking at that list with the benefit of hindsight, I had surprisingly little idea who I was talking to, or about what. Worse yet, I recognized that to a certain degree I too had bought into the very myth I had come to unveil. With all due respect to scholarly method and presumption, little did I imagine that the story that was about to unfold before me would transport me on a journey through time following its own itinerary, and that my job as messenger was to encourage that to happen.

Oral historians are generally not from the inner circle of the culture that they are studying. In order to establish myself as a credible conversation partner and put the interviewees at ease, proficiency in the language and a background in gastronomy was not sufficient. I needed to be fluent in their points of reference, conversant in their values, self-assured in the framework and jargon of their youth. Furthermore, I had to be knowledgeable about how these varied in each context from north to south, from rich to poor, from city to town to village to farm.

It is therefore crucial, as well as exciting, to develop an interview structure and style that is flexible enough to allow for unexpected and alternative excursions. And it is also crucial, as the Italians say, to know your chickens. I had gone to those first interviews with the wrong tools, greedily digging for diamonds. I quickly realized that the diamond was of little worth without the rough; indeed it is hard to say which of the two is more valuable. In this case study, an investigation about food as socio-historical phenomenon, the object in question became a vehicle from which a more dynamic and comprehensive history was fleshed out. It brought a black and white photo into full Technicolor.

The Interview

In order to put the participants at ease, I began by telling them that they were free not to answer anything that they did not want to talk about, and that after the interview they could rescind anything they had said. In a professional writing consultancy, I was chided that good journalists dig and pick for the information they are looking for and do not stop until they get it. Firstly, I was not about to dig and pick at women in their nineties, and secondly, an oral historian is not a journalist. By listening to the playback of the colloquia (as I did each time before moving on to the next), I discovered that less was definitely more. The less I poked and prodded, the more vividly they were able to envision the landscape of their memories. With each interview, and with continual research, I was able to orchestrate an increasingly fluid exchange. Loosely structured prompts and a minimum of suggestions generally sufficed to set everything in motion and keep the conversation on a flexible but focused path.

Initially, I had thought that the interview would be best if conducted one on one. My belief was that it would create an intimate environment conducive to the evocation of memory. But fortunately, here too, I discovered early on that the presence of family helped on various levels. Firstly, when necessary, they helped rephrase my questions, so that they were more easily digestible, or they shouted the questions if hearing was a problem. Secondly, their intervention often rekindled memories: 'Mamma, you remember when you told us about…'. Thirdly, their presence made the woman feel needed and important. Spurred on by the attention, she tended to put in her best effort; in some cases the family members were hearing these stories for the first time themselves, and so her account was addressed as much to them as to me, adding to, and not detracting from, the intimacy. Given the communal nature of the interview, family members, too, were encouraged to interject so long as the focus remained on the interviewee. It was a poignant moment for all involved, reminding me of the English Renaissance madrigal 'The Silver Swan':

> The silver swan, who living, had no note,
> when Death approached unlocked her silent throat.
> Leaning her breast against the reedy shore,
> thus sung her first and last, and sung no more.[8]

In order to further valorize their experience, I asked, whenever conditions permitted, if we could prepare a dish together of their choosing that harkened back to Italian food as they had experienced it. I took ample photographs, and for some it was the next best thing to being on a TV food program. Regardless of whether or not we cooked together, I asked each participant to contribute at least one recipe that had special significance for her in representing what food from 'the old days' was, in order to illuminate how conceptions of standard Italian fare have changed.

Memory as Object

While selective memory can be called into question for scrutiny in any oral account, and the lucidity of the mind when one is in their nineties may be tentative, there are further extenuating circumstances affecting the memory of the subjects who lived out their formative years during the Ventennio.

A built-in part of fascist ideological indoctrination was the systemic generation of ignorance; the patriotic slogan encouraging blind faith 'Believe, Obey, Fight' was so thoroughly ingrained that it was even written in cookbooks. One learns not to question what is safe, and to implicitly trust that what you are told is true, for the sake of the collective good. How much of that can be undone, however, is a question regarding the individual. During the Ventennio, two other forces were at work that kept females, in particular, in the grip of ignorance. In accordance with folkways, girls did not need any more than four years of schooling. Although it ran contrary to the law, most girls did not finish elementary school and almost none went on to middle school. The cost of keeping girls in school was deemed a frivolous or implausible expense for many families. Furthermore, most of the population resided in rural enclaves. These were particularly isolated with little influx of news. Information based on hearsay and propaganda, repeated and unquestioned, fossilized over time as truth. As such, memory itself becomes the object of oral histories, together with memories.

For the purposes of oral history, what subjects believe happened is as valid as what did happen because the former expresses how they lived those events and determines how that memory was carried on through time. Events and conditions perceived at the time as perfectly normal, even laudable, may later have become a basis for intense shaming, and/or identity annihilation for reasons not always fully understood by the interviewee, as was the case with the fall of fascism. Therefore, while the individual's aim is always truthfulness, her personal truth may be tinged by fear, embarrassment or confusion, resulting in concealed details or distorted disclosures. To illustrate the gravity of the matter, there is a constitutional law dating back to 1952 explicitly establishing that it is a felony to 'publically praise the exponents, principles, facts, or methods of fascism or its antidemocratic ends'.[9] (The constitution also guarantees freedom of expression; the extreme Right has advanced a formal proposal to revoke the 1952 law.) It is debatable, even unlikely, that any of the women knew about the law, but nevertheless, they were part and parcel of the environment in which it was spawned, and the changing tides of the new collective directive would not have gone unnoticed. Only two participants requested that their surname not be used, for which reason I did not include anyone's surname. For others this was a disappointment. Given the objectives of my project, the interviews that made the final cut for the book were based on how effectively they represented a given context and category in the broader examination of food as social phenomenon; as such, surnames were immaterial.[10]

Most oral histories are collected in the distant aftermath of an incident, giving time for the dust of trauma to settle and allowing for benefit of hindsight. At that remove, in most cases the women seemed comfortable sharing not only their memories of daily life from the fascist era, but also their views regarding the positive and negative points of fascism itself. In a consultation I had with a leading historian of fascism, he was shocked enough by the blatant partiality of their memories and their historical 'inaccuracies' to suggest I write a disclaimer in my introduction.

Packaging the Text

In crafting and packaging the final product to be presented to the public, the oral historian faces many options and wears many hats. In deciding on the form the text would take, I started by identifying my target audience. Anniversaries in remembrance of the First and Second World War now peppering the media tend to focus on the men who made history and the various markers of the wars themselves, rather than the lives lived on the home front. Part of my mission was to counter this trend and bring the unsung voice of the women of the Ventennio to the widest possible audience. There is a weighty sense of responsibility that is common to oral historians when they become the custodians of memory. In my case, I felt as though the women were entrusting me with the urn of their youth, passing on to me the spent embers of what were once burning flames. As I said my good-byes and left their house, I felt as if I had stolen something precious from them. As such, releasing their story to the public was all the more pressing.

The three questions at hand were: Who did I want to bring this work to? Who would be most receptive? And how might I pique and hold the interest of those who might not naturally gravitate to the topic? There were many considerations to take into account in preparing the text for my target audience. With this in mind, I devised a unique way of layering the information that respected the integrity of the women's accounts and gave the reader an enlightening, entertaining reading experience. It had to be historically robust yet accessible, diverting yet substantially informative, without becoming a history tome, a dumbed-down bit on fascism or an exercise in navel gazing.

I choose a compendium format, as opposed to an analytical overview or a first person narration of *my* experience with them. I wanted each entry to stand on its own, to allow each individual voice to sing, and in the end, create a mosaic rendering a significant portrait of daily life in the Ventennio. As linguist, I translated each account into an analogous cross-section of American English, as that is the linguistic palette that is closest to my own experience. As raconteur/dramatist, I extracted my part from the original oral history interview and transposed each account into a single voice narration, honing and crafting with a focus on individuality, so as to bring the reader as close as possible to the stream of the original experience, albeit freed from the interviewer's intervention. As anthropologist/gastronome, I bridged the gaps of information between narrator and reader reasserting my voice through non-intrusive interpolations posited within the narration itself. These asides offer clarifications, related lore, factoids, historical extensions and other incidental information in lieu of formal academic annotations. They are graphically distinguished from the interviewee's narration, and as such respect its integrity and overall flow. This structural technique sets up a permeable triad between reader, narrator (interviewee) and interpreter, which augments the reading experience. As historian/essayist I separated each narration with an engaging intermezzo illuminating a particular aspect of the Ventennio drawing on the commonalities of the narrators' lives, from fascist youth groups to the sacred ritual of pig slaughter to the black market to fascist cookbooks.

The compilation concludes with an epilogue by Dario Cecchini, the 'mad butcher of Panzano', who offers his no-holds-barred interpretation of how Italy arrived at the present state of affairs, and where it might go in the future if he gets his druthers.

Notes

1. Anthony Portelli, 'What Makes Oral History Different', in *The Oral History Reader*, ed. by Robert Perks and Alistair Thomson (London: Routledge,1998), pp. 63-74 (p. 64).
2. Portelli, p. 67.
3. Paul Thompson, 'The Voice of the Past: Oral History', in *The Oral History Reader*, pp. 21-28, (p. 24).
4. Ronald J. Grele, 'From the Intimate Circle to Globalized Oral History', *Words and Silences: Journal of*

the International Oral History Association, 4.1-2 (November 2007-November 2008), pp. 1-4 (p. 1).

5. Mark Feldstein, 'Kissing Cousins: Journalism and Oral History', *The Oral History Review*, 31.1 (Winter-Spring, 2004), pp. 1-22 (p. 5).

6. Thompson, p. 27.

7. See Mary Kay Quinlan, 'The Dynamics of Interviewing', *The Oxford Handbook of Oral History*, ed. by Donald A. Ritchie (New York: Oxford University Press, 2011), pp. 23-36 (p. 26).

8. Orlando Gibbons, *First Set of Madrigals and Motets of 5 parts* (London: Thomas Snodham, the Assigne of W. Barley, 1612), p.1.

9. *Legge Scelba*, n. 645, 20 June 1952.

10. See Quinlan, p. 26.

The Author, the Reader, the Text: Literary Communication of a 1611 Spanish Cookbook

Carolyn A. Nadeau

In 1611 Francisco Martínez Montiño, head chef of the kitchens for both Philip III and Philip IV of Spain, published what would become the most recognized Spanish cookbook before the twentieth century: *Arte de cocina, pastelería, vizcochería y conservería* [*The Art of Cooking, Pie Making, Pastry Making and Preserving*].[1] The publisher for this work, Luis Sánchez, chose as an illustration for the title page a moral emblem of a hand with eyes floating above each finger (see Figure 1).[2] By highlighting the senses of sight and touch, Sánchez weighs in on the Humanist debate of the banquet of the senses by privileging touch together with sight as ways to acquire and achieve knowledge. He echoes the thoughts of the Humanist Fray Luis de Granada who wrote, '*usando de la industria de las manos en las cosas de naturaleza, habemos venido a fabricar otra nueva naturaleza*' [using the industry of the hand in the things of nature, we have come to produce another, new nature].[3] In this way, Luis Sánchez communicates to readers of this court cooking manual the task of all who aspire to cook well, that through selecting the right ingredients, preparing them under the right conditions and serving them perfectly, they transform nature into something new and better.

Martínez Montiño is also incredibly sensitive about how he communicates with his diverse readers and certainly uses images of sight and touch to explain how best to recreate his recipes. However, his primary focus is on taste, and throughout his 502-recipe collection he continually reminds his readers – made up of apprentices, cooks, and other master chefs – that the taste of the diner also plays a key role in this

296

Figure 1. Title page of Arte de cocina, pastelería, vizcochería y conservería. *Photo by author, courtesy of the Lilly Library, Indiana University, Bloomington, Indiana.*

transformative, culinary process. This essay examines Martínez Montiño's attentiveness to his readership and the descriptive language that he used to achieve the best results from his personal recipes. It then turns to the communicative challenges of bringing this cookbook to the twenty-first century and particularly to an English-speaking audience. How can I account for the inevitable lack of accuracy with regards to specific ingredients for an audience that is separated from the original text by centuries and, in some cases, continents? What information needs to be shared regarding quantities when amounts are unspecified and cooking times are practically non-existent? What are the ways to best explain some of the cultural factors that enter into the different recipes?

A Brief Overview of Martínez Montiño and His Cookbook

As with so many cooks of the early modern period, little is known about Martínez Montiño's life. He was possibly Galician and worked his entire life in kitchens, beginning as a humble kitchen boy before moving his way up to head chef for the Spanish Habsburgs. In his opening pages Martínez Montiño alludes to having served in the kitchens of Philip II's sister, Doña Juana, in Portugal. María de los Ángeles Pérez Samper notes that he then moved to the royal kitchens in Madrid and began serving Philip III in 1585. He then worked for Philip IV until his retirement or death in 1629 when records show he was replaced by another chef.[4]

Martínez Montiño's cookbook is separated into two chapters – one on cleanliness of the kitchen and staff, on how to serve banquets and on suggested banquet menus, and the other which consists of 449 recipes for all types of sweet and savoury dishes and two memoirs on conserves and jellies with twenty and thirty-three recipes, respectively. The cookbook was published throughout Spain, ten times in the seventeenth century, ten times in the eighteenth century and six times in the nineteenth century until 1823. It was published again in 1982 when Tusquets printed a facsimile version, and again in Valencia, 1994 and 1997. Recently three new facsimiles have surfaced: Valladolid, 2006; Seville, 2008; and Madrid, 2009. The first three facsimiles are based on the 1763 edition and the latter two on the 1778 edition.

The book is organized, much as the title suggests, into various sections on cooking, pies, pastries and preserves. The cooking section begins with roasts, both meat and poultry, and continues with one-pot meals and stews. The savoury pies follow and include torts, empanadas, puff pastries and other wrapped food. There are also recipes for wild game, veal, sweets, goat, pork, poultry and rice. Martínez Montiño then includes abstinence and partial abstinence recipes for vegetables, fish, organ meats, nuts and eggs. He then returns again to grain-based recipes, including several for cous cous (the only ones that appear in a Spanish-language cookbook before the twentieth century), game and other meat and vegetable dishes before a modest section on food for the sick. His next section on pastries contains some sixty recipes. He closes this part of the cookbook with instructions for carving and serving different types of meat. The last section of the cookbook focuses on jams, jellies, gelatines and pickling food. Martínez

Montiño's collection also includes regional and international dishes, primarily from Portugal but also from Geneva, Germany, England, Cataluña, Aragon and dishes that reflect Spain's Hispanic-Muslim heritage.[5]

Martínez Montiño's Readership that Extends Beyond the Court Kitchen

Throughout the cookbook, Martínez Montiño addresses his audience in brief side comments. This attentiveness to his audience is clear from the very beginning:

> *y si en alguna cosa hubiere falta, suplico al discreto Lector lo supla, que como hombre me habré descuidado, que ya sé que los grandes Oficiales no han menester Libro: mas con todo eso por ser todos tan amigos míos, tendrán en algo mis cosas, y todavía hallarán alguna cosa nueva: y los Aprendices si hicieren lo que yo ordeno, entiendo que no podrán errar. Y así los unos por aprender, y los otros por curiosidad, todos se holgarán de tener mi obrecilla.*
>
> [And if there were a mistake somewhere, I beg of my discreet reader to fix it, because as a man I may have been a little neglectful, and I know of course that master chefs don't need this book. But in spite of this and because they are all good friends of mine, I hope they might get something out of my ideas and even find something new. And if apprentices do what I put forth here, I am certain they will not err. And thus, for those who are learning and for others out of curiosity all will delight in having my little work.] (pro)

From the very start, Martínez Montiño is very aware of his diverse audiences and their different purposes.

Sometimes he targets the age or gender of his specific audiences. In one section he explains, '*Quiero poner aquí algunas potagerías de legumbres: y esto hago (como tengo dicho) <u>para los mancebos, y mugeres, que sirven a algunos señores, y no saben estas cosas</u>, aunque parecen muy faciles*' [I want to write down here some vegetable dishes and I'm going to do this (as I have said) *for apprentices, and women, who serve lords and do not know these things* even though they seem so easy] (pp. 227-28). In another instance he focuses exclusively on women: '*Estos Flaones, o pasteles de leche <u>si hubiere alguna mujer que no los sepa hacer</u>, podrá echar este batido en una cazuela untada con manteca, y meterla en el horno a fuego manso, y se cuajará como si fuera pastel*' [These *flaones*, or custard pies *in case some woman does not know how to make them*, she could put this batter into a pan that has been greased with lard, and put it in the oven on low flame, and it will congeal as if it were a pie] (p. 387).

He also writes directly to a type of kitchen personnel. In '*Como se ha de salar el jabalí*' [How to salt boar], he first explains how to debone and cut the meat, then how to salt and dry it and, finally, what to serve it with. As a transition to treating deer meat, he offers the following explanation: '*con esto dejaré de tratar del jabalí, y diré algo del venado. Y esto todo importa mucho saberlo los Pasteleros, porque de esto saben mucho menos que los Cocineros*' [With this I am finishing [the section] on boar and will now discuss venison. And all this is very important for pastry cooks to know because generally they know much less about this than cooks do] (p. 179).

Often times his sensitivity to his readers is communicated in terms of the taste of the person being served. In one recipe he allows for a diner's sweet tooth: '*Tambien podrás mezclar este relleno, <u>si fuere amigo de dulce tu Señor</u>, con un poco de pasta de mazapán mezclado con yemas de huevos duros, y mezclado con el relleno de la carne*' [You could also mix into this stuffing, *if your lord had a sweet tooth*, a little bit of marzipan paste mixed into the hard-boiled egg yolks and then mixed into the meat stuffing] (p. 65).

And still other times he makes certain assumptions knowing that his reading audience does have a certain level of culinary knowledge. In the recipe, '*Otros palominos ahogados*' [More drowned squab dishes], he describes how to prepare the herbs and spices by relying on his readers' knowledge: '*picarás un poco de verdura, peregil, yervabuena, y cilantro verde, ó seco con un pedacito de pan duro, y echale medio grano de ajo, y unos pocos de cominos, pimienta, y nuez, y picalo muy bien, tanto como para salsa de peregil*' [chop up some herbs, parsley, spearmint, and cilantro or coriander with a little piece of dry bread. Add a half clove of garlic, some cumin, pepper, and nutmeg, and mince it up very fine, as you would for parsley sauce] (p. 79). In this example, Martínez Montiño acknowledges that those reading his recipe will already know how to prepare parsley sauce.

In the recipe '*Fruta de frisuelos*' [Large funnel cakes], Martínez Montiño's attentiveness to his audience draws upon visual images from beyond the kitchen to facilitate the cook's understanding of how to cook this sweet treat to perfection: '[*Y] para estar la fruta como ha de estar… por la parte de abajo ha de parecer un garvín de mujer con muchos granillos redondos, como perdigones de arcabuz, que parecen muy bien*' [And for the funnel cake to turn out as it should… the bottom should look like a woman's laced bonnet with many little, round seeds, like buckshot from an harquebus. That would look just right] (pp. 267-68).[6] In this case, Martínez Montiño uses both feminine and masculine images to convey the blistering of the fried dough that indicates it is done. These two very different visual cues allow for increased audience reception to best achieve the outcome of the recipe and demonstrate Martínez Montiño's sensitivity to his readers.

Sensitivity to the King's Palette and Those of Others

Apart from the conscientiousness of attuning to his readership, Martínez Montiño is also sensitive to the king's palette and to those of future diners for whom these recipes may be prepared. At times he specifically includes what the King and Queen like. For example, from reading through the recipes we know that Philip III regularly eats roast pheasant with an egg-oil emulsion, that he prefers meatballs made from poultry, that he likes spices but only in moderate amounts, and that he likes his chicken pinwheels, which are normally filled with hard-boiled egg yolk seasoned with mint, pepper, nutmeg, ginger and a little lemon juice, on the sweeter side. For this reason Martínez Montiño adds sugar, cinnamon and even a touch of marzipan to the mixture. And for dessert, he prefers sponge cake and of the different types, he prefers flourless.

Throughout the recipe book he remains attentive to conforming to the diner's taste. Martínez Montiño often provides an either-or variation on a recipe and reminds cooks that their choice of preparation is dependent upon their lord:

'*Una olla podrida en pastel*'[:] *Se les suelen echar aceitunas fritas, y algunas castañas: mas algunos señores no gustan de ello.* (pp. 165-66)

'*Otras almojábanas de cuajada diferentes*'[:] *Lo que pretendo en las otras en pasarlas por el suero, es, que salgan muy tiernas, y en éstas pretendo que salgan muy tiesas, porque algunos señores gustan de las unas, y otros de las otras.* (p. 203)

'*Potaje de habas*'[:] *A estas habas se suele echar un poco de eneldo, mas algunos señores no gustan de él.* (p. 240)

['A pie of hodgepodge stew'[:] Fried olives and some chestnuts are often included, but some lords do not like them.

'Other, different fried cheese pastries made from milk curds'[:] What I am trying to do in the others by dipping them in whey is to have them come out tender and with these I want them to come out firm because some lords like them one way, and others, the other way.

'Fava bean stew'[:] It is common to add dill to these beans, but some lords do not like it.] (p. 240)

Other times, however, he leaves these detail-oriented decisions to the discretion of the head chef. For example, in deciding whether to make a medium or a large pig's feet pie and how much sugar to add, Martínez Montiño insists that it be left up to the chef: '*Esto se queda al albedrío del Oficial*' [This is up to the discretion of the cook] (p. 323).

When addressing issues of taste, Martínez Montiño weighs in on issues of class and nationality in no uncertain terms. In describing an omelette made with honey and beef fat, he insists that these eggs are better for '*frailes, y gente ordinaria, que para señores*' [monks and regular people than for lords] (p. 330). Through his comments we learn that Germans prepare and serve trout in ways different from and not necessarily agreeable to Spaniards. According to Martínez Montiño Spaniards are more moderate in their use of salt and vinegar and prefer their fish served whole as opposed to in pieces as if they were folded like a napkin (p. 280).

Questions of the diner's taste not only involve decisions about ingredients but also how to serve the dishes. In several shellfish recipes Martínez Montiño includes how to serve them and insists that the shell be left intact. In '*Langosta rellena*' [Stuffed lobster], the visual image is delightful: '*luego harás una sopilla, y pondrás la concha rellena en medio, y pondrás alrededor las piernas con sus conchas, porque gustan los señores de partirlas*' [next, make sops and put the stuffed lobster in the middle and put the legs in their shell around it because lords like to crack them open] (p. 316).

Descriptive images such as those used to communicate the pleasure of dining fill the pages of *Arte de cocina*. Non-cooking imagery often helps to describe the desired visual effects of a given dish (like the bonnet or buckshot described above). In *'Huevos hilados'* [Spun egg yolk threads] Martínez Montiño explains that the eggs should come out looking like stands of fine thread or silk (p. 326). In many recipes, including *'Memoria de los bizcochuelos'* [Memoir of little sponge cakes], he uses the *'gordor de un dedo de la mano'* [thickness of a finger] (p. 432) to explain the size of the cake. In other pastry recipes he compares texture or size to certain types of bread rolls with which others are very familiar: *'lisos como panecillos de San Nicolás de Tolentino'* [smooth like Saint Nicholas of Tolentino rolls] (p. 440) or *'cantidad de un panecillo de los de Madrid'* [the quantity used for Madrid rolls] (p. 228).

At times one can also pick up on a sense of humour in his work. For example, in *'Otro plato de huevos hilados'* [Another dish of spun egg yolk threads], Martínez Montiño creates every day objects out of spun eggs and marzipan. He describes how to create a scene of frying fat back on a grill (marzipan) with flames coming up from under (strands of spun egg yolk) or how to recreate eggs so that anyone seeing them would not know the difference between the real thing and these imitations without tasting them. Here he comments, *'todo lo que lleva es otra cosa de lo que significa…Esos son para adornar algunos platos, y para hacer burla'* [Everything on it is something other than what it signifies…These are for garnishing dishes and playing a joke] (pp. 328-29).

Bringing the Cookbook to a Twenty-First Century, English-Speaking Audience

Switching to the communicative challenges of today, the attentiveness to my readership is equally present but my concerns differ. I will limit my comments to three areas: identifying ingredients, quantities of ingredients and cooking times. Foodstuffs from four hundred years ago and a different continent pose multiple problems. Beginning with vegetables, the many varieties are difficult to identify and, even if we could identify a specific type, how relevant are the flavours of four hundred years ago to today's palette? When Martínez Montiño describes eggplant or carrots, for example, he mentions different varieties by size or colour: *'berenjenas, si fuesen pequeñas, que son las mejores'* [eggplants, if they are small, which are the best] (p. 245) and *'las acenorias para ensalada, se han de buscar de las negras'* [for a carrot salad, look for the purple ones] (p. 98). These clues can point a twenty-first century reader in the right direction but selecting the right ingredient is still somewhat of a guessing game. Visual clues from paintings of the same time period, and here the works of Juan van der Hamen y León (1596-1631) and Luis Meléndez (1716–1780) have proven beneficial, can also help to target a specific variety. The same is true for all animal products. How animals are raised has a tremendous affect on their flavour. One need only consider an egg from a chicken raised on one's own farm to that of a commercial egg to know how different the two are in terms of wateriness, colour and richness of flavour.

Another challenge is bringing to a contemporary audience the rich variety of animal products consumed. In his recipe for quince sauce, Martínez Montiño explains it can be used with a variety of wild fowl. In addition to *'ánades, y zarcetas'* [duck and teal] it can be served with '*sisones, y alcarbanes y pluvias, y gangas, y otros pájaros salvages*' [little buzzards, stone curlews, plovers, and pin-tailed sand grouses] (p. 33). Other poultry dishes include doves, partridges, orioles, thrushes, cranes, squabs, pigeons, capons, hens, chickens, turkeys and turtledoves. Apart from the bird aficionados, most readers of this translation and critical edition will require a brief explanation of the types and varieties of fowl. It would also be appropriate to inform readers of the social status of consuming each bird. According to the research of Francisco Valles Rojo, among the farm-raised birds the preference from highest to lowest is as follows: '*capón cebado, capón, polla cebada, polla, pavo, gallina, gallina cebada, pollo*' [fattened capon, capon, fattened (female) chicken, (female) chicken, turkey, hen, fattened hen, (male) chicken], all of which are found among Martínez Montiño's pages. However, among game fowl the hierarchy of preferences is as follows: '*perdices, francolín, perdigón, buchón, ansarón, ánsar, astarna, zorzal*' [partridges, francolin, young partridge, pigeon, gosling, goose, grey partridge, thrush].[7] Surprisingly, five of these eight birds never appear in the king's cookbook. Questions of personal preferences of either the cook or the king might be at play here, or perhaps it has to do with hunting practices of those who supplied wild birds to the court. I've used poultry here as an example of the complexities involved in understanding different types of fowl that are in the cookbook, but the same is true for many of the cuts of meat, organs meats, and fish that are also among its pages.

In terms of quantities of ingredients, more times than not, Martínez Montiño does not specify exactly how much is needed. Occasionally he measures in ounces. This is particularly true with sugar where specific measurements appear thirty times, five times more than some of the other ingredients measured in ounces like almonds, cinnamon, wheat flour and at times different waters.[8] But considering that sugar appears hundreds of times in the cookbook, more times than not the quantity goes unspecified. In fact, Martínez Montino's favourite measurement is '*un poco de*' [a little bit of] which appears 849 times throughout the 502 recipes. This is almost always the case with spices and herbs.

His most common spice mix is '*todas especias*' [all spices] which includes black pepper, cloves, nutmeg, ginger and saffron. However, within this mix itself, there is no mention of quantities. When Chad Sanders, a professionally trained chef, and I recently prepared '*Carnero verde*' [Green mutton stew], we used one teaspoon of black pepper, ½ teaspoon each of clove, nutmeg, and ginger and a pinch of saffron. However, the clove overwhelmed the flavouring, and for future recipes we have decided to reduce its amount to ¼ teaspoon.

Another complication regarding measurements is the use of the *maravedi*. This small monetary unit was the basis upon which other coins were measured and was minted in 1, 2, 4 and 8 *maravedi* denominations and varied in size. In his cookbook Martínez Montiño uses this term six times to explain how much black pepper (4 mvs. and 8 mvs.), honey (8 mvs.), wine (2 mvs.), anisette (2 mvs.) and caraway (1/4 mvs.) is needed in their respective recipes. In '*Memoria de las berenjenas en escabeche*' [Memoir of pickled eggplant] he provides the following measurements: '*tomarás una onza de canela, y otra de clavos, y ocho maravedís de pimienta, y un cuarto de alcaravea'* [add an ounce of cinnamon and another of clove, eight maravedis of black pepper and a quarter of caraway]. Most likely the measurement refers to how much of each spice could fit on a certain size coin.[9] But, what is the relationship between ounces and *maravedis*? I am hopeful that future investigation will reveal the answers to this type of prickly question.

Another fascinating source of inquiry in writing a critical edition and translation of a seventeenth-century Spanish cookbook is the concept of time. Martínez Montiño's work helps to reveal how time was understood in the palace kitchens. It is well documented that the Spanish Hapsburgs were interested in the mechanization of time. Philip II owned several clocks, mostly imported from the Low Countries or Germany. Coinciding with Martínez Montiño in the palace was the official clock caretaker, Claudio Gribelín. Together with other clock conservationists, Jennin Cocquart, Gaspar Enríquez, Antonio Matheo and Lorenzo de Evalo, he was paid a handsome salary and ate daily food from the Royal Kitchens.[10]

For the most part time is inferred through the desired stage of the cooking process. Phrases like, *'hasta que esté en punto'* [until it is just right], *'hasta que estén bien cocidos'* [until they are completely done], *'hasta que esté la carne perdigada'* [until the meat is browned], *'hasta que esté la masa bien cocida'* [until the dough is completely cooked], *'cuezan hasta que se apure el caldo'* [boil until the stock reduces] and *'ándalo a una mano, hasta que venga a hacerse una crema un poco espesa'* [stir continually until it becomes creamy], are found throughout the cookbook.

Of the 502 recipes, only about ten per cent state time in terms of hours. In no instance are minutes or seconds acknowledged; however hours are sometimes given in fractions, for example ½ hour or a ¼ of an hour. In one instance, time is highlighted in the very title of the recipe: *'Cómo se manen las aves en dos horas'* [How to tenderize fowl in two hours]. And in the recipe, *'Cazuela de arroz sin dulce'* [Unsweetened rice casserole], Martínez Montiño states an actual time of day. He first explains to soak rice, rinse it in warm water, spread it out on a cloth, cover it, and leave it overnight but if that isn't possible and the process begins in the morning, he offers an alternative option: *'Y* déjalo allí hasta la mañana, o desde la mañana *hasta las once del día'* [and let sit until morning, or from early morning *until 11:00 a.m.*] (p. 237, my emphasis). This specific hour implies that some clock was available to the kitchen staff and that cooks were not just aware of time but of the actual hour as well.

Transmitting information about food preparation and presentation from a different time period, with a different historical context, and a different language inevitably raises questions about all aspects of the communicative process. In this essay I have focused primarily on the author's sensitivity to his contemporary audience and on my own sensitivities and series of challenges as I bring this work to my contemporary audience. At times the project is daunting and although I have raised many questions, I have not yet been able to answer them all. Additionally, I have intentionally left for another moment questions of appliances, utensils, kitchen spaces, cooking processes, and a

303

myriad of cultural references. As I move forward with the project, cultivate sources from academics, chefs, other translators and enthusiastic gastronomes and try out many of the recipes, I hope that the fruits of my labours, this critical edition and translation, will enrich our understanding of food preferences of the Spanish Hapsburgs and their affects on a wider Spanish audience.

Notes

1. Francisco Martínez Montiño, *Arte de Cocina, pastelería, vizcochería y conservería* 1611 (Valencia: Librerías París-Valencia, 1997). Subsequent references are cited parenthetically. All translations in this essay are my own.

2. This emblem was first published in 1576 in Christóbal Pérez de Herrera's *Proverbios morales, y consejos christianos, muy provechosos* [*Very Beneficial Moral Proverbs and Christian Advice*] (Madrid: Los herederos de F. del Hierro, 1733).

3. Fray Luis de Granada, *Introducción del símbolo de la fé* [*Introduction of the Symbol of Faith*] ed. by José María Balcells (Madrid: Cátedra, 1989), p. 489.

4. María de los Angeles Pérez Samper, *La alimentación en la España del Siglo de Oro, Domingo Hernández de Maceras, 'Libro del arte de Cocina'* [*Food in Golden Age Spain, Domingo Hernández de Maceras, 'Book on the Art of Cooking'*] (Huesca: La Val de Onsera, 1998), pp. 29-30.

5. Recipes '*a la Portuguesa*' include soup, fish, spinach, rice and fowl. There is a recipe for '*Sopa de Aragón*' [Aragonese soup] (p. 423), '*Una empanada inglesa*' [English pie] (pp. 196-98), '*Capón a la Tudesca*' [Capon, German style] (pp. 60-61), '*Ciruelas de Génova*' [Genoese plums] (p. 483) and '*Fruta de Fartes*' [Fartes fritters] (pp. 411-12). Recipes with clear ties to Spain's Muslim heritage include several for cous cous (pp. 360-64), '*Bollo Maymon*' [Maimon roll] (pp. 136-37), '*Cazuela mojí de berenjenas*' [Eggplant stew, Mojí style] (pp. 245-47), '*Gallina morisca*' [Morisco hen] (pp. 63-64) and '*Gallina a la morisca*' [Morisco-style hen] (p. 407). Inés Eléxpuru writes about the Arab influences seen in Martínez Montiño in *La cocina de al-Andalus* [Cooking in Al-Andaluz] (Madrid: Alianza Editorial, 1994), p. 132).

6. As a side note, the mere translation of this title presents its own challenge as *frutas de sarten*, literally *fruits of the frying pan*, are commonly translated as *fried dough* or *funnel cakes*. The word *frisuelo*, which comes from the latin *foliolum*, diminuitive of *folium*, offers little in terms of translation opportunities, But, these funnel cakes are substantially larger than the usual ones and thus, can best be translated as *large funnel cakes*.

7. Julio Valles Rojo, *Cocina y alimentación en los siglos XVI y XVII* [*Cooking and food in the Sixteenth and Seventeenth Centuries*] (Valladolid: Junta de Castilla y León, 2007), p. 238.

8. I suspect that sugar may be measured more often than other products because it was so closely tied to medicinal remedies where it is very common to have exact amounts of herbs, waters and all ingredients used.

9. I am grateful to Barbara Ketcham Wheaton for clarifying what a '*maravedi*' measurement is in her 'Reading Historic Cookbooks' seminar, 31 May-5 June 2015, Schlesinger Library.

10. Most of Philip II's clocks were destroyed when the Alcázar burned down but one, made in 1583 by Hans de Evalo, still survives today and is the oldest of the royal collection in Spain. For more information see '*Relojes*', *Centro Virtual Cervantes* (Spain: Instituto Cervantes, 1998-2015), <http://cvc.cervantes.es/actcult/patrimonio/relojes/introduccion.htm> [accessed 20 May 2015].

The Squander Bug: Propaganda and its Influence on Food Consumption in Wartime Australia

Diana Noyce

'The Fate of Nations depends on how they are fed.'– Brillat-Savarin, 1825[1]

On 3 September 1939, the then Prime Minister of Australia, Robert Menzies (1894-1978), made a national radio broadcast: 'My fellow Australians. It is my melancholy duty to inform you, officially, that, in consequence of the persistence by Germany of her invasion of Poland, Great Britain has declared war upon her, and that, as a result, Australia is also at war.'[2]

Thus began Australia's involvement in the six-year global conflict.

The idea of war as a titanic clash of men and machines has meant that histories of Australia's part in the Second World War generally focus on its military contribution in Greece, Crete, Syria, Northern Africa and New Guinea. No matter how valiant Australian efforts in battle, these campaigns were peripheral in the defeat of both Germany and Japan. The more effective and less known Australian contribution to the war effort was the supply of food: 'Australia supplied more food per head of population to the allied larder than did any other country.'[3] This unprecedented demand for food led to food rationing of the civilian population which in turn affected the national diet. A massive propaganda campaign was launched intended to ensure that people supported rationing and had enough to eat, that nutrition levels were maintained and that morale was kept high. The fate of a nation is never more dependent on how its people are fed than in wartime. It was food that was 'the highway to victory'. The 'food front' was essential in the struggle against the enemy, and yet it is an often overlooked dimension to our understanding of global conflict. In examining the role propaganda played in altering and influencing Australian eating habits in wartime, this paper begins to address this shortfall.

Food is one of the first casualties of war. Securing a food supply became a central preoccupation for all the countries drawn into the conflict. Failure in the food supply would impact not only the army, but also war industries and more diffusely the civilian population. Shortages would lead to civil unrest. In Australia there was an unprecedented demand for food, not only for the troops overseas and the people at home, but also for the allied nations. Britain particularly relied on food imports from Australia, mainly sugar, butter, cheese and meat. From 1941, when Japan entered the war and brought the war almost to Australia's doorstep, thousands of American troops arrived in Australia to fight the war in the Pacific, and they too had to be fed. For the next four years American troops were a continuous presence in Australian cities.[4] Australia's population in 1938 was 7.5 million. By 1942, Australia had committed to feed almost double her population.[5] Australia had become a food arsenal for the allied world.

306

Figure 1: 'We must Share our Food.'
Australian War Memorial, ARTV02569.

Not every Australian embraced the war effort. The war, however, demanded every person's full commitment, and persuading the public to support the war effort became a wartime industry just as important as producing bullets and planes. To communicate the government's objectives and to galvanize the support for the government initiatives, propaganda was extensively used. According to T.E Lawrence (Lawrence of Arabia, 1888-1935), the idea of propaganda was to 'arrange' men's minds – 'not only our own men's minds, though them first: the minds of the enemy, so far as we could reach them: and thirdly the mind of the nation supporting us behind the firing-line'.[6] Over the course of the war the Australian government (like all combatant nations) waged a constant battle for the hearts and minds of its people. In its broadest sense, World War II 'propaganda' in this paper is just about any form of communication aimed towards influencing the attitude and behaviour of the population towards food consumption. It was through the propaganda machine that food was thrust to the forefront of national consciousness as the national diet became the business of government.

Austerity

In April 1942, the Minister for War Organisation of Industry, John Dedman (1896-1973) launched the 'Austerity' campaign designed to discourage spending on consumer goods, particularly black market goods. The real reason for the campaign, of course, was to raise money for the war effort by encouraging Australians to invest their money in war savings schemes rather than consumer goods. The war was costing Australia up to 50,000 pounds an hour.[7] To garner Australians to support the austerity scheme, artists, filmmakers, actors, writers and scientists were recruited to take the government's objectives and turn them into a propaganda campaign. Various mediums were brought into play, including pamphlets, posters, billboards, newspapers, magazines, film and radio broadcasts.

The 'Squander Bug' became the central symbol in the austerity campaign to encourage people not to waste or misuse scarce resources. To do so would be disloyal. Australians could fight the Squander Bug by investing their money in the war savings schemes, rather than consumer goods. The message was 'Save and Save Australia'. Originating in Britain, the character developed an international reputation, and an adapted version was used in Australia, where the Squander Bug was given a Japanese appearance. In September 1942, the then Prime Minister John Curtin (1885-1945), who led Australia through much of the war, made a national broadcast stating, 'Austerity calls for a pledge by the Australian people to strip every selfish comfortable habit, every luxurious impulse, every act, word and deed that retards the victory march.' In particular, he hoped the austerity campaign would discourage people from squandering their money on 'beer and betting', specifically at the racetrack.[8] Australians mostly fell into line with the austerity campaign, except perhaps for the latter request.

Figure 2: The Squander Bug. Australian War Memorial, RC02347

Figure 3: Food as a Weapon of War. Australian War Memorial, ARTV00161

Feeding Her Allies

The unprecedented demand for food placed huge demands on Australian agricultural producers and manufacturers. As more and more rural workers were recruited into the armed services, labour supplies in the rural industries had fallen by more than twenty per cent, and little attention was paid to maintaining stocks of agricultural machinery, manufacturers of which had been diverting their energies to making munitions. But food had now assumed an importance equal to that of munitions; in fact it had been officially declared 'a munition of war'. Manufacturers returned to their previous activities, and many machines such as tractors and bulldozers were imported from the United States. However, under the provisions of Lend-Lease, Australia was required to provide whatever machinery it was capable of making. Moreover, the United States sent processing technicians as well as experts in management and agriculture to Australia to improve agricultural production and increase manufacturing.[9]

Women made up the shortfall in labour in the manufacturing sector as more and more entered the workforce. And the Australian Women's Land Army (AWLA), an organization created in July 1942, made up the deficit in labour shortages in the farming sector. The Australian food industry became a war industry as it passed through a stage of technical and economic development surpassed by few other countries during this period. And despite the fact that a large proportion of the most active young men were in the Services, Australia was able to supply more food per capita to the Allied larder than any other country.[10]

However, in spite of every effort to increase production of food, Australia could not meet all its commitments to the allies without restricting consumption of food by the civilian population. With so many extra mouths to feed, for the first time since the earliest days of British settlement in Australia it became necessary to ration food.

Figure 4: Propganda poster aimed at encouraging people to support food rationing

Rationing

Rationing came under the umbrella of the Austerity Campaign and was administered by the Rationing Commission through the issuing coupons to consumers. The use of ration coupons was applied to clothing, tea, sugar, butter and meat. From time to time eggs and milk were also rationed under a system of priority for vulnerable groups, such as children and expectant mothers, during periods of shortage. Rationing in Australia was less harsh than in the United Kingdom: the North Atlantic blockade by German U-Boats caused huge shortages of food materials, leading to heavy rationing regulations imposed on the British population. At no time were the same drastic conditions seen in Australia. Nevertheless, it was imperative that the nation supported rationing. Propaganda posters with their bold colours, blocky typography and stark imagery were used extensively to gain support for government initiatives. The posters were designed to either threaten or frighten people to make a point.

Film was also extensively used to secure the support of the population. A propaganda film clip made in 1943 entitled *Give Us This Day* takes its title from a phrase in the

Lord's Prayer: 'give us this day our daily bread'. The film illustrates the effective use of contrasting personal experiences of food, comparative scales of hunger and opposing perspectives on food rationing to draw out the argument for rationing's introduction. The scenarios at home pit one person's perspective against another; the argument that wins out, however, is the one that supports food rationing.

The film opens with an injured soldier in the jungles of New Guinea struggling as he runs out of food. An aircraft drops food rations nearby. Meanwhile, back in Australia, two female volunteers package the emergency food parcels to be sent overseas. Back in New Guinea, three servicemen share a tin of emergency rations. One of them points out that 'an army always marches on its stomach'. Another man imagines what a big juicy steak would be like.

Back in Australia, two men in a restaurant complain that they haven't had a steak for six days. Their waitress gently notes that some of the troops stationed in New Guinea haven't had a steak in six months, saying 'if we go a little short, maybe they'll get a break'.

Inside a parlour at the bar, another man complains about the food rationing and asks why he should have to go without. The bartender gives him an earful, pointing out that the English have been on hard rations for four years, that we have two armies to feed (meaning the US army as well as the Australian) and that the millions of people starving in Greece are lucky if they own a cat – because they can eat it.[11]

The Nation's Diet

The government had to ensure that rationing would not be detrimental to the health of the nation. 'Health brings Victory', so the slogan went.[12] Health and nutrition were vital new areas for research and still in their infancy as far as public awareness was concerned. However, Dr Philip Muskett, as far back as 1893, equated nutrition, and thus health, with certain foods; he noted severely that Australian 'consumption of butcher's meat and of tea is enormously in excess of any common sense requirements and is paralleled nowhere else in the world'. Moreover, market gardening was 'deplorably neglected' and salads were 'conspicuous by their absence' in the Australian diet.[13] Forty years on, and nothing had changed in Australia's food culture.

A Commonwealth Advisory Committee on Nutrition had been established in 1936 (it was reconstituted as a committee of the National Health and Medical Research Council (NH&MRC) in 1939) because of fears that the Depression was harming the health of low income families, a fear that was later borne out in a survey of the diets of 1800 families in Australian capital cities. It was found that diets contained an excessive amount of fat and meat and were deficient in vegetables, fruit, eggs and dairy products. Milk was viewed merely as a necessary addition to their tea. The survey revealed that though most families consumed enough energy-rich foods, they did not get enough of the 'protective foods' that provided the necessary vitamins and minerals essential for growth and well-being. It is not easy to generalize about diet and nutrition, but to some extent the dietary defects discovered in the survey reflected the influence of national food habits.[14]

A 1925 Green and Gold Cookery Book I found on my bookshelf provides some indication of these dietary habits. The recipes for Cornish pasties; Irish stew; meat joints accompanied by Yorkshire pudding; the plethora of puddings baked, steamed or boiled; and the absence of rice in recipes except for rice pudding reflected Australia's transported British culinary traditions. Potatoes rule the vegetable section with cabbage a close second, followed by beans and parsnips. Salads are confined to potato salad, beetroot salad or potato and beetroot salad. Lettuce – when it appears – is boiled rather than served fresh. There is little mention of herbs beyond parsley and mint, and apart from curry powder there are no taste enhancers like garlic or soya sauce. Recipes for cakes, pastries and biscuits dominate the index. Overall, it appears that Muskett was right – salads are 'conspicuous by their absence' and the rather plain diet was high in fat, sugar and meat.[15]

By 1942, Australians still ate more meat than anyone else in the world, beating even the Americans almost twofold, with an average 212 lbs (96 kg) a year and drank more tea than the British, averaging 7lbs (3.2 kg) per head.[16]

Rationing and shortages, however, as will be seen below accounted for real changes in people's diet. Altering a person's tastes and food habits is one of the hardest things to achieve. We are wedded to what we eat (and drink) for food is very much part of our culture. There are two principal ways, says food historian Barbara Santich, of effecting change in people's diets – by targeting either the food supply or the people.[17] Rationing targeted the food supply; it was up to the propaganda machine to persuade people to choose differently and prepare food differently to change their diet.

Tea was rationed from 6 July 1942 due to the Japanese occupation of Malaya, the Dutch East Indies and Java – the prime tea producers for Australia. For Australians who were used to having tea with all meals and several extra cups throughout the day and night, an allowance of 1.6 ounces (45 grams) per week reduced consumption to three cups a day.[18]

Australian's beverage of choice apart from tea was beer. However, in 1941 the government directed that production be reduced by one-third. For many Australians the beer shortage caused the greatest inconvenience, but it also created social change. Many men began to drink spirits, which increased drunkenness, and as bottled beer was virtually unattainable from hotels to be taken home and consumed, women began drinking publically in hotels and bars, traditionally a male preserve in Australia.[19]

From 31 August 1942, many Australians drank their tea unsweetened too, because sugar rationing had been introduced. Each adult Australian was entitled to one pound of sugar (almost 500gm) a week – a figure that gives further indication of Australian's passion for sweets and puddings. Generous as this ration may seem today, it was increased in the summer months, on request, to allow for jam making and preserving. Apparently Australians regarded only a pound a week as a serious hardship because there were bitter complaints.[20]

In June 1943, butter rationing came into force, not because of any shortage in Australia, but to ensure that people in Britain received as much as possible. The Australian ration of eight ounces (226 grams) per person per week ensured that Britons should each receive two ounces (50 grams) per week. In 1944 the Australian ration dropped to six ounces per week. Australians again complained bitterly about the lack of butter.[21] Apart from the principal ingredient in cakes, scones, biscuits and puddings, butter was spread heavily on bread at all three meals, and housewives used butter liberally in preparing vegetables, soups, grills and when frying food, a habit which this author can attest continued well into the 1960s.

Meat rationing came into operation in January 1944, again to permit more meat to be exported to the United Kingdom. Consumers accepted meat rationing more readily. Sausages, ham, bacon and rabbits were not rationed. It was common to see the 'rabbit-o' walk the streets selling rabbits and skinning them for customers on the spot. Nor were poultry and fish rationed, in an attempt to encourage Australians to eat more of these foods. Consumers, too, learned to revert to the ways of their grandparents and use previously unpopular cuts, and, like the rabbit, offal such as mutton flaps, cheeks and hearts, brains, tripe, livers and kidneys made a comeback. These more readily available animal parts formed a significant part of people's diets during the war and for several years after. They also cushioned the effect of rationing and facilitated the sale in these forms of otherwise unsalable meats.[22]

312

Figure 5: A rather evocative image of meat being loaded onto a ship at a wharf and a family outside a bomb damaged house in Britain. Australian War Memorial, ARTV00260.

One of the most notable changes in Australia's food production was the great increase in the area devoted to growing vegetables, especially potatoes, cabbages, peas, tomatoes, carrots and beetroot. The area allocated to grow vegetables nearly doubled over the war years; the area committed to growing potatoes alone was increased from 99,000 to 242,000 acres. The great increase in production of vegetables was to some extent a reflection of the fact that American troops were accustomed to larger amounts of vegetables and fresh fruits, especially fruit juices, in their diets than were Australians. Much of the vegetables were processed, either canned or dehydrated to feed the troops in the Pacific.[23]

Despite the enormous efforts to produce more fruit and vegetables to feed two armies, the American 'invasion' meant fruit and vegetables were often in short supply and therefore expensive. Instead of rationing fruit and vegetables, Australians were encouraged through billboards, newspapers and magazines to grow their own vegetables – 'be wise, be advised, eat them daily', so the slogan went.[24] Many Australians turned their lawns and garden beds into vegetable patches as well as raising their own chickens for eggs.

Figure 6: Billboard. 'Grow your own vegetables, raise your own fowls and help the farmers feed our fighting forces.' National Archives of Australia, C2829.

The Art of Persuasion

As the convention of the times dictated, women were considered the main consumers – they did the household shopping – and homemakers, and as such much of the propaganda was directed at women. There was a constant stream of literature, films and radio broadcasts aimed at women to explain the reasons for rationing, and a good deal of advice on making the best use of rations (especially meat), on planning family meals, on food choices and in particular on food preparation and storage. **The NH&MRC Nutrition Committee's contribution towards the improvement of national health was to publish a book,** *Diet and Nutrition for the Australian People*, **which appeared in four editions between 1941 and 1945. The book gave advice on preserving and cooking food to prevent deterioration and wastage, encouraged the consumption of wholemeal bread instead of white bread, and urged more consumption of the 'protective foods' (a compiled list of foods and their vitamin content was given to encourage women to make appropriate food choices) and less consumption of cakes and biscuits.**[25]

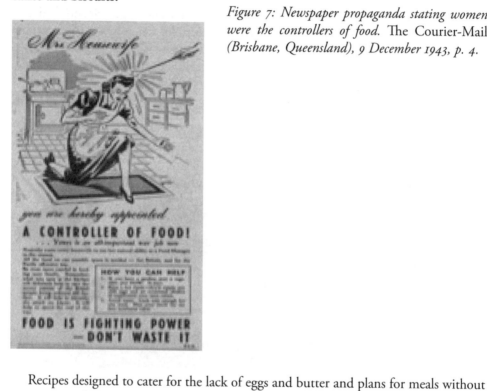

Figure 7: Newspaper propaganda stating women were the controllers of food. The Courier-Mail *(Brisbane, Queensland), 9 December 1943, p. 4.*

314

Recipes designed to cater for the lack of eggs and butter and plans for meals without meat appeared in newspapers and women's magazines on a regular basis.[26] Recipe books at the time did their best to make cooking sound challenging and exciting despite the short supply of many items. *The Truth and Daily Mirror Cookery Book* (1943) gave a recipe for wartime cream buns, which used egg powder and margarine along with mock 'cream' whipped up out of cornflour, milk, margarine, sugar and vanilla. The book contains a large section of 'Austerity Menus', with recipes for meat cuts that Australians were now expected to eat: for example, surprise patties (made with three sets of brains and half a pound of mince) and 'meatless dishes' such as vegetable roast. Austerity potatoes, made with half the usual quantity plus soaked breadcrumbs, and austerity fruit cake, made without eggs and with dripping instead of butter, were also part of the fare.[27]

Radio broadcasting was seen as highly important in influencing opinion and behaviour during the Second World War and was viewed as a more durable medium than print-based sources. Originating in Britain, *The Kitchen Front* programme in Australia ran for five minutes from Monday to Friday and ten minutes on Sundays. The talks emphasized simple, easy and appetizing methods of preparing food. The public was also offered the latest information on nutritional principles, diet and food preparation, in particular on appropriately cooking vegetables to retain their nutrition. Eating of salads dressed with oil and vinegar was also encouraged. The broadcasts were so popular that requests from listeners for printed copies of various talks were so numerous that a compilation was published.[28]

Austerity menus to help consumers plan meals, particularly for their food value, were also broadcast by way of a series of radio talks entitled, *What Shall We Have for Dinner*. The talks were likewise later compiled into a book. Menus were given for a thirteen-week period and included dinner and cold luncheons for adults as well as dinner and supper menus for children.[29] As can be seen below, meals were simple but provided variety in the diet and, with the inclusion of brown bread, fruit and milk for children, were considered nutritious. However, by today's standards the diet is heavily meat-based, and there is very little variety in the vegetables. (See p. 316 - 317 for a sample Menu Plan for One Week.)

Appropriate storage of food was seen as essential to prevent waste. An article from *The Australian Women's Weekly* dated 12 February 1944 offered tips on how to store food in the fridge and pantry, and how to store items if you didn't have a fridge.[30] Not everyone had a fridge in the 1940s; most had ice chests and some used a Coolgardie safe instead, a very basic form of fridge which worked on the simple principle of evaporative cooling, developed from the old meat safe.

Finally, food was also to be recycled – **a**pple peel could be boiled to make a lemon substitute in jams or drinks; bacon rinds provided fats for cooking meat or were used for flavouring soups; stale bread went into puddings or was used to make stuffing. Other scraps fed the animals. (Australians today throw out $8 billion worth of edible food each year, and local councils have launched the 'Too Good to Waste' campaign. Councils are asking residents to change their behaviour to reduce landfill and save precious resources.)[31]

The Second World War ushered in a period of change in Australian's culinary culture. Although Australians thought they ate well at the time, the wartime propaganda campaign led Australians to consider what they were eating more closely than ever before. At the very least Australians generally were made aware of the necessity of a balanced diet and the importance of nutrition. The era of 'vitamania' in Australia, as one 1940s journalist called it, had begun.[32] Moreover, many of these messages – intended to directly influence the culinary behaviour of civilians during the war – are being recycled today: eat less meat; reduce sugar consumption; don't waste food; grow your own vegetables; improve the way you store (including preserving), prepare and cook food; recycle; and strive for healthy nutrition. However, it was not until thousands of immigrants from war-torn Europe made Australia home that substantial change occurred in Australia's culinary traditions, change that the Second World War made possible.

		CHILDREN'S		
	DINNER	DINNER	SUPPER	COLD LUNCHEONS
Tuesday	Thick Celery & Sago Soup Triangles of Toast Boiled Corned Beef & White Sauce Carrots, Turnips, Parsnips Boiled Jacket Potatoes Stewed Nectarines & Cream	Steamed Brains White Sauce Toast Bananas Brown Bread Butter Milk	Thick soup Toast Stewed Nectarines Cream Home-made buns Milk	Corned Beef Celery Cheese Home-made Buns Fresh Fruit
Wednesday	Pea Soup Fried Bread Curried Rabbit & Rice Jacket Potatoes & Cauliflower White sauce Stewed Plums, Boiled Custard	Cold Corn Beef Vegetable Salads Fruit Salad, Cream Home-made Buns Milk	Pea Soup Fried Bread Stewed Plums Boiled Custard Home-made Biscuits Milk	Corned Beef Mashed Curried Rabbit Tomato Lettuce Home-made Cake Fresh Fruit
Thursday	Mulligatawny Soup Fingers of Toasted Brown Bread Cold Corned Beef Lettuce and Potato Salad Mayonnaise Dressing Beetroot in Vinegar Plum Pie and Cream	Rabbit, Cauliflower Potato White Sauce In Casserole Tomatoes Brown Bread Butter Milk	Soup Toasted Brown Bread Home-made Buns Cocoa	Eggs Lettuce Beetroot Cheese Home-made Buns Fresh Fruit
Friday	Lentil Soup, Fried Bread Boiled Trout, Parsley Sauce Green Peas, Mashed Potatoes Banana Custard	Boiled Fish White Sauce Boiled Carrots Fruit Salad Oatcake Milk	Lentil Soup Fried Bread Banana Custard Home-made biscuits Milk	

316

Saturday	Oyster Soup Toasted Sippets Crumbed Veal Cutlets Brown Gravy Vegetable Marrow White Sauce Boiled Jacket Potatoes Oatcake, Butter, Celery, Cheese	Fish Kedgeree Toast Fresh Peaches Brown Bread Butter Milk	Fish Soup Toast Fruit Salad Cream Oatcake Celery Milk	
Sunday	Roast Leg of Mutton Mint Sauce, Brown Gravy French Beans Baked Potatoes Queen Pudding	Share Adult Dinner	Milk Sago Pudding Jam Celery Brown Bread Milk	Cold Mutton Mint Sauce Tomatoes Home-made Buns Fresh Fruit
Monday	Gravy and Macaroni Soup Fingers of Toast Cold Mutton Mint Sauce, Apple Jelly Potato & Lettuce Salad Mayonnaise Dressing Beetroot in Vinegar Peach Pie, Cream	Cold Mutton Vegetable Salad Queen Pudding Milk	Soup Brown Bread Toast Fruit Salad Cream Home-made biscuits Milk	Cold Mutton Chutney Beetroot Lettuce Home-made Buns Fresh Fruit

Notes

1. Jean-Anthelme Brillat-Savarin, *The Physiology of Taste* (London: Penguin, 1970), p. 13.
2. Frank Crowley, *Modern Australia in Documents 1939-1970*. (Melbourne: Wren Publishing, 1973), p. 1.
3. Lizzie Collingham, *The Taste of War: World War Two and the Battle for Food*. (London: Allen Lane, 2011), p. 443; D.P. Mellor, 'The Role of Science and Industry', *Australia in the War of 1939-1945*, vol. 5 (Canberra: Australian War Memorial, 1958), pp. 573-611 (p. 610) <https://www.awm.gov.au/images/collection/pdf/RCDIG1070371--1-.pdf> [accessed 1 March 2016].
4. Americans opened major Australian cities to a new culture and made a substantial impact on the local economy. They were welcomed with open arms, at least initially. However, resentment built over time as many Australians considered the Americans to be *over-sexed, over-paid and over-fed receiving* thirty-nine items in their rations compared to the Australian soldier's twenty-four. The acquisition of new tastes in food during the war, however, is inextricably linked with the presence of the American forces in Australia. Americans drank coffee instead of tea. Coca Cola, hamburgers, hot dogs, sundaes, ice cream sodas and cold fruit drinks, tinned spaghetti and spam were all readily accepted by Australians. Americans were introduced to meat pies and, reluctantly, dim sim. The American influence on Australia's food culture requires a paper in itself.
5. Mellor, p. 582.
6. T.E. Lawrence, 'The Evolution of a Revolt', *Army Quarterly and Defence Journal* 1.1 (October 1920), reprinted by Combat Studies Institute, p. 11 <http://usacac.army.mil/cac2/cgsc/carl/download/csipubs/lawrence.pdf> [accessed June 2014].
7. Michael McKernan, *Australians at Home: World War II* (Victoria: Five Mile Press, 2014), p. 168.
8. McKernan, p. 168.
9. Mellor, p. 582; p. 589.
10. Mellor, p. 597; p. 610.
11. Cinesound Productions for the Department of Information and National Films Council, *Give Us This Day*, 1943. National Film and Sound Archive <http://aso.gov.au/titles/ads/give-us-this-day/≥ [accessed 16 May 2015].

12. Sydney Health Week, *Health Brings Victory: Health, Milk and National Fitness Week,* 24 October to 1 November 1941.

13. Philip E. Muskett, *The Art of Living in Australia* (Sydney: Kangaroo Press, 1987 [London, 1893]), p. 1. Muskett was firmly in favour of fish and salads and a variety of vegetables to alleviate the potato and cabbage fixation of the times.

14. Mellor, p. 581.

15. Combined Congregational and Baptist Churches of South Australia, *Green and Gold Cookery Book* (Adelaide: Vardon and Sons Ltd, 1925).

16. Special Service Division, Services of Supply, United States Army, *Instructions for American Servicemen in Australia* (Washington, DC: War and Navy Departments, 1942), p. 16. Reprinted 2007 (Oxford: Bodleian Library) <http://www.army.gov.au/-/media/Files/Our%20history/AAHU/Primary%20Materials/World%20War%20Two%201939-1945/Training%20Materials/Instructions%20for%20American%20Servicemen%20in%20Australia%201942.pdf> [accessed 1 March 2016].

17. Barbara Santich, *What the Doctors Ordered: 150 Years of Dietary Advice in Australia* (Victoria, Hyland House, 1995), p. 113.

18. McKernan, p. 157.

19. McKernan, p. 162.

20. McKernan, p. 157.

21. McKernan, p. 159.

22. S.J Butlin and C.B Schedvin, 'War Economy, 1942-1945', *Australia in the War of 1939-45*, vol. 4 (Canberra: Australian War Memorial, 1977): pp. 286–309 (p. 307) <https://www.awm.gov.au/images/collection/pdf/RCDIG1070665--1-.pdf> [accessed 1 March 2016].

23. Mellor, p. 586.

24. Sydney Health Week, p. 74.

25. 'Diet and Nutrition for the Australian People,' Nutrition Committee of the National Health and Medical Research Council of Australia, ed. by F W Clements (Australia: Angus and Robertson Ltd. in conjunction with the Commonwealth Department of Health, 1941).

26. 'Meals without Meat', *The Australian Women's Weekly*, 4 March 1944, pp. 22-23.

27. Michael Symons, *One Continuous Picnic: A Gastronomic History of Australia* (Melbourne: Melbourne University Press, 2007), p. 192.

28. Australian Broadcasting Commission, *The Kitchen Front: Selections from Talks Broadcast by the Spokesman of the Australian Broadcasting Commission's Nutrition Advisory Committee* (Sydney: ABC, 1943).

29. W A Osborne and Elizabeth Howell, *What Shall We Have for Dinner?* (Melbourne: Albright & Wilson, n.d.), pp. 28-29.

30. *The Australian Women's Weekly,* 12 February 1944, pp. 27-28.

31. Manly Council, *Manly Council Weekly eNews Bulletin*, 23 March 2015 <http://www.manly.nsw.gov.au/council/email-newsletters/> [accessed 30 March 2015].

32. Catherine Price, 'Vitamania', *Sydney Morning Herald*, 4-5 April 2015, p. 32.

I Am What I Don't Eat: Food and Eating as a Form of Communicating Distinction in the Jewish Literature of the Second Temple Period

Harriet Publicover

Dietary laws and practices present an opportunity to express one's identity through the medium of food. As much today as in antiquity, how we eat communicates a great deal about our social position and religious affiliation. In this paper I will illustrate how certain examples of Jewish literature from the Second Temple period demonstrate a move towards abstaining from the food of non-Jews in pursuit of piety. This, as I will show, constitutes a departure from ancient Israelite practice, and from biblical dietary law. I will argue that this phenomenon was a response to the Hellenization of *Eretz Israel* (the land of Israel) and that it came about as a result of the need to communicate a clear distinction between 'us' and 'them'.

I

The Jews of the Second Temple period (530 BCE–70 CE) followed the dietary laws that were laid down in the Torah (the first five books of the Hebrew Bible), primarily in the books of Leviticus and Deuteronomy. These laws permit only the consumption of the following kinds of animal: land mammals that have cloven hooves and chew the cud, fish with fins and scales, 'clean' birds and fowl, and certain kinds of locust.[1] In some instances certain species of animals are expressly forbidden or permitted, while in others only the description of the category is given. The Torah also specifically prohibits eating animals that have died of natural causes, the cooking of a kid in its mother's milk and the consumption of blood.[2] As far as crops are concerned, the laws also require that grain, wine and oil are correctly tithed, such that one tenth is appropriately given away.[3]

However, nowhere in the Bible does it state that 'foreign food' (that is to say, food prepared by and eaten in the company of non-Israelites) is forbidden. Indeed, the Bible contains a great many narratives in which Israelites consume the food of other peoples.[4] One example is Aaron and the elders of Israel eating food provided by Jethro, the Midianite father-in-law of Moses.[5] Another such example is the story of the prophet Elisha, who is said to have eaten frequently at the house of a Shunammite woman.[6] Given the lack of concern with which our biblical characters eat foreign food, we may assume that the ancient Israelites considered such food fit for consumption, provided that it was prepared in accordance with the biblical dietary restrictions.

The inhabitants of *Eretz Israel* in late antiquity ate a largely vegetarian (vegan) diet composed of bread, wine, pulses, fruit, vegetables and olive oil. This was supplemented by fish, eggs, dairy products, locusts and grasshoppers, as well as occasional meals of meat. This was the medium through which Jewish dietary restrictions were practiced, and through which Jews could communicate their identity by abstaining from foreign food. This is especially relevant to the present discussion, as much of the foreign food that pious Jews refused would surely have been composed of bread and lentils, rather than suckling pig.

The Second Temple period witnessed the initial movement among Jews towards abstention from the food of the other. As we shall see, this is illustrated through a number of different literary sources. Although we cannot claim that these texts reflect popular practice, there is no doubt that they present a particular common ideology in which piety was expressed through abstaining from non-Jewish food and wine. This may have served in part to prevent the possibility of table-fellowship among Jews and non-Jews, and thus to prevent Jews from accidentally engaging in idolatrous practices. However, while the Hebrew Bible is greatly concerned with idolatry, it appears indifferent to the question of eating foreign food. Preventing this table-fellowship may rather have been an effective method of making interaction with non-Jews practically impossible, and thus of preserving the closed nature of the Jewish circle. The practice speaks of a people who felt threatened by assimilation, and who placed a wall around their everyday lives to keep outsiders out.

The custom of abstaining from foreign food developed in a Hellenized environment (from 332 BCE), in which Jews may have felt their identity to be challenged. This situation continued following the Roman conquest of Judea in 63 BCE, which ultimately led to the destruction of the Second Temple. Greek identity was a very fluid concept, and one could, in many ways, 'become Greek' through education and lifestyle. Previously, Jews had lived in *Eretz Israel* under Persian rule, according to which they were recognized and treated as a separate and distinct nation. It may be that the fear of losing an identity distinctive from that of the dominant power led certain Jewish groups to attempt to separate themselves from others in all behaviours, including common meals and shared food. Eating only food prepared by Jews was a sure way to communicate one's Jewish identity and to remain separate from one's surrounding environment.

II

The following texts present examples of pious Jewish characters who abstain from foreign food. If read in the light of the context in which they were composed, these passages of text may be illustrative of two aspects of Jewish dietary practice in the Second Temple period. First, some Jews were eating non-Jewish food (and perhaps adopting non-Jewish practices). And second, piety-minded Jews opposed this practice. These piety-minded Jews, the authors of our texts, may have been relatively few in number, but their opinions have been preserved in numerous writings. For the large part our authors use Hebrew and Aramaic, though it is interesting to note that Greek was also used, even to oppose Hellenistic influence on Jewish society.

Jubilees

The Book of Jubilees is a Jewish text that retells episodes from Genesis and Exodus. It was originally composed in either Hebrew or Aramaic and is thought to date from the middle of the Second Temple period. The author of Jubilees places a declaration regarding abstention from non-Jewish food into the mouth of Isaac, who quotes a saying of his father Abraham: 'Now you, my son Jacob, remember what I say and keep the commandments of your father Abraham. Separate from the nations, and do not eat with them. Do not act as they do, and do not become their companion, for their actions are something that is impure, and all their ways are defiled and something abominable and detestable' (Jubilees 22.16).[7]

This saying naturally has no basis in biblical sources, and is a reworking of the narrative designed to bring Second Temple standards of piety into the historical context of the biblical patriarchs. This passage makes plain the reason for avoiding non-Jewish food, stating clearly that Jew and non-Jew should not become 'companions'. We may thus infer that the movement towards abstaining from non-Jewish food was the product of a desire to keep Jews socially separate from non-Jews. It is interesting that the 'actions' and 'ways' of non-Jews are described in Jubilees as being impure, though their food itself is not. There is no suggestion that eating with non-Jews will lead one to break a commandment (through consuming forbidden foods, for example) but rather that it might encourage close relations. The author of Jubilees appears to be warning against social interaction at all levels, which itself may be interconnected with the fear of accidentally engaging in idolatry.

321

Additions to Esther

The Book of Esther tells the story of the salvation of the Jews in Persia, who were threatened by Haman, the advisor to the king. Esther is a Jewish woman who becomes the queen of Persia; together with her cousin Mordecai, she prevents the downfall of her people. Although the Hebrew text of the Book of Esther (composed in the third or fourth century BCE) does not mention abstaining from non-Jewish food, its Greek translation dating from the first or second century BCE contains an addition to the original text that reflects this practice. In one additional passage, Esther prays to God saying:

> You have knowledge of all things, and you know that I hate the splendour of the wicked and abhor the bed of the uncircumcised and of any alien. You know my necessity – that I abhor the sign of my proud position, which is upon my head on days when I appear in public. I abhor it like a filthy rag, and I do not wear it on the days when I am at leisure. And your servant has not eaten at Haman's table, and I have not honoured the king's feast or drunk the wine of libations. (Esther 14.15-17)[8]

Just as Abraham and Isaac are rewritten in Jubilees, so too is Esther's character transformed in order to conform to new standards of pious practice. It is not surprising that the Book of Esther should receive this treatment, since the Hebrew original makes no mention whatsoever of God. In order to establish Esther's identity as a pious Jewish woman, she is thus required to pray, and to mention that she does not touch the Persian food and wine of her household. This passage appears to present non-Jewish food in association with idolatry, as specific reference is made to the ritually poured 'wine of libations'. Non-Jewish wine is consistently forbidden in rabbinic literature for precisely this association. The additions to Esther in the Greek translation attempt to portray the heroine as despising the other and attaining some form of social separation though dietary practice.

Tobit

In addition to the revision of older narratives and texts, new texts and stories were also composed in the Second Temple period displaying a clear rejection of foreign food. The Book of Tobit tells the story of a pious Jew who is taken into captivity in Nineveh during the reign of the Assyrian king Shalmaneser. It is commonly believed to have been composed shortly before the Maccabean period (164-63 BCE), though scholars have variously placed its composition between the seventh century BCE and the second century CE.[9] D. N. Freedman has suggested that from its earliest stages the book may have existed in both Aramaic and Hebrew.[10] In the opening chapter of this work, the author states clearly that he refrained from eating non-Jewish food while in exile, though his fellow Jews did not: 'After I was carried away captive to Assyria and came as a captive to Nineveh, everyone of my kindred and my people ate the food of the Gentiles, but I kept myself from eating the food of the Gentiles. Because I was mindful of God with all my heart, the Most High gave me favour and good standing with Shalmaneser, and I used to buy everything he needed' (Tobit 1.10-13).

It should be noted that the 'food of the Gentiles' mentioned here (and elsewhere) does not necessarily fall outside the prescribed biblical diet. In this sense, Jews could be keeping biblical law (by eating only those animals that are permitted according to the Torah, and by abstaining from blood and animals that had died of natural causes) but breaking with custom by eating food prepared by non-Jews. This practice, as we have seen, could easily lead to unintentional idolatrous actions. Just as God rewards Esther and the Jewish people, so too is Tobit rewarded by God for abstaining from non-Jewish food. This is a theme that is often repeated in texts that date from the first and second centuries BCE.

Daniel

The Book of Daniel tells the story of a pious Jew who is held captive by the Babylonian king. It is commonly argued to have been composed in the second century BCE (in

Hebrew and Aramaic), and it provides a further example of the practice of abstaining from non-Jewish food.[11] In this instance Daniel refuses to eat the food that the Babylonian king provides, preferring vegetables and water:

> But Daniel resolved that he would not defile himself with the royal rations of food and wine; so he asked the palace master to allow him not to defile himself. Now God allowed Daniel to receive favour and compassion from the palace master. The palace master said to Daniel, 'I am afraid of my lord the king; he has appointed your food and your drink. If he should see you in poorer condition than the other young men of your own age, you would endanger my head with the king.' Then Daniel asked the guard whom the palace master had appointed over Daniel, Hananiah, Mishael, and Azariah: 'Please test your servants for ten days. Let us be given vegetables to eat and water to drink. You can then compare our appearance with the appearance of the young men who eat the royal rations, and deal with your servants according to what you observe.' So he agreed to this proposal and tested them for ten days. At the end of ten days it was observed that they appeared better and fatter than all the young men who had been eating the royal rations. So the guard continued to withdraw their royal rations and the wine they were to drink, and gave them vegetables. (Daniel 1.8-16)

This passage specifically states that Daniel refuses the king's food and wine because he does not wish to defile himself. As in the other texts that we have seen, no mention is made regarding the content of the food allowance itself, and we thus cannot say whether or not it constitutes food that is forbidden according to biblical law. However, Daniel chooses to consume only vegetables and water for fear of defilement. This text may also reflect a fear of association with idolatry (through unwittingly eating the meat of sacrifices or drinking the wine of libations). In any case, Daniel and his companions cannot truly separate themselves from the other, though refusing foreign food may be a symbolic way of enacting and communicating such a practice.

Judith

The Book of Judith in many ways revolves around the question of dietary law. Carey A. Moore believes the text to have been composed during the Maccabean period, and he argues for a Hebrew original on the basis of the Septuagint (the first Greek translation of the Hebrew Bible, completed in the second century BCE), suggesting that the Greek gives evidence of direct translation from Hebrew.[12] The book presents the story of Judith, a piety-minded Jew, who defeats the Assyrian general Holofernes and thus defends her town and people. Many elements of the narrative revolve around food. When Judith first goes to the Assyrian camp, having made herself so beautiful that none can resist her, she takes with her the basic staples that she will require: 'She gave her maid a skin of wine and a flask of oil, and filled a bag with roasted grain, dried fig cakes, and fine bread; then she wrapped up all her dishes and gave them to her to carry' (Judith 10.5). Judith then tricks the general, telling him that he will be able to conquer the town when its people give in to their hunger and break their dietary law by eating and drinking forbidden foods. She states that the people will eat 'all that God by his laws has forbidden them to eat', including the first fruits and tithes set aside for the priests in Jerusalem; 'things it is not lawful for any of the people even to touch with their hands' (Judith 11.12-13). Judith thus presents this impious disregard for biblical law as incurring the wrath of God to such an extent that the Jews will be overcome by the Assyrian armies. This reverses the motif we have seen before, in which piety in dietary law is rewarded by God.

Judith herself, however, is a model of piety. When offered food and wine by the general she declines, on the grounds that it may be an 'offense':

> Then he commanded them to bring her in where his silver dinnerware was kept, and ordered them to set a table for her with some of his own delicacies, and with some of his own wine to drink. But Judith said, 'I cannot partake of them, or it will be an offense; but I will have enough with the things I brought with me.' Holofernes said to her, 'If your supply runs out, where can we get you more of the same? For none of your people are here with us.' Judith replied, 'As surely as you live, my lord, your servant will not use up the supplies I have with me before the Lord carries out by my hand what he has determined.' (Judith 12.1-4)

There are a number of significant things to note about this passage of text. Firstly, Judith uses her own appearance of piety in order to gain the trust of Holofernes, who will remark that she is observant in the matter of dietary law (unlike the Jews of her town, whom she appears to be betraying). Secondly, the food of the Assyrians is considered to be an 'offense' according to Judith's standards of piety. As in the other texts that we have seen, there is no reason given for this except that it is the food of non-Jews. And thirdly, Holofernes himself remarks that if Judith were to run out of food there would be none of her people to prepare more. This reaffirms the idea that the only food that was considered fit for Jewish consumption in this period was food prepared by Jews.

III

As we have seen, in Second Temple literature, abstaining from foreign food became a widely used means of communicating one's pious Jewish identity. This identity was projected backwards onto biblical characters such as Abraham, Isaac and Esther. It was also used in the description of certain characters who were later rewarded for their piety by God. This practice may have been founded on the desire to avoid engaging in accidental idolatry (through eating or drinking sacrificial offerings). However, although this may have formed one strand of the overall intention, it seems more plausible that pious-minded Jews primarily wished to avoid becoming Greek. The very existence of this particular model of piety suggests that many ordinary Jews were eating like Greeks and with Greeks. Had this not been the case, there would surely have been no need for such pious characters as Tobit and Esther to present an alternative example. Consciously eating and drinking separately was an effective way of communicating the boundaries of 'us' and 'them', and one that could be put into practice on a daily basis.

It should be noted here that the Second Temple period also witnessed the distinction of Jew from Jew in table fellowship. Food and eating could be used not only to communicate one's Jewish identity, but also the identity of the specific group to which one belonged. This further development likely occurred during the Hasmonean period (140-37 BCE), during which major shifts in political and religious identity took place.[13] During this period Judean identity became less a question of ethnicity; one could politically become a member of the Judean state, or religiously accept the God worshipped in the Jerusalem Temple. As Shaye Cohen states, 'outsiders could become insiders.'[14] This naturally led the insiders to distinguish themselves from one another in a number of different ways.

One example of distinct sectarian dietary practice is that of the Qumran community, the authors of the Dead Sea Scrolls, who appear to have been extremely strict in separating themselves from outsiders (both Jewish and non-Jewish). As the Community Rule scroll states, new members of the group were only permitted to partake in communal food after one year and in communal drink after two.[15] Furthermore, outsiders were also forbidden from gathering the harvest, lest their impurity be transferred directly to the crops.[16] Archaeological evidence suggests that the Qumran community also ate from individual dishes, rather than sharing food among many.[17] This may indicate that their heightened purity laws required a greater separation of foods, or else of people eating them.

The New Testament also provides an interesting insight into Jewish attitudes to table fellowship in the late Second Temple period. The synoptic gospels record how the Pharisees censure Jesus for eating with sinners and tax collectors, members of the Jewish community who were rejected from communal meals with the Pharisees.[18] This indicates that the Pharisees refused to eat with Jews they considered 'impure'. It also suggests that Jesus took the opposite approach to table fellowship, eating with Jews regardless of their social status. In the Gospel of Luke, Jesus commands his disciples to eat what is put before them when they visit the neighbouring towns of the Galilee.[19] The controversy that arises from this statement is not that Jesus' followers are eating non-Jewish food but that the food may not have been prepared according to certain stricter regulations of oral law and custom. Furthermore, members of the household may also fall into the category of 'sinners', making communal eating abhorrent for those Jews of the first century that followed sectarian practices.

Following the destruction of the Second Temple by the Romans in 70 CE and the advent of rabbinic Judaism, abstention from non-Jewish food and wine became an integral part of Jewish dietary law (*kashrut*). Just as other food laws were expanded upon at length, so too were certain rules laid down regarding the boundaries demarcating non-Jewish food. The following statement is taken from the Mishnah, a rabbinic document believed to have been redacted around the beginning of the third century CE, and clearly illustrates the process of establishing these rules: 'These things of the gentiles are forbidden [...] milk which a gentile milked when no Israelite watched him; their bread and their oil [...] stewed or pickled vegetables into which it is their custom to put wine or vinegar' (Mishnah Avodah Zarah 2:6).[20] This practice reflects the fragile nature of post-Second Temple Judaism; threatened with obliteration, the authoritative Jewish circle closed itself off entirely to outsiders. Furthermore, Christianity was a growing presence, and Jewish and Christian communities were constructing their identities in opposing directions. Where Christianity was inclusive, rabbinic Judaism was exclusive. Christianity allowed one to eat virtually anything with anyone, while rabbinic Judaism limited table fellowship to one's own group, and even provided a distinction between the class of sages and their families and that of ordinary Jewish people.

The Jewish legal codes written in the medieval period further formulated these rules. *Shulchan Arukh*, a legal code written in 1563 by Yosef Karo, gives us many such rulings relating to dietary law. It is widely used and consulted to this day. The following statement is taken from *Kitzur Shulchan Arukh*, a condensed version of this code, which was compiled by Shlomo Ganzfried in the nineteenth century: 'Something that is not eaten raw, and which is also served at a kings' table to go with bread or as a small dish, which is cooked or roasted by a non-Jew, even in the dishes of a Jew or the house of a Jew – it is forbidden because it is cooked by a non-Jew' (*Kitzur Shulchan Arukh* 38.6).[21] To this day, a kosher chicken cooked using kosher utensils is not suitable for Orthodox Jews to eat if prepared by a non-Jew. Likewise, bottle of kosher wine ceases to be kosher according to Orthodox law if it is opened and poured by a non-Jew. I bring these examples to illustrate that abstaining from foreign food (and even foreign contact with Jewish food) was not a phenomenon of the Hellenistic period that disappeared as the Jewish religion evolved and grew. Rather, the rabbinic and medieval periods cemented this attitude and formulated rules for its practical implementation that continue to be followed to this day.

Communicating otherness and distinction through food has thus been a feature of certain forms of Judaism for over two thousand years. Food is the means by which an individual's status may be communicated, and abstention from that individual's food creates the intended gulf between Jew and non-Jew. It is my belief that our Second Temple literature is an early illustration of rejecting assimilation and of enacting this rejection through separation from others in matters of food and eating.

Notes

1. See Leviticus 11 and Deuteronomy 14.
2. See Deuteronomy 14.21, Exodus 23.19, 34.26 and Leviticus 17.10.
3. See Deuteronomy 14.22-29.
4. On this subject see David Freidenreich, *Foreigners and their Food: Constructing Otherness in Jewish,*

Christian and Islamic Law (Berkeley: University of California Press, 2011), p. 18.

5. Exodus 18.12.

6. II Kings 4.8.

7. *The Book of Jubilees*, trans. by James C. Vanderkam (Lovanii : E. Peeters, 1989), p. 131.

8. Unless otherwise stated, all biblical quotations (including those from the Apocrypha) are taken from the New Revised Standard Version.

9. *Tobit: A New Translation with Introduction and Commentary*, trans. by Carey A. Moore (New Haven: Yale University Press, 1996), p. 40.

10. *Tobit*, p. 34.

11. The more traditional view of the dating of Daniel does not challenge its historical authenticity, and places it composition in the sixth century BCE. Scholars such as J. A Montgomery consider the first part of Daniel to predate the second, which is attributed to the reign of Antiochus IV (175-164 BCE). See 'Daniel', *Encyclopaedia Judaica*, Second Edition, Vol. 5 (Jerusalem: Keter Publishing House Ltd., 2007), p. 422.

12. *Judith: A New Translation with Introduction and Commentary*, trans. by Carey A. Moore (New Haven: Yale University Press, 2008 [1985]), p. 67, p. 66.

13. On this subject see Shaye Cohen, *The Beginnings of Jewishness: Boundaries, Varieties, Uncertainties* (Berkley: University of California Press, 1999), pp.109-10.

14. Cohen, p.110.

15. See Hannah K. Harrington, 'Keeping Outsiders Out: Impurity at Qumran', *Defining Identities: We, You and the Other in the Dead Sea Scrolls: Proceedings of the Fifth Meeting of the IOQS in Gröningen*, ed. by *Florentino García Martínez and Mladen Popović* (Leiden: Brill, 2008), p. 189.

16. Harrington, p. 189.

17. Jodi Magness, *Stone and Dung, Oil and Spit* (Grand Rapids, MI: William B. Eerdmans Publishing, 2011), pp. 83-84.

18. See Mark 2.15-16, Matthew 9.10-11, Luke 5.29-30 and Luke 15.1-2.

19. Luke 10.8.

20. *The Mishnah*, trans. by Herbert Danby (Oxford: Oxford University Press, 1933), p. 439.

21. Translation my own.

Looking Good: Picturing Food in Early Books and Prints

Marcia Reed

Have you ever wondered when food started to look good? After searching in vain for detailed images of feasts and food in illuminated manuscripts and early books in the course of research for the 2015 Getty exhibition, 'The Edible Monument: The Art of Food for Festivals', I did wonder. Accustomed as we are to the enticing images in contemporary cookbooks, food magazines and the internet, the lack of detailed depictions of food in the Middle Ages and the Renaissance was initially both remarkable and completely unexpected. Without having actually investigated images in manuscripts and early printed books, I was certain that I would find interesting images of legends and religious narratives focused on food. In fact, it was puzzling to search for precursors to contemporary visualizations of food and come up so short!

In medieval and Renaissance illuminated manuscripts and paintings of feasts, although the narratives were said to be ancient, the settings tended to be contemporary, from the period when the art was created. Illuminations and early prints provided little information about the meal on the table. In a fourteenth-century French Book of Hours, the drollery for January of the two-faced god Janus feasting is expanded into three faces, drinking on the left, eating on the right (Figure 1). While the illumination has an ornate multi-coloured gothic frame, the food is barely sketched out, making it difficult to discern what Janus is eating. Typically, the tabletop shows goblets and ewers, platters or trenchers, a round roll or bit of bread, fish and perhaps a roast, all roughly outlined in the shapes of the vessels and dishes. Occasionally there is a pig on a platter, or a bird mounted on pastry. Table settings are always schematic. These are certainly not scenes of dining pleasure, with guests eating enthusiastically.[1]

Figure 1. Janus feasting, a drollery on the leaf for January. Ruskin Hours 83.ML.99 (Ms. Ludwig IX, 3), fol. 2v. About 1300, Northeastern France. J. Paul Getty Museum.

Paintings and illuminated manuscripts do depict scenes of dining to illustrate Biblical parables, yet there are few details about the food. Heavenly nourishment falls upon the hungry Israelites like snowballs in the miracle of Manna in the Wilderness; it melts at their feet as they gather it as quickly as they can.[2] The story, told in Exodus 16, describes quails dropping from the sky as well as the manna, a white flaky substance that falls after the dew, like hoarfrost. More concretely, it was said to resemble coriander seeds and taste like honey wafers. A significant number of Biblical parables focus on hunger or deprivation. Problems coming from the lack of food are solved by miracles, and the stories become the substance of legends.

At least since the classical tale of the Judgement of Paris and the golden apple that sparked the Trojan War, weddings have provided consummate paradigms for parties. With possibilities of uninvited guests or excessive consumption, there is the looming prospect that the food will run out. Giotto's early fourteenth-century fresco of 'The Marriage of Cana' in the Scrovegni Chapel features large containers of wine in front of a prim group around the table. In Veronese's painting of this same subject, Jesus becomes the most welcome kind of guest as he performs what is called his first public miracle, turning jugs of water into wine to provide sufficient amounts – of the best quality – for the party which had run out.[3] Now in the Louvre, it is notable that the painting was commissioned in 1562 by the Benedictine Monastery of San Giorgio Maggiore in Venice, Italy for its refectory. Shown as a contemporary Venetian feast, this Biblical artwork was created for a dining space where monks ate in silence. The oversize painting gives a wonderfully detailed picture of lavish service and over-the-top enjoyment. It conveys the social distinctions embedded in food service and eating.[4] The theatrical scene becomes a stage for depicting conspicuous consumption with dual levels of food preparation and consumption: high above and below. There are the ever-present canines, a staple presence at very grand banquets. Remarkably, party dogs are almost always in attendance at feasts, happily helping to clean up the table.

The miracle of the Wedding at Cana was a popular image for sixteenth-century European painters from Italy to the Netherlands. Gerard David, Giorgio Vasari, Marten de Vos, and Tintoretto all composed more restrained images than Veronese. Wine jugs are always featured. The table is a central element, yet there is relatively little food. Veronese's work was exceptional in its inclusion of food. However, it was a painting made for a specific space, and thus did not circulate except in copies and prints. Harking back to the famous scene of Adam and Eve tempted by the forbidden fruit in the Garden of Paradise, the depiction of the Wedding at Cana indicates how banquets often serve as moralizing scenes, presenting reminders of the price of vice and rewards of virtue, often portraying the sin of gluttony or the social gaffe of drunkenness. Table manners are more important than actual dining or food. The diners' demeanours and their physical appearances provide lessons about the appropriate conduct of life. An illustration from a mid-fifteenth century manuscript of Biblical stories, *Barlaam and Josaphat,* shows a less propitious wedding scene (Figure 2). There is a modest depiction of food: drinking goblets, fish on platters, a small centrepiece and knives for utensils. The image concerns decorum, illustrating the fate of a less than well-dressed guest. He is kicked out, not only thrown out the door but down into the mouth of a monster.[5] Enlarged versions of a similar monster who eats people or fools show a comical but also cautionary element of the Schembart carnival festival floats called Hells in medieval Nuremberg.[6] Being eaten is associated with being sent to Hell. Rather than communicating information about what people ate, this is a lesson about monstrous appetites. The Schembart festival is staged just before the Lenten fasts, and the monster is an outsize glutton who consumes the foolish.

Figure 2. A Royal Wedding Feast; An Unsuitably Dressed Guest Cast into Darkness, from Barlaam and Josaphat. (Ms. Ludwig XV 9), fol. 88v. J. Paul Getty Museum

330

The Biblical parable of Lazarus and Dives presents a portrait of conspicuous consumption and self-indulgence. Displaying the effects of over-eating, the red-faced rich man has a double chin and considerable girth. Dressed splendidly in furs and jewellery, he is seated at a table laden with dishes in a richly appointed dining space with silver platters displayed on the credenza; drinks are chilling beneath it. What we don't see are the elements on the banquet table. Poor Lazarus comes to the door begging for a few scraps from his table and is refused; ironically, the house dogs run outside and lick Lazarus' sores. After Lazarus starves to death, two angels appear to receive his soul. Typically in Biblical narratives like this story of Lazarus, scenes of lavish secular feasts are the bad examples used to present instructive, corrective narratives as parallels to virtuous deeds or lifestyles. Dining is shown emblematically as sinful, elaborating on one of the rich man's sins, gluttony, and pointing out the misdirections of his lifestyle centred on the material world. Luxury and feasting are not shown as good things, certainly not an enjoyable celebration. Rather they are signposts of a sinful life.

For Christianity in the Middle Ages and Renaissance, the signal symbolic depiction of a shared meal is the Last Supper, foretelling the religious sacrament of Communion (Figure 3).[7] By now it is not surprising to learn that the food shown on the table is remarkably simple. Scenes of the Last Supper usually, and most appropriately, show only goblets and small hunks of bread in front of the disciples, who are not eating. In contrast with the lavish meal of Dives, the scenes of the Last Supper point away from the evils of gratifying the senses toward the virtues of a disciplined, almost ascetic and humble dietary regimen. It parallels the simple meals of peasants and the poor.

Medieval and Renaissance manuscripts and paintings reveal that even when the didactic narrative concerns sustenance or focuses on a meal, there is no detailed description of food in the accompanying texts. In most cases, the reference to food is vague: is it an apple that Adam eats in the Garden of Paradise or some other kind of fruit? What exactly is manna? The lack of textual detail about food is one possible explanation for the absence of representations of real food. In general, what is depicted is the opposite, a spare hint at a meal guaranteed neither to stimulate the senses nor even make your mouth water. While there are numerous sensual and sensuous depictions in manuscript illuminations, especially in the margins, scenes of edible pleasure are not among them.

Popular prints from the sixteenth and seventeenth centuries are surprisingly more concrete in their visions of food. Unlike deluxe manuscripts and paintings, they are made for a different audience. These were people who did not have grand feasts, nor much variety or sensual pleasure at all in their daily experience of dining. The myth of Cockaigne (in Italian, Cuccagna) envisions a paradise where almost everything is made of food.[8] Based on folktales and legends, it is a land of leisure and self-indulgence where '[h]e who works the least earns the most'. Miracles of food and other fantasies are everywhere, humorously depicted for people who had very little for their daily bread. It rains pearls and diamonds; there are ships loaded with mortadella and salted meats, a lake of meatballs and pasta and another with all kinds of cheeses and a cave of ravioli. Plants produce cakes and pastries; a marsh is filled with sweet rolls. A fountain flows with Malvasia; a cannon shoots off flasks of Moscato. In the centre of Cuccagna prints, there is an enormous steaming, overflowing pot of macaroni or stew. While Cuccagna prints are schematic vernacular depictions, somewhat like medieval comics, they do show and name many different kinds of foodstuffs. We can understand what might have looked appetizing and good in these visions of food shown in the landscape of legend for the poor and hungry peasants. Italian prints reference Cuccagna festivals and monuments, but there also were versions in France known as 'The Island of Bust-Belly' and in Germany 'Schlarraffenland' was the Land of Milk and Honey.[9] Cuccagna festivals were often connected with Carnival celebrations, the time before Lenten fasting, or with saints' days. An important, indeed essential, part of these festivals was the food distributed to the people. There were ephemeral monuments decorated with breads, cheeses and salami, made to be sacked as the food was carried away. There were beverages – wine and water – and roasts in the streets. Cuccagna prints have some of the most substantial and mouth-watering descriptions of festival foods.

No doubt food was on people's minds. Miniatures and border decorations in Books of Hours and calendars organized by the months show signature agricultural activities, seasonal employments and occupations: sowing, harvest, roasting meats and cooking. This is where images of food begin to creep in, not so much in scenes of elaborate dining or actual food service, but rather as single images of produce, frequently shown in the margins. Here too luscious fruits and sensuous vegetal forms are employed as moralistic or emblematic vignettes in which artists took the opportunities to display their newly acquired talents for observing nature. Joris Hoefnagel's gouache and gilded illustrations to the model book of writing samples, *Mira Calligraphiae Monumenta* (1591-1596), take a new direction for appreciation of edibles depicted on paper.[10] Fruits, vegetables and nuts are shown fully ripe, harvested, picked or plucked from their trees or bushes, neatly cut in half or split open. They seem ready to be eaten. Molluscs are split open, and delectable crayfish are bright coral, sympathetically shown cooked rather than their natural grey colour. Hoefnagel's work is a stellar example of the tendency to show nature as enticing and even potentially delicious, like still life paintings, especially by Netherlandish artists. Yet, these are still not composed images of food intended for table presentations.

Indeed, it was still life painting that should have opened the door to illustrations of food. These were artful arrangements of natural and other objects, often including items of food, especially fruit, vegetables and game. The genre is most often seen in paintings, but other media have been used for still life such as mosaics and frescoes in antiquity. Although in fact they are carefully composed, the groupings are made to seem as if they are drawn from life, shown with casual reportage that is reinforced by their placement in a domestic setting. Still life emerged as a popular genre only in the seventeenth century, especially in the Netherlands, but also in France, Spain and Italy. The Italian artist Giovanna Garzoni's modest chipped bowl holding an overflow of citrons cleverly depicts stages in the life cycle of the fruit which was appreciated for its intense taste and strong smell.[11] Like oranges that could have been the golden apples of the Hesperides, the leaves and the blossoms of citrons recalled gardens of paradise. Flowers and leaves provided assurance of forthcoming fruits, that is, fertility.

Stressing the meaning of 'life set still', in the Netherlands still life paintings were often called by names of meals such as *ontbijtje* [small breakfast], *banketje* [little banquet] and frequently they were kitchen scenes crowded with food. Dutch still life paintings show nature, gathered and ready to be prepared and eaten, but not yet on the table.[12] Countering the meagre table settings of earlier prints and illuminations, abundance is the optimistic message of bowls of apples, peaches and pomegranates and dead animals and fowl hung above and piled below. Nature is subdued and put to service in nourishing life. More commonly, particularly when a skull is included in the composition, a still life painting is known as a '*vanitas*'. The message is to seize the day, and perhaps eat your heart out, since everyone will eventually die. In French, still life is nature *morte* [dead nature]. Interestingly for the food connection, in seventeenth-century Spain such images were called *bodegones*, after the lower-class inns and eating-places they were painted for.

Similar to Biblical depictions, still life painting was further complicated by the symbolic meanings of the natural products and creatures depicted, as well as the physical effects ascribed to them since antiquity. There was often a complex story attached, based on folklore or the appearance of the animal, vegetable or mineral, and associated with moral lessons as well. Until a considerable assist came from photography, and from the developing sciences of botany and chemistry that also informed the art and science of cooking and food preparation, foodstuffs were not much appreciated independently and in themselves, but rather for their symbolic meanings and their properties.

Publishing Food

In the middle ages, properties of fruits and vegetables could be found in texts that supplied wise advice and provided regimens for physical well-being. These described the characteristics of different foods, diagnosing and forecasting their affects in bodily humours. *Tacuinum Sanitatis* [*The Table of Health*] is the Latin translation of an eleventh-century Arabic text that recommended or offered cautions about different substances. A number of illuminated manuscript versions survived and were the basis for the earliest printed edition.[13] The first part addresses different foods and how they affect the bodily humours. While illuminated manuscripts of the *Tacuinum* show occupations, the printed edition focuses on foodstuffs with small woodcuts of at the bottom of pages, pointing to a new interest in the significance of the material. For each vegetable or foodstuff depicted, the author describes its nature, optimal state, uses, dangers and effects. Suggestions on how to prepare the foods and other natural products are, in essence, recipes. Acorns should be fresh and large; it is best to eat them roasted, with sugar. Asparagus has a positive influence on intercourse and removes occlusions, yet it is bad for the stomach lining. It should be boiled and seasoned with salted water. The best kind of sugar is white and clear; it purifies the body, and benefits the chest, kidneys and bladder. The best pasta is that which is prepared with care. Very nourishing, it is good for the chest and throat, yet it is harmful to weak intestines and the stomach. Allied to herbals and receipt books that provide some of the same information, the *Tacuinum Sanitatis* is formidable source book for folk remedies, early medical advice and dietary practice. It is significant as a precursor of self-help guides and, of course, cookbooks.

Handwritten or printed, annotated and passed down, cookbooks have been known since the Greeks. They imply certain health regimens, maintaining a balanced mind and body, providing preventives to illness.[14] Published cookbooks, plans for menus, and guides to table settings developed from the practical literature that circulated in the middle ages and Renaissance. These sources included books of secrets, receipt books, artisanal manuals and herbals. What is now seen as a historical body of knowledge concerning food was drawn from diverse types of know-how and practical knowledge taught by masters and passed down to their apprentices. Initially, the knowledge of food

333

circulated orally among itinerant 'experts' and artisans. When their expertise and lore was assembled and began to be printed, relatively late in the history of printing, cookbooks were resources and tools, supremely instructive, but not intended to be beautiful finely produced editions. One can assume that like other educational printed works, there were far more editions than we know today, because they were used, excerpted, torn apart, but not collected. The great puzzle is that, although other practical manuals and handbooks of this ilk did have instructive images, cookbooks did not. Compare them, for example, to artist's and architect's manuals, herbals and garden manuals. Just from a practical standpoint, prior to eating, it is enjoyable to look at food in an anticipatory way. Indeed, several of the famous feasts mounted for seventeenth century festivals in Versailles and Rome had viewing days prior to the time of the banquet. Yet for centuries, cookbooks did not illustrate the results of their instructions and the practical wisdom they promulgated. Visualizations of cooking and serving must have been experienced or learned firsthand, rather than communicated by texts and images.

Part of the reason may be due to cooks' professional status. In general, the social status of culinary professionals was in ascendancy. We see tantalizing glimpses of significant culinary occupations in fifteenth- and sixteenth-century manuscripts; yet, only a few names have come down to us. The professions of the *scalco* [carver] and the pastry chef were articulated and their status recognized in the sixteenth and early seventeenth centuries with printed manuals, some well-illustrated, like Bartolomeo Scappi's *Opera* (1570) and in seventeenth-century prints such as The Pastry Shop by Abraham Bosse. In Scappi and in the *Encyclopédie* in the mid-eighteenth century, we are shown the preparatory spaces and utensils; in Scappi, we even see the cook and the carver; in the Bosse print, the pastry cook. Divisions and specifics of culinary knowledge – making bread, butchering, roasting, pastry-making and sugar-refining – were articulated and illustrated in the eighteenth-century *Encyclopédie*. Still, when compared to the centuries-old studies of law, medicine or theology, culinary science was an emergent field.

In the early modern era, the work of the mind and the work done by hand were very different categories. Culinary expertise fell into the latter category. With a few exceptions, notably the illustrations in Scappi's book and Bosse's engravings, until the nineteenth century it was very difficult to know how food should look when being prepared and served. Lacking models, food in books and prints were not described or crafted to look good. During this important period for the development of culinary science, there are parallel, but not interactive, paths of communication. The practical literature comprised recipes, menus and views of table settings, while festival books and prints showed images of actual feasts and banquet settings as they were staged. Very different kinds of publications for different users, these remained remarkably separate while obviously informing each other in practice. In fact, however, neither genre showed the food as it was prepared and served at the table.

Alan Davidson's entry on 'Cookery' in the *Oxford Companion to Food* offers some useful distinctions that are helpful to considering the ways of codifying of the knowledge surrounding food. He describes the 'art view', 'the skill view' and the 'science view'.[15] Borrowing his concepts and placing them in the context of the literature of food history, one can see that the early development of describing cooking processes and what cooks made was simply not visualized in terms of an 'art view'. Rather this knowledge, the 'skill view', is artisanal and learned on the job from masters, who then were spurred to write the first manuals which promoted not only themselves and their patron-employers but also the court or ecclesiastical settings where they worked. Infused by such culinary artisans, the published knowledge proceeded from situational practice towards recognized levels of skill or expertise. This was then illuminated by the studies and experiments of science, becoming the 'science view'. By the eighteenth century we can see the results in the systemized knowledge published and illustrated in the *Encyclopédie*, a scholarly enterprise that notably included food production, its preparation and cooking techniques. There was still considerable emphasis on methods and tools at the expense of the materiality of food products. Finished or accomplished versions of the latter are not shown in context, as in banquets or feasts, nor in detail but rather very schematically as elevations or bird's-eye views.[16]

Depicting Feasts

The elaborate programs for late Renaissance and early modern era court ceremonies such as coronations and weddings routinely featured grand banquets with artistically designed table pieces. Here again, it was difficult to find detailed images of the food, even in well-known paintings of feasts such as Giovanni Bellini's Feast of the Gods (1514-29) or in Veronese's Marriage at Cana (1563). Realistic renderings of edibles had survived in antique frescos, yet during the Middle Ages and Renaissance these seem to have been forgotten. There are isolated examples of specific foods, such as a pretzel shown in a German illuminated fourteenth-century manuscript (Figure 3). As we now know, there was no established iconography for the substance of feasts.

Figure 3. The Last Supper, An Ottonian Benedictional (Ms. Ludwig VII 1, f. 28) Regensburg, Bavaria, Germany, ca. 1030–1040. J. Paul Getty Museum

335

Figure 4. Antoine Trouvain, The Sixth Room of the Apartments, 1698. Los Angeles, Getty Research Institute.

Food finally started to look good when court entertainments became the height of fashion. Towards the second half of the seventeenth century deluxe visions of food presentations began to appear in print. They appeared in large folios such as those of the Cabinet du Roi, describing the festivals of Louis XIV at Versailles.[17] The Versailles fête books illustrate the cosmic staging of festivals, including the banquets – Feasts of the Gods and a procession of the Four Seasons – which were depicted in spacious ornamental garden landscapes. They accompanied scenes of theatre and dance, fountains and fireworks in the impressive books. Texts described the offerings of food and related decorations, putting special emphasis on the extraordinary orange trees for their sensory and symbolic qualities. Circulating in the same way as fashion prints, festival banquet prints set a new standard for distant courts. In Rome, Bologna, Stockholm and Vienna, interior scenes framed central banquet tables with glittering silverware, tapestries and candelabra; some were obviously designed in imitation of Versailles. Like French fashion plates of this same period, news of spectacular parties travelled fast, and food could be part of a fashion statement. One of Antoine Trouvain's 1698 printed set of 'Apartment' scenes, again from Versailles, shows a group of well-dressed men socializing at a dessert buffet serving chocolate, pastries, and tasteful pyramids of fruits (Figure 4).[18]

Significantly, it was in this same period that the new genre of cookbooks and serving manuals commenced. Initially they had no illustrations; gradually they included smaller prints and fold-outs depicting table settings for different occasions and numbers of covers.[19] More like maps or plans, these had no images of real parties, showing guests in attendance or actually eating. Cheaply made simple books, these manuals were practical guides; quite often prints did not match the size of text pages and were just sewn in or ganged together at the back of the book.[20] Coincidentally, the new culinary professions were staking out their social status. They were depicted by some of the same popular printmakers who created French fashion plates. Satirical portraits of food vendors, butchers, cooks and pastry chefs dressed in the tools of their trades appeared the printed series known as 'Cries' or 'Trades'. From nameless and faceless toilers, certain personalities emerged: the uncouth sweaty cook, the debonair and manly carving master and the confident nattily attired pastry chef (Figure 5).[21]

Figure 5. Abraham Bosse, The Pastry Shop, Netherlands, seventeenth century. Los Angeles, Getty Research Institute.

Figure 6. Recipe for venison pie, Conrad Hagger, Neues saltzburgisches Koch-Buch (Augsburg: Johann Jacbon Lotter, 1719), pls. 8 and 9. Los Angeles, Getty Research Institute.

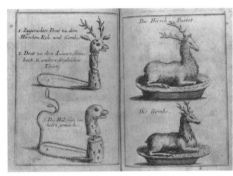

337

Depictions of both grand ceremonies and daily rituals of food were initially intended as journalistic images, focusing on how to do it, what should happen and who was there. Artists seemed not to know how to show the results of accomplished recipes and table service in prints of banquets illustrating festival books. Perhaps the mundane aspects of consumption were not seen as important to record, except in lists and menus. Food was essential, but made to be chewed, not viewed in reproductions on paper by others at distances of time and space. The ephemeral paintings and edible sculptures created expressly for festivals and celebrations as well as fireworks and water features were often depicted. Pastry, both savoury and sweet, led the way as the most artistically depicted genre, but it is not illustrated on the table (Figure 6). In general, the sparse number of images for recipes and culinary presentations in early printings demonstrate that these images were not considered essential. Cookbooks and related culinary works such as carving manuals and serving guides were printed and disseminated as guides intended for use and transmission. But, they were on the low end of the publishing spectrum; not scholarly or erudite, not intended to be collected and preserved as fine books or prints. What turned the corner was colour. Finally, in the nineteenth century came spectacular chromolithographs like Gouffé's and Urban Dubois' illustrated volumes, and inevitably, photography. Finally, the promising proposals of recipes could be envisioned and the details of the celebratory foods could be shown. While they are somewhat unsatisfying because of what they do not show or tell, the precursors to contemporary culinary literature are still significant documents which reveal the historic role of culinary practice, providing the back-stories to significant events, and most importantly, the essential place of food in cultural history.

Notes

1. A companion exhibition to the Getty Research Institute's 'The Edible Monument' was shown at the Getty Museum from 13 October 2015 through 3 January 3 2016. 'Eat Drink and Be Merry: Food in the Middle Ages and the Renaissance' displayed a selection of illuminated manuscripts made for elite patrons at the high end of the social spectrum. I want to acknowledge the ideas concerning images of seasonal foods, meal preparation and dining practices which curator Christine Sciacca shared to inform this section of my paper.

2. Anonymous artist, 'The Israelites Collecting Manna from Heaven', in Rudolph von Ems, *World Chronicle Welt-Chronik* (Regensburg: *c.* 1400-1410), Ms. 33, fol. 81v, J. Paul Getty Museum.

3. John 2:1-11; Paolo Veronese, The Wedding at Cana, 1562-1563, Paris, Musée du Louvre.

4. See Kate H. Hanson, 'The Language of the Banquet: Reconsidering Paolo Veronese's Wedding at Cana', *Invisible Culture*, 14 (2010), pp. 32-50.

5. Follower of Hans Schilling, from the Workshop of Diebold Lauber; Rudolf von Ems, Workshop of Diebold Lauber, A Royal Wedding Feast; An Unsuitably Dressed Guest Cast into Darkness, from *Barlaam and Josaphat*, Ms. Ludwig XV 9, fol. 88v, J. Paul Getty Museum.

6. *Schembard Büch*, Nuremberg, sixteenth-century manuscript, Getty Research Institute, 2009.M.38, f. 66 recto. The monster is called '*ein Narrenfresser*' [a fool-eater].

7. Carolin C. Young, 'Depictions of the Last Supper', in *Food in the Arts: Proceedings of the Oxford Symposium on Food and Cookery 1998*, ed. by Harlan Walker (Totnes: Prospect Books, 1998), pp. 223-236.

8. In the Foreword to the revised edition of *The Joy of Cooking*, Marion Rombauer Becker writes that the word 'Cockaigne' was added to favorite recipes. She clarifies that this was 'a mythical land of peace and plenty' in medieval times, as well as the name of their country home (Indianapolis: Bobbs-Merrill, 1964), p. viii.

9. 'Isle de Crevepance', *The French Renaissance in Prints*, ed. by Karen Jacobson (Los Angeles: Grunwald Center, 1994), p. 400-01. The German version of this pleasurable Utopia is mapped satirically on *Accurata Utopiae tabula* published by Matthäus Seutter (Nuremberg, *c.* 1730) Getty Research Institute, 2015.PR.43.

10. *Mira Calligraphiae Monumenta*, a sixteenth-century calligraphic manuscript, inscribed by Georg Bocskay, illuminated by Joris Hoefnagel, ed. by Lee Hendrix and Thea Vignau-Wilberg (Malibu: J. Paul Getty Museum, 1992).

11. Giovanna Garzoni, Bowl of Citrons, painting on vellum, late 1640s, J. Paul Getty Museum.

12. Frans Snyder with Jan Boeckhorst, Kitchen Still Life with Maid and a young boy, mid-seventeenth century, J. Paul Getty Museum.

13. Ibn Butlân, *Tacuini sanitatis* (Strassberg, 1518).

14. Roy Strong, *Feast* (London: Jonathan Cape, 2002), pp. 10-11.

15. Alan Davidson, 'Cookery', *Oxford Companion to Food* (Oxford: Oxford University Press, 1999), p. 212.

16. Juan de la Mata, *Arte de reposteria* (Madrid: Por Antonio Marin, 1747).

17. André Félibien, *Les plaisirs de l'isle enchantée...* (Paris: Imprimerie royale, 1674), pl. 5-6.

18. Antoine Trouvain, *Sixième chamber des appartements*, 1698.

19. François Pierre La Varenne's *Le cuisinier françois* was issued almost every year from 1651 through 1715, coinciding closely with the time of notable banquets during reign of Louis XIV.

20. See La Mata with its smaller size etchings, bound into the volume as fold-outs.

21. Abraham Bosse, The Pastry Shop (*c.* 1635).

Whitebait or *Blanchailles?*
Cuisine and Chaos in Britain, 1865-1914

Laura Shapiro

In the winter of 1902, the London-based journal *Food and Cookery* reported on a troubling rumour: the King now wished his menus to be written in English instead of French. For gastronomes like the editors of *Food and Cookery*, this wasn't just a bit of gossip, it was an affront to everything they cherished about fine cuisine – and, for that matter, everything they cherished about King Edward VII, whose devotion to French cooking had been warmly applauded in the pages of the journal since his years as the Prince of Wales. 'At Marlborough House and at Sandringham, the cuisine is almost entirely French, for the Prince and Princess are great lovers of French dishes,' the journal reported in 1898.[1] Two years later: 'There is probably no man in England who has mastered the art of dining so completely as the Prince of Wales.'[2] In 1901, upon Edward's ascension to the throne: 'The King is not only a lover of good cheer, but also an accomplished connoisseur. As Prince of Wales he captivated Paris by his knowledge of how to concoct a *recherché* salad [...]. We could wish no better gastronomic leaders than King Edward and Queen Alexandra.'[3]

One reason for this determined loyalty to the monarch's epicurean tastes was that Juste Ménager, a Frenchman and the long-time royal chef, was, as the journal liked to put it, 'Our Chairman' – he headed the Universal Cookery and Food Association, which published *Food and Cookery*.[4] The Association, founded in 1897 to support culinary training and promote British *haute cuisine*, had a distinguished swath of noble names among its official patrons; Queen Alexandra herself became a patron after Edward came to the throne. Hence the journal had good inside sources on whether the rumour about the King was true or not, and the editors hastened to emphasize that it was baseless. Nothing would change; French would continue to dominate the highest table in the land:

> All the Royal menus are composed in French, with the exception of certain typical English or German dishes, which appear in their respective language. French being the accepted and recognised *langue de cuisine*, just as much as it is that of diplomacy, that language has been adopted at the English Court, and throughout other countries where cookery and gastronomy reign supreme.[5]

But if gastronomy reigned supreme in Britain during these years, as the editors so fervently insisted, it did so uneasily. Like some Shakespearean pretender to the throne, forced to spend all his time fending off the rightful heir, British high-end cookery was struggling to assemble an identity grand enough to justify its rule. Thanks to a century marked by a French culinary invasion coupled with a very British wave of class anxiety, the usual signs and symbols indicating the social context of a particular meal were in disarray. Sometimes the food was French, sometimes it was British; most often it was a tangle of the two. Yet everyone knew that the French occupied the highest realms of cuisine, while the very notion of British cuisine was, as the London chef Charles Elmé Francatelli put it in 1846, 'a by-word of ridicule'.[6] Chefs, restaurateurs, cookbook writers and the public had no trouble accepting a culinary hybrid when it showed up on a plate. What stymied them was what to call it. The warring cultural associations seemed impossible to reconcile: '*Pouding à la Victoria*'? 'Strawberries in Surprise *à l'Anglais*'? '*Jambon d'York*'? '*Côtelettes* with Tomato Sauce'?[7] One of the enduring mysteries of upper-class life as the Victorians and Edwardians practiced it is why they were so convinced that neither English nor French was fully capable of capturing the whole truth about dinner.

Food and culture always live in close quarters, though often, it seems, without speaking to each other. It was the British, after all, who decided that the national dish of India was something they named 'curry', even though no such culinary category existed in the subcontinent. Throughout the life of the empire they busily incorporated Indian ingredients and flavours into British cooking, yet few epicures of the time would have proudly announced that the new language of cuisine in Britain was Hindustani. The foreign elements were safely absorbed into traditional tastes, and Britannia ruled. But the French offered a different and more complicated set of challenges. Thousands of French chefs were working in British homes, clubs, hotels and palaces by the late nineteenth century. Escoffier himself moved to London 1890 and spent the rest of his career there, in charge of renowned restaurants first at the Savoy Hotel and then the Carlton. In 1913, when he was president of the London branch of the *Ligue des Gourmands*, an international association of distinguished French chefs, London had sixty members – the largest branch in the world. Paris came in second, with forty-three. London was a world capital for French cuisine, and British-born chefs needed French training if they hoped to reach the heights of their profession.

But whether they were French or British, the chefs at work in the nation's most prestigious kitchens were using British ingredients, overseeing British staff and preparing dishes to please British tastes. Hence what had emerged over the years was a flexible cuisine more true to the spirit of accommodation than to orthodox tradition on either side. When it came to writing menus, the array of choices left menu-writers floundering. '*Jambon Braisé aux Epinards*' sent one message; 'Braised Ham and Spinach' sent another. '*Chapon en Bechemelle*' and 'Capon *à la Béchamel*' and 'Capons Bechamelle' all had the same pedigree; 'chicken in white sauce' manifestly did not, even if the ingredients were similar.[8] 'A very vexed question amongst cooks is the language that should be used on the Menu, French being usually adopted, or a mixture of French and English, with some very amusing results,' observed Theodore Garrett, whose *Encyclopaedia of Practical Cookery* set forth the entirety of Victorian cuisine in eight wonderfully readable volumes. He suggested that cooks follow 'the character of the dinner' – 'if purely English, the Menu should be in that language as far as possible; if French, then French throughout'.[9] But as a practical matter, the food was never going to be much use as a guide: it was the culinary equivalent of an unreliable narrator. Even Escoffier, who reportedly refused to learn English and rarely allowed it on his pristine French menus, prepared *'Beefsteack-Pies et Puddings de Boeuf à l'Anglaise,'* and allowed 'Roly-Poly Pudding' to slip into his repertoire untranslated.[10]

What's more, there were other considerations bearing on menu language, and they had nothing to do with the kitchen. Virginia Woolf complained that women writers were plagued by 'the angel in the house', that persistent, Victorian image of ideal femininity, hovering over their shoulders and guiding their pens along lines of sweet, accommodating propriety.[11] Menu-writers had a watchful angel, too, and it looked a lot like 'The Ancestor', the name King Edward gave to Sargent's portrait of Lord Ribblesdale dressed for the hunt, the very model of confident, impeccable aristocracy. Class was as demanding as cuisine when it came to writing a menu – more so, in fact, according to the journalist Edward Spencer Mott, who published culinary essays under the name 'Nathaniel Gubbins'. He attributed the rise of French cuisine in Britain not to the excellence of the food but to the aspirations of newly-rich hostesses like 'dear Lady Thistlebrain', whose place in society was assured the moment she hired a French chef: 'It is extremely probable that, could it be arranged to feed our starving poor, beneath the public gaze, on *sole Normandes, cotelettes à la Reform*, and *salmi de gibier truffe*; to feast our workhouse children on *bisque d'ecrevisses* and *Ananas à la Creole*, the upper classes of Great Britain would soon revert to plain roast and boiled.'[12]

Lady Thistlebrain (who started as a laundress, explained Gubbins, but married well) was a cartoon version of the new money disrupting many of the verities of the British class system in the decades around the turn of the twentieth century. People whose parents never dreamed of such advancement were gaining access to education, opportunity and wealth. Their affluence fuelled the hotels, theatres and shops of a glamorous, magnetic London, and the most conservative among the old-money classes had to close ranks vehemently if they wanted to avoid associating with Jews, or foreigners, or savvy, ambitious tradesmen. Then as now, there was no simple way to define social class in Britain – birth, education, accent, manners, taste and income all contributed, and only the first of these was immutable. Who belonged? Who didn't? More nerve-wracking yet, who might belong next week or next year, given a little luck or the right fiancée?

Trollope, that excellent authority on Victorian class anxiety, made a point of identifying it with culinary anxiety in his novel *Miss Mackenzie*, published in 1865. Several characters assemble for a dinner party at the home of the heroine's sister-in-law, Mrs Mackenzie, who is so eager to stage this affair properly that she hires a butler named Mr Grandairs to supervise the food and service. Mrs Mackenzie chooses the increasingly fashionable *service à la Russe* – the food to be offered in courses rather than set out on the table all at once – and each course is a disaster. The soup, purchased from a shop and laden with Marsala, arrives at the table cold. The fish, 'very ragged in its appearance,' is also cold; and the melted butter has become 'thick and clotted'. Then come three of the fanciful little preparations known as *entrées* – 'so fabricated, that all they who attempted to eat of their contents became at once aware that they had got hold of something very nasty' – followed by the 'inevitable' saddle of mutton and boiled fowls. These were badly carved and bare of sauces, which didn't appear until they were too late to be of use. After all that, Trollope writes, 'Why tell of the ruin, of the maccaroni, of the fine-coloured pyramids of shaking sweet things which nobody would eat [...] the ice-puddings flavoured with onions? It was all misery, wretchedness, and degradation.'[13]

And yet, as Trollope emphasizes, Mrs Mackenzie is not trying to better herself with that pretentious dinner. She never dreams of attempting to pass for a duchess: 'Her place in the world was fixed, and she made no contest as to the fixing. She hoped for no great change in the direction of society.' She stages such a dinner simply because that is how well-bred people are supposed to entertain, and since she doesn't have the money or the experience to do it properly, she does it badly. At this point Trollope, who had clearly eaten more than his share of misbegotten dinners, breaks out of his narrative and addresses his readers directly. Why oh why, he demanded, couldn't 'the ordinary Englishman' with a middle-class income simply offer his friends a little fish and a leg of mutton, rather than a pathetic imitation of a grand banquet? 'Unless the question can get itself answered, ordinary Englishmen must cease to go and eat dinners at each other's houses,' he concluded – a heartfelt declaration of independence from a cuisine he would not, alas, outlive.[14]

Food needed help. It was moving into a position of prominence during Trollope's dinner-going years, bolstered by French influence, but it couldn't possibly articulate the ambitions of hostesses, guests and cooks when so many of them lacked the proper background and when so much was at stake. Menus had to speak up when the food could not. Written descriptions of the meal had to express nuances of class, power and exclusivity that guests might not taste, but that they certainly absorbed. Accuracy mattered less than atmosphere. Language hovered beyond the reach of logic. Menu-writers tried English, they tried French, they tried both, they tried to interlace the two languages, they tried to translate; sometimes they wedged a chunk of one language under the other like a shim to keep the whole edifice steady. Nobody wanted the food to simply announce itself. Chaos was preferable to projecting the wrong class.

French, of course, prevailed as the language of culinary prestige, which meant that the most powerful symbols of British identity, British values, British history and British tradition hastily retreated behind a flourish of French when it was time to eat. Indoors or out, wherever the royal family or their guests picked up a menu – Buckingham

Palace, Ascot, a box at the Opera – it was written in French. Even the royal breakfast menus were in French, including the bacon and eggs ('*Bacon a l'Anglaise*', '*Oeufs pocher*').[15] Members of the King's Guard who ate in the dining room reserved for them at St James's Palace ordered from a French menu. The menu of the restaurant in the House of Commons was French. When the High Sheriff of Lancashire gave a dinner for the grand jury in 1895 (thirteen courses, eight wines), he set a French menu before them. And on those full-dress occasions when Britain celebrated the long and glorious history of the crown itself, bands playing and colours flying – Queen Victoria's Diamond Jubilee, the Coronation of King Edward – the menus were French and proud of it. Monarchs dined at the top of the culinary hierarchy, where the whole world could see them. After all, the whole world understood the difference between 'Soups' and '*Soupes*' even when the former was 'Clear Turtle' and the latter was '*Tortue Claire*'.

Nonetheless, there were times when patriotism tinged with nostalgia demanded an allegiance to English. Restaurants that wanted to evoke a sense of deep-rooted tradition – the Compleat Angler, for instance, an old-fashioned inn on the river outside London, or the Mitre, a restaurant at Hampton Court – kept their menus in English. The Great Eastern Railway Hotel on Liverpool Street upheld the use of English in its menus, and so did the railway's dining car. Simpson's-in-the-Strand, renowned for the joints of beef and mutton wheeled up to the table and carved while guests looked on, was so resolutely British that the only sightings of French in the restaurant were on the wine list. The Royal Bath Hotel in Bournemouth seemed determined to uphold as much English as a first-class dining room reasonably could: the menus for breakfast and lunch were written entirely in English, and only gave way to French at dinner. Even then, while the individual dishes appeared in French, the names of the courses – 'Soups', 'Fish' and so forth – were in English. (An exception had to be made for '*Entrées*', a word with no English equivalent, since it hadn't yet come to mean 'main courses' and the usual translation – 'made dishes' – hardly did justice to a choice between *Escalopes de Ris de Veau Trianon* and *Supremes de Caneton Richelieu Froid*.) As for the two 'Soups', they bore proper French names while still projecting national character: one honoured a royal residence (*Consommé Windsor*) and the other the Queen (*Crème Alexandra*).[16]

Translation problems were the bane of a bifurcated cuisine. When Urbain Dubois's *Cosmopolitan Cookery* appeared in 1870, the author included a sampling of exemplary menus printed in English and French on facing pages. Understandably enough, the translator was helpless in the face of '*quenelles*', '*timbales*' and '*au bleu*', all of which remained French. But he was also at wit's end over '*poulards*' and retained the French there as well, as if 'chickens' could not be entrusted with the task. '*Noix de veau*' became 'veal-cushion', '*foie gras*' was given the inelegant 'fat-liver' and like every other menu-writer he left '*à l'Anglaise*' exactly as it was, suggesting that no conceivable arrangement of English words could begin to convey the meaning of such a term.[17]

Tutoring in French, of course, was once a standard feature of an upper-class childhood. But more and more of the British were dining out – or instructing their cooks – without that benefit. The anonymous author of *Party Giving on Every Scale*, a handbook that listed all the most fashionable dishes and their prices, explained that he was naming every dish in French to make it easier for hostesses to order the menu they wished to serve. 'Some ladies make laughable mistakes when writing out a *menu* in French,' he added, before himself going on to place 'Sweetbreads *à la Financière*' right alongside '*Ris de Veau à la St. Cloud*' as if sweetbreads were immune to translation in one dish but not the other.[18] The Adelphi Hotel in Liverpool was one of the few to confront the problem openly, printing its dinner menu with both languages side by side on a single page – 'at the request of numerous patrons'.[19]

Most often, English and French seem to have been interspersed on the basis of whim or desperation. An otherwise all-French lunch menu at the Grand Hotel resorted to '*Pommes* Chips'; and the writer behind an otherwise all-English dinner menu at the New Welcome Club tried valiantly to translate '*mauviettes en surprise*', only to end up with 'Surprised Larks'.[20] When the Prince of Wales hosted a dinner celebrating the Derby Day races in 1900, a much-loved British sweet appeared on the menu as '*Macedoines de Fruits à la Eton*' – more dignified, presumably, than 'Eton Mess'.[21] By 1908 standards had relaxed, and 'Eton Mess *aux cerises*' was served to the King at an Ascot picnic.[22] But why did the Savoy Hotel, where the *haute cuisine* was exemplary, allow a luxurious French menu to start off with a soup labelled 'Real Turtle'?[23] Turtle soup was standard at upper-class dinners, though the preparation was so laborious that chefs unequal to the task sometimes bought it ready-made – even tinned, if necessary. More déclassé yet was the popular substitute Mock Turtle soup, made with a calf's head. The Savoy seems to have wanted no confusion on this point: the restaurant's turtle soup was made fresh, and it had come from a turtle. Apparently French could not underscore this point strongly enough.

There were also foods deemed so sacred to British gastronomy that chefs sometimes refused to translate them out of respect, the way 'G-d' appears in Jewish texts. Both Ménager and Escoffier had a deep reverence for whitebait, a tiny, definitively local fish that was caught in the Thames amid much seasonal acclaim. A viable French translation existed (*blanchailles*), but Escoffier and Ménager, the most important French chefs in London, insisted on the original even when they had to give it a French tag for descriptive purposes ('Whitebait *Naturel et* à *la Diable*').[24] Similarly, an otherwise all-French menu from the Grand Hotel gave 'Marrow Bones' its own space on the menu, respectfully set off between the *Ris de Veau à la Renaissance* and the *Filets de Boeuf à la Richelieu*.[25] Beef, too, was a word that demanded careful handling. It often appeared as *boeuf*, but there were some occasions when only English would do. Queen Victoria's Jubilee Day dinner featured *saumon, cailles, poulardes* – and 'Roast Beef'.[26] At Ascot, King Edward regularly ate '*Boeuf Rôti*' and '*Boeuf Pressé*' but always 'Derby Beef'.[27] Banquets at the Guildhall, the official headquarters of the Lord Mayor of London, were elaborate affairs that often included a spectacular double sirloin roast known as a baron of beef – a legendary cut that could weigh more than a hundred pounds and was tantamount to showcasing Britain itself on a platter. The catering firm Ring and Brymer was often responsible for the food at these banquets, and typically the dishes were named in French – but not this one. Standing tall in its capital letters, 'BARON OF BEEF' cast a staunchly British identity over the meal even when flanked by *Cailles, Pâtes* and *Petits Turbans Parisiens*.[28]

All this pomp and extravagance did not survive World War I. French-trained cooks, fine ingredients, experienced kitchen staff and the rich themselves were in short supply after the war, and even when conditions eased, tastes and styles had changed. French held on through the 1930s, but it was losing its monopoly on British culinary prestige, and gradually, after more than a century of ignominy, English came into its own as an acceptable medium in which to discuss expensive food. Today the elaborate menus of the Edwardians are relics for collectors and historians – what libraries call 'ephemera'. Gazing at them, it seems impossible to penetrate the bilingual fog that still hangs damply over the food. Perhaps these menus can be most usefully imagined not as guides to food at all, but as outposts in the literature of sentiment, like Victorian poetry. Escoffier took great pride in a dish he called '*Nymphs à l'Aurore*' – 'Frogs at Dawn' – an arrangement of frogs' legs coated in sauce and displayed on a bed of champagne jelly with more champagne jelly to cover. Fresh herbs were tucked here and there to represent 'water-grasses', and the whole thing was served in a block of ice. What moved Escoffier to create this was his conviction that the British only refused to eat frogs because the very word 'frog' was so unpleasant. He thought '*nymphs*', with its genteel air of the mythological, would offer a more appealing image, and when he included the recipe in the *Guide Culinaire* he reported with satisfaction that his new word for 'frog' had been 'universally adopted'.[29] This last was wishful thinking, but the dish itself won many admirers – perhaps for its excellence, and surely because it came from Escoffier. Guests at the Carlton expected to eat the finest food in the world, and there can be no better seasoning in any language than an appetite primed for bliss.

345

Notes

1. 'Cuisine Notes and Notions', *Food and Cookery*, November 1898, p. 300.
2. 'Hors d'Oeuvre', *Food and Cookery*, July 1900, p. 196.
3. *Food and Cookery*, March 1901, p. 67.
4. 'Our Chairman', *Food and Cookery*, August 1898, p. 223.
5. 'Hors d'Oeuvre', *Food and Cookery*, December 1902, p. 420.
6. Charles Elmé Francatelli, *The Modern Cook* (London: Richard Bentley, 1846), p. vi.
7. C. Herman Senn, *Recherché Luncheon and Dinner Sweets* (London: The Food and Cookery Publishing Agency, 1906), p. 16; A.B. Marshall, *Mrs. A.B. Marshall's Larger Cookery Book of Extra Recipes* (London: Marshall's School of Cookery, 1891), p. 464; 'Our Menu Album', *Food and Cookery*, August 1898, p. 233; *Party Giving on Every Scale* (London: F. Warne and Co., 188-?), p. 192.
8. Menu, 'Luncheon by the London Chamber of Commerce', 7 June 1901, Buttolph Menu Collection, New York Public Library (NYPL); Menu, 'City Déjeuner to Their Majesties, The King and Queen, Saturday, October 25th, 1902', in *The Epicure*, November 1902, p. 367; Menu, 'Royal Luncheon at the

Guildhall on Saturday, October 25th, 1902', Buttolph Menu Collection, NYPL.

9. Theodore Garrett, *The Encyclopaedia of Practical Cookery*, 2 vols (London: L.U. Gill, 1898), vol. I, p. 932.

10. Auguste Escoffier, *Le Guide Culinaire* (Paris: 1903), p. 383; *A Guide to Modern Cookery* (London: William Heinemann, 1907), p. 738.

11. Virginia Woolf, 'Professions for Women', in *The Death of the Moth and Other Essays* (New York: Harcourt Brace Jovanovich, 1974), p. 237.

12. Edward Spencer, *Cakes & Ale* (London: Grant Richards, 1897), pp. 74-75.

13. Anthony Trollope, *Miss Mackenzie* (London: Chapman and Hall, 1865; repr. New York: Dover, 1986), p. 97; p. 99; p. 101.

14. Trollope, p. 102.

15. Gabriel Tschumi, *Royal Chef* (London: William Kimber, 1954), p. 103.

16. 'A Hotel de Luxe of the South', *Food and Cookery*, September 1903, p. 329.

17. Urbain Dubois, *Cosmopolitan Cookery* (London: Longman's, Green and Co., 1895), pp. xxvii, xiv, xxvii; p. xiv; pp. ix, xv, xix.

18. *Party Giving on Every Scale*, p. 178.

19. Menu, Dinner, Adelphi Hotel, Liverpool, 31 August 1906, Buttolph Menu Collection, NYPL.

20. Menu, Lunch, Grand Hotel, London, 15 June 1898, Buttolph Menu Collection, NYPL; 'Our Menu Album', *Food and Cookery*, March and April 1898, p. 119.

21. 'Our Menus', *Food and Cookery*, July 1900, p. 211.

22. Tschumi, p. 115.

23. Menu, Lunch, Savoy Hotel, 21 February 1900, Buttolph Menu Collection, NYPL.

24. 'Our Chairman', p. 224; Escoffier, *Memories of My Life*, trans. by Laurence Escoffier (New York: Van Nostrand Reinhold, 1997), p. 127.

25. Menu, Dinner, the Farmers' Club, Grand Hotel, London, 22 March 1898, Buttolph Menu Collection, NYPL.

26. 'The Royal Menu', *Food and Cookery*, September 1897, p. 9.

27. Menu, Box at Ascot Races, 21 June 1906, Buttolph Menu Collection, NYPL.

28. Menu, Visit of Colonial Prime Ministers, Déjeuner in the Guildhall, 16 April 1907, Buttolph Menu Collection, NYPL.

29. Escoffier, *Guide to Modern Cookery*, p. 152.

The Rhetoric of Salmon: The War of Words, Images and Metaphors in the Battle of Wild-caught vs. Farmed Salmon

Richard Warren Shepro

Salmon breeding breeds controversy. Traditionally, indigenous species of salmon returning from the ocean to the rivers where they were born were fished in those same rivers and eaten locally. But change has created stress. Salmon stocks have been declining in most regions for centuries, perhaps millennia.[1] Fishing methods developed, allowing salmon to be tracked and captured before they enter their rivers.[2] In the late nineteenth century, artificial breeding and raising of salmon in hatcheries, originally called 'fish factories', placing juvenile salmon ('smolts') in rivers and flushing them to the ocean became common in a possibly misguided effort to replenish stocks.[3] The use of hatcheries has grown to the point where every year many billions of hatchery salmon are placed in rivers leading to the North Pacific and North Atlantic oceans, more by weight than all the adult salmon, wild or hatchery, that return.[4]

Fish farming, in which hatchery salmon are transferred to salt-water pens and raised in captivity to maturity, became commercially feasible in Norway in the 1960s and quickly dwarfed the fishing industry in number of salmon caught.[5] Developments in the international market in fresh fish ensured that fresh wild-caught and farmed salmon could both be distributed around the world.[6]

The magnitude of these transformations has challenged people's traditions, taste memories and preferences, and can destroy or ensure their livelihoods and enhance or bankrupt their communities. It can also lead to dramatic ecological change. Extensive arguments have been advanced about the effects of hatchery salmon and farming on wild salmon and, in turn, of the effects of the decline of salmon (for whatever reason) on other fish, and even on forests, birds and land animals.[7]

This paper concerns perception, argument and marketing in communications, largely by fishers and farmers. Some scientific sources will be useful in examining claims, but for the most part the paper tries to emphasize rhetoric and argument rather than who is right and who is wrong. The rhetorical battleground includes all communications tools, pictures as well as words.

* * *

You all sat here and chowed down on farmed salmon and obviously you don't give a shit about what you're putting into your body. You know what a farmed salmon is? It's filled with toxic chemicals.

> David Suzuki, Canadian environmentalist, speaking to a luncheon audience at the National Press Club of Australia, 2006[8]

I like to use quality Scottish [farmed] salmon fed on as natural a diet as possible. I get this from Loch Duart.

> Gordon Ramsay.

I believe they are the gold standard of farmed fish.

> Raymond Blanc.

This is the closest thing I have ever seen to a wild salmon.

> Rick Stein.[9]

The crystal-clean flavour of wild Atlantic salmon has become almost as rare as the fish itself [.... I]ts replacement, farmed salmon, is as different to it as grouse is to chicken. One has tasted the wild and tastes of it; the other is all about domesticity: less exercised, less adventurous and, in the case of salmon, the poorer for it.

> Rose Prince, 10 August 2011, *The Telegraph*[10]

The purity of the wild Alaska salmon is based more on myth than reality [...]. And while Alaskans look down their noses at salmon farming (it's not allowed), they encourage salmon ranching – a variation on salmon farming that sees fish raised in pens until they are big enough to fend for themselves, and then let go into the wild. The creme de la creme of Alaskan wild salmon is the Copper River run, and every year its arrival on the market in May is greeted with the same enthusiasm and hoopla applied to the arrival of Beaujolais wine from France. But guess what – it's laced with PCBs.

> Don Whitely, The Washington Fish Growers Association.[11]

Real salmon don't eat pellets.

> Fishing industry slogan

* * *

I focus on two species key to gastronomy, *Salmo salar* (known as 'Atlantic salmon') and *Oncorhynchus tshawytscha* (a Pacific salmon known as 'King' or 'Chinook'), because they have similar flesh and are often viewed as culinary substitutes for each other. A more plentiful Pacific salmon, *Oncorhynchus nerka* (usually known as 'Sockeye'), a very different tasting fish with different cooking properties, is occasionally discussed. Traditionally canned, it has increased in popularity as a fresh fish.

UN Statistics reflect 'global capture' and 'global aquaculture product'. By 1986, considering Atlantic and King salmon, farmed Atlantic salmon already had the leading market share:

Farmed Atlantic salmon: 58,979 metric tons (64% of total)
Wild-caught King: 21,187 (23%)
Wild-caught Atlantic: 11,727 (13%)
Farmed King: 698 (less than 1%)
TOTAL: 92,591

Farming has grown exponentially, while wild-caught fish catch has declined. For 2012:

Farmed Atlantic: 2,066,560 metric tons (99% of total)
Farmed King: 14,085 (less than 1%)
Wild-caught King: 8072 (less than 0.4%)
Wild-caught Atlantic: 2580 (about 0.1%)
TOTAL: 2,091,297[12]

Even if Sockeye and Coho salmon, many times more plentiful than King, were included in the wild-caught totals, the wild-caught percentages would remain minuscule. Farmers won the economic battle decades ago; rhetorically, the battle continues, with farmers facing an uphill battle.

A Short Salmon Primer

Thinking there are only two kinds of salmon, 'wild' and farmed, is a serious mistake. Many people generalize about the differences between wild-caught and farmed salmon without acknowledging, often without realizing, that they are usually comparing different kinds of fish, not just different species but fish from different genera.

Biologically, there are eight species of salmon across two genera. In the wild, one genus, with only one salmon species, *Salmo salar,* is found in the north Atlantic and rivers that empty into it. This is the salmon that led to such words as 'salmon', 'saumon', 'salmo' and 'salmone' in English, French, Catalan and Italian. All the others are from the north Pacific, from a different genus, *Oncorhynchus,* that also includes most trout.

Salmon are anadromous, meaning that they are born and develop in fresh water, move in a later stage of life to the sea, and eventually return to fresh water to spawn. Atlantic and Pacific salmon have a different life cycle: Pacific salmon spawn and then die. Atlantic salmon have a chance to spawn and return to the ocean. Different species look and taste different.

Salmon can reproduce naturally in riverbeds, or they can be conceived and raised in a hatchery. Hatchery salmon can either be released to rivers ('ranched') near the completion of their fresh water stage, or reared in captivity ('farmed'). A salmon caught by a fisherman cannot easily be identified as wild, ranched, or escaped from a farm, hence the common euphemism, 'wild-caught'.

An Uncommon Historical Comparison

Atlantic salmon, *Salmo salar*, is now rare in the wild in North America and seriously depleted in Europe. Because most farmed salmon is *Salmo salar*, comparisons of wild versus farmed salmon are usually also comparing *Salmo* to *Oncorhynchus*. As a result, it might be instructive to examine historical comparisons of Atlantic and Pacific salmon made before farming became widespread, in order to isolate the differences created by the type of fish. Unfortunately, few informed commentators in the past seemed to have experienced both, so they wrote with an enthusiasm not clouded by comparisons.[13] Most who did know both seem to have been Americans familiar with both coasts, and the consensus seems strongly to favour *Salmo salar*.

James Beard (1903-1985) grew up in Oregon, later established his career in New York, and eventually had cooking schools on both coasts. He grew up with Pacific salmon, seems to have loved all salmon, but largely treats salmon as just salmon: 'There are several varieties of Pacific salmon – Chinook is perhaps the best known-and the meat varies in color from very pale pink to reddish. Eastern salmon is usually paler than the western salmon found in the markets, and some people contend that the flesh is not so firm.'[14]

Waverley Root (1903-1982), who made his reputation as a connoisseur more than as an instructor, was not quite so accepting:

> The most important influence on taste [...] seems to be the species. Nobody disagrees with the judgment that the Atlantic salmon, *Salmo Salar* [...] is the best [...]. Pacific salmon are in general ranked below Atlantic salmon for flavor [...]. In the descending order of flavorfulness they are as follows: 1. The Chinook salmon, *O. tshawytscha*. Its tastiness is legitimately won [...] 2. The sockeye salmon, *O. nerka* [...] 3. The coho salmon, *O. kisutch* [...] 4. The pink salmon, *O. gorbuschka* [...] 5. The chum salmon, *O. keta*, is little valued for its flesh, which is yellowish or an unappetizing pink.[15]

Root's rank order of Pacific salmon is generally accepted today.

The chef and *New York Times* writer Pierre Franey (1921-1996) and his restaurant critic colleague, Bryan Miller, were equally unequivocal, noting the availability of salmon from both coasts and declaring, 'Atlantic salmon is recognized as the best in flavor and texture, with top honors going to those from the rivers of Ireland and Scotland; they are also the most costly.'[16]

Today, the phrase 'Atlantic salmon' has become sullied, a reason for rejection by some consumers as an indication that the fish has been farmed, but these same place names, now indicating a farming location, are still used to attract consumers, along with new locations that sound attractive enough for marketing, such as the Faroe Islands, Tasmania and New Zealand. 'Norwegian salmon', in contrast, seems to be a dirty word in England, a bit more accepted in France and a positive in some parts of the United States, where people may see the name and believe it to be wild.

Changes in supply often shape preferences and judgments. A flood of inexpensive farmed *Salmo salar* has made some people disdain Atlantic salmon, formerly a luxury product, perhaps because of negative rhetoric but perhaps because it has become common. Some in North America, looking for differences between wild and farmed fish, are beginning to think the exemplar of wild salmon is Sockeye, possibly because it is cheaper and more plentiful than King, possibly because it looks and tastes so different from *Salmo salar* that 'this must be what wild salmon is'.

However, for those who recognize the differences in genus and species and prefer the taste of *Salmo salar*, quality farmed salmon may be their best opportunity to continue that experience.

Appeal to Authenticity: The Call of the Wild

There is drama and majesty to these fish. The first stanza of Robert Lowell's important poem, 'Waking Early Sunday Morning' (1967), reads:

> O to break loose, like the chinook
> salmon jumping and falling back,
> nosing up to the impossible
> stone and bone-crushing waterfall –
> raw-jawed, weak-fleshed there, stopped by ten
> steps of the roaring ladder, and then
> to clear the top on the last try,
> alive enough to spawn and die.

Lowell, a Boston Brahmin, gives a heroic narrative to the Pacific salmon, describing its tribulations caused by damming of rivers. The dramatic life-cycle of the wild fish, spawning and dying, becomes a hero to best the worst industrial society can provide, a dam, blocking the upstream return to the spawning grounds, creating the bone-crushing waterfall and offering well-intentioned but ineffectual fish ladders.

Farmers and fishers both claim this majesty by association with wild waters and the nobility and vitality of the fish. Fishers emphasize their connection to the wild with photographs of bears eating salmon in the wild, and gorgeous landscapes. With encouragement from marketing materials, consumers are free to imagine their wild salmon as caught by a solitary fisherman in waders standing in a river with a rod and reel.

But farmers? For them, a key theme is purity of water and nobility of surroundings, beautiful photographs of seacoast near mountains. Here from a French website about a prized type of farmed salmon that has been awarded the *Label Rouge* designation – accompanied by glistening photographs of the Scottish Highlands:

> This harsh and inhospitable climate for humans becomes a stomping ground for the breeding of *Salmo salar*, particularly the Label Rouge Scottish Salmon. Mountain water in the streams and rivers provide ideal resources for the growth of young fish in freshwater ponds until transfer to the sea. Cold-water salty lochs take over. Brewed by currents and tides, this dynamic environment encourages salmon to swim constantly, helping to ensure their firm flesh and lean bodies, contributing to superior quality.[17]

Like Melville's Captain Ahab, fish farmers can peer into the souls of the sea and its creatures. The website for 'Skuna Bay' (a trademark, not a place) Atlantic salmon farmed in British Columbian *Onchorynchus* country boasts photographs of Vancouver Island's rocky coastline with workers dressed like fishermen and proclaims, 'The Skuna Bay craftsman farmer stands alone in the teeth of mother nature, using his experience and judgment to raise good fish.' Scottish Development International, a government agency, asserts in promotional material that the fish farmer 'instinctively knows and understands his fish'.

Other farmers consider this expansive rhetoric to be 'green-washing', and the same environments are described by detractors – such as salmonfarmingkills.com and *gaaia. org/fishyleaks* ('the watery world's response to WikiLeaks') – as creating the 'Silent Spring of the Sea', a chemical cesspool producing fish unfit for human consumption, despoiling the environment for wild fish.

The nice smoked salmon sold by 'Ducktrap River of Maine' ('Naturally Smoked in Maine') is indeed smoked in Maine, and its advertisements emphasize unspoiled seacoast and the forests of Maine, even bragging about the local types of wood used for the smoking. The salmon itself is farmed in Chile by the Norwegian company, Marine Harvest, which owns Ducktrap and is the largest farmer of salmon in the world.

Attacks on the Authenticity of The Other

There is a certain amount of regional pride (or prejudice) that can lead people to say of other regions' fish, 'That is not salmon. Period.' I experienced a person from British Columbia referring to salmon-obsessed Seattle and Portland: 'Southerners don't know about salmon. Do salmon runs even exist south of the border?' Europeans may not know that the Pacific salmon genus even exists. These are conventional regional prejudices, resulting in part from a lack of information. But with a little more knowledge, one person's 'environmentally caring fish farm' becomes another's 'industrial factory'.

Wild-caught Pacific salmon are derided as 'hatchery-based' and not wild at all. In the Columbia River in the US Pacific Northwest, 'greater than 80% of the outmigrating smolts [...] are of hatchery origin.'[18] In Prince William Sound, Alaska, and Iturup

Island, Russia, more than 50% of salmon caught come from hatcheries.[19] Yet 'Wild Alaska Salmon' is the constant phrase in both private and Alaska government materials. Use of hatcheries, if mentioned, is termed 'salmon enhancement', just giving the species a little boost. Fish farming is illegal in Alaska, but shellfish farming is not. The word 'aquaculture' is too connected to fish farming so shellfish farming in Alaska is known as mariculture.

'Wild' is assumed to be the reference point, so simply using the term is a key fisher strategy, as is emphasizing the term 'Atlantic salmon' as a synonym for farmed, inauthentic and inferior.

The colour of farm-raised salmon is attacked as an indication of inauthenticity. In the wild, flesh colour depends on the locale and the species: some salmon eat more or less of foods, such as krill, that give their flesh a rose-coloured or red hue. Unlike most fish, salmonids store carotenoids in their flesh. A key carotenoid is astaxanthin, the pigment that gives lobsters and shrimp shells their colour. Farmed salmon get their carotenoids from their feed. These are not just colorants: they 'are essential for their proper growth and survival' and also important to success with consumers.[20] Critics of farming call these carotenoids 'dye', a highly coloured word. One prominent sport fisherman goes a step farther: 'Most people know now that farm salmon are pink owing to in-feed dye and that without it they would be the same grey as the sludge underneath the places they were reared.'[21] Use of the term 'dye' has led many people to imagine colour is sprayed or injected into the dead fish after processing. Colour fans, a paint-chip-style numbering system used by egg, poultry and salmon businesses to standardize their products, seem to be viewed as a particularly cynical salmon-farming device, and pictures of the 'DSM SalmoFan' went viral on the Internet following a 12 March 2015, blog that asserted, fancifully, that 'pigmenting supplements are the most expensive component of the farmed salmon diet, constituting up to 20% of feed costs'.[22]

Meanwhile, an albino variety of King salmon cannot metabolize carotenoids and winds up whitish grey. These off-colour salmon sold at lower prices than normal King until they were rebranded 'Ivory King'.[23]

Ecosystem/Biosphere Health

Management and restoration of salmon populations is a thorny problem even in the absence of hatcheries and salmon farming. Growing human population and accelerating industrialization simply are not in the interests of salmon. Dams producing electricity restrict access to rivers; logging, housing and industry disturb the ecosystems of the rivers. More fresh water for humans means less for salmon.

Some argue you need to eat the fish to save them. The argument is: only if the fish are perceived as valuable will anyone work to improve conditions. The opposite argument is: we should not eat wild salmon until stocks recover. A leading proponent of this approach is Orri Vigfússon, who founded the North Atlantic Salmon Fund in part to pay fisherman not to fish for salmon and to help them find new jobs. Fishing,

353

or 'overfishing', use of hatcheries, and farming all can deplete the supply of wild krill, squid and other bottom-of-the-food-chain fish, reducing the availability of food for wild salmon and other fish.

Hatcheries compound the problems by introducing genetic issues. Overuse of hatcheries can result in the loss of adaptive genetic variation in the wild. Hatchery fish compete and may breed with wild fish, reducing biodiversity. Hatchery operators even call competing indigenous fish 'feral fish' and deride their impact on their hatchery stocks; one said, 'feral salmon in a river were a disease threat to fish in a nearby fish factory [hatchery] and so the feral fish should be destroyed.'[24]

Raising hatchery fish to adulthood – farming – adds additional ecological issues. Where there is a native salmon population, fish farms add one more human development to interfere with salmon runs. Escaped farmed fish may breed with wild stocks, just like hatchery fish. Farms in areas without native salmon (including all the Southern Hemisphere) introduce a non-native species that could cause unintended consequences. Open net-pen marine salmon farming is a relatively new business, with many potential problems and a lot of experimentation in technique. Responsible farmers try to prevent escapes, sea lice and algal blooms.

Hatchery and farmed fish, living in open pools, produce considerable waste. Some farming regions, such as the Faroe Islands, emphasize their strong ocean currents that flush out salmon cages. As with any animal husbandry, confinement in too close quarters fosters disease, and salmon farmers, like chicken farmers, vary in how much space they allow. At times, farmers have tried to fight disease with antibiotics, but a better long-term solution is to give the animals more room. Use of antibiotics, a troublesome issue already at hatcheries, is even more troublesome if antibiotics are dropped into open pens in the marine environment, particularly if a large excess flows out of the pen. Some farming jurisdictions, such as Norway and the Faroe Islands, prohibit use of antibiotics. Elsewhere, pressure from customers and desire for rating organization approval (discussed below) eliminate or restrict antibiotics' use.

Fish farmers don't seem to deny any of these potential issues, responding like free-range chicken farmers: We're trying, and it's the other guy who causes these problems, not me. If pressed, they may say wild salmon are disappearing because of their real enemy, the world ecosystem. Leave wild fish alone to recover. But people are hungry, wild salmon is scarce, and through our responsible efforts we can feed the world, cheaply.[25]

The serious discourse about health of fish and the environment carried out by scientists and government bodies is not mirrored by newspaper and popular writing, where problems identified decades ago, to which there is a response, are simply repeated as reasons to avoid eating farmed salmon. An inflammatory, ill-informed, out-of-date blog by 'investigative food journalist' Barry Estabrook, 'Five Things I Will Not Eat', which made its way into *Best Food Writing 2014*, posits insoluble problems and deadens the appetite:

A salmon farm [...] is [...] a floating feedlot. Excrement, uneaten food, and dead fish fall into the ocean, along with a witch's brew of drugs and disease organisms that can kill wild salmon unlucky enough to swim in the vicinity. Farmed salmon are susceptible to infectious salmon anaemia, aquaculture's answer to highly contagious hoof-and-mouth disease [...]. Captive salmon also spread sea lice to wild fish. The parasites feed on the mucous, blood, and skin and can kill young salmon.[26]

Appeals Regarding Human Health

Testaments to the health benefits of omega-3 fatty acids found in all salmon lead to arguments about whose salmon has more. There are debates, too, concerning adulterants and contaminants that can come from diet or water pollution and raise purity issues for both wild-caught and farmed fish, so there is ample room for both improvement and invective. Levels of impurities are monitored and vary greatly by location, sometimes higher in one source than another but for salmon, unlike some other fish, generally within accepted (and, of course, debatable) government guidelines.

Health is a frequent media topic, and comments by nutritionists may be less than fully informed. One, on CNN, extolled the virtues of omega-3 in farmed salmon but urged boiling it 'to cut down on the fat' (the only place omega-3 fatty acids are found). Estabrook again exemplifies the inflammatory rhetoric that encourages blogosphere repetition: 'Studies have shown that farmed salmon contains significantly higher levels of chemicals known to cause everything from neurological damage to cancer than wild salmon.'[27] But which farmed salmon? 'Cause everything'? What type of cancer? Which wild salmon from what area? And, of course, whether levels in any salmon are high enough to worry about. Estabrook writes in the style of activists who describe poor practices at 'factory' chicken farms to argue against eating chicken altogether. He urges substituting tilapia, a tasteless fish, or 'Wild salmon from Alaska [...] its taste will remind you why you wanted to eat salmon in the first place' (which will not be true for those who were looking for the taste of *Salmo salar*).[28]

Media reports raising health issues have significant effects on farmed salmon purchases, at least in the short term.[29] In contrast, even some investigators raised under the Pacific Northwest 'theology' that 'farmed salmon is a blasphemy', have revised their views after visiting and studying farms. One such food safety expert observed, 'Most of what people think they know about aquaculture salmon is obsolete, or wasn't true in the first place.'[30]

Public health scientists worry less about fine differences favouring fish from a particular farmer or fishery, and more that fear of contaminants leads consumers to avoid salmon: Omega-3 health benefits for any kind of salmon are said to dwarf the effects of contaminants.[31] Where PCB contamination is present but within government guidelines (typical with both farmed and wild-caught salmon), an analysis from the

Harvard School of Public Health estimates that if 100,000 people ate salmon twice a week for seventy years, 'the extra PCB intake could potentially cause 24 extra deaths from cancer – but [the salmon] would prevent at least 7,000 deaths from heart disease.'[32]

Communities

Salmon farming can change the economic dynamic of sparsely populated coastal towns. On the one hand, there is investment and employment. Although some of the most celebrated and award-winning salmon farms are small, the industry is dominated by a handful of corporations of significant size, the largest of which is Marine Harvest. (Though often described by opponents as giant multinationals, even Marine Harvest is considered a 'mid-cap' company, not huge compared to, say, the largest poultry producers, which are about three times its size.)

Fishermen and environmental activists generally oppose any new fish farm through the courts and governmental agencies, particularly in areas where fishing and farming would coexist. A key battleground has been British Columbia.[33] Some argue that farming drives fishermen's prices down, 'forcing thousands of wild-salmon fishermen off the water,' turning 'small independent fishermen into low-paid factory workers at the local salmon farm'.[34]

On the other hand, some view farms as a response to declining wild stocks, not a cause, and celebrate the benefit to local communities. Loch Duart, a highly regarded independent farm in Scotland, argues its presence builds local communities:

> The ecological imperative [...] suggests a need to preserve a way of life and preserve traditional rural values, but of a way of life that has actually just begun. As our fishing fleets dwindle and the days of the "sea hunter" decline, the future of fish protein as a source of food for us is under threat. Unless we find efficient ways to farm in the sea, we will remove the option for most people to eat fish [.... T]his form of farming must become a way of life for coastal communities, otherwise they too will decline as they have for the last 50 years. Sea fish farming has to become a tradition, just like all the other rural professions – or we will lose these communities.[35]

A line of U.S. court decisions affirms special fishing rights for native peoples, allowing, however, regulation by Federal and state governments.[36] In some cases, native people have a near-monopoly on the product, such as on the long Yukon River, whose wild King salmon are prized but increasingly rare. Through their marketing arm, Kwik-pak Fisheries, the Yupik are able to communicate the remarkable quality of their product, the care they take in harvesting, and the significance of the fish to their people over the past several thousand years. However, with quotas and restrictions on timing of fishing aimed at preserving the fish, they struggle economically.[37]

Appeals by Association with Those Who Know

Few rhetorical devices are as powerful as guilt or praise by association. Savvy salmon farms have obtained endorsements from respected chefs, particularly chefs known well in places where both wild-caught and farmed salmon are found. Chefs appreciate reliable, uniform products, so high-quality farmed salmon appeals to them (though many like the word 'wild' on their menu so much it appears even when the fish is farmed). On 24 September 2014, The Wall Street Journal presented a large feature story entitled, 'Top Chefs, Grocers Choose Farmed Salmon: Even Fish Snobs Are Ordering Better-Tasting Varieties From New Sources'. But nofarmedsalmon.com ('No farmed salmon, […] Just say NO! Pass this site to every chef you know. Don't Eat Farmed Salmon At All.') takes an opposite approach, fingering chefs who previously opposed farmed salmon and now embrace it.

Publicly available information about the economics of endorsement is rarely available, but in 2004 the office of the Governor of Alaska announced the initial success of a $10 million application of state marketing funds that 'positions Alaska salmon as a premier product' at Legal Sea Foods' thirty restaurants from Boston to Florida, quoting Roger Berkowitz, Legal's CEO: 'We […] have always appreciated Alaska wild salmon as the finest in the world.'[38] Today, Legal Sea Foods features Faroe Islands farmed salmon, and its web site states, 'We think […] aquaculture that utilizes the highest levels of sanitation, environmental safeguards and is antibiotic-free should be supported'.[39]

The development of rating organizations whose approval farmers and fishers seek may be improving both farming and fishing practices. These organizations rate fisheries and farms based on 'sustainability', and ratings can improve if practices change. The most followed organizations are the Seafood Watch program of the Monterey Bay Aquarium in California and a pair initiated by the World Wildlife Fund: the Marine Stewardship Council ('MSC') for fishing and the Aquaculture Stewardship Council ('ASC') for farming. Seafood Watch has been sceptical of farming (other than in contained, recirculating water pens) but in November 2014 gave its highest rating ('*Best Choice*') for the first time to a salmon farming community, the freshwater hatcheries and open net marine pens used to raise King salmon in New Zealand; on the wild side, only salmon from Alaska and the Fraser River received this rating. Other wild fisheries have been rated '*Good Alternative*', along with a single farm producer, the Verlasso salmon farms in Chile, run by the Chilean company AquaChile (which is itself partially owned by Marine Harvest). All other farms are still rated '*Avoid*'.

The MSC, unlike Seafood Watch, has been sceptical of hatchery salmon in Alaska, and Alaska's troubled relationship with the MSC led Alaska to withdraw from the certification program in 2012, returning in 2015. A mysterious, anonymous web site, *alaskasalmonranching.com*, emphasizes the MSC's concern: 'What we take issue with is dishonest promoters of Alaska seafood who insist on covering up the fact that the Alaskan salmon industry heavily relies on aquaculture.' A newer rating organization, the Sustainable Fish Partnership, has a more complex rating system, aimed more at helping fisheries improve sustainability and less at consumers. It does not rate farms and presents concerns about hatcheries.

Farms eager for sustainability credentials have been working to gain ASC endorsement. In 2014 a salmon farm (Villa Arctic AS Jarfjord Farm in Norway) gained ASC certification for the first time. By June 2015, there were forty-six farms, in Australia, Canada, Chile, the Faroe Islands, Norway and Scotland, that had received an ASC certificate. The 'Global Salmon Initiative' of seventeen companies representing over 70% of global salmon farming, has committed to ensuring that its members' farms all meet the ASC Salmon standard by 2020.

Minds do change. One wild salmon fish store now 'promotes one brand of farm-raised Atlantic salmon' from the Faroe Islands and 'one brand' of King, farmed in New Zealand, while continuing to urge its customers to boycott other farmed salmon as 'farmed and dangerous'.[40]

Freshness is rarely discussed, but farms have a tremendous advantage because they can control feeding and the timing of slaughter (or 'harvest,' the word they prefer) to minimize bacterial contamination from the guts of the fish, then chill, pack and deliver the fish immediately.[41] Farms may be loath to trumpet their advantages for fear of playing into the vision of industrially-produced fish. Cooks have been more likely to recognize the benefits. James Peterson describes his first encounter with hyper-fresh Norwegian farmed salmon with enthusiasm like Keats first looking into Homer: 'when I opened the Styrofoam box I saw a beautiful fish, bright silver with black clear eyes, still slippery from the sea, and smelling like an immaculate beach.'[42] Julia Child 'fumed' at 'romantics', who 'feel we should eat wild instead of farmed salmon, even though you don't know the condition of the salmon on the line'.[43] Alaskan and other fishermen have been making efforts to improve fishing and handling processes to provide comparably fresh fish.[44]

Flavour and Taste

Flavour is implied more than written about, through photographs of raw and cooked salmon, and by association with the concept of 'the wild' mentioned above. 'Wild' proponents posit 'complex' flavour – difficult to describe – and sometimes say farmed salmon is 'greasy', but acclaim Yukon river salmon, the fattiest of all.

A 2013 'blind tasting' described in *The Washington Post* claimed 'judgments [...] definitive, and surprising. Farmed salmon beat wild salmon, hands down [.... W]e could not consistently tell which was which'.[45] The article made quite a stir, although it was comparing three different species without acknowledging the complications that adds. The author of the study later said, sensibly, 'The conclusion here isn't that farmed salmon invariably tastes better than wild, it's that we think there's good reason to stop saying that wild salmon invariably tastes better than farmed.'[46] Other comparative tastings have been less careful, introducing more extraneous variables, but are intriguing (and amusing) because of the rhetoric involved: what, after all, is the line between 'creamy and rich' and 'greasy', or between 'full-flavored' and 'fishy'?[47]

Among serious authors, James Peterson, an appreciator of farmed salmon, notes the greater variability of wild fish: 'I still eat wild salmon [...] because it's different, not because it's necessarily better. True, I occasionally happen upon a fish that has a celestial flavor but every fish is slightly different, an element of unpredictability that makes eating wild salmon more interesting.'[48] Paul Johnson, a true wild fish expert, writes similarly: 'Wild salmon, like my wild blackberries, changes with the weather and the season. It's not always perfect, but when it is, you sit up straight and take notice.'[49]

Rating organizations eschew discussion of taste as too subjective, except for the French government-sponsored assurance of quality, *Label Rouge*. In 1994, Scottish salmon farmers achieved the first *Label Rouge* for seafood, and the first for a non-French product. In France, where Pacific salmon is rare, the top fish merchants tout their *Label Rouge* (now extended to Norwegian producers) or salmon certified as 'bio' (*biologique* [organic]). The requirements for these designations are mutually exclusive. Loch Duart salmon, aiming for the *Label Rouge,* imitates the diet of wild salmon, with at least 75% natural seafood products. Irish organic salmon needs to keep natural seafood under 50% of the feed so that a majority of the feed can be certified 'organic'.[50]

Decades ago, James Le Coquet, food editor of *Le Figaro*, found a farmed salmon 'perfectly insipid [...] no longer a hard-bellied athlete. You could sink a finger into its flesh as if it were an eiderdown coverlet'. He concluded, 'Salmon are like men: too soft a life is not good for them.'[51] This is no longer the French view.[52] *Saumon Label Rouge* is now appreciated in France not only for the low-density of the pens and the quality of the feed but most of all for the taste: '*c'est la certitude d'un poisson ferme mais fondant, à la chair de couleur soutenue et modérément grasse, au goût délicat.*'[53]

Sport fisherman and severe critic of farming James Wigan, well acquainted with the taste of wild *Salmo salar*, has his own response to Le Coquet: he actually approves of a particular salmon farm in the Scottish Hebrides and gives his test for farming density. In crowded 'feedlot' farms, 'all the fish swim in the same direction, wide-eyed zombies on invisible circuits'. When there are only four hundred fish in a nine cubic meter cage, 'there is room to swim both ways. They glide about, as in an aquarium. . .they taste better'.[54] Low-density farms in water with strong currants have a similar advantage.[55]

Conclusion

A report published by the World Wildlife Fund in 2007 to examine economic and policy issues related to wild and farmed salmon in North America concluded by urging 'government, scientists, the wild and farmed salmon industries [...] and the press' to avoid 'misinformation [...] or overstating the degree of certainty of scientific knowledge', in part to keep consumers from losing confidence in all salmon. Focusing its advice on the 'wild' salmon industry, it urged moving away from 'the simplistic perspective that policy makers and consumers face a choice between wild salmon and farmed salmon', and to 'recognize the role of hatcheries'.[56] There is a gulf still between rhetoric and science, possibly more today in journalism than even in advertising.

Peaceful coexistence may be the proper response, recognizing that aquaculture and hatchery practices need to continue to improve methods and practices and that fishermen should continue to improve handling, processing and delivery methods, all with a focus on environmental sustainability.

Notes

1. Frank Jensen, 'Synopsis on the Abundance of Atlantic Salmon (Salmo salar L.) since the Last Ice Age', *Millennium Report of the Museum of Natural History* (Aarhus, Denmark: Museum of Natural History, 1991), qtd. in Paul Greenberg, *Four Fish: The Future of the Last Wild Food* (New York: Penguin 2010), pp. 267-68.
2. Jim Lichatowich, *Salmon Without Rivers: A History of the Pacific Salmon Crisis* (Washington, D.C.: Island Press, 1999), pp. 95-110.
3. Peter Coates, *Salmon* (London: Reaktion, 2006), pp. 85-95.
4. Jim Lichatowich, *Salmon, People and Place: A Biologist's Search for Salmon Recovery* (Corvallis: Oregon State University Press, 2013), p. 3; Colin E. Nash, *The History of Aquaculture* (Ames: Wiley-Blackwell, 2011), pp. 51-78, p. 145.
5. There is also a small industry raising hatchery salmon in salt-water inland tanks, which many environmentalists approve of as causing a minimum of interference with natural fisheries. AquAdvantage, a much publicized and feared or welcomed Atlantic salmon, genetically modified with a growth-hormone gene from King salmon, was under review by government authorities in the US and Canada for over two decades and was approved in 2015 by the US Food & Drug Administration only for production in inland tanks (U.S. Food & Drug Administration, 'Questions and Answers on FDA's Approval of AquAdvantage Salmon', 19 November 19 2015 <http://www.fda.gov/AnimalVeterinary/DevelopmentApprovalProcess/GeneticEngineering/GeneticallyEngineeredAnimals/ucm473237.htm> [accessed 15 May 2015]).
6. Richard Shepro, 'Degrees of Freshness: The Contemporary International Market for Hyperfresh Seafood', in *Food & Markets: Proceedings of the Oxford Symposium on Food and Cookery 2014*, ed. by Mark McWilliams (London: Prospect Books, 2015), pp. 372-83.
7. See e.g. Dale Stokes, *The Fish in the Forest: Salmon and the Web of Life* (Berkeley: University of California Press, 2014).
8. 'Eeewww!! Toxic Fish in Gourmet Lunch' *<https://www.youtube.com/watch?v=UN1locZloYQ>* *[accessed 15 May 2015]*.
9. 'A Lock Duart Salmon Is Like No Other', Lock Duart, Ltd *<http://lochduart.com/taste-the-difference/>* *[accessed 15 May 2015]*.
10. Rose Prince, Wild Salmon from the Faroe Islands', *The Telegraph*, 10 August 2011 *<http://www.telegraph.co.uk/foodanddrink/recipes/8691401/Wild-salmon-from-the-Faroe-Islands.html>* *[accessed 15 May 2015]*.
11. Don Whiteley, 'Wild Alaska Salmon Isn't as Pure as Advertised', Washington Fish Growers Association, 18 May 2004 *<http://www.wfga.net/issues.php?ID=60>* *[accessed 15 May 2015]*.
12. *Species Fact Sheets*, UN Food and Agriculture Organization
13. People like to remember Izaak Walton's massive1653 book, *The Compleat Angler Or the Contemplative Man's Recreation* (Oxford: Oxford University Press, 1915), as having denominated salmon 'the King of Fish'. He actually wrote, 'The Salmon is accounted the King of fresh water-Fish' (p. 134). It was known in 1653 that salmon were born in rivers and then they went to sea, and then came back to spawn, but the life of salmon outside rivers was largely unknown. Walton, Europeans and those on the east coast of America knew only the Atlantic salmon, *Salmo salar.* The vast genus of Pacific salmon was unknown to them.

14. James Beard, *James Beard's Fish Cookery* (New York: Little, Brown and Company, 1954), p. 143.

15. Waverley Root, *Food: An Authoritative and Visual History and Dictionary of the Foods of the World* (New York: Simon and Schuster, 1980), p. 434.

16. Pierre Franey and Bryan Miller, *The Seafood Cookbook: Classic to Contemporary* (New York: Times Books, 1986), p. 152. A dissenter expresses a contrary view: 'Atlantic salmon are dry and tasteless' compared to 'a rich fish such as Pacific salmon', though no species is specified (*Don Holm's Book of Food Drying, Pickling and Smoke Curing* (Caldwell: Caxton, 1978), p. 82).

17. 'Une contrée sauvage', *Saumon Écossais Label Rouge* <http://www.saumonecossais.com/fr/provenance/une-contre-e-sauvage> [accessed 15 May 2015].

18. James A. Lichatowich, et al., 'Artificial Production and the Effects of Fish Culture on Native Salmonids,' in *Return to the River: Restoring Salmon to the Columbia River*, ed. by Richard N. Williams (London: Elsevier, 2006), p. 444.

19. N. Portley, et al., *Global Sustainability Overview of Pacific Salmon Fisheries* (Honolulu: Sustainable Fisheries Partnership Foundation, 2014) <www.fishsource.com> [accessed 15 May 2015].

20. Iciar Martinez, 'Revision of Analytical Methodologies to Verify the Production Method of Fish', in *Seafood Research from Fish to Dish: Quality, Safety and Processing of Wild and Farmed Fish*, ed. by J.B. Luton et al. (Wageningen: Wageningen, 2006), p. 546.

21. Michael Wigan, *The Salmon: The Extraordinary Story of the King of Fish* (London: William Collins, 2013), pp. 313-14.

22. Grant Warkentin, 'Facts Left Behind in Race to Repost 'Viral' Farmed Salmon News Posts', Cermaq Canada <http://www.cermaq.com/wps/wcm/connect/msca-content-en/mainstream-canada/news/blog/facts+left+behind+in+race+to+repost+viral+farmed+salmon+news+posts> [accessed 15 May 2015].

23. Tammy Davis, 'White King Salmon: Greenbacks, Gustatory Preference and Genetics', *Alaska Fish & Wildlife News* (Alaska Department of Fish and Game, October 2006).

24. Lichatowich, *Salmon, People and Place*, pp. 108-09.

25. See Nancy Harmon Jenkins, 'Chilean Salmon Farming's Amazing Comeback', *Zester Daily*, 31 July 2013 <http://zesterdaily.com/world/chilean-salmon-farmings-amazing-comeback/> [accessed 15 May 2015].

26. In *Best Food Writing 2014*, ed. by Holly Hughes (Boston: Da Capo Press, 2014), pp. 21-25 (p. 24).

27. Estabrook, p. 24.

28. Estabrook, p. 25.

29. Nathan Young and Ralph Matthews, *The Aquaculture Controversy in Canada: Activism, Policy, and Contested Science* (Vancouver: University of British Columbia Press, 2010), p. 7.

30. Ross Anderson, 'Theology of Salmon: Wild or Farmed?' *Food Safety News*, 1 May 2012.

31. D. Mozaffarian and E.B. Rimm, 'Fish Intake, Contaminants, and Human Health: Evaluating the Risks and the Benefits', *Journal of the American Medical Association*, 296:1885-99 (2006).

32. 'Fish: Friend or Foe', *The Nutrition Source*, T.H. Chan School of Public Health, Harvard University <http://www.hsph.harvard.edu/nutritionsource/fish/> [accessed 15 May 2105].

33. Peter Robson, *Salmon Farming: The Whole Story* (Surrey: Heritage House, 2006).

34. Paul Johnson, *Fish Forever* (Hoboken: Wiley, 2007), p. 251.

35. 'Loch Duart: A Modern Tradition', *A View from the Water's Edge*, Loch Duart Ltd, 9 January 2015 <http://lochduart.com/2015/01/loch-duart-a-modern-tradition/> [accessed 15 May 2015].

36. See *Washington* v. *Fishing Vessel Assn.*, 443 U.S. 658 (1979), and cases cited therein.

37. Greenberg, pp. 21-68.

38. 'Governor Reports "Alaska Wild Salmon" Marketing Success: Legal Sea Foods Campaign Making Big Splash on East Coast', Press Release, State of Alaska, 27 September 2004.

39. 'Sustainable Seafood', Legal Sea Foods <http://www.legalseafoods.com/index.cfm/page/Sustainable-Seafood/pid/44745>

40. '"Farm-raised" Salmon', Prime Seafood LLC, 17 October 2012 <http://www.primeseafood.com/farm_raised_salmon.html> [accessed 15 May 2015].

41. Shepro, pp. 379-80.

42. James Peterson, *Simply Salmon* (New York: Stewart, Tabori & Chang, 2001), p. 7.

43. Bob Spitz, *Dearie: The Remarkable Life of Julia Child*, (New York: Vintage, 2013), p. 490.

44. See Shepro.

45. Tamar Haspel, 'Farmed vs. Wild salmon: Can You Taste the Difference?', *The Washington Post*, 24 September 2013.

46.. Rebekah Denn, 'Does the Best-tasting Salmon Come from Costco?' *Seattle Times*, 9 October 2013 <*http://blogs.seattletimes.com/allyoucaneat/2013/10/09/does-the-best-tasting-salmon-come-from-costco/*> *[accessed 15 May 2015]*.

47. See e.g. Nancy Nichols, 'Jammin' with Wild Salmon Blind Tasting Report', *Side/Dish*, 28 May 2009 <http://sidedish.dmagazine.com/2009/05/28/jammin%E2%80%99-with-wild-salmon-blind-tasting-a-report/> [accessed 15 May 2015] and Valerie Phillips, 'Utah Tasters Put Salmon to the Test', *Deseret News*, 16 June 2004 <*http://m.deseretnews.com/article/595070562/Utah-tasters-put-salmon-to-the-test.html?pg=all&ref=https%3A%2F%2Fwww.google.com%2F%3Fref%3Dhttps%3A%2F%2Fwww.google.com%2F*> [accessed 15 May 2015].

48. Peterson, p. 13.

49. Johnson, p. 250.

50. Discussion with Karim Machi, 'Poissonnier' at CleanFish, a distributor of 'artisan' farmed and fished products, at Seafood Expo North America, Boston, 15 March 2015.

51. Qtd, by Root, p. 435.

52. Jean-Pierre Coffe, however, is highly critical of certain farming practices (*Arrêtons de manger de la merde!* (Paris: Flammarion, 2013), pp. 81-87).

53. Marie-Hélène Baylac, *Dictionnaire gourmand: Du canard d'Apicius à la purée de Joël Robuchon* (Paris: Omnibus, 2014), p. 1313.

54. Wigan, p. 316.

55. Discussion with Árni G. Olsen, Marketing Manager of Bakkafrost, a leading producer in the Faroe Islands, at Seafood Expo North America, Boston, 15 March 2015.

56. Gunnar Knapp, et al., *The Great Salmon Run: Competition Between Wild and Farmed Salmon* (Washington: World Wildlife Fund, 2007), p. xxix.

The Comté Aroma Wheel: History of an Invention, Ethnography of a Practice – A Look at the Early Years.

Christy Shields-Argelès

Introduction

Comté, a cooked and pressed Protected Designation of Origin (PDO) cheese, made with raw milk, is produced in the *Jura Massif* region in eastern France. Today, Comté is widely recognized as an exemplary place-based food, in part because the supply chain has succeeded in preserving traditional modes of production and a strong collective organization while integrating select technological innovations and gradually increasing production volumes. However, if the proof is in the pudding, then, in the Jura, the proof is also in the cheese because while Comté is the largest PDO cheese in France (with 64,179 tons produced in 2014), no two wheels of Comté taste alike. This variability is seasonal, but more importantly, it is place-based and built into the organization of the supply chain itself: there are 160 village-based *fruitières* [cheese-making facilities] spread throughout the region, each owned cooperatively by the farmers who contribute their milk to it. The diversity of tastes is also assured by a number of strict production rules aimed at maintaining the links between place and product.

Several scholars have examined the Comté model in an attempt to identify the features responsible for its success. Among these, the strong valorization of *terroir* within the supply chain is consistently highlighted. The '*Terroir* Program', a collaborative scientific program, initiated by the Interprofessional Committee for Gruyère of Comté (CIGC) and led by food scientist Florence Bérodier, has played a central role in this valorization. Throughout the 1990s, scientists working within the frame of this program drew together soil maps, assessments of climatic conditions, inventories of plant species and sensorial characterizations of the cheeses in an effort to characterize the 'milk basins' of twenty volunteer *fruitières*. The resulting publications successfully linked the tastes of Comté cheese to place, thus providing scientific data in support of *terroir* and guiding development and communication efforts over the last two decades.

The Comté Aroma Wheel was first published in a scientific journal in 1997 (Bérodier et al.) within the frame of this program. It presents, categorized into six aromatic families, the eighty-three aromatic descriptors most frequently found in Comté cheese by the *jury terroir*, a panel of trained volunteer tasters from the Comté supply chain (e.g. farmers, cheese technicians, CIGC administrative staff) and from the region (e.g. local culinary school instructors, local cheese mongers). The wheel continues to be used in the *jury terroir*, which meets monthly to describe the tastes of Comté cheeses from the different *fruitières* of the region, and their results are published bi-monthly in the newsletter *Les Nouvelles de Comté*. The wheel is also used today, in a variety of ways, as an external communication tool.

I am currently working on an ethnographic research project focused on the Comté Aroma Wheel and the practice of taste within the supply chain. To date, I have completed two phases of the project. First, in the winter and spring of 2013, I carried out twelve in-depth interviews with the actors involved in the development of the wheel, including members of the first *jury terroir*. Second, in 2013 and 2014, I attended six sessions of the *jury terroir* as participant-observer and interviewed ten of the current participants. For this paper, I focus on the birth of the Comté Aroma Wheel (approximately 1989-1993), a moment when the *jury terroir* was first put into place. In so doing, I propose to approach taste as a communicative, and ultimately transformative, practice.

In her work on Comté, sociologist Sarah Bowen (2011) argues that a widely shared belief in *terroir* – spoken of in terms of 'diversity' – represents an important form of 'vertical embeddedness' that unites Comté supply chain actors in the face of the disembedding forces of globalization. Bowen attributes this shared belief to innovative programs such as the *Terroir* Program, but also to larger contextual frames such as national political institutions and French culture itself. Building upon Bowen's work, I explore the manner in which this shared belief stems from a particular form of taste practice introduced to the supply chain in the early 1990s.

Paradoxically, while taste has been identified as central to *terroir* – indeed it is translated into English in Trubek's influential work as 'the taste of place' – it has received relatively little sustained attention from social science scholars. With this research project I hope to contribute to the literature by focusing on taste, though I am not as interested in 'the taste of place', where taste is understood as the quality of an object, as I am in 'tasting place', where taste is approached as dialogical practice.

In her recent work on American artisanal cheese makers, anthropologist Heather Paxson suggests that tasting, based on a shared vocabulary and an interactive exchange, is an important activity that helps both producer and consumer recognize and express the moral value of craft production. While Paxon argues that tasting in this way stems from American cultural traits, and contrasts these to French *terroir*, her observations actually echo those made to me by actors involved in these early years who describe the interdependent development of a particular form of tasting and a shared belief in *terroir* as a process that ultimately allows the supply chain to connect 'quality in taste to quality in production methods' (2012: 192).

Therefore, in the following pages, I recount, largely as it was told to me, the development of a taste language and practice, first as a response to a difficult context, then as a journey that moves from doubt to discovery and belief. I was initially inspired by Shapin's suggestion that Anne Noble's Wine Aroma Wheel (which served as one of the models for the Comté wheel) should be understood as a 'homespun intersubjectivity engine' (Shapin 2012: 178) that helps taste communities unite by providing them with shared words for describing individual taste experiences. In this paper, I explore the descriptive nature of this shared language, and then, drawing from the work of Hennion and Teil, consider taste as a collective and co-constructive activity.

A Challenging Context

For both Jean-Jacques Bret, the director of the CIGC at the time, and Florence Bérodier, the food scientist responsible for the *jury terroir*, this project was initially elaborated in response to a set of formidable challenges. In the late 1980s, according to Bret, Comté cheese was highly criticized: first, for its unpredictable and often poor quality, and second, for its taste variability. Despite a renewed interest in traditional products, industrial cheeses had made great strides in the previous decades and remained 'the example to follow'. Bret illustrates: 'at the time, a well-known consulting agency published a study stating that the future belonged to traditional products, but with a uniform taste.'

While improving the quality was easy enough to envision, obtaining a uniform taste was impossible within the supply chain's village-based *fruitière* system. Correspondingly, according to Bret, 'in the 1980s, the *fruitières* were highly contested. [...] That was the past! To make 40,000 tons of Comté, there should be two to three factories. Period. And then the cheese would all be the same.' This logic was also linked to a vision of milk itself; Bret continues: 'at the time, there was an expression in the dairy industry, including the AOC sector, which was "all milk is white"'. Of course the movement towards rationalization and standardization did not concern Comté producers alone, but characterized much of the post-war Western world, including France (Delafosse 2007).

When talking about these early years, Bérodier begins with a memory of Yves Goguely, a Comté dairy farmer and the president of the CIGC at the time. She remembers his angry return from a regional council meeting where he had presented three Comté cheeses to a silent room:

> He said to us [me and Mr Bret]:
>
> 'do you realize how humiliated I was? I tried to present the product [...] and when they asked me what cheese-making facilities they came from, I didn't know what to tell them! We only knew the name of the cellar [...] it could have come from my own dairy and I didn't know it!' And that really irritated him [...] and he continued, '[...] the winemakers [...] spoke about the soil, production techniques [...] they were inexhaustible, and we had nothing to say!' [...] And I can still see him saying: 'you manage it however you want, but find a way for us to talk about our cheese!'

Goguley's anger does not stem from doubts about the quality of the cheese itself, but from his inability, first, to know precisely which *fruitière* it came from, and second, to communicate this quality to others. As suggested here, Bérodier and others within the supply chain initially looked to the wine world's *terroir* model for guidance.

The reader, however, should understand that such *terroir* talk was not at all common to the Comté supply chain at the time. While many knew empirically that tastes varied (according to season, *fruitière*, etc.), this knowledge was rarely framed or spoken of as *terroir* per se. Moreover, while tasting and speaking about taste existed within the supply chain prior to the 1990s, it was largely the domain of key professionals such as cellar masters or cheese technicians, who carried it out in a different way, making use, for example, of an evaluative vocabulary focused on finding and correcting defaults. More importantly, in these early years, many in the supply chain were suspicious of taste and tasting practiced in this way, assuming that it was 'elitist' or 'nonsense' or simply not applicable to a cheese. Indeed, many of the original jury members, individuals Bérodier refers to as *défricheurs* [trailblazers], were initially quite sceptical: 'Well, I remember when Mr Puisais came here and he said "we can find this and that in your Comté" [...] and I thought "but this is just nonsense, what on earth is he doing?"' (cheese technician).

Bret and Bérodier turned to oenologist Jacques Puisais for help. Founder of the *Institut Français du Goût* and *Les Classes du Goût*, Jacques Puisais was also well known for his work with AOC products. Puisais offered to do a series of sensorial characterizations with a small team of trained tasters in Tours. In the fall of 1989, Florence sent them a selection of cheeses from three different seasons and 24 different *fruitières*. Following their analysis, Puisais and his team sent back a series of sensorial characterisations, which took the form of lists of descriptors ordered in accordance with the successive stages of the tastings. According to Bérodier, initially 'people were struck by the sheer number of words' which seemed to suggest the probability of the improbable: that a cheese, too, could have the tastes of *terroir*.

A Descriptive Language
While the number of words is initially striking, the nature of the words is even more important. Indeed, drawing from Ferguson's paper in these *Proceedings*, I suggest that the jury's 'taste talk' plays a key role in transforming the individual into the collective. Like anthropologists, jury members use a descriptive language in their practice that fits with the desire to formulate, translate – indeed, give voice to – the worldview of a particular group.

To begin, the words sent by Puisais (a portion of which are finally included in the wheel) are referred to as 'descriptors'. As Bérodier remarks in an early conference paper (1992): these descriptors are not technical words (e.g. *propionique*) and do not name defaults (e.g. rind taste). Bérodier realized early on that much of the vocabulary used in the supply chain focused on naming defaults, which then shaped the manner in which people approached both the tasting and the cheese. In using 'descriptors', she aimed at 'providing a different idea: a cheese is a quality cheese only if its qualities outnumber its defaults.' Moreover, descriptors are never 'hedonic' (e.g. good, agreeable) or 'closed'; Bérodier writes: 'I will join Mr Puisais, no closed descriptors like the word "characteristic", because it represents a conclusion and not a description' (1992: 12). 'Closed' words represent either a judgement or an interpretation, whereas the point here (and for the anthropologist too) is to avoid both because they introduce individual or cultural perspectives as analytical frames.

Instead, 'descriptors' are meant to be 'open'. This means several things. First, the language is available to non-specialists. This can mean the consumer, but also, especially in this early phase, actors within the chain, like farmers, who do not typically use a taste language. The vocabulary is also 'detailed', thus allowing the taster to talk about cheese in a more in-depth manner, but also to identify individual cheeses (and eventually their *fruitières*, *terroirs*, etc.) as unique. For example, the descriptor *doux* [mild], one of the general descriptors used in the supply chain prior to the *jury terroir*, could become in one instance 'notes of butter, milk caramel, hazelnut and a little vegetable' (Bérodier 1992: 12). Of course, this quest for depth is also bound to an understanding of the 'totality' because this set of unique entities is understood to be part of a larger whole committed to such values as diversity. An original member (and farmer) confirms: 'the *jury terroir* is there to speak of all the richness in the tastes of a Comté, or, I should say, Comtés. [...] This is important in a supply chain that wants a diversity of tastes.' Lastly, the descriptors that appear on the wheel are the words of the *terroir* itself. According to both Bret and Bérodier, the most precious words of advice given to them by Puisais was that it was of the utmost importance that the members of the supply chain and the region reappropriate these words and make them their own.

A Collective Taste Practice

To reappropriate the words, Puisais suggested that they set up a *jury terroir,* and he provided key suggestions concerning its composition and practice. First, he proposed that the jury's membership reflect the diversity of the *terroir* itself by including an array of people from the supply chain and the region. Second, despite their differences, all the jury members were (and continue) to be 'amateurs' or 'Comté lovers'. Indeed, Bérodier and jury members alike consistently use the term 'amateur' in this way when speaking of the jury: 'I think that the team, the people who come here are all amateurs, Comté lovers, and they really hope things go well for the Comté chain, and I feel good here with these people' (farmer).

French sociologists Hennion and Teil argue that taste needs to be understood as an activity, and not a passive or determined state. To elaborate their perspective they focus on amateurs, a set of actors they locate between professionals, with their cool, analytical, 'certified expertise', and laymen, with 'their lack of attention to what they eat' (2004: 19). For Hennion and Teil, the amateur consciously builds attachments to a repertoire of loved objects she values, and during this process, evolves along with the object itself. That the *jury terroir* is consciously populated with amateurs suggests not only that Hennion and Teil's model is an appropriate analytical choice, but that it could potentially be extended to imagine how a particular kind of actor (an amateur, or food lover) along with a particular kind of tasting practice (one that is framed, reflexive and collective) can help to elaborate and communicate the value of artisanal products in an industrial world.

Hennion and Teil's work is extensive so I will only isolate two points here that speak to the *mise en place* of the *jury terroir*. First, Hennion and Teil stress the centrality of the collective in amateur practice:

> Amateurs know well that there is no amateur as long as one is alone in front of some good things to taste. Amateurism begins with the confrontation with others' tastes [...]. Far from being mere *snobbishness*, this collective production of a common elaborated taste is a very powerful way of experiencing the stability, durability and various types of *respondance* – that is, the ability to respond – that objects of love may have and, conversely, of producing the collective ability to perceive these differences and give them more and more worth (2004: 31).

In other words, this form of taste practice is focused on dialogical interactions among tasters, but also between tasters and the object tasted, which result, and this is the second point, in the co-construction of both taster and tasted: the first improving their ability to perceive and the second gaining in value.

Certainly the taste practice put into place in these early years can be understood (and indeed has very much been presented to me) in such terms. Puisais had two other forms of contact with Bret, Bérodier and the new *jury terroir*: he came twice with colleagues to offer a series of 'training sessions', and he participated in two local conferences on the topic. Interviewees retain few specific memories of these events, and I have yet to find a written account of the trainings, but a few points can be made safely. The first is that interviewees refer to the trainings as an important moment of 'sensibilization' that introduced them to basic categories, terms and methods. One aspect of the training, and this echoes Shapin's observations, was the development of a common set of references. In an early publication, Florence speaks about Puisais' training sessions in the following manner: 'Certainly, in the beginning, the cultures were so different that we had the impression that we were not all speaking about the same thing. But after a year of unique training, we all acquired a general culture on the fringes of our own specialisations that enabled us to describe and exchange about the taste of Comtés' (Bérodier 1992: 13).

So, the transmission of a common set of references is important, but so is the elaboration of a certain dialogical stance with the product. One of the early jury members, an instructor from the local culinary school, remembers the following from his encounter with Puisais at the training sessions: 'So, words are for communicating, right? Well, Mr Puisais, I'll always remember, he said: "this wine wants to talk with you. He wants to say, I was born there, experienced this, spent my adolescence here in this place, and now I am mature." Really, he wants to speak with you? Well, let's do it, let's communicate! It's communication!' This attendee refers to wine, but any artisanal product would do, and typically a variety of artisanal products were integrated into such training sessions. It suggests again that the first dialogical interaction to be had is between taster and tasted. Such a relationship is about attending to an attachment (rather than an evaluation), but it also makes the cheese an agent in its own right. The cheese here, as Hennion and Teil suggest, 'responds', and, in the end, it is precisely many unique, individual cheeses that motor the 'discussions' taking place in the *jury terroir*.

And finally, Puisais told them to taste together, to talk with one another and exchange. This guiding principle finds structural form in the *jury terroir* today. For example, the jury works around an open table, instead of within individual boxes; Bérodier states, 'When we went to see Mr Puisais […] he explained that tasting should not take place in boxes […] like you see everywhere, but at a convivial table so that participants could, in a shared space, taste in silence and then communicate; talk about their emotions, talk about what they thought about the product.' The *jury terroir* is also organized, as this citation suggests, around an open exchange. This practice is referred to as the *mise en commun*; a difficult term to translate into English, it means something like 'the sharing, pooling together or placing in common'. Indeed, throughout the proceedings, individuals taste alone first, working with and filling out a tasting sheet, and then share their thoughts with the others. These sharing sessions are framed by a set of rules, both spoken and unspoken, that work towards treating participants, and their subjective experiences of food, inclusively and equally. These rules include, for example: sharing words, taking turns and remaining open to and respectful of others' sensory worlds.

369

Figure 1. The Wheel

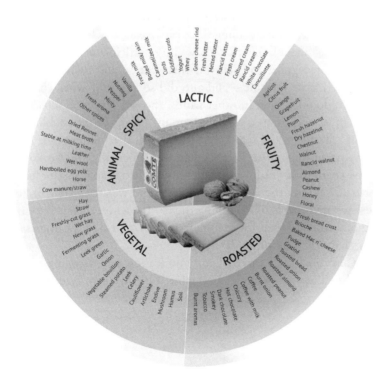

To return to the birth of the wheel, then, informants refer to this experience of working together as key to their conversion:

> And after [the training sessions], working in a group [was also important]. I think that if each of us had been in our own little corner, in boxes [...] it wouldn't have worked. I think I would have given up. I would have told myself 'I don't know what I am doing'. [...] Whereas by taking turns and speaking around the table, we started to find things in common and that was encouraging and made it worthwhile (cheese technician).

Indeed, trailblazers' narratives of learning to taste are similar to those of novices who have only recently joined the jury: they move from suspension and incomprehension to belief and attachment by learning a descriptive language, a set of shared references and a new collaborative practice.

Conclusion

Of course, the reader must understand that this article recounts only a small part of a larger story. In this short space, I did not relate additional textures of the time; nor did I identify and explore tensions or shortcomings within the project. And, of course, I focus almost exclusively on the early years: so, if my final research objective is to trace the manner in which a strong shared belief in *terroir* came to be, here, to some extent, we only witnessed the discovery that *terroir* in Comté could be. What we have done, however, is identify a particular form of taste practice, put into place at the very onset of the project, that consists of a descriptive language and a set of framed, dialogical interactions among a diverse group of 'amateurs' from the supply chain and the region, but also between these amateurs (or Comté lovers) and Comté cheese (as loved object).

If, in the end, I spent so much time detailing these early years, it is because this often overlooked taste practice provides a frame that allows jury participants (and eventually the supply chain itself) to recognize and reinvest their cheese and their production practices as artisanal, and thus as valuable – and also did so at a time when they were very much encouraged to do otherwise. In other words, the *jury terroir*, as a particular form of taste practice, must also be seen as an important means of (re)establishing a worldview and sense of self in times of rapid change. Indeed, Bret understands this to be one of its most important functions: 'I think that, fundamentally, the work of the *jury terroir* allowed the chain to lay claim to its identity, to better appropriate its own values. We are an artisanal cheese, the tastes are different, and we are capable of being proud of this, because we are capable of describing them.' The wheel then is important because it presents the vocabulary used for such descriptions, and thus incarnates core values like the supply chain's dedication to diversity.

Today the wheel is also used as an external communication tool. Coming across it for the first time, in a brochure for example, I imagine it could easily be dismissed as mere marketing tool. But to do so would be to misunderstand it as only a hollow form of transmission communication, whereas I suggest, in concert with Bret's observation, that the wheel be approached, especially when considering its development in the *jury terroir*, as a form of ritual communication: so, as a practice 'directed not toward the extension of messages in space but toward the maintenance of society in time; not the act of imparting information but the representation of shared beliefs' (Carey 1992: 18).

Returning to Bowen's argument, then, that a shared belief in *terroir* acts as a form of vertical embeddedness for the supply chain, I suggest that the *jury terroir*, understood also as ritual practice, aids not only in the co-construction of both producer and cheese, but also acts to embed both producer and cheese in place. For example, several jury members identify the sharing of memories, experiences and expertise within the *jury terroir* as one of its most rewarding aspects. In this way, Bret remembers Maurice Bressoux, the son of a cheesemaker who sat on the first *jury terroir* as a seasoned cellar master:

> I can still see Mr Bressoux explaining to us [the *jury terroir*] that when he was a young cheesemaker [...] he knew the Comté would be good when the *rognure* [leftover trim after pressing] smelled like fresh hazelnut. So, you see, it is in this sense that Jacques Puisais was really helpful to us, because the aroma wheel was not created artificially as a commercial communication tool [...], but connected to a *savoir-faire*, a history, *voilà*.

Bret's example illustrates that the words on the wheel are embedded in local knowledge and history, but also that the *jury terroir* – as a ruled, collective, repetitive and also symbolic activity – provides a frame for the transformation of personal memories into collective memory and group identity. As ritual practice, then, the *jury terroir* also allows participants to transcend relations with other jury members and particular cheeses, and feel part of a larger whole that extends into the past, reaches across the landscape and integrates the practices of a region.

However, the reader should not understand the *jury terroir* as a quaint cultural gathering that only serves to commemorate an idealized past: instead, the words and practice of the *jury terroir* also act to embed local actors because their language and knowledge move within and outside the supply chain, allowing for dialogue across fields of activity and expertise. For example, as cited at the onset of this paper, the wheel was first published in a scientific paper: the work of the *jury terroir*, guided by food scientist Bérodier and combined with her statistical analysis, is also a scientific language and form of expertise. Similarly, the *jury terroir*'s results are linked with those of other disciplines within the frame of the *Terroir* Program. For example, one study (Monnet, Bérodier et al. 2000) demonstrates an 85% overlap between eight environmentally defined regions and nine sensory groups (identified by the *jury terroir*), thus proving the link between the tastes of Comté and the places of production. If our sense of self is produced in and through our relations with others, as many social scientists have demonstrated, then here too a strong sense of self within the chain is reinforced when scientific authorities recognize the language and practice through which it is formulated.

Similarly, and most importantly for the people with whom I spoke, this knowledge is reintegrated into the quality development efforts of the supply chain, especially those that span the 1990s and focus on the *fruitière*. Bret states:

> [The wheel] is not a communication sort-of-thing like 'taste me, there are several families' and all that. That's not very interesting. Well, I need to weigh my words. What I mean is, that kind of approach does not lead to development. [...] By development I mean that the sensorial reflection must be integrated into the techniques of the *fruitière*. In other words, the diversity of aromas is an integral part of our quality research, one of our main concerns. So if we have starter cultures, heating techniques, mixing techniques, etc. that reduce diversity, we are making a mistake. Each *fruitière* must keep its own personality. It is in this sense that the sensorial approach remains at the heart of the concerns of those who produce the milk and make the cheese. And it must remain so!

In short, the wheel is perhaps most interesting because of its malleability: at once a language of self identity and communication with others, of scientific research and technical expertise as well as a symbol of a production system based on the *fruitière* and a cooperative framework, it spans the nebulous expanse that artisanal products must always navigate between modernity and tradition.

372

Bibliography

Bérodier, F. 1992. '*Notion de Cru en Terroir de Comté*', Unpublished paper presented at *Les Mots pour Dire le Goût*, Dole, 16 November 1992.

Bérodier, F., C. Stèvenot and P. Schlich. 1997. 'Description of the Flavour of Comte Cheese', *LWT-Food Science and Technology*, 30.3: pp. 298-304.

Bowen, S. 2011. 'The Importance of Place: Re-territorialising Embeddedness', *Sociologia Ruralis*, 51.4: pp. 325-48.

Carey, J. 1992. *Communication as Culture: Essays on Media and Society* (London: Routledge).

Delafosse C. 2007. *La France fromagère (1850-1990)* (Paris: La Boutique de l'Histoire Editions).

Hennion, A., and G. Teil. 2004. 'Discovering Quality or Performing Taste? A Sociology of the Amateur', in M. Harvey, A. McMeekin and A. Warde (eds.), *Qualities of Food* (Manchester: Manchester University Press), pp. 19-37.

Monnet, J.C., F. Bérodier and P.M. Badot. 2000. 'Characterization and Localisation of a Cheese Georegion Using Edaphic Criteria (Jura Mountains, France)', *Journal of Dairy Science*, 83.8: pp. 1692-1704.

Paxon, H. 2012. *The Life of Cheese: Crafting Food and Value in America* (Berkeley: University of California Press).

Shapin, S. 2012. 'The Sciences of Subjectivity', *Social Studies of Science*, 42.2: pp. 170-84.

Trubek, A. 2008. *The Taste of Place: A Cultural Journey into Terroir* (Berkeley: University of California Press).

'What if I smell your peanuts and die?' Communicating Fact and Fiction about Peanut Allergy

Matthew Smith

Introduction

In August 2009 the venerable rockers AC/DC were scheduled to play Edmonton, Alberta's 60,000-seat Commonwealth Stadium. A few days before the concert the *Edmonton Journal* published some tips for fans, including a list of prohibited items. Included were many of the usual suspects, including guns, knives, drugs, alcohol, pets and glass containers, but heading the list was a more unexpected hazard: peanuts.[1]

The ban had been instituted after the mother of a young peanut allergy sufferer wrote to complain that her son felt anxious about the peanuts consumed at Edmonton Eskimo football matches held at the stadium. Previously, unshelled peanuts had been a popular snack. Leaving an event involved shuffling through millions of peanut shells, which created a low-lying cloud of dust, a daunting prospect for those who might go into anaphylactic shock when exposed to even a few milligrams of peanut. The City of Edmonton, owners of the venue, acted promptly, prohibiting peanuts from all Stadium events.

There was little outcry at first. Canadian football fans are a considerate bunch, and given how terribly the Eskimos had been playing, most were more concerned about the lack of form on the field, rather than what was being consumed off it. But that all changed in 2009 when AC/DC came to town. The list of banned items had AC/DC's fans, predictably, split down the middle. In one corner were allergy sufferers, who felt that the risks they faced were unappreciated. In the comments that followed the *Edmonton Journal's* article, one angry fan retorted that those who thought the ban was too drastic:

> need to learn about allergies! I am so allergic to peanut products that I will swell up like a balloon [...]. Once on a plane trip to France, some bonehead decided to eat a peanut butter sandwich [...] we had to make an emergency landing [...]. You know, I could have died on that plane and now these 'boneheads' want to bring peanuts to the concert [...]. What if I smell your peanuts and die? Huh what if???[2]

Others argued that, while an allergic reaction could be fatal, the ban certainly did not mean 'the end of the world' for those who used to enjoy peanuts at the stadium; fans who did not like the restrictions could simply 'stay home' if they wanted peanuts so badly. Another person sensibly asked, 'since when do you need peanuts to enjoy an ACDC concert? I could understand if the[y] banned alcohol, but seriously peanuts?'[3]

Such arguments did not faze the ban's opponents. Responding to the claim that peanut allergy could be triggered by smell, one fan retorted: 'You can't have a [*sic*] allergic reaction to the smell of peanuts. Go back to your doctor and get the real facts.' Another questioned why peanut allergy sufferers could not 'bring a medical kit', complaining that he was 'so sick and tired of situations where 60,000 people have to change what they do because one person can't be bothered to look after themself [*sic*] and be prepared. Sorry you're allergic but enough already. The world isn't turning only for you'. Still others expressed the very black humour inherent in the situation. While one fan complained dramatically that if 'I can't enjoy a good bag of peanuts while I listen to AC/DC then I might as well end it all', another ominously warned, 'I'm bringing peanuts in, and nobody can stop me.'[4]

Although the language used by AC/DC fans has tended to be less formal than that used by allergists, nutritionists and health policy makers in discussing peanut allergy, the fundamental issues have been identical: 1) Are the risks posed by peanut allergy real or imagined? and 2) Should the general public sacrifice their right to eat what they want in order to safeguard the allergic? In what follows, I provide some historical background for such disputes, arguing that open and honest communication about peanut allergy – and what to do about it – has been hampered by virulent and longstanding debates within the medical community about 1) how to define food allergy, 2) how much patient accounts of their symptoms should be trusted, and 3) how best to generate knowledge about food allergy. With these debates left fermenting during the years prior to the peanut allergy epidemic, those involved in dealing with the condition and communicating about it have tended to talk past each other, or ignored their detractors altogether, rather than engage dispassionately about peanut allergy and, most importantly, why it has emerged so rapidly in the past quarter century.

Another Person's Poison

Many of the debates about food allergy have revolved simply around a very basic question: what is an allergy? The term allergy was coined in 1906 by Austrian pediatrician Clemens von Pirquet (1874-1929) as 'any form of altered biological reactivity'. Long before von Pirquet's definition, however, physicians had recognized that their patients could have bizarre and sometimes frightening reactions to certain foods.[5] None other than Hippocrates (c. 460-370 BCE) observed that 'cheese does not harm all men alike; some can eat their fill of it without the slightest hurt, nay, those it agrees with are wonderfully strengthened thereby. Others come off badly'.[6] Other physicians, ranging from Galen (c. 130-210 A.D) and Maimonides (1138-1204) to John Floyer (1649-1734) and William Cullen (1710-1790) described similar reactions.[7] Richard III was even said to have exploited his susceptibility to strawberries for political gain. After surreptitiously consuming 'a messe of strauberies', Richard duly broke out into hives, and then blamed it on witchcraft orchestrated by one of his political opponents, Lord Hastings, who was summarily beheaded.[8]

By the eighteenth century, the term idiosyncrasy was being used to describe such strange reactions. Cullen defined idiosyncrasy as 'a peculiarity of temperament in a particular part of the system', listing honey, egg and crab as possible excitants.[9] Such idiosyncrasies could be triggered by an enormous variety of foods and could cause an array of symptoms, including asthma, migraine and a host of skin complaints.[10] But, as with the AC/DC fans, physicians debated about the legitimacy and extent of such reactions. Although English physician Edward Liveing (1832-1919) agreed that diet could play a role in what he described as 'megrim', he also believed that both physicians and patients had exaggerated its role. Dietary explanations were so common that Liveing was surprised when one of his other patients was 'never […] able to trace an attack to any indiscretion in diet or to any particular kind of food'.[11] Opinions were even more divided regarding dermatological symptoms, particularly those suffered by children. While many physicians attributed childhood eczema to dietary error, others firmly rejected such associations. In 1896, London physician Stephen Mackenzie, for instance, complained that he and his colleagues 'constantly find ascribed to faults in diet – too early or excessive use of starchy food, the premature use of meat or gravy, insufficient or deteriorated quality of the mother's milk, or the use of preserved milk. All these no doubt bring evils of their own, but there is no evidence to connect them with eczema as cause and effect'.[12] Diet might have been a common explanation for strange symptoms, but similarly to today, proving such associations was both difficult and divisive.

One might have thought that von Pirquet's definition of allergy, published a decade after Mackenzie's comments, would have clarified matters. It did not. Part of the problem was that another term had been concocted four years earlier, in 1902, which appeared to describe a similar phenomenon. Anaphylaxis, literally defined as 'against protection', was coined by French physiologist and soon-to-be Nobel Laureate Charles Richet (1850-1935) following his research on the variable effects of venom from sea creatures, such as sea anemones or Portuguese man o' war.[13] Richet found that some of his laboratory dogs exhibited severe, even fatal, shock responses having being injected a second time with such toxins. Other dogs failed to present such symptoms. Using the term anaphylaxis to describe such shock responses, Richet quickly equated such reactions to those long associated with food:

It has long been known that some people are sensitive to cheese or to strawberries or to fish or to shellfish or to eggs or even to milk. Now the symptoms […] are analogous to the effects of anaphylaxis: acute stomach pains, vomiting, diarrhoea, colic, erythema, urticaria, severe itching and sometimes cardiac troubles and fever.[14]

375

For the first two decades of the twentieth century, the two terms were used interchangeably, anaphylaxis being much preferred to allergy.[15] By the time of von Pirquet's death in 1929, however, the use of the term allergy became more popular and, moreover, the terms were differentiated.[16] Anaphylaxis was restricted to instances of shock-like symptoms, exemplified today in peanut allergy reactions, which were accompanied by swelling, breathing problems, nausea and cardiac difficulties occurring almost immediately after ingestion. By the 1930s, virtually all physicians, including those representing the new speciality of allergy, would know an anaphylactic reaction when they saw one.

The use of the term allergy, however, was much more contested, especially when it came to food allergy. For some allergists, who came to be known as orthodox allergists, a reaction could only be described as a food allergy if the involvement of the immune system in eliciting the reaction could be demonstrated. In cases of hay fever and other allergic diseases, this was determined by conducting skin tests: a small amount of the suspected allergen, for example pollen, was injected under the skin; if the site swelled into a wheal, the patient was deemed to be allergic.[17] Following diagnosis by skin test, desensitization therapy would begin. This involved injecting patients with minute particles of allergen and building up the patient's resistance over time. Food allergy, however, was not so straightforward. On the one hand, anaphylactic reactions to food, such as those today associated with peanut allergy, were immediate and severe, thus making diagnosis simple. On the other hand, foods were also thought to trigger delayed, lingering and chronic reactions (ranging from asthma and eczema to gastrointestinal problems and migraine), and these were much more difficult to trace. When skin testing was attempted in these cases, many allergists complained that it resulted in too many false positives and negatives. Skin testing, along with desensitization, could also be dangerous in cases of food allergy, even causing some fatalities.[18]

For this reason, allergists who would come to describe themselves as food allergists would use other means to test for such reactions. Although a number of tests emerged, the most common type was the elimination diet, first designed by Albert H. Rowe (1889-1970) in Oakland during the late 1920s. By starting patients out on a basic, bland diet and then reintroducing foods to see if they triggered symptoms, food allergists determined which foods were causing the allergies. Such tests helped to convince food allergists not only that food allergies were very common and could be caused by almost any type of food, but also that the involvement of the immune system in such reactions was either difficult to determine or absent altogether. As such, food allergists employed a broad definition of food allergy, very much in keeping with von Pirquet's idea of 'any form of altered biological reactivity'. With this expansive definition in mind, some food allergists, including Warren T. Vaughan (1893-1944) and Arthur F. Coca (1875-1959), estimated that upwards of sixty per cent of the American population were allergic to one food or another.[19] Orthodox allergists scoffed at such figures. A review of one of Rowe's textbooks, for example, criticized the Oakland food allergist for his 'didactic positiveness' and labelled any physician who followed him a 'disciple'. The root cause, according to the reviewer, was not only that Rowe's cases were 'inadequately studied', but also 'the broad interpretation of the definition of allergy'.[20]

Exacerbating such differences was more metaphorical use of the term allergy. As early as the 1930s, the term was commandeered by authors to describe a pronounced distaste for something. While one author cautioned that those who watched war movies were 'not allergic to the suggestions implied and expressed by the screen', another claimed that 'Genghis Khan was allergic to cities', thus explaining his predilection for destroying them.[21] Such loose use of the word allergy may have indicated that it had fully entered the popular lexicon, but did little to clarify what the word actually meant. Rather than coming to a compromise, food allergists and orthodox allergists preferred to entrench their positions in the decades following the Second World War, each side meaning something very different when they uttered the word 'allergy'.

From the Patient's Mouth

The disagreements between food allergists and orthodox allergists about how to define allergy also extended to their respective attitude towards their patients and, specifically, patient accounts of their symptoms. As mentioned above, the skin testing used by orthodox allergists to diagnose allergies to pollen or animal dander were believed by food allergists to be ineffective, who used elimination diets instead. Whereas skin testing and the resulting desensitization therapy required patients to be the passive recipients of diagnosis and treatment, effectively sitting back and letting the allergist get on with the poking and jabbing, elimination diets were reliant on both patient testimony and participation. Patients had to provide a comprehensive and accurate history of their symptoms and diet, adhere religiously to the elimination diet, add foods precisely when required and take meticulous notes of whatever symptoms arose in a diet diary. Food allergists, therefore, developed symbiotic, cooperative and trusting relationships with their patients. As Albert Rowe declared, 'the absolute determination of all the allergenic causes of many allergic manifestations requires the intelligent and understanding cooperation and analysis of the patient.'[22]

Most importantly, when the allergenic foods were identified, patients were wholly responsible for avoiding them. As one food writer ruefully observed, 'Doctors consider their work done when they have played detective and uncovered your food enemies. They can't go into the kitchen and cook for you, too.'[23] Nevertheless, patients were grateful for food allergists' explanations for their symptoms and the solutions they offered. This was especially the case when such dietary advice appeared to work, but also because many food allergists (including Rowe and Coca mentioned above) claimed to suffer from food allergies themselves.

The relationship between orthodox allergists and their patients could not have been more different. Since orthodox allergists employed a restricted definition of food allergy, they viewed individuals who came into their office rather sceptically. This was especially so during the middle years of the twentieth century when psychosomatic theories of allergy were prevalent.[24] In other words, many orthodox allergists viewed their patients' symptoms as evidence of underlying mental disorder, rather than an immunological dysfunction. As one such allergist bemoaned, 'It is unfortunate that allergists rarely consider the psychosomatic side of human behavior [...] permanent relief is obtained when a thorough study of his home environment and of his many mental problems is made, and when these all-important factors are adjusted.'[25]

Given that many food allergists believed that food allergies could manifest themselves in neurological symptoms, ranging from depression to hyperactivity, psychosomatic theories of allergy were particularly contentious.[26] But possibly more significant was that, whether orthodox allergists prescribed desensitization or psychotherapy, it was the patient that needed to be fixed.

Food allergists, in contrast, refused to blame their patients for their allergies; it was the environment that was at fault and which needed adjustment. For some patients, the solution could be as simple as more comprehensive and accurate food labels, so that they could avoid harmful foods more easily. But following the Second World War, when processed foods (such as refined sugars and corn) and food additives were targeted more readily by food allergists as potential allergens, addressing the so-called 'chemical environment' was also part of the remedy.[27] People who were hypersensitive to such chemicals were like canaries in a coal mine, reacting to substances that would ultimately prove harmful to all.[28]

Food Allergy Knowledge

Related to how orthodox allergists and food allergists perceived their patients and the causes of their patients' symptoms was how their clinical experiences informed their knowledge of food allergy. For orthodox allergists, the best knowledge about food allergy was that which was derived deductively, through the application of immunological theory by means of experimentation. As such, an allergy was only an allergy when it was proved to be so, usually through a trusted skin test or similar laboratory procedure. Food allergists, in contrast, trusted in inductive knowledge, that which was acquired over time through hundreds or even thousands of clinical encounters. It was the gradual build-up of such anecdotal evidence over time that reinforced food allergists' faith in a broad definition of allergy, their trust in their patients' testimony and, more generally, their belief that food allergy was a far more common cause of chronic health problems than most physicians admitted.[29]

For orthodox allergists, however, such reliance on induction was the primary reason why allergy was regarded by some as 'witchcraft, a fad, or racket'.[30] Any success claimed by food allergists, they countered, was likely the result of placebo, not least if the patient's mental state was truly the nub of the problem. Such was certainly the case when San Francisco allergist Ben F. Feingold (1899-1982) popularized his food additive-free diet for children with hyperactivity during the 1970s.[31] While Feingold, who was a self-described orthodox allergist prior to his epiphany about food additives and hyperactivity, acknowledged that placebo-controlled trials of his diet would have been useful, he argued that they would be too complex to design and would take too long to conduct. Instead, he relied on the accumulation of clinical observations, which proved to him, and many of his followers, that such dyes, flavours and preservatives could cause behavioural problems in children. Feingold's detractors responded by claiming that any positive benefit from the diet was down to placebo and designed dozens of placebo-controlled trials to test his hypothesis. Although most of the trials were, as Feingold predicted, poorly designed, most physicians by the early 1980s had taken from them the message that the Feingold diet had little effect. The accumulation of anecdotal evidence in support of Feingold, however, continued, and by the late 2000s, food regulatory agencies, such as the European Food Safety Authority, were issuing warnings on labels about the behavioural effects of food dyes, and food manufacturers had voluntarily begun removing such additives from their products.

In the case of the Feingold diet, it was largely parent organizations, such as the Feingold Association of the United States, and not physicians, that provided advice and support for people concerned about the effects food additives might have on behaviour. Similarly, since the emergence of the Internet, it has become much easier for patients and parents to discover alternative explanations for chronic health problems that focus on food. Less willing to trust physicians and their pharmaceutical remedies, health consumers have turned to other experts, including other patients with whom they might only interact via the Internet.[32] As a result, it is likely that more people self-diagnose themselves with food allergy, as well as a host of food intolerances (for example to lactose, gluten or yeast). While many of these self-diagnoses might well be completely accurate, the absence of medical authority in these determinations has raised additional questions about the legitimacy of food allergy and intolerance more generally.

379

Conclusion

As the comments made by some of the AC/DC fans suggest, similar scepticism has extended to peanut allergy. To a degree, such suspicions are surprising. Unlike chronic food allergies, the causes of which are difficult to trace and which trigger symptoms associated with other conditions, peanut allergies produce immediate and severe anaphylactic reactions that are easily attributable to peanuts and can cause fatalities, often in children and young adults. Because of this, even orthodox allergists have readily accepted such allergies. Nevertheless, doubts remain about both the epidemiology of peanut allergy and what to do about it, and not just among fans of AC/DC. While peanut allergy has been treated seriously enough to warrant peanut bans in schools, airplanes and sports stadiums, to elicit changes in food production and marketing, and to warrant legislation requiring schools to keep an adequate stock of epinephrine injectors as an emergency response, others downplay its significance, adding that such measures are both unnecessary and possibly counterproductive.[33]

What is more concerning is how, amidst such division, will questions about the ultimate cause of the peanut allergy epidemic be answered. Unlike many other food allergies, peanut allergy is a relatively recent phenomenon, with the first fatal cases being reported in medical journals during the late 1980s.[34] If food allergy was not controversial enough in itself, some of the purported theories for the rise of peanut allergy have included breastfeeding practices, excessively clean domestic environments and even the ingredients found in certain vaccines.[35] With the various sides in the food allergy debates unable to agree on what an allergy is, whether or not to trust their patients and how to derive knowledge about allergy, it is difficult to see how agreement about the causes of peanut allergy will ever be determined. The role for history in such debates is not to resolve them, but rather to explain why they emerged in the first place.

Notes

1. Anonymous, 'City Offers Tips', *Edmonton Journal*, 23 August 2009.

2. Anonymous.

3. Anonymous.

4. Anonymous.

5. Clemens von Pirquet, 'Allergie', *Münchener Medizinische Wochenschrift*, 30 (1906), pp. 1457-58.

6. Hippocrates, *Ancient Medicine*, Part 20, Greek Text and Translations <http://perseus.uchicago.edu/cgi-bin/philologic/getobject.pl?p.196:29.GreekFeb2011> [accessed 1 May 2015].

7. Vivian Nutton, 'Galen and the Traveller's Fare', in *Food in Antiquity*, ed. by John Wilkins, David Harvey and Mike Dobson (Exeter: University of Exeter Press, 2003), pp. 359-70; Mark Jackson, *Asthma: The Biography* (Oxford: Oxford University Press, 2009), pp. 33-35; John Floyer, *A Treatise of the Asthma* (London: R. Wilkin, 1698), pp. 90-99; William Cullen, *Lectures on the Materia Medica* (London: T. Lowndes, 1773), pp. 52-53, pp. 148-49.

8. Sir Thomas More, 'Richard III: Statesmen, Strawberries, History and Hives', in *Excerpts from Classics in Allergy*, ed. by Sheldon G. Cohen, 3d ed. (Bethesda, MD: National Institutes of Allergy and Infectious Disease, 2012), pp. 44-45; J. Rawson Lumby, *More's History of Richard III* (Cambridge: Cambridge University Press, 1883), pp. 46-47.

9. Cullen, *Lectures*, p. 20.

10. Henry Hyde Salter, *On Asthma: Its Pathology and Treatment* (London: Churchill, 1860); John Fothergill, 'Remarks on that Complaint Commonly Known under the Name of the Sick Head-Ach', in *Medical Observations and Inquiries*, ed. by the Society of Physicians of London (London: T. Cadell, 1784), pp. 103-43; McCall Anderson, 'A Lecture on Nettle Rash', *British Medical Journal* 1197 (1883), pp. 1107-09.

11. Edward Liveing, *On Megrim, Sick-Headache, and Some Allied Disorders* (London: Churchill, 1873), p. 6.

12. Stephen Mackenzie, 'The Inaugural Address on the Advantages to Be Derived from the Study of Dermatology', *British Medical Journal* 1830 (1896), pp. 193-97.

13. Paul Portier and Charles Richet, 'De l'action anaphylactique de certains venins', *CR Societé biologie* 54 (1902), pp. 170-72; Ilana Löwy, 'On Guinea Pigs, Dogs and Men: Anaphylaxis and the Study of Biological Individuality, 1902–1939', *Studies in History and Philosophy of Biological and Biomedical Sciences* 34 (2003), pp. 399-423.

14. Charles Richet, 'Nobel Prize Lecture', December 11, 1913. <http://www.nobelprize.org/nobel_prizes/medicine/laureates/1913/richet-lecture.html> [accessed 1 May 2015].

15. Mark Jackson, *Allergy: The History of a Modern Malady* (London: Reaktion, 2006), pp. 40-42.

16. Von Pirquet had less success with his term 'nem', which was intended to replace the term calorie as a measure of food value (*An Outline of the Pirquet System of Nutrition* (Philadelphia: Saunders, 1922)).

17. Jackson, *Allergy*, p. 42, pp. 46-47.

18. H. J. Gerstenberger and J. H. Davis, 'Report of a Case of Anaphylaxis Following an Intradermal Protein Sensitization Test', *Journal of the American Medical Association* 76 (1921), pp. 721-23. Allergists are currently trialling desensitization in cases of severe peanut allergy; see Matthew Smith, 'Another Person's Poison', *Lancet* 384 (2014), pp. 2019-20.

19. Warren T. Vaughan, 'Minor Allergy: Its Distribution, Clinical Aspects, and Significance', *Journal of Allergy* 5 (1935), pp. 184-96; Arthur F. Coca, *Familial Nonreaginic Food-Allergy* (Springfield, Ill: Charles C. Thomas, 1943), p. 11.

20. Leslie N. Gay, 'Review of *Elimination Diets and the Patient's Allergies: A Handbook of Allergy*', *Quarterly Review of Biology* 20 (1945), p. 183.

21. Albert Benham, 'War or Peace in the Movies', *Public Opinion Quarterly* 1 (1937), pp. 109-14 (p. 114); Homer Hoyt, 'Urban Decentralization', *Journal of Land and Public Utility Economics* 16 (1940), pp. 270-76 (p. 271).

22. Albert H. Rowe, *Elimination Diets and the Patient's Allergies: A Handbook of Allergy* (London: Kimpton, 1941), p. 33.

23. Helen Morgan, *You Can't Eat That!* (New York: Harcourt Brace, 1939), p. 7.

24. Mark Jackson, '"Allergy con Amore" Psychosomatic Medicine and the "Asthmogenic Home" in the Mid-Twentieth Century', in *Health and the Modern Home*, ed. by Mark Jackson (New York: Routledge, 2007), pp. 591-603.

25. Gay, p. 183.

26. For example, see Francis Hare, *The Food Factor in Disease* (London: Longmans, Green 1905); T. Wood Clarke, 'Neuroallergy in Childhood', *New York State Journal of Medicine* 42 (1948), pp. 393-97; Ben F. Feingold, *Why Your Child is Hyperactive* (New York: Random House, 1974); Richard Mackarness, *Not All in the Mind* (New York: Pan Books, 1976).

27. Theron G. Randolph, *Human Ecology and Susceptibility to the Chemical Environment* (Springfield, IL: Charles C. Thomas, 1962).

28. Peter Radetsky, *Allergic to the Twentieth Century* (Boston: Little, Brown and Company, 1997).

29. For instance, see Arthur F. Coca, *The Pulse Test for Allergy* (London: Parrish, 1959).

30. William G. Crook, Walton W. Harrison and Stanley E. Crawford, 'Allergy – The Unanswered Challenge in Pediatric Research, Education, and Practice', *Pediatrics* 21 (1958), pp. 649-54 (p. 649).

31. Matthew Smith, *An Alternative History of Hyperactivity: Food Additives and the Feingold Diet* (New Brunswick, NJ: Rutgers University Press, 2011).

32. Harry Collins and Robert Evans, *Rethinking Expertise* (Chicago: University of Chicago Press, 2007). See also Michelle Murphy, *Sick Building Syndrome and the Problem of Uncertainty* (Durham, NC: Duke University Press, 2006).

33. Nicholas A. Christakis, 'This Allergies Hysteria is Just Nuts', *British Medical Journal* 337 (2008), p. 1384.

34. Susan Evans, Danna Skea and Jerry Dolovich, 'Fatal Reaction to Peanut Antigen in Almond Icing', *Canadian Medical Association Journal* 139 (1988), pp. 231-32.

35. Heather Fraser, *The Peanut Allergy Epidemic* (Toronto: Skyhorse, 2011).

381

Communicating Gourmet Values in Japanese Popular Media

Nancy Stalker

The Solitary Gourmet [*Kodoku no gurume*] is the chief character of a popular Japanese TV series that aired for five seasons from 2012 to 2015. Like many popular shows, *The Solitary Gourmet* is based on a long running manga comic, first serialized in 1994. Each episode follows a formula: our middle-aged protagonist, Inogashira Goro, arrives at a humble Tokyo neighbourhood to conduct a sales call for his one-man tableware importing business. Suddenly seized with hunger, he desperately searches for a restaurant that suits his preferences: working class establishments serving high quality home-style or traditional foods with a nostalgic air. The next sequence reveals Goro's interior monologue as he passionately relishes the dishes he orders. The final portion of the show features the author of the original manga, Qusumi Masayuki, visiting the place featured in the episode, as the TV series and manga both highlight actual restaurants in Tokyo, blending fact and fiction in a manner not usually seen in American food-based TV programming.

Foodie-ism is in full swing in Japan, and mass media there appears even more obsessed with food than even American media, with a wider scope of offerings, as seen in the hybrid form of *The Solitary Gourmet,* offering reviews of little known dives in a fictional format. In a seminal 2005 essay on masculinity in Japanese TV, T.M.J. Holden claimed that, in Japan, 'Food is present on virtually every channel every hour, every day of the week throughout the broadcast day.'[1] Like the US, Japan has scores of TV shows that feature cooking instruction or competition, culinary travel and restaurant critique. On variety shows, game shows and talk shows, celebrity chefs – or just plain celebrities – offer culinary tips and cooking demonstrations. In addition, however, food also represents a regular theme in fictionalized narratives on TV, including both live and animated series, to a much larger extent than in the US.

Since the late 1980s, food-themed *gurume manga* comics have proliferated, beginning with *Oishinbo* [*The Gourmet*] (1983-2014), about the adventures of a culinary journalist, and *Cooking Papa* (1985-2014), depicting a beefy salaryman who likes to cook for his family but hides this 'feminine' interest from co-workers.[2] Both are among the longest running series in manga history. Like *Solitary Gourmet, Cooking Papa* mixes fiction and nonfiction, featuring full recipes for the dishes Papa makes at the end of each chapter. Both were adapted into animated TV series [*anime*], and their success spawned masses of imitators. The number of *gurume*-themed TV shows and anime has spiked even higher recently, perhaps due in part to UNESCO's official recognition of Japanese cuisine [*washoku*] as an intangible cultural treasure and related government investment into the promotion of *washoku* as part of its Cool Japan campaign.[3] A recent online search for '*gurume manga*' turned up hundreds of titles, dozens of which have already been made into anime or live-action products designed to appeal to a variety of audiences. On one hand, for fans of machismo, there is the anime *Toriko*, named for its lead character, a hyper-virile hunter of rare animals he wishes to eat, or the 2011 indie film *Gokudou meshi* [*Criminal Grub*] about a group of prisoners competing to tell the most mouth watering story. On the other hand, there are the beautiful boys of *Seiyo kotto yōgashiten* [*Antique Bakery*], attracting female fans of so-called Boy's Love semi-erotic comics (or *yaoi* comics).[4] According to one website, in addition to anime there have been over forty food-centric live-action television series and at least eighteen food-themed feature films in the past decade.[5]

This diverse range of Japanese food media can convey hegemonic or emerging messages about food and food culture in a different manner and arguably more effectively than the instructional, critical or competitive non-fictional food media that dominate in the US. Using narrative and emotional appeal, this media coaxes viewer-consumers to approach their food practices in ways that conform to prevailing or emerging attitudes toward proper gender and social roles. As suggested by Holden, food is a powerful component of gender identity, and TV is a prominent media for disseminating gendered food ideals.[6]

Since *gurume manga*, the source of many programs, targets a mainstream male readership, it focuses on male protagonists, portraying women, if at all, as housewives in the home kitchen or as unmarried young women fond of sweet treats and fashionable foreign restaurants. This androcentric focus has carried over to TV series, where a common storyline features a young male slacker who transforms himself in order to succeed as a chef or to save a family restaurant, often featuring either French or Italian cuisine (e.g. *Bambino* (2007), *Hungry* (2012), *Monsieur* (2013) and *Dinner* (2013)). In most of these series, male main characters embody or aim at embodying authority, power and expertise as a professional chef in the kitchens of top-notch restaurants. In past decades, male gourmets and gourmands were stereotypically portrayed as foppish fans of French cuisine and other expensive delicacies. In the deluge of recent *gurume* TV dramas, however, some have begun to shift rigid associations between gender and food roles, occasionally presenting female main characters as culinary apprentices or head cooks (e.g. *Osen* and *Ando Natsu*, both 2008) and masculine male characters preparing or celebrating home-style foods.

In this paper, I focus on new representations of culinary masculinity in several popular *gurume* TV dramas. I both challenge and extend scholarship on gender in US food TV programming, such as Rebecca Swanson's analysis of the Food Network or Signe Rousseau's *Food Media* which find that, on balance, with a few emerging exceptions, US programs tend to uphold a gender binary, with female 'cooks' in home kitchens and male 'chefs' in professional kitchens and competitive arenas.[7] Furthermore, I update Holden's 2005 work on masculinity in Japanese food TV, which was limited to game shows and variety shows. Holden argued that the emblematic figure of Japanese masculinity, the salaryman, an urban, middle class, white collar worker, was entirely absent from food TV but that the men who appeared – a diverse collection of transvestites, athletes and entertainers – still embodied hegemonic, patriarchal conceptions of Japanese masculinity represented by the salaryman in their demonstrations of authority, expertise and possession.[8] In contrast, I demonstrate that the male protagonists in several popular *gurume* dramas today are often salarymen-types who embody new patterns in masculine relationships with food that conform with Japan's changing social landscape. In short, the declining marriage rate and the purported loss of young male interest in women and sex, which I will later elaborate, means that men are increasingly responsible for their own meals and often eat alone; this situation is reflected, even celebrated, in current food TV.

As examples of changing male food norms, I've selected shows that originated as manga and were adapted into TV series that ran for multiple seasons on major networks, indicating a wide and diverse viewership. In these shows, bachelors roam the urban landscape seeking solace or identity through consuming or producing customary or home-style comfort foods. These recent incarnations are portrayed as stoic yet suave: tough, iconoclastic traditionalists who smoke, routinely pay their respect to the gods and say little but demonstrate critical food-based skills, invoking a 'silent samurai' archetype of masculinity. This new form of culinary masculinity challenges received images of chefs dressed in professional white uniforms or of men as dandified connoisseurs. In the newly gendered food environment 'real' men cook, serve and eat comfort food, making no apologies for their interests, tastes and indulgences.

The Solitary Gourmet [Kodoku no gurume]

During the opening sequence of *The Solitary Gourmet*, a deep, authoritative voiceover proclaims: 'Whatever their society, when a man indulges in satisfying his hunger, he will become selfish and be liberated for a moment without being disturbed by anyone. To eat freely is an act of aloofness – this act is the best comfort given to any man.' Goro's solitary nature is revealed in the first episode. When he contemplates opening his own antique shop, he quickly rejects the idea: 'It's just like a marriage, open a shop and you'll add more things that you must protect and life becomes more complicated. I'm a man who basically prefers to be light and free.' He works alone at his import business to spare himself from 'annoying interpersonal relations'. Most of the narration is voiceover, representing Goro's interior monologue. There is little dialogue, and Goro becomes uncomfortable around overly chatty female clients, who comment on his perpetually sour countenance.

The biggest problem Goro faces is the daily decision of what to have for lunch. He favours shabby restaurants with good cheap food that cater to male clientele. Episodes are named after the dishes he eats, like the Boiled Fish Set Meal [*nizakana teishoku*], Chicken and Egg Rice Bowl [*oyakodon*] or Spaghetti Neapolitan. Food appears to be the main source of his emotional life, the only thing that can bring a smile to his face. As he considers which restaurant to choose that day he often muses, 'What do I need to put in my stomach right now? Don't think – Feel it!!' His unspoken comments often reflect a pseudo-romantic relationship with food: for example, 'The sauce has permeated the fish so well that its taste has permeated my heart' and 'Meeting a good eatery is a once in a lifetime opportunity – it must be fate'. When faced with a difficult choice between two restaurants, he thinks, 'I feel like I'm deciding between two beautiful women.' Choosing one, he bows and apologizes to the rejected shop, promising that he'll 'come there next'.

Indeed, food even acts as a substitute for sex for Goro. As he eats there's often a loud drumbeat increasing in tempo, and he audibly gasps, grunts and moans, while his interior monologue excitedly proclaims, 'Yes! Yes! Mmmm…Mmmmm', or makes suggestive double entendres. For example, at an eatery where customers grill their own foods, his organ meats sizzle away as he thinks, 'Finally I can hear the cry of the meat I'm going to eat.' Or, while eating braised pork belly from Japan's tropical southernmost islands, he thinks, 'Yum! Yum! Let's have an Okinawan festival all by myself.' It is clearly no accident that the word used for festival, *omatsuri*, is also slang for sex. In one over-the-top episode he finds his grilled seafood appetizer 'Plump, plump yet delicate…Yes! Yes! Like I thought – the milk of the sea!' and receives the main course with 'Hot! Hot! Good! Good! Mmm, this taste, this taste! So good, so good!' Following a satisfying meal he sometimes runs out of the restaurant for a seemingly post-coital cigarette or notices the 'good sweat' he has worked up.

Given this sexualisation of eating, it seems important that viewers learn that Goro is not gay through a flashback: he was once in love with an actress named Sayuki while both were living in Paris, but he refused to marry her. In another episode, he encounters a friend he hasn't met for twenty years. Now a gay transvestite, the friend urges Goro to fall in love, but Goro blurts back, 'Please live your life in the way you want – I…am hungry!' as he rushes out to find lunch.

While his profession and obsession – tableware and comfort food, respectively – might mark him as metrosexual or feminine, Goro's strong, silent demeanour exudes masculinity. Tall and handsome, with a slight pompadour, he is attractive to women. We also learn that he is highly competitive in an episode where he plays the chess-like game of *shogi* with old men in a neighbourhood park. Rejecting personal relationships, he is most passionate about meals, and he elevates everyday foods prepared unpretentiously to objects of worship, demonstrating that men do not have to eat delicacies or frequent fancy foreign eateries to acquire *gurume* consciousness. Learning to appreciate quality ingredients and preparation in down home eateries is enough to confer a sense of masculine confidence and self-sufficiency, implying that every man has the resources to cultivate culinary capital. Eating alone at restaurants is not undesirable, but rather an opportunity for self-indulgence and deep self-satisfaction.

Soldier of Food [Shoku no Gunshi]

The Solitary Gourmet proved so popular that a different series based on another of Qusumi's *gurume manga* premiered in April 2015. The protagonist of *Soldier of Food* [*Shoku no Gunshi*] is Hongo Ban, another single salaryman in a trench coat and suit, who approaches eating like a battle, with strategies and tactics designed to prove himself superior to opponents. In many restaurants serving traditional foods, such as sushi, tempura, yakitori and oden (a kind of stew), customers are seated at counters in front of the cook and do not order all at once, but as they go along. Through the sequence and content of orders, diners demonstrate talent and knowledge – a cool savoir-faire demonstrated by men known favourably as *tsu* in Japanese. Hongo is assisted in his battles by a famous third-century Chinese military general, Kongming (Zhuge Liang, 181-234 AD), who resides in his subconscious and provides strategic advice.

Hongo aspires to be a *tsu*, but he is neither suave nor stoic. He is an arrogant fool who childishly breaks into a skip and song when nearing target restaurants, leers pervertedly at women, overdrinks and ends many episodes waking from a drunken stupor in his tiny quarters, feeling humiliated by his defeat at the hands of his rival, Kaoru Rikishi, a handsome, younger man who always wears a simple grey hoodie. It is actually Rikishi who represents the culinary samurai and desirable *tsu*, a self-possessed expert who chooses his words sparingly but outperforms Hongo in ordering the best dishes in the most optimal sequences at every venue.

Soldier of Food promotes the pursuit of detailed food knowhow as a masculine ideal, but cautions against the vulgarity and excess faux masculinity displayed by Hongo. Its vision of connoisseurship of traditional foods offers another contrast to the received image of male gourmets as voluble, foreign-food oriented dandies. Rikishi's restrained, masculine appearance and demeanour highlights his perfect command of food knowledge and timing, which earn him the respect of cooks and other aficionados that is so craved by the more flamboyant Hongo.

Late Night Diner [Shinya Shokudō]

Late Night Diner [*Shinya Shokudō*] was broadcast for three seasons in 2009, 2011 and 2014 and released as a feature film this year. The story centres on a rundown *izakaya* open from midnight to 7:00am with a sordid and eclectic clientele of gangsters, hookers, police detectives, poets and bitter middle-aged spinsters. The sign hanging outside simply proclaims *meshi* [grub], a masculine term for food and the menu, posted on the wall, contains just four cheap items: *tonjiru* [pork and miso stew] and three kinds of alcohol: beer, sake and *shochu*, a strong white liquor. But the mysterious owner, known only as Master (a common appellation in Japan for men running small businesses), will, if he can, prepare any dish a customer requests. Like *The Solitary Gourmet*, each thirty-minute episode is named for a simple comfort food, like wieners, pickles or cream stew, that the Master makes for a given customer, who is the central character of that episode. Each episode ends with that character explaining the recipe while we see Master cooking the dish: the show is another hybrid form combining drama and instruction.

Master exudes calm, confident masculinity, but also a strong sense of both melancholy and nostalgia, heightened by a wistful soundtrack. He invariably wears a deep blue *samue*, the manly attire of artisans and craftsmen, with traditional *geta* wooden clogs, and he sports a large scar across his left eye that hints at a criminal past. Though frequently acknowledging orders with an authoritative '*haiyo!*' ['Coming right up!'], he speaks little, only occasionally offering philosophical nuggets that address customers' problems. We know nothing of his personal life, but he appears unattached romantically, without personal relationships other than his clients.

In contrast with the male characters described earlier, Master's identity does not revolve around what he consumes, but rather around what he produces: homey foods that customers often proclaim taste like Mom's cooking. Master thus represents a gender reversal, dedicating his life to providing comfort foods for the denizens of the night, just as the idealized Japanese housewife dedicates herself to supplying such foods for her family. Here, food is not a substitute for sex or sociality for Master; instead, he himself is a substitute for home and family, providing a 'feminine' space of succour and nourishment for quirky souls battling life in the gritty city. Furthermore, his attentive and sincere hospitality, a key value known as *omotenashi* in Japanese culture, is more often associated with largely feminine roles, such as the mistress and attendants at traditional inns or hosts of tea ceremonies. *Omotenashi* includes the ability to create an intimate, relaxing environment for guests through unobtrusive service, just as Master provides at his diner. He demonstrates a new gender ideal – the masculine nurturer: manly yet considerate, someone who exudes cool yet can also cook, and who embodies traditional values that are often deemed feminine.

387

Contextualizing New Culinary Masculinities

Several factors help explain the emergence of these new forms of culinary masculinity in Japanese TV and film. For one, they accompany increased consumption of food publications and cooking lessons targeted specifically towards men, including glossy magazines like *Danshi Shokudo* [*Men's Cafeteria*] and *Otoko no Ryori* [*Masculine Cuisine*] and dedicated schools like *Danshi honkaku ryōri kyōshitsu* [*Men's Kitchen* or *Men's Basic Cooking Classroom*], not to mention male-only classes at Japan's largest chain of cooking schools, ABC Cooking Studio, which claims to have taught over 10,000 male students from teens to 'active seniors' at its over 130 locations.[9]

More fundamentally, however, media and consumer trends reflect demographic changes and economic conditions that have affected patterns of eating. Marriage rates have declined dramatically over the past decade. According to one article, an astounding 47% of Japanese man between the ages of 30 and 34 are unmarried today, in comparison with around 21% in 2005. The percentage of unmarried women of the same age bracket has jumped from 9% to over 34% in one short decade.[10] Since wives are stereotypically responsible for preparing home meals and bento lunches for their husbands, the decline in marriage rates means more men have increased responsibilities for choosing and preparing their own food. This situation is unlikely to change in the near future. Earlier this year, a survey by the Japan Family Association determined that more than 20% of men between the ages of 25 and 29 expressed little interest in sex or in relationships with women leading to marriage.[11]

Such individuals have been widely dubbed 'herbivores' [*soshoku danshi*] in the media, a term coined by cultural critic Fukasawa Maki in 2006 to describe men in their 20s and 30s who were less interested in sex than previous generations.[12] According to one marriage consulting company's survey in 2012, of 400 single men around the age of 30, a full 75% were self-proclaimed herbivores.[13] These men are typically said to take keen interest in fashion and personal appearance; they would rather be friends with women than be in sexual relationships with them. The *New York Times* described herbivores as 'metrosexuals without the testosterone'.[14] The Japanese media also claims herbivore men are quiet and submissive, traits associated with femininity, and often blame their increase on the growth of 'carnivorous women' [*nikushoku joshi*], reportedly due to new economic opportunities and lifestyle options. Such women are deemed loud and aggressive, masculine traits undesirable for women.

Some social critics, however, point to economic causes for the declining interest in sex and marriage and the increase in self-proclaimed herbivores. Men growing up in the era of the burst bubble economy of the 1990s have had less economic opportunity than their fathers. With a weak economy, low salaries and long work hours, young men are too tired or too broke to take women on dates, though they may wish to eventually marry. Architect Kikuchi Rintaro provides another explanation for the high rate of celibacy and disinterest in sex: namely, that the average urban apartment, although expensive, is tiny, dark and depressing. Averaging 430 square feet, they are barely large enough for one and an embarrassing deterrent to inviting guests over.[15] Kitchens are too small for practical cooking, which, incidentally, also increases the number of individuals dining out alone or purchasing ready-to-eat meals.

All of these factors mentioned– consumerism, demographic change and economic opportunity – have changed masculine relationships with food and created new male archetypes in the media, such as the Solitary Gourmet, the Food Soldier and Master. These new characters first became popular with largely male readers of *manga*, but as they are transformed into network TV programs the new norms of culinary masculinity are widely disseminated among mainstream audiences. The sexy, stoic heroes of these shows, the '*gurume* samurai', become role models that empower ordinary men to similarly pursue new relationships with food as companionless consumers, cooks, and connoisseurs.

Notes

1.   T.M.J. Holden, 'The Overcooked and Underdone: Masculinities in Japanese Food Programming', in *Food and Culture: A Reader*, ed. by Carole Counihan and Penny Van Esterik, 3rd edn. (New York:

Routledge, 2012), pp.119-34.

2. Lorie Brau, 'Oishinbo's Adventures in Eating: Food, Communication, and Culture in Japanese Comics', *Gastronomica,* 4 (Fall 2004), pp. 34-45.

3. See, for example, the episode entitled 'Washoku' from the NHK series *Cool Japan,* first broadcast in February 2014.

4. See Anonija Cavcic, 'From Dashing to Delicious: The Gastroorgasmic Aesthetic of Contemporary BL Manga', *The Asian Conference on Cultural Studies Official Proceedings* (Murdoch University, Australia, 2013), pp. 278-85.

5. MyDramaList.com, 2015 < http://mydramalist.com> [accessed 3 March 2015].

6. Holden, p. 119.

7. See Rebecca Swenson, 'Domestic Divo? Televised Treatments of Masculinity, Femininity and Food', *Critical Studies in Media Communication,* 26:1 (2009), pp. 36-53 and Signe Rousseau, *Food Media: Celebrity Chefs and the Politics of Everyday Interference* (London: Berg, 2012).

8. Holden, pp. 130-32.

9. 'Men Cooking', ABC Cooking Studio <https://www.abc-cooking.co.jp/board/men-cooking/> [accessed 2 June 2015].

10. Julian Ryall, 'The Japanese Apartment Designed to Boost your Libido', *The Telegraph,* 14 February 2015 <http://www.telegraph.co.uk/news/worldnews/asia/japan/11412278/> [accessed 1 June 2015] .

11. Julian Ryall, 'Nearly 50 per cent of Japanese Adults "Not Having Sex"', *The Telegraph,* 20 January 2015 <http://www.telegraph.co.uk/news/worldnews/asia/japan/11357201/> [accessed 1 June 2015].

12. Morgan Neill, 'Japan's 'Herbivore Men' – Less Interested in Sex, Money', *CNN.com,* 8 June 2009 <http://edition.cnn.com/2009/WORLD/asiapcf/06/05/japan.herbivore.men/index.html?eref=edition.> [accessed 1 June 2015].

13. 'From Carnivores to Herbivores', *Japan Today.com,* 16 February 2012 <http://www.japantoday.com/category/lifestyle/view/from-carnivores-to-herbivores-how-men-are-defined-in-japan> [accessed 1 June 2015].

14. Ben Schott, '*Soshokukei Danshi*', *New York Times,* 10 November 2009 <http://schott.blogs.nytimes.com/2009/11/10/soshokukei-danshi/> [accessed 3 June 2015].

15. Ryall, 'The Japanese Apartment'.

Crossing the Kosher Food Barrier:
Outside Influences on Talmudic Food

Susan Weingarten

In this paper I look at some of the foods Jews ate in the ancient Near East, as reflected in the Talmudic literature. It is usual to think of the Jewish table as a dividing one – the kosher laws divide Jews from their neighbours and often make it impossible for them to share a meal. Modern scholars, indeed, have looked at how this division has functioned in the establishment of a separate Jewish identity, though it has also been pointed out that Jewish eating practices have as often distinguished Jew from Jew as much as Jew from non-Jew.[1] I wish to show the opposite side of the coin. Although Greek and Roman writers created the figure of the barbarian who differed from themselves in many ways including food and drink, this figure was often more rhetorical than real.[2] In observing the kosher laws, Jews created real food differences, but even these were not totally impermeable to outside influences. The extent to which the Talmudic sources reflect the sharing of food and foodways between late antique Jews and their surrounding cultures is the subject of this paper.[3]

It is clear that neither in Greco-Roman Palestine nor in Sasanian Babylonia did Jews live in a culinary cultural vacuum. There was some degree of communication from the wider majority cultures to the minority Jewish culture of both foods and eating habits. For example, in both Palestinian and Babylonian Talmudic literature we find foods referred to by their local, non-Jewish names. People must have been aware of what their neighbours were cooking and eating. One of the mechanisms is described in Mishnah Tohorot. The Mishnah claims that a woman left to take care of a pot on her neighbour's stove can never withstand the temptation of lifting the lid and looking to see what she is cooking:

> If a woman went out and found her neighbour raking coals under a cooking pot [...] Rabbi Akiva declares [the contents of the pot] unclean, but the rabbis declare it clean [...]. But why did Rabbi Akiva declare it unclean [...]? Because women are insatiable: for a woman is suspected of uncovering her neighbour's cooking pot to find out what she is cooking' (M Tohorot vii, 9).

On the most basic level, there was communication of names for foods, even if not the foods themselves. Greek food-names are common in the Palestinian Talmud, for by the time this was written down *provincia Palaestina*, the Roman province, had long been under Hellenistic influence. We can identify Hellenistic influences in local architecture and political structures, and the same is true of foods. So, for example, we have lists of bread names in the Jerusalem Talmud (tractate Hallah) which include

Greek bread names: *isqaritin*, from the Greek *escharites*, hearth-bread and *meligala*, honey-bread, from *meli*, honey and *gala*, milk (JTHallah i,6: 57d-58a). Elsewhere the Hebrew and Aramaic terms for the bitter herbs to be used on Passover are identified by their equivalent Greek names: *entubon*, wild endive, and *troximon*, raw vegetables (JTKilayim i, 27a). Greek, indeed, was the main language of the Hellenized Roman Near East, and Latin food-names are less frequent in the Talmudic literature: when they do occur there are hints that they may have arrived with the Roman army. There is a graphic description in the Jerusalem Talmud (tractate Sanhedrin) of Roman soldiers turning up in a Jewish village and demanding fresh bread, presumably with threats (JTSanhedrin iii, 21b). The rabbis rule that in this sort of situation Jews were allowed to break the Sabbath laws and bake bread for the soldiers. It is hardly surprising, then, that the source from the Jerusalem Talmud mentioned above (tractate Hallah) includes one bread word among the Greek terms, *buqarlata*, which appears to derive from the Latin *bucellatum*, the dried or toasted bread that was used by the Roman army on long journeys. In another case, the word used for a sausage in a version of the Jerusalem Talmud is *luqaniqa*, which clearly derives from the Latin *lucanica*, sausage. The first century Roman writer Varro associates this kind of sausage with the Roman army, saying they brought it from Lucania to Rome.[4] So it is possible that this sausage was brought by the army to Palestine as well.

Sometimes attitudes towards certain foods were communicated together with the name. An artichoke in Greek is *kinara* or *kynara*, which becomes *qinras* in Talmudic Aramaic. They were carefully cultivated by the Romans who valued them highly, unlike most other vegetables. Indeed, both Pliny the Elder in first century Rome and Galen in third century Pergamon in Asia Minor describe artichokes as 'overvalued'. Pliny goes into details of how the Roman aristocracy spent huge sums of money, importing artichokes from afar.[5] We see them still clearly highly valued in a mosaic from Antioch from the fourth century, where they sit on a silver dish as a first course for dinner.

391

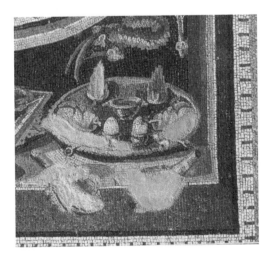

Figure 1: F Cimok (ed.) Antioch mosaics (Istanbul, 1995), by permission

The same attitudes seem to have reached Roman Palestine. A mosaic with what look like artichokes accompanied by a silver bowl dated to the third century have been found recently in ancient Jerusalem – or rather the Roman city of Aelia Capitolina.[6]

And the Babylonian Talmud notes that a very large quantity of artichokes were sent from afar by a rich man called Bonios to Rabbi Judah haNasi. Rabbi Judah haNasi (often known simply as 'Rabbi') was the *nasi* or patriarch, the head of the Jewish community in Palestine and well-known for his close relations with the Roman authorities: the Talmudic sources express this by relating many stories about his friendship with 'Antoninus', a Roman emperor. Scholars now think these stories are not to be taken literally, but are there to express his unusually close links with the higher representatives of Roman rule in Palestine and his own powerful status as their familiar. One of the ways in which Rabbi's status was likened to that of 'Antoninus' was through food. It was proverbial that the emperors went to great lengths not just to import desirable foods, but also to cultivate them. Pliny tells us that the emperor Tiberius was so partial to cucumbers that he had them specially cultivated for him in glass frames, so he could have them in season and out of season, both summer and winter (*NH* 19,64). Similarly, in comparing 'Antoninus' and Rabbi, the Babylonian Talmud tells us that cucumbers (and lettuce and radishes) were never absent from their tables, summer or winter (BT Berakhot 57b). Thus the status of the Jewish patriarch in Palestine is compared to that of the Roman emperor through what contemporaries would have seen as their amazing ability to manipulate the seasons and have desirable food on their table all through the year, as well as having expensive foods brought from afar.

But it was not only the names of foods and attitudes to them that were communicated from Greco-Roman to Jewish tables. There is also evidence of possible communication of knowledge about systems of scientific thought, in particular the classification of edible plants. The third-century Mishnah, quoting second-century rabbis, discusses different types of plants that may be eaten in the sabbatical year, when it was forbidden to cultivate the land and only wild plants were permitted. Mishnah Shevi'it ix,1 identifies some wild plants by their habitat: it lists herbs, including 'hill-coriander, river-celery and eruca from the dry fields'.[7] At first sight it looks as if the rabbis here are identifying these wild plants by their topographic places of growth, as a result of simple observation. However, later in the same chapter (M Shevi'it ix, 2), they go on to discuss different local geographical areas where different animals are found and various trees and other plants grow: in the upper and lower Galilee and the valley, and in the hill country, the middle-territory and the valley in Judaea. These ecological classifications do appear to be the results of local observation in Judaea and Galilee, and as such are somewhat different from the more general classifications in M Shevi'it ix, 1 of the types of places where the herbs mentioned above grew. In fact, it would seem that the mishnaic description of the habitats of the edible herbs in M Shevi'it ix, 1 was not simply a matter of observing where they grew, but seems to have been influenced by a Greek system of classification of plants.

This system distinguishes between wild and cultivated plants, and plants which exist in more than one variety, classified according to their natural habitats. Thus Theophrastus, colleague of Aristotle and an influential Greek writer in the fourth century BCE, writes: 'Horse-celery, marsh-celery and mountain-celery differ from one another and from the cultivated kind.' Here he is clearly distinguishing these three kinds of wild herbs from the cultivated kind. This description is developed by the Roman first century CE writer Pliny the Elder who writes:

> Basil, sorrel, spinach, cress, eruca, orage, coriander and dill are plants of which there is only one kind, as they are the same in every locality and no better in one place than another [...] on the other hand plants we have mentioned [...] have several varieties and particularly celery. The celery that grows wild in damp places is called [in Greek] *helioselinum*, marsh-celery [...] a celery growing in dry places is horse-celery, *hipposelinum*; a third kind is mountain-celery *oreoselinum*. Moreover cultivated celery also has differences in the leaf [...].

Thus Pliny distinguishes cultivated from wild plants, and classifies the different varieties of wild celery as growing in wet places, dry places and mountainous places, just as Mishnah Shevi'it ix,1 had classified the wild plants from hills, rivers and dry fields.[8] This tradition of classification clearly continued, and we find it still extant in Palladius, a Latin writer of the fourth or fifth century CE, who also writes of *hipposelinum* in dry places, *helioselinum* in wet places, and *petroselinum*, rock celery or parsley, which grows in rough places.[9] Thus there is a continuous Greco-Roman scientific tradition about these wild and cultivated plants from the fourth century BCE to the fourth or fifth century CE, to which the rabbis of the Mishnah and later the Jerusalem Talmud seem to relate. Celery is mentioned in both the Greco-Roman and the Jewish sources, and the habitats are the same: hills/rocks, wet places/rivers and dry fields.[10] If pagan foods were suspect to the rabbis, making it undesirable to share a table with pagan people, pagan philosophy was similarly suspect.[11] But pagan science appears to have been acceptable.[12] When the rabbis wanted to discuss which plants were wild or cultivated in their discussion of the sabbatical year, or to classify plants according to their usual habitat, they used the Greco-Roman system.[13]

It is possible, too, that medical beliefs about the properties of foods were communicated from the Greco-Roman world to Jews. A number of Talmudic sources write about the problems of going to non-Jews for treatment of illnesses. The borders between medicine, magic and religion were not well defined in late antiquity, so that the rabbis had an interest in sharpening them in order to keep out alien influences. It was permitted in time of need to transgress central precepts, such as observing the Sabbath, in order to save life, but a Jew had to be prepared to die rather than participate in pagan worship. Stories are reported of rabbis who preferred to die of snakebites, rather than have a pagan or heretic healer whisper incantations over their wounds (BTAvodah Zarah 27b). But just as with the apparently permeable barrier of the kosher laws, it

393

would seem that some foreign medical beliefs connected to the powers of foods were adopted by Jews from the surrounding Hellenistic culture. Thus the biblical book of Exodus (12.5-8; 14) prescribed what Jews were to eat on their redemption from slavery in Egypt: they were to slaughter their paschal lamb, and eat it with unleavened bread and bitter herbs, and to do this again every year in memory of the Exodus, in the place where God tells them. Presumably Jews did as they were told for many hundreds of years: there is certainly evidence from both Josephus and the later talmudic sources that they went up to Jerusalem to celebrate Passover in the Temple courts.

The talmudic literature discusses exactly which herbs should count as bitter herbs, including bitter lettuce and endives (MPesahim ii,6). However, by Roman times some bitter herbs were perceived as being unhealthy to eat just by themselves. The Roman cookery book attributed to Apicius tells us that lettuce and endives are bad but could be corrected by dipping them into a digestive sauce called *oxyporium* or *embamma*. The idea that these bitter herbs, lettuce and endives, could be harmful is repeated some hundreds of year later in the Babylonian Talmud, where the *embamma* is given its Hebrew name of *haroset*, and the bitter herbs are said to be dipped in it to counteract their '*qappah*'.[14] It is unclear from the Talmud what *qappah* is, exactly, but it is clear that it was seen as something intrinsically harmful in the bitter herbs, which needed dipping in the *haroset/embamma* to counteract it. Thus this Greco-Roman medical concept of the harm done by bitter juices in the lettuce which needs to be corrected seems to have been communicated to contemporary Jews, who thus added *embamma/haroset* to their commemorative eating of bitter herbs on Passover – and *haroset* is still there on the Passover table to this very day.[15]

Many scholars have pointed out the resemblances between the Jewish Passover meal (*seder*) and the Greek formal banquet known as the *symposium*, and it is clear that dining-habits, at least at some formal meals, were also communicated from the prevailing Greco-Roman and Babylonian cultures.[16] There is a description of a dinner in the Tosefta, a collection of laws probably from the third or fourth century, which clearly echoes Greco-Roman dining practices – with the addition of Jewish blessings.

What is the order of the meal?
As the guests enter, they are seated on benches or chairs until everyone assembles.
Once everyone has arrived, they give them [water] for their hands, and each one washes one hand.
They mix [wine] for them in the cup, and everyone makes the blessing for himself.
They bring them side-dishes, and everyone makes the blessing for himself.
They get up [on couches] and recline, and they bring them [water for washing] their hands, and even though each has already washed one hand, he now washes both hands.
They mix the cup for them, and even though each one has already said the

blessing over the first, he says the blessing over the second.

They bring them side-dishes, and although each one has made the blessing over the first, he makes the blessing over the second, but [now] one person makes the blessing for everyone. Someone who arrives after three [courses] of side-dishes, is not allowed to come in. (TBerakhot iv,8)

In the next chapter of Tosefta Berakhot we find:

5 What is the order of reclining? When there are two couches, the leader reclines at the head [of the first], the one second to him below him (etc) and when there are three couches, the leader reclines [at the head of the middle one], the one second to him [reclines] above him, and the third below him and this is how they progressively ordered it.

6 What is the order [of handwashing? ...]

7 The order of the mixing of the cup [....] (TBerakhot v,5-7)

These descriptions do not appear to be relating to Passover *seder* meals, although there are a number of resemblances – reclining, ritual hand-washing, cups of wine, ordered blessings, a leader of ceremonies – but what is clear is the reception into Palestinian Jewish society of at least some Greco-Roman dining practices.[17] This is all the more noteworthy because the rabbis disapproved of many of the practices associated with the *symposium*, in particular the sexual mores, as is clear from this source from the Babylonian Talmud, quoted in the name of a rabbi who moved between Palestine and Babylonia:

Rav Yehudah said in the name of Rav: the men of Jerusalem before the destruction of the Temple were promiscuous. A man would say to his fellow, what is at the meal today? Bread of well-worked dough or bread not of well-worked dough? White wine or red wine? A wide couch or a narrow couch? Good company or bad company? Rav Hisda said: It was all for prostitution (BTShabbat 62b-63a).

So far we have looked mostly at evidence for Greco-Roman foods and foodways crossing the kosher barrier, but the same seems to have been true, to some extent at least, of local habits in Babylonia, where there was a large Jewish community in Late Antiquity, which eventually produced another version of the Talmud. The Babylonian Talmud (BT) contains evidence of the trickle-down of some aspects of non-Jewish Babylonian and Persian aristocratic customs into Jewish society. In Babylonia the *resh galuta*, the exilarch, was the head of the Jewish community, in parallel to the *nasi*, the patriarch, in Palestine. We know from Herodotus that Persian kings had been proverbial in the Greek world for the extravagances of their table. So too there are hints in the Talmudic literature that the table of the *resh galuta* surpassed even that of the Palestinian Rabbi Judah haNasi in the exotic foods served: the BT sources note both duck (cooked whole in a coating of dough) and gazelle.[18] On one occasion, we are told, the gazelle was hunted by a non-Jew on a Jewish festival, and then ritually slaughtered for the festive table of the exilarch. Hunting animals – boars, lions but also gazelles, deer and rams – was an important part of court life in Sasanid Iran, where royal hunts appear frequently in local art, particularly on decorated silver plates.[19]

Figure 2: Los Angeles County Museum of Art, public domain image

It is clear from this that gazelle meat would have been seen as royal food. Thus just as we saw that the Palestinian Talmudic sources noted that R. Judah haNasi had the same food as the Roman emperor on his table, so the exilarch is shown in the BT sources with the same food as the Sasanian king. In another case, Rav Nahman (the exilarch's son-in-law) also has the same food as the Persian King Shapur on his table, *etronga*, an *etrog* or citron. This fruit was taken into Jewish cultic use at an uncertain date as the interpretation of the biblical 'fruit of a goodly tree,' *pri etz hadar*, on the festival of Sukkot, where it is still used today. In the BT scenario, quoted from the time of Shapur I (241-272) and applied to the time of Shapur II (309-379), Rav Nahman is criticized by other rabbis for being too Persianized in his habits, and using the Persian name *etronga*, rather than the Hebrew or Aramaic. It would seem that there were limits to what was happily received from the surrounding culture. Was it seen as over-identifying with Persian high culture to use the Persian rather than Aramaic foodname? Did the lesser rabbis resent the house of the exilarch? It is difficult to tell. The high status of the *etrog* as food is conveyed in yet another source from the BT where King Shapur himself is recorded as cutting slices from it.[20] As with the Palestinian sources about Rabbi, these stories have legendary elements: King Shapur is portrayed as being knowledgeable about the Jewish laws related to the knives used in cutting up the *etrog*, which would seem most unlikely. Presumably one of the functions of the story here is to increase the status of the *etrog* by stressing the royal connections of the fruit used in Jewish ritual.

The Babylonian Talmud also includes two descriptions of banquets held in the house of the exilarch which seem to imply the survival of an unusual drinking-vessel used at banquets in Sumerian culture, also in Babylonia, millennia before the BT was written.

This was the *qenishqenin*, a pot with multiple tubes or spouts.[21] The two BT sources which mention this pot relate that Rabbah b R Huna visited the exilarch who drank from a *qenishqenin*, but he did not disapprove. In one case the potential disapproval was because this style of dining might have been seen as too luxurious after the destruction of the Temple, and in the other because pagans were drinking together with Jews through tubes or straws, so that there was danger of contamination in the communal vessel. It is clear from this that a *qenishqenin* was seen by the rabbis as an exceptional luxury vessel, and it appears to have been one from which several people could drink at once. It seems possible that we can identify it with the very much earlier banqueting vessel seen in second millennium BCE Babylonian cylinder seals at royal banquets.[22]

Figure 3: Banquet scene, seal of Pu-abi. © Trustees of the British Museum.

This earlier Babylonian vessel belonged to a beer-drinking culture, where the straws would help the drinkers drink from the clear liquid in the middle of the pot, thus avoiding the sediment at the bottom, and the scum and floating husks on top.

Many hundreds of years elapsed between the ancient Babylonian vessels and the Talmudic *qenishqenin*, but there is some evidence for its continued existence during the years in between. The Greek general Xenophon in the fourth century BCE writes that 'barley-wine' was drunk in a similar way when his army of Greek mercenaries, having failed to conquer Persia, retreated and arrived in Armenia.[23] Xenophon describes

Greeks and Armenians drinking together from a single vessel through straws. This is interesting, in view of the BT source which describes Jews and pagans drinking together from the same *qenishqenin*. In both cases people from disparate groups are able to drink together across barriers of suspicion and custom, and the long straws mean each could get near to his neighbour – but not too near. The BT sources both speak of drinking wine rather than beer, but perhaps they are referring to what Xenophon called 'barley-wine' (*oinos krithinos*), or perhaps they are influenced by the verse they quote from the biblical book of Amos which talks about wine. Talmudic dictionaries have been unable to trace the origin of the word *qenishqenin*, although perhaps the last element is related to *qaneh* (pl. *qanin*), a reed or a straw. Thus this object appears to have been communicated to Babylonian Jewry from the surrounding culture, a relic of a culture many hundreds of years older.

Thus not only can we see evidence of communication of food-names, attitudes to food, plant classifications, medical beliefs and eating habits from the surrounding cultures to kosher Jews, but in one case at least the Babylonian Talmud shows evidence for the survival of a table practice which appears to have survived over many hundreds of years from a much earlier culture.

Notes

1. On eating practices and the creation of Jewish identity, see D. Kraemer, *Jewish Eating and Identity through the Ages* (New York: Routledge, 2007); J. Rosenblum, *Eating and Identity in Early Rabbinic Judaism* (Cambridge: Cambridge University Press, 2011); N. MacDonald, *Not Bread Alone: The Uses of Food in the Old Testament* (Oxford: Oxford University Press, 2008); S.D. Kunin, *We Think What We Eat: Neo-Structuralist Analysis of Israelite Food Rules and Other Cultural and Textual Processes* (London: Bloomsbury, 2004); G. Schäfer and S. Weingarten, 'Celebrating Purim and Passover: Food and Memory in the Creation of Jewish Identity', in *Celebrations: Proceedings of the Oxford Symposium on Food and Cookery, 2011*, ed. by M. McWilliams (Totnes: Prospect Books, 2012), pp. 316-25. On eating practices separating Jew from Jew, see Kraemer, p. 4.

2. Peter Garnsey points out that, among the Greeks, local rivalries between Athenians, Spartans, Cretans, etc. were a more present reality than the Greek/barbarian opposition, and food and foodways formed part of this opposition of identities (*Food and Society in Classical Antiquity* (Cambridge: Cambridge University Press, 1999), p. 64).

3. I am grateful to my colleague Yuval Shahar for discussions of this subject.

4. See my paper 'Ancient Jewish Sausages', in *Cured, Fermented and Smoked Foods: Proceedings of the Oxford Symposium on Food and Cookery 2010*, ed. by H. Saberi (Totnes: Prospect Books, 2011).

5. Pliny, *Natural History*, 19.43.

6. See now R. Talgam, *Mosaics of Faith: Floors of pagans, Jews, Samaritans, Christians and Muslims in the Holy Land* (University Park, PA: Penn State University Press, 2014), pp. 48-49. Talgam interprets the bowl as a fish-shell.

7. *Eruca*, garden rocket, (which in spite of its name is a wild plant, as opposed to the related field rocket, which is the cultivated variety) is the identification of I. Loew, *Die Flora der Juden* (Hildesheim: Olms, 1967 [1928]); S., Z. and H. Safrai prefer *diplotaxis erucoides*, white wall-rocket (*Mishnat Eretz Israel: Tractate Shevi'it* (Ramat Gan: Bar-Ilan University Press, 2014), p. 282).

8. For a discussion of the actual meaning of the Hebrew term *afar* which I have translated here as dry fields, see Safrai, p. 282.

9. Greek writers did not distinguish between parsley and celery, seeing them as varieties of the same plant (A. Dalby, 'Celery', in *Food in the Ancient World from A to Z* (London: Routledge, 2003), pp. 77-78).

10. Pliny also mentions coriander and eruca in this context.

11. On the rabbis and Greek wisdom, see M. Vidas, 'Greek Wisdom in Babylonia', in *Envisioning Judaism: Studies in Honour of Peter Schäfer on the Occasion of his Seventieth Birthday*, ed. by R.S. Boustan *et al.* (Tübingen: Mohr Siebeck, 2013), pp. 287-305.

12. In at least one case Rabbi is cited as preferring pagan science to Jewish: BT Pesahim 94b

13. For the suggestion that the rabbis of the Mishnah made use of Greco-Roman classifications of foods in other contexts, see Y. Furstenberg, 'Early Redactions of "Purities": A New Look into Mishnah Source-

Criticism', *Tarbiz* 80 (2012), pp. 507-37 (in Hebrew).

14. *Embamma* is given as the translation of the Hebrew term *haroset* in a mishnaic glossary found in the Cairo Genizah (N. de Lange, *Greek Jewish Texts from the Cairo Genizah* (Tübingen: Mohr Siebeck, 1996), p. 304 no.16, l. 12).

15. For more detail, see my paper, 'How Do You Say Haroset in Greek?' in *Judaea-Palaestina, Babylon and Rome*, ed. by B. Isaac and Y. Shahar (Tübingen, 2012) with bibliography.

16. On this connection, see S. Stein 'The Influence of Symposia Literature on the Literary Form of the Pesah Haggadah', *Journal of Jewish Studies* 8 (1957), pp. 13-44. For opposing views, see B. Bokser, *The Origins of the Seder: The Passover Rite and Early Rabbinic Judaism* (Berkeley: University of California Press, 1984); P.F. Bradshaw, L.A. Hoffman (eds.), *Passover and Easter: Origin and History to Modern Times,* Two Liturgical Traditions Vol. 5 (Notre Dame, IN: University of Notre Dame Press, 2000) and *Passover and Easter: Origin and History to Modern Times: The Symbolic Structuring of Sacred Seasons,* Two Liturgical Traditions Vol. 6 (Notre Dame, IN: University of Notre Dame Press, 1999); D. Smith, *From Symposium to Eucharist: The Banquet in the Early Christian World* (Minneapolis: Fortress, 2002). For the Greek symposium see A. Dalby, *Siren Feasts: A History of Food and Gastronomy in Greece* (London: Routledge, 1997).

17. See Rosenblum.

18. On duck, see BT Pesahim 74b; on gazelle, see BT Eruvin 39b.

19. P.O. Harper, *Silver Vessels of the Sasanian Period* (New York: Metropolitan Museum of Art, 1981)

20. BTQiddushin 70a. There is no mention of the high status of the *etrog* in Palestinian sources.

21. *qenishqenin/z*: BT Shabbat 62b; Avodah Zarah 72b. qv TA II 280 641 n 237.

22. In *Die Bankettszene: Entwicklung eines 'überzeitlichen' Bildmotivs in Mesopotamien von der Frühdynastischen bis zur Akkad-Zeit* (Wiesbaden: Franz Steiner Verlag, 1983), Gudrun Selz suggests connecting these banquets to the *marze'ah* of the biblical book of Amos (6.7). Note that the description of the *qenishqenin* in BT Shabbat 62a comes as an exegesis of the previous verse in Amos (6.6) where wine is drunk from bowls *hashotim mimizreqe yayin*. The word for bowl *mzrq* is also used for the Temple bowls from which wine was sprinkled, and in the BT can be used for large veins.

23. *Anabasis* iv, v 25. I am grateful to Nawal Nasrallah and Andrew Dalby for their help over this identification.

399